THE
SOVIET ECONOMY
A BOOK OF READINGS

THE IRWIN SERIES IN ECONOMICS

Consulting Editor
LLOYD G. REYNOLDS
Yale University

THE
SOVIET ECONOMY
A BOOK OF READINGS

Edited by

MORRIS BORNSTEIN
Professor of Economics

and

DANIEL R. FUSFELD
Professor of Economics

Both of the University of Michigan

1970
Third Edition

RICHARD D. IRWIN, INC., Homewood, Illinois
IRWIN-DORSEY LIMITED, Georgetown, Ontario

Third Edition

First Printing, January 1970

Library of Congress Catalog Card No. 73–98247

Printed in the United States of America

PREFACE

THE STUDY of planned economies, particularly that of the Soviet Union, can be undertaken for two reasons. We may want to understand planned economies as such: how they operate, how they are organized, their successes and failures, their problems and achievements. Or they can be studied because of the information they provide about the basic economic principles applicable to any modern economy. Contrast and comparison with the American economy throw those basic principles into sharp focus. Courses in comparative economic systems in American colleges have long had these goals.

In recent years the clash of ideologies and the world rivalry of the Soviet Union with the United States have created both greater interest in the Soviet Union and a greater need for more students to understand its economy and how it compares with ours. Courses in comparative economic systems and the Soviet Union and its economy have multiplied. Most textbooks on economic principles have a chapter on the subject— usually very general in nature and tacked on at the end—which is brought into the course almost as an afterthought. The subject demands more effective treatment.

At the same time that interest has been growing, a large volume of research on the Soviet economy has become available. Much of the research has been presented in articles which make admirable supplementary reading for courses on the Soviet economy, courses in comparative economic systems, and introductory courses in economic principles. It is the purpose of this volume to present material that would be particularly appropriate for such use.

Part I examines some fundamentals: the strategy of planning, Stalin's rationale for the policy of rapid growth as he stated it in 1928, and a summary view of the principles by which resources are allocated.

Part II goes into greater detail about the operation of the Soviet planned economy. Three articles discuss economic planning, its "tautness," and problems of consistency. They are followed by discussions of prices, finance, management, labor, agriculture, and foreign trade.

Part III deals with the macroeconomics of growth. A brief evaluation of Soviet statistics is followed by an analysis of the sources of economic growth in the U.S.S.R. and two studies of consumption and living standards.

Part IV is devoted to the recent economic controversies and reforms. A summary article is followed by the key proposals made by Yevsei Liberman, three criticisms by other Soviet economists, Kosygin's 1965 announcement of reforms in planning and management, and an American evaluation. An analysis of concurrent changes in Soviet agriculture and a summary of economic reforms in Eastern Europe help to fill out the picture. The last selection considers the question of "convergence" of the Eastern and Western economic systems.

Of the 26 articles in this third edition, only seven appeared in the second edition and only two of those survived from the first. In part this reflects the rapid changes taking place in the Soviet economy and the advances in Soviet studies of recent years. It is also due to the many suggestions made by the users of earlier editions. The editors are grateful to them for their invaluable help.

Wherever possible full articles have been included. The editors feel that students benefit from seeing how a scholar wrestles with the implications of his topic. Except for excessively technical matters, references to foreign language sources and other minor deletions, and some outdated material, the articles have been left as the authors intended. At the same time, we have selected only articles, written in a lucid style, which get to the essential matters effectively.

Ann Arbor, Michigan   MORRIS BORNSTEIN
December, 1969   DANIEL R. FUSFELD

CONTENTS

I

BASIC FEATURES OF THE SOVIET ECONOMY

When the Bolsheviks attained power in Russia in 1917 they took over a nation which was largely agricultural, with a backward technology and illiterate peasantry. Yet, according to their ideology, a large wage-earning working class was essential to the building of a society based on social ownership of the means of production. If only for ideological reasons, the leadership was bound to push for large-scale industrialization and the creation of an urban working class. In addition, the economic basis for national power had to be created, the working class of the rest of the world had to be convinced of the superiority of socialism, and economic abundance ultimately had to be achieved as the basis for a fully communal society. Considerations of both ideology and power brought the Soviet leadership to advocate large-scale industrialization as rapidly as possible.

By the mid-1920's, when the economy had largely recovered from war and revolution, a lively public policy debate broke out over the proper growth strategy for the country. Out of that debate, and the political rivalries it involved, came the growth policies which have characterized the Soviet economy ever since. They involved high rates of saving and investment, the mobilization of an economic surplus to be used to achieve the national purpose, and a deliberate effort to hold back consumption. These objectives required economic planning, for the normal adjustment mechanism of a consumer-oriented market system would not ordinarily be expected to achieve these goals. The added requirement of maximum speed in economic development meant that the economy had to be driven forward as fast as possible—that planning had to be "taut."

The Soviet leaders also chose planning for ideological reasons. Their socialist orientation and Marxist beliefs meant rejection of capitalist institutions and substitution of planning for the market system. But, in many ways, the solutions to problems facing the Soviet leadership were practical ones, rooted in everyday reality, rather than in ideology.

The three articles in this section examine these basic aspects of the

Soviet economic system. The first analyzes the problems facing the Soviet leadership and the strategy of economic development which was adopted. The second presents Stalin's own rationale for the strategy. The third examines the fundamentals of the decision-making process. Together, they provide an overview of the goals, strategy, and operation of the Soviet planned economy.

1| NATIONAL ECONOMIC PLANNING: THE SOVIET EXPERIENCE

Paul A. Baran

Any planned economy must make a series of strategic decisions about the choice of long-range goals, the speed of their attainment, and the manner in which the goals are to be achieved. The growth goals selected by the Soviet leadership implied strong checks on consumption and living standards, with the sacrifices to be distributed between the urban and rural populations. This article discusses the way these issues were perceived and the methods used to resolve them, including the collectivization of agriculture; wage, price, and tax policies; the distribution of investment; and the use of various "national economic balance sheets" to allocate resources.

Paul A. Baran, now deceased, was Professor of Economics at Stanford University. This selection is reprinted with permission from American Economic Association, *A Survey of Contemporary Economics,* Vol. II, ed. Bernard F. Haley (Homewood, Ill.: Richard D. Irwin, Inc., 1952), pp. 387–403.

IT IS PERHAPS the very limited extent to which economic theory can offer help to a Central Planning Board engaged in the administration of a system in the throes of economic development and in transition from capitalism to socialism that accounts for the conspicuous paucity of theoretic publications on economic planning on the part of Soviet economists. Indeed, an economic science that has drawn its inspiration from the study of the "coordinating operation of the market and at times the failure of the market to achieve a coordination of decisions"[1] is not geared to deal with problems confronting an economy in which the coordination of decisions is a function of a central political body. Nor are possibly other branches of social sciences which are designed to study the processes taking place in capitalist (and precapitalist) societies as yet in the

[1] Oscar Lange, "The Scope and Method of Economics," *Review of Economic Studies,* Vol. XIII, (1945–46), p. 26.

position to provide insight as to the regularities characterizing the behavior of such an authority.[2]

It could hardly be otherwise. Although the basic philosophy of the Central Authority may determine the goal of its activities, its concrete policies are shaped by the specific circumstances prevailing at any given time. Even if it were possible to establish some regular pattern of the authority's reaction to any set of specifiable economic and political conditions, an attempt at a general theory of its policies would be necessarily jeopardized by the impossibility of anticipating adequately domestic and international developments determining, and *themselves determined by*, its actions.

Thus the experience of Soviet planning has lent itself very little to theoretical summaries; and most useful writing on the subject has been by necessity of a historical character.[3] Whether in monographs dealing with relatively short periods and with special aspects of the Russian planning effort or in larger treatises seeking to encompass the entire period since the Revolution—students of Soviet planning have had to analyze the policies of the Russian government as caused by, or themselves causing, specific economic and political constellations. It is by no means fortuitous therefore that effort at a comprehension of Soviet economic reality in terms of conventional economic theory reached their apex in the years of the New Economic Policy, i.e., at a time when the "coordination of economic decisions" was still largely entrusted to the market mechanism, and have become increasingly rare and unrewarding in the ensuing two decades, in the years in which economic planning has become the effectively governing principle of Soviet economic life.

A brief consideration of the problems that the Soviet planners are called upon to solve may serve to render the foregoing more explicit.

1. The Determination of the Long-Run Goal of Economic and Social Development. It goes without saying that decisions under this heading represent the bases of all plans and policies pursued by the Soviet government. Although strongly affected by the ideology (and social basis) of the ruling party—and to that extent explicable in its terms—they are powerfully influenced by the specific conditions under which they have to be made. The tasks confronting the Soviet government have turned out to be quite different from what was anticipated in earlier Marxist thought.

---

[2] See, however, Nathan Leites, *The Operational Code of the Politburo* (New York, 1951), for an attempt to establish a pattern of *political* conduct of the Soviet leadership, an attempt that illustrates, if anything, the sterility of the generalizing formalism characteristic of much of modern social sciences.

[3] "The methodology of Soviet planning has grown with the practice of administering the socialized economy. This discipline is not taught in a single university in the world. One cannot find it in any text. The Soviet practitioners have had to learn the science of planning from their errors and omissions which they have had to discover and rectify." Stanislas Stroumiline, *La Planification en U.R.S.S.* (Paris, 1947), p. 29 [translated from the French by the editor].

Indeed, although political developments in Russia permitted the seizure of political power by a socialist party, the economic and social prerequisites for a socialist order were entirely absent. Fully aware of this contradiction, the Bolsheviks had no intention of immediately establishing socialism (and comprehensive economic planning) in their hungry and devastated country.[4]

Their plan was rather to resist all internal and external attempts to overthrow the socialist regime and to preserve political power until the victory of socialism in Europe's leading industrial nations. All economic measures in the years immediately following the Revolution were subordinated to this basic purpose.[5] Once socialism had prevailed in the advanced countries of the world, the fortress of Russia's economic and social backwardness was expected not to be stormed by a frontal assault but to succumb to a carefully planned flanking operation. Aided by highly developed socialist countries such as Germany and Great Britain, socialist Russia was to approach slowly, although much faster than before, the levels of productivity and welfare attained in the Western world. "The achievement of socialism was . . . thought of by Lenin at this time primarily in terms of world revolution."[6]

The New Economic Policy that followed the phase of War Communism was still merely a set of temporary measures, designed to promote a recovery of the national economy from the catastrophic depths into which it had been plunged by war, foreign intervention, and revolution. The purpose of those policies was not, any more than that of the earlier ones, the introduction of a socialist economic system, but the creation of transitional conditions that would permit the socialist government to retain political power until the triumph of socialism in the West.

The picture changed drastically in 1924. The failure of the last revolutionary attempt in Germany (the Hamburg uprising in the fall of 1923)

---

[4] "Not 'introduction' of socialism is our *immediate* task, but *immediate* transition merely to control by the Soviets of Workers' Deputies over the social production and distribution of products." Lenin, "On the Tasks of the Proletariat in the Present Revolution" (April 7, 1917), as translated in E. H. Carr, *The Bolshevik Revolution 1917–1923* (London, 1950), p. 80.

[5] "The Party proclaimed the country an armed camp and placed its economic, cultural and political life on a war footing. . . . It took under its control the middle-sized and small industries in addition to large-scale industry, so as to accumulate goods for the supply of the army and the agricultural population. It introduced a state monopoly of the grain trade, prohibited private trading in grain and established the surplus-appropriation system under which all surplus produce in the hands of the peasants was to be registered and acquired by the state at fixed prices, so as to accumulate stores of grain for the provisioning of the army and workers. Lastly it introduced universal labor service for all classes. . . . All these measures which were necessitated by the exceptionally difficult conditions of national defense and bore a temporary character were in their entirety known as War Communism," *History of the Communist Party of the Soviet Union (Bolsheviks); Short Course* (Moscow, 1949), pp. 282 ff.

[6] Carr, *op. cit.*, p. 107.

placed the Soviet government face to face with an essentially new situation. It had become clear that the expectation of an early victory of Western socialism was erroneous, that socialism in Russia was isolated. This implied, however, that the Soviet regime in Russia, considered earlier as an essentially provisional arrangement for the duration of the "holding out" phase, had to stabilize itself for an indefinite period separating it from the world revolution, and to build "socialism in one country."[7]

Such stabilization was predicated upon a number of crucial conditions. First, the regime had to be able to meet Russia's urgent need for economic development—without any significant foreign assistance;[8] secondly, the economic growth of the country had to be so directed as to render it as immune as possible to economic blockade or outright military aggression deemed probable under conditions of "capitalist encirclement"; and third, the living standards of the population had to be improved and the internal political and economic basis of the socialist regime strengthened and broadened.

These objectives became the guiding principles of the Five Year Plans of which the first was enacted in the spring of 1929.[9]

2. The Determination of the Speed of Attainment. The policies followed at any given time are only partly determined by long-term goals. The other coordinate is provided by the decision concerning the *tempo* at which the realization of these ends is sought. To be sure, the speed with which the long-term goals are to be attained is far from independent of the nature of the goals themselves. Indeed, the development of an integrated economy independent of foreign markets and able to support technically no less than economically its own further growth calls primarily for expansion of basic industries. This in itself necessitates certain minimum rates of advance. In the absence of an already existing elaborate framework of an industrial economy, every major industrial project requires outlays far in excess of its own cost. These outlays have to be synchronized if waste is to be avoided; plants consuming electric power have to be built at the same time as power stations are erected, coal mining has to be expanded simultaneously with the construction of blast

---

[7] Cf. Stalin's *Report to the XVIII-th Congress of the CPSU* on March 10, 1939, where he developed also his modification of the theory of the "withering away" of the state under socialism. The meaning of that new orientation is frequently misunderstood. As Rudolf Schlesinger points out, "What was really discussed was not whether it was possible to build an ideal type of Socialism in one country but whether what could be built in one country should be supported or opposed." *The Spirit of Post-war Russia, Soviet Ideology 1916–1946* (London, 1947), p. 103.

[8] For a short review of the foreign economic relations of the USSR, cf. P. A. Baran, "The U.S.S.R. in the World Economy," S. E. Harris (ed.), *Foreign Economic Policy for the United States* (Cambridge, Mass., 1948).

[9] For the history of the planning effort at that time see Friedrich Pollock, *Die Planwirtschaftlichen Versuche in der Sowjetunion, 1917–1927* (Leipzig, 1929), *passim;* and Maurice Dobb, *Soviet Economic Development since 1917* (London, 1948), pp. 230 ff.

furnaces, and dwellings for workers have to be built where new factories are established.[10]

What is more, prevailing technological standards impose indivisibilities that have to be taken into account in the determination of the investment program of any given year. Neither automobile factories nor hydroelectric plants can be acquired piecemeal or in such sizes as might be convenient. Even if adoption of units smaller than technologically optimal, or of a technology less capital intensive than the most advanced should appear rational at any particular moment, such policy might prove to have been myopic in the longer run.

At the same time, the nature and the rate of investment decided upon for the initial period of the program exercises a powerful influence upon the speed of expansion in ensuing periods. The basic industries constructed during the first period produce the investment goods to be used in the next; the volume of saving needed in the next period is thus greatly influenced by investment decisions made earlier.[11]

If the goal of expansion of basic industries necessarily implied rather high rates of speed in the execution of the development program, the Soviet government's appraisal of the international situation and of the dangers threatening Russia's external security suggested even higher *tempi* of growth.[12]

To some extent the accelerated preparation for defense coincided with the general industrialization program. Calling for emphasis on basic industries and mining as the essential prerequisites for current and potential expansion of military output, it reinforced the reasoning underlying the Soviet broad plan of economic development. On the other hand, suggesting dispersal of industry, erection of parallel plants, and the industrialization of the more distant areas of the Soviet Union, it prevented full utilization of available "external economies" and thus increased the magnitude of the required investment. It stimulated, however, the development of the backward regions of the USSR—highly desirable on its own account.

No such harmony, tentative as it may have been, existed with regard to the third fundamental objective: strengthening of the internal basis of the regime and improvement of the standard of life. That goal would have pointed to an altogether different strategy and to altogether different rates of development.

---

[10] Cf. Dobb, *loc. cit.*

[11] Correspondingly, a program directed towards economic development via consumers' goods industries implies automatically not only smaller initial investment but also much lower rates of subsequent growth.

[12] "We are 50–100 years behind the advanced countries. We have to traverse this distance in ten years. We will either accomplish it or else we will be crushed." Joseph Stalin, *Problems of Leninism* (11th ed.; Moscow, 1939), p. 329. (Translated from the Russian by the writer.) It is interesting to note that this statement was made on February 4, 1931, i.e., exactly ten years prior to Germany's invasion of Russia.

What is necessary in such a situation is a decision on the magnitude of the "economic surplus" that can be used for investment (and defense) purposes in any given period. If great urgency is attached to the attainment of the developmental (and/or defense) goals, consumption standards may be fixed at "rock bottom." This "rock bottom" is indicated by the need to preserve health and productive efficiency of the population and to maintain political stability.

It goes without saying that the reduction of current consumption to such "rock-bottom" levels is highly undesirable. Under conditions of strain that would inevitably result from such "belt tightening," even small hitches in production, let alone crop failures, may easily give rise to major difficulties.[13] Moreover, the political and economic costs of mobilizing the marginal amount of the "surplus" may be entirely out of proportion to the advantages that can be derived from it for the developmental program. Thus the First Five Year Plan, although programming extremely high rates of expansion, was very far from scheduling a reduction of consumption to "rock-bottom" levels. In actual fact it anticipated an increase of consumption by as much as 40 percent over the quinquennium.[14]

The decision on the magnitude of the "economic surplus" extractable from the economy for investment purposes is thus of an eminently political and socio-psychological nature. It has to take into account not only the "margin of social and political tolerance" but also the effect of any level of consumption on incentives and efficiency. It has to depend, moreover, on the possibility and the cost of securing control over the "economic surplus" by the governmental authorities.[15]

3. The Mobilization of the "Economic Surplus." The authorities can secure the resources needed for investment, defense, social services, administration, and the like in a number of alternative ways. Some of the criteria by which the choice has to be made are purely technical—the reliability, convenience, and cost of various procedures. Where the resources involved represent a large share of an absolutely low aggregate income, as is the case in the Soviet Union, political considerations assume prime importance. The mobilization of the "surplus" has to be so organized as to minimize the political resistance to what is bound to be an

---

[13] This is the reason for the stress placed by the Soviet authorities on the accumulation of sizable reserves of all important consumers' goods.

[14] Dobb, *Soviet Economic Development*, p. 235. This increase did not materialize in view of unexpected difficulties associated mainly with the peasants' resistance to collectivization.

[15] On the share of national product devoted to investment, cf. Abram Bergson, "Soviet National Income and Product in 1937," *Quarterly Journal of Economics*, Vol. LXIV (May and August, 1950), pp. 208–41, 408–41; also P. A. Baran, "National Income and Product of the U.S.S.R. in 1940," *Review of Economics and Statistics*, Vol. XXIX (November, 1947), pp. 226–34. [The share of investment in national product since the Second World War is discussed in Selection 16, below.—The Editors.]

unpopular policy. At the same time the distribution of the burden of the program among various social groups and classes has to be calculated so as to strengthen the social and political basis of the regime. Much of the controversy in Russia in the late twenties and early thirties centered around this issue.

The best procedure for withdrawing from the population the share of its money income which is required to meet the government's outlay is an income tax. Under the conditions prevailing in the Soviet Union prior to the industrialization period this method of raising revenue was beset with considerable difficulties. As far as the urban population was concerned, the tax could be readily assessed and collected. Matters were much less simple with regard to the rural sector of the economy. Neither the assessment of income accruing in agriculture nor the collection of the tax from subsistence farmers appeared to be a manageable task. The fiscal authorities were confronted with strong resistance from peasants—only recently freed of Czarist tax and rent burdens of the Czarist days—and measures of enforcement of the tax assessments, such as removal of produce in kind or confiscation of livestock, were bound to provoke profound hostility against the government and were politically intolerable.

Another method of securing the resources needed for the realization of the governmental program is the expansion of the earnings of the government-owned and operated sector of the economy (industry, transportation, trade, etc.). This could be accomplished by keeping industrial prices low in relation to prices of agricultural products—combining, however, such a price policy with a wage policy leaving large profits in the hands of the nationalized enterprises. Such a course, favoring the agricultural population, would place the burden of the program upon the shoulders of industrial workers. Even if it could have been made to yield sufficient revenue—a doubtful assumption in view of the relative smallness of the government sector of the economy prior to its expansion under the Five Year Plans—it would have been politically wholly unacceptable.

The accumulation of profits in the governmental sector of the economy could be brought about not merely by an appropriate wage policy but also by raising the prices charged for its output. The obvious advantage of this procedure as compared with relying on industrial wage policy alone is that it distributes the burden of the accumulation process between the urban and the rural sectors of the population.[16]

Yet this strategy, involving the "opening of the scissors," i.e., a shift in relative prices in favor of industry, could be and was effectively counteracted by the "kulaks," i.e., peasants in possession of marketable surpluses, who refused to exchange on terms proposed by the government. While

---

[16] This policy could be and was—actually not according to plan—reinforced by inflationary developments accompanying almost the entire period of the first two five-year plans.

rural demand for some products of the nationalized sector was sufficiently inelastic to enable the government to obtain for them certain quantities of agricultural produce, the general tendency of those agricultural producers that mattered was either to reduce their output or to increase their own consumption of agricultural produce, rather than to trade on terms below what they considered to be a "parity" ratio.

At the peril of overemphasizing one aspect of the problem at the expense of others, it may be said that the collectivization of Soviet agriculture was motivated to a large extent by the necessity of overcoming this crucial hurdle. To be sure, expansion of agricultural output and release of agricultural manpower for industrial employment—possible only through transition to large-scale farming and mechanization of agriculture—were by themselves objectives of tremendous importance. However, without a reorganization of the agricultural economy assuring the possibility of "syphoning off" agricultural surpluses, progress in agricultural production would have only slowly affected the volume of agricultural output available for nonrural consumption.

By transferring the disposal of agricultural output from individual peasants to government-supervised collective farm managements, collectivization destroyed the basis for the peasants' resistance to the accumulation policy. From now on the share of agricultural output consumed on the farm could be fixed by direct apportionment to collective farm members, while farm consumption of nonagricultural commodities could be regulated by fixing the prices paid by the government for the marketed share of agricultural output and charged by the urban sector of the economy for goods supplied to the farm population. The way was thus open for wage and price policies to become the main instruments for mobilization of the "economic surplus." The total of wages paid (including the apportionment in kind to collective farm members) is calculated to absorb the share of total product allotted to consumption, while the government secures control over the part of national income to be devoted to investment, defense, social services, administration, etc., through the profits of the government-controlled enterprises.

These profits could be transferred in their entirety to the government, which could use them to defray its planned outlays. In fact a more complicated procedure is employed. A large share of the profits is paid over to the government in the form of an "advance." This "advance," called "turnover tax," is contributed to the State budget immediately following the marketing of the factory's products, *independent of cost accounting.*"[17] The balance of the profits—the difference between the wholesale price net of turnover tax and cost—appears as profits *sensu strictu.* A share of these profits is paid to the government at the end of the

---

[17] M. I. Bogolepov, *The Soviet Financial System* (London, 1945), p. 9 (italics supplied).

accounting period as "deductions from profits," while the remainder is left with the enterprises for various stipulated purposes.[18]

There are a number of reasons for the employment of this cumbersome device. One is that "the State cannot wait for periodical balance sheets to be issued in order to determine how much a given establishment has accumulated."[19] Payment (or nonpayment) of the turnover tax serves thus as a rapidly reacting indicator of the extent to which productive plans are fulfilled by the individual enterprise. Equally important perhaps is the consideration that "flooding" of individual enterprises with vast profits not to be surrendered until the end of an accounting period would generate an atmosphere of "quasi-prosperity" in their managerial offices and exercise an adverse effect upon the effort to assure economical conduct of plant operations. Moreover, this arrangement prevents accumulation of "artificial" profits generated *within* the industrial system and not representing a withdrawal of "economic surplus." ". . . Since a very large part of what is produced by heavy industry is consumed by State-owned industry . . . prices of industrial equipment either do not include the turnover tax or only at a very low rate. . . ."[20]

This is not the place for a detailed description of the Soviet financial system.[21] Suffice it to add that the "turnover tax" and the "deductions from profits" account for the bulk of the "economic surplus" generated in the country. The balance appears in the form of small amounts of profits reinvested locally, the even less significant income taxes, various minor business taxes, loans from the public, and the like.

4. The Allocation of the "Economic Surplus." Most of the "economic surplus" is channeled through the government budget into a variety of purposes. While a share of it serves to support the military establishment, governmental administration, and social and cultural undertakings, the balance is used to carry out the investment program.

Two types of problems have to be solved in determining the use of these investment funds. The *total* must be divided among different industries, and a choice has to be made concerning the technical form that investment should take in any particular case.[22] The former issue is to a large extent prejudged by the decisions concerning the goal and tempo of the developmental program. Once these decisions are made, "the problems of economic planning seem to acquire a resemblance to the problems of

---

[18] Approved local investment, payment of bonuses to employees, erection of welfare establishments (work canteens, rest homes, etc.).

[19] Bogolepov, *loc. cit.*

[20] *Ibid.*, p. 10.

[21] Good treatments of the subject will be found in Bogolepov, *op. cit.*; Dobb, *Soviet Economic Development*; Alexander Baykov, *Soviet Economic System* (Cambridge–New York, 1947). [See also Selection 8, below.—The Editors.]

[22] Maurice Dobb, "A Note on the Discussion of the Problem of Choice between Alternative Investment Projects," *Soviet Studies,* Vol. II (January, 1951), p. 291.

military strategy, where in practice the choice lies between a relatively small number of plans, which have in the main to be treated and chosen between as organic wholes, and which for a variety of reasons do not easily permit of intermediate combinations."[23] This choice between "a relatively small number of plans" seems to be made by an appraisal of the feasibilities and implications of the available alternatives. Certain specific bottlenecks——shortages of steel or machine tools or transportation facilities—may dictate the selection of a plan calling for the least quantity of the critical item. The need to concentrate scarce talent on one construction project rather than dissipating it on a number of undertakings may dictate the preference for a certain technological process.

Such a preference, in turn, may temporarily preclude investment even of relatively small quantities of resources in other branches of the economy, although the advantages that such investment may promise could be large. "The economic plan singles out each time the leading branches of the national economy, the crucial links that have to be grasped for the entire chain of economic development to be pulled up."

The consecutive plans are thus characterized by the nature of the "link" singled out. "The crucial link of the first Five Year Plan was the heavy industry with its heart piece—machine building. The decisive links in the second and third Five Year Plans were the leading branches of the heavy industry—metallurgy, machine building, fuel, energetics, chemistry. Under the conditions of the Patriotic War the crucial link in the plan was military production." It is this concentration upon the highest priority tasks that gives the Soviet economy the character of a "target economy." At any particular time certain highest priority objectives command exceptional attention. This frequently results in transitory "disproportionalities." The fulfillment of one target is accompanied by lags in the attainment of others. The next period witnesses, then, a shift of emphasis to the backward "links" that have to be pulled up for the "chain" to be straightened out.

This strategy of local advances followed by a subsequent consolidation of the conquered terrain is dictated, however, by the specific conditions of the Russian economy, and may well represent a particularly effective method for a rapid development of underdeveloped countries. Where slow growth rather than urgent structural change should constitute the guiding principle of the economic effort, the pattern of "campaigns" and "targets" may be inappropriate, and investment could be allocated in relatively small portions among different branches of the economy with a view to equating their productivities on the margin.

However, the decision about the production targets and the distribu-

---

[23] Dobb, *Soviet Economic Development*, p. 6. "Much substitution in production arises through shifts in the extent to which alternative processes are used, rather than through variation in factor combinations in the individual process." T. C. Koopmans, "Efficient Allocation of Resources," *Econometrica*, Vol. XIX (October, 1951), p. 455 ff.

tion of the investment funds among different *branches* of the economy leaves unanswered the question how to choose between different *modes* of producing the desired output. The solution of this problem suggested by conventional theory (the ratios of costs of factors to their respective marginal value products should be the same for all factors) would provide no succor to the planning authority. Even if sufficient continuity of substitution could be assumed, the Planning Board would have to consider not only the *social* costs involved in the employment of an additional quantity of a factor, but also—and this is most important—take into account the impact of its own activities on the future relative scarcities of factors.

Thus the existence of a large rural surplus population may have suggested (and still suggests) that in Russia strong preference should be given to techniques employing much labor and little capital. Yet such advice would overlook the large social cost of transferring a man from the village into industrial occupation. The additional industrial worker must be provided with urban dwelling space. Paid the going industrial wage, he must be assured of the quantity of food, clothing, etc., that is usually consumed by industrial workers.[24] Even if his product in the new occupation should exceed the cost of his sustenance in the city, it may be impossible for technical and/or political reasons to extract the requisite additional food from agriculture. True, the "disguised unemployed" had contributed previously nothing or little to total agricultural output while consuming a certain quantity of food. That food came, however, from his family's table and constituted no drain on the sparse "marketed share" of agricultural output.

Since the expansion of agricultural output and the increase of agricultural supplies available to the cities require not only large-scale investment but also a considerable amount of time, the physical limitations on the amount of food that could be placed at the disposal of the urban population may by themselves call for the selection of capital-intensive rather than labor-intensive techniques of production.

The same conclusion may be arrived at if it is considered that the abundance and "cheapness" of currently available labor is only a temporary condition *preceding* the realization of any given stretch of the developmental program. The Planning Board, aware of the aggregate demand for labor entailed by its own plans, has to bear in mind therefore that relatively soon, during the life-span of the equipment that is to be installed, labor may turn from a relatively ample to a relatively scarce factor.

5. The Balance Sheet. The investment decisions of the Central Authority as well as of managements on lower (plant and regional) levels are combined with the estimates of the magnitude and composition

---

[24] This quantity itself is largely influenced by political considerations!

of consumers' goods supply and checked for mutual consistency in the so-called "national-economic balance sheets." To describe the procedure involved, it may be best to present an extensive quotation from the work of a Soviet economist:

The balance sheets and distribution plans as drawn up at the present time include: firstly, material balance sheets (in kind) showing the proportions of the material elements of reproduction; secondly, value (price) balance sheets showing the proportions in the distribution of financial resources and ensuring proper proportion in the distribution of the social product in respect of its material form and its value; thirdly, balance sheets for labor power.

Material balance sheets (in kind) consist of the following: 1) balance sheets of industrial products which, considering the main purpose for which they are to be used, represent the elements of the fixed funds of the national economy that ensure fulfillment of the construction program of the national-economic plan (equipment and building materials), 2) balance sheets of industrial and agricultural products, which considering the main purpose for which they are to be used, represent the elements of the circulating funds of the national economy that ensure fulfillment of the production program of the national-economic plan (metals, fuel, electric power, chemicals, agricultural raw materials), 3) balance sheets of industrial and agricultural products, which, considering the main purpose for which they are to be used, represent articles of individual consumption.

The material balance sheets and distribution plans, which are approved by the Government, cover products of national-economic importance as well as products which require centralized distribution because of their shortage. During the war the number of items of funded products, i.e. products distributed by the center, had to be considerably enlarged.

Value balance sheets consist of the following: 1) balance sheet of the population's money income and expenditure, 2) the State Bank's cash plan, and 3) the state budget.

The income side of the balance sheet of the population's money income and expenditures covers the wage fund of the workers and office employees and other incomes of the urban population; the expenditure side covers expenditure by the population in buying goods at state and cooperative stores, paying for services and other money expenditures. The chief purpose of this balance sheet of the population's money income and expenditure is to ensure proper proportion in planning the volume of trade, the wage fund and the money income of collective farmers. This balance sheet serves as a basis for drafting the trade plan and also for planning the wage fund in the national economy.

The State Bank's cash plan serves as an important means for planning money circulation. The income side accounts for money received by the State Bank from trade turnover and payments by state organization; the expenditure side accounts for payments made against the wage fund and other money expenditures. The State Bank's cash plan makes it possible to determine the volume of currency emissions required for the ensuing period.

The state budget is a most important financial balance sheet which determines the distribution of the bulk of the national income. The main items of revenue in the state budget are accumulations of the socialist economy in the form of profits and turnover tax, and money received from the population in payment of taxes, subscriptions to state loans, etc. The expenditure side of the state budget consists of disbursements made in financing the national economy (production and capital construction), social and cultural development, administrative expenses and expenditures on defense. The function of the state budget is to ensure the financing without deficit of the national economy with the aid of the country's internal financial resources.

The labor power balance sheets include: 1) the balance sheet for labor power in the state economy, which determines the demand for labor power and skilled personnel in the various branches of the national economy, and the principal sources for recruiting labor for it (training in the state labor reserve schools, organized hiring of labor), 2) the balance sheet of labor power in the collective farms, which determines the utilization of collective-farm labor resources for carrying out the plan of agricultural production and for work in industry.

The balance sheets system in the national-economic plan makes it possible correctly to solve the problem of planning resources, consumption and distribution in the national economy.[25]

The method thus briefly sketched represents a merely formal solution of the task of maintaining a general dynamic equilibrium of the Soviet economy. Whether it assures a smooth functioning of the economic system depends obviously on the magnitudes that are entered in that generalized "input-output" matrix.[26] The degree of accuracy that is attained in the estimation of the shape of the technological transformation functions, of the volume of actual production in individual plants, and of consumption of various goods by the consumers, determine the extent to which the plan is able to avoid disproportionalities and waste.

There can be no doubt that both have characterized the working of Soviet planning—particularly in its earlier phases. Yet the causes of these deficiencies may have been primarily associated with the historical setting of the Russian planning effort rather than with the principles underlying it. The breakneck speed of the "target-economy" calling for the "leading links" strategy accounted for continuous occurrence and recurrence of major successes in some parts of the economy and equally serious "gaps" in others; the poverty of the country made it impossible until the late thirties to accumulate sufficient reserves to permit a rapid plugging of those "gaps"; and the lack of personnel scientifically trained for planning

---

[25] A. D. Kursky, *The Planning of the National Economy of the U.S.S.R.* (Moscow, 1949), pp. 129 ff. The remainder of the chapter from which the above is cited contains additional valuable information on the methodology of Soviet planning.

[26] The problems involved in elaborating such a matrix are akin to those discussed in W. W. Leontief, *The Structure of the American Economy, 1919–1929* (Cambridge, Mass., 1941), in particular p. 34, although the difficulties that have to be overcome in the planning practice may not be quite as stupendous as suggested by Leontief's analysis. It may be sufficient for the "central" matrix to include only the "leading links" of the economy, leaving a great deal to the functioning of the decentralized economic units.

work on all levels caused avoidable mistakes in the preparation of the estimates determining the relationships embodied in the plan.

The "hitches" that occur in the functioning of the system become less frequent and less costly as their causes gradually disappear. Slowing down the speed of industrialization, filling the "pipelines" of the economy with the indispensable stocks of food, raw materials, fuel, etc., the availability of adequately prepared planning officials, combined with growing levels of literacy and civic responsibility on the part of the population, lead to a progressive improvement of the actual performance of the economic system.[27]

As Maurice Dobb points out, ". . . the notion that successful development from one economic situation, with its given combination of resources and configuration of demand, to another might be a more crucial test of the contribution made by an economic system to human welfare than the attainment of perfect equilibrium in any given situation seldom commanded attention."[28] Such attention, on the part of social scientists, is however urgently called for by the problems faced by many relatively advanced nations, but faced especially by the multitudes living in the world's underdeveloped countries.

Very little of what constitutes the main body of our customary economic theorizing would seem to be of much help in solving these perplexities. What the Soviet experience strongly suggests is the need for concrete historical research into the social and political prerequisites for economic growth and development. The "standards of perfection" evolved in the writings on "economics of socialism" offer no guidance in the effort to conquer backwardness, squalor, and oppression. "The advocacy of impossible changes is advocacy of no changes at all." The contribution that economic science can make to the solution of the problems of a planned economy is more likely to be found on the lines suggested by Wassily Leontief and "linear programming" than in the refinements of "optimum conditions" pertaining to an imaginary world. This contribution would be amply rewarded—by the continuous "feedback" linking realistic economics with the demands and issues of reality. What this implies, however, is that in a rationally organized society the economist of our days would be one of the "disguised unemployed" to be transferred to the position of "social engineer" helping to understand and to create the conditions for economic and social progress.

---

[27] An impressive testimonial of efficiency was the rapid conversion and reallocation of the Russian industry during the war, as well as its reconversion and growth during the postwar years. On the latter, cf. Abram Bergson, J. H. Blackman, and Alexander Erlich, "Postwar Economic Reconstruction and Development in the U.S.S.R.," *The Annals of the American Academy of Political and Social Science*, Vol. CCLXIV (May, 1949), p. 52 ff.; as well as the more recent statements on the "Results of the Fourth (Postwar) Five Year Plan," *New Times*, Vol. XVII (April 25, 1951 (Suppl.).

[28] *Soviet Economic Development*, p. 3.

2| THE RATE OF DEVELOPMENT OF INDUSTRY

Joseph Stalin

In the 1920's a great debate raged in the Soviet Union over the strategy of economic policy. It ended with the rise of Stalin as the dominant political figure and adoption of the program of maximizing industrial growth. In this selection, Stalin speaks about the goals of the first Five-Year Plans and presents their rationale. Three points should be particularly noted: (1) the effect of the USSR's international political position on the thinking of the leadership, (2) the problem of peasant agriculture (the decision to collectivize had not yet been made), and (3) the creation of "tension" in plans that would strain the economy's resources to the utmost.

Stalin presented these views in a speech on "Industrialization of the Country and the Right Deviation in the CPSU" at the Plenum (assembly) of the Central Committee of the Communist Party on November 19, 1928 as part of the discussion of goals of the first year of the First Five-Year Plan. It is reprinted from Joseph Stalin, *Works*, Vol. 11 (Moscow: Foreign Language Publishing House, 1964), pp. 256–266.

OUR THESES proceed from the premise that a fast rate of development of industry in general, and of the production of the means of production in particular, is the underlying principle of, and the key to, the industrialization of the country, the underlying principle of, and the key to, the transformation of our entire national economy along the lines of socialist development.

But what does a fast rate of development of industry involve? It involves the maximum capital investment in industry. And that leads to a state of tension in all our plans, budgetary and non-budgetary. And, indeed, the characteristic feature of our control figures in the past three years, in the period of reconstruction, is that they have been compiled and carried out at a high tension. Take our control figures, examine our budget estimates, talk with our Party comrades—both those who work in the Party organizations and those who direct our Soviet, economic and co-operative affairs—and you will invariably find this one characteristic feature everywhere, namely, the state of tension in our plans.

The question arises: is this state of tension in our plans really necessary for us? Cannot we do without it? Is it not possible to conduct the work at a slower pace, in a more "restful" atmosphere? Is not the fast rate of industrial development that we have adopted due to the restless character of the members of the Political Bureau and the Council of People's Commissars?

Of course not! The members of the Political Bureau and the Council of People's Commissars are calm and sober people. Abstractly speaking, that is, if we disregarded the external and internal situation, we could, of course, conduct the work at a slower speed. But the point is that, firstly, we cannot disregard the external and internal situation, and, secondly, if we take the surrounding situation as our starting-point, it has to be admitted that it is precisely this situation that dictates a fast rate of development of our industry.

Permit me to pass to an examination of this situation, of these conditions of an external and internal order that dictate a fast rate of industrial development.

External Conditions.   We have assumed power in a country whose technical equipment is terribly backward. Along with a few big industrial units more or less based upon modern technology, we have hundreds and thousands of mills and factories the technical equipment of which is beneath all criticism from the point of view of modern achievements. At the same time we have around us a number of capitalist countries whose industrial technique is far more developed and up-to-date than that of our country. Look at the capitalist countries and you will see that their technology is not only advancing, but advancing by leaps and bounds, outstripping the old forms of industrial technique. And so we find that, on the one hand, we in our country have the most advanced system, the Soviet system, and the most advanced type of state power in the world, Soviet power, while, on the other hand, our industry, which should be the basis of socialism and of Soviet power, is extremely backward technically. Do you think that we can achieve the final victory of socialism in our country so long as this contradiction exists?

What has to be done to end this contradiction? To end it, we must overtake and outstrip the advanced technology of the developed capitalist countries. We have overtaken and outstripped the advanced capitalist countries in the sense of establishing a new political system, the Soviet system. That is good. But it is not enough. In order to secure the final victory of socialism in our country, we must also overtake and outstrip these countries technically and economically. Either we do this, or we shall be forced to the wall.

This applies not only to the building of socialism. It applies also to upholding the independence of our country in the circumstances of the capitalist encirclement. The independence of our country cannot be upheld unless we have an adequate industrial basis for defense. And such an industrial basis cannot be created if our industry is not more highly developed technically.

That is why a fast rate of development of our industry is necessary and imperative.

The technical and economic backwardness of our country was not invented by us. This backwardness is age-old and was bequeathed to us by the whole history of our country. This backwardness was felt to be an evil both earlier, before the revolution, and later, after the revolution. When Peter the Great, having to deal with the more highly developed countries of the West, feverishly built mills and factories to supply the army and strengthen the country's defenses, that was in its way an attempt to break out of the grip of this backwardness. It is quite understandable, however, that none of the old classes, neither the feudal aristocracy nor the bourgeoisie, could solve the problem of putting an end to the backwardness of our country. More than that, not only were these classes unable to solve this problem, they were not even able to formulate the task in any satisfactory way. The age-old backwardness of our country can be ended only on the lines of successful socialist construction. And it can be ended only by the proletariat, which has established its dictatorship and has charge of the direction of the country.

It would be foolish to console ourselves with the thought that, since the backwardness of our country was not invented by us and was bequeathed to us by the whole history of our country, we cannot be, and do not have to be, responsible for it. That is not true, comrades. Since we have come to power and taken upon ourselves the task of transforming the country on the basis of socialism, we are responsible, and have to be responsible, for everything, the bad as well as the good. And just because we are responsible for everything, we must put an end to our technical and economic backwardness. We must do so without fail if we really want to overtake and outstrip the advanced capitalist countries. And only we Bolsheviks can do it. But precisely in order to accomplish this task, we must systematically achieve a fast rate of development of our industry. And that we are already achieving a fast rate of industrial development is now clear to everyone.

The question of overtaking and outstripping the advanced capitalist countries technically and economically is for us Bolsheviks neither new nor unexpected. It was raised in our country as early as in 1917, before the October Revolution. It was raised by Lenin as early as in September 1917, on the eve of the October Revolution, during the imperialist war, in his pamphlet *The Impending Catastrophe and How to Combat It*.

Here is what Lenin said on this score:

The result of the revolution has been that the *political* system of Russia has in a few months caught up with that of the advanced countries. But that is not enough. The war is inexorable; it puts the alternative with ruthless severity: either perish, or overtake and outstrip the advanced countries *economically as well.* . . . Perish or drive full-steam ahead. That is the alternative with which history has confronted us.

You see how bluntly Lenin put the question of ending our technical and economic backwardness.

Lenin wrote all this on the eve of the October Revolution, in the period before the proletariat had taken power, when the Bolsheviks had as yet neither state power, nor a socialized industry, nor a widely ramified cooperative network embracing millions of peasants, nor collective farms, nor state farms. Today, when we already have something substantial with which to end completely our technical and economic backwardness, we might paraphrase Lenin's words roughly as follows:

"We have overtaken and *outstripped* the advanced capitalist countries *politically* by establishing the dictatorship of the proletariat. But that is not enough. We must utilize the dictatorship of the proletariat, our socialised industry, transport, credit system, etc., the cooperatives, collective farms, state farms, etc., in order to overtake and *outstrip* the advanced capitalist countries *economically* as well."

The question of a fast rate of development of industry would not face us so acutely as it does now if we had such a highly developed industry and such a highly developed technology as Germany, say, and if the relative importance of industry in the entire national economy were as high in our country as it is in Germany, for example. *If that were the case,* we could develop our industry at a slower rate without fearing to fall behind the capitalist countries and knowing that we could outstrip them at one stroke. But then we should not be so seriously backward technically and economically as we are now. The whole point is that we are behind Germany in this respect and are still far from having overtaken her technically and economically.

The question of a fast rate of development of industry would not face us so acutely if we were not the *only* country but *one of the countries* of the dictatorship of the proletariat, if there were a proletarian dictatorship not only in our country but in other, more advanced countries as well, Germany and France, say.

If that were the case, the capitalist encirclement could not be so serious a danger as it is now, the question of the economic independence of our country would naturally recede into the background, we could integrate ourselves into the system of more developed proletarian states, we could receive from them machines for making our industry and agriculture more productive, supplying them in turn with raw materials and foodstuffs, and we could, consequently, expand our industry at a slower rate. But you know very well that that is not yet the case and that we are still the *only* country of the proletarian dictatorship and are surrounded by capitalist countries, many of which are far in advance of us technically and economically.

That is why Lenin raised the question of overtaking and outstripping the economically advanced countries as one of life and death for our development.

Such are the *external* conditions dictating a fast rate of development of our industry.

Internal Conditions. But besides the external conditions, there are also internal conditions which dictate a fast rate of development of our industry as the main foundation of our entire national economy. I am referring to the extreme backwardness of our agriculture, of its technical and cultural level. I am referring to the existence in our country of an overwhelming preponderance of small commodity producers, with their scattered and utterly backward production, compared with which our large-scale socialist industry is like an island in the midst of the sea, an island whose base is expanding daily, but which is nevertheless an island in the midst of the sea.

We are in the habit of saying that industry is the main foundation of our entire national economy, including agriculture, that it is the key to the reconstruction of our backward and scattered system of agriculture on a collectivist basis. That is perfectly true. From that position we must not retreat for a single moment. But it must also be remembered that, while industry is the main foundation, agriculture constitutes the basis for industrial development, both as a market which absorbs the products of industry and as a supplier of raw materials and foodstuffs, as well as a source of the export reserves essential in order to import machinery for the needs of our national economy. Can we advance industry while leaving agriculture in a state of complete technical backwardness, without providing an agricultural base for industry, without reconstructing agriculture and bringing it up to the level of industry? No, we cannot.

Hence the task of supplying agriculture with the maximum amount of instruments and means of production essential in order to accelerate and promote its reconstruction on a new technical basis. But for the accomplishment of this task a fast rate of development of our industry is necessary. Of course, the reconstruction of a disunited and scattered agriculture is an incomparably more difficult matter than the reconstruction of a united and centralized socialist industry. But that is the task that confronts us, and we must accomplish it. And it cannot be accomplished except by a fast rate of industrial development.

We cannot go on indefinitely, that is, for too long a period, basing the Soviet regime and socialist construction on two *different* foundations, the foundation of the most large-scale and united socialist industry and the foundation of the most scattered and backward, small commodity economy of the peasants. We must gradually, but systematically and persistently, place our agriculture on a new technical basis, the basis of large-scale production, and bring it up to the level of socialist industry. Either we accomplish this task—in which case the final victory of socialism in our country will be assured, or we turn away from it and do not accomplish it—in which case a return to capitalism may become inevitable.

Here is what Lenin says on this score:

> As long as we live in a small-peasant country, there is a surer economic basis for capitalism in Russia than for communism. This must be borne in mind. Anyone who has carefully observed life in the countryside, as compared with life in the towns, knows that we have not torn out the roots of capitalism and have not undermined the foundation, the basis of the internal enemy. The latter depends on small-scale production, and there is only one way of undermining it, namely, to place the economy of the country, including agriculture, on a new technical basis, the technical basis of modern large-scale production. And it is only electricity that is such a basis. Communism is Soviet power plus the electrification of the whole country.

As you see, when Lenin speaks of the electrification of the country he means not the isolated construction of individual power stations, but the gradual "placing of the economy of the country, *including agriculture,** on a new technical basis, the technical basis of modern large-scale production," which in one way or another, directly or indirectly, is connected with electrification.

Lenin delivered this speech at the Eighth Congress of Soviets in December 1920, on the very eve of the introduction of NEP, when he was substantiating the so-called plan of electrification, that is, the GOELRO plan. Some comrades argue on these grounds that the views expressed in this quotation have become inapplicable under present conditions. Why, we ask? Because, they say, much water has flown under the bridges since then. It is, of course, true that much water has flown under the bridges since then. We now have a developed socialist industry, we have collective farms on a mass scale, we have old and new state farms, we have a wide network of well-developed cooperative organizations, we have machine-hiring stations at the service of the peasant farms, we now practice the contract system as a new form of the bond, and we can put into operation all these and a number of other levers for gradually placing agriculture on a new technical basis. All this is true. But it is also true that, in spite of all this, we are still a small-peasant country where small-scale production predominates. And that is the fundamental thing. And as long as it continues to be the fundamental thing, Lenin's thesis remains valid that "as long as we live in a small-peasant country, there is a surer economic basis for capitalism in Russia than for communism," and that,

---

* My italics.—*J. St.*

consequently, the danger of the restoration of capitalism is no empty phrase.

Lenin says the same thing, but in a sharper form, in the plan of his pamphlet, *The Tax in Kind,* which was written *after* the introduction of NEP (March–April 1921):

If we have electrification in 10–20 years, then the individualism of the small tiller, and freedom *for him* to trade locally are not a whit terrible. *If* we do not have electrification, a return to capitalism will be inevitable *anyhow.*

And further on he says:

Ten or twenty years of correct relations with the peasantry, and victory on a world scale is assured (even if the proletarian revolutions, which are growing, are delayed); otherwise, 20–40 years of the torments of whiteguard terrorism.

You see how bluntly Lenin puts the question: either electrification, that is, the "placing of the economy of the country, including agriculture, on a new technical basis, the technical basis of modern large-scale production," or a return to capitalism.

That is how Lenin understood the question of "correct relations with the peasantry."

It is not a matter of coddling the peasant and regarding this as establishing correct relations with him, for coddling will not carry you very far. It is a matter of helping the peasant to place his husbandry "on a new technical basis, the technical basis of modern large-scale production"; for that is the principal way to rid the peasant of his poverty.

And it is impossible to place the economy of the country on a new technical basis unless our industry and, in the first place, the production of means of production, are developed at a fast rate.

Such are the internal conditions dictating a fast rate of development of our industry.

It is these external and internal conditions which are the cause of the control figures of our national economy being under such tension.

That explains, too, why our economic plans, both budgetary and non-budgetary, are marked by a state of tension, by substantial investments in capital development, the object of which is to maintain a fast rate of industrial development.

3| HOW DOES THE SOVIET ECONOMY FUNCTION WITHOUT A FREE MARKET?

Z. M. Fallenbuchl

Americans are so familiar with the functioning of our market economy that we find it hard to understand how any other system might work effectively. The tendency of a market economy, operating through the motive of profit maximization by producers, to produce the commodities demanded by consumers, has an internal logic which has been recognized for centuries. Yet this "consumers' sovereignty" has been replaced by a "planners' sovereignty" in the Soviet Union.

The following article explains how the Soviet system has been made to work through a series of interrelated policy decisions on the part of the planners, without relying extensively on the market mechanism as a means of making basic economic decisions. The author is Professor of Economics at the University of Windsor (Canada). The article is reprinted with permission from *Queens Quarterly*, Vol. LXX, No. 4 (Winter, 1964), pp. 559–75.

IN A FREE enterprise economy the basic economic problems of what to produce, how to produce, and for whom to produce are decided through the operation of a market. In the Soviet-type economy these problems are solved through a combination of administrative commands, and market forces which are allowed to operate within certain limits in respect of some economic activities.

Administrative commands can effectively be applied because the state and the party exercise an enormous degree of control over the economy. This control is based on the three main institutional features of the system.

There is, first of all, the totalitarian political power and the state monopoly of information and education which give the leaders a considerably greater freedom of decision than that which would ever be possible under political democracy, at least in peace time.

Another feature is the state ownership of the great majority of the means of production. The state sector is responsible for about 92 percent of the gross value of industrial output. All of the land is owned by the state and 16 percent of the total area under cultivation belongs to state farms while over 80 percent of the area is allocated to collective farms over which the state has complete control. In addition, the government has at its disposal nationalized banking and finance, transportation, the monopoly of international trade, domestic wholesale trade, and over 90 percent of the retail outlets.

The third feature of the system is centralized planning with economic plans which are enacted as law and which are therefore backed by legal sanctions, supplemented by various kinds of administrative pressures and numerous economic and non-economic incentives.

This institutional framework enables the leaders to make some basic economic decisions in accordance with their own scales of preferences and to ignore, up to a certain point, the preferences of the consumers. It is impossible to understand the working of the Soviet economy without realizing that dictatorial objectives are the dominant force determining the direction of a great deal of economic activity.

However, not even the most autocratic leaders and the best planners can solve millions of detailed economic problems in a completely centralized way. Moreover, an excessive centralization and bureaucratization have serious drawbacks. The maintenance of an extensive bureaucratic machine is expensive, rigidity and inertia tend to develop, and economic efficiency of the system declines. Hence the perennial dilemma of the Soviet economic organization: how to decentralize some economic activities without losing the control over the economy and the possibility of central planning.

Some decentralization on a regional basis was introduced by the industrial reorganization of 1957 but the majority of basic economic decisions are still highly centralized. It is possible that Professor G. Grossman is correct in saying in *Value and Plan* that "from the regime's point of view the feasibility of any further overall decentralization in economic affairs rests largely on the degree of spontaneous and complete commitment to the official values on the part of the executants or, in Soviet parlance, on state discipline." On the other hand, one can expect that with the improvement of the system of material incentives and the development of more sophisticated planning methods a greater degree of decentralization will be possible.*

CONSUMER CHOICE

The communists have rejected consumers' sovereignty but they have left consumers with some degree of free choice in the market for consumption goods. Contrary to the early communist dreams, the consumers

---

* Editors' note: These possibilities are discussed below in Selections 18–22.

receive their incomes not in the form of allocation of various consumption goods but in money form. They are free to decide what they want to buy within the limits imposed by the existing quantities of commodities which have been produced in accordance with the planners' decisions.

Two problems are involved here. The first is the maintenance of an overall balance between the effective demand of the population, i.e., the sum of personal incomes which are likely to be spent on consumption, and the aggregate supply of consumption goods available. Any discrepancy between the two can be eliminated by adjustments in the general price level which can easily be effected by changes in the rates of the sales tax, in the total wage bill, or in the aggregate supply of consumption goods, if the authorities are prepared to do it.

The second problem is that of maintaining balance between demand for and supply of particular commodities. If there are discrepancies, then adjustments in relative prices, changes in the production plans, and, in the case of some serious shortages, rationing can be introduced.

Although the consumers are free to choose among the produced consumption goods, they have only a very limited opportunity to influence the production pattern, which is mainly determined by the planners. The planners decide whether or not the consumers should have more textiles or electrical appliances, for example. They can assess the strength of demand on the basis of changes in the stocks of particular commodities and they can order changes in the production plans, but the process is lengthy and clumsy. The managers of the state enterprises can possibly adjust the product mix, but the system by which demand is transmitted to the producers is very inadequate. Not only has the wholesale trade organization no material incentive to effect the required adjustments, but even if it would report the pattern of demand, the state enterprises have usually no material incentive to make changes in the product mix which would lead to an underfulfillment of the gross output plan or, at least, to additional efforts and complications.

How is it possible for the Soviet planners to leave the freedom of choice to consumers and, at the same time, to deny them the power to decide the pattern of production?

The answer can be found in the maintenance of a permanent state of full employment on the one hand and the ability to control inflation on the other. In all communist countries the leaders try to achieve the fastest possible economic growth by directing a huge proportion of resources to investment while, at the same time, they tend to increase "communal consumption" (education, health, social welfare, entertainment, public administration) and to maintain a high level of defense expenditures. As a result of this policy, there is a chronic shortage of producers goods in relation to the amounts which are needed. The producers goods industries have permanently more than sufficient demand for their output.

A relatively small proportion of resources is left for consumption and this relative shortage creates sellers' market conditions. Under these conditions the possibility of insufficiency of the overall effective demand for consumption goods is eliminated, and the maintenance of balance is reduced to guarding against inflation, i.e., an excess effective demand in relation to the aggregate supply of consumption goods. The problem is not how to stimulate effective demand but how to reduce it without reducing the output of capital goods by not providing incentives to work in the form of satisfactory wages and the ability to spend them on consumption goods.

The existence of the sellers' market makes it easy to sell anything which has been produced, and the planners do not have to fear any serious overproduction of individual commodities. Although cases of the overproduction of some particular commodities have occurred from time to time in the Soviet Union, and other communist countries, so far these cases have been relatively insignificant under the conditions of general scarcity.

The degree of scarcity has now slowly been reduced, but so long as the communist countries maintain their determination to achieve highest possible rates of growth, to have a relatively large proportion of total consumption in the communal form and to spend a large proportion of their national income on armaments, space programs, and similar types of expenditures, the planning of the production of consumption goods will remain relatively easy.

It is only when there is a saturation of the market with consumption goods that the planners have to take fully into consideration consumers' tastes to avoid both an overall relative overproduction and unsold quantities of some particular commodities. But as soon as the planners start to consult the consumer, the plans are likely to be upset by unexpected changes in demand. The planners have to depend then on estimates of the future changes in demand. Mistakes are possible and the economy may find itself with an overcapacity in one industry and an undercapacity in another.

One can venture a hypothesis that two alternative situations are possible in the future. One is that the West will be faced with a more or less permanent cold war, peaceful or less peaceful competition, and a gigantic Soviet space program. The second alternative is that, if political changes in the Soviet Union induce a transfer to a mass consumption economy in that country, the Soviet economy will experience oscillations and disturbances not unlike those known in the West, although perhaps somewhat more moderate in the absence of other sources of instability which are present in a free enterprise economy.

The policy of over-committing the resources eliminates the danger of insufficiency of aggregate demand and reduces the importance of overproduction of particular commodities, but it also has its disadvantages.

First of all, it implies a relatively low standard of living. It creates inconvenience for the consumers who are faced with various shortages, delays, and difficulties. In addition to these there are also some serious dangers involved.

Although the danger of balance of payments difficulties which is usually associated with such conditions is not great in the case of the Soviet Union because of its self-sufficiency and the state monopoly of international trade, the danger of inflation is always present. There have been periods of open inflation in the Soviet Union and other communist countries, but as the planners have some effective means to fight inflation, it is a suppressed inflation rather than an open inflation which is more typical for the Soviet-type economy. The anti-inflationary means include a complete control over almost all prices and a high degree of control over wages. The danger of a cost-pushed inflation is therefore relatively unimportant. As a British economist, A. K. Cairncross, has observed, "the Soviet authorities can afford to ignore the side of wages as opposed to the side of demand. They can, therefore, allow demand to press supply to a degree that would be highly explosive in this country (i.e., Britain) except perhaps in war-time."

The existence of suppressed inflation is, however, responsible for a number of inefficiencies. It leads to hoarding of machines and raw materials by state enterprises, to a deterioration in the quality of both consumers' and producers' goods, to bottlenecks and interruptions in the productive process, and to the "take it or leave it" mentality in the distribution process.

PLANNING

The communists have rejected not only consumers' sovereignty but also the maximization of consumers' satisfaction (at least the present consumers' satisfaction) as guiding principles for the planners, and they have rejected maximization of profits as a guiding principle for productive enterprises.

Stalin in his last work on economics referred to the "highest form of lasting and permanent profitability" which replaced profitability of individual enterprises. This concept, which has not been denounced by his successors until now, stresses that planning of production and investment should be based on long-run macroeconomic considerations instead of short-run microeconomic ones or, as Stalin has expressed it, "profitability is seen not from the point of view of individual enterprises or branches of production, and not in the context of a single year, but from the point of view of the whole national economy and in the context of, say, 10–15 years . . ."

Instead, planning is based on some general decisions as to the rate of growth of the economy as a whole and its structure, as well as various political, military, and other non-economic considerations.

These decisions are expressed in general directives and tentative long-run targets which form a part of the Party program. On this basis the general plans are constructed, representing a fairly detailed, and integrated list of output targets, and the investment program to create the productive capacity necessary for the achievement of these targets.

Since 1928, when the planning era began, there have been seven such plans. Six of them were of five years duration and the most recent one covers the period of seven years. Four five-year plans were completed: the first (in four years), second, fourth and fifth. The third plan was interrupted by the Second World War and the sixth was abandoned in 1958 and replaced by the seven-year plan.

The operational orders are prepared in the form of annual, quarterly, and monthly plans, which represent subdivisions of the five- or seven-year plans with such changes as may be necessary to improve planning. These short-run plans attempt to coordinate the production process in various sectors of the economy. They are very detailed and their preparation has sometimes been delayed with the result that enterprises were given their production plans and allocation of inputs after the beginning of the planning period.

The method which is used in the preparation of the plans is the so-called "planning by material balances"—a crude input-output process expressed mainly in physical terms.

Because of the enormous practical difficulty of considering all interrelationships within the economy, the planners' approach has been, until now, to concentrate on certain key branches of material production which are selected by the Party leaders as the priority branches. The whole plan is built around output goals and investment projects in these key branches. The other branches of the economy are developed only to the extent which is required in order to achieve the main goals. This approach was recommended by Lenin who called it the principle of "decisive links." It simplifies planning and makes sure that the most important goals are achieved. Whenever their implementation requires more resources than have been planned for, the low-priority sectors are sacrificed. At the same time when plans were fulfilled, or even over-fulfilled in heavy industry, such branches of the economy as agriculture, housing and light industry were seldom able to fulfill their plans, although these plans were usually less ambitious than those for the high-priority branches of the economy.

In this way some serious errors in planning were often cushioned by the existence of such non-priority branches and this seems to be the main reason why relatively unsophisticated methods are sufficient to enable the economy to function.

As a result, the Soviet economy has been developing through a series of leaps forward with successive concentration of the main efforts on some particular sectors, maintaining always, however, the priority of the production of producers' goods, and eliminating successive bottlenecks. The process has been very uneven and wasteful, but it has worked, and it resulted in very high rates of growth.

The following description of Soviet pre-war planning by a Polish Marxist, Professor O. Lange, explains very well the nature of the process which has not changed since.

The Soviet economy was planned not for the harmony of the different branches, but for one single purpose, namely the most rapid industrialization and preparation of effective national defense . . . The fact that over-fulfillment of the production plans is regarded as a virtue, instead of an upsetting of the general economic plan, shows clearly that Soviet economic planning did not serve the objectives of a harmonious socialist welfare economy, but served political and military objectives to which all other aspects of economic planning were sacrificed.[1]

The Soviet economy is often referred to as "a war economy" because of this concentration on a few major goals, breaking of successive bottlenecks, general scarcity, and the mobilization of all efforts and resources irrespective of costs. Just as it happens during a war in any country, decisions of central authorities in respect of major goals and corresponding resource allocation are decisive throughout the whole economy.

This type of economic system is well adapted to achieve the selected goals but it cannot usually secure economic efficiency. In other words, it can solve the problem of "what to produce" in accordance with the planners' scale of preferences but it is not completely successful in solving the problem of "how to produce" the required product mix.

INCENTIVES

Whereas prices of consumption goods are usually adjusted to eliminate discrepancies between demand and supply, prices of producers' goods are used as accounting prices and as indicators of the planners' wishes as to the use of inputs by the state enterprises. In this way the planners can induce the solution of the problem of "how to produce." Prices are utilized, for example, to spread new technology, to economize scarce raw materials or even simply to cover the costs of inefficient plants.

As it is impossible for the central planning office to specify all details concerning the desired assortment and methods of production, a certain number of decisions have to be left to the management of the productive enterprises.

---

[1] O. Lange, "The Working Principles of the Soviet Economy," *The USSR Economy and the War* (New York, 1943), p. 43.

The manager's first duty is to maximize gross value of output and also to fulfill other tasks specified by the plan, such as, for example, reduction of costs, increase in labor productivity, and others. There is a whole system of material incentives, the purpose of which is to induce enterprises to conform to the plan.

Piece rates and bonuses are used to induce greater efforts by workers. A certain percentage of planned and a somewhat higher percentage of extra profits are left within the enterprise in the form of the so-called "enterprise fund," while enterprises expected to make losses receive part of any saving resulting from the reduction in the planned loss. This fund can be used in part for small investments within the enterprise, improvements in working conditions, housing and amenities, and in part for the payment of bonuses. It was, however, one of the findings of Professor J. S. Berliner in his study of informal organization of the Soviet firm, that "profits play a rather secondary role as incentive to Soviet plant management." Fulfillment of the planned profit target, which is fixed as the residual between the planned value of sales and planned costs of production, is only one of the several criteria according to which the performance of the firm and its manager is assessed. The other "quantitative indices," like volume of output and total wage bill, and "qualitative indices," like reduction in costs and increase in labor productivity, are equally or even more important.

For the achievement of planned tasks and, above all, for the fulfillment of output plans, managers receive bonuses which form a considerable proportion of their total incomes. In addition to material incentives there are a number of non-economic incentives and administrative pressures.

Evaluating the effects of the existing system of incentives, Berliner concludes that it "has created a corps of managers dedicated to their work and responsive to the production demands made upon them" by the planners, but that at the same time certain features of the system are "directly responsible for motivating management to make a variety of decisions contrary to the intent and the interest of the state."

Together with excessively high targets and general full employment conditions, the system induces some undesirable changes in the product mix (for example, when the target is expressed in tons there is a tendency to produce a heavier product), the concealment of the real productive capacity of enterprises (to make the fulfillment of high targets easier), and the falsification of reports and the deterioration of quality.

The system, as it exists now, tends to encourage the largest possible output but it does not provide a sufficient inducement to ensure the most efficient ways of producing this output.

In a free enterprise economy a product which is better from the users' point of view will sell at a higher price and will bring a higher profit to the enterprise, encouraging in this way production of this product. In the Soviet-type economy the preferences of the users of producers' goods will not be transmitted through the price mechanism to the producer. As a result, the users have often to produce with equipment and raw materials which may not be the best from the users' point of view but which bring the highest bonus to the enterprises producing them. This practice obviously has an adverse effect on the efficiency of the enterprises using this equipment and raw materials.

The system also induces waste of raw materials. When, for example, the enterprises producing a variety of products have their plan targets expressed in value terms, the incentive system works in such a way as to induce the use of more expensive materials as the cost, plus a fixed margin of planned profit, will add up to a higher price in this case and will automatically increase the value of production, thus helping fulfill the plan.

The induced changes in the product mix may lead to shortages of some types of producers' goods. The following description of the situation by a Polish economist explains this effect of the bonus system:

The plan must not only be fulfilled, but it must even be surpassed . . . In such a case the plan, and not production, becomes the aim of the enterprise. The management makes great efforts in order to reach 100 percent of the plan, or even 103 percent (a greater excess does not bring a bonus and it leads to an increased target in the future . . .). This system is responsible for a situation where everybody has fulfilled the plan, but there is a shortage of those goods which were planned. Some goods . . . have been produced in excess . . . whereas other goods are missing, creating slowing down effects in many interrelated branches of the economy or making satisfaction of many urgent needs impossible.

Another illustration may be quoted from the experience of East Germany:

In spite of overfulfillment of the plan, in spite of an increase of production by a fifth, there is much that is not in order. Neither the plan of final production nor of the production of spare parts was fulfilled either in timing or as to assortment. What good is it if an additional D.M. 5 million worth of more spare parts is produced but not in the desired assortment?[2]

The communist leaders are now aware of the problem and economists are discussing the ways in which the system could be made more efficient. At least some economists are sceptical whether any solution other than introduction of the principle of profitability will give the required results.

The distortion of the price mechanism is another factor which tends to reduce efficiency of production. As prices of producers' goods are fixed at artificially low levels, they do not reflect real costs of production of these goods and they do not induce their economical use. There is no reason, for example, why an enterprise should increase its labor costs in order to eliminate a wasteful use of a particular raw material which is inexpensive

---

[2] W. F. Stolper, *The Structure of the East German Economy* (Cambridge, Mass.: Harvard University Press, 1960), p. 7.

from the enterprise's point of view, although it may be expensive to produce.

Also the differentials between prices of various producers' goods do not reflect their relative scarcities. In the absence of the market for producers' goods, and because prices of these goods have been often used to achieve various goals, the price system in the Soviet Union and other communist countries cannot be used as a guiding device for efficient allocation of resources.

The distortion of the price system is now officially recognized as a great obstacle to efficient planning and it has been admitted that "an improvement in price formation is of great importance."

Some other factors adversely affecting efficiency of production are the practice of allocating funds for fixed and, partly, for working capital of enterprises in the form of free grants, limiting the use of the rate of interest to relatively unimportant bank loans and even less important private savings, fixing low depreciation reserves, and not utilizing the concept of land rent.

Especially difficult under these conditions is the choice among alternative investment projects, and among different methods of production, as well as replacement of old machines and equipment by new. For this reason, these problems have been discussed in the Soviet Union and other communist countries for years. The great debate concerning the methods of calculation of the economic efficiency of investment started in the late 1940's and despite a mass of articles, numerous conferences, and the publishing of several official instructions, it has not resulted in finding a completely satisfactory solution. A planning device similar to the rate of interest has finally been introduced, although this interest is not actually charged to the enterprises, and some further improvements in investment planning will probably be introduced in the future.

Although some serious mistakes have been made in the field of investment planning, the importance of the inefficiency of the system should not be overestimated. The Soviet economy has not been fully efficient, but it works and it has been able to produce very high rates of growth. One can only speculate that with improved efficiency these rates would have been even greater.

INCOME DISTRIBUTION

The problem of "for whom the economy produces" is again solved mainly by leaders' decisions in accordance with what they believe is in the interest of the nation and partly by market forces operating within certain limits.

The division of national income into accumulation fund and consumption fund is basically a political decision in the Soviet-type economy, although a number of important economic factors have to be taken into consideration.[3] This division determines how big a proportion of the annual total production is used for current needs and how much will be devoted for the expansion of the total product in the future.

The accumulation fund is, in turn, divided into (a) investment in the so-called "productive sphere" (i.e., funds for the expansion of productive capacity in industry, agriculture, and transportation), (b) investment in the "unproductive sphere" (funds for the expansion of building and equipment in connection with education, health, social welfare, research, the arts), and (c) the state reserves.

The consumption fund is divided into (a) the wage fund of those employed in material production, (b) current expenses on education, health, art, and similar activities, (c) the social insurance fund (pensions, benefits etc.), and (d) the state administration fund.

The decisions concerning the division of the consumption fund determine the proportions of the total product which are produced for those who work in the "productive sphere," those who are employed in the "unproductive sphere," and that which is used by the state for its administrative expenses.

Within the "productive sphere" the distribution of income among the state sector, collective sector, and a rather insignificant private sector, composed mainly of private plots of collective farmers, some craftsmen and professional people, is effected through budgetary grants and loans, the manipulation of prices, the rates of turnover tax, and deductions from profits. In this way, considerable funds have been transferred from collective farmers to the state industry and from light industry to heavy industry.

The distribution of income among members of the industrial labor force depends on the wage scale, which is sharply differentiated in accordance with the relative scarcity of a particular skill, the importance of an industry (the high priority industries have higher wage scales than the low priority industries), and the geographical area (higher wages are paid in remote areas).

In agriculture, workers employed by the state farms receive wages based on the same principle as industrial wages, while members of collective farms receive their remuneration in accordance with the nature of the work, which determines the allocation of work-day units.

Although the general level of wages and wage differentials are determined by the central authorities, a certain flexibility exists in practice.

Under the 1940 decrees, unauthorized leaving of a job, as well as absenteeism or lateness, were treated as criminal offenses punishable by imprisonment, forced labor, or fines. These decrees were not, however,

---

[3] Z. M. Fallenbuchl, "Investment Policy for Economic Development: Some Lessons of the Communist Experience," *The Canadian Journal of Economics and Political Science* (February 1963).

applied in practice after 1953 and they were cancelled in 1956. At present the labor market is free in the sense that people can move to enterprises which offer higher wages. There is a penalty, however, if someone leaves his job and does not take another one within a month. Labor does not have the right to strike or to collective bargaining for wage increases.

Market forces operate in reality in a stronger way than it would appear on the basis of the study of existing regulations. In various ways managers are able to compete for better workers or scarce skills by offering higher wages than the official rates. This is often done by reclassifying upward a particular worker or by manipulation with bonuses and piecework arrangements. There exists, therefore, a discrepancy between official and actual rates.

The labor market is, however, highly imperfect. There is usually only very limited knowledge of existing openings elsewhere. Geographical mobility is limited by housing shortages, the rigid system of housing allocation, and administrative restrictions imposed on moving to some areas. In addition, moving is complicated by the fact that usually more than one member of the family is working.

As a result of the imperfections of the market, workers with exactly the same skill have different wage rates in different industries, different geographical areas, or even within the same industry and within the same area.

CONCLUSIONS

Summarizing, we may say that the decisions of the central authorities determine, to a considerable extent, the solution of what? how? and for whom? These decisions are mainly enforced by direct controls, but market forces are also utilized in some areas to strengthen these orders or, sometimes, to replace them. In some cases market forces act, however, against the wish of the planners and create undesirable results.

On the whole the Soviet-type economy can solve the problem of "what to produce" rather well in the sense that it secures the priority of the production of producers' goods and high rates of growth. It makes possible the concentration of huge resources on some selected goals and, in general, the required composition of output is produced, although some distortions of the product mix of both consumption and producers' goods tend to occur.

The solution of the problem of "how to produce" seems to be much less satisfactory. The system involves considerable waste and inefficiency, some of which will, no doubt, be eliminated in the future with a further improvement in planning methods, decentralization of economic administration, and introduction of a better system of material incentives.

The problem of "for whom the system produces" is solved well in the sense that the state can secure for investment, communal consumption, public administration, and defense a very high proportion of national income. It does not seem to secure to labor, however, that part of the value of the total product which labor contributes and it does not always secure equal pay for equal skill and equal effort.

As quite a lot has been said about the defects of the system, wastes and inefficiencies, it is perhaps necessary to comment on how, despite all these drawbacks, the Soviet economy has been able to achieve such high rates of growth, and spectacular scientific and technological achievements.

The main reason for fast Soviet economic growth is the channeling of as large a part of income as possible into productive capital investment. This is the result of an ability to reduce consumption to an extent which would not be possible under a democratic political system. Until now the Soviet Union has also been able to borrow foreign technology from the more advanced countries, at least in the majority of fields. The natural possibilities of the country have also to be taken into consideration. Russian rates of growth at the end of the 19th century and the beginning of the 20th century were also very high. Perhaps the most important factor is, however, a firm determination to catch and surpass the capitalist countries and to enforce fast economic growth, whatever the cost in terms of human suffering and economic waste.

The well known scientific and technological achievements can, similarly, be explained by the determination of the government and the possibility of concentrating huge resources in this field, refusing at the same time any more significant improvement in consumption. The level of technology is extremely uneven in the Soviet Union. While in some high-priority sectors the most advanced technology, sometimes the best in the world, is used, the majority of non-priority sectors are very backward. The Soviet Union leads in the space program and, at the same time, very primitive methods are used, for example, in building-construction. It is pioneering in space travel and, at the same time, it has an extremely poor road system.

In conclusion it can be said that with time the impact of factors adversely affecting efficiency will probably tend to decline, although certain features of the system make improvement difficult. On the other hand, it may not be possible to maintain present high rates of accumulation and the present pattern of investment allocation with the increasing maturity of the country and political pressure for a higher standard of living.

What the net result of these two forces will be is difficult to foresee. Although there are some grounds for expecting that Soviet rates of growth will perhaps be lower in the future than in the past, they will still remain relatively high.

II
HOW THE SOVIET
ECONOMY OPERATES

In a capitalist economy such as that of the United States, prices guide economic activity in response to market forces. "Economic planning" in such a system plays only a supplementary role, taking the form of government efforts to stabilize the level of national income, employment, and the price level; to develop less developed areas; to promote economic growth; and to modify income distribution. To accomplish these objectives, the government relies primarily on instruments of monetary and fiscal policy. Planning therefore tends to be partial, aggregative, and indirect.

In contrast, in the Soviet socialist economy planning is comprehensive, highly detailed, and direct. The government owns the means of production and closely controls almost all aspects of economic activity. Economic plans are supposed to achieve the goals of the Communist leadership and are executed primarily through administrative "commands" such as output quotas, input norms, and allocation orders. Prices, markets, and the financial system play important but supporting roles, assisting in the implementation of the plan.

The articles in Part II were selected to provide insights into Soviet planning and its problems that go beyond the usual textbook treatment. The first three deal with the system of administrative planning. Other articles deal with prices in the Soviet economy, the financial system, management of enterprises, labor, agriculture, and foreign trade. The themes that run through these articles are the combination of "command" and "market" factors in Soviet planning and the ways in which the planning system seeks practical solutions to the basic economic problems.

4| ECONOMIC PLANNING IN THE USSR

R. W. Davies

Comprehensive central planning and administrative control were adopted in the USSR in the late 1920's to mobilize resources for rapid industrialization. The planning process embraced the allocation of material inputs and outputs, the regulation of money flows, and the use of the labor force. While these methods worked imperfectly, they did succeed in achieving some of the main objectives of the Soviet regime. However, after the death of Stalin in 1953, it became increasingly evident to the Soviet leadership, as well as to Soviet economists and administrators, that this "mobilization" model was less suitable for the more "mature" contemporary Soviet economy. In an attempt to adapt the economy to meet its current problems, the Soviet government has altered resource allocation, economic organization, and planning techniques. Economic reformers have advocated even more drastic changes, but there are a number of obstacles to further improvements in Soviet economic planning and management.

This selection provides a critical historical survey of the evolution of Soviet planning. It explains why comprehensive planning was adopted, the forms it took, and its advantages and disadvantages. It shows why the "Stalinist model" had to be modified and discusses the changes adopted. It concludes with a discussion of factors affecting the future development of Soviet economic planning.

R. W. Davies is Professor and Director of the Centre for Russian and East European Studies at the University of Birmingham, England. The selection, which is reprinted by permission, was originally published as "The Soviet Planning Process for Rapid Industrialization," *Economics of Planning,* Vol. 6 (1966), No. 1, pp. 53–67, and "Planning a Mature Economy in the USSR," *Economics of Planning,* Vol. 6, (1966), No. 2, pp. 138–52.

THE SOVIET PLANNING PROCESS FOR RAPID INDUSTRIALIZATION

An Outline of the System

THE SOVIET government set itself the objective of a more rapid rate of industrialization, with a greater investment in capital-consuming industries and processes, than could be achieved within the framework of the market economy of the 1920's. The main objective was achieved, but with a much slower increase in living standards (consumer goods, agricultural output) than had been intended. To enforce its priorities, the Soviet government abandoned the major assumptions of its earlier policy:

1. A market relationship with the peasant was replaced by administrative or coercive control over his output. The centers of economic and political resistance in the rural commune were destroyed, and hundreds of thousands of *kulak* families were expelled from their home villages. Twenty-five million individual peasant farms were combined into 250,000 collective farms (*kolkhozy*), one or several to each village. The old boundaries and strips were destroyed, and most land and cattle were pooled and worked in common. Agricultural machinery was gradually made available from several thousand state-owned Machine and Tractor Stations (MTS). The *kolkhoz* was required to supply a substantial part of its output to the state collection agencies at low fixed prices in the form of compulsory deliveries. These supplies were then used by the state (*a*) to make available a minimum amount of foodstuffs to the growing urban population, and (*b*) for export. Exports of grain fell from 9 million tons in 1913 to 2 million tons in 1926–27 and 178 thousand tons in 1929; they rose (temporarily) to 4.8 million tons in 1930 and 5.1 million tons in 1931, and this increase was used to pay for imports of equipment and industrial materials. . . .

2. Inflation was permitted to develop: The wages of the expanding industrial and building labor force were partly met by increasing the flow of paper money. Prices began to rise, but the inflation was partly repressed through price control in both the producer goods market and the retail market (private shops and trading agencies were taken over by the state to facilitate this). For several years (1929–35) a rationing system was introduced in the towns, supplemented by state sales of goods above the ration at high prices. In this way, the available supply of consumer goods and foodstuffs was distributed over the old and the new urban population, and consumption per head in the towns was forced down. This was then an extreme form of the "regime of economy."

3. Within industry, the system of physical controls which had already existed during the 1920's was greatly extended. Prices were fixed, and there was no market for producer goods; instead, materials and equipment were distributed to existing factories and new building sites through a system of priorities, which enabled new key factories to be built and bottlenecks in existing industries to be widened. The plan set targets for the output of major intermediate and final products, and the physical allocation system was designed to see these were reached.

To sum up these first three points: the policy of 1928–32 enabled a new allocation of GNP to be imposed on the economy. The discussions of the 1920's had assumed that savings would be made by the state within the framework of a dynamic equilibrium on the market between agriculture and industry. This placed a constraint on the proportion of GNP which could be invested, and on the allocation of that investment (investment in consumer goods industries would need to be sufficient to enable the output of consumer goods to increase at the rate required for equilibrium). Now this constraint was removed; urban and rural living standards could be temporarily depressed, and physical controls used to divert resources to the establishment of new capital-intensive industries and techniques which gave no return during the construction period and were relatively costly in the medium-term. This method of obtaining forced savings through physical controls resembled the wartime planning controls used in capitalist economies to shift resources towards the end product of the armament and maintenance of the large armed forces. In the Soviet case, the end product was the capital goods industries and the maintenance of the workers employed in building and operating them. But in both cases a shift in the allocation of resources which could not easily be achieved through manipulating the market mechanism was achieved through direct controls.

4. However, the system was not one simply of physical controls. Within a few years, the following features, stable over a long period, supplemented the system so far described:

a) Each peasant household was permitted to work a private plot and to own its own cow and poultry. After obligations to the state had been met, the separate households and the *kolkhoz* as a unit were permitted to sell their produce on the free market ("collective farm market"), on which prices were reached by supply and demand. Here an important part of all marketed foodstuffs was bought and sold.

b) With some important exceptions, the employee was free to change his job. A market for labor existed, if a very imperfect one, and wage levels were formed partly in response to supply and demand. A corollary of this was that cost controls and profit-and-loss accounting were introduced in industry to supplement the physical controls.

c) Rationing of consumer goods was abolished, and an attempt was made to balance supply and demand on the consumer market, as a whole and for individual goods, through fiscal measures, notably a purchase tax (the "turnover tax") differentiated according to commodity.

5. A large variety of unplanned and even illegal activities between firms supplemented and made feasible the rather crude controls of the central plan and must be considered as part of the logic of the system.

The Planning Process

We have so far established that Soviet plan controls may be divided schematically as in Figure 1. Each enterprise receives a set of output targets and input allocations with which to fulfill them; at the same time its monetary expenditures are controlled by financial or cost plans, which are less important to it than its output plan, but which come into operation if the pressure from above for higher output leads the enterprise to increase its money expenditures excessively.

FIGURE 1

Principal Planning Controls Over Industrial Activity

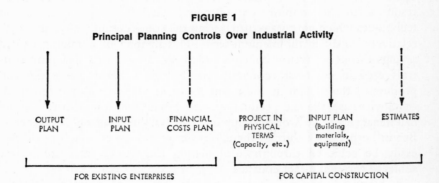

Disaggregation. A key problem for the central planners is to disaggregate their major decisions so that they will be enforced at the plant level and to aggregate information and proposals so as to be able satisfactorily to take into account the effect of their past and present decisions on different parts of the economy. In Soviet planning, this has normally been dealt with in the following ways:

1. Economic organization is adapted to handle this problem.

   a) Factories are placed under the control of ministries or subministries, each of which is responsible for a particular group of products (e.g., iron and steel, motor vehicles). Each ministry is given very considerable control over its enterprises. The government is therefore to a considerable extent concerned only with handling transfers *between* industries.

   b) Smaller factories producing low priority items are placed under the control of the government of one of the constituent republics, or under local authorities. In the past, the government tended not to bother with them, and to treat allocations to them as a residual.

   c) Within the State Planning Committee (Gosplan), which is an advisory body to the government, and within each ministry or subministry, departmental organization mirrors the planning arrangements. In the iron and steel industry, for example, there are separate departments of the ministry responsible for sales of the industry's product, for supplies to the industry, for production plans of iron and steel works, and for capital construction. Within Gosplan, there are separate departments concerned with production, alloca-

FIGURE 2

Central Economic Administration

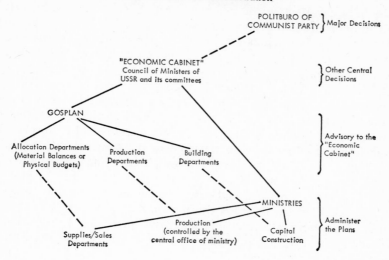

tion, and construction. This is illustrated schematically in Figure 2.

2. The time-horizon is divided so as to disaggregate. Five-year plans set broad rates of growth for GNP by sector of origin and end use, state output targets for important intermediate and final products, and list the location and intended capacity of all major construction projects. Annual plans (known as "operative" plans) handle the detailed application of these longer term plans in a particular year; quarterly and even monthly partial plans handle particular industries or aspects of planning.

3. Planning procedures are designed so as to enable more or less systematic aggregation and disaggregation. We give the procedure for the annual plan as an example:

FIGURE 3

Procedure for Annual Planning

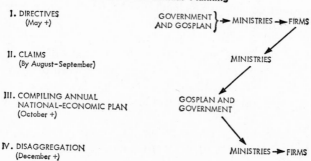

Stage I. Gosplan possesses a mass of data on past performance, and it or the government issues a statement about the principal economic magnitudes to be aimed at for the following year. These directives indicate the main proportions and principal production targets, the proposed investment allocation for each ministry, and proposals for the growth of output per man-year ("labor productivity," in Soviet terminology) and the reduction of costs.

Stage II. Ministries have already prepared a skeleton production program and set of claims for materials and equipment; this is now adjusted in the light of the directives and of information received from the firms. The forms on which claims are submitted are approved by Gosplan: The products itemized generally correspond to the nomenclature of the national production and supply plans, which have included up to 5,000 product groups. There are usually substantial differences between the ministries' output proposals and supply claims and the original directives.

Stage III. Gosplan now has the job of fitting together the ministry plans and its own draft plans: We enter the "period of coordination and reconciliation," in which the heads of firms and ministries negotiate with the government in Moscow. From this there emerges the national economic plan, with its constituent production, supplies (allocation), and investment plans. This whole negotiation is conducted in terms of, say, 30 times as many major indicators as were set out in the original directives.

Stage IV. The ministries now disaggregate the national economic plan to firm level.

4. These aggregation and disaggregation procedures are assisted by two important sets of what might be termed "control coefficients":

a) Output targets (or success indicators). The fulfillment of these has been the main driving motive of the Soviet firm and even ministry (managerial promotions and salaries tended to be related to success in fulfillment of output targets). Output targets were given for very broad groups of products at the national level, and they were supplemented by the sales departments of each ministry, whose disaggregation of the planned output target for a product group is supposed in theory to be binding on the firm. We return to the difficulties involved here later.

b) Norms or consumption standards. At the shop-floor level, hundreds of thousands of specific consumption standards are used to control the production process and to cut down waste. But at the plant level, discussion already proceeds on the basis of aggregated standards; a further aggregation takes place between plant and ministry. Gosplan uses overall input coefficients to check the claims of ministries, and many of these are incorporated in the plan. These may be of the form

x physical units of input of A for y physical units of output of B; e.g., tons of crude steel per ton of rolled steel.

or

x physical units of input of A for y value-units of output of B; e.g., tons of cement per 1 million rubles' building and assembly work.

Different consumption standards will be applied to different processes and even to different plants; these are probably quite reliable as a rough measure of efficiency and of reliability of claims, and a useful device for handling complex production activities centrally.

Coordination. The outline so far given of the planning process is unrealistic, for it assumes much smoother control than is possible in practice. Smooth planning has been vitiated by:

1. Uncertainty. Innovations, mistakes, and bottlenecks were not predicted with any accuracy; future proportions of coal and oil output, for example, were quite wrongly predicted even after World War II.

2. "Tight" planning. The plan was used as an instrument for forcing up production, and all targets were deliberately strained, all stocks minimized. This reinforced uncertainty and encouraged the emergence of unexpected bottlenecks. (In the early 1930's annual as well as five-year plan targets were sometimes wildly exaggerated.)

Moreover, we have so far been writing as if planning started from a clean sheet with each planning period. In fact, of course, planners work *at the margin*. Of a steel output of 12 million tons, as much as 10 million tons in an annual plan may be irrevocably committed to existing activities. Even in a five-year plan, possible shifts may be small: during the second five-year plan, for example, most capital investment was devoted to completing projects already started during the first plan or earlier.

The "coordination and reconciliation" activities undertaken by Gosplan in drawing up the annual plan are therefore limited by uncertainty, by the consequences of tight planning, and by existing commitments. Gosplan has two functions here. First, it seeks to balance programs by eliminating existing or potential bottlenecks due to the excess of demand over supply. To do this it follows a regular procedure and uses a list of priorities. Thus it may cut cement supplies to housing in order to have enough to push through a crash program to complete a steel foundry needed to produce certain types of steel required by priority industries. Second, it tries to inject into departmental programs the priorities and investment programs favored by the government. Thus it may increase cement supplies to the constructors of new chemical factories which are regarded as urgent.

In the coordination procedure, a great deal of use has been made by Gosplan of "material balances" or physical budgets, showing supplies and requirements for different product groups or types of equipment. These physical budgets were adjusted by the appropriate Gosplan through a fairly crude procedure of rule-of-thumb iteration. These were not input-output tables, for no technical coefficients had been calculated; sometimes a rough allowance was made for indirect outlays (e.g., of steel needed to make more machinery for motorcar factories if the output of motorcars was increased, as well as direct outlays of steel on the motorcars themselves). The procedure was therefore slow and inexact. At present, input-output tables and the traditional "material balances" are used side by side.

Financial Planning

1. Our account so far has been primarily concerned with physical planning. But as we have seen, a money flow corresponded to all the physical flows, and some of the money transactions in the system (e.g., wage payments, sales on the collective-farm market, sales on the retail market generally) were not accompanied by physical controls. Once the inflationary process had led to the initial reallocation of GNP in 1928–30, financial equilibrium was a subsidiary goal of the government. What was required was that money payments to the population (wage payments by the state, payments by the state to *kolkhozy* which were then distributed to their members, etc.) should not exceed the value of the supply of commodities available on the state-controlled market at fixed prices and on the collective-farm market at market prices. As outpayments by the state included the earnings of persons employed in the investment goods industries, in the social services, and in the armed forces, a gap existed between the cost-price of consumer goods (equal to the cost of wages in that sector and the materials, etc., it employed) and the total monetary demand.

This gap needed to be covered by taxation, and could be met in principle in one or all of three ways: (*a*) by direct taxation, (*b*) by allowing the profits of enterprises to rise and then taxing them, or (*c*) by an indirect tax: this could be an equiproportional markup on all goods, or imposed only on consumer goods.

a) Direct taxation has been of minor importance: there are no incomes uncontrolled by the state available to tax, and high income tax on state employees is regarded as undesirable.

b) Profits tax has been of some importance, but in the early stages the authorities feared that the monetary pressure on the retail market would lead to very high profits in the consumer goods industries (this pressure was not held back after 1935 by the rationing procedures which still operated in the case of producer goods).

c) The misnamed "turnover tax" therefore became the main source of tax: it is a markup on the wholesale price of consumer goods and the low delivery price of foodstuffs. The markup is differentiated by product for social reasons and to bring about a rough equality between the supply and the demand for each product. It was argued that a high level of tax on producer goods, which were mainly sold to the state, would only require the state to reimburse itself from a still higher tax rate on consumer goods.

Figure 4 illustrates the principal money flows in the system.

FIGURE 4

Soviet Financial Planning: A Simplified Picture (not to scale)

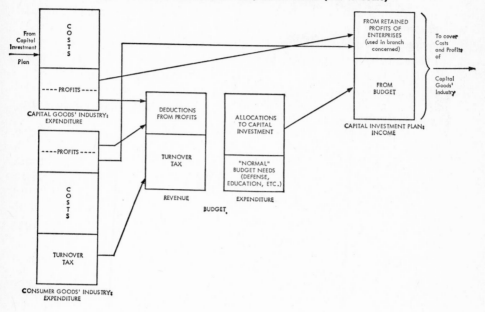

2. Prices in the producer and the consumer goods industries therefore had a common base; they were reached as follows:

 a) costs of production, including wages, the cost of materials, overheads, a small allowance for depreciation, but no interest charge on capital;

 b) a small markup for profits;

 c) trade and transport costs.

To these was added in the case of consumer goods

 d) turnover tax (differentiated by product) to reach the retail price.

Profits are partly taxed, partly retained by the firm or industry; a high proportion of profits in excess of the plan is placed at the disposal of the firm in the "Director's Fund" (now the "Enterprise Fund").

It will be noted that the prices of producer goods are unresponsive to supply and demand, and could remain stable for many years. Each industry receives a price for its product equal to average costs for the industry plus a small margin for profit; but the industry itself can pay differential prices, offering high prices to high-cost firms and low prices to low-cost firms. However, prices include no systematic allowance for the varying richness of the capital stock of firms producing similar products. In practice, the rate of profit earned on different products varies enormously, owing to the hit-and-miss way in which prices were fixed.

3. Elaborate arrangements are made to control the flows of (*a*) short-

term loans (for seasonal stocks, goods in transit, etc.), (*b*) wages, (*c*) allocations to investment (mainly financed by the budget), and (*d*) cash through the State Bank (responsible for working capital) and specialized investment banks (responsible for allocations to fixed capital). All these devices aimed at maintaining the financial equilibrium, which was secured through balancing money incomes against money expenditures through the fiscal system. In the end, inflation was repressed over a short period before the World War II (1935–37) and in a more systematic way after the war (1948–   ). Between 1948 and 1953, retail prices were even substantially reduced.

Labor and Labor Controls

1. The following are the principal devices used by the government to control the urban labor force:

   a) Once unemployment had been absorbed (by about 1932), recruitment of labor from the villages to the towns was organized systematically on contract with the collective farms.

   b) Training and education of semiskilled, skilled, and technical manpower are systematically planned.

   c) At various stages (particularly in the war and postwar years from 1940 to 1951), scarce grades or types of manpower were restricted in their movement or even subject to allocation.

2. In spite of these measures, labor was highly mobile, particularly in the early 1930's, and both central planners and factory managements utilize money wages to influence the allocation of labor—hence a form of labor market emerged, though recent studies of Soviet production functions have confirmed that it was highly imperfect:

   a) The government approves national scales for different grades and types of labor in different areas, and adjusts these from time to time to take account of demand and supply; there is a high differential for skill.

   b) There is an elaborate piece-rate and bonus system to encourage higher productivity.

   c) Management can in practice manipulate bonuses and classifications to attract scarce kinds of labor.

3. Unskilled and even semiskilled labor are not basically a scarce factor of production (owing to the existence of a large stock of labor in the countryside). There has therefore been a recurrent tendency to substitute labor for capital.

4. The need for labor coupled with the pressure to fulfill the output plan encouraged management to overspend its allocation for wages and made for an inflationary situation. Control by the State Bank over wage payments is the most important single element in maintaining wage stability.

5. Government control over trade unions has greatly assisted wage policy. The central wage bargaining process was very tenuous from 1929 onward. At the same time, a policy of cutting the rate for the job as techniques and organization improved was systematically enforced, so that money wages rose *less* rapidly than output per man.

6. But the government, as well as firmly controlling wage rates, also took responsibility for social conditions. Hours of work were restricted to seven to eight hours daily. Pensions, sickness and maternity benefits, holidays with pay, and welfare services (crèches, factory clubs, canteens), largely administered through the trade unions, were more generous than was the case in many Western countries at a similar stage of industrialization. These social benefits (particularly housing tied to the factory) were used to influence the movement of labor (high priority factories tended to have better facilities and housing; benefits were partly dependent on length of service at the particular factory).

Strengths and Weaknesses of the Soviet Planning System

No adequate "cost-benefit analysis" of the Soviet system or its constituent parts has yet been attempted. Here we simply list some of its principal achievements and failures:

Advantages. 1. The system succeeded in enforcing allocation of a very high proportion of GNP to investment over a long period; within this allocation resources were concentrated on the growth-inducing producer goods industries, which were transformed from high-cost to low-cost industries. In general, it is possible with this kind of mechanism to enforce successfully high priority crash programs (e.g., the sputniks).

2. A high degree of centralization enabled the planners to inculcate the latest technology, imported from more advanced economies, into the whole economy at a rapid rate: project institutes, such as *Gipromez* (the State Institute for Projects of Iron and Steel Works), were able to plan large-scale technological advance for a whole industry on a national scale. For many major technological problems, the Soviet system of centralized research also carries great advantages at a more advanced stage of development (e.g., nuclear research).

3. Considerable economies of scale (including economies from standardization) and economies of effort are possible in nationally planned industries.

4. The output drive from above, characteristic of Soviet planning until recently, provides a powerful instrument for enforcing high capacity utilization, and for keeping management and men working at a high pace.

Disadvantages. 1. The cost of concentrating resources on producer goods industries was very high. Thus the policy adopted towards the peasantry led to a drastic decline in peasant holdings of working livestock and forced the state in fact to reallocate unexpected resources to the agricultural equipment industry and hence to the high-grade steel industry. It also had a drastic long-term effect on peasant morale.

2. When the central planners make a *wrong* technological choice, the cost (because the policy is carried out on a national scale) is proportionately heavy; for example, there has been overinvestment in the coal industry and underinvestment in oil and chemicals.

3. When controls are highly centralized, initiative and innovation at the plant level are cramped. But decentralization of a system of administrative planning is difficult. If the success indicators are not very detailed, managements will produce what it is easier to produce rather than what is wanted. Control of quality through success indicators is very difficult. The sellers' market which was coupled with Soviet administrative planning reinforced these difficulties. At the same time it led to the tendency for each industrial ministry to become a self-contained "empire," carrying out wasteful backward integration in order to control its supplies. If advertising and inflated sales organizations are a high cost of modern capitalism, inflated supplies organizations were (and are) a high cost of Soviet central planning.

To sum up with an example: Central planning enabled the emergence of steel foundries and rolling mills, using home-manufactured equipment, which are technologically as good as those in the United States and are worked at a much higher capacity. It also produced a situation where Soviet bedsteads were the heaviest in the world (because planned in tons), were produced on too small a scale (because made under several ministries) and therefore costly, and owing to the sellers' market could be made of iron, when the consumer would have preferred something more modern.

This is a mere list of factors. Economists need to ask themselves: *how* costly and beneficial were these various factors? How far were the advantages and disadvantages of the system inextricably tied together? Could the Soviet strategy for rapid growth, or some features of it, be employed without the disadvantages? How many of the unsuccessful features were due to the special conditions of Russia (including the difficult external and internal position of the government) and to the inexperience and imperfect knowledge of the people who made the system?

PLANNING A MATURE ECONOMY IN THE USSR

Economic Theory and the Soviet Economy

1. Traditional economic theory contrasts two types of system: the competitive or market system, with its "ideal type" of perfect competition, and "command economy," or "planning under a dictator." These are treated as two possible alternative methods of allocating resources.

a) The *market economy* is divided into competing units: a large number of individual consumers bargain with a large number of producers on the market. The goal of the producer is to maximize his profit; the goal of the consumer is to maximize his satisfaction. The resulting demand and supply are equated through price.

The decisions on the consumer market are reflected back into the factor market, where a similar bargaining process settles the distribution of incomes between factors and the distribution of the factors.

As a result, resources in such an economy are allocated "rationally," by which the economist means "in accordance with the desires of the consumers."

b) In the *command economy* (often referred to as "*planning under a dictator*"), final demand is determined not by individual consumers but by the decision of the central authority, as "dictator's preferences" or "planners' preferences" replace "consumers' preferences." The central authority also controls the allocation of all factors of production and the distribution of income. The system is completely centralized: its difficulty lies in the ability of the "dictator" to work out the "thousands of equations" involved in transforming his preferences into practical economic decisions.

2. How far does this theory provide an effective framework of analysis for contemporary capitalism and for Soviet planning?

a) The development of economic analysis in the past forty years has involved a number of realistic modifications of the original theory as applied to modern capitalism:

　i) In many cases free entry into industries will be restricted and a state of imperfect competition will exist; at equilibrium, output may be lower and price higher than under perfect competition. However, economies of scale may make for lower costs in a highly organized oligopolistic industry: advantage and disadvantage must be carefully examined.

　ii) While consumer *choice* exists, advertising, imperfect knowledge, and the power of initiative of the large firm mean that consumer *sovereignty* is quite restricted.

　iii) The assumption of permanent equilibrium in the system is a microeconomic one. At the level of macroeconomics, supply does not create its own demand and hence the possibility of underemployment of factors exists. Macroeconomic equilibrium requires government intervention.

　iv) The large government sector requires separate analysis. Nationalized industries produce as monopolies, but often with their "maximum profit" goal constrained; and as consumers they control a large part of the market for certain intermediate goods (e.g., an electricity board purchasing power-station equipment). The defense, education, and health departments of central and local governments are also large buyers and often act as oligopsonies. State fiscal and monetary and tariff policy regulates the market.

v) The view that a firm's economic behavior can be understood solely in terms of aiming at maximum profit in response to market price is an insufficient one. Within the large firm, decisions will be taken administratively (through the hierarchy) or by a cooperative or bargaining process; and much interfirm behavior may also be explained in this way. Industry is not an infinite number of atoms responding to price, but a finite number of blocs: The bloc as a whole reacts to price, but also has dealings with other blocs which are to be explained in terms of organization theory rather than of the price mechanism; and bargaining and administrative processes help to explain economic behavior within each bloc.

However, even with these modifications the orginal theory retains much validity:

i) If firms do not always aim at maximizing their profits, they are concerned with making a satisfactory level of profits ("satisficing").

ii) There is consumer choice, and a market process also operates for intermediate goods and (partly) on the factor market.

iii) In spite of the considerable role of the government, a large segment of investment is still determined by the decisions of individual entrepreneurs (or entrepreneurial firms).

b) These developments of Western economic theory are of direct relevance to our understanding of the Soviet system:

i) Physical planning is not something unknown in capitalist economies. In the Soviet economy, relationships between firms are regulated by administrative and bargaining processes; in a competitive system they are largely regulated by the market. But analogies to all the administrative and bargaining processes described in the section on "the planning process" above may be found within the capitalist firm, and within the government sector (compare the process for making fiscal estimates in a market economy with the procedures for plan compilation in Soviet industry). The "thousands of equations" of Western economic theory are simplified by the existence of "administrative decentralization": subsystems of economic administrators share decision making with the Council of Ministers; and bargaining and pressure from lower units assist the decision-making process. Moreover, like decisions by private entrepreneurs, planners' decisions are made only "at the margin."

ii) Some important economic activity in the USSR is to be explained in terms of a market mechanism, though most Soviet markets are highly imperfect. As we have seen, there is a partial market for labor, a fixed-price market for retail consumer goods, a free market for part of retail food sales; and various unofficial or illegal markets operate in practice.

Modern capitalist economies are imperfectly competitive and have important elements of administrative control; the Soviet economy is not entirely "planned from the center," and imperfect markets exist for certain purposes.

The Soviet Economy as a Special Case of Planned Economy

The Soviet planning system of the 1930's–1950's is not the only possible form of planned economy. In Soviet experience alone, at least two other forms of planning system have existed. In the period of *War Communism* (1918–20), industry was nationalized and industrial output was allocated physically. Owing to inflation the economy was virtually moneyless; labor was directly controlled, consumer goods were rationed and agricultural output subject to requisition. However, peasants continued to work their own land and no serious attempt was made to socialize agriculture. This system was the closest approach in principle to the "ideal form" of the command economy in the history of the Soviet system. In the period of the *New Economic Policy* (1921–29), as in present-day Poland, state ownership of industry was combined with private agriculture through a regulated market. The effectiveness of planning was constrained by the existence of the market, but central goals were to some extent enforced.

A considerable variety of forms of central planning is to be found in Eastern Europe.

The systematic study of forms of economic organization has so far been little developed. One may distinguish two basic ways of classification.

Ownership. A planned economy is unlikely to be one in which all economic activity is nationalized. It will be a "mixed economy," combining private ownership with state ownership and possibly embracing different forms of state ownership (very varied forms of public ownership have been experienced, incorporating different degrees of state, consumer, and workers' control). In this spectrum, the Soviet economy lies considerably toward the "state" end, particularly as far as industry is concerned. Nearly all industrial activity is nationalized, and since 1918 forms of syndicalism or "guild socialism" have been firmly rejected in favor of "one-man management" by administrators appointed by the state and liable to instant dismissal. The argument for this has always been in terms of economic efficiency and of the need to enforce a central state policy.

Allocation of Resources. Various forms of "market socialism" are in principle conceivable, and have been much discussed among economists (especially in Poland and Yugoslavia). To what extent can a scale of preferences (of planners or individual consumers or a combination of both) be put into effect through a market, on which state firms aim to maximize their profits in simulation of private enterprises? In a variation of this, suggested by Kornai and others, the state would use its regulatory powers only to counter inefficient decisions due to the existence of state monopolies. Prices in "market socialism" might be formed freely, or might be fixed by the planners, but would, of course, need to reflect the chosen preference-scale more or less exactly, as they would indicate to the producer what he should produce, and how he should allocate resources (including investment). In its extreme form, the economic behavior of "market socialism" ought not to differ from that of a private market economy.

The alternative approach is the one followed by the Soviet government: to allocate resources by direct physical controls, and to allow some degree of decentralization in decision making to other controllers at industry, region, or plant level.

Planning systems might be classified (*a*) by the relative strengths in them of the "market principle" and the "physical planning principle," (*b*) by the degree to which, within the market sector, the government regulates the market (imposes its preferences), and (*c*) by the degree to which decision making is decentralized within the physical planning sector.

We have not made any allowance for the *effectiveness* of controls. Should not the degree of planning be measured not only by the all-embracingness of the planners' goals and the detailedness of their controls but also by the extent to which the planners succeed in fulfilling their goals in the actual allocation of resources? For instance, War Communism was in principle a highly centralized system. But in practice central decisions were usually ineffective; illegal barter and local quasi markets tended to dominate economic life: what was the "real" economic system? Again, where was there more planning—industry under War Communism, where detailed orders were not enforced, or in agriculture under the New Economic Policy, where indirect controls succeeded to some extent in moving agriculture in the direction desired by the central government? Further, good planners of course incorporate their knowledge of their objective possibilities into their goals: but is a planner whose goals are very limited, but successfully achieved, as "effective" as, say, the Soviet planners in 1929–31, who set quite impossible goals but did succeed in reallocating resources very drastically in the desired direction?

Planning a More Mature Economy

The basic allocation decisions and the planning process in the USSR in 1928–53 probably had stronger "functional" elements than "dysfunctional" elements in the stage of moving the Soviet economy from a semiagrarian economy to an industrialized economy. But as the economy matured, the "dysfunctional" elements certainly became more prominent. The changed context may be summarized as follows:

1. Industrial output per head is now above the British level and moving towards the U.S. level for some important producer goods. The economy is vastly more complex than it was in the 1930's.

2. The Industrial Revolution has been accompanied by major social changes:

  a) In 1928, two thirds of the population were illiterate; now, nearly everyone can read and write.

  b) In 1928, some 3 million persons were employed in industrial labor; it is now (1965) over 25 millions.

  c) In 1928, some 5 percent of the state-employed labor force (i.e., excluding peasants and collective farmers) had received professional or semiprofessional education; the figure now (1965) is about 15 percent.

3. The technological situation is different: as the economy becomes more mature, the amount of technological borrowing it can do tends to decline, and the amount of innovation required increases. This is reinforced by the long-term trend for labor to become a more scarce factor of production: the economy must increasingly come to rely on higher labor productivity and hence on more capital-intensive production (and/or on technical progress) rather than on increasing the industrial labor force.

In this new situation, changes in both allocation and organization are required. It is not easy to demonstrate that industrial efficiency is hampered by a relatively low standard of living (the Soviet average real wage is probably about a quarter that of the United States, but labor productivity may be over half the U.S. level). But in any case political and social pressures have dictated a shift in resources towards consumption. Such a shift requires a much greater output of food; and in agriculture it is very probable that the low return to the peasant for the output of the collective farm has held down productivity. And certainly as the economy has grown, the highly centralized planning structure has become less efficient and less workable.

Here we summarize the principal changes so far made in both respects since 1953.

Allocation of Resources.   1. There has been a relative and absolute increase in the resources devoted to consumer goods (manufactures, manufactured foodstuffs). In the 1930's and in 1946–50, the output of producer goods increased much more rapidly than that of consumer goods; the gap is now much narrower.

2. A much higher proportion of total investment has been allocated to urban housing construction.

3. In 1953–58, the prices paid by the state for agricultural products were very substantially increased; according to official figures, the money incomes of collective farms rose from 5 billion new rubles to 13.2 billion new rubles between 1953 and 1958. At the same time, the total annual investment in agriculture (state plus collective farm) increased from 2.1 to 5.1 billion new rubles. This double shift was accompanied by a rapid rise in agricultural output—by some 50 percent, according to official figures (i.e., a greater increase than in 1928 to 1953).

Between 1958 and 1965 agriculture tended to stagnate (even ignoring the bad harvest of 1963). Recent studies have shown that this stagnation has occurred simultaneously with a falling-off in peasant incomes and in the rate of growth of investment in agriculture. It seems likely that agricultural difficulties are at least in part due to the failure of the state to allocate a share of GNP to agriculture adequate enough to enable the goals of the planners to be achieved (organizational weaknesses may also have played a part).

4. There has been a significant shift in the distribution of income. The incomes of peasants tended (until 1958) to increase more rapidly than those of the urban population. Within the urban population, there has been a process of leveling up: the minimum wage has been increased, wage differentials have been narrowed, social benefits such as pensions have been substantially increased.

5. Nevertheless, the priorities have not been reversed. It seems certain, however the measurement is done, that a higher proportion of GNP is allocated to net investment than in the U.S., and that a higher proportion of this investment is allocated to the producer goods industries. As a result, the rate of industrial growth has remained high (7–9 percent a year), though less high than a decade ago.

Organization. Attempts to improve the working of Soviet planning have followed two main lines simultaneously: (1) improvements in central planning; (2) attempts to decentralize.

1. Improvements in central planning. Central decision making has undoubtedly tended to be more consistently thought out, and to become more logical and consistent.

Long-term technological decisions have been reconsidered, and a bold policy of technical change has been embarked upon. Thus oil has been given preference to coal, and the transfer of the railways to the diesel has been undertaken; this reverses previous policy. The development and manufacture of prefabricated reinforced concrete components and other building materials have been given preference over traditional materials like brick and timber. Plastics are being developed in preference to steel and other metals.

In the discussions about all these changes, most of which had previously been undertaken in capitalist economies in response to market criteria, there has been a great deal of emphasis on economic arguments.

The question of the appropriate criteria to use in making investment choices has been predominant here. Thinking has moved in the direction of adopting a single rate of return for the whole economy (the rate of return is, of course, the inverse of the so-called "recoupment period"): the standard formula now used is

$$\frac{I_1 - I_2}{C_2 - C_1} \leq R.P.$$

where I_1 and I_2 are the investment alternatives being compared and C_1 and C_2 are the costs of production in the two alternatives, and $R.P.$ is the maximum permissible period in which the investment may be recouped. (This has tended to vary by industry, from 4–5 years in light industry, i.e., a rate of return of 20–25 percent, to 16–17 years in electric power, i.e., a rate of return of about 6 percent.)

The adoption of a standard rate for all industries would require the use of something like a cost-benefit analysis if the social welfare problem is to be taken into account; Soviet thought is moving cautiously in this direction.

A stumbling block to consistent macroeconomic decision making is the inconsistency of the prices in which goods are valued. Investment decisions, and indeed all multiproduct decisions, have to be discussed not in physical terms but in value terms. As we have seen, Soviet prices are an inadequate indicator of real costs; they do not include a capital charge (so capital-intensive production is relatively undervalued), they do not vary with the scarcity or abundance of the goods, the rent element for use of natural resources is inconsistent, and the price incorporates a profit markup which is more or less arbitrary. Rule-of-thumb adjustments are made by the central planners, but decisions are clumsy and often inaccurate.

A second line of approach to the improvement of central planning has been the attempt to improve knowledge at the center by use of mathematical methods. Technical coefficients have been worked out so that the consequences of alternative production policies may be taken into account more systematically; national and some regional input-output tables have been constructed (among the largest is the 438-sector matrix for planning purposes of 1964–65). The central planning of supplies and requirements seems still to be carried out by rule-of-thumb methods, but these are now supplemented by improved information. At the same time various methods of mathematical programming, such as the transportation algorithm, have been used to improve traffic flows (e.g., truck transport in Moscow, scheduling of Baltic steamers, timber and coal hauls), bringing savings of about 10 percent in costs for each problem.

2. Attempts at decentralization. Three major attempts have been made since 1953 to devolve some of the decision-making powers of the central authorities. But these attempts have been conducted within the frame-

work of the physical planning system, rather than representing an increase in the market sector of the economy.

a) 1954–56: "step-by-step" decentralization. The Gosplan-Council of Ministers central organization attempted to shed some of its powers by reducing the number of indicators in the national output, supply and capital investment plans; thus product groups, for which output targets were laid down, were made more aggregative. The intention was that each ministry, possessing more flexibility itself, would devolve some of its authority to its departments, which in turn would increase the decision-making powers of economic units.

The reform was on the whole unsuccessful. Ministries failed to pass down their powers to the factory; instead, they tended to use their increased authority to bind their own "empires" more closely together. At the same time, the reduction in the number of central output targets (success indicators) revealed clearly a dilemma inherent in administrative planning. The enterprise is required to maximize its output in terms of the output targets. If the targets are broad or loose, it will try to follow the "easiest" course within the target. If the target is merely for "tons of nails shorter than 2 inches" the factory will try to produce all $1\frac{9}{10}''$ nails, because this is easiest. If it is for "numbers of nails," the factory will try to produce all $\frac{1}{2}''$ nails. But if the plan is set in terms of $\frac{1}{2}''$, $1''$, $1\frac{1}{2}''$ and $1\frac{9}{10}''$ nails, there will be overcentralization. If the target is set in terms of gross value of output, the factory will maximize its use of materials and semifabs and minimize the net value it adds to each product (this has been dealt with by using a new indicator of "standard cost of work done to the product," but this has involved further—if smaller—difficulties).

b) 1957–65: regionalization. In 1957, industry was "regionalized": the industrial ministries were abolished, 104 regions were set up and all factories in each region were put under the regional economic committee. However, much of the central machinery was retained, particularly the sales organizations which control product mix, and gradually committees for each industry were reestablished, with research organizations attached. What emerged was a mixture of area-by-area and industry-by-industry control. This probably gave the factory manager greater effective power, if only because he no longer had one unambiguous boss; it also led to the breakup of the ministerial "empires" and a more effective consideration of regional factors in central decision making. But it also made economic administration very much more complicated.

c) September, 1965– : more authority to the factory. The reforms introduced by Kosygin contained two main elements. First of all, they abandoned the attempt at regional organization and returned to control by industrial ministries. More important, they made the first serious attempt to increase greatly the powers of the factory management. The most important measures are the following.

i) The importance of profits as a success indicator is intended to be greatly increased. Profits retained by factories are to be large and will be related to planned profit (if achieved) rather than actual profit so as to discourage firms from trying to keep their plan low. Bonuses to management and workers will be paid from and related to the amount of profit.

ii) Various measures are to be adopted to encourage the efficient use of capital investment.

iii) The powers of the factory management to determine the way in which it spends the total allocation for wages are greatly increased; the manager may divide up the total allocations as he wishes between classes of employee—he may, for instance, reduce the total number of persons employed in order to increase the portion of highly paid workers.

iv) The main global indicator of output is to be "actually marketed production" rather than "gross production"; it is hoped that this will force factories to produce goods for which there is a high demand.

However, the main physical indicators are retained, including both the plan of supplies in physical terms and the itemization of production items in physical terms in the national-economic plan; Kosygin merely expressed the hope that the degree of detail would be gradually reduced. The success of the reforms in moving away from administrative planning will depend on the extent to which a linear relationship can be established between the preferences of the planners and the profits earned by the factory; if such a linear relationship exists, and the factory aims at maximizing its profit, then the desired pattern of production will be achieved without administrative orders.

But the achievement of such a "linear relationship" requires a radical reform of the price system. The main suggestions for reform have been: make turnover tax into an equiproportional markup on the wholesale price (or value added) of all products; give higher profits for scarce products and negative profits for surplus products; include an interest charge on capital stock. But so far only the last of these proposals appears to be likely to be achieved in the near future.* The prices which the planners are to establish have not been worked out in detail, and even the method by which they could be reached is unclear. Kosygin has announced an impending price reform, but it seems unlikely to be a radical one.

Three things seem to block a major price reform: (1) fear that an

---

* Editors' note: Such a change was introduced in 1967.

increase in market forces, or the use of profit as a "universal regulator" in a socialist economy, may diminish the control of the center over the allocation of resources; it is for this reason that proposals permitting a kind of "market socialism" to develop have been firmly rejected; (2) a feeling that profit will not be so powerful an incentive to managers to increase output as output targets in physical terms have been; and (3) inability (as yet) to arrive at the actual prices required.

The weakness of the reforms of the planning system we have so far discussed is, then, that they do not tackle the problem of *valuation* systematically or integrally. The reforms are essentially *ad hoc*. Thus all the proposals for improving the allocation of investment incorporate a required rate of return which is arrived at more or less empirically or even arbitrarily: The choice between investments is not consistently interwoven with long-term production planning. The result is likely to be that the approved pattern of planned investment is not entirely compatible with the approved production targets, so that adjustment by rule-of-thumb will still need to follow. Similarly even the most radical reforms proposed for short- and medium-term production and supply planning depend on the availability of a system of prices which systematically reflect the aims or preferences of the planners; prices must favor a production pattern which not merely widens present bottlenecks but also makes its contribution to the dynamic goals of the planners.

A far-reaching proposal such as Liberman's could worsen the operation of the system rather than assist it, if put into effect without an appropriate set of prices being available. This does not mean that the partial reforms which have been proposed or undertaken would not improve the operation of the present system. Waste and inconsistency have been reduced both by the use of better investment criteria and by the application of linear programming techniques to partial problems.

One general solution—much discussed and partly attempted in Poland and Yugoslavia—is for the required scale of prices to be reached by permitting state enterprises to compete on a market. The central planners would restrict themselves to controlling the general level of investment and to intervening in order to ensure that the market was as perfect as possible. The principal economic objection to this solution is that it would incorporate into the planned economy most of the disadvantages of modern capitalism, in a situation in which the imperfections of the market would be more considerable than in a privately owned economy.

Mathematical methods. An increasingly influential school of Soviet economists holds that with the application of mathematical methods and the use of the computer the major dilemmas of central planning can be solved. Computers make it possible to examine the properties of a very large number of economic variables: With the aid of appropriately designed mathematical models, economic processes can be simulated on the computer so that plan variants can be tested for feasibility and consistency. The core of the method is that objective functions are set up which indicate what is to be maximized or minimized within a system of constraints. The functions yield a system of imputed values (efficiency prices or shadow prices), and these for the problem concerned are the consistent system of prices which, as we have seen, the nonmathematical proposals lacked.

Soviet mathematicians and mathematical economists believe that this technique can be applied to the planning of the entire economy. What is proposed is a "unified and automatized system of national economic planning and management" which would seek to optimize the achievement of goals set by the government. The economy would be divided for planning purposes into a number of blocs or subsystems (both by area and by sector); for each bloc an appropriate programming model would attempt to optimize subgoals consistent with and integrated with the overall national goals, which would in turn be incorporated in a macro-model for the economy as a whole. For each bloc, a set of shadow prices would emerge which would indicate its "best" economic behavior in the planning period. A measure of decentralization is inherent in the system: The elements in each subsystem would be free to move so as to optimize their subgoals within constraints obtained from the larger bloc of which the subsystem formed a part.

A requirement for the efficient working of the new system is the establishment of a consistent computerized system of information flows. All economic information (for instance, all inputs and outputs) will need to be classified by a unified system for the entire economy, so that data may be processed in forms suitable for feeding in to the planning models on which the system is to be based. A chain of computer stations is being established for assembling and processing economic information. (This is a long and arduous business; it is likely to take about 10 years.)

For the efficient operation of the system, actual economic forms need to be adapted as far as possible to the solutions found on the computer (inflexibilities in institutions and arrangements constitute constraints on optimization). In particular, actual prices, it is hoped, will be made to correspond more closely to the shadow prices obtained from the computations. This does not mean that all prices would necessarily need to be fixed by the state; actual market arrangements in a subsystem could be made consistent with the larger economic models (in principle, a private and uncontrolled sector could be incorporated as a stochastic element in the overall system).

·If prices thus correspond to the preferences stated in the models, they would be appropriate for Liberman's proposal that profit should indicate to an economic unit how it should behave. But in the light of Western studies of the behavior of the private firm, it seems likely that the Soviet firm cannot be expected to behave as though maximizing profits were its sole goal; as part of the restructuring of planning, an appropriate system of incentives would be needed to ensure that decisions are executed.

So far we have spoken simply of models which would optimize the achievement of government-fixed goals; we have evaded the problem of the preference functions which would convert those goals into meaningful quantities. At present, the goals of the Soviet government are stated in terms of a long series of targets for investment goods, intermediate goods, and final consumption goods. These targets, as we saw earlier, are reached both for five-year and for annual plans as the result of a long bargaining process and reflect both the need to overcome expected bottlenecks and the major investment projects and priorities which the government intends to encourage. To optimize the achievement of these targets (as is for example the aim in Hungary) is only to maximize the achievement of a network of decisions reached by a rule-of-thumb process. The alternative is to persuade the politicians to reformulate their goals in more general or more operational terms. A satisfactory outcome will obviously only be achieved as a result of a long and difficult dialogue between the politicians and the mathematically trained planners. One element in this dialogue must be a discussion on the extent to which the preference functions of the planning models should incorporate the preferences of the individual consumer. Some Soviet and East European economists would be prepared to go a very long way in the direction of consumer sovereignty; others have suggested that zones of state influence, individual influence, and mixed influence would need to be determined. One considerable weakness of present Soviet discussions is that they have paid little attention to techniques such as cost-benefit analysis which are needed in order to bring social and other noneconomic factors more consistently into the considerations of planners and politicians: the rationale of economic policy making has not been carefully considered, and hence goals may remain inconsistent or ill-defined.

Conclusion

Few of the techniques of planning we have now been considering were available to the Soviet economist during the period of intensive industrialization; those which were available were worked out only in elementary form. In any case, the gap between the goals of the politicians and the assumptions of the economists was so great that little dialogue was possible. The politicians, and the politically minded economists, undertook the elaboration of their own system of planning and their own rule-of-thumb methods of quantifying their goals to make them operational. In doing this, they acquired a rich fund of valuable experience about the problems of development through central planning; the lessons from this experience, both successful and unsuccessful, could save resources in other economies where central planning is being used for development. Unfortunately, it is information about formal mechanisms for planning and financial control which has until now tended to be communicated from the Eastern bloc to the developing countries, rather than a realistic account of problems and achievements. For the developing countries, the further question exists: now that the new techniques for planning are available, can they be coupled with planning for a high rate of growth in conditions of rapid social change? If so, some of the successes of Soviet-type central planning may be achieved at less cost.

5 | PRESSURE AND PLANNING IN THE SOVIET ECONOMY

Herbert S. Levine

A distinctive feature of Soviet central planning is the "tautness" which results from the regime's pressure to set and strive for very ambitious targets which intentionally strain the ability of the economy to achieve them. In this selection, Levine argues that the pressure imposed on and built up within the economic system, rather than centralized planning as such, accounts for many of the observed characteristics of the Soviet economy. He explains the sources of pressure on enterprises and the effects, including distortion of managerial incentives, inadequate inventories, and a sellers' market. He concludes by evaluating the prospects for planning without pressure.

Herbert S. Levine is Professor of Economics at the University of Pennsylvania. The article is reprinted by permission from Henry Rosovsky (ed.), *Industrialization in Two Systems: Essays in Honor of Alexander Gerschenkron* (New York: John Wiley & Sons, Inc., 1966), pp. 266–85, with the omission of some references to Russian-language sources.

I. INTRODUCTION

THIS PAPER is about the Soviet experience with centralized planning and the significance of this experience for our general understanding of the functioning of economic systems. Building on a well-known Gerschenkronian hypothesis about Russian economic history, the paper argues that because Soviet centralized planning is so enmeshed with the exertion of pressure on the internal economy by the Russian State, it is difficult clearly to ascribe causes to observed effects. Therefore, the Soviet experience should be used with care by economists in discussions of the characteristics and consequences of centralized economic planning. The argument is to some extent modified toward the end of the paper owing to the possibility that there may exist a somewhat general joint-productness about pressure and centralized planning. But more about that in awhile.

Among the "hypotheses" of Professor Gerschenkron—those broad,

64

insightful generalizations so cautiously wrung from masses of carefully collected empirical evidence—there is one describing a pattern of Russian economic development which is observable on a number of occasions in the course of Russian history.[1] The history of Russia, for the past five hundred years, is dominated by the theme of territorial expansion: from the small principality of Muscovy just emerging from Mongol rule, Russia grew to its present great size. During this process of expansion, the Russian State frequently came into contact and conflict with Western nations more advanced and more powerful than she. Such confrontations forced upon the leaders of Russia the painful realization that they would not be able to attain what they wanted to attain because of the extreme backwardness of the Russian economy. In such situations, Gerschenkron asserts, the Russian State would take on the role of initiator of economic development. The State would apply pressure to the internal economy to get it to grow rapidly and thus be able to support the foreign policy aims of the State in as short a period as possible. This relationship between military affairs and economic growth was the cause of the fitful nature of economic development observed in Russian economic history. When the military needs of the State were pressing, the economy was pressured into rapid growth. When a degree of power parity was reached, the need for further rapid growth subsided and the State removed its pressure for growth. Because so much growth was compressed into such short periods, the burden of sacrifice borne by the people living in Russia during those periods was great. To exact this sacrifice, extremely oppressive means and institutions were employed. The increase of pressure and the exaction of sacrifice were often so intense that they led to the exhaustion of the internal population; consequently, a period of rapid growth was very likely to be followed by a long period of little or no growth.

This was the pattern of Russian economic development described by Gerschenkron. It should be added that he was careful to point out that the pattern was intended as a framework for understanding the forces at work in Russian economic growth and was not meant to describe "some iron law of evolution" through which Russian development had to proceed:

What is implied is that the actual development seems to conform to a certain pattern and that such conformities and uniformities as can be observed do help us understand the course of events . . . That the development followed a certain course does not preclude the possibility of alternative routes, but it does suggest that the forces which propelled the Russian economy along its actual course must have been strong indeed.[2]

The pattern is most clearly and fully seen in the period of Peter the Great. It is also observable in the period of rapid growth of the 1890's,

---

[1] See Alexander Gerschenkron, *Economic Backwardness in Historical Perspective* (Cambridge, Mass.: Harvard University Press, 1962), pp. 17–18.

[2] *Ibid.*, p. 157.

although this spurt of development is not followed by a long period of relative stagnation.[3] Finally, it is seen in the massive industrialization drive launched under the Soviets.

This last period is still in progress, and, whereas it remains to be seen whether future events will conform to the pattern, it is evident that the course of past events, since the end of the 1920's, does clearly conform.[4] The key role played in the pattern by the conflict between military needs and economic backwardness is graphically illustrated in a famous speech delivered by Stalin, at the beginning of the industrialization drive, in which he said:

> One feature of the history of old Russia was the continual beatings she suffered for falling behind, for her backwardness. She was beaten by the Mongol Khans . . . the Turkish beys . . . the Swedish feudal lords . . . the Polish and Lithuanian gentry . . . the British and French capitalists . . . the Japanese barons. All beat her . . . for her backwardness: for military backwardness, for cultural backwardness, for political backwardness, for industrial backwardness, for agricultural backwardness. . . . Do you want our socialist fatherland to be beaten and to lose its independence? If you do not want this you must put an end to its backwardness in the shortest possible time . . . We are fifty or a hundred years behind the advanced countries. We must make good this distance in ten years. Either we do it, or they crush us.[5]

In the Soviet industrialization drive, the State has been the initiator and controller of economic growth. To force the speed of this growth, it has applied pervasive pressure on the entire internal economy. Cruelly oppressive means have been used to exact severe sacrifice from the Russian people.

Soviet economic development and Soviet economic institutions can best be understood against the background of this pattern in Russian economic history. Stalin's use of collectivization is in many ways a functional analogue of Peter the Great's use of serfdom. Centralized planning is the means by which the State exerts its control over the economy and through which it transmits pressure for rapid growth.[6] To see Soviet collectivization merely as a device to increase production is to miss its vital function in exaction of sacrifice from the peasantry. Further,

---

[3] For discussion, see *ibid.*, pp. 130–42.

[4] *Ibid.*, pp. 147–51.

[5] J. Stalin, *Selected Writings* (New York: International Publishers, 1942), p. 200.

[6] This is not the place for a full discussion of the definition of the term *centralized planning*. Briefly speaking, what is meant is a system wherein the major economic decisions are made by central authorities and are communicated to the periphery by means of directives; the units at the periphery act in response to these directives, or "commands," rather than in response to parameters such as prices. See Janusz G., Zielinski, "Centralization and Decentralization in Decision Making," *Economics of Planning*, Vol. 3, No. 3 (December, 1963), pp. 196–208, and Gregory Grossman, "Notes for a Theory of the Command Economy," *Soviet Studies*, Vol. XV, No. 2 (October, 1963), pp. 101–23.

to see Soviet centralized planning merely as a Marxian device to eradicate the disproportions resulting from the anarchy of market systems is to miss its role both in giving the political leaders control over the course of Soviet development and in giving them a means of forcing rapid structural change on the economy, in order to modernize it and so bring it up to parity with the West.

The Soviet economy in the Plan Era is often taken as *the* case study of centralized planning, and the operating characteristics of the Soviet economy (as described in the works of Berliner, Granick, Nove and others)[7] are often taken as *the* necessary consequences of centralized planning. It is the argument of this paper that such views of the economic significance of the Soviet experience with centralized planning ignore the background of the Soviet use of centralized planning. They ignore, specifically, the role played by pressure, that pressure exerted on the economy by the political leaders through the means of centralized planning. It will be argued that the observed operating characteristics of the Soviet economy can be said to be as much if not more a result of the pressure in the system than they are of the mechanism of centralized planning itself.

II. SOURCES OF PRESSURE

When the Russian economy, at the end of the 1920's, had reattained its pre-World War I levels, the Soviet leaders turned away from the loose policies of the NEP period and toward the highly centralized means of economic planning and control which have marked the Plan Era. Undoubtedly, centralized planning had certain political and ideological attractions for the Soviet leaders,[8] but it also had important economic attractions. Having made the decision to embark upon forced draft industrialization—to close the "fifty to one hundred year-gap" between Russia and the advanced nations of the West in ten years—the regime needed economic organization methods appropriate to the task. In a situation wherein the aim of the State is to make a rapid and massive structural change in the economy, when this aim is clearly the dominant aim and when the priorities, the things that have to be done to accomplish the aim (the concentration on basic industrial commodities and machinery), are also clear, then direct centralized planning commends itself.[9] In such

---

[7] Joseph S. Berliner, *Factory and Manager in the USSR* (Cambridge, Mass.: Harvard University Press, 1957); David Granick, *Management of the Industrial Firm in the USSR* (New York: Columbia University Press, 1954), and "An Organizational Model of Soviet Industrial Planning," *Journal of Political Economy*, Vol. LXVII, No. 2 (April, 1959), pp. 109–30; and Alec Nove, *The Soviet Economy: An Introduction* (New York: Frederick A. Praeger, Inc., 1961), chap. 6 and *passim*.

[8] See Alexander Gerschenkron, *The Stability of Dictatorships* (Harvard Lecture, Yale University, April 3, 1963); and Abram Bergson, *The Economics of Soviet Planning* (New Haven, Conn.: Yale University Press, 1964), pp. 173–74.

[9] Compare the United States' and United Kingdom's uses of centralized techniques during World War II.

situations, indirect, decentralized methods of economic organization and control, relying on the price mechanism and marginalist calculations, can be said to work too slowly, moreover, not very effectively. When concentration is on new products, new industries, and new regional complexes, the constants needed to make close marginal decisions are themselves variables. Uncertainty runs rampant, and externalities, which cannot easily be internalized by individual decision makers, become of major importance.[10] Under such circumstances, centralized planning offers the state in some ways a more promising means of effectuating its control over the economy, for it is both a means of directly concentrating economic efforts on high priority sectors and diverting the impact of mistakes onto low priority sectors and a means of transmitting pressure and urgency to the economy.

The pressure transmitted by the Bolshevik regime to the Soviet economy was essentially of two different types. One was the pressure on the living standards of the Russian people, which was manifested in the rising rate of investment out of GNP, falling rate of consumption, and, for long parts of the Plan Era, falling levels of per capita consumption.[11] The second was the pressure exerted on the producing units in the economy to increase output. This pressure for more output per unit of input, this search for reserves of productivity was ubiquitous, and it was supported by a multitude of economic, social, and political incentives: the monetary rewards for surpassing production targets, the red banners for victory in interplant competitions, the political promotions (or demotions) for production successes (or failures). It imparted to all the producing units in the economy a constant and omnipresent condition of excess effective demand.

Although it is the first type of pressure, the pressure on the living standards of the people, which is of major interest to Gerschenkron in his pattern of Russian economic development, it is the second type of pressure, the pressure on the productive capacity of the basic enterprises, which is of major interest in this paper.

"Taut" Planning

The pressure on producing units was a result not only of the conscious policy on the part of the regime; it was also intensified, consciously and unconsciously, in the process of plan construction and implementation. A Soviet plan is not intended as a tool to achieve harmonious operation of the economy, but as a tool to mobilize resources for the attainment of a rapid rate of growth.

---

[10] See Tibor Scitovsky, "Two Concepts of External Economies," *Journal of Political Economy*, Vol. LXII, No. 2 (April, 1954), pp. 143–51.

[11] See Janet G. Chapman, "Consumption," in Abram Bergson and Simon Kuznets (eds.), *Economic Trends in the Soviet Union* (Cambridge, Mass.: Harvard University Press, 1963), pp. 236–44.

State plans established for the enterprises must mobilize all workers, manual and professional, in the struggle for the plan, in the movement forward toward the conquering of difficulties and the attaining of new growth in the national economy.[12]

Therefore, at the very beginning as a matter of policy, the intention is to give the enterprise a "taut" plan.[13] There is to be little slack between the full productive capacity of the enterprise and the output demanded of it. In fact, the intention is to set the target somewhat beyond the "full capacity" so as to force the enterprise to seek out reserves of increased output.

In the process of plan construction—speaking now of the annual plan, and primarily of the industrial plan—the conscious policy of putting pressure on all producing units is embodied in the control figures, the preliminary aggregate targets constructed by the state planning committee (Gosplan)[14] after consultation with the political leaders, and communicated by Gosplan down through the planning-control hierarchy to the producing units.[15] The input norms used in the construction of the control figures are highly optimistic ones, in this way imparting a significant degree of tautness to the plan at its inception.[16] This pressure is undoubtedly relieved somewhat in the counterplanning and bargaining as the plan comes back up the planning-control hierarchy. The enterprises seek to implant protective fat in the plan; although the superior organs do cut out some of the fat, they are restrained somewhat by the "family relationship" which exists between the superior body and the enterprises subordinate to it.[17] A considerable amount of pressure is reinstated in the plan when it comes back into Gosplan, for the central planners are not

---

[12] *Pravda*, March 1, 1947, p. 1.

[13] See Holland Hunter, "Optimal Tautness in Developmental Planning," *Economic Development and Cultural Change*, Vol. IX, No. 4 (July, 1961), Part I, pp. 561–72.

[14] We will use the term *Gosplan* to refer to the central planning body responsible for the construction of the annual plan even though at various times a different organization had this responsibility.

[15] For a description of the process and chronology of plan construction, see Bergson, *The Economics of Soviet Planning*; Herbert S. Levine, "The Centralized Planning of Supply in Soviet Industry," in United States Congress, Joint Economic Committee, *Comparisons of the United States and Soviet Economies* (Washington, D.C.: U.S. Government Printing Office, 1959), Part I, pp. 151–76; and Herbert S. Levine, *A Study in Economic Planning* (Unpublished Ph.D. thesis, Harvard University, 1961).

[16] In actuality, the conscious policy of pressure appears even earlier than the control figures in the chronology of plan construction. In the first stage, that of preparing the statistical base, done in the first part of the planning year, the planners have to project available data to the end of the planning year, that is, to the eve of the planned year. To assure the discipline of the plan, this projection should be done on the basis of all the growth rates planned for the (planning) year, but by the time these projections are undertaken, some knowledge is available on how the plan for the planning year is going. Thus, to the extent that current failures are ignored in the statistical projections, the plans for some sectors and some enterprises are extra taut.

[17] The aspect of the "family relationship" important here is that the performance of the superior organ is a sum of the performances of the subordinate enterprises.

part of the same family as are those directly responsible for production, and therefore they are free to bargain for the degree of tautness in the now much more detailed plan that they had originally put in the aggregate plan when it first began its journey down the administrative hierarchy. We would probably be safe to assume that when the plan is accepted back into Gosplan, it is in general less taut than when it began but not substantially so.

At this point, it is the task of Gosplan to work out the internal consistency of the plan. The method used is that of the material balances, in which an accounting balance, listing planned sources and uses of a product, is constructed for each of a large number of major products. The consistency of the plan is achieved by forging a balance between planned sources and uses in each and every material balance.[18] The material balances are often said to resemble aspects of input-output tables. This is true, although it should be noted that a material balance is similar to a row, not a column, of an input-output table and thus does not explicitly reflect the production technology of the economic plan.

The material balance method and Soviet planning practice do have a spiritual kinship with the input-output approach insofar as the assumption of fixed input coefficients is concerned (or, in the Soviet case, at least temporarily fixed coefficients). The production function used in the construction of a Soviet plan is of the following nature:

$$X_k = \min \left(\frac{x_{1k}}{a_{1k}}, \frac{x_{2k}}{a_{2k}}, \ldots, \frac{x_{ik}}{a_{ik}}, \ldots, \frac{x_{nk}}{a_{nk}} \right),$$

where, X_k = the planned output of the kth good,

$\quad x_{ik}$ = the planned flow of the ith good to the kth sector,

$\quad a_{ik}$ = the planned input of the ith good per unit of output of the kth good.

This function states that the output of any good is equal to the smallest ratio of an input flow divided by that input coefficient.[19] Aside from questions of inventory planning, it is the aim of planners to get all the relevant ratios equal to each other and equal to the desired level of output.

If the planned level of output of, say, the kth good turns out, on first inspection of the kth good's material balance, to be less than the planned uses of the kth good $\left(\sum_{i=1}^{n} x_{ki} \right)$, as is generally the case, how do Soviet planners achieve the required balance? That is, how do they increase the planned output of k and/or decrease the planned uses of k? One possible approach is to increase X_k by increasing each x_{ik} (in pro-

---

[18] This process is discussed in the sources in Footnote 15 above. The number of material balances has varied in the postwar period from approximately 760 to 1600.

[19] For example, if, $x_{1j} = 10$, $a_{1j} = 2$, $x_{2j} = 28$, $a_{2j} = 4$; then, $X_j = \min (10/2, 28/4) = 5$. (This means that 8 units of x_{2j} are in "excess" supply.)

portion to each fixed a_{ik}) and/or to decrease Σx_{ki} by decreasing all or some of the x_{ki}s. This approach, however, requires that a multitude of subsequent changes be made. As each input flow into $k(x_{ik})$ is increased, each input into each input (x_{vi}) has to be increased, and this has to be done a number of times before each material balance in the set will be sufficiently balanced (and similarly, *mutatis mutandis*, on the down side). I have argued in detail elsewhere that, although Soviet planners do go back a few levels when the output of a key product is increased, this iterative approach is not the sole nor probably even the primary method they use to attain a consistent set of material balances.[20] Briefly put, the computational requirements of the iterative approach, given the form of the material balances and the computational technology in use (desk calculators at best), make it clear that this is an infeasible approach, and it is confirmed by the Russians' own statements.

Adjusting Imbalances

How, then, are the output levels of deficit products increased and/or demand requirements decreased?[21] It appears that much reliance is put on methods which avoid the necessity of making secondary changes, thus avoiding reverberation of a change through the entire set of material balances. Output levels are increased, without increase in inputs; planned distributions to users are decreased, without decreasing the output levels of the user sectors. The approach is not to change the x_{ik}'s and the x_{ki}'s, but to change the input coefficients, the a_{ik}'s and the a_{ki}'s. This adds to the tightness of the plan, to the pressure on the producing enterprise. This increased pressure may at times be applied where protective fat still exists, and thus it may not be undesirable or unrealistic pressure. However, since buildup of pressure at this stage is not a result of conscious effort to remove fat but, rather, a by-product of a primitive planning technique used by harried planners to hammer out consistency in the plan, it must be assumed that in many instances it will be applied where there is not an ample layer of fat. That this is so is attested to by the statements of many Soviet authorities, including an official statement of the Communist Party to the effect that planned input relationships are often unrealistic, leading to "excess tension in the fulfillment of plans." Furthermore, it should not be thought that perhaps the excess pressure on some enterprises is "balanced off" by the excess fat of others. The pressure on an enterprise is not easily relieved by the presence of fat at another enterprise because

---

[20] See Levine, "Centralized Planning of Supply. . . ," pp. 163–67. For a somewhat divergent view, see J. M. Montias, "Planning with Material Balances in Soviet-Type Economies," *American Economic Review*, Vol. XLIX, No. 5 (December, 1959), pp. 963–85.

[21] The phrase "deficit product" is used here to mean a product for which demand is greater than planned supply during the process of plan construction.

in an atmosphere of heavy pressure an enterprise jealously guards whatever surplus resources it might have in anticipation of needing them itself someday (soon).

There are several other nonsecondary effect steps taken to reduce imbalances in the material balances which are worth discussing. Planned levels of input stocks are often cut down excessively in an effort either to increase the output of a deficit product into which the stock in question is an input or to reduce the demands on a deficit input. In practice, stocks actually held are usually significantly greater than planned levels. The proclivity of Soviet enterprise managers to hoard inventories is well known, and we will discuss this further on. However, here we wish to point out that one reason Soviet managers hold above-norm stocks is simply that the planned levels of these stocks are set too low. At times when inventories of input materials are even twice as high as planned levels, these inventories prove to be insufficient to prevent production stoppages. Actually, Soviet inventory levels (related to flow of output) should be higher than those in say the United States. This is so because to a certain extent inventories and unused productive capacity are substitutes for each other and because under Soviet conditions of general plan tightness there is a relative unavailability of excess productive capacity in the Soviet economy. Another balancing technique which avoids secondary effects is to accelerate the introduction of new productive capacity and include its planned output flow in the material balance of a deficit product. Under the best of conditions, the precise scheduling of the introduction of new capacity is difficult to accomplish; but under Soviet conditions, it is well nigh impossible, for with the tightness of plans, the consequent unreliability of supply, and the general deficiencies of excessive centralization (see below), the introduction of new capacity is almost always held up for want of one or another needed material or piece of equipment. Under such conditions, the reliance on output from new capacity to be introduced during the planned year, a fortiori when the introduction schedule is artificially speeded up, constitutes an element of "paper consistency" and thus adds to the pressure built up in the plan.

Further pressure is put on the enterprise by certain indirect ways of reducing input coefficients. For example, the planned flow of materials to be used in maintenance work is often reduced below required levels. Thus, when the need for maintenance becomes pressing, the enterprise must shift materials from direct production work to maintenance, in this way increasing the pressure in its production plan.

The buildup of pressure in the process of plan construction does not end with the working out of the internal consistency of the plan but continues into and through the stage at which the plan is officially reviewed and confirmed and also in the stage wherein the confirmed plan is brought down through the administrative hierarchy to the producing unit.

When the draft of the plan has been reviewed and altered by the political leaders it is not clear whether the changes made are mostly increases or decreases in outputs—whether they are intended to increase or relieve pressure on the specific sectors involved. Perhaps the approach varies both at a given time and over time. What is clear, however, is that when the political leaders make changes in outputs, it is hardly possible for the planners, in the short time they have at this stage (normally about two weeks), to work out the indirect consequences of these changes. Therefore, even if they were able to forge a consistent draft of the plan to present to the political leaders, it comes back unbalanced and remains unbalanced. To the extent, then, that the plan is more inconsistent than it was, the pressure in it is further increased.

The confirmed plan contains output, input, and other types of commands addressed primarily to the high-level administrative bodies. Before 1957 these were the ministries; at this writing they are mainly the administrative-planning bodies at the republic level (also the remaining and recreated ministries and the state committees). In the pre-1957 period, for which the picture is clearer than now, the relevant parts of the plan were sent to the ministry involved, and the ministry and its intermediary organs were supposed to subdivide the ministerial output targets and input allotments among the subordinate enterprises. In order to give themselves more maneuverability and thus more protection, the ministries practiced what the Russians call reinsurance planning and reserving.[22] Reinsurance planning describes the ministerial practice of assigning output targets to subordinate enterprises so that the total assignments totaled more than the ministerial output assignment. By increasing targets in this way, the ministries put pressure on all enterprises to produce at higher levels (with lower targets, they might have stopped at producing at lower levels), thus giving themselves more of a protective cushion against the possibility that some of their enterprises would not fulfill even the lower targets. This practice was officially recognized by the government, which set a limit of 10 percent on the amount by which the sum of assignments to enterprises could exceed the ministerial output assignment.

Reserving was another form of ministerial self-protection. This refers to the practice whereby a ministry did not distribute to its subordinate enterprise all the input allotments it received. The ministry reserved to itself a part of the allotments which it could then dispatch to trouble spots as they appeared during the course of the planned year. This practice too was officially recognized by the government, which permitted the ministry the right to reserve no more than 5 percent of the total ministerial allotment.

Although these practices added to the maneuverability of the ministry

---

[22] Reinsurance planning is what Berliner refers to as clearance planning. See Berliner, *op. cit.*, pp. 83–85, 257–259. It is to be assumed that these practices were continued by the relevant administrative bodies after the 1957 reorganization.

and in this way may have reduced the pressure on it, they added substantially to the pressure on the enterprise. They may be viewed as a means of redistributing some of the slack the ministry previously permitted enterprises to retain (in the bargaining process when the plan was coming up the hierarchy). By these methods such slack was transferred from the individual enterprises to the ministry as a whole, leaving the enterprise in a more highly pressured condition.

III. IMPACT OF PRESSURE

The question now to be faced is how all this pressure built up in the system leads to the observed characteristics of the Soviet economy. In this discussion, we do not intend to deny the role played by centralized planning itself and its many deficiencies. However, many of the characteristics, although related to the deficiencies of centralized planning, have been brought to their observed intensity by the presence of pressure in the system, and in addition there is a set of observed characteristics which are more directly related to pressure than they are to the presence of centralized planning.[23] We will examine the impact of pressure on Soviet economic activity under three major headings: the incentive system, the empty economy, and the seller's market. These are not three separate, airtight compartments, nor do they all operate at the same analytical level. They are at best loose classifications, and their effects are in many ways interrelated. But they are, nevertheless, useful categories with which to develop the argument.

Before proceeding to an analysis of the impact of pressure, let us look first at the impact of the direct deficiencies of centralized planning. The Soviet economy suffers from many ills of overcentralization, of which the major cause is that the planners at the center do not know and indeed cannot be expected to know all the details of the real situations at the basic producing units.[24] The information required by central planners in the Soviet system of centralized planning is monumental.[25] Moreover, because the information which the enterprise supplies has an important effect on the tasks and resources given to the enterprise, the enterprise will distort the information; for example, it will "pad" its requests for materials (this is of course a generally observed characteristic of bureaucracies which operate under analogous conditions). It appears that Soviet central planners at times try to avoid confrontation of masses of informa-

---

[23] Somewhat similar ideas are discussed in Granick, "An Organizational Model . . ."

[24] See Bergson, *Economics of Soviet Planning*, pp. 331-32; and Leon Smolinski, "What Next in Soviet Planning?," *Foreign Affairs*, Vol. 42, No. 4 (July, 1964), pp. 602-13.

[25] As an extreme example, to supply the information requested by its supply administration for the central construction of input norms, the Ural Machine Building Factory submitted a document 17,000 pages long.

tion, of doubtful reliability at that, and try to conduct their business without being burdened by too much information from the enterprises. Under such conditions plans are constructed with even less knowledge of real conditions at the periphery. As a result of the limited knowledge at the center, enterprises often receive detailed plans which do not take into account either the actual production capabilities and specialities of producing-enterprises or the specific input needs of consuming-enterprises. There is a frequent lack of coordination among the different plans (outputs, inputs, deliveries, finances, etc.) given to the enterprise by different superior planning organs. It is commonplace to see complaints in Soviet economic literature about enterprises' being given delivery assignments which are greater than their output targets, or allocations of input materials without sufficient allocation of financial means to purchase them. Moreover, this problem is aggravated by the great number of changes in the plans for enterprises made by superior organs during the course of the planned year (see below), for it often happens that changes are made in one set of plans without compensating changes being made in the others. All this creates a general condition of unreality in plan assignments and unreliability of planned inter-enterprise relationships.[26]

In addition to the above, centralized planning visits upon the Soviet economy the multitude of maladies flowing from the overgrowth of bureaucratic administration: red tape, delays in reaching decisions and getting things done, multiplicity of paper work, conflicting and overlapping lines of authority, and so forth.

There are other disadvantages directly attributable to centralized planning, but these are the most important ones. Keeping them in mind, let us go on to our argument that it is the pressure imposed on and built up within the economic system rather than centralized planning per se that to a significant extent accounts for many of the observed characteristics of the Soviet economy.

Incentive System

The pressure in the plan is communicated to the directors of enterprises through the application of the system of rewards and penalties. The

---

[26] The following blistering attack is by a prominent Yugoslav economist, quoted in Bela A. Balassa, *The Hungarian Experience in Economic Planning* (New Haven, Conn.: Yale University Press, 1959), p. 79:

The balancing of supply and demand in a centrally planned economy occurs in offices where a few people unaware of the real effects of their authoritarian plan become the supreme judges of the destinies of all producers and consumers through their bureaucratic machine. From this source of authority, plans lead further down to smaller bodies, splitting unrealistic averages into still smaller averages, according to norms born in offices which, when they reach the enterprise level, have little resemblance to the conditions of actual life.

(Perhaps centralized planning in the Soviet Union was not quite so bad as it apparently was in Yugoslavia—H.S.L.)

Soviet incentive mechanism, with its high rewards for successful fulfillment and overfulfillment of plan assignments and its monetary and position penalties for failure, is clearly geared to transmit the pressure in the plan. And since bonus rewards for plan fulfillment are not an insignificant part of managerial income, accounting for about 40 percent of that income, the incentive system transmits the pressure in an intensified way.[27] Its impact is pervasive, but closely interwoven with the operation of the other categories we will consider, and thus often difficult to distinguish. Nevertheless, many of the things discussed by Berliner and Granick are clearly related to the pressure transmitted by the incentive system.[28]

First of all, there is the search for safety. Since success is a function of performance relative to expected (or commanded) performance, rewards can be acquired not only by performing on a high level, but also by being assigned low expectations. Therefore, the pressure on the enterprise in the plan, magnified by the incentive mechanism, greatly intensifies the general bureaucratic tendency to seek out ways of increasing security by understating productive capacity, by overstating input requirements, and by hoarding hidden inputs. Furthermore, the pressure transmitted by the reward and penalty system leads also to a group search for safety, the protective family circle.

Another aspect of the search for safety in the face of pressure from the incentive system is the operation of the "ratchet principle":[29] the enterprise manager tempers his rate of plan overfulfillment in order not to get too high a plan the following year, and he resists innovation (which always entails some risks) because the penalty for failure is great, and the reward for success short-lived.

Many familiar operating characteristics of the Soviet economy are primarily responses to the pressures communicated by the incentive system. The pressure to fulfill the dominant physical output plans is so great that enterprises ignore costs, "storm" at the end of the accounting period, falsify output data, skimp on quality, distort the planned output mix by emphasizing those outputs where the bonus per unit of available resources is highest.[30]

"Empty Economy"

The second of our categories is the "empty economy." The heavy pressure leads to a situation of general tautness in the Soviet economy. There is an absence of slack, and reserve stocks of resources are not easily

---

[27] See especially Berliner and Nove in Footnote 7 of this chapter.

[28] See Footnote 7 of this chapter.

[29] Berliner, *op. cit.*, pp. 78–79.

[30] This distortion of the product-mix is associated with the absence of a meaningful price system in the centralized economy. However, the enterprise's need to engage in such activity is greatly intensified by the pressure in the system.

available. This condition is what Hicks referred to as the "empty economy" when describing the post-World War II English economy. In such a situation, he said, the economy becomes accident prone, and minor mishaps become major crises.[31] This is just what happens in the Soviet economy; since there are insufficient protective reserves, even a minor shortage of an important material often becomes a major bottleneck.[32] This not only calls for the pursuit of bottlenecks in the construction of Soviet plans, but also leads to the great number of changes which are made in the operating plans during the course of the planned year in an effort to attack bottlenecks as they appear. The unavailability of reserves coupled with frequent unrealistically tight plans, leads to the unreliability of the Soviet materials supply system and its consequences: work stoppages, use of inferior but available substitute inputs, and the enterprise's network of expediters searching for needed inputs in all parts of the country. It also intensifies the tendency toward the hoarding of input materials, and it encourages producing units to integrate vertically, to produce as many of the needed inputs as possible; thus the economy loses the potential economies of specialization.

Sellers' Market

The pressure in the system and the way rewards are established in relation to the physical output plan have led to a chronic condition of sellers' market in the Soviet economy. This term means simply the situation wherein demand, under the given "rates of exchange," is consistently greater than supply.

This seller's market has had a marked effect on the operation of the Soviet economy. Moreover, its impact was intensified during the pre-1957 period (and to some extent afterward) by the strategic role of producers' organizations in the construction of the central plan. It was the sales administration of the producing ministry which, in the final stages of plan construction, was responsible for setting the highly detailed production plans for enterprises within its ministry and for establishing detailed product flows from producing-enterprises to consuming-enterprises, all within the bounds set by the official annual plan. (After the 1957 reorganization these tasks were performed by Gosplan organs, entitled main administrations of interrepublican deliveries and based upon the former ministerial sales administrations.) This arrangement intensified the influence of the sellers' market because the ministerial sales organs were

---

[31] J. R. Hicks, "The Empty Economy," *Lloyds Bank Review*, No. 5 (July 1947), pp. 1–13. I am indebted to Prof. F. Holzman for calling my attention to this article. See also H. K. Charlesworth, *The Economics of Repressed Inflation* (London: Macmillan, 1956).

[32] Shortages may arise because enterprises failed to operate properly or because the plans themselves were unrealizable.

concerned with interests of the producers, the group with strong market power, rather than with the interests of the purchasers, the group with weak market power, thus in many situations adding a contributing force to the sellers' market rather than a countervailing one.

Given the sellers' market and the dominance of the physical output targets, the Soviet enterprise does not have to worry at all about being able to sell its output; it can concentrate its efforts on getting its needed inputs and making sure it is able to meet its output targets. Among other things, this accounts for the Soviet enterprise's greater aversion to innovation in products than to innovation in processes. Under the conditions stipulated, the producing-enterprise has no incentive to improve its product in order to make it more useful to the consuming-enterprise (as we saw before, it has little incentive to improve its production processes because of the operation of the "ratchet principle"). Furthermore, it is not pressed to do so by the sales administration of its ministry because the sales administration is more concerned with the production problems of its own ministry than with the needs of consumers.

The producer's one-sided concern with its own production needs and lack of concern for the needs of consuming enterprises lead also to a lowering of the quality of output and to a failure to produce the output assortment most needed by the users, the producer concentrating on the output mix most easy to produce and yielding the highest bonus. In addition, the sellers' market affects the timing of output and deliveries. Soviet steel-rolling mills, for example, tend toward long, uninterrupted runs of individual items of their output mix, which is fine for meeting their output targets but is highly detrimental to the interests of, say, a machine plant customer who needs a number of different types of rolled steel to produce a machine. Finally, because of the lack of attention paid by the sales administration of the producing-ministries to the needs of individual consumers, a consuming-enterprise is often assigned an irrational array of suppliers; its orders are spread out among a large number of them rather than concentrated in a few, and it also is often assigned different suppliers from year to year. This contributes further to the unreliability of inter-enterprise relations in the Soviet economy.

Before leaving this question, let us look briefly at some of the methods which are used to counteract the deleterious effects of the sellers' market. One important method is vertical integration but here with a slightly different focus from the one we discussed in relation to the "empty economy." Here the aim is to make sure that the quality and mix of inputs are in accord with the needs of the consumer. Furthermore, it is sometimes used to foster product innovation as was done when the coal ministry produced its own coal cutting machinery.

Another method is the fairly frequent use of wholesale prices established f.o.b. point of destination, that is, one price for all consumers or for all consumers in a given region.[33] By including transportation charges in the price, an incentive for achieving a rational geographic distribution of orders is given the producers rather than the consumers. This is wise, both because it is the sales administrations of the producers that play the dominant role in fixing producer-consumer ties and because under conditions of a sellers' market, purchasers may be willing to buy from any producer no matter what the extra transportation cost, whereas sellers, if they have to cover transportation costs, might be more apt to try to minimize these costs.

The most formal effort to counteract the uneven market power of sellers and buyers is the attempt to gain legal protection of the rights of buyers through the use of legal contracts enforced by the system of arbitration courts. However, its effects are somewhat reduced by the reluctance of buyers to apply contractual sanctions against suppliers violating these contracts, because of the fear of antagonizing suppliers they may be dependent upon in the future.

IV. PLANNING WITHOUT PRESSURE?

The hypothesis put forth in this paper has concerned the role and impact of pressure in the Soviet economy. It has been argued that the pressure on the basic producing units exerted by the political leaders and built up in the process of plan construction is manifested through and intensified by the incentive system, the "empty economy," and the sellers' market, and is responsible to a great extent for many of the observed characteristics of the Soviet economy frequently attributed to the mechanism of centralized planning itself.

The hypothesis has been argued; what is needed to test it are some observations on the operation in the Soviet economy of a system of centralized planning without pressure. Is such a situation possible? More practically, is it to be expected?

Theoretically it appears feasible, although some problems of incentives would need discussion. In the realm of Marxian theory, it fits well with what Marx and Engels seemed to have had in mind on the rare occasions when they spoke of planning in a socialist society. To Marx, the aim of having a central plan was the eradication of anarchy and the gearing of the economy to the wants of society.[34] There was no thought of using it to apply pressure to the economy.

---

[33] See Morris Bornstein, "The Soviet Price System," *American Economic Review*, Vol. LII, No. 1 (March, 1962), p. 77, and the sources listed there.

[34] "(Labor's) apportionment in accordance with a definite social plan maintains the proper proportion between the different kinds of work to be done and the various wants of the community." Karl Marx, *Capital*, Vol. I (Moscow: Foreign Languages Publishing House, 1954), p. 79.

After the death of Stalin and especially after his removal from the ranks of the deities in 1956, Soviet leaders began to talk about the reduction of pressure on producing units. In discussing the draft of the Seven Year Plan, Khrushchev said that "the Seven Year Plan is being drawn up in such a way that it can be implemented without overstrain," and he went on to describe some of the negative features of overly tight plans. Others have also spoken about the dangers of overstrain and complained of its presence, but at the same time, complaints are also heard about excessive looseness in the plans. The debate continues and it is not clear yet to what extent there has been a change in the amount of pressure in the plan.

By extending the Gerschenkron pattern of Russian economic development, with which this paper began, to the present period, it might be argued that the time is ripe for the removal of pressure. Russia has built up its economic base. It has achieved a state of military parity with the West. There is no longer the gnawing tension between what the State wants to do and what it can do because of a relatively backward economy, for the economy is no longer so relatively backward. Furthermore, the leader associated with the economic development drive is dead, and his political influence removed. In the past workings of the pattern, it was after the death of Peter the Great and after the removal of Count Witte, that the State withdrew its pressure from the economy. Perhaps such political events are important for changing the atmosphere. The period of pressure has been long, and it has included a terribly destructive war; certainly the people must be exhausted. There are signs now that the pressure on the standard of living of the Russian people has been reduced. For example, consumption levels have grown significantly in the decade of the 1950's,[35] and now many notable Russian political figures and economists are calling for a relative increase in the growth of consumption. Perhaps one of the strongest statements and most pertinent for our purpose was made recently by a leading Soviet economic official:

> In the period of the construction of the material and technical base of socialism, the industrialization of the country entailed sacrifices; it was necessary to economize on everything, including personal consumption. Today our economy is so healthy and industry is so well developed that we have every possibility of successfully solving the problem of creating the material and technical base for communism and, on this basis, strengthening defenses and simultaneously stepping up the personal consumption of the Soviet people.[36]

It must be noted that Professor Gerschenkron has never, to our knowledge, extended his pattern of Russian economic development to the point

---

[35] Chapman, *op. cit.*

[36] Academician A. Arzumanian in *Pravda*, February 24, 1964, as translated in the *Current Digest of the Soviet Press*, Vol. XVI, No. 8 (March 18, 1964), p. 4.

of using it to indicate the strong possibility of the Soviet political leaders' withdrawal of pressure from the economy. The extension is the author's. Gerschenkron has in fact put forth an hypothesis on dictatorships which to a significant extent runs counter to this. In his 1963 Harvard Lecture at Yale University, he argues that modern dictatorships must continuously legitimatize themselves in order to remain in power. They do this by (among other things) the "maintenance of a permanent condition of stress and strain," and by the "incessant exercise of dictatorial power."[37] He does not go so far as to deny that the Soviet leaders have not or may not reduce stress and strain but to the extent that they do, he argues, their power will erode.[38]

Do the recent signs of the reduction of pressure indicate that nonpressure centralized planning in the Soviet economy is just around the corner? We do not think so. At the same time the degree of pressure may be changing, the forms of planning and control are also changing. This is so not only because the Soviet economy today is larger and more complex and thus more difficult to plan, but also because there has been change in economic focus. Centralized planning has accomplished what its use was intended to accomplish: the radical and rapid structural transformation of the Soviet economy. On almost all counts (with the exception of proportion of labor force in agriculture and also, perhaps, the overall level of technology), Russia is today a highly industrialized nation. The aim now is to improve the efficiency of the economy, to get more output per unit of input, and to change the product mix in a slower and not altogether predetermined way. This is not a situation in which the brute force methods of centralized planning recommend themselves. When the task is to improve economic efficiency, decision making must be moved to the level of the producing units, and useful choice parameters (prices) must be provided so that relative benefits and costs can be compared and economically meaningful choices made.

That this situation calls for an increase in decentralized methods of planning and control is apparent, and it is also apparent from the current discussions (Libermanism, and so forth) and from some current actions that this is the direction the Soviets are taking. However, since the Soviet leaders undoubtedly want to maintain control over the general path and pace of development (including avoidance of glaring disproportions, maintenance of full employment, and so forth), reform will undoubtedly stop far short of complete decentralization. At a minimum, the political leaders will retain control over the amount and direction of investment. Also, they will most likely retain some power to assure aggregate sectoral balancing and the production and inculcation of major elements of tech-

---

[37] Gerschenkron, *Stability of Dictatorship*, p. 5.
[38] *Ibid.*, pp. 34–36.

nical change.[39] The development of computers and computer techniques for data collection, processing, and use will help the centralized aspects of such a mixed system operate more effectively than would be the case in the absence of these computational devices.

What is in store, then, is a Soviet economy with perhaps less pressure but also with less centralized planning. It appears that we may never get to observe real nonpressure centralized planning in the Soviet economy. For that matter (and for similar reasons), the entire subspace of economies with nonpressure centralized planning may be empty. Thus we are left with an hypothesis about the separate effects of the separate components, pressure and centralized planning, when in reality the two components may be a joint product. They appear together, both in relation to dynamic, determinate structural change, and they fade together when the economic focus switches to the channels of slower growth, less determinate and more moderate structural change. The analysis presented here is, hopefully, of analytical interest, but to the extent that pressure and centralized planning do operate as a joint product, the value of treating them separately may, we regret to say, be somewhat limited.

Before closing, a word on non-joint responsibility. We have in this paper used—or misused—some of the hypotheses of Professor Gerschenkron. It should be clear, however, that all responsibility for what has been said here lies with the author. It is the task of the apprentice to learn the master's methods, but the master should never be held responsible for the foolishness of the apprentice. A wrathful God once spoke of *poked awon avoth al banim*, but even he did not countenance, *poked awon banim al avoth*.[40]

---

[39] The power to assure aggregate sectoral balancing and sectoral technical change may require the reintroduction of branch line ministries. This may appear to be a contradiction of decentralization, but it is not necessarily so.

[40] For those who, unlike Alexander Gerschenkron, cannot handle a multitude of foreign languages: A wrathful God once spoke of "visiting the sins of the fathers upon the sons," but even he did not countenance "visiting the sins of the sons upon the fathers."

6| THE CONSISTENCY
OF SOVIET PLANS

Michael Ellman

A basic test of good planning is "consistency"—whether supplies and uses of resources balance without shortages or surpluses. Consistency is a necessary condition for "efficiency"—obtaining the maximum output from given resources and technology. In turn, "optimality" in planning involves selecting, from among a number of alternative "efficient" variants of the plan, the variant which best satisfies the ruling social preferences. A common criticism of Soviet planning is that it fails to achieve consistency and thus, also, efficiency and optimality. Despite this, the planners may still succeed in accomplishing important governmental objectives, such as rapid industrialization and national power. However, because of shortcomings in the planning process, they use resources less effectively and fulfill targets to a lesser extent than if resource allocation were guided by consistent, efficient, and optimal plans.

This article analyzes the obstacles to attaining consistency in Soviet planning. After a careful definition of consistency, it examines the two main instruments used in seeking consistency in Soviet planning—material balances and input-output methods. It explains the nature of these tools, their limitations, and their use in the USSR. It concludes that although the application of input-output has not by itself greatly reduced inconsistencies in planning, the related introduction of mathematical models and modern computing techniques may significantly improve planning in the future.

Michael Ellman is Lecturer in Political Economy at the University of Glasgow. The article is reprinted by permission from the *Scottish Journal of Political Economy,* Vol. XVI, No. 1 (February, 1969), pp. 50–74, with the omission of citations to Russian-language sources.

I. INTRODUCTION

THERE ARE a number of questions which can be asked about a national economic plan. What are its objectives? Were they achieved? Is the plan comprehensive? Is the plan optimal? A question which is often asked and which seems prima facie to be rather important is that of whether the plan is consistent, i.e., are its various sections compatible with one another? The purpose of this paper is to examine the consistency of Soviet plans. This question is very closely linked with the classic debate on the economics of socialism.

In a famous paper Barone argued that the Ministry of Production in the Collectivist State would have to solve the millions of equations of the Walrasian general equilibrium system, that this would be extremely difficult, and that there was not much point in abolishing capitalism as capitalism automatically solves the equations. In addition the collectivist solution would be very costly (employing an army of bureaucrats) and for the sake of rationality would have to employ the same instruments of economic calculation (e.g., the rate of interest on capital) as capitalism.[1]

An examination of the consistency of Soviet plans leads the present author to the conclusion that Barone and Robbins[2] were right to emphasize the difficulty of drawing up even consistent, let alone optimal, central plans, but that the moral that they drew from this was false. Planning and the market are not alternative roads to the same destination. Planning is advocated by those who wish to achieve a very different distribution of goods among the population than would have been achieved by the market, and to allocate resources, in a dynamic economy, in a direction which the market, left to itself, would not have chosen. The market, left to itself, will allocate resources in a direction determined by the preferences of individuals weighted by the distribution of income and wealth, by the preferences of firms weighted by the distribution of initiative and assets between firms, and by technology. Planning is advocated by those who want to allocate resources in some other direction. Soviet planning has been primarily concerned with the rapid industrialization and modernization of a backward country, and the only sensible way of judging its record is by analyzing its achievements in this field and their costs. The question of the consistency of the plan is much less important than the question of the goals of the plan and their achievement. Nevertheless, the question of the consistency of Soviet plans is of interest in itself, and it is to this question that the present paper addresses itself.

One of the conclusions that is arrived at is that Soviet plans are normally inconsistent. It should be borne in mind that this only means that the plans for at least some of the many thousands of centrally planned commodities are in fact inconsistent, and that the plans for at least some of the many thousands of enterprises are in fact inconsistent. It does not mean that the main proportions of the plan are inconsistent with each other (a subject outside the scope of this paper). Neither does it mean

---

[1] E. Barone, "The Ministry of Production in the Collectivist State," in F. A. Hayek (ed.), *Collectivist Economic Planning* (London: Routledge & Kegan Paul Ltd., 1935), pp. 245–90.

[2] Robbins repeated the Barone argument in his book, *The Great Depression* (London: Macmillan, 1934).

that it is unimportant for countries with a very highly aggregated frame-work plan to try and ensure that this plan is consistent.

II. THE PROBLEM

Consider an output plan

$$a_{11} \ a_{12} \ ... \qquad\qquad a_{1n}$$
$$m \longrightarrow \infty$$
$$.....................$$
$$n = 200,000$$
$$a_{m1} \ a_{m2} \ ... \qquad\qquad a_{mn}$$

where each column represents the productive activity of an enterprise, and each row represents a separate commodity, so that a_{ij} is the output of the ith good produced by the jth enterprise.

Consider a supply plan

$$b_{11} \ b_{12} \ ... \qquad\qquad b_{1n}$$
$$m \longrightarrow \infty$$
$$.....................$$
$$n = 200,000$$
$$b_{m1} \ b_{m2} \ ... \qquad\qquad b_{mn}$$

where each column represents the input requirements of an enterprise, and each row is a commodity, so that b_{ij} is the amount of the ith good required by the jth enterprise.

Consider a delivery plan

$$c_{11} \ c_{12} \ ... \qquad\qquad c_{1n}$$
$$m \longrightarrow \infty$$
$$.....................$$
$$n = 200,000$$
$$c_{m1} \ c_{m2} \ ... \qquad\qquad c_{mn}$$

where c_{ij} is the amount of the ith good delivered to the jth enterprise.

The problem of compiling a consistent plan can be represented as the problem of choosing

    a) A matrix a_{mn} $m \longrightarrow \infty$
                                   $n = 200,000$

    b) A matrix b_{mn} $m \longrightarrow \infty$
                                   $n = 200,000$

    c) A matrix c_{mn} $m \longrightarrow \infty$
                                   $n = 200,000$

such that

    1) $c_{ij} = b_{ij}$ $i = 1 \ ... \ \infty$
                                 $j = 1 \ ... \ 200,000$

i.e. each enterprise should receive the goods it requires.

    2) $a_{ij} \leq \bar{a}_{ij}$

where $\bar{a}_{ij}$ is the full capacity output of the ith good by the jth enterprise. i.e. no enterprise should receive a plan to produce more of a good than is possible.

$$3) \quad \sum_{j=1}^{n} a_{ij} = \sum_{j=1}^{n} b_{ij}$$

i.e. the output of each good should equal requirements.

A plan that meets these requirements is "consistent" in only the weakest of Stone's seven senses of the word.[3] Soviet plans are often inconsistent even in this sense. According to the late Academician Nemchinov, the doyen of Soviet economists, "The plans for production, labor, finance, and supply are often inconsistent."

The chief difficulties in compiling a consistent plan are:

1. Collecting the necessary data. Accurate data on capacity and input requirements are hard to obtain in an economy where enterprises have an incentive to minimize capacity and maximize output needs in their reports to the center.

2. Aggregation. The process of aggregation and disaggregation is a major source of inconsistencies. The author has analyzed this elsewhere.[4]

3. Processing the necessary data. A limited number of officials, divided into numerous departments, and armed with abacuses, pens and telephones—or more sophisticated equipment—have only a limited time to solve the problem, which is excessively complicated both because of its huge dimensions and because the variables are interrelated. When, during the course of plan calculations a_{ij} altered, its input requirements b_{ij} ($i = 1 \ldots \infty$) are altered, which alters the necessary outputs of other enterprises.[5]

---

[3] Richard Stone, "Consistent Projection in Multi-sector Models," in E. Malinvaud and M. O. L. Bacharach (eds.), *Activity Analysis in the Theory of Growth and Planning* (London: Macmillan, 1967), pp. 232–44.

[4] Michael Ellman, "Aggregation as a Cause of Inconsistent Plans," *Economica*, Vol. XXXVI, No. 141 (February, 1969), pp. 69–74.

[5] A prominent Soviet economist has explained that: ". . . very year it becomes more difficult to balance the economy, to compile a plan for its development, to control it . . .

. . . the chief difficulty is that with the existing system of planning and control, based on manual calculations and the perception of a limited amount of information by a planner, it is difficult not only to find an optimal solution to the development of an economy, but physically impossible to balance the plan. For the compilation of such a plan for the tens of thousands of products for which the USSR state plan sets targets, requires the carrying out of billions of calculations (mathematically this is a problem of solving a system of linear equations), whereas a man equipped with a desk calculator can do 1,000–2,000 calculations per day. Even if the infinite splitting up of the work were possible (which is impossible with these relationships) the whole apparatus of Gosplan could not do one hundredth part of the necessary calculations for this group of plan indices."

III. MATERIAL BALANCES

Nature

An essential requirement for successful government regulation of an economy is a statistical picture of the economy arranged in a way compatible with the instruments of regulation which the government uses. In Britain such a statistical picture is provided by the national accounts, which provide the information necessary for the regulation of the economy by fiscal means. In the Soviet Union the necessary statistical information is arranged in a series of "balances," the "balance of the national economy" and its subdivisions. The nature of the Soviet planning system in which the central authorities give detailed orders for the production of specific items to the enterprises, and allocate to them specific quantities of goods, is such that the most important subdivision of the balance of the national economy is the set of "material balances." These are the instruments used to ensure consistency, i.e., a state of affairs in which producers produce the quantities of goods required by consumers, without shortages or waste.

A material balance shows, on the one hand the economy's resources,

TABLE 1

Material Balance for Product X for 1968
(million tons)

Resources	Distribution
1. Production (subdivided by republics)	1. Production needs (subdivided by republics and by ministries)
2. Imports	2. Free market allocation
3. Other sources	3. Exports
4. Stocks at suppliers at beginning of plan period (subdivided by republics)	4. Other needs
	5. Stocks at suppliers at end of year
	6. Reserves

and on the other hand the economy's needs, for a particular product for a specified period of time. A material balance can be arranged schematically as in Table 1.

The entries are reasonably self-explanatory. The free market allocation is the amount of the good which goes outside the state sector, e.g., to collective farms or to consumption.

The material balances are used in the following way. In April–May of the year preceding the planned year (the planning year) Gosplan, after consultation with the republican gosplans and the USSR ministries, drafts a preliminary plan. It usually contains between 110 and 170 commodities, the exact number varying from year to year. In August, Gosplan compares its preliminary plan with the counter plan that has emerged from below. It draws up material balances for 1,300–1,500 products, to ensure consistency and spot any glaring disproportions. At the end of the year about 2,000 material balances are worked out by Gosplan, and many more disaggregated balances by the State Committee for material-technical supply and its chief administrations. The precise details of the system are in continual flux. Until 1963 there were 24,790 centrally planned products. Of these, Gosplan itself worked out the plans and balances for 3,308, various USSR ministries and departments for 1,331, the union republics for 704, and the chief administrations for interrepublican supply worked out the plans and balances for 19,447 commodities. After the September (1965) Plenum the number of centrally planned commodities was reduced.

The crucial problem in material balance methodology is the equation of planned resources and planned distribution. Usually at the beginning of the balancing work, the prospective demand for a product is greater than the prospective supply. What steps are taken in these circumstances? The basic principle is that the plan is not reduced to accommodate a bottleneck. ("Don't plan on the bottleneck, plan to widen the bottleneck," was a familiar slogan of the 1930's.) This is regarded by the planners and Party leaders as sheer opportunism. What is done is that the corresponding industrial department attempts to increase the supply of the deficit commodity. One way of doing this would be to reduce stocks held by suppliers. Another would be to raise planned imports. The major effort is directed to increase current production by more efficient use of resources. Sometimes the planned introduction of new capacity is speeded up. Remorseless pressure will be transmitted to the enterprises to raise efficiency.

Simultaneously the summary department is attempting to decrease the demand for the deficit material. The basic principle is to accomplish this without lowering the output targets of the users. Pressure is applied to decrease the norms. Another possibility is the substitution of non-deficit materials for the deficit one. Throughout the balancing process, the priority principle is at work, for the emphasis is on guaranteeing the supply of goods to the priority sectors. It is the sectors of secondary importance that have their allocations cut, or are called on to use substitutes. (As a result of the multiplication of objectives from the middle of the 1950's onwards, strict application of the priority principle had perforce to be relaxed, with consequent difficulties.) When a summary department makes a change which reduces the flow of the deficit commodity to other sectors, it notifies the corresponding industry department, and vice versa.

The process of concurrent adjustment of the supply and demand for each balanced commodity ends with the "closing" of the balance, when the sum total of the allocations matches the total planned supply. Before all the balances can be closed simultaneously, it is often necessary to go up and down the administrative hierachy several times. (The process is similar to that in the UK Ministry of Supply in World War II.)

Problems

The method of material balances suffers from a number of weaknesses:[6]

1. Material balances are not worked out for all goods. This reduces the dimensions of the problem from millions of equations to thousands of equations, but it means that there may well be shortages or waste in non-balanced commodities.

2. Often material balances do not cover the entire output of the good in question. For many kinds of products material balances embrace little more than 60 percent of production. When commodity A is produced as a subsidiary product of enterprise X belonging to industry B, then X's output of A may not be known to the central planners or to the sectoral planners responsible for the A industry. Consequently, even when the balance is closed on paper, the plan may well be inconsistent.

3. If the compilers of different balances use different assumptions, then inconsistencies will result.

4. Most of the data on stocks which the center has are on the stocks of producers. Its data on consumers' stocks are scanty and unreliable.

5. It is well known that the concept of "capacity," data on which are basic to the construction of material balances, is imprecise. The data available to the planners is of doubtful reliability because the enterprises have an incentive to minimize their capacity in reports to the center.

6. When output is measured by the "gross-value-of-output" index, its volume depends, *inter alia*, on the degree of vertical integration.

7. Input norms are basic to the calculations. These too, the enterprises have a direct incentive to falsify.

8. When during the course of the material balance calculations, the output of one product is altered, it is necessary to alter the outputs of all the products that, directly or indirectly, are used in the production of that product. For example, an increase in the production of cars entails an increase in the production of steel, which in its turn entails an increase in the production of electricity, which in its turn requires an increase in the production of coal, which in its turn . . . In practice, however, Efimov has explained that:

Because of the great labor intensity of the calculation of changes in the material balances and the insufficiency of time for the completion of such work in

---

[6] For a discussion of the problems of the material balance technique, see N. K. Chandra, *Some Problems of Investment Planning in a Socialist Economy with Special Reference to the USSR and Poland* (Unpublished Ph.D thesis, London, 1965).

practice, sometimes only those balances which are linked by first order relationships are changed. As regards relationships of the second order, and especially of the third and fourth order, changes in the balances are made only in those cases where the changes are conspicuous.

In other words, whereas consistency requires the evaluation of the convergent series

$$X = (I + A + A^2 + A^3 \ldots)Y$$

the traditional Soviet practice is to approximate X by considering the first two terms only. In view of the fact that the process of calculation is often cut short, inconsistencies are to be expected, in principle. The practical importance of this depends on the ratio of full inputs to direct inputs, and the number of iterations required for consistency. The Soviet Central Statistical Administration, working on the 1959 input-output table for the USSR in value terms, found that usually this ratio was between 1 and 2, but that much larger values occurred quite frequently, ranging up to 54.7! The number of iterations required has been estimated by Levine at between 6 and 13.[7]

On the other hand, it has been shown, using Soviet data, that in most cases two rounds of iteration were enough to bring direct input norms quite close to full input norms. Furthermore, the number of iterations required is reduced by the existence of bottlenecks. The planners can arrive at a consistent plan without matrix inversion, through iterations, provided that the outputs in the excess capacity sectors are adapted to the potentials of the bottleneck sectors.[8] Furthermore, in practice the planners can use the experience of previous years to offset the difficulties listed above. In addition, if the planners have available to them an input-output table, they can use the full input coefficients derived from it in their calculations.

IV. INPUT-OUTPUT

Nature and Problems

An input-output table is a way of arranging the national accounts which focuses attention on productive relationships between industries. In Soviet statistical practice an input-output table is regarded "as an organic part of the balance of the national economy, as its further development,

---

[7] Herbert S. Levine, "The Centralized Planning of Supply in Soviet Industry," in United States Congress, Joint Economic Committee, *Comparisons of the United States and Soviet Economies* (Washington, D.C.: U.S. Government Printing Office, 1959), Part I, pp. 151–76.

[8] See John Michael Montias, *Central Planning in Poland* (New Haven: Yale University Press, 1962), pp. 339–45, and J. M. Montias, "On the Consistency and Efficiency of Central Plans," *Review of Economic Studies*, Vol. XXIX, No. 4 (October, 1962), pp. 280–90.

and above all as the development and disaggregation of the balance of the production, consumption, and accumulation of the social product and the national income."

The concept of an economy as a circular flow of commodities goes back to Quesnay's *Tableau Economique*. The first set of national accounts providing data on productive relationships between industries was compiled by the Soviet Central Statistical Administration in the 1920's. Leontief, aware of the Soviet work,[9] subsequently developed in the United States a mathematical model which provides a convenient way of arranging, and a useful method for analyzing and extrapolating, statistics on inter-industry relations. Soviet work on input-output in summarized in the Appendix table.

The construction of input-output tables gives rise to numerous problems. "The most complicated and labor intensive part of the work on an ex post input-output table is to obtain and process the necessary statistical information." As the statistical information which enterprises send to the Central Statistical Administration is inadequate, the necessary additional information is obtained by sample surveys. The existing data on the production and consumption of agricultural products produced on private plots by collective farmers and others, are not very reliable.

Economic activity takes place in enterprises, which are grouped into administrative units (firms in capitalist countries, economic ministries in the USSR). As input-output is concerned with data about technological relationships between industries to be used in planning, it is desirable that data be collected about the enterprises, and not about the administrative units into which they are grouped.[10] Where an enterprise produces, in addition to its main product, subsidiary products, it is desirable that the subsidiary output, and the inputs necessary to produce it, be transferred to the appropriate industry.[11] (The proportion of "foreign" output depends on the detail of the classification.) In this way it is possible to arrive at a "commodity-commodity" table. Call the method of classification which does not take into account the fact that enterprises may produce more than one commodity, the "industry-industry" classification. The difference between the two can be very great, as the following table (p. 92), which refers to Lithuania in 1961, clearly shows.

Either those inputs which come to the enterprise from outside, or all inputs regardless of whether they come to the enterprise from outside or from an earlier stage of production within the enterprise itself, can be considered as inputs. (In Soviet statistical practice, the former is known as

---

[9] He reviewed it in a German journal. There is an English translation in Nicolas Spulber (ed.), *Foundations of Soviet Strategy for Economic Growth: Selected Soviet Essays, 1924–1930* (Bloomington, Ind.: Indiana University Press, 1964), pp. 88–94.

[10] Richard Stone, *Input-Output and National Accounts* (Paris: Organization for European Economic Co-operation, 1961), pp. 34–35.

[11] *Ibid.*, pp. 35–36.

TABLE 2

The Relationship Between a "Commodity-Commodity" and "Industry-Industry" Calculation of the Outputs of Particular Industries, with a 239 Industry Classification

(1) *Industry*	(2) *Volume of Production of the Industry's Product Produced in Enterprises Belonging to the Industry Itself*	(3) *Volume of Production of "Foreign" Products Produced by Enterprises Belonging to the Industry, as a Percentage of Column (2)*	(4) *Volume of Production of the Given Industry Produced by Enterprises Belonging to Other Industries, as Percentage of Column (2)*
Wine making............	100	0.5	139.9
Non-alcoholic drinks......	100	—	128.0
Yeast...................	100	1.9	92.4
Medical instruments and equipment.........	100	331.2	90.4
Concentrated feeds........	100	—	87.0
Equipment for the building materials industry..............	100	202.3	81.0
Electricity and thermal power generation.......	100	1.3	66.7
Tractors and agricultural machinery........	100	40.6	64.0
Constructural engineering...............	100	72.8	48.2

the "gross output" (*valovaya produktsia*) method, the latter as the "gross turnover" (*valovoi oborot*) method.) Input coefficients calculated from statistics gathered using the former method are determined not only by technology, but also by the extent of vertical integration, and therefore the latter method is preferable for planning.

In general, it is desirable that statistics for input-output purposes be collected from enterprises and not from groups of enterprises, that they allocate subsidiary activities correctly, and that the gross turnover method is used. These points are more important in the USSR than they would be in say, the UK, because Soviet enterprises are less specialized. All Soviet input-output tables are based on data collected from enterprises and are "commodity-commodity" tables rather than "industry-industry" tables. In some cases the gross output method is used, in others the gross turnover method. The latter is favored by most economists in this field and by the Central Economic Mathematical Institute (TSEMI), the former by the Central Statistical Administration.

The question of which prices to use in value input-output tables, has been much debated in the Soviet Union. The Central Statistical Administration uses the prices actually paid by consumers. TSEMI prefers producer prices (i.e., costs plus profits and turnover tax but excluding trade and transport expenses). The use of value input-output tables will only result in the compilation of consistent plans if the prices in which the tables are compiled reflect relative consumers' valuations.[12] Soviet prices often do not.

Another problem concerns the units to be used in physical input-output tables. In the input-output model it is assumed that each industry produces only one product, and that every product is uniform, and therefore it is possible to sum the rows in physical units. In all the input-output tables which it is feasible to construct, however, each industry produces a physically heterogeneous collection of goods. In Soviet practice, output is measured not only in natural physical units, but also in conventional physical units, and money. Conventional physical units (e.g., the measurement of various fuels in tons of coal equivalent) are used where it is clear that natural physical units do not reflect consumers' valuations. As a Soviet expert in this field puts it, "Physical measures (weight, volume, area, and so on) often cannot reflect quantitatively the consumers' value of goods. . . . The establishment of conventional units for the measurement of output, which convert physical measures to volumes of consumers' value has a progressive significance. Such indices are widely used in the input-output table."

Where the output of an industry is very heterogeneous, e.g., the engineering industries and the furniture industry, output is measured in money, using constant prices. In general, the use of physical input-output tables composed of "commodities" aggregated in this way will not lead to the compilation of consistent plans.[13,14]

The input-output model assumes that all inputs are proportional to outputs. In fact in many industries this is not so, as a number of writers have pointed out.[15] In some of the Soviet regional tables attempts have been made to isolate the non-proportional inputs.

The input-output model assumes that each output is produced by only one technique. In fact many goods are produced by several techniques, e.g., electricity from coal, oil, or uranium. Similarly the input structures of the extractive and agricultural industries vary according to the location of the industry. This can be allowed for by setting out each tech-

---

[12] Ellman, *op. cit.*

[13] *Ibid.*

[14] In accordance with normal Soviet practice, the top left hand quadrant of Soviet input-output tables only embraces "material production," and excludes "non-productive" branches of the economy. (A recent booklet has argued, however, that "all work in a socialist society is productive, that there are no unproductive classes or social groups." An approving reviewer comments that "from the point of view of optimal planning the division of labor into productive and simply socially useful is senseless. All kinds of labor, satisfying a social need, i.e., making a definite contribution to the criterion of optimality, receive shadow prices corresponding to the quantity of their contribution.")

[15] Hollis B. Chenery and Paul G. Clark, *Interindustry Economics* (New York: John Wiley and Sons, Inc., 1959), p. 144.

nique in a column of its own and expanding the matrix from a square into a rectangle.

The compilation of ex ante input-output tables raises a number of further problems: how to estimate future technology, future personal consumption, future capital investments, and future exports and imports. The task of projecting the technological coefficients is rendered much easier by the fact that the vast majority of them are either zero or of negligible importance. "Calculations by the Economic Research Institute of the State Economic Council showed that in the ex post input-output table 10–15 percent of the coefficients in each industry embraced 90–95 percent of all the inputs."[16] Gosplan's Economic Research Institute analyzed the input coefficients of the 83 × 83 1959 all-Union table to find out by what percentage it was necessary to alter the input coefficients of each industry in order to produce a 1 percent change in the output of that industry. It turned out that 86 percent of the non-zero coefficients had to be altered by more than 100 percent to produce such a 1 percent change in the output of the industry concerned.

There are three methods of projecting the important coefficients: by extrapolation,[17] by the use of a model which embodies some theory of how technology may be expected to alter,[18] or by direct estimation by experts in the different technologies. The third method is the one normally used in Soviet practice. For example, when calculating the 1970 all-Union input-output table, more than 200 industrial research and project institutes were asked to estimate future technology in their industries. Experience has shown that the big problem in projecting the technical coefficients is not in estimating technical progress in the production of goods already in production, but in estimating changes in the structure of production, i.e., the "birth" of new products and the "death" of old ones.

The volume and assortment of future final product is determined partly by political choices and partly by technology. To assist in determining the volume and structure of final product for the Union as a whole, 20 variants of the 1970 all-Union input-output table were drawn up (of which two were selected for further study). The main differences between these variants were the result of different assumptions as to the volume and structure of final output. Similarly, when working out the 1970 input-output table for Estonia, 15 variants of final product were tried.

---

[16] The reference is to the 1959 all-Union table in value terms.

[17] See for example Cambridge University, Department of Applied Economics, *A Programme for Growth*, Vol. 3: *Input-output Relationships 1954–1966* (London: Chapman and Hall, 1963); or C. B. Tilanus, *Input-output Experiments: the Netherlands 1948–1961* (Rotterdam: Rotterdam University Press, 1966).

[18] L. L. Pasinetti, "A New Theoretical Approach to the Problems of Economic Growth," in *The Econometric Approach to Development Planning* (Amsterdam: North-Holland Publishing Co.; Chicago: Rand McNally, 1965), pp. 571–688.

The structure of personal consumption is arrived at using the methods of extrapolation, rational consumption norms,[19] and elasticity coefficients. The projections for social consumption, on the other hand, are based on plan estimates. These are based on plan norms, for example the number of hospital beds required per thousand inhabitants.

Accurate estimation of future capital investment is particularly important in a country where gross capital formation amounts to 35 percent of the national income. The input-output projections used are based on plan estimates. Calculation of the physical composition of investment is considerably simplified for those regions for which capital stock matrices have been compiled. Trade projections are based on plan estimates.

Input-output tables are a valuable source of information about the structure of an economy. They give a vivid picture of inter-industry flows, the commodity composition of imports and exports, and the commodity structure of accumulation and consumption; and they indicate the main proportions of the economy. Analysis of the 1961 input-output table for Lithuania, for example, showed that only a very small proportion of Lithuanian industrial production flowed into Lithuanian agriculture. Since Lithuania is a mainly agricultural republic, it was decided that this was unsatisfactory and that the proportion ought to be increased. The all-Union tables have provided data for an analysis of the efficiency of production and for price calculations.

Use in Soviet Planning

Economic planning is a hierarchical, or multi-level, process. At the top, the time path of a few summary indicators, e.g., national income, is decided; at the bottom, the expansion plans of every enterprise. The calculations made at every stage can be summarized in a model, which indicates the assumptions made, the data required, and the steps in the process. The strategy of development can be decided with the help of an extremely aggregated growth model. A classic case is the Feldman model, which brings out clearly (on the assumptions made) the advantages of concentrating on heavy industry.[20] More recently, Mikhalevsky has attempted to use a number of tools borrowed from Western economic

---

[19] Rational consumption norms (an approach which H. S. Houthakker has termed "the technology of consumption" in "The Present State of Consumption Theory: A Survey Article," *Econometrica*, Vol. 29, No. 4 [October, 1961], pp. 704–40) are extensively used in projecting personal consumption. In one variant of the Estonian calculations, norms of the consumption of food products, suggested by the Laboratory for the Study and Planning of Nutrition of the Academy of Sciences of the USSR, and consumption norms of non-food products recommended by the Scientific Research Institute of Trade and Social Nutrition, corrected for Estonian conditions, were used.

[20] [A translation of Feldman's model appears in Spulber, *op. cit.*, pp. 174–99 and 304–31. —The Editors.]

thought (e.g., production functions) to explain past Soviet economic growth and lay the foundation for planning the macrosummary indices. Input-output is a tool to be used at a lower level of the hierarchy to plan the relations between the various industries. It forms a link between plans for the basic national economic indices and the plans for separate industries and regions. The use of input-output in planning is illustrated in Figure 1.

FIGURE 1

The Use of Input-Output in Economic Planning

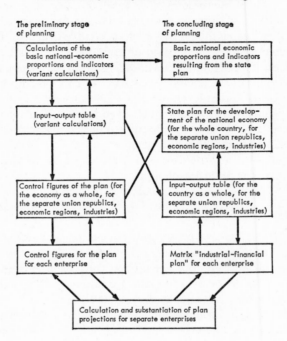

At the present time, both the underlying economic system and the techniques used to plan it are in a state of transition. On the one hand, the September (1965) Plenum inaugurated the transition from the administrative allocation of commodities to inter-enterprise trade. On the other hand, the balance of the national economy and the material balances are still being compiled, an ex ante input-output table in physical terms is drawn up annually by Gosplan's Chief Computing Center to assist in current planning, and ex ante input-output tables in both monetary and physical terms for some years ahead are drawn up by Gosplan's Research Institute and Gosplan's Chief Computing Center to assist in perspective planning.

The use of input-output has important advantages when compared to traditional planning methods:[21]

1. It shows clearly the relationship between the macroeconomic summary indicators and the physical structure of production.

2. Being a mathematical method which can be solved on a computer, it is much less laborious than traditional methods, enabling consistency to be achieved in a shorter time and many plan variants to be experimented with. These plan variants can be compared with regard to the values assumed by a number of important economic indices, and the best one picked.

In principle, the use of input-output in current planning promises to improve the consistency of plans and the use of input-output in perspective planning promises to improve the planning of the relative sizes of different industries in the national economy. In practice, the use of an ex ante input-output table for 1970 in drafting the five-year plan for 1966–70 for Lithuania, to check the consistency of the projected national income of the republic with the projected industrial outputs, appears to be something of an exception. In connection with the 1966–70 all-Union five-year plan, a lot of work has been done in drawing up an input-output table for 1970. At a meeting in July 1966, Professor Alter correctly pointed out that this was the first time that ex ante coefficients for an input-output table had been compiled on such a wide scale, not only in the Soviet Union but in the world as a whole. At the same meeting, however, the head of Gosplan's Input-Output Subdepartment stated that the practical significance of this table has not been very great.

The integration of input-output into the planning mechanism gives rise to numerous problems:

1. The results of input-output calculations may be irrelevant to planning because the indices of the plan and those of the input-output table are non-comparable.[22] For example:

a) Input-output tables include all the output of particular products. Plan calculations ignore the small industrial enterprises of state

---

[21] For a comparison of the traditional balances and input-output as techniques for arriving at a consistent plan, see S. S. Ahluwalia, "Balancing Versus Input-Output Techniques in Ensuring the Internal Consistency of a Plan," in Warsaw Center of Research on Underdeveloped Economies, *Essays on Planning and Economic Development*, Vol. 2 (Warsaw: Polish Scientific Publishers, 1965).

[22] The input-output tables may themselves be non-comparable because different methods are used in their compilation. The all-Union tables compiled by the Central Statistical Administration are in consumer prices. The input-output tables for the Baltic Republics, compiled under the aegis of the Central Economic Mathematical Institute, are in producer prices. The compilers of the 1959 all-Union value and physical tables used different methods of calculating inputs. In the value table, only those inputs were calculated which came from outside the enterprise concerned, whereas in the physical table all inputs, including those produced within the enterprise itself, were included.

farms; building, trade, and transport organizations; collective farms; and consumer cooperatives.

b) The product classification of the plan and the input-output table may be different. When comparing the 1959 all-Union physical input-output table with the basic indices of the seven-year plan, it was found that only 77 products were comparable, 80 products in the input-output table were not in the plan nomenclature, and 33 products in the plan nomenclature were not in the input-output nomenclature.

It is clearly necessary for the Central Statistical Administration and Gosplan to agree on a single industrial classification which will provide control over enterprises and which will be used in planning and in compiling input-output tables.

c) Plans and input-output tables are calculated in different prices. Enterprise wholesale prices + turnover tax = producer prices (industry wholesale prices). Producer prices + trade and transport costs = final consumer prices.

According to a 1966 Soviet source:

In plan calculations, output is calculated in enterprise wholesale prices, and social product in industrial wholesale prices. The method of compiling ex ante input-output tables used at the present time is such that in them products are reckoned in those prices at which were calculated the ex post input-output tables. Because the first, and last, ex post input-output table was worked out by the Central Statistical Administration in final consumer prices of 1959, all the ex ante input-output tables are calculated in those prices. In this way, as a result of using different prices, "output" in the input-output calculations exceeds "output" in the plan calculations by the extent of turnover tax and the trade-transport markup.

Consequently, the volume of output of an industry for the planned year arrived at by input-output calculations must be translated from final consumer prices of 1959 to producer prices of 1959, and finally, to enterprise wholesale prices of that year, the prices of which are accepted as comparable to those of the planned period. (Up to 1966 comparable prices for the measurement of the gross output of industry are the enterprise wholesale prices of July 1, 1955.) Such a three-stage re-estimation of the volume of output can scarcely avoid lowering the reliability of the results.

Bringing the prices used in the regional input-output tables into line with plan prices is simpler because the former are in producer prices.

d) Soviet input-output tables are based on a "commodity-commodity" classification, whereas plans are drawn up for industries (where by "industry" is meant a totality of enterprises) and for enterprises. This is a more serious difficulty in the Soviet Union than it would be in Britain because the Soviet industry is less specialized.

e) In planning, a group of industries (sewn goods, footwear, woollens, cotton cleaning, wool scouring, artificial leather, celluloid materials) have their gross outputs calculated differently from all other industries, certain items (raw materials, basic already processed materials, and profits) being excluded.

f) There are also other differences between input-output indices and those used in planning practice. "At the present time to liquidate fully the inconsistencies between the indices of the ex ante input-output table and the national economic plan, which have been mentioned, is extraordinarily difficult in connection with the lack of the necessary ex post and ex ante information."

2. A major difficulty in reconciling input-output with the traditional system of planning by material balances, let alone superseding the latter by the former, is that the latter are worked out for many more products than the former. The Soviet economist Shvirkov wrote in 1963:

At the present time the USSR Council of Ministers approves in the annual plan for the development of the national economy the volume of production in physical terms of more than 600 types of industrial output. Moreover, about 400 indices which are subdivisions of these 600 products are confirmed in addition. Thus Gosplan USSR must calculate the volume of production of more than 1,000 products for submission to the Council of Ministers of the USSR. Naturally, the volume of production of these products must be coordinated. Such balancing can most effectively be carried out with the help of an input-output table.

Pursuing this line of thought would require an input-output table of order 1,000 × 1,000. Shvirkov suggests 800 × 800 on the ground that this is the upper limit possible with existing computer technology. This approach seems unsatisfactory. Such tables would be difficult to compile and invert. In addition, it would leave open the relationship between Gosplan's input-output table and the many thousands of material balances compiled at lower levels of the planning hierarchy. A much more promising approach has been outlined in an important paper by Dudkin and Yershov. They suggest an iterative method by the use of which it is possible to arrive at a consistent plan for all the products for which material balances are compiled. They do not prove, however, that the iterative process must speedily converge, merely providing an arithmetical example which happens to do so. This approach has been developed further in a book by Dudkin. There is no evidence that these ideas have had any impact on planning in the USSR.

3. There has been a tendency in input-output calculations to use "progressive" coefficients, regardless of the production possibilities for "progressive" goods in short supply, resulting in impossibly high outputs of some goods in the input-output calculations. For example, comparison of necessary output levels as calculated using the physical input-output tables and using the traditional methods in 1962 and subsequent years generally showed close agreement. Where there were divergencies, this

generally showed not the inadequacy of the traditional methods but the folly of using input coefficients for mineral fertilizers into agriculture, or aluminum into cables, which reflected a desirable, but unfeasible input structure. This problem arises from the fact that in the input-output model technology is fixed and output levels flexible, whereas in planning practice technology is flexible and output levels constrained by resource availability.

4. In order that the enterprise plans be consistent with the national or regional input-output tables, it is desirable that the enterprise plans be drawn up in matrix form using the same statistical conventions as are used in compiling the input-output tables.

5. There is a shortage of economists competent in this field.

6. The most important practical obstacle to the use of physical input-output tables in planning is that the ones so far compiled fail to account for a large proportion of the output of important products. For example in the plan table for 1963 one-third of electricity went to "other productive uses."

7. The input-output model assumes that constant returns to scale prevail throughout the economy. In fact, however, increasing returns to scale are normal in manufacturing industry, diminishing returns to scale in extractive industry, and agricultural production is heavily dependent on "chance inputs" (e.g., rain, wind, and sunshine). Consequently it is not normally possible to rely on an input-output coefficient when the output under consideration is substantially different from the output for which the coefficient was calculated.

One important difference between planning by material balances and planning by input-output is that the former is concerned with gross production and gross consumption of commodities, and focuses attention on supply bottlenecks, whereas the latter focuses attention on the net output available for final consumption. As Dadayan has remarked, "The production and consumption of coal and steel are significant not in themselves, but only to the extent that they provide for the production of products intended for final consumption. . . . Society does not become one iota richer if the industrial apparatus devours not 300 but 500 million tons of coal or 90 and not 50 million tons of steel."

The use of input-output has provided interesting data on inter-industry relations, which has been of use in economic analysis and policy-making, which has improved the planning of inter-industry proportions, and which supplements existing methods of checking the consistency of highly aggregated plans.

The construction of input-output tables on varying assumptions leads to an immense accumulation of data on possible worlds, and this, together with experiments on inter-industry models, has served to emphasize the need for, and potential utility of, optimal planning. The main gain from the use of input-output in Soviet planning has not been its contribution to reducing inefficiency, but the fact that it has introduced mathematical models and modern computing technology into Soviet planning and that important gains in efficiency may well follow from this.

V. CONCLUSION

It has not been possible to ensure that the plans for all the many thousands of centrally planned commodities and all the many thousands of enterprises are consistent, using material balances or input-output or a combination of these techniques. How, it may be asked, does the economy manage if the plans are normally inconsistent?

The answer seems to be as follows. The last stage of the process of planning supplies is the conclusion of contracts between supplier and user. This stage gives the supplier and user the possibility of bringing the plan into line with real possibilities and needs. One of the features of the reform inaugurated by the September (1965) Plenum is the increased emphasis placed on these contracts and generally on direct contacts between suppliers and users, often of a long-term nature. Furthermore, scarce inputs can often be obtained from those who have them by direct contacts outside the formal planning system, by activities of a quasi-market type. Impossible output plans can generally be avoided by understating possibilities in reports to the center, by representations to the center when impossible output plans are received, or by some mixture of the two strategies. Both of them are customary gambits in the long process of "planning and counter-planning" (i.e., the negotiations between the center, intermediate bodies such as the industrial ministries, and the enterprises over preliminary drafts of the plan, which precede the compilation of the final version of the plan). During the year as inconsistencies come to light, the plans can be, and frequently are, altered, sometimes repeatedly. Frequent alterations to the plan during the "planned" period are often attacked in the Soviet press, but they would seem to be an integral part of a system of inconsistent central planning. Moreover, it is important to remember that the enterprises do not start off each year *ab initio*. Most enterprises produce this year very much what they produced last year, relying on the same suppliers. The changes to the previous year's output envisaged in the plan are normally only of a marginal character. The planners themselves expect inconsistencies to arise. In the annual plan, part of the output of each product is allocated to reserves and as shortages become apparent during the course of the year, the planners allocate these reserves to the priority enterprises. Furthermore, the material balances are most detailed for those products in which the planners are most interested, reducing the dangers of inconsistency in commodities important to the planners.

Although Soviet plans have normally been inconsistent, this has not prevented the economy's flourishing. The planners have not been much troubled by the consistency problem, as they were primarily concerned with strategic problems, for example the relationship of industry to agriculture, the allocation of investment between industries, and the development of specific products (e.g., tanks), specific plants (e.g., the Dnieper and Bratsk hydro stations and the Magnitogorsk iron and steel complex), of specific programs (e.g., the space program), and of specific industries (e.g., oil). In all these their successes were striking. (It was the non-priority sectors that suffered from inconsistencies.) Compared to these crucial questions the calculations necessary to ensure consistency were regarded as a mere "game with figures." [23] The annual plan for the production and distribution of commodities serves to coordinate the plans of individual enterprises and projects. The primary objective of the planners is to fulfill the plans for these separate enterprises and projects, or at any rate for the priority ones among them, and if the annual plans for the production and distribution of commodities are inconsistent, then this does not matter to the planners provided that the priority projects do not suffer and the shortages are felt by non-priority sectors, such as personal consumption. By the 1960's this traditional attitude had begun to alter. The economy had become so complex that the gains from the administrative allocation of resources to the key sectors began to be rivaled by the losses from the misallocation of resources throughout the economy. Furthermore, the planners began to attach importance to the satisfaction of consumers. Hence the discussion of reform, the very limited reforms introduced by the September (1965) Plenum, and the experiments in replacing the centralized administrative allocation of resources by inter-enterprise trade.

It is no more surprising that the Soviet economy functioned and in a number of respects performed extremely well, when the plans were inconsistent, than that the British economy has been as stable as it has in the post-war period given the crudity of the instruments of control used.

In summary:

1. The important thing about a plan are its objectives, whether or not they are attained and whether or not there existed a more efficient way of attaining them than that chosen by the planners. Consistency is a secondary matter.

2. To ensure that the plans are consistent, Soviet planners have traditionally used material balances and now supplement this with input-output.

3. These techniques have been unable to ensure consistency, and Soviet plans have always been inconsistent.

4. Traditionally the inconsistency of the plans has not worried the planners very much as they were primarily concerned with the achieve-

---

[23] The phrase is Stalin's. See J. Stalin, *Pravda*, December 29, 1929, translated in *Works*, Vol. 12 (Moscow: Foreign Languages Publishing House, 1955), p. 178.

ment of the plan for specific, priority sectors of the economy. The administrative allocation of resources, the core of the traditional economic system, greatly facilitated the concentration of resources according to the priorities of the planners. The inconsistencies of the plans were felt by non-priority sectors about which the planners were not much concerned.

5. The inconsistency of Soviet plans is relevant to discussion of economic reform.

Area	Date	Units of Measurement	Ex Post or Ex Ante	No. of Industries	No. of Positions in 2nd Quadrant
USSR	1959	Consumer prices	Ex post	83	n.a.
USSR	1962	Consumer prices	Ex ante	83	n.a.
USSR	1970	Consumer prices	Ex ante	130[b]	n.a.
USSR	1959	Physical	Ex post	157	n.a.
USSR	1962	Physical	Ex ante	346	n.a.
USSR	1963	Physical	Ex ante	435	n.a.
USSR	Annual	Physical	Ex ante	n.a.	n.a.
USSR	1970	Physical	Ex ante	600[b]	n.a.
USSR	1959	Man years	Ex post	83	n.a.
Armenia	1963	Consumer prices	Ex post	91	n.a.
Byelorussia	1962	Consumer prices	Ex post	500	n.a.
Latvia	1961	Producer prices	Ex post	239	13[e]
Lithuania	1961	Producer prices	Ex post	239	13[e]
Lithuania	1962	Producer prices	Ex post	180	n.a.
Estonia	1961	Producer prices	Ex post	239	13[e]
Kaliningrad oblast	1960	n.a.	Ex post	15	n.a.
Karelia	1961	n.a.	Ex post	75	n.a.
Mordovia	1958	Consumer prices	Ex post	14	n.a.
Mordovia	1959	Consumer prices	Ex post	86	11[f]
Tataria	1959	Consumer prices	Ex post	165	6[g]
Tataria	1960	Consumer prices	Ex post	150	n.a.
Tataria	1961	n.a.	Ex post	56	n.a.
Tataria	1962	n.a.	Ex post	56	n.a.
Tataria	1963	n.a.	Ex post	56	n.a.
Latvia	1970	Producer prices	Ex ante	150	n.a.
Lithuania	1970	Producer prices	Ex ante	150	n.a.
Estonia	1970	Producer prices	Ex ante	150	n.a.
Estonia	1961	Producer prices	Ex post	150	Capital stock matrix
Estonia	1970	Producer prices	Ex ante	150	Capital stock matrix
Chemical industry	1960	n.a.	Ex post	n.a.	—
Chemical industry	1962	n.a.	Ex ante	n.a.	—

Notes:

   n.a. = not available
   — = not applicable
   CSA = Central Statistical Administration
   TSEMI = Central Economic Mathematical Institute
   SRI Gosplan = Gosplan's Scientific Research Institute
   SRI Chemical Industry = Scientific Research Institute for technical-economic research in the chemical industry
   CCC = Chief Computing Center

   [a] A reconstruction of the entire table is in Vladimir G. Treml, "The 1959 Soviet Input-Output Table (As Reconstructed)," in United States Congress, Joint Economic Committee, *New Directions in the Soviet Economy* (Washington, D.C.: U.S. Government Printing Office, 1966), Part II-A, pp. 257–70.

No. of Positions in 3rd Quadrant	Method of Calculating Inputs	Compiled By	Method of Calculating Region's Imports and Exports	Were Nonproportional Inputs Isolated?	Were Alternative Techniques Distinguished?	Date of Publication
n.a.	Gross output	CSA	—	No	No	1961[a]
n.a.	n.a.	SRI Gosplan	—	No	No	Unpublished
n.a.	n.a.	SRI Gosplan	—	No	No	Unpublished
n.a.	Gross turnover	CCC Gosplan	—	n.a.	n.a.	Unpublished
n.a.	Gross turnover	CCC Gosplan	—	n.a.	n.a.	Unpublished
n.a.	Gross turnover	CCC Gosplan	—	n.a.	n.a.	Unpublished
n.a.	Gross turnover	CCC Gosplan	—	n.a.	n.a.	Unpublished
n.a.	Gross turnover	CCC Gosplan	—	n.a.	n.a.	Unpublished
n.a.	n.a.	CSA	—	n.a.	n.a.	1962
n.a.	Gross output	CSA Armenia	n.a.	n.a.	n.a.	Unpublished
n.a.	n.a.	n.a.	Balance	n.a.	No	Unpublished
10[d]	Gross turnover	TSEMI	Direct	No	Yes	Unpublished
10[d]	Gross turnover	TSEMI	Direct	No	Yes	Unpublished
n.a.	Gross turnover	TSEMI	Balance	No	No	Unpublished
10[d]	Gross turnover	TSEMI	Direct	No	Yes	Unpublished
n.a.	n.a.	n.a.	Mixed	n.a.	No	Unpublished
n.a.	n.a.	n.a.	Balance	n.a.	No	Unpublished
n.a.	n.a.	TSEMI[e]	Balance	n.a.	No	1962
8[d]	Gross turnover	TSEMI[e]	Mixed	Yes	Yes	Unpublished
7[d]	Gross turnover	Tatar Sovnarkhoz	Mixed	Yes	Yes	Unpublished
n.a.	Gross turnover	Tatar Sovnarkhoz	Mixed	n.a.	No	Unpublished
n.a.	Gross turnover	Tatar Sovnarkhoz	Balance	n.a.	No	Unpublished
n.a.	Gross turnover	Tatar Sovnarkhoz	Balance	n.a.	No	Unpublished
n.a.	Gross turnover	Tatar Sovnarkhoz	Balance	n.a.	No	Unpublished
n.a.	Gross turnover	TSEMI	n.a.	n.a.	n.a.	Unpublished
n.a.	Gross turnover	TSEMI	n.a.	n.a.	n.a.	Unpublished
n.a.	Gross turnover	TSEMI	n.a.	n.a.	n.a.	Unpublished
—	—	Institute of Economics, Estonia	—	—	—	Unpublished
—	—	Institute of Economics, Estonia	—	—	—	Unpublished
—	—	SRI Chemical Industry	—	—	—	Unpublished
—	—	SRI Chemical Industry	—	—	—	Unpublished

[b] Approximate.

[c] Excluding imports and exports and error. Of the 13 columns, three were for accumulation and 10 for consumption.

[d] Excluding competitive imports and including amortization.

[e] This table was compiled under the aegis of the Laboratory for Economic-Mathematical Methods, which subsequently became TSEMI.

[f] Excluding imports and exports and error. Of the 11 columns, two were for accumulation and nine for consumption.

[g] Excluding imports and exports and error. Of the six columns, four were for accumulation and two for consumption.

7 | SOVIET PRICE THEORY AND POLICY

Morris Bornstein

In a market economy, the level and composition of production, the allocation of resources, and the distribution of income and output are determined primarily by market forces whose decisions are expressed through prices. In this sense, "the price system" and "the market" are often used interchangeably to explain the operation of the economic system. In the Soviet planned economy, the role of prices is much more limited, reflecting the prevalence of planners' (rather than consumers') sovereignty and the reliance of the planners on physical planning and administrative commands to execute their decisions.

This selection examines the functions of prices in the Soviet economy and the characteristics of the major types of wholesale and retail prices. It analyzes recent proposals for reforms in the price system and evaluates the measures actually taken.

Morris Bornstein is Professor of Economics at The University of Michigan and one of the co-editors of this volume. The selection is a revised version of his "Soviet Price Theory and Policy," in United States Congress, Joint Economic Committee, *New Directions in the Soviet Economy* (Washington, D.C.: U.S. Government Printing Office, 1966), Part I, pp. 65–94. Citations of Russian-language sources are omitted.

IN THE SOVIET UNION, as in all modern, complex economies, prices play an important part in the guidance of economic activity.[1] However, their role in the Soviet economy is different both from their role in a capitalist market economy and from their role in the socialist market economy described in the theoretical models of Lange, Taylor, and Lerner.[2] In the

[1] This paper is based in part on research supported by The University of Michigan Center for Russian and East European Studies, whose assistance is gratefully acknowledged.

[2] Oskar Lange and Fred M. Taylor, *On the Economic Theory of Socialism*, ed. Benjamin E. Lippincott (Minneapolis: University of Minnesota Press, 1938), and Abba P. Lerner, *The Economics of Control* (New York: Macmillan, 1944).

Soviet economy (and in the Soviet-type economies of Eastern Europe and Communist China), prices are not an autonomous force determining production, resource allocation, and consumption. Instead, prices are manipulated by the central authorities as one of various instruments intended to accomplish their planned goals.

Following a summary view of the various functions of prices in the Soviet economy, this paper deals in turn with the three major subsystems of the Soviet price system: industrial wholesale prices, agricultural procurement prices, and retail prices. The discussion focuses on current pricing practices, theoretical controversies among Soviet economists about price reforms, and recent and pending changes in price policies. Certain types of prices—such as wages, transportation rates, and foreign trade prices—are not considered here. The paper also does not treat in any depth such aspects as the historical evolution of the price system in the 1930's and 1940's, narrowly technical aspects (such as the construction of price lists), or minor types of prices (such as those which collective farms charge their members).

I. ROLE OF PRICES IN THE SOVIET ECONOMY

The functions of the Soviet price system may be classified under three very broad headings: control and evaluation, allocation, and income distribution.[3]

Control and Evaluation

Prices are used by the central planners to secure compliance by enterprise managers with the plans elaborated by the former, and to evaluate the performance of the managers in the execution of their assigned tasks. Although resource allocation is determined by the planners largely in physical terms, it is necessary for them to express complex input and output targets for the enterprise in value terms in order to have a common denominator for physically dissimilar units of raw materials, labor, and capital goods. Thus the enterprise plan contains targets for the value of output, sales, cost, profits, tax payments, etc.

Allocation

Although physical allocation by administrative commands predominates in the Soviet economy, prices do influence the allocation of resources, and thus the pattern of production, in various ways.

1. At the central planning level, prices are used to construct macro-

---

[3] Here and elsewhere in this paper I draw upon Morris Bornstein, "The Soviet Price System," *American Economic Review,* Vol. LII, No. 1 (March, 1962), pp. 64–103.

economic balances, such as national product and intersectoral accounts, and capital-output ratios to supplement the basic physical planning tools. In addition, the relative pricing of substitutes may have some influence on the selection of technological coefficients for physical planning, as the planners substitute more abundant for scarcer materials during the successive iterations of the balancing process. Finally, project designers use value calculations in choosing among alternative variants of a given-output investment project and in assessing the benefits of modernization or innovation.

2. It is impossible for the central authorities to specify in complete detail the inputs and outputs of each enterprise. As a result, managers have a limited range of choice regarding both inputs and outputs. The relative prices of inputs and outputs influence the choices which managers make in trying to increase the value of output, sales, and profits.

3. Prices affect both the total supply of labor and its distribution. The state relies on low real wages, resulting from the relationship of money wages and consumer prices, to evoke a high rate of participation of the population in the labor force. Wage differences, in turn, are the principal means of securing the distribution of the labor force (by skill, industry, enterprise, and geographical location) desired by the planners.

4. In the collective farm sector, the central authorities use prices, along with delivery quotas, to influence the allocation of resources to certain crops and products in preference to others. (In addition, prices are used, along with delivery quotas, to stimulate total output, but in this case the aim is primarily to raise the productivity of given resources engaged in agriculture, by increasing real compensation and thus incentives.)

Income Distribution

In the Soviet economy, the basis of income distribution is the "socialist" principle of unequal monetary compensation according to labor services rendered, rather than the "communist" principle of distribution according to need; and the promise of unequal monetary compensation is the basis of production incentives. The wage (i.e., price) system—together with transfer payments and income taxes—determines the distribution of (disposable) money income. The Soviet government endeavors to make the distribution of real income less unequal than the distribution of money income by two chief methods. One is a broad program of "free" health and education services financed from general budget revenues. The second is to fix relatively low prices for mass consumption goods and relatively high prices for luxury goods by means of differentiated turnover taxes. The distribution of real income is also made less unequal than the distribution of money income through the administrative allocation of housing and through the informal rationing of queues and empty shelves when retail prices are fixed below the market-clearing level.

II. INDUSTRIAL WHOLESALE PRICES

Nature and Trends

Industrial wholesale prices are those at which goods are transferred or evaluated within the state sector of the Soviet economy.[4] The term covers prices of producer goods, including raw materials, semifabricates, and machinery, as well as manufactured consumer goods. It excludes prices at which agricultural products are obtained by the state from collective farms but includes prices at which procurement agencies sell agricultural products to state enterprises for processing or to trade organizations for retail sale without further processing. It also excludes foreign trade prices, although it includes the prices at which foreign trade organizations buy from and sell to Soviet enterprises. Since 1958, collective farms have been permitted to buy various producer goods at wholesale prices, rather than at retail prices, as previously.

The Soviet industrial wholesale price system is composed of three types of prices. The "enterprise wholesale price" is the price at which a producing enterprise sells its output. The "industry wholesale price" is paid by the state-enterprise buyer and includes, in addition to the enterprise wholesale price, (1) the turnover tax, if any, on the product; (2) the markup of the branch sales organization; and (3) transportation charges if these are borne by the sales organization rather than the buyer. Finally, a settlement or "accounting price" is used in some branches where production costs diverge widely, notably the extractive branches. Individual enterprises or groups of enterprises receive different settlement prices, rather than a single, uniform enterprise wholesale price, from the branch sales organization. The latter, however, sells to customers of the branch at a single industry wholesale price.

Enterprise wholesale prices are composed of the planned branch average cost of production (*sebestoimost'*) and a profit markup. The former has no exact equivalent in Western cost accounting. It includes direct and indirect labor, materials (including fuel and power), depreciation allowances, and various overhead expenses, but excludes both rental and capital charges. The profit markup is supposed to provide a "normal" profit, which until the 1967 wholesale price reform (discussed below) was planned at 5 to 10 percent of *sebestoimost'*. This profit markup is not intended to allocate resources among alternative uses, but rather is to provide a source of "net income" or accumulation to the state, to serve as an instrument of financial control, and to promote the "businesslike" operation of Soviet enterprises.

Another source of accumulation is the turnover tax, which is levied

---

[4] *Ibid.*, p. 69, and Morris Bornstein, "The Soviet Price Reform Discussion," *Quarterly Journal of Economics*, Vol. LXXVIII, No. 1 (February, 1964), pp. 18–19.

primarily on consumer goods and included in the wholesale prices of the light and food industries, and thereby in retail prices. As a result, there is a great disparity between producer and consumer goods in the relationship between their "costs" and their wholesale prices. In 1967, for example, in heavy industry, production and marketing costs accounted for 79.4 percent of the value of output in industry wholesale prices; profit, 15.5 percent; and the turnover taxes, 5.1 percent. In contrast, the corresponding figures for the light and food industry branches were 70.1, 7.8, and 22.1 percent.

The main trends in Soviet industrial wholesale prices from 1949 to 1967 are shown in Tables 1 and 2. In the price reform of January 1, 1949, heavy industry prices were raised sharply (on the average by 58 percent above the 1948 level) to eliminate most subsidies and to remove the turnover tax from all producer goods except electric power, natural gas, and petroleum products. As a result of subsequent cost reductions, heavy industry prices were later reduced through comprehensive price revisions in 1950, 1952, and 1955, and through more limited adjustments in particular industries from 1958 to 1966. A comprehensive revision of light industry prices was undertaken in two installments, on October 1, 1966, and January 1, 1967, but the aggregate effect was relatively small. In contrast, the reform of heavy industry prices introduced on July 1, 1967, significantly raised the average level of heavy industry prices and of all industrial production.[5]

A comparison of Tables 1 and 2 shows how the cushion of the turnover tax makes it possible to alter enterprise wholesale prices without equivalent changes in industry wholesale prices. In the food industry, enterprise wholesale prices (Table 1) have been raised several times since 1952 to cover higher costs from successive increases in agricultural procurement prices. Industry wholesale prices (Table 2) do not show a corresponding rise, however, because these cost increases have been largely offset by reductions in turnover taxes, intended to prevent the higher agricultural procurement prices from affecting industry wholesale prices and thus retail prices. Similarly, the enterprise wholesale prices of refined petroleum products rose 43 percent from 1966 to 1967 (Table 1), in connection with the partial introduction of marginal cost pricing and rental payments, but industry wholesale prices increased less than 8 percent (Table 2). A cut in turnover taxes permitted this increase in prices received by producers without a corresponding increase in prices charged consumers.

---

[5] The increase was greater than appears from Tables 1 and 2, in which the figures for 1967 are averages of the first half of the year at old prices and the second half at new prices. A more precise measure of the increase is provided by a comparison of prices in the second half of 1967 with those prevailing in 1966. The comparison shows that enterprise wholesale prices rose 9 percent for industry as a whole and 17.5 percent for heavy industry, while the respective increases in industry wholesale prices were 7 and 15 percent.

TABLE 1

Indexes of Soviet Industrial Prices: Enterprise Wholesale Prices (Excluding Turnover Tax), Selected Years, 1950–67

(1949 = 100)

Commodity Group	1950	1952	1955	1958	1962	1966	1967
All industrial production......	83	72	68	67	71	71	77
Heavy industry............	80	68	61	58	57	55	65
Chemical industry.......	84	76	67	67	67	64	65
Ferrous metallurgy.......	71	63	60	60	60	60	90
Coal industry...........	100	91	84	84	84	84	152
Petroleum refining.......	85	72	65	65	63	63	90
Electric power..........	92	82	74	70	61	61	83
Machine-building and metal-working........	76	60	52	45	44	40	40
Timber industry.........	85	85	85	107	107	107	127
Cellulose and paper industry..............	81	68	65	65	65	65	81
Construction materials industry..............	82	67	57	57	57	57	68
Light and food industry.....	91	82	86	93	110	114	113
Light industry...........	91	83	80	80	81	84	84
Food industry...........	91	81	91	104	135	140	139

TABLE 2

Indexes of Soviet Industrial Prices: Industry Wholesale Prices (Excluding Turnover Tax), Selected Years, 1950–67

(1949 = 100)

Commodity Group	1950	1952	1955	1958	1962	1966	1967
All industrial production......	80	69	61	60	61	59	63
Heavy industry............	80	68	61	59	59	57	66
Chemical industry.......	84	76	67	67	67	62	62
Ferrous metallurgy.......	71	64	60	60	60	60	89
Coal industry...........	100	91	84	84	84	84	152
Petroleum refining.......	85	72	65	72	66	66	71
Electric power..........	92	82	74	70	70	69	80
Machine-building and metal-working........	76	61	52	45	45	42	42
Timber industry.........	85	85	85	107	107	107	125
Cellulose and paper industry..............	81	68	65	65	65	65	80
Construction materials industry..............	79	67	57	57	57	57	68
Light and food industry.....	80	70	59	61	61	60	59
Light industry...........	88	88	70	70	70	67	67
Food industry...........	77	62	54	57	59	58	57

Price Reform Discussion

In the lengthy discussion on price reform which began in 1956, Soviet economists have criticized the industrial price system on various counts and have advanced different proposals for price reform.[6]

---

[6] Bornstein, "The Soviet Price Reform Discussion."

Criticisms. The chief criticisms include the following:

1. Many Soviet economists believe that producer goods prices do not properly reflect their "values," in the Marxian sense of the term. In Marxian value theory it is possible for the actual prices of commodities, whether determined by market forces or administratively, to differ ("deviate") from their values, which in a long-run, "normal" sense are regarded as determined by the amount of past and present socially necessary labor embodied in them. ("Socially necessary" labor is the amount used with average skill, intensity of work, and conditions of production.) According to Marxian value theory, the value (*stoimost'* in Russian) of a commodity is regarded as composed of three parts: (a) the value of past labor embodied in the materials and that portion of plant and equipment (as measured by depreciation charges) used up in producing the commodity, (b) the value of current labor for which workers receive compensation in the form of wages, and (c) the value of current labor for which workers are not compensated ("surplus value" or "surplus product"). In Marxian terminology, these components of value are designated, respectively, c for constant capital, v for variable capital, and m (or s) for *mehrwert* (or surplus value or product).

In applying this value $= c + v + m$ formula to the Soviet economy, Soviet economists usually take *sebestoimost'* as equivalent to the sum of c and v, and they regard the sum of total profits and turnover taxes as equal to total surplus product or aggregate m. One criticism of industrial price formation is that, because (as noted above) prices of producer goods contain significantly less profits and turnover taxes (m) in relation to *sebestoimost'* ($c + v$) than do prices of consumer goods, producer goods as a group are "priced below their value." In addition, this criticism asserts, because surplus value is not properly distributed in the prices of different commodities, relative prices of producer goods do not correspond to their relative values. That is, both the level and the structure of producer goods prices are held to deviate from their Marxian value.

2. In turn, because producer goods prices fail to correspond to their values, either in some aggregate sense or relative to each other, they furnish unreliable guides for choices by planners and enterprise managers. If relative prices are not correct, then incorrect choices will be made regarding alternative inputs and outputs. Because producer goods as a group are considered underpriced relative to consumer goods, in the calculation of production expenses both materials and machinery are undervalued relative to labor—whose wage rates are related to the price level of consumer goods—leading to the unjustified substitution of materials and machinery for labor. Similarly, the shortcomings of producer goods prices distort the comparisons of internal and external prices on imports and exports which are made in planning foreign trade.

3. The defects of industrial wholesale prices impede the effective use of value targets in the control and evaluation of enterprise operations. For

example, they cause differences in the level or rate of profits (or losses) which are unrelated to the performance of enterprises or their contribution to the economy.

4. Soviet economists agree that this scheme of industrial pricing causes part of the value created in producer goods branches of industry to be "realized" in the prices of consumer goods. Thus, the calculation of various macroeconomic relationships using these prices does not give an accurate picture of the structure and development of the economy. For instance, the share of heavy industry is understated in the distribution of national income by sector of origin, while the share of accumulation (i.e., investment) is understated relative to consumption in the distribution of national product.

Reform Proposals.   On the issue of what reforms should be made in the industrial price system, Soviet economists are divided into three main schools: a traditionalist school, a surplus product markup school, and an opportunity cost school.

1. Traditionalist school. One group upholds the essentials of the traditional scheme of industrial price formation but suggests relatively modest adjustments in order to improve the structure of producer goods prices without altering their level significantly. It believes that the use of prices as instruments of economic control requires many deviations of price from "value," in order to promote the efficient operation of enterprises, recognize supply and demand factors in certain cases, promote or discourage consumption of certain goods, etc. The traditionalists see no justification for a large increase in the overall level of producer goods prices to incorporate more "surplus product" in them. Instead, they stress selective adjustments in the structure of producer goods prices to eliminate losses and excessive profits, establish the "correct" price relationships between substitutes, encourage the introduction of new models of machinery, etc.

2. Surplus product markup school. Another group of Soviet economists favor pricing on the basis of "value" by adding a uniform, proportional surplus product (m) markup to *sebestoimost'* ($c + v$) to derive a price equal to value (i.e., to the sum of $c + v + m$). They propose to raise the level of wholesale prices of producer goods without altering the general level of wholesale prices (or retail prices) of consumer goods. This would be accomplished by a partial shift of surplus product (profits and turnover taxes) from consumer goods prices to producer goods prices in order to raise the latter relative to the former.

The members of this school differ among themselves, however, on the manner in which surplus product should be distributed in the prices of goods. One view favors using labor cost as the base to which the markup would be applied; a second, *sebestoimost'*; a third, capital; and the fourth, a combination of labor cost and capital. Each of these will be discussed briefly in turn.

The most orthodox position advocates relating the surplus product markup to labor cost—i.e., the wage bill—in order to obtain prices that are truly based on "labor value" (*trudovaia stoimost'*). It proposes a uniform surplus product markup related to the wage bill, according to the following formula:

$$p = c + v + v\frac{M}{V} = c + v\left(1 + \frac{M}{V}\right) \tag{1}$$

where p represents the price of a commodity, c the branch average materials costs (including also depreciation charges) per unit of the commodity, v the branch average wage cost per unit of the commodity, M the total surplus value to be distributed among goods, and V the total wage bill for workers engaged in "material production." The prices of the material inputs (and capital equipment to be depreciated) in c would themselves be calculated in the same way.

Another formula relates the markup to total *sebestoimost'* ($c + v$) rather than to labor cost (v) alone. With p, c, v, M, and V defined as before and C representing the total materials cost (including also depreciation) of aggregate "material production,"

$$p = c + v + (c + v)\frac{M}{C + V} = (c + v)\left(1 + \frac{M}{C + V}\right) \tag{2}$$

This formula resembles the traditional price-setting practice in relating the surplus product markup to *sebestoimost'*, but it differs from it in calling for the uniform application of the same percentage markup to all producer and consumer goods.

A third position relates the markup to capital. With p, c, v, and M defined as before and k representing the average amounts of fixed and working capital per unit of the commodity and K the total fixed and working capital used in "material production," the corresponding formula is

$$p = c + v + k\frac{M}{K} \tag{3}$$

The supporters of this position hold that the magnitude of surplus product depends not only on the quantity of live labor used in production but also on its productivity, which in turn depends on the capital with which it is equipped. They believe that capital investment should be reflected in prices in order to promote the economization of capital in choices between more and less capital-intensive goods and methods of production. Likewise, enterprises should pay capital charges to the State, because such charges would lead them to request less fixed and working capital and to use more effectively the capital they have.

A fourth position, which has evolved in the past few years, offers a compromise between the first and third formulas, by relating part of the surplus product markup to labor cost and part to capital. According to this position, with p, c, v, k, and K defined as before and M_1 representing the part of surplus value to be distributed in proportion to the wage bill and M_2 the part of surplus value to be distributed in proportion to capital,

$$p = c + v\left(1 + \frac{M_1}{V}\right) + k\frac{M_2}{K} \tag{4}$$

It is suggested that M_1 correspond to the portion of the total "surplus product" devoted to "social-cultural expenditures" (health, education, and social welfare measures) and that M_2 correspond to the portion devoted to investment, defense, and general administration. In some variants of the formula, an additional price-forming element D is added to include differential rent on natural resources. Also, some proponents favor a single rate for the capital charge M_2/K, while others prefer a charge differentiated by branches of industry according to the structure of capital and the rate on return of capital.

It should be noted that all of these formulas are cost-oriented, neglecting demand as a basic element in value and price. They do not recognize a connection between value and allocation. The allocation of resources would still be accomplished by directives in physical terms, supplemented by selected divergences of price from the "value" result yielded by the particular formula—for example, in order to secure the correct relative price structure for substitute fuels or machines.

3. Opportunity cost school. The members of this school, in contrast, advocate, explicitly or implicitly, efficiency prices which reflect relative scarcities and include capital and rent charges. These prices would, ideally, be the shadow prices obtained from the formulation of an "optimum" plan by input-output and other mathematical programming techniques. Such an optimum plan would achieve as fully and as efficiently as possible a set of final output goals specified by the political leadership. The members of this school recognize that such a plan, and its shadow prices, cannot be formulated at present because of the absence of the necessary detailed information on many millions of economic relationships and the lack of the necessary data processing and computing facilities to handle this information if it did exist. However, they believe that it is still possible at present to improve the existing price system by incorporating, if only imperfectly, some of the features of the ideal prices of the optimum plan.

The advocates of this approach—particularly V. V. Novozhilov and L. V. Kantorovich—have been attacked on the ground that they reject the Marxian labor theory of value by recognizing land and capital as factors of production, relating value to scarcity, and using the "notorious" bourgeois marginal analysis. However, Novozhilov and Kantorovich steadfastly deny any deviation from Marxian value theory, asserting that their prices are different from capitalist prices, that land and capital are considered only insofar as they affect the productivity of labor, etc.

Recent Changes

1961–64 Price Revision. The July 1960 Plenum of the Central Committee of the CPSU called for a revision of heavy industry prices and freight rates during 1961–62, with the aim of introducing the new prices in 1963. The main features of the revision, as disclosed while the work was in progress, indicated that it would conform to the views of the traditionalist school.

The principal objective was to adjust prices and costs (i.e., *sebestoimost'*) in heavy industry to provide a "normal" level of profitability, in relation to *sebestoimost'*, of about 9 percent. The general level of wholesale prices for heavy industry was to remain virtually unchanged, being reduced by only about 3 percent. However, the structure of heavy industry prices was to be altered markedly, by price increases in most extractive branches and price reductions in the secondary branches, such as machine building and chemicals. The revision thus sought to recognize and ratify wage and cost increases in the extractive branches, on the one hand, and productivity gains and cost reductions in the manufacturing branches, on the other, since the last general price revision in 1955. In some cases (e.g., coal and petroleum), relative prices of substitutes were to be changed to adjust demands on the part of users to the planned supplies. The effects of the producer goods price revision on other sectors of the price system—such as wholesale prices of consumer goods, agricultural procurement prices, and retail prices—were to be negligible.[7]

Work on the price revision was not completed on schedule, however, because of the huge volume and great complexity of the work. One source estimates that the total volume of price lists amounted to 38,400 printed pages containing several million prices. By the end of 1962, price lists had been completed for raw materials and fuels, chemicals, construction materials, and electric power, but not for machine building, in which, because of technological developments some 40 percent of the entries in the price lists were new items. Nevertheless, it appears that by late 1963 or early 1964 the new price lists were ready, as instructions were issued in June 1964 to recalculate the 1964 plan and budget in the new prices, as a basis for calculating the 1966 plan and budget and the five-year plan for 1966–70 in the new prices.

The actual promulgation of the new heavy industry price lists was successively postponed, however. According to S. G. Stoliarov, Chief of the Department of Price Statistics of the Central Statistical Administration, one reason was the opposition of critics of the traditional scheme of price formation, particularly those who favored the surplus product markup approach instead. After the ouster of Khrushchev in October

---

[7] Morris Bornstein, "The 1963 Soviet Industrial Price Revision," *Soviet Studies*, Vol. XV, No. 1 (July, 1963), pp. 43–52.

1964, the adoption of new prices was delayed while the new leadership formulated its economic program, including the decisions on economic planning and management announced in Kosygin's speech to the Central Committee on September 27, 1965.

1966–67 Price Reform. The principal features of the reform of industrial management are as follows. (1) Sales and profitability, rather than total output, are now the main enterprise performance indicators. (2) To encourage enterprises to economize on capital, they are required to pay a charge on fixed and working capital, their profitability is now calculated in relation to capital rather than cost, and a large part of new investment is to be financed from bank credits instead of budget grants. (3) Enterprises will retain a larger share of their profits for investment and the payment of bonuses to both workers and management. (4) Enterprise managers have been granted additional authority over the composition of labor inputs.

To implement these objectives, industrial wholesale prices were revised effective October 1, 1966, and January 1, 1967, in light industry and July 1, 1967, in heavy industry.[8] The main aim in fixing the new prices was to enable most enterprises to cover production costs and earn enough profit to pay a 6 percent charge on capital, establish incentive funds, and expand their capital. In general, prices are intended to cover branch average costs of production, plus a "normal" profit markup, estimated, for industry as a whole, at approximately 12–15 percent on fixed and working capital. However, profit rates vary by branch of industry. For example, in heavy industry, in order to cover costs in the coal industry and at the same time secure the proper relative prices for substitute fuels, accumulation (in the form of both profits and turnover taxes) must be higher in the petroleum and gas industries than in the coal industry. In light industry, accumulation (particularly in the form of turnover taxes) will be higher on alcoholic beverages and tobacco than on other products. In the extractive industries, two methods were used to deal with large differences in costs due to natural conditions. In iron ore and coal mining, group settlement prices vary by regions. In the petroleum and gas industries, on the other hand, a type of marginal cost pricing was introduced, under which prices are based on the costs of high-cost enterprises, and rents are charged producers with lower costs and higher profits. Finally, in most industries prices were adjusted to encourage enterprises to improve quality and to adopt new technology.

The revision of industrial wholesale prices was not accompanied by changes in the level or structure of retail prices. Likewise, the prices of industrial producer goods sold to agriculture were not altered, so as not to affect the terms of trade for agriculture. Instead, turnover tax rates were

---

[8] The "several million" new prices were published in 679 price handbooks. The main features of the reform are summarized in Gertrude E. Schroeder, "The 1966-67 Soviet Industrial Price Reform: A Study in Complications," *Soviet Studies*, Vol. XX, No. 4 (April, 1969), pp. 462–77.

reduced, or the differences were charged to various budget accounts. However, the losses in budget revenue from turnover tax reductions are to be recovered from increased profits taxes and rental payments by enterprises.

The price reform was conducted by a new State Price Committee (SPC) under the USSR State Planning Commission (Gosplan), created late in 1965 by the merger of the Price Bureau of USSR Gosplan with the Commission on Prices of the Presidium of the USSR Council of Ministers. The new Committee is a union-republic body with counterparts in the republic Gosplans and departments for prices in the provincial and city planning commissions. Its functions are to establish the principles for fixing all types of prices, to direct the actual setting of prices, and to supervise the enforcement of prices once established. The SPC itself fixes the wholesale prices on all important producer and consumer goods, including 75–80 percent of the value of output of heavy industry and about 50 percent of the value of output of the light and food industries. Price committees in the republics set prices covering nearly 20 percent of the value of output in heavy industry and over 40 percent in consumer goods industry. Enterprises themselves may set prices only for goods whose prices are not fixed by higher organs. In practice, this means that enterprises can negotiate prices with customers only on some kinds of new products and special orders. However, enterprises do have some influence on the prices fixed by the price committees because the enterprises prepare the initial cost estimates on which final prices are based.

The wholesale price reform was successful in making all major branches of industry profitable and in reducing the spread in profitability among industries and enterprises within industries. However, the new prices have been criticized in the Soviet press on many counts, including the following. (1) For many goods, the costs on which prices are based are incorrectly calculated, and often inflated. (2) Relative prices of different varieties frequently conflict with the pattern of production specified in the enterprises' "assortment" plans. (3) Quality differentials are imperfectly reflected in price differentials. (4) Relative prices of substitutes often do not promote consumption in the same proportions as outputs are produced. (5) The SPC has not established the methodological guidelines needed to permit ministries and even enterprises to fix more prices themselves.

The new prices represent an improvement over the previous prices, set in 1955, because they incorporate changes in labor and materials costs which have occurred since then, thus permitting the reduction or elimination of subsidies. In addition, as a result of the inclusion of explicit, though arbitrary, capital charges—and in some cases rents—prices now reflect total costs to a greater, though still incomplete and imperfect, extent. However, the new prices are still largely based on average rather than marginal costs and are not intended to be scarcity prices capable of allocating resources in an efficient way. Thus, they will not contribute much to improving those choices which enterprise managers, seeking sales and profits, are able to make regarding current inputs and outputs and investment. Nor are they likely to enhance significantly the ability of higher administrative authorities to evaluate enterprise performance. In short, the price reform, like the reform of industrial management, is of restricted scope, and its beneficial effects will also be limited.

III. AGRICULTURAL PROCUREMENT PRICES

Agricultural procurement prices are those at which collective and state farms sell to state procurement agencies. Collective farm market prices, at which agricultural producers sell to households, are analyzed in the following section on retail prices.

Nature and Trends

Collective Farm Prices. In setting procurement prices for collective farms, the Soviet government has pursued two conflicting objectives: (1) to fix the terms of trade for the collective farm peasantry so as to make it bear a large share of the burden of industrialization, and (2) to provide incentives to produce. The former objective clearly dominated during the Stalin era. Since 1953, the latter has been more characteristic of collective farm price policy.

The terms of trade and real income of the peasantry depend on the relationship between agricultural procurement prices paid to the collective farms, on the one hand, and prices paid by collective farms for material inputs and prices paid by collective farmers for consumer goods, on the other. The terms of trade for the peasantry were extremely unfavorable during the Stalin era. Procurement prices for grain remained almost unchanged from 1929 to 1953. Livestock prices doubled from 1929 to 1940 but remained unaltered from 1940 to 1953. Over the same period, retail prices (at which collective farms also bought many of their industrial inputs) rose many fold. In 1952, the level of retail prices was 10 times the 1940 level. Grain and livestock production was very unprofitable, and the price of potatoes did not even cover the cost of delivery to the city. For technical crops, such as cotton, sugar beets, and tobacco, the situation was more favorable, as procurement price increases after 1940 had kept pace with increases in the prices of consumer goods and industrial inputs.[9]

---

[9] On trends in prices and terms of trade from 1928 to 1953, see Jerzy F. Karcz, *Soviet Agricultural Marketings and Prices, 1928–1954*, RM-1930 (Santa Monica, Calif.: RAND Corporation, 1957); and Nancy Nimitz, "Soviet Agricultural Prices and Costs," in United States Congress, Joint Economic Committee, *Comparisons of the United States and Soviet Economies* (Washington, D.C.: U.S. Government Printing Office, 1959), Part I, pp. 249–55. For an accurate picture of the peasantry's terms of trade one must, of course, also consider trends in prices of collective farm market sales, which account for an important share of the incomes of producers of meat, milk, eggs, fruits, and vegetables.

One of the first steps taken by Stalin's successors in 1953 was to embark on a broad program to increase agricultural output, involving changes in planning and administration, delivery obligations, taxes, investment, and prices. The changes in agricultural procurement prices included a large increase in the general level of prices, regional differentiation of prices, a revision in the relative price structure in favor of food crops, a greater effort to relate prices to costs, and the unification of multiple prices into single procurement prices for each crop. Major price increases were made in 1953, 1956, 1958, 1962, 1963, and 1965. Table 3 shows the trend of collective farm procurement prices from 1952 to 1966. More recent data unfortunately are not available.

TABLE 3

**Indexes of Soviet Agricultural Procurement
Prices, Selected Years, 1953–66***
(1952 = 100)

Commodity Group	1953	1954	1955	1956	1958	1962	1965	1966
All agricultural products	154	207	209	251	296	332	404	412
Grain†	236	739	553	634	695	840	1024	1113
Technical crops‡	115	111	117	147	143	143	174	169
Sunflowers	528	626	987	928	774	859	1046	1122
Fruits§	119	135	138	192	179	167	165	157
Potatoes	316	369	368	814	789	1043	1374	1299
Cattle	385	579	585	665	1175	1523	1980	2103
Milk	202	289	303	334	404	434	521	528
Eggs	126	135	152	155	297	339	342	343
Wool	107	146	158	246	352	346	379	376

* Average state procurement-purchase prices on agricultural products procured from collective farms and private plots.
† Wheat, rye, barley, oats, maize, millet, buckwheat, and rice.
‡ Raw cotton, flax fiber, hemp fiber, sugar beets, and tobacco.
§ Including wine grapes.

In 1953 the government increased sharply both obligatory delivery prices and state purchase prices. The former applied to the delivery quotas fixed for each farm, and the latter to additional sales to the state above the quota. Although state purchase prices were higher than obligatory delivery prices, they were still below collective farm market prices, and hence sales at state purchase prices were in most cases not voluntary but compulsory. In addition to increasing both types of prices, the government further raised average realized prices on vegetables and potatoes by reducing obligatory delivery quotas, thereby releasing more of their output for sale at the higher state purchase and collective farm market prices. In 1956, procurement prices were again increased, and in some cases the differential between the basic and the higher incentive price was reduced.

Prices were again changed in 1958, when multiple pricing was replaced by a single state purchase price for each product. Concurrently, the machine-tractor stations (MTS's) were abolished and their machinery sold to the collective farms. For the first time, prices of all crops were revised at the same time, providing an opportunity for a comprehensive adjustment of relative prices. However, the new prices could not be accurately related to costs (even if this had been intended) because of a lack of appropriate cost data. For decades, as long as average procurement prices were extremely low, reference to costs was politically inexpedient, and collective farms did not calculate their production costs. The notion was even widely accepted that the concept of cost was not applicable to collective farms. Only in 1955 did the state begin to investigate the level and structure of collective farm costs, and only in 1958 did farms begin to calculate their costs.[10] The 1958 prices were therefore not based on costs. Instead they were set on the principle that the total bill to the state for procurements from the collective farms should not exceed the previous bill for procurements plus the bill for MTS operations and investment. Thus, basically, the existing terms of trade between the agricultural and industrial sectors were left unchanged; as one Soviet economist put it, "only the channels of exchange were altered."[11]

In the case of livestock products, it was not intended that the 1958 prices should cover costs. Instead it was "supposed" that collective farm losses on livestock products would be covered from earnings on grain, sunflowers, and other crops. The ratio of prices to costs in 1960, for example, was 155 percent for grain (excluding corn), but only 65–67 percent for meat and eggs and 86 percent for milk.[12] This relative price-cost structure provided little incentive to collective farms to increase livestock production, and they instead emphasized the more profitable plant crops. In 1962, the government raised purchase prices on cattle and poultry by an average of 35 percent. It also took the politically unpopular step of raising retail prices of meat products by an average of 30 percent and of butter by 25 percent. However, despite the substantial increase in livestock prices, they still failed to cover costs.

---

[10] The calculation of collective farm costs was, furthermore, complicated by the question of how to value labor inputs, which were reckoned not in money wage payments or even man-days, but in "labor-day" accounting units. The payments made in money and in kind per labor-day varied widely from one farm to another, and from year to year on the same farm. Moreover, since payments for a labor-day were greater on the more successful farms, to use actual labor-day payments would make it appear that the more efficient farms had higher costs. For purposes of comparison, therefore, it was decided to assign a fixed notional value to collective farm labor inputs, namely, to value them at state farm wage rates. Some Soviet economists, however, favored valuation of collective farm labor inputs at actual labor-day payments. See Nimitz, *op. cit.*, pp. 256–57, and Frank A. Durgin, Jr., "Monetization and Policy in Soviet Agriculture since 1952," *Soviet Studies*, Vol. XV, No. 4 (April, 1964), pp. 389–91.

[11] Another Soviet economist reports that the 1958 prices took into account only state expenditures on the current operations of the MTS's, excluding state investment in them.

[12] In these figures collective farm labor inputs are valued at state farm wage rates.

In 1965, as part of the broad Brezhnev-Kosygin agricultural program, prices for milk, livestock, and grain were raised, and above-quota premium prices were re-established for wheat and rye, cotton, and sunflowers. Table 4 shows the ratio of the new prices to the average of costs in 1963–65 on collective and state farms. These figures indicate that for all collective farms as a group the new prices made production of cattle barely profitable, while milk, eggs, and vegetables must still be produced at a loss.

In addition to these changes since 1953 in the level and structure of procurement prices, the terms of trade of collective farm agriculture have been improved through reductions in the prices of industrial inputs and in

TABLE 4

Ratio of 1965 Prices to Average 1963–65 Production Costs* of Selected
Commodities on Soviet Collective Farms and State Farms
(percent)

Commodity	Collective Farms	State Farms
Grain.........................	184	118
Potatoes......................	153	114
Vegetables....................	99	125
Sugar beets...................	140	107
Sunflowers....................	589	430
Raw cotton....................	157	131
Milk..........................	98	93
Cattle[†]......................	109	87
Sheep[†].......................	113	98
Pigs[†]........................	104	96
Poultry.......................	118	98
Eggs..........................	83	112
Wool..........................	134	114

* *Sebestoimost'*, including material inputs, depreciation, and labor costs.
† Weight gain.

the prices of consumer goods sold to the peasantry. Until 1958, machinery, trucks, spare parts, and fuel were available to collective farms only at retail prices, while state farms bought these goods at much lower wholesale prices. In 1958, uniform wholesale prices for state and collective farms were established on trucks, machinery, and spare parts. But this concession was offset, at least in part, by an unpublicized increase in the same year in the wholesale prices of farm machinery and spare parts and in the retail price of gasoline. This measure was reversed in 1961, when the government reduced retail prices on gasoline and wholesale prices on trucks, machinery, and spare parts. In 1962 it authorized collective farms to buy construction materials at wholesale, rather than retail, prices. Prices of trucks, farm machinery, and spare parts were again reduced at the beginning of 1966.

Though no precise calculations are available, it is evident that successive increases in agricultural procurement prices, together with adjustments in prices of industrial inputs and of consumer goods, have markedly improved the collective farm peasantry's terms of trade since 1953. The general price increases from 1953 to 1958 helped, in conjunction with other measures, to bring about a large increase in agricultural output. Subsequent price increases have been more selective, focusing on lagging commodities, particularly livestock products. It is by no means clear, however, that the 1965 price increases, whose magnitude was limited by the decision not to raise retail prices, will be sufficient to cover costs (including reasonable compensation for collective farm labor) and make livestock production sufficiently profitable.

State Farm Prices.   State farm delivery prices have been essentially different in nature from the prices paid to collective farms. State farms are "factories in the field" similar to state enterprises in industry, transportation, trade, etc. Their employees receive money wages on a piece-rate basis, and they calculate cost of production (*sebestoimost'*) in essentially the same way as other state enterprises. If—as has commonly been the case—sales revenue failed to cover *sebestoimost'*, the deficit was met by redistributions of profits within the state farm network or by operating subsidies from the budget. (In addition, investment has been financed by budget grants.) Because state farm costs are reimbursed by the combination of delivery prices and subsidies, the failure of prices to cover costs does not restrain output. In contrast, for the collective farms, prices are the sole source of compensation for production expenses and productive effort.

Until 1954, state farm prices were based on (but were lower than) the corresponding state purchase prices for collective farms. As these prices did not cover production costs, a subsidy was planned for each type of state farm output. In 1954, with the announced objective of eliminating subsidies, state farm delivery prices were raised and differentiated by geographic zones. The new prices were supposed to yield an overall profit of 7.7 percent on *sebestoimost'*, although it was expected that livestock would still be produced at a loss, to be covered from earnings on crops. But by 1956 the overall profit rate was only 5.6 percent, and by 1958 crop profits failed to cover livestock losses, resulting in an overall loss rate of 1 percent. By 1960, net losses of the state farm system covered by budget subsidies amounted to 600 million rubles (in terms of "new" rubles after the 1961 monetary reform). To eliminate these subsidies, the government in 1961 reduced the state farms' input prices and raised their output prices. State farm costs were cut by about 300 million rubles per year through a reduction of prices on machinery, spare parts, and fuel. State farm revenues were augmented by 500 million rubles through higher prices for livestock products, grain, sugar beets, and fruits. In 1962, state farm livestock prices were raised again, concurrently with the increase in collective farm livestock prices. However, the new prices still failed to cover costs for cattle, pigs, poultry, and eggs. In 1963, along with collective farm prices, state farm prices were raised on cotton, sugar beets, and certain vegetables.

The state farms also benefited from price increases under the new agricultural measures announced in 1965, although their prices remained below collective farm prices by 10 percent on meat, 15 percent on wool, 17 percent on cotton, 39 percent on grain, and 55 percent on sunflowers. As Table 4 shows, the new prices failed to cover costs, and losses were therefore planned, for meat and dairy production.

The principles of the industrial reforms announced in 1965 were first applied to state farms in 1967, when, by way of experiment, 390 of the most profitable state farms (out of a total of more than 12,000) were transferred to the new system of management. These state farms were paid collective farm prices for their deliveries, in order to provide them profits to finance not only all current expenses but also most of their investment expenditures. The experiment was considered successful; a second group of 400 farms was shifted to the new system in 1968, and the gradual transfer of other farms has been promised.

Price Reform Discussion

Beginning in 1958, defects in agricultural procurement prices have been criticized and suggestions for improvement have been advanced at scholarly conferences and in Soviet economic journals and newspapers.[13] The agricultural price reform discussion has been more cautious than the industrial price reform discussion, because agricultural price changes are politically sensitive measures which directly affect the distribution of income between the rural and urban populations. Changes in industrial prices, in contrast, primarily affect financial relationships within the state sector.

Criticisms. The principal criticisms concern price-cost relationships for different products, defects in geographical differentiation of prices, and the failure of prices to promote a rational pattern of specialization.

1. One criticism is that both the level and the structure of procurement prices have been set without adequate regard for production costs (including reasonable compensation for the labor of collective farm members). As a result, incentives to expand collective output are lacking, and collective farmers instead devote as much effort as possible to their private plots. On the one hand, more accurate calculations of costs are needed. On the other, the government should fix prices so as to make the produc-

---

[13] For a comprehensive discussion of the issues and reform proposals, see Morris Bornstein, "The Soviet Debate on Agricultural Price and Procurement Reforms," *Soviet Studies,* Vol. XXI, No. 1 (July, 1969), pp. 1–20.

tion of each product profitable, rather than expecting profits on plant products to compensate losses on livestock products.[14]

2. Prices of individual crops are differentiated geographically in an effort to skim off differential rents arising from more favorable natural conditions. However, the variation in prices is not as great as the variation in costs in the different zones.[15] As a result, the profitability of a given crop varies greatly from zone to zone. For some crops, such as potatoes, flax, and wool, prices are not differentiated geographically, even though they are produced in different areas with widely varying costs. In addition, there are large differences in costs and profitability within price zones, some of which cover a very large area. For example, grain price zone IV stretches from the shores of the Arctic into southern Siberia, comprising an area 10.3 times that of France, with extreme variations in soil, rainfall, temperature, and length of growing season. One consequence of these defects in price zoning is large differences in the incomes of collective farmers in different regions, and even in the same region, due to natural conditions, rather than to differences in equipment, productive effort, or managerial skill. Another consequence is that the state does not obtain the maximum results from a given total expenditure on agricultural procurements. By increasing prices in some zones and reducing them in others, the state could secure a net increase in the volume of procurements without any increase in total procurement expenditures.

3. Many collective and state farms operate at low profitability or losses because they are required, by their delivery plans, to produce products for which they are not suited. It is not unusual for collective farms to receive procurement plans for 15 or 20 different products, some of which they are expected to produce at a loss. Often the quotas exceed the farm's capabilities, forcing it to request loans in kind for seeding or planting purposes. In part, the lack of rational specialization is the result of the low level of agricultural production: the state is afraid to reduce or eliminate delivery plans from low-yield areas lest it lose badly needed supplies. On the other hand, the requirement that farms produce and deliver products for which they are not suited prevents them from specializing in those crops on which their yields would be much higher.

Reform Proposals. Various proposals have been advanced to deal with shortcomings in the level, structure, and regional differentiation of agricultural procurement prices. They include the following: (1) basing

---

[14] According to some recent estimates, profitability rates of 40 to 60 percent on *sebestoimost'* (including reasonable compensation to collective farm members) would be necessary if collective farms are to pay income taxes, make contributions to pension and welfare funds, and carry out planned expansion of fixed and working capital.

[15] According to one estimate, the differences in *sebestoimost'* in different natural zones range from 180 to 600 percent for different agricultural products, while the maximum differentiation of procurement prices is 116 percent (for rye).

prices on marginal rather than average costs, (2) revising the boundaries of price zones, (3) using instruments other than price differences to take differential rent, and (4) varying prices in accordance with harvest fluctuations.

1. At present, the zone price of a product is supposed to be based on the average cost of production in that zone. As a result, collective farms with higher than average costs for the zone have difficulty covering expenses, and the incomes of their members are correspondingly low. The supporters of marginal cost pricing argue that if the state requires a farm to produce and deliver a commodity, the state should pay the farm a price adequate to cover costs (including reasonable compensation for the labor of its members) and provide a profit for expansion. Although a few members of the marginal cost school favor basing price on the national marginal cost of the product, most accept the principle of zonal price differentiation and urge instead that price be based on the marginal cost of the zone. More precisely, they advocate basing the price on the cost of production of farms with the worst land in the zone (in terms of fertility and location) but with average conditions of production in regard to mechanization, labor productivity, and managerial efficiency. The differential rent accruing to farms with better land would be taken by taxation.

Prices based on marginal costs would, of course, mean a much higher bill for state procurements—double, or for some products or zones even triple, the bill with prices based on zonal average costs. However, there need not be a corresponding increase in wholesale and retail prices. As noted, additional tax revenues would be collected on the differential rent of farms on inframarginal land. These revenues would be allocated to subsidies to the light and food industries and the trade network intended to keep wholesale and retail prices below the level of procurement prices. Opponents of this approach object that it is undesirable to set retail prices below procurement prices, as this situation encourages farms to buy agricultural products at retail prices in order to resell them to the state at procurement prices. Critics also point out that it would be difficult to determine the correct amount of differential rent to be taken through taxation from all but the highest cost farms.

2. Suggestions for improving price zoning include the following. The number of zones should be increased to make them more homogeneous and to reduce intrazonal differences in cost and profitability. Zone prices should be introduced for such crops as potatoes, flax, and wool. The revision of zone boundaries should consider both natural factors (such as soil, temperature, precipitation, topography, etc.) and economic factors (such as the structure of output, extent of mechanization, income per acre and per man-day, etc.). Price zoning should promote rational specialization through higher profitability for crops in the zones most suited to them, but prices should be high enough to cover costs and provide a profit even in the less suitable areas.

3. Even with improvements in the delineation of price zones, intra-zonal differences in cost and profit would continue to exist. To take some of the differential rent of farms with better than average, or better than marginal, land in the zone, income taxes and/or land taxes are recommended. An income tax has been levied on collective farms for a number of years, not only to take differential rent but also to exert control over the fulfillment of production and financial plans. However, the tax has been levied on gross income (including labor-day distributions to members) rather than on net income, and with virtually no progression in rates. Reform proposals have recommended using net rather than gross income as the base and introducing a progressive scale of rates. In 1965, the base was shifted to net income, and an element of progression was introduced through the exemption from taxation of the first 15 percent of net income. An alternative, or supplementary, method of taking rent is direct money rent payments varying with the quality of the land. However, this method requires a land cadaster, which is not likely to be available for many years.[16]

4. Another reform proposal is that, instead of keeping prices stable despite variations in harvests, the government raise them temporarily when harvests are especially poor. Under this proposal, in bad harvest years both agricultural procurement prices and state retail prices would be increased. The 1958 agricultural price revision was supposed to have introduced flexible procurement prices varying with harvests, but in practice flexibility operated in only one direction: prices were reduced for very good harvests but not raised for bad harvests.

1965 Revisions.   The 1965 agricultural price revisions reflect these reform proposals only to a very limited extent.[17] Prices are still based on zonal average costs, except in the case of grain procurements in the main grain areas, where the new prices seem to be related to cost conditions on farms located on the least favorable land. While some price zone boundaries were altered, there was no comprehensive revision based on a careful study of natural and man-made factors affecting costs. The nature of the collective farm income tax was significantly improved, but it is still an imperfect instrument for taking differential rent—inferior to explicit rental payments, which are precluded by the absence of a land cadaster. Prices are not to vary inversely with the size of the harvest. Rather, the reintroduction of premium prices for above-plan deliveries of wheat, rye,

---

[16] Despite several conferences and much discussion in the technical literature, Soviet economists are not agreed on the basic principles of the cadaster, the concrete steps to compile it, or the uses to be made of it.

[17] For a detailed discussion of the 1965 agricultural program, see Jerzy F. Karcz, "The New Soviet Agricultural Programme," *Soviet Studies,* Vol. XVII, No. 2 (October, 1965), pp. 129–61; and Roger A. Clarke, "Soviet Agricultural Reforms since Khrushchev," *Soviet Studies,* Vol. XX, No. 2 (October, 1968), pp. 159–78. [The latter is reprinted in this volume, pp. 409–27 below.]

cotton, and sunflowers will make their average realized prices higher when harvests are good.

On balance then, the 1965 price changes appear to be another desirable, but still relatively modest, step on the road to guiding Soviet agriculture through prices and monetary incentives, rather than administrative commands. Soviet agriculture still lacks sound prices capable of securing rational specialization of production through decentralized decisions of farm managers. Moreover, it is important to recognize that although higher prices, properly related to costs, can stimulate production, the development of Soviet agriculture also requires a steady and adequate flow of industrial inputs (including investment goods) at reasonable prices and on reasonable credit terms, as well as adequate and guaranteed remuneration for farm members.

IV. RETAIL PRICES

Nature and Trends

There are two principal types of retail prices at which goods are sold to households in the Soviet Union: state retail prices and collective farm market prices.[18]

State Retail Prices. The state retail price is charged by state retail stores, consumer cooperative stores, and state and cooperative service establishments, such as restaurants, laundries, theaters, etc. The consumer cooperatives, which operate primarily in the rural areas, are closely supervised by the state, which determines their number, size, location, etc.; allocates goods to them; and establishes sales plans for them. Of total state, cooperative, and urban collective farm market sales in 1967, the respective percentage shares of the three types were 67.9, 29.1, and 3.0.

State retail prices supposedly are fixed with the aim of clearing the market both in aggregate terms and for each commodity. In aggregate terms, the objective is to set the general level of state retail prices so that total retail sales at that price level will absorb the money income which the population is expected to want to spend at state and cooperative retail outlets. For individual goods, the objective is to fix the price of each at a level which equates planned supply and expected demand.

The general level of retail prices depends upon both tax and wage policies. The Soviet government relies primarily on price-increasing taxes, namely the turnover and profits taxes, to finance investment, military programs, and social services. As a result, the general retail price level is higher than it would be if direct taxes on households were used to a greater extent. Planned increases in private consumption can be distrib-

---

[18] The following discussion draws on Bornstein, "The Soviet Price System," pp. 88–97.

uted among households by reducing retail prices or by increasing money incomes (or by a combination of the two). The first method distributes the increase in consumption among the population as a whole, while the second is more selective. With stable retail prices, money incomes of different segments of the population can be increased by different degrees (and at different times) to provide selective incentives for increased production and for occupational and geographical shifts.

The first method was used from 1948 to 1954, when retail prices were

TABLE 5

Indexes of Soviet State Retail Prices, Selected Years, 1952–67
(1950 = 100)

Commodity Group	1952	1955	1958	1962	1963	1967
All commodities	87	74	76	76	76	75
Food	82	70	73	75	75	74
Meat	74	60	66	78	85	85
Fish	88	79	77	76	76	70
Butter	74	64	65	76	83	83
Vegetable oil	84	65	65	65	65	65
Sugar	91	80	80	77	75	74
Bread and bread products	73	60	59	59	59	59
Potatoes	n.a.*	n.a.	92	100	112	106
Vegetables	n.a.	n.a.	88	84	90	86
Alcoholic beverages	88	78	94	94	94	94
Non-food commodities	95	81	80	79	78	75
Cotton fabrics	98	71	71	71	71	68
Woolen fabrics	97	92	92	89	89	82
Silk fabrics	99	91	89	80	77	68
Clothing	98	90	90	86	86	81
Knit goods	99	88	87	87	87	86
Leather footwear	98	81	81	82	83	81
Rubber footwear	99	76	75	76	76	74
Tobacco products	87	82	81	82	82	82
Watches	86	82	79	54	54	46
Bicycles	87	78	78	60	60	57

* Not available.

reduced each spring. As Table 5 shows, since 1954 the state retail price level has been relatively stable, although there have been adjustments in the prices of individual goods. In addition to a moderate rise in the general wage level,[19] there have been selective increases in the money incomes of particular segments of the population, through increases in agricultural procurement prices, pensions, minimum wages, and the wages of selected occupations (miners, teachers, etc.).

Under planners' sovereignty in the USSR, the basic method of eliminating a disequilibrium in the market for a particular good is to adjust

---

[19] Average monthly wages of workers in the state sector rose from 71.5 rubles in 1955 to 103.4 rubles in 1967.

demand to supply, in contrast to the adjustment of supply to demand which characterizes the response under consumers' sovereignty. The latter kind of adjustment occurs in the USSR only to a limited extent when, in response to evidence in the form of shortages or surpluses at the prevailing prices, planners modify the composition (types, models, etc.) of the output of the various kinds of consumer goods which can be produced with the resources which they have allocated to those lines of production.

On some goods, retail prices are set with other objectives which conflict with the aim of clearing the market. One such additional objective, stemming from administrative considerations, is to avoid changing prices very often. This objective clearly conflicts with the aim of balancing demand with supply.

Another objective is to make the distribution of real income less unequal than the distribution of money income. To do this, the government fixes lower prices for mass consumption goods (such as basic foodstuffs) which predominate in the budgets of lower income groups, and higher prices for goods (e.g., consumer durables and luxury foodstuffs) which are relatively more important in the budgets of higher income groups. In pursuit of this objective, prices of some food products, such as meat, have been deliberately set below the equilibrium level (even below the corresponding agricultural procurement prices in some cases), as persistent shortages attest. In this way, the informal rationing of queues and empty shelves helps to modify the distribution of real income from the initial distribution of money income.

Relative prices are also used to pursue other objectives of social policy. For example, low prices are set on books in order to promote indoctrination and education, and on children's apparel in order to aid large families, while high prices are intended to curb the consumption of vodka.

The turnover tax, which now provides about one third of total budget revenue, is the principal device used by planners to secure the desired level and structure of retail prices. The principal components of the state retail price are (1) the enterprise wholesale price (or the agricultural procurement price plus the markup of the procurement agency), (2) the turnover tax, (3) the wholesale trade margin, and (4) the retail trade margin. In addition, there are transportation charges. The wholesale and retail margins are intended to cover expenses and provide a profit at the respective stages. The respective shares of enterprise wholesale prices, turnover taxes, and the two trade margins in the total value of state retail sales in recent years may be estimated very roughly at 60, 30, and 10 percent. Their relative importance in the prices of individual goods differs markedly, however, precisely because the turnover tax is used to fix the retail price at the desired level.

The turnover tax thus serves as a cushion which separates the retail prices paid by households and the wholesale prices received by producing enterprises in industry and agriculture. It permits the planners to alter consumer prices without changing producer prices correspondingly, and vice versa. Retail price reductions need not be accompanied by wholesale price reductions, and wholesale price increases need not be followed by retail price increases. The turnover tax separates not only the levels but also the structures of consumer and producer prices, since the different rates of taxation on different goods cause their relative retail prices to differ from their relative wholesale prices. For most goods the turnover tax is set as a specific ruble amount, and there are separate wholesale and retail price lists. For a limited group of goods, chiefly intended for local markets, the turnover tax is levied as a percentage of the enterprise wholesale price. These goods include some types of haberdashery, household items, and recreational and educational items. For certain nonfood consumer goods, the turnover tax is calculated as a percentage of the retail price. This scheme is used for consumer goods produced by the paper, chemical, and radio industries, as well as for sewn and fur items.

Collective Farm Market Prices.   The collective farm market price of goods is determined by supply and demand in the individual collective farm markets, varying from market to market and from day to day in the same market. There are about 7,300 collective farm markets, approximately 70 percent of them in towns of various sizes and 30 percent in rural areas. The markets occupy designated trading areas and are equipped with a varying number of stalls, benches, tables, storage bins, meat and milk control points, etc. Sellers are charged a small daily fee for the right to offer their wares. About 600,000 peasants are estimated to participate in the markets each day.

Although urban collective farm market sales represented only about 3 percent of total state, cooperative, and urban collective farm market sales in 1967, their importance in Soviet retail trade is greater than this figure suggests. In relation to total trade of the three channels in the same food goods, the collective farm market share in 1967 was 9 percent. In some important cities the collective farm markets account for 20 to 40 percent and more of total sales of major food products.

Collective farm market prices are set by supply and demand, but both supply and demand are strongly influenced by the state. Demand on the collective farm market depends on the extent to which the state retail network is able, with available quantities at the established prices, to satisfy the effective demand of households. The excess purchasing power remaining after household expenditures in the state retail trade sector finds an outlet in the collective farm market. The supply offered by agricultural producers (collective farms, peasants, and urban workers with garden plots) depends on the amount of output they have left after selling to state procurement agencies.

In contrast to the relative stability of state retail prices (see Table 5), collective farm market prices fluctuate with the size of the harvest,

TABLE 6

**Indexes of Soviet Collective Farm Market Prices,
Selected Years, 1958–67***

(1950 = 100)

Commodity Group	1958	1960	1963	1967
All commodities, including cattle..............	109	108	131	131
All commodities, excluding cattle..............	107	107	129	127
Bread products.........................	67	64	100	77
Grains..............................	67	62	89	74
Flour...............................	53	49	91	62
Groats..............................	63	63	97	69
Potatoes...............................	119	119	170	159
Vegetables.............................	131	119	158	167
Cabbage............................	146	148	193	209
Onions.............................	124	91	130	89
Fruits.................................	118	115	124	117
Vegetable oil...........................	70	67	68	68
Meat and meat products...................	105	109	121	122
Beef................................	126	127	148	144
Pork................................	88	92	100	101
Poultry.............................	120	129	146	183
Milk and dairy products..................	92	96	116	113
Milk................................	84	88	108	98
Butter..............................	87	86	102	99
Eggs..................................	96	96	112	107
Cattle.................................	132	126	150	189

* Based on data for 251 large cities.

increasing sharply when harvests are poor and supplies are reduced in both state stores and collective farm markets. Table 6 shows the trend of collective farm market prices during recent years.[20] Collective farm market prices exceed state retail prices on the same commodities by substantial amounts, although the extent varies from item to item. In part the difference reflects below-equilibrium pricing in state stores, but in part it also reflects a premium paid for better quality and freshness in the collective farm market.

Price Reform Discussion

At scholarly conferences and in the economic literature of the last few years, Soviet economists have criticized a number of aspects of retail price formation and have advanced suggestions for changes.

Criticisms. Among the criticisms of retail prices are the following: (1) prices diverge from a market-clearing level, (2) prices are set without adequate study of demand, (3) rural price differentials are unjustified, and (4) price lists are outdated and too complex.

---

[20] For a careful appraisal of the statistical data on collective farm market sales and prices, see Jerzy F. Karcz, "Quantitative Analysis of the Collective Farm Market," *American Economic Review*, Vol. LIV, No. 4 (June, 1964), Part 1, pp. 315–34.

1. For decades, many state retail prices have been too low, and demand has exceeded supply, giving rise to shortages and queues. Among the causes responsible are the effort to modify income distribution in favor of lower income groups, underfulfillment of ambitious production plans, and the failure to meet assortment plans. In addition, local shortages often exist because of errors in the distribution of goods by the trade network. A general situation of excess demand was even justified by Stalin on the ground that it was a "law" of socialism that demand should outstrip supply.[21] This position has now been condemned as theoretically unsound and undesirable in practice. Nevertheless, prices remain below the market-clearing level for various goods, particularly meat and certain consumer durables, and for certain services, notably housing.

While there are shortages of these goods, at the same time there are large excess inventories of yard goods, clothing, footwear, cameras, bicyles, watches, and sewing machines. In part, these surpluses are due to overpricing, but they also are due to poor estimates of demand and to the failure to adjust production to changes in consumer tastes. Thus, sharp price cuts on sewing machines and outmoded clothing failed to liquidate excess stocks.[22]

2. If it is intended to strive for market-clearing prices, then accurate estimates of current and future demand are essential. But such studies of consumer demand are lacking. Only in the last few years has serious attention been devoted to demand studies, and work on the subject is still relatively primitive. In particular, demand estimates are too aggregative, covering excessively broad categories of goods and very large geographic areas, and neglecting differences in the demands of different income groups. There has been little application of mathematical techniques to the analysis of retail trade problems.

3. Since 1949, prices on various goods in rural areas have exceeded urban prices for the same items by about 7 percent. This differential has been justified on the ground that marketing and transportation costs are higher for rural trade. However, the price differential tends to divert peasant purchases from rural to urban retail outlets, and to encourage "speculation," i.e., resale of goods bought in the city to other peasants at higher prices.

4. Many retail price lists are out of date. Retail price lists on some goods, especially fabrics and sewn goods, were fixed in 1954 on the basis of 1939–40 prices. In 1963, the RSFSR price list on sewn goods contained 100,000 prices, of which about one-fourth pertained to items long since

---

[21] Abram Bergson, *The Economics of Soviet Planning* (New Haven, Conn.: Yale University Press, 1964), p. 70. For an evaluation of Soviet retail prices from the standpoint of welfare economics, see *ibid.*, chap. 4.

[22] Marshall I. Goldman, "The Reluctant Consumer and Economic Fluctuations in the Soviet Union," *Journal of Political Economy*, Vol. LXXIII, No. 4 (August, 1965), pp. 372–73.

removed from production. Retail price lists are so numerous and so complex that only a small group of specialists understands them. For example, there are over 90,000 price lists for clothing and over 7,000 for footwear.

Reform Proposals. Various suggestions to improve retail prices have been advanced, including (1) more intensive study of demand, (2) greater flexibility of prices, (3) more decentralization of price fixing, and (4) wider use of the two-price-list scheme.

1. As a basis for improved price-setting, consumer demand studies should be intensified. In particular, attention should be devoted to income as well as price elasticities of demand, rural versus urban demand, and the long-term evolution of demand and prices. The work of the various research institutes studying different aspects of demand should be more closely coordinated.

2. Price flexibility should be increased in various ways. Clothing and footwear prices should be raised more often and more quickly on fashionable items in high demand, and reduced on slow-moving, out-of-style items. To adjust production to sales, wholesale prices of producers should be varied in the same direction as retail prices. Seasonal prices, now used for a limited number of food products (such as eggs, fruits, and vegetables), should also be applied to yard goods, clothing, and footwear. When harvests are poor, both retail and agricultural procurement prices should be raised.

3. Since 1957, the union republic and regional authorities have been responsible for fixing retail prices on a group of goods accounting for about 45 percent of retail sales. This group includes sausage and confectionery articles, eggs, milk, sewn goods, furniture, toys, and non-alcoholic beverages. The central authorities in Moscow set prices on the remainder of retail trade, including such important goods as bread, meat, fish, butter, cloth, footwear, knit goods, tobacco, vodka, and most consumer durables. It has been suggested that further decentralization of price-fixing is desirable, in order to increase price flexibility and bring prices closer to a market-clearing level. In particular, it has been proposed that producing enterprises, in conjunction with the trade network, fix prices on new items in line with prices on analogous existing items.

4. In the case of sewn goods, china and earthenware, glass articles, and pots and pans, it is proposed that the two-price-list scheme be adopted instead of the present arrangement of levying the turnover tax as a percentage of the retail price. When the tax is levied as a uniform percentage of the retail price for an entire class of goods, the relative structure of retail prices also determines the relative structure of enterprise wholesale prices. In many instances, items which are more complex and more expensive to manufacture do not have correspondingly higher retail and wholesale prices. As a result, the profitability of different items to the producing enterprise varies, and it is inclined to depart from its

assortment plan by producing more of the "advantageous" items and less of the "disadvantageous" items. By adopting the two-price-list scheme— that is, by fixing the turnover tax as a specific ruble amount for each item —the government could adjust the wholesale price structure independently of the retail price structure and thus reduce or eliminate differences in the profitability of producing different items in the assortment. To adopt this scheme in the case of clothing, however, it would be necessary to shift the turnover tax, now levied on the cloth rather than on the finished garment, to the final product.

Recent Changes

Recent measures in the sphere of retail price formation show a limited response to these criticisms and recommendations. For example, in 1965 the State Committee on Trade of the USSR Council of Ministers was instructed to establish an All-Union Scientific Research Institute to study the demand for consumer goods and the problems of trade fluctuations, with branches in the union republics. Organizations to study demand have been created in trade organizations, republic ministries of trade, and at various levels of the consumer cooperative system.

In 1963 a scheme of temporary prices was established under which temporarily high prices are set for new fabrics, clothing, footwear, and furniture in high demand. At the end of one year (or sooner if the demand declines), prices are reduced to their "permanent" level. The temporary surcharge of 10 to 15 percent applies to enterprise wholesale prices as well as to retail prices, because the enterprise wholesale prices of these goods are set as a percentage of their retail prices. This scheme has been criticized because of lengthy delays in setting the new prices, which are fixed at the republic level. Another criticism is that the resulting enterprise wholesale prices do not always make the new goods as profitable to produce as the older items which they replace, causing the enterprise's profits to fall.

In the now famous Bolshevichka-Maiak experiment, the pricing of new goods was decentralized to the enterprise level. The RSFSR Ministry of Trade authorized the factory and its retail outlets jointly to establish retail prices on new garments, on the basis of prices of existing goods but with due recognition of demand factors and additional costs incurred in producing the new garments. Because there is no turnover tax on clothing, enterprise wholesale prices were increased in the same proportion as retail prices. However, the factories found that the new models were less profitable to produce than the old ones, and their profits declined. While price setting (on new goods) was decentralized to the enterprise level during this experiment, when the scheme was extended to a large part of the light and food industry in 1965, enterprises were not given the right to fix prices on new products, and this right was taken away from the two experimental firms. This retreat from decentralized price setting was not publicized or explained in connection with the announcement of the "success" of the experiment and its extension to other enterprises.

Other developments in retail pricing worthy of brief mention are the elimination of the rural price differential and the revision of long-neglected prices on services. As part of the effort to improve the peasantry's terms of trade, beginning in 1959 the rural price differential was successively eliminated on a number of products and was abolished completely in 1966. During 1962–65, a comprehensive revision of prices on personal services (laundry, haircuts, clothing, shoe and appliance repairs, etc.) was conducted in the Ukraine, and it is apparently to serve as a guide to similar revisions in other areas.

These measures indicate a new interest on the part of the Soviet government in setting better retail prices—an interest stimulated by the dramatic buildup of unsold goods, after a long period of excess demand conditions when improper relative prices could be tolerated. However, the government has been reluctant to move toward more flexible prices responsive to supply and demand conditions. The use of temporary prices has been limited, and the decentralization of price fixing to the enterprise level, tried in the Bolshevichka-Maiak experiment, has been rescinded. In sum, it appears that the central authorities are much more concerned about retail prices than ever before, but they are hesitant to surrender control over retail prices to the enterprise and through it to the market.

V. CONCLUSION

Soviet economists, planners, and political leaders have been devoting growing attention to prices as the Soviet economy slowly moves toward a greater role for market forces and money flows, rather than administrative commands in physical terms, in guiding production and resource allocation. A broad critical discussion of industrial prices, at scholarly conferences and in the economic press, began in 1956. Similar, though more cautious, discussions of agricultural and retail prices started a few years later. These discussions have exposed many defects in the price system and have produced a wide variety of suggestions for improvements, ranging from minor technical revisions to sweeping changes of a basic character.

It is clear that the highest levels of the Communist Party and the government are now concerned with price problems. Yet the central authorities have shown great reluctance to embark on major reforms in the price system in order to secure prices which reflect scarcity and can allocate resources efficiently. One reason, surely, is resistance to such reforms by members of the planning and administrative bureaucracy, who are used to, and comfortable with, command economy methods which do not depend on sound prices. They have a personal stake in the preservation of the traditional approach to resource allocation. They also genuinely distrust moves toward reliance on market forces and scarcity prices, fearing that they inevitably will bring inflation, on the one hand, and unemployment, on the other.

Because the political leadership and the central planners are unwilling to surrender control over the economy to consumers' sovereignty, they hesitate to let flexible scarcity prices determine output, allocate resources, and distribute income. Thus, it is not surprising that, despite the changes in enterprise performance indicators, managerial powers, and incentives, in Kosygin's "new economic model" price setting remains centralized and will largely follow traditional patterns. As a result, the planners will continue to be faced with the impossible task of regulating the eight to nine million prices in the Soviet economy.

8 | FINANCE AND BANKING IN THE USSR

George Garvy

In the Soviet economy, money is supposed to be "neutral" or "passive" rather than "active." Soviet planners endeavor to adjust financial flows to carry out physical plans for allocating resources and distributing output. The budget implements macroeconomic decisions about the division of national product among investment, consumption, and military programs, as well as microeconomic decisions about the allocation of investment among different branches of the economy and regions of the country. The main functions of the banking system are to finance planned inventories at various levels of production and distribution, and to supervise the adherence of enterprises to their plans (i.e., to exercise "control by the ruble"). Thus, the banking system plays a derivative, supporting role, and there is no independent monetary policy.

This selection provides both a general survey of the financial aspects of the Soviet economy and a more detailed study of the banking system. The first part analyzes the nature of financial planning, monetary policy, and the relationship between the banking system and its clients. It points out the many differences in these respects between the Soviet economy and regulated capitalist market economies in the West. The second part examines in detail the organization and activities of the Soviet banking system, Soviet monetary theory, and recent changes connected with the current economic reforms.

George Garvy is Economic Adviser at the Federal Reserve Bank of New York. The selection is reprinted by permission from his monograph, *Money, Banking, and Credit in Eastern Europe* (New York: Federal Reserve Bank of New York, 1966), pp. 12–27 and 122–36, with the omission of citations to Russian-language sources.

I. FINANCIAL CHARACTERISTICS OF THE CENTRALLY PLANNED ECONOMY

ALL THE COMMUNIST countries of Eastern Europe are now attempting, in various degrees, to make use of the market process. Many of the

138

changes are being introduced only gradually, however, and in most countries details are still to be worked out for some of the most significant changes. In the meantime, the basic features of centrally planned economies remain intact. Production targets, formulated mainly in physical terms, are set by the central government and embodied in specific directives, usually cast in the form of output plans. Designated governmental agencies specify for each enterprise, or group of enterprises, the kinds and sources of inputs and the destination of outputs. Since all basic planning is in real magnitudes ("material balances"), the role of money is mainly to provide a common denominator (*numéraire*) for aggregation and projection. The allocation of resources is determined by the central plan and not through the price system. All prices are set by authority, and wage rates and total payroll costs of individual enterprises are strictly controlled. Consumer prices and transfer prices among producers are seldom changed because stable prices facilitate global planning and an orderly distribution and redistribution of the national product. Administrative decisions, and not market adjustments, are relied upon to correct disequilibria and deviations from plans. Until experiments with more flexible policies were begun in recent years, individual enterprises in the government-owned sector of the economy (which, in each country, accounts for all but a small percentage of total output outside agriculture) had little scope for deciding between production alternatives or for making investment decisions.

The Central Role of the Budget

All financial flows in the Eastern European countries, whether related to the movement of goods or to the flow of investment, are influenced by output plans and by direct controls over funds spent. They are not market determined and, indeed, there are no credit or capital markets. Instead the budget of the national government assumes the key role in the distribution of the national product. All major macroeconomic decisions —such as the division of current output between investment and consumption—are embodied in the government budget. In particular, the financial counterpart of the flow of real resources into investment is for the most part channeled through the budget. The national budget also fulfills an important allocative function with regard to investment flows (between industry and agriculture, among industries and regions), which in the free market economies is performed largely through the market process.

The budget is thus the most important funnel for all payments flows and the most important component of overall financial planning. Receipts of the state-owned enterprises in excess of expenditures for direct costs (mainly labor and materials) are siphoned off into the budget, either through taxes or by the transfer of profits (except for a relatively small part to be invested or spent for collective consumption by the enterprises themselves). About half of the national income of each country flows through the budget, a much larger proportion than in the United States and the other leading industrial countries of the West. This higher proportion results primarily from two facts: first, the channeling through the budget of the bulk of all investment (in working as well as fixed capital), and, second, the financing of a very large part of expenditures of all lower units of government through transfers from the national budget. Moreover, the bulk of "collective consumption"—which includes not only free educational, health, and other services, but also subsidies for housing, transportation, and the like—is budget financed.

Financing of investment in the government sector of the economy involves essentially transfers from the accounts of enterprises to the budget (and vice versa). Voluntary savings provide a very minor though growing counterpart of real investment. The, in effect forced sale of government bonds to the population, resorted to in various communist countries in the first postwar years (in the Soviet Union until 1957–58), must be regarded as a measure for preserving monetary equilibrium by reducing consumption, rather than as a normal means of financing investment.

The Separation of Payments Flows

A considerable part of the activity of the banking system centers on the administration of a two-circuit payments mechanism: cash and "noncash." Currency is used for virtually all payments between the government (including the state-owned enterprises) and the population (as wage earners but also as entrepreneurs, to the extent that farming and some other activities remain in private hands). Practically all consumer expenditures are made in currency. The flow of purchasing power to consumers is planned to match the available supply of goods and services, plus an estimated increase in cash balances (supported by an increase in currency in circulation). Savings accounts (and, in some cases, bonds issued by savings banks or by the government) and hoarding of currency are the only means open to the population for accumulating financial assets. In contrast, all payments among enterprises, organizations, and the government (except very small and strictly limited amounts) involve transfers on the books of the banking system; this noncash circuit is best thought of as the counterpart of check circulation in Western countries. The relationship between the two circuits corresponds to separate markets for consumer goods and producer (including raw material and intermediary) goods.

Separation of the two circuits not only facilitates control but also makes it easier to detect disequilibria, bottlenecks, and various shortfalls in the execution of economic plans. Because of the separation of the payments stream into two watertight compartments, and the considerable differences between the functions of balances in the two sectors, the concept of the total money supply has very limited analytical significance in the countries of Eastern Europe.

Equilibrium through Planning

Maintenance of equilibrium conditions and achievement of growth objectives are supposed to result from proper overall planning of material resources and not through influencing, indirectly, aggregate pecuniary demand and its structure or the cost and availability of money and capital. From its very origin, Soviet financial planning has been "derivative"— based on material balances, in which specific kinds of physical resources are allocated to achieve growth under conditions of overall equilibrium. Monetary flows are planned as the counterpart of physical flows and adjusted to changes in such flows. Equilibrium between supply and monetary demand for consumer goods and services is to be attained by production, price, and wage decisions taken by the planning authorities. Equilibrium in the cash circuit is achieved when wage and other payments to the population equal the monetary value of the consumer goods and services that are to be produced by the economy at established prices, which, ideally, remain stable for relatively long periods of time. Adjustments needed to maintain such an equilibrium are taken by the planning, not by the monetary, authorities.

Planning for growth under conditions of overall equilibrium of monetary demand and supply takes the form of an interlocking system of financial plans. In effect, these plans are projections, in the form of balances, of sources and uses of funds in the various sectors of the economy. They vary in their makeup—some flows are on a gross, others on a net basis and a few are drawn up in stock terms. Some are, in effect, detailed operating plans while others are more in the nature of broad guidelines for the use of policy-making bodies. There are also considerable differences among countries in the number and articulation of such plans and in the extent to which the plans represent merely internal working documents or approach the status of binding operational directives. Moreover, the role of financial planning itself has been undergoing important changes in recent years.

Whatever the official status of the monetary plans, actual performance measured against plan figures provides a day-to-day check on the working of the economy—indeed the only overall check. Monetary flows in the socialized sector, recorded through the banking system (by entries in the appropriate accounts), reveal deviations from planned real flows and thus mirror disequilibria and bottlenecks in the real processes. Money thus performs an important signal function, but it is not relied on to any significant degree as an adjuster. Remedial action normally comes through direct intervention by the authorities in charge of production and distribution ("the economic organs") and through fiscal and pricing policies and other tools intended to change output levels and patterns directly. Much of what appears to be monetary action is rather the exercise of administrative functions by the banking system in support of policies formulated elsewhere in the planning structure.

The control of individual enterprises is shared among national, regional, and local authorities. As a general rule, enterprises producing basic materials, capital goods, or consumption goods for the national market are subordinated to a ministry. The other enterprises, which tend to be smaller, are responsible to regional political entities (federated republics in the Soviet Union) or to municipalities (which typically have jurisdiction over such enterprises as local retail and service establishments, bakeries, utilities, or movie theaters). Several enterprises of national significance, or even all units in the same industry, are frequently joined for administrative purposes into organizations variously called trusts, combines, groups, firms, aggregations, associations, and the like. (For the sake of consistency, these will hereafter be uniformly referred to as associations; they are normally subordinated to a ministry in charge of a given group of industries.)

The Roles of Money and Credit

Because of the basic reliance on planning in terms of real flows, and the central importance of the national budget for financial planning, the functions of money and credit in Eastern Europe are radically different from the roles they play in free market economies. Ownership of money does not give an absolute command over resources. The individual can acquire only consumer goods and strictly limited categories of property for personal use. Small service establishments, artisans, and independent farmers also can acquire producer goods—and this is of some importance in countries like East Germany and Poland; but these nonsocialized sectors are not significant (with the major exception of agriculture in Poland). In the state sector, money may be used only in conformity with the plan; credit gives command over resources only if acquisition of the resources is foreseen in the plan, while plan allocation of resources carries with it an almost automatic claim on credit. The role of monetary flows is to implement the planners' intentions, not to invoke response or to correct movement away from equilibrium ("neutral money"). The power of money to influence real processes is severely limited by direct administrative controls. Attempts to use monetary incentives in order to guide economic activity have been made in recent years, but so far on a limited scale only.

The countries of Eastern Europe know no credit-granting institutions other than banks. To a very limited extent, banks have been used since the mid-1950's to finance certain minor kinds of fixed investment, but the main role of credit under the standard system is to provide the bulk of the financing of inventories at the various levels of production and distribution. Consumer credit and financing of cooperative and individual home building have become important only in recent years. Where a significant part of agriculture remains in private hands, notably in Poland, some efforts have been made since the mid-1950's to provide credit to farmers, both for seasonal needs and for improving technology. Except in East Germany, Czechoslovakia, and Poland, practically no credit is available to private enterprise in the other sectors of the economy. Changes of a rather marginal nature in credit policy and techniques, intended to provide somewhat greater flexibility, were made in the Soviet Union after the death of Stalin in 1954. These were also copied in the other countries, although in some cases in a modified form, and some changes were introduced for which there was no Soviet example. Until very recent years, however, such divergences involved chiefly techniques and details, rather than a fundamental reappraisal of the potentialities of monetary and credit policy.

The aggregate volume of credit is determined almost automatically by the production and distribution goals set in real terms. The proper amount of total working capital and the extent to which it consists of the enterprises' own resources (designated as "own funds") are determined by the central authorities for each individual industry. Thus changes in the volume of credit are, for the most part, the counterpart of changes in the volume of inventories, unless planning authorities decide to change the relative share of enterprise funds and bank credit in the carrying of inventories. Under the standard system, the granting of credit is almost automatic, once the borrower's output plan has been approved, and the mechanics of credit granting is geared to rigid rules. Changes in the cost and availability of credit are not relied on as the means of achieving changes in resource use, although in recent years differentiation in interest rates has been increasingly used to achieve greater efficiency and to favor socially desirable activities. The prevailing official view is that the essential function of the credit system is the redistribution of cash balances (temporarily redundant enterprise balances, budget surpluses, and consumer savings) rather than credit creation.

During the first 25 years after the credit reforms of 1930–32, the credit policy of the Soviet Union was concerned exclusively with providing the payments counterpart of the movement of real goods through the production and distribution process. The other countries originally copied the Soviet credit system to the smallest details. In very recent years, however, at least some of the countries have begun to explore the possibility of adapting credit administration techniques as instruments of active credit policy.

Liquidity Position of Enterprises

Since the ability of enterprises to acquire goods depends, theoretically at least, on the planners' intent and not primarily on liquidity, the liquidity position of the enterprise sector is ostensibly of no concern to credit policy. In effect, however, administrative and financial controls have not proved sufficient to prevent "unplanned" spending: enterprises have frequently made use of their financial resources to support their operations, as dramatically evidenced in several instances of inflationary outbursts—especially in 1950–53—in all the smaller communist countries with the exception of East Germany. Thus, while the monetary system has no way of influencing the liquidity of the socialized sector on a day-to-day basis, some countries have at times resorted to the device of temporarily sterilizing (blocking) enterprise balances or imposing limitations on their use.

The individual enterprise, which under the standard system has very limited latitude in managing its working capital, is rarely confronted with liquidity problems in the same sense as firms in capitalist countries. Its liquidity position has no direct bearing on its fixed investment plans, since these are, with negligible exceptions, implemented by financing from budgetary resources. Loans are made automatically on bills of lading to cover the standard collection period, and usually provision is made for easy access to bank credit in order to finance unforeseen expenditures, such as bulges in inventories of raw materials due to deliveries ahead of or beyond schedule. At the same time, considerable emphasis is placed on "improving the payments discipline," since failure to pay on time is tantamount to extending interunit credit; it disrupts the circular flow of capital and creates payments difficulties all down the line.

While the management of an enterprise has usually little difficulty in temporarily replenishing working funds through bank loans, its ability to use its own bank balance is strictly circumscribed. In communist countries the absolute order to pay is unknown; all payments must be documented as consistent with the applicable plan, and the purpose of the payment is normally verifiable from the underlying documents. Interenterprise payments are usually made not by check but on the basis of drafts supported by documents related to the shipment of goods, and collection of payments for shipments (or services rendered) requires time-consuming movement of documents. Claims arising from production and distribution are nonnegotiable and nonassignable: they can give rise only to deposit transfers (settlements) between the accounts of the actual buyer and seller.

A shortage of funds normally results in difficulties of one sort or another, but the accumulation of free funds (excess liquidity in Western terms) confers little advantage, since it does not in itself entitle the enterprise to purchase additional resources. It may actually lead to a loss of working capital (if the superior economic authority directs the enterprise to relinquish the excess to other enterprises), or failure to obtain an additional allocation ("replenishment") of working capital from the budget next year, or even a permanent reduction of allotted working capital. Policymakers in communist economies have an interest in keeping the enterprises' own working funds at a minimum, so that extension of credit would give the bank a greater lever to exert tighter controls over each enterprise.

Indeed, the total volume of credit does not have the same significance that it has in the Western countries. The dividing line between credit and working capital owned by the individual enterprise is fluid and not of great significance in itself. The choice between more "own" capital and more credit hinges on overall policy considerations, embodied in industrywide "norms" (prescribed standard ratios). Since all capital in the state enterprise sector is owned by the government and is merely assigned to individual enterprises, a working-capital shortage in any given enterprise can be remedied either by granting it more credit or by adding to its capital (through budgetary resources or through transfers from other enterprises administered by the same ministry or from other "higher echelon" organizations in the economic administration). In principle, all state enterprises operate in part with borrowed funds, mainly because it is desired to increase control by the banking authorities, but the precise share of loans in working funds varies.

The Role of the Banking System

Even before he took power, Lenin envisaged the banking system as becoming the backbone of the socialist state's administrative apparatus. Nationalization of private banking and establishment of a government monopoly of all foreign exchange transactions were among the first economic measures taken by the Bolshevik government in 1917. In the other Eastern European countries, foreign exchange transactions were virtually a government monopoly at the time the communists obtained a dominant position, and nationalization of banks and other financial institutions was uniformly one of the first actions of the new governments. Centralization of bank credit appeared to be a logical concomitant of centralized planning and management of production and distribution.

The particular form of banking organization developed originally in the Soviet Union combines in the state bank most of the attributes of a central bank with those functions of commercial banking that are relevant in the communist economy, and also with a wide range of activities related specifically to the characteristics of such economies. The term "monobank" fits well this type of banking institution. The monobank is supplemented by a small number of banks that serve special functions, including an investment bank, which is a key institution for channeling funds into fixed capital.

In specific terms, the monobank is the *bank of issue* and is responsible for the regulation of note circulation. It manages the gold and foreign exchange reserves, in close cooperation with (and in some cases under the direction of) the Ministry of Finance and the Ministry of Foreign Trade (which in all countries of Eastern Europe is responsible for administering the foreign trade monopoly). In most of the countries, the financing of foreign trade, and even of related domestic activities, has in recent years been shifted to special foreign trade banks.

The monobank (along with the other banks, to the limited extent that they extend short-term credit) is the sole *source of short-term credit*, as the extension of direct interenterprise ("commercial") credit is forbidden. The bank is not the ultimate but the only lender. Since control of credit is exercised directly, the monobank is not concerned with the same problems (such as controlling the reserves or liquidity of independent commercial banks) or activities (such as discounting and open market operations) as central banks in Western countries. As there are no financial markets or instruments (except savings bonds held by individuals), authorities do not have to worry about the prices of financial assets.

The monobank services the *currency needs* of the entire economy, including the savings banks and all specialized banks, where these exist as separate entities. Its offices act as *agents for specialized banks* in localities where these are not represented.

Since all payments within the socialized sector are transfers on its books, the monobank is the one and all-encompassing *settlements and clearing center* of the country. It keeps the accounts of the national government and of all subordinate government units, and performs all the usual *fiscal agency functions* carried out by central banks in Western countries (e.g., the collection and disbursement of revenue to support regular government activities, the issue and redemption of public loans). Of the proceeds deposited at the monobank from the sale of goods by the state enterprises, a part is paid out in cash for wages and the remaining part is credited to various accounts through book transfers. Thus it functions as a *social accounting center*, which not only keeps track of payments flows but, in many cases, also allocates single payments among several special-purpose accounts.

Because payments flows are planned and tied to plan fulfillment, all such monobank operations as cash withdrawals, book transfers, and credit extensions involve an *audit function* to check conformity of payment to underlying authorization. This important activity—essential to what is called "control by the ruble" (or the forint, or the koruna), which is a basic feature of centrally planned economies—entails more than financial supervision; indeed, it makes the monobank a key part of the policy and administrative apparatus of the communist state.

In view of its manifold functions, it is logical that the monobank is an active participant in all phases of economic planning. It is also a major, and frequently the main, channel through which any failures in the meshing of gears come to the attention of the authorities. But the monobank raises the flag without cracking the whip; when the signals it transmits require corrective action, this is normally taken through policy measures that emanate from the higher authorities of the state.

The difference between the monobank and both the central and the commercial banks of capitalist countries is reflected in the structure of the balance sheet. The assets side of the monobank's balance sheet consists mainly of loans to the various segments of the economy (possibly including a small amount of housing loans to individuals), in addition to gold and foreign exchange; it contains no government or private securities. Among the monobank's liabilities (in addition to capital accounts and note liabilities) are the free balances of its clients—the counterpart of demand deposits in capitalist countries. These balances are owned mainly by economic or governmental units and, to a lesser extent, by cooperative farms and nonprofit organizations. The only counterpart of the interbank balances held by banks in Western countries is the uncommitted deposits of specialized banks. There are no time deposits and only a negligible amount of deposits of individuals.

The monobank's activities have some similarities to those of central banks in underdeveloped countries, with their rudimentary or nonexistent money and capital markets, their reliance on government for the bulk of capital formation, the relatively large volume of lending either by the central bank directly or through development banks, and largely fixed or stable rates of interest. Differences between Eastern Europe and the West in regard to the functions of money and credit and the central bank are considerable and basic.

Sources of Bank Funds

No state bank of any country of Eastern Europe currently publishes data on the liabilities side of its balance sheet. It is known, however, that funds available for lending are acquired each year from a combination of the following sources (disregarding any resources of foreign origin): cumulative budget surpluses of previous years (a main means of achieving equilibrium in the economy), an increase in capital resources (from profits or transfers from the budget), an increase in note circulation, funds held at the state bank by the specialized banks, reserves of social insurance funds (where they exist as separate entities, as in Czechoslovakia), deposits of savings banks (particularly where, as in the Soviet Union, they have no lending business of their own), and an increase in balances of enterprises and organizations. The last of these, being strictly controlled and kept at a minimum, is likely to be of greater significance from a seasonal than from a longer run point of view. In the Soviet Union, for instance, such balances at the beginning of 1965 stood at 12.1 billion rubles which, in relation to the value of industrial output, is considerably below the ratio between the level of commercial bank balances maintained by United States corporations and the value of the corporate product.

Even though the banking literature of the communist countries keeps repeating that the state bank can make loans only within the limits of resources at its disposal, and though considerable day-by-day efforts are made to attract ("mobilize") additional resources (for instance, by inducing farm cooperatives to keep their free funds with banks), the implied analogy with commercial banks in capitalist countries is misleading. The state bank cannot lose funds to any other bank, since it accounts for 95 percent or more of total credit and is the depository of the uncommitted funds of all other banks. Issue of additional currency may be, and almost certainly will be, the result of any additional lending, but this merely represents a shift in the composition of the liabilities that match the loans added to the assets side of the balance sheet. The real, indeed the only, limit to the extension of bank credit in communist countries—where bank liabilities are not subject to reserve requirements and there is full administrative control of foreign payments—is determined by macroeconomic decisions made by the political and planning authorities and embodied in the financial plans.

The Bank and its Clientele

The relationship between the monobank and its clientele also bears little resemblance to the corresponding relationship in capitalist countries. Rather than being an agent of the depositor, the monobank, when dealing with the individual enterprise, is, in fact, the representative of the state; the population at large has no direct contact with it. It protects the interests of the state by debiting from the depositor's account—in most cases, automatically—the various payments due the treasury. If necessary, it extends credit to meet such payments. More generally, criteria that the bank applies in relations with its clientele are tied to the borrower's execution of the economic plan, to which the meeting of the borrower's financial obligations to the bank is subordinated. Each enterprise, unit of government, or nonprofit (voluntary) organization has to bank with the single office in whose territory it is located. This arrangement obviously provides no incentive for the management and personnel of any unit of the banking system to improve service in order to retain or attract depositors.

Until the emergence of new trends in recent years, the bank and its customers were merely involved in a web of impersonal accounting relationships, embracing set, uniform, and rigid rules, few alternatives, a minimum of flexibility, and supervision that reached into the minute details of an enterprise's activities and amounted in effect to a continuous and detailed audit of physical and financial performance. The monobank used no other criterion for measuring performance than the degree of success with which an enterprise discharged its current financial obligations (maintained a sufficient balance to pay bills and loans when due) and avoided exceeding norms—most importantly, the inventory norms—imposed from the outside by planning authorities and various economic administrations, including ministries.[1]

Monetary Policy in a Planned Economy

From the foregoing brief summary it is clear that the functions of monetary policy in planned economies are very different from those it serves in the West. In the communist countries, as elsewhere, the basic objective of economic policy is to achieve optimum growth rates without exposing the existing price structure to pressures caused by imbalances between the flow of consumer purchasing power and the availability of consumer goods. And the underlying analysis of capabilities—in terms of available real resources—and of the required changes in money supply, credit, and financial flows resulted in procedures not much different from those used in making macroeconomic projections in Western countries. But in formulating and implementing monetary policies that will serve their objectives, the two types of economies differ completely, reflecting their fundamental differences in capital ownership, economic organization, and political and social philosophy.

In Western countries the formulation of monetary policy is a continuous process, responding flexibly to changes in the performance of the market economy. In communist countries, monetary policy is embodied in all-embracing financial plans, which carry final authority and are changed only at fixed intervals. Although one can identify the nature of credit and note issue policies pursued by a communist country, and show what policies it follows with regard to encouraging personal saving, providing financing for small-scale capital improvements, or managing foreign exchange reserves, it is difficult to tie these separate aspects into something that would add up to a socialist monetary policy. But in all such matters the banking system acts merely as a vehicle for the execution of broader government decisions as embodied in the detailed plans; monetary action is not geared to the market but is determined by administrative processes centered on the planned allocation of resources. The familiar tools of monetary policy available to Western central banks are irrelevant. In communist countries, monetary policy is concerned primarily with assuring the efficiency of currency circulation and of the payments mechanism and with facilitating the economic performance of enterprises, while fiscal policy is heavily relied upon to assure balance between aggregate demand and supply.

---

[1] See Robert W. Campbell, *Accounting in Soviet Planning and Management* (Cambridge, Mass.: Harvard University Press, 1963), pp. 205 ff.

In fact, one would look in vain in the writings of Soviet economists, who so far have been setting the tone in the other countries of Eastern Europe as well, for an explicit discussion of monetary policy. Typically, Soviet textbooks and treatises merely discuss the various functions of credit in the socialist economy. The more sophisticated treatment makes a distinction between the "functions" and the "role" of credit, reserving the first term for the place of credit in the socialist economy and equating "role" with the results achieved in accelerating growth and output. Economic literature in Eastern Europe deals with the practical problems of controlling monetary circulation, crediting production and trade, and financing capital investment, usually under separate headings, but it does not discuss monetary policy, as such, or its relationship to fiscal policy, even though in the communist countries the two are closely integrated and the relationship between the monobank and the Ministry of Finance is at least as close as between central bank and government in Western countries. Similarly, banking officials, in their published speeches and articles, typically focus on how the state bank can best implement the economic plan or party decisions. Such statements clearly reflect the implementary nature of the monobank's activities and characteristically treat the monetary aspects of those activities (credit, currency circulation) on the same footing as routine operations (mutual offsets) or control functions (control over payroll disbursements).[2]

Even though the monobank plays essentially the role of an implementing agency, it has significant functions in the central administration's efforts to influence aggregate demand and stimulate growth. It contributes—to an extent that varies from country to country—to the determination of realistic plan targets and of the proper magnitudes that will "correctly" implement them, as well as serving indispensably in furthering the proper execution of the various financial plans. The monobank's role in economic administration is enhanced by an organizational advantage: in contrast to the various ministries, organized on an industry principle, and to regional economic bodies, it has a close and continuous contact, not only with specific branches or areas, but with the entire economy.

---

[2] In the authoritative Soviet two-volume *Dictionary of Finance and Credit* (issued by the official publishing house specializing in financial literature), there is no entry for "monetary policy." "Credit policy" is defined as "a system of measures in the area of credit, designed to secure the economic interests of the ruling class." There is no definition for a socialist economy, but a short review of the tasks of credit policy is prefaced by the statement that "In the Soviet Union credit policy corresponds to the tasks that the government places before the country in each phase of the construction of socialism and communism." "Credit restrictions" are described as "limitations or reductions in the volume of credit, which are put into effect by capitalist banks and the bourgeois state," and correspondingly, "credit expansion" is "enlargement of credit, put into effect by capitalist banks and the bourgeois state, which exceeds the growth of production, stimulates overproduction and the coming about of economic crises." There is no reference to a possible role of either process in a socialist economy.

Nevertheless, the fact remains that, when the level and distribution of spending power do not conform with the underlying plan, the means used to correct the disequilibria are not changes in the cost and availability of credit but administrative improvisation by the monobank—unless the matter is so serious that higher echelon government or party authorities step in with a change in the ground rules. The monobank is an adjuster, not a steerer; its role, to borrow Robert V. Roosa's terminology, coined in a different context, is defensive rather than dynamic.

Communist countries have no effective means of controlling the excess liquidity of the population sector and its threat to price stability, except through the harsh and dramatic measures of currency conversions and upward price adjustments (and in some cases, until the mid-1950's, through forced loans placed with the population).[3] Thus a primary objective of financial planning and action is to prevent excess liquidity of consumers from coming into existence and in general to avoid inflation, both overt and repressed (though the word "inflation" is banned from the vocabulary of Soviet economists, at least in relation to their own economy). Nevertheless, inflationary pressures have recurrently arisen in all the countries of Eastern Europe. To combat inflationary tendencies, to remove their causes, and to re-create conditions favorable to maintenance of price stability, centrally planned economies rely on a combination of fiscal, price, wage, foreign trade, and monetary and credit measures, and also on administrative shifts in the allocation of resources (and, if necessary, changes in planned targets).[4]

The nature of the monobank's role in monetary policy has been clearly stated in an interview given by Dr. O. Pohl, General Director of the State Bank of Czechoslovakia: "Of decisive importance for the expansion of an active financial policy is a structurally sound and well-balanced plan. Once the material resources have been incorrectly employed, the bank will be too late with whatever measures it could take." Increased bank

---

[3] The experience of currency conversion, common to all these countries in the first postwar years, left few fond memories, though the 1947 conversion in the Soviet Union, and some others, did produce a more favorable ratio of exchange for small savings and for certain groups of account holders. See Edward Ames, "Soviet Bloc Currency Conversions," *American Economic Review*, Vol. XLIV, No. 3 (June, 1954), pp. 339–53.

[4] Even a cursory review of the Eastern European countries' efforts to neutralize the inflationary overhang of World War II and to combat the subsequent succession of inflationary threats would exceed the limits of this study. Fortunately, adequate accounts of these developments are readily available. See John M. Montias, "Inflation and Growth: The Experience of Eastern Europe," in Werner Baer and Isaac Kerstenetzky (eds.), *Inflation and Growth in Latin America* (Homewood, Ill.: Richard D. Irwin, Inc., 1964), pp. 216–50; also Franklyn D. Holzman, "Soviet Inflationary Pressures, 1928–1957: Causes and Cures," *Quarterly Journal of Economics*, Vol. LXXIV, No. 2 (May, 1960), pp. 167–88. For an (unorthodox) communist view of this problem, see Bronislaw Oyrzanowski, "Problems of Inflation under Socialism," in Douglas Hague (ed.), *Inflation* (New York: St. Martin's Press, Inc., 1962), pp. 332–41, and the several papers by Oyrzanowski and other Polish authors cited by Michael Kaser in his comments on the Montias article (*Inflation and Growth in Latin America*, pp. 276–83).

participation in the preparation and drawing-up of the plan is desirable, he said, "to enable the bank to step in with its own knowledge and demands when there is still time to influence the anticipated employment of material means, in other words to strengthen the preventive character of the bank's role." After the plan is accepted, the monobank's efforts are directed toward keeping the monetary variables in line with the projections that relate changes in credit and currency circulation to real targets. Within the framework of the plan, credit policy can help bring about a more efficient use of the resources than the plan provides, and thus contribute to lowering costs. But the monobank will automatically validate any of the plan's misjudgments and shortcomings that are binding for it. And although it is expected to prevent spending in excess of stipulated amounts—particularly for wage disbursements and inventory building—it can do little to bring inadequate spending to target levels.

Toward Greater Reliance on "Economic Levers"

With the new policies that began to emerge in the post-Stalin era but which became generally accepted throughout Eastern Europe only by 1965, the role of the banking system has begun to change. In general, the new developments involve a downgrading of physical indicators and an elevation of profitability to a position as an indicator of success—in other words, a differentiation between good and poor performers; a more liberal treatment of the former; increased stress on financial performance, as compared with physical output; and greater reliance on initiative and on material incentives. Although the new policies that have been taking shape in recent years give greater latitude to the local bank official, they by no means change his position as agent of the state: the difference lies in a shift from the state's exclusive reliance on administrative controls to a system that makes increasing room for "steering by self-regulation," in which "economic levers" are assigned an active role.

The degrees to which the individual countries have at this writing moved away from the Soviet prototype vary greatly. It is clear that much greater variety in institutional arrangements and policies is developing as each country's specific conditions and experience, as well as the differing views on the way in which a communist economy can make use of the market mechanism and dispense with detailed administrative controls, are gradually being embodied in new banking legislation and regulations. It appears that any further moves in individual countries toward greater reliance on the impersonal mechanism of the market for achieving a more rational and more effective allocation of resources and greater efficiency in their use will be accompanied quite generally by an increased role assigned to financial criteria (including profits) and incentives. Credit policy is likely to play a greater and, in some respects, different role, losing much of its purely implementary character. In this process the bank official will become less concerned with the interpretation of regulations and gauging plan performance and more with evaluating the profitability of alternative uses of credit.

II. BANKING AND CREDIT IN THE USSR

The monetary and credit system of the Soviet Union was rebuilt from scratch after the victory of the Bolshevik revolution. One of the first acts of the new government was to nationalize all domestic and foreign banking institutions, their head offices in the capital having been taken over by armed detachments on a single day, December 14, 1917. Subsequently the monetary system underwent a series of radical changes. These included: attempts during 1918–21 to abolish money; the introduction in 1924 of a uniform and stable currency, after the astronomical inflation and monetary disorganization of the civil war and the following years; and a reform in 1947 designed to mop up the excess consumer liquidity resulting from World War II. The revaluation of the ruble in terms of the dollar in 1961 was, however, of little practical significance. Fundamental credit reforms in 1930–32 put an end to the substantial circulation of trade bills and direct extension of interunit credits and centralized practically all short-term credit activity in the Gosbank. Since then the credit system, though it has undergone further developments, has remained basically unchanged. There has been, however, a good deal of organizational restructuring of banking, reflecting the changes over the years in economic policy and organization and persistent efforts to tighten the Gosbank's control over payments flows.[5]

The development of Soviet financial arrangements has been hampered all along by adherence to theoretical views derived from the writings of Karl Marx, which relate to a capitalist financial environment of a century ago. The checkered history of the banking system over half a century of evolution can be viewed as a struggle to forge an effective tool for monitoring the fulfillment of economic plans and to preserve price stability by controlling payments flows. Although that system served as a model for all communist countries, the Soviet Union has lagged behind the others in the attempts to make money and credit play a more active part in the transformation of the economy away from a rigidly centralized form.

The standard system discussed in Part I is, in essence, the system originally developed in the Soviet Union. All that need be added is a brief description of the evolution of its banking structure, of the modifications that have occurred in recent years, and of those that are currently under way.

---

[5] The history of developments before World War II is readily available in English; see Arthur Z. Arnold, *Banks, Credit, and Money in Soviet Russia* (New York: Columbia University Press, 1937).

The Banking System

Since World War II there has been a strong tendency in the Soviet Union toward consolidation of banking institutions. Even before the war, notably in 1932 and 1936, various banks were consolidated that had been originally created to finance capital formation in specific economic sectors, including agriculture. Subsequently, in 1959, further mergers and reassignment of activities occurred, and as a result the Investment Bank (Stroibank) emerged as the single conduit of budgetary appropriations into fixed investment. And since the beginning of 1963 the savings bank system, with over 70,000 branches (including agencies in factories, offices, and farms), has been part of the Gosbank, operating as a separate department that is also in charge of selling government bonds. Apart from the Gosbank and the Investment Bank, the only other banking institution now in existence is the Bank for Foreign Trade (Vneshtorgbank),[6] whose scope of operations was considerably increased in 1961. Originally, it was concerned mainly with currency exchange for tourists and diplomatic missions and with remittances, since payments for commercial transactions with foreigners were handled by the Gosbank. After its reorganization the Foreign Trade Bank has been handling all foreign settlements and also the crediting of foreign trade. Since the Investment Bank is essentially an administrative organization supervising the disbursement of government budget grants, and the Foreign Trade Bank is actually only a headquarters organization, the Gosbank is the purest example of a monobank, as it virtually alone services the cash, credit, and payments needs of a country with a population exceeding 230 million.

In its organization the Gosbank corresponds to the standard type of monobank. In addition to its policy-making head office and its principal offices in the various republics, it has two levels (in some of the smaller republics, only one level) of regional office and a network of about 3,500 local branches which are its main points of contact with enterprises, collective farms, and lower level government units. To service the urban population it maintains nearly 2,000 collection offices (originally part of the network of communal banks abolished in 1959), which receive payments for rent and service bills, taxes, and other compulsory payments and contributions. The office network also includes a small number (currently fewer than thirty) of special cash service agencies in large industrial establishments and construction projects. Seasonal agencies are operated at remote points where large purchases of farm products are made.

Little statistical information is available on the operations of the Gos-

---

[6] See M. Poliakov, "USSR Bank for Foreign Trade," *American Review of Soviet and East European Foreign Trade*, Vol. 1, No. 1 (January-February, 1965), pp. 63–67.

bank. Its more than 150,000 employees service about 1.2 million clients: the bulk of all banking operations is with the approximately 250,000 enterprises that operate on the basis of cost accounting, or *khozraschet* (enterprises that have their own working capital, prepare a balance sheet and an income statement), and borrow regularly or occasionally. There are about 40,000 collective farm accounts. Nearly half a million are various government units and organizations (such as party, trade union, and cultural organizations) that have no access to credit. Most accounts held by individuals are loan accounts for home financing, which number around 400,000; in addition, there are a negligible number of individual savings deposits.

Aggregate balances maintained by Gosbank clients are small in comparison with cash balances held by business and government units in the United States. At the beginning of 1961, total balances in accounts of all *khozraschet* organizations amounted to less than 4.7 billion rubles[7] (compared with 3 billion rubles five years earlier), and all other current accounts came to only 1.6 billion rubles. It is not known how the sum of these two amounts (which corresponds approximately to demand deposits in the United States, including Treasury deposits at Federal Reserve and commercial banks) compares with note circulation data, as these are considered a state secret.

The operation of a centralized payments system poses many problems in a country the size of the Soviet Union, with its diverse economy and its comparatively small degree of industrial integration. The system is based in the main on documentary drafts and involves processing a large number of items. In very recent years this operation has begun to be automated, but the use of electronic equipment is still very limited.

The rapid increase in transactions by individuals—which has occurred even though consumer loans are extended by stores rather than by banks —has been a consequence of rising incomes, a rise in savings, provision of facilities for depositing wages in savings accounts and making periodic payments from them, and the growing importance of housing loans and of tourism. Since savings bank offices handle virtually all accounts and transactions of individuals, the great increase in these transactions seems to have been a main reason for the incorporation of the savings bank system into the Gosbank.

Of even greater importance as an operating problem has been the rise in transactions involving the collective farms. The relationship between the collective farms and the state, and between the farms and their members, began to be monetized in 1953. Under the system hitherto in force, the collectives paid in kind for the services performed by the state-owned tractor and farm machinery stations and had to deliver a large part of their output to the state at relatively low prices fixed by the

---

[7] All amounts in this chapter are in post-1961 reform rubles.

government, which were in fact a form of taxation. In connection with the changes that started in 1953, the tractor and machinery stations were liquidated and their equipment was sold to the collectives. The farms then had to pay in cash for all machinery and fuel, as well as for building materials, fertilizer, and other supplies; on the other hand, they could sell their output to the state on contract, at significantly higher prices.

Since the early fifties, a gradual shift has been made toward remunerating members of collective farms in cash, rather than in kind, even though until recently they received their income annually, after the end of the crop year. In 1953 only one third of the compensation for work contributed by members was in cash; five years later the proportion had risen to more than half, and it was nearly three fourths in 1963. Since the beginning of 1965 the flow of money income to the farm population has been further increased by the introduction of state pension payments to the aged members of collective farms. The introduction in the summer of 1966 of minimum monthly payments to the members of collective farms will result in greater use of money in the farm sector.

The substantial growth of payments flows and bank lending in rural areas and the need to service an ever-growing clientele in villages have added to the complexity of Gosbank operations, traditionally geared to the needs of industry and government which are concentrated in urban areas. Thus the Gosbank has continuously attempted to simplify payments procedures. Efforts to speed up payments through local and industrywide compensation arrangements—whereby mutual claims were offset —have not been successful, and separate compensation offices were abolished in 1955. Other forms of compensation arrangements are now in effect, and local and regional offices have been experimenting on and off with a variety of procedures for accelerating payments, at least for certain categories of transactions. Yet the Soviet banking and economic publications continue to devote much space to the need to improve the settlements mechanism, which seems to represent one of the major operating problems of the Gosbank.

The activities of the Gosbank are not limited to purely financial operations. Despite recent changes in other communist countries, the Soviet economy still does not provide the managers of enterprises with direct and powerful incentives or rewards for maximum performance. In fact, managers have no authority to innovate or even to make quite small modifications in established technology and procedures, as they are confronted with bureaucratic hurdles if they attempt any change, however small it may be. In such a system, a considerable part of improvements must be initiated by persons or organizations outside the enterprise. Ever since the creation of the Soviet regime, various techniques have been tried to provide such outside "assistance" for improving performance. In recent years the emphasis has shifted somewhat from party organs to "voluntary citizens' organizations" to serve this purpose, and "public bureaus of economic analysis" have been created at many enterprises and state farms. These organizations consist of several members of the enterprise staff who are directly engaged in production and administration (engineers, foremen, accountants) as well as economists from the various government agencies.[8] A large number of Gosbank economists are engaged in such "voluntary" activities in addition to their regular duties; in the Ukraine, for instance, at the beginning of 1965 there were nearly 5,000 bureaus, and more than 2,000 economists on the staffs of local and regional offices of the Gosbank participated in the work of these bureaus. Professional employees of the Gosbank also take active part in "voluntary" and auxiliary control organizations attached to the lower territorial units of the government and the party. In the words of an article in the bank's official publication:

Economists of the Gosbank are widely used by the control organs of the party and of the government to check the state of affairs in trade, in public eating places, in various establishments that service the population, and in the development of the network of movie theaters, and to conduct complex investigations of the business and financial activities of enterprises and organizations in the fields of production, trade, procurement, and other branches of the economy.

Credit Planning and Practices

Little need be added here to the discussion of planning above. Credit planning in the Soviet Union goes back to 1924, immediately after the introduction of a stable currency but several years before the extension of short-term credit became a monopoly of the Gosbank. The form and structure of the various monetary plans in use in the Soviet Union have changed little over time, but such changes as have taken place reflect in the main administrative changes rather than attempts at integration or at increasing the analytical value of the plans. In recent Soviet economic literature one encounters increasing recognition that financial planning involves more than mere balancing of accounting statements, and that the interrelationship of all financial accounts does not necessarily mean they are either integrated among themselves or consistent with the underlying physical balances. Some contemporary Soviet writers on banking subjects are aware of the need to extend financial analysis to deposit money, to the factors that determine the demand for such balances, and to money flows and velocity. So far, however, monetary planning has been limited, in effect, to currency circulation and, in view of the prevailing monetary

---

[8] In Eastern Europe the word "economist" has a much broader connotation than in the West, in terms of both training and occupation. In all agencies concerned with the administration of economic activities, a large proportion of the professional staff are classified as "economists."

arrangements, this is equivalent to saying it has been confined to the consumer sector.

Soviet economists have generally denied the monetary nature of bank deposits. Most of them consider such balances to be merely a settlement fund, a liability of the Gosbank, or a potential claim of the depositor to currency.[9] The relationship between credit and money creation is only dimly perceived, and the view is widely held that resources of the Gosbank determine its ability to expand credit. The "real bills" doctrine continues to be extolled, and great pains are taken to explain any departures as consistent with it. In Soviet monetary literature the relationship between the balance of international payments and domestic monetary equilibrium and money supply is generally ignored. Only recently a leading authority had to plead for recognition of the fact that the sale of foreign exchange proceeds by exporters, or their purchase by importers, may lead to a change in the volume of money in circulation.

The heavy burden of orthodoxy is evident in the Gosbank's lending activities. Since the end of the Stalin era there has been some tendency toward greater flexibility, but the bank's credit practices have been conservative and unimaginative when compared with those of most other communist countries. Until the announcement of more significant changes in the fall of 1965, progress was mainly in reducing the excessive compartmentalization of lending and in simplifying accounting procedures. Little was accomplished, even tentatively, toward using credit as a constructive tool for influencing the processes of production and distribution, rather than merely as an implementation of higher level decisions. It is difficult to say to what extent this lag vis-à-vis the other countries reflects a hesitancy resulting from the cumulative experience of disastrous effects from sudden and frequent changes in economic policy and organization, and how far it reflects a reluctance to give up monetary and credit theories that the Soviet Union itself has generated and elevated to the status of inviolability.

The present loan administration is a patchwork of procedures introduced to supplement the original system of gearing credit to financing the movement of real assets through the economic system. The proliferation of separate "objects of crediting," originally accompanied by the opening of a separate loan account, began almost with the establishment of the Gosbank: "production credit for specific purposes" made its appearance in the bank's balance sheet in 1922. Subsequently, whenever a new pressing need was identified, a new object of crediting was added. As a result, many items of small quantitative significance emerged in Gosbank statistics, including such entries as "loans for the construction of movie theatres." The trend toward compartmentalization of loans was not reversed

---

[9] An attempt by Professor Kronrod to have bank balances at least recognized as "money of the banking circuit" (the term "deposit money" apparently being avoided because of its capitalistic ancestry) met with widespread opposition.

until the midfifties. Since then the loan and current accounts of some enterprises have been merged, and various other simplifications that have increased the flexibility of credit administration have been adopted. Credit on the basis of "norms" established for specific categories of inventories, with a specific ceiling for each, has now been replaced by loans for broad inventory categories, in most cases without specific upper limits. The more recent tendency toward crediting on the basis of total sales turnover makes funds available to pay for deliveries, as attested by shipping documents, with credit no longer being dependent on inspection reports based on actual visual checking of the level of inventories. In fact, this new method of crediting makes bank loans available for the financing of all production costs, including wages. At the beginning of 1965, however, still less than 11 percent of total short-term credit outstanding in industry was on a turnover basis.

At the end of 1964, the latest year for which data are available, the total volume of short-term credit outstanding amounted to 63 billion rubles, compared with 17 billion rubles in 1950 (see Table 1). Loans directly secured by physical collateral accounted for three-fourths of the 1964 total, and with the addition of credit documents in process of collection (covering goods shipped) the figure rises to over nine-tenths,

TABLE 1

Short-Term Credit Outstanding in the USSR, 1950 and 1964

	Year-end 1950	Year-end 1964
Total Outstanding (in billions of rubles)	17.3	63.2
By type of loan (in percent of total):		
Secured by real assets	62.5	74.7
Raw materials and fuel	16.7	18.9
Goods in process	2.7	1.8
Finished goods	4.2	4.5
Construction equipment	0.9	1.8
Trade inventories	36.7	45.6
Wholesale trade	6.5	7.6
Procurement of farm products	2.4	6.9
Retail trade	25.7	28.8
Other inventories	2.1	2.3
Other real assets	1.3	2.1
Secured by items in process of collection	28.8	18.8
Other types of loans	8.7	6.5
By economic sector (in percent of total):		
Industry	40.3	33.4
Agriculture (including collective farms)	3.3	6.7
Transportation and communications	1.3	0.8
Construction	3.5	4.8
Wholesale trade	14.9	12.0
Procurement of farm products	4.4	8.2
Retail trade	31.7	33.2
Other sectors	0.7	0.8

leaving less than 7 percent for all other types of credit. These percentages are very close to those for the immediately preceding years, and not much different from the corresponding proportions at the end of 1950. The head of the credit department of the Gosbank does not expect this percentage to change materially even after the introduction of the new credit policies described below.

Industry and retail trade each accounted for one-third of the total volume of short-term credit outstanding at the end of 1964, and most of the remaining third was divided between wholesale trade and agriculture. More than 45 percent of the short-term credit to industry, after subtracting the loans to finance collection float, was for carrying inventories of agricultural origin. Both cooperative and state farms are heavily dependent on credit, which currently meets about two-thirds of all their produc-

TABLE 2

Long-Term Credit in the USSR, 1964
(in millions of rubles)

Type of Loan	Outstanding at Year-end	Loans Granted during Year
Loans to collective farms...............................	4,404	1,251
For construction of farm buildings......................		412
For equipment..		485
For electrification....................................		85
For other purposes....................................		269
Loans to the population................................	718	
Urban..	289	
Rural..	429	
Loans to state and cooperative enterprises and organizations...	892	
Total..	6,014	

tion expenses apart from labor costs. Advance payments by state purchasing agencies account for a large part of the production credit extended to cooperatives, including (to the extent that the farms have shifted to the payment of money wages) the credit needed to finance the cost of labor. A gradual shift toward direct Gosbank lending to the cooperatives—for labor as well as other costs—is now under way, as will be seen in the subsequent section.

Long-term credit has so far been available mainly to agriculture, where it is the main means of financing capital formation in collective farms, and for home construction. At the end of 1964 (see Table 2) the outstanding amount of such credit extended by the Gosbank and the Investment Bank, combined, was less than one-tenth of the outstanding short-term loans, a proportion that has prevailed during most of the years since 1950. Certainly, the amount of credit extended to stimulate capital investment in agriculture is pitifully small in relation to needs. By the beginning of 1965,

2,700 new construction and building-material-producing enterprises had been created for the specific purpose of promoting the construction of farm buildings (particularly barns), but the aggregate amount of credit made available to them in the preceding year amounted to only 38.4 million rubles. However, the total volume of long-term loans increased sharply in 1965, including credit to agriculture.

Changes under Way

Since the early 1960's, Soviet credit administration has been gradually modified in some respects, and toward the end of 1965 a number of further changes were announced as a result of the Communist Party deliberations held in September and October. The proposed reforms represent, in effect, an adaptation of loan procedures to the new economic policy, which gives greater latitude to managers and aims at substituting economic incentives for administrative command. The reforms have been influenced by changes first introduced in Hungary in 1961, and to a certain degree in Poland, in connection with the reorientation of economic policies that followed the insurrectionary events of 1956. The new Soviet measures range over the Gosbank's entire field of activity and represent new departures as well as measures to simplify and improve existing procedures, notably those pertaining to the payments mechanism and credit sanctions. Of particular importance for the future activities of the banking system is a move away from budget financing, at least as regards investment projects with a relatively short recoupment period.

Various measures have been taken to alleviate the credit burden on agriculture which, it is admitted, has resulted to a considerable degree from policies now considered faulty. About 1.5 billion rubles of collective farms' long-term debt, and over half a billion of their short-term debt, have been written off; and other obligations too have been canceled or postponed. Farm production credit will become available directly from the Gosbank instead of through advances of state purchasing agencies. This shift to direct lending by the Gosbank entails large-scale experimentation with alternative methods of crediting, involving about 3,000 collective farms that differ in size, profitability, and location.

Moreover, in an attempt to encourage individual initiative where state and collective farms have conspicuously failed, credit is now being made available to increase ownership of cattle. For a loan to buy a cow (the maximum loan amount is 300 rubles for one cow per family, or 150 rubles for a calf) a request must be addressed to the state or collective farm, or in rural or suburban areas where cattle can be raised as a sideline by urban workers, to the enterprise or government unit where the individual is employed. The employer (administrative official of the farm or general manager of the enterprise) decides whether the loan should be granted, and then submits the application to the appropriate bank office. The employer guarantees the loan, acts as collection agent for the bank by withholding the amounts needed for monthly amortization and for interest payment (2 percent annually), makes sure that the proceeds are actually spent for the stated purpose, and collects the balance due if the animal is sold or slaughtered. These procedures are typical of the bureaucratic handicaps involved in the extension of credit to individuals and the terms—including the amortization over a period of seven years, after one year of grace to repay a $330 loan—reflect the low level of incomes.

In an effort to enourage the manufacture of new products and improved models, loans will become available to acquire raw materials and carry goods in process above the levels stipulated in the original plans. Experiments are under way for extending credit on a global basis, rather than for designated purposes and with specific collateral, and for letting the individual enterprise use these funds at its discretion, without detailed planning and control by the Gosbank. In an endeavor to prevent working capital from being impaired because of buyers' failure to meet obligations on time, loans of up to thirty days are to be made available to pay suppliers; such loans are to be repaid in the same order of preference as those secured by real assets.

Other changes in credit practices, such as introduction of lending on the basis of total turnover, are designed to reduce the required "documentation" (detailed verifications and other paperwork) and to provide greater flexibility in the use of borrowed funds in accordance with changing needs.

In connection with the greater latitude permitted to plant managers, there will be a reduction in the role of the authorities interposed between the individual enterprise and the relevant ministry. Thus enterprises will themselves determine their working-capital requirements, and these requirements, once approved by the higher echelon authorities, cannot be changed during the year, unless the production plan is modified. As a result, the higher level authority will no longer be able to take away or transfer to some other enterprise working capital that it judges to be excessive. For enterprises whose working capital has been impaired because of losses or less-than-projected profits, the shortfall will no longer be made good through budgetary appropriations but will have to be rebuilt from future profits.

The partial shift to loan financing of fixed capital formation has been under discussion at least since 1957, with the old guard arguing that it would weaken planning.[10] The present plans call for gradual moves. Enterprise managers will have more independence in determining plans and financing plant expansion, modernization, and repair. The individual enterprises will accumulate resources for such expenditures in "funds for

---

[10] See, for instance, K. Plotnikov, "Certain Problems of the Development of Finance and Credit in the Process of Building Communism," *Problems of Economics,* Vol. 7, No. 10 (February, 1965), pp. 31–40.

the development of production"—constituted from retained earnings, part of depreciation allowances, and the sale of redundant equipment and miscellaneous sources—to be used primarily for the improvement of technology. In some cases, industrywide investment funds will be formed from part of these resources. Whatever additional investment funds the enterprise may require will be supplied on a repayable credit basis by the Investment Bank, which has recently been doing this on a limited experimental basis, provided the loan can be amortized within six years from the time the new facility begins to operate. Even entirely new factories will receive Investment Bank financing if the loan can be retired within a relatively small number of years from the projected cash flow of the new plant. Only projects for which the internal flow of funds will not permit full loan retirement within six years will continue to be financed through budget grants, and each such allocation will require the approval of the Council of Ministers. For some time, however, budgetary financing will continue to be important; over the next several years, self-financed investment in industry is not expected to exceed 20 percent of the total, and apparently considerable differences of opinion exist with regard to the proportion of total investment which should or, in effect, will be financed through loans.

In combination with the partial shift from budget to loan financing, there will be a charge—for the benefit of the budget—on the fixed and working capital of enterprises, in order to equalize the cost of using new and existing investment. The role of the Gosbank in financing fixed investment will not be increased significantly, but there will be a liberalization of the conditions on which it makes loans for new and improved technology and for enlarging the production of mass consumption goods. One half of the turnover tax levied on consumer goods, instead of being channeled into the budget, will be used as a source of funds for loan repayment.

One of the ideological hurdles that Soviet officials have great difficulty in overcoming is the role of interest in allocating resources. As one of the vice chairmen of the Gosbank wrote recently, "Up to now, interest rates and their differentiation did not result in any serious influence on the economic and financial activity of enterprises." Practically uniform interest rates on short-term credit still prevail, with higher rates automatically charged as a penalty for overdue loans.

Interest has not played a significant role since the credit reforms of 1930–32. Until then, rates were as high as 8 percent, and were differentiated according to purpose and maturity (though not the financial condition of the borrower). Under the system that has been in existence for the last thirty-five years, virtually uniform rates are applied to all short-term loans, irrespective of borrower or purpose, with interest serving mainly the purpose of raising enough revenue to cover the expenses of the Gosbank. Loans to facilitate settlements carry a nominal rate of 1 percent, and on all other short-term loans the annual charge is 2 percent. For overdue loans there is a penalty rate of 3 percent to collective farms, 5 percent to all other economic enterprises. The several distinct purposes for which long-term loans can be obtained carry annual interest charges ranging from ¾ of 1 percent to 2 percent. It is not yet clear how much interest rates will be differentiated in the future, this being one of the major issues still unresolved, but the principle has been established that bank funds should be more expensive than the charge on "own" working capital, and that borrowing made necessary by management shortcomings (excessive inventories, for example, or impaired working capital) should carry higher rates than loans to finance normal needs. It appears that penalty rates for overdue loans and for late payments will be increased and their collection more vigorously enforced. The levels at which rates on loans for investment purposes and equivalent charges on existing capital are to be set are still under discussion.

The changes announced in the fall of 1965 not only will require considerable modification in the old systems and procedures of financial planning, settlements, accounting, and control,[11] but will also entail substantial internal reorganization, increase in the scope of the activities of lower echelon offices (hitherto confined largely to putting into effect instructions received from above), and more importantly a change in the thinking and attitude of the Gosbank operating staffs. Up to now, according to the official publication of the Gosbank, many of the bank's territorial offices "have proceeded by bureaucratic rote and have regarded paperwork and the issuance of innumerable instructions, orders, and regulations as their basic method of exercising leadership." The head of the Gosbank, in discussing the implications of the new policies, is quoted as commenting that the bank must now "free itself from imposing tutelage down to minute details on economic units and from administrative forms and methods of dealing with the economy, and give as much scope as possible to the action of economic and material stimulants."

The specific measures to implement the new policies are now being worked out in detail. A first step has already been made to provide credit on the new basis to the first group of enterprises which have been experimentally shifted to the new system of management at the beginning of 1966. If and when the new policies are fully put into effect, the resulting changes will add up to the most significant development in the Soviet credit system since the reforms of 1930–32. The success of these changes will depend, in the last analysis, on the further development of the recently initiated changes in economic policy.

----

[11] For instance, control over expenditures for wages and salaries is to be exercised on a quarterly basis instead of on the basis of five- or ten-day periods, as in the past.

9 | MANAGERIAL INCENTIVES AND DECISIONMAKING: A COMPARISON OF THE UNITED STATES AND THE SOVIET UNION

Joseph S. Berliner

Within the scope and limits of the plan for the enterprise, the Soviet manager has a substantial area of authority and responsibility. His assignment from the state is to achieve or surpass the plan targets for the enterprise, using the resources allocated to him by the plan. The rewards for successful performance are large. However, because the plan targets are very ambitious the Soviet manager finds himself much more concerned with acquisition of inputs and production levels than his American counterpart. American managers, on the other hand, are judged by profits and are more concerned with marketing and the long-run investment strategy of the firm.

The following article examines the recruitment, position, motivation, and behavior of the Soviet enterprise manager. It compares him with his American counterpart, showing both striking differences and similarities in their behavior.

Joseph S. Berliner is Professor of Economics at Brandeis University. This article is reprinted from United States Congress, Joint Economic Committee, *Comparisons of the United States and Soviet Economies* (Washington, D.C.: U.S. Government Printing Office, 1959), Part I, pp. 349–76.

THE REWARDS in income and prestige in the United States and Soviet economies are such that a larger proportion of the best young people in the USSR turn to careers in heavy industry, science, and higher education, whereas in the United States a larger proportion of the best talent flows into such fields as heavy or light (consumer goods) industry, finance, commerce and trade, law, medicine, etc. Higher education, particularly technical, is more of a prerequisite for the attainment of a top business career in the Soviet Union than in the United States.

The principal managerial incentive in Soviet industry is the bonus paid for overfulfillment of plan targets. The incentive system is successful in the sense that it elicits a high level of managerial effort and performance. But it has the unintended consequence of causing managers to engage in a wide variety of practices that are contrary to the interests of the state. Managers systematically conceal their true production capacity from the planners, produce unplanned types of products, and falsify the volume and quality of production. In the procurement of materials and supplies they tend to order larger quantities than they need, hoard scarce materials, and employ unauthorized special agents who use influence and gifts to ease management's procurement problems. The incentive system causes managers to shy away from innovations that upset the smooth working of the firm.

Since American managers operate in a different economic environment, their problems and therefore their practices differ from those of Soviet managers. But in those aspects of economic life in which the U.S. economy approximates the operating conditions of the Soviet economy, American managers develop forms of behavior similar to those of Soviet managers. The separation of management and ownership characteristic of the modern corporation leads to conflicts of interest between managers and stockholder-owners, and management's pursuit of its own interest leads to activities similar to those of the Soviet manager striving to defend his interests against those of the owner-state. The spread of legislation constricting the freedom of operation of the American firm leads to the evasion of laws and regulations characteristic of the Soviet economy, though on a larger scale there. Finally, under wartime conditions the burgeoning of government controls and the dominant role of the government as customer alters the operating conditions of the U.S. economy in such ways that it closely approximates some of the normal operating conditions of the Soviet economy. The change is accompanied by black-market operations, hoarding, quality deterioration, and the use of influence, practices which are normal in the peacetime Soviet economy.

MANAGERIAL INCENTIVES AND RECRUITMENT

The most important decision a manager has to make is made before he ever becomes a manager; namely, the decision to prepare for a managerial career. The factors influencing this decision are of vital importance for our industrial society. Imagine the consequences if no one aspired to become a manager, or if young people chose management only as a last resort, or if other careers were so attractive that management got only the last pickings of each year's crop of youngsters. It might therefore be appropriate to begin with some reflections on the incentives that the United States and the USSR offer their young people to choose a managerial career rather than some other.

The factors motivating young people to choose one or another occupation are probably not vastly different in the two countries. Family tradition is often decisive; many a youngster chooses a career simply because he wishes to be like his father (or mother). Special talents such as those of the artist, or early conceived deep interests, like the boy who must be a scientist, account for the career choices of some others. But most teenagers have no clear idea of what they would like to be. It is with respect to these youths that it is most interesting to speculate upon the incentive-pulls that the two systems offer for the choice of one career or another.

Education and Career Choice

The role of higher education in career choice is different in the two nations. Higher education is very much more of a prerequisite for the prestigeful and high income occupations in the USSR than in the United States. To be sure, the person with a high school education or less has an increasingly difficult time entering the managerial ladder of the large American corporation. But in such fields as trade, commerce, construction and in small business in general, the opportunities are still vast for a financially successful career. College, and education in general, is not of decisive importance. And the brute fact is that a college diploma can always be obtained somewhere in the United States, with very little effort or ability, by just about anyone who can pay the tuition and write a semiliterate paragraph. Those who don't aspire to a managerial position or who fail to make the grade can, as workingmen, nevertheless enjoy a standard of living that is the envy of the world. The point is that the young American who is not inclined toward academic work need not feel that he is out of the competition for our society's best rewards.

This is not true in the USSR. A number of conversations with young Soviet people have convinced me that to be a "worker" is something devoutly to be shunned by most young people who have reached the high school level. There are at least two reasons for this attitude, which seems so anomalous in a "worker's state." The first is the enormously high prestige that Russian (and European) culture has always placed upon the "intelligent," the learned man, the man who works with his mind instead of his hands. The Soviet regime has striven hard to make manual labor respectable, and it undoubtedly has succeeded in endowing the worker with a social position relatively much higher than before the revolution. But the young person who has reached the educational level at which he can choose between being a worker or an "intelligent" would, other things being equal, choose the latter without question.

Other things are not equal, however. In particular, the income possibilities of a worker are far smaller than those of a college graduate, and this is the second reason for the desperate, and sometimes pathetic, drive for a higher education. Of course, a person must have reached the high school level before he can even begin to think about choosing between the career of a worker or an "intelligent." The steady annual expansion in the high school population has had the effect of presenting ever-increasing numbers of young people with the choice, and few of them would freely choose to be workers. If the expansion of the school population had continued, giving more and more young people the opportunity to avoid being workers, it would have raised serious problems for the recruitment of the labor force. The radical reform of the educational system by Khrushchev was undoubtedly motivated, in part, by the wish to avoid that problem.

Thus, the undesirability of a career as a worker has intensified the desire for higher education. Add to this the fact that there is no private enterprise, no small business in which a man could pull himself out of a worker's status and reach a position of prestige and income comparable to the self-made American businessman. I do not wish to state that the door is completely closed. By dint of hard work, ability, and certain other qualities, a Soviet citizen without the college diploma can from time to time rise to an important position in some economic hierarchy. But his chances are about as good as those of an equivalent person in a progressive American corporation. And the young person evaluating the importance of higher education understands this.

Finally, the Russian teenager who decides he has to get a college diploma has very few easy ways out. He can't buy his way into college, as the American student can if he has the money. There are no private colleges that can set whatever standards they wish. To be sure there are instances of bribery or influence, but they are certainly the exception. If the Soviet student wants a college diploma very badly, he has to work hard to gain admission and to be graduated. The very intensity of the drive for education, and the competition of many applicants for the limited number of admissions, permits the high schools and colleges to maintain high standards of performance. Moreover the colleges are financially independent of student tuitions: not only are there no tuitions but most of the students earn stipends. The consequence is that the typical Soviet student works harder and has to meet higher standards of performance than the typical American student. The standards are different in the two countries, of course, because of differences in the philosophy of education. But there is no doubt that study is a much more serious business for the young Soviet student than for the American.

One final note on education and incentives. The quality of the managerial (and technical) manpower of a nation depends on the proportion of the population comprising the pool from which the managers are drawn. That is, if half the population were for some reason excluded from the pool, the quality of the managers would be lower than if the whole population comprised the pool. Both nations suffer in this respect from the fact that rural educational facilities are poorer than urban, which reduces the pool of the potential college group. Since the Soviet rural population is larger percentagewise than that of the United States, and since their rural educational facilities are probably relatively worse than ours, they suffer more than we from this loss. But there are other ways in which our pool is curtailed more than the Soviet. First is the fact that the private cost of education keeps a substantial portion of our talented young people in the lower income groups out of college. I admit that this fact puzzles me. With our network of free state universities and with a fairly abundant scholarship program, I don't fully understand why any competent student who really desired it could not get a college education. It is my impression, however, that systematic studies generally show that we are losing an unfortunate number of young people to higher education for financial reasons. If this is so, we are worse off than the Soviets in this respect, for their education is absolutely free, and most students of any merit earn stipends besides. Lower income young Soviet people may nevertheless be unable to go off to college if the family needs their earnings. A young Soviet woman told me, in reply to my question, that this was why she never went on to college. She is not a very good illustration of my point, however, for she went on to say that she really wasn't very smart anyhow.

The second group that is largely lost from America's pool of potential managerial manpower is the Negro and some other racial minorities. It may well be that the proportion of college graduates among some of the Soviet national minorities is smaller than for the Slavic nationalities; I have seen no data on this. But I would doubt that their loss from racial discrimination is as large as ours.

The third and largest group lost from our pool comprises exactly half our population—the female half. Sex discrimination certainly exists in the Soviet economy, probably more in management than in science and technology. But undoubtedly the female population enlarges the pool of technical and managerial manpower much more in the USSR than in the United States. The difference in the role of women in the two countries must, I think, enter into the balance I am trying to strike, but it is not a subject on which I would recommend that your committee consider writing corrective legislation. For one thing it is not perfectly clear which way sex discrimination works in the United States. Women discriminate against working about as much as jobs discriminate against women.

Let me summarize briefly this discussion of the relationship of education to career choice. Education, and particularly higher education, is more important in the USSR than in the United States as the gateway to a prestigeful and highly remunerative career. Competition is keener for higher education, the cost of education to the individual is less, and the standards of admission and performance are higher in the USSR. Both nations lose part of the potential pool of managerial talent, the USSR because of its large rural population, the United States because of financial burdens and racial and sex discrimination.

Competition among Careers

How does a managerial career compare with the attractiveness of other careers in the two nations? The young American not dedicated to some particular field, but motivated by a roughly equal desire for prestige and money, might select some field such as law, medicine, business, or engineering. He would decidedly not go into education or science. An equivalent young Soviet person would make a somewhat different choice. He would certainly not select law, which has been assigned a most humble role in Soviet society. Nor would he select medicine, for while the prestige is high, the income is low. On the other hand, higher education or science would be an excellent choice. The very title of "Professor" or "Scientific Worker" would assure him one of the highest places of honor in the society. And an outstanding career in either of those fields would assure him an income ranking in the upper 10 percent or perhaps even 5 percent (data are hard to come by) of the population. The difference in the economic and social position of the scientist and teacher in the two countries is of fundamental importance in the matter of career recruitment.

The American who decides to choose a career in the business world has a much wider range of choice than his Soviet counterpart. A great variety of fields offer roughly equivalent rewards in prestige and incomes: advertising, accounting, finance, commerce, trade, sales, light manufacturing, heavy industry. Of all these fields, it is only the latter that would exert a great pull on the young Soviet person. For 40 years the government and party have hammered home the central role of heavy industry, children are instilled with an admiration of technology, and heavy industry has been endowed with an aura of glamour that exceeds even our American fascination with technology. The ideological cards are stacked, in varying degree, against all other branches of the economy. In keeping with the ideology, the prestige and income possibilities in heavy industry are decidedly greater than in the other branches.

Not only will the student be attracted to heavy industry, but he is likely to choose engineering as his path of entry into whatever branch of heavy industry he selects. He would be attracted to engineering for the educational reasons discussed above. Engineering is, moreover, the most direct line of approach to a managerial career.

The Soviet engineering graduate will find his first job opportunities rather different from those of his American counterpart. If he is at the top of his class, the best offers will come from the research institutes, with top starting salaries and opportunities for graduate work. The poorer students will find lower paying jobs in industry. In the United States the situation is quite the reverse. The most successful students will be snapped up by recruiters from the large corporations, with the best starting salary offers.

Some of the top students will, to be sure, spurn the attractive job offers and go on to further graduate work, but I suspect that many of those who go immediately into graduate work are the men who didn't get the good job offers. To be sure, many of the top American students who join the corporations are put immediately into research and development, but as many of them will be working on new passenger car or dishwasher design as will be working on electronic development and automation technique. The Soviet researcher is more likely to be working on the latter than the former.

The young Soviet engineer who goes into industry starts at the bottom of the managerial ladder, as chief of a production shop, or the design or maintenance departments of the enterprise. As new job opportunities develop, he faces the choice of continuing in direct production or taking one of the staff jobs in the enterprise, such as the planning department. If he stays in production proper, his career path may lead to chief engineer of an enterprise or to one of the higher economic agencies. If he moves into staff work, his career may lead to the directorship of an enterprise or of one of the higher organs. Either career leads to the pinnacle of Soviet management.

The paths that are least likely to lead to top management are finance or sales. I would guess the proportion of top management in the United States who started in such fields as finance and sales is much larger than in the USSR. There are no "colleges of business administration" in the Soviet Union. The ambitious youngster who wants to work for the top of the Soviet business world studies engineering, not personnel and marketing.

Summarizing, industry in the United States has to compete with a wide variety of other branches of economic activity for its share of the best potential managerial talent. In the USSR the values and the rewards are concentrated in relatively fewer fields, and industry is far more attractive than most others. Science and higher education, which scarcely compete with industry in the United States, are strong competitors of industry in the USSR. Among the various branches of industry, in the United States the light and consumer goods industries compete very effectively for both managerial and engineering talent. In the USSR light and consumer goods industries are much less attractive than heavy industry. And finally the nature of industrial recruitment is such that technical education is much more important as part of the training of a would-be manager in the USSR than in the United States.

My conclusion is that heavy industry, science, and higher education attract, by and large, a better and more competent crop of young people in the USSR than in the United States. Moreover, the competition for education is keener in the USSR, so that they get a more rigorously trained (trained in different ways, to be sure) corps of managerial, engineering, scientific, and university personnel. On the other hand, such branches of the economy as sales, advertising, finance, trade and commerce, light industry, and law attract a much more competent group of people in the United States than in the USSR. Most of the outstanding people in these fields in the United States would, if they were Soviet citizens, have enjoyed successful careers in heavy industry, science, technology, or higher education. There is, after all, nothing startling in this conclusion. It is but another way of saying that each society gets what it pays for.

MANAGERIAL INCENTIVES AND DECISIONMAKING

Material Incentives

The incentives that attract people into management are not necessarily the same incentives that motivate managers to do their jobs and do them well. What are the goals of the manager? What are the considerations that impel him to make one decision rather than the other?

The moving force of our economic system is the pursuit of private gain. The worker chooses the higher paying job, the businessman accepts the more profitable contract, the investor buys the higher interest security. The usual exceptions must of course be made; the laws must be obeyed, public opinion may sometimes require that one decision must be made rather than another, people make wrong decisions, a short-run loss may be accepted for a longer term gain. But by and large—"other things being equal," as the economist likes to say—it is private gain that determines economic decision.

The Soviets have at various times experimented with other forms of incentive, for it did not at first seem quite appropriate that a socialist economy should stress private gain. But practicality won out over dogma, and private gain has for the last 25 years been the keystone of the managerial incentive system. To be sure, we still find references to various social incentives such as communist enthusiasm. But we are also reminded that while enthusiasm is well and good, communism, as Lenin used to say, must be built "not directly on enthusiasm but with the aid of enthusiasm born out of the great revolution; [communism must be built] on private interest, on personal incentive, on businesslike accounting." Moreover, the incentive of private gain will be with us for a long time. According to the eminent labor economist E. Manevich, it will not disappear until the day of general overabundance arrives, until the differences between country and city are eliminated, and until the differences between mental and manual labor vanish. We are safe in saying that for the next several decades at least, private gain will be the central economic inventive in both economic systems.

The form that material incentives take is of some importance. For the American businessman it is clearly profit. If you ask why did he take on this contract rather than that, why did he order this machine rather than that, why did he ship by truck rather than train, the answer would normally be, "because it's cheaper that way," or what comes to the same thing, "because he would make more money that way."

For the private businessman managing his own business, profit is clearly the guide to his actions. But most American business is not managed in this way. The men who actually run the firm are salaried managers, hired by the stockholders' representative body, the board of directors. The profit of the business does not belong to the manager but to the stockholder-owners. The fact is that the private interest of the manager need not necessarily coincide with that of the stockholder. In order to bring the manager's private interest into closer coincidence with that of the owners, most corporations have instituted some kind of bonus system, on the assumption that if the manager has a direct stake in the profit of the enterprise, his decisions are more likely to be those that will earn more profit.

In fashioning an incentive system for its managers, the Soviet government faced a problem similar to that of the American corporation. For all Soviet enterprises are run by salaried managers. If the Soviet manager's income consisted solely of his salary, it was conceivable that his private interest would not coincide at all points with the interest of the government. Accordingly a considerable variety of supplementary bonuses are available to the managerial staff. The bonuses are designed to motivate managers to make those decisions that the government considers to be in its own interest.

. . . .

But incentive for what? This is surely the crucial question. For we can readily imagine an incentive which was extremely successful in motivating action, but action of an undesirable kind. The test of an incentive is therefore not only its motivating power, but the extent to which it leads to the desired kind of decision.

Before proceeding to the relationship of incentives to decisionmaking, let me clarify the sense in which I use the term incentive. By incentive I mean that consideration which explains why one decision was made rather than another. If a young person decides to find employment in the electrical machinery industry rather than in the furniture industry, the difference in basic salaries in the two industries may well have been the decisive consideration. In this case salary is the effective incentive. But once in the job, the salary does not vary according to whether one operating decision is made rather than another. When the manager decides to put one order into production ahead of another, or to substitute one material for another, it is not his salary he is thinking about. It is usually the size of the month's bonus that will depend on the decision taken. It is in this sense that the bonus is the principal incentive in the operational decisions of the Soviet enterprise.

Production Decisions

Two generations ago people debated the question of whether a socialist economy could possibly work. History removed that question from the agenda. The last generation changed the question to whether the Soviet economy could work at all efficiently. That question has also been answered. These hearings would not otherwise be taking place. My discussion takes for granted that the Soviet economy is reasonably efficient and that the question at issue is how efficient.

There is little doubt that the system of managerial incentives, broadly viewed, has created a corps of managers dedicated to their work and responsive to the production demands made upon them. Like their American counterparts, they are deeply involved in their work, they worry about production quotas, they demand results from their labor force. As hired managers, they are aware that if their performance is not satisfactory, there are always other persons spoiling for a chance at their jobs. I have no way of knowing whether the intensity of managerial life is greater in the USSR than in the United States; in both countries there are variations from industry to industry. But there are two reasons why industrial life probably proceeds at a faster tempo in the USSR than here. The first is that the absence of free trade unions makes it difficult for workers to resist pressure for intense operation. The second is that industry is under constant exhortation from government and party for ever-increasing levels of production.

But the question as indicated above is not whether management is motivated to work hard. It is rather whether the incentive system motivates them to do what the state wishes them to do; whether, in other words, they get as much mileage out of their effort as they might get.

One of the most interesting conclusions of the study of Soviet managerial incentives is that the bonus system is directly responsible for motivating management to make a variety of decisions contrary to the intent and the interests of the state. The decisions to be described go far back in the history of the Soviet economy and have resisted countless efforts by the government to eliminate them. Most of them have survived the great organizational changes in industrial organization of the past several years. They are clearly deeply rooted in the soil of Soviet economic organization.

First, consider the matter of the reporting of information. In a planned economy it is vital that the central planners have as accurate information as possible about the productive capacity of enterprises. The bonus system, however, acts as a prevailing motivation for managers to understate their real production capacity. The reason is that the most important of the bonuses available to managers depends on the extent to which the production target of the enterprise is overfulfilled. If the manager honestly reports his full production capacity, and if for some reason something goes wrong in the course of the month, then he and his staff will lose that month's bonus. It is safer therefore to report a smaller capacity than really exists, in order that the production target will be kept low enough to allow for emergencies. The Russians call this "insurance" or "security." The consequence is that the planners can never be sure that their plans are based on accurate figures. The government is aware of the problem: "This is fully understandable," writes a Soviet economist, "because the lower the plan, the greater the opportunity to fulfill and overfulfill it. . . ."

Because the higher state agencies cannot trust management's reporting of its productive capacity, various techniques have been fashioned for setting targets high enough to force the firms to operate as close as possible to capacity. One of these techniques is the arbitrary increase of targets over last year's production. As a prominent state planning commission economist put it, "they take as the base magnitude the level of production achieved during the preceding period and raise it by some percentage or other." Sometimes this technique helps flush out the manager's "hidden reserves," but in other cases the arbitrary increase in targets leads to impossibly high tasks. Indeed, the spirit of planning is reflected in the systematic use of high targets as a device for keeping managers working at as fast a tempo as possible. In the past targets have been set so high (deliberately, one suspects) that one third of all enterprises failed to fulfill their annual plans. . . . The intense pace of plant operation has its distinct advantage from the state's point of view: it elicits from management a high level of effort that might not be forthcoming if the plans were set at a more modest level. But the price paid by the state is the manager's effort to defend his enterprise by concealing his full capacity.

When the target has been set, the manager's bonus depends on the success with which he fulfills it. Most of the firm's production does indeed follow the lines laid down in the plan. But when the end of the month rolls around and, as often happens, production is far short of meeting the month's target, then managers turn to a host of time-tested techniques of meeting—or seeming to meet—the targets. In certain types of production, such as metals, the target is expressed in tons; in such cases the manager might order his shops to curtail the production of relatively lightweight products (special and quality metals) and to throw more men and materials into the production of the heavier products. In textile production we read that the practice of setting targets in "running meters" (that is, in measures of length, without regard to width) causes managers to overproduce narrow-width cloth and underproduce broad width. In firms with a considerable variety of products, the production targets are expressed in value units—so many millions of rubles of production. In such cases managers tend to overproduce those products that have high fixed prices (all prices are fixed); they may deliberately use more expensive materials in order to drive up the value of production. These are some of an endless variety of ways in which managers "violate the planned assortment of production," to use the official expression of disapproval.

How widespread are these practices? We really don't know. From time to time individual managers are publicly excoriated for such practices, and figures are published to show how widely the planned assortment of production had been departed from. But these may well be extreme cases, and it would be unwise to generalize from them. Occasionally, however, the results of special studies are published, and they give us some idea of the magnitude of the problem. The state planning commission recently released the results of a survey of the production practices of 63 enterprises. Of the total production by these enterprises in excess of the plan targets, only 43 percent consisted of the basic products normally produced by them; 26.5 percent consisted of "products not included in the plan when it was originally confirmed," 20 percent consisted of "other production," and 7 percent consisted not of finished products but of an increase in semifabricated parts and goods-in-process. While these data are not precisely in the form in which we would want them, they do provide a good indication of managers' tendency to produce those products that are best from their own enterprises' point of view, rather than those products that the state would most wish to have produced.

Two other consequences of the bonus system (and the pressure of high targets) should be noted. One is the simple falsification of reported production. "Thus, for example," we read in a Soviet article, "if the plan is fulfilled 99 percent, the managerial and engineering personnel receive no bonus. But if the enterprise fulfills the plan 100 percent, they receive bonuses of from 15 to 37 percent of their salary." Quite a lot of money hinges on that last percentage of production, and it is no wonder that management may succumb to the temptation to "fudge" the report a bit in order to earn the bonus. Again, the techniques of covering up for falsely reported production are myriad. To cite only one, production is "borrowed" from next month. That is, production that is expected to occur next month is reported as having been produced this month. If things go well next month, the "borrowed" output is "repaid"; if not, the manager may get into trouble.

More serious than falsification, however, is the deterioration of the quality of production. The poor quality of much of Soviet consumer goods production is well known. In other types of production the danger of detection is greater, and quality standards are less readily violated. But the explanation of management's tendency to shave on quality is the same: the high production targets are so often not attainable, and the manager wants to keep his job. Much of the quality shaving is of a kind that is not easily detected: fewer stitches in the garment, fewer screws in the piece, greener lumber in the building, more impurities in the metal. But if the pressure is keen enough, more extreme forms of quality deterioration will be adopted.

Summarizing, the bonus system is an effective device for eliciting a high level of managerial effort, but in the context of excessively high production targets, it induces management to make certain types of decisions that are contrary to the intent of the state. The production of unplanned products, the concealment of production capacity, the falsification of reports, and the deterioration of quality are the unintended consequences of the system of managerial incentives.

Procurement Decisions

The high level of production targets is but half the problem facing the Soviet manager. The other half is the perpetual shortage of materials and supplies. In order to get the greatest possible production from the available stocks of materials and supplies, the state employs a variety of devices to minimize the use of materials in production and inventory. Undoubtedly these devices have served to control wasteful use of resources, and they have also helped channel the flow of resources in the direction most desired by the state. But they have been self-defeating to some extent for they have forced managers to make certain kinds of decisions which frustrate the intent of the state.

The core of the matter is that managers simply don't trust the planning system to provide them with the supplies and materials they need in the right quantity and quality, and at the right time. . . . For all important materials the manager must still obtain an allocation order from his home office, which must in turn get the allocation order from the republican or all-union planning commission.

Thus, we still read of the "existing complicated system of obtaining allocation orders, under which every enterprise must submit detailed requisitions to Moscow a long time before the new planning quarter is to begin." Because plans are not always finally set at the time the planning period is to begin, enterprises sometimes start with "advance allocations," that is, temporary allotments of resources designed to keep them operating until the final allocation orders are available. . . . Perhaps even more serious than the complex supply planning system is the large percentage of enterprises that regularly fail to fulfill their plans, or fulfill them by producing the wrong products or substandard products. Since the production of these enterprises constitutes the planned supplies of other enterprises, the supplies of the latter are delayed or simply not available. Perhaps enough has been said to explain why "managers of enterprises did not have confidence in the possibility of getting their materials on time and having them delivered to the factory by the supply depot's trucks."

What does the manager do to make sure he gets his supplies? Just as he "secures" his production plan by attempting to conceal the existence of some production capacity, so he "secures" the flow of supplies in various ways. He overorders, in the hope that if he doesn't get all he ordered, he may at least get as much as he needs. He also orders excessively large amounts of some supplies in order to be able to buy directly from the producer, instead of having to go through the maze of jobbing depots. A survey of 15 Moscow enterprises showed a 10.4 percent overordering of metals for just this reason. Sometimes management's boldest efforts to obtain supplies are unsuccessful: ". . . over 300,000 construction workers undergo work stoppages daily because of the absence of materials at the workplace." In other cases their padded requisitions are accepted and they receive more than they need of some materials. The consequence is the piling up of hoards of supplies of all kinds, one of the most enduring problems of Soviet industrial organization. The government has waged a long-standing war against hoarding. One of the weapons by which it attempts to hold hoarding within bounds is through the use of quotas of working capital; that is, for its annual production program the enterprise is allowed to keep on hand at any one time no more than so many tons of coal, so many board feet of lumber, so many rubles worth of inventory. These quotas must be negotiated between enterprise and government, and the enterprise's interest demands that they be set as high as possible. The mutual attempt at outguessing the other leads to a familiar bureaucratic game: ". . . enterprises try to 'justify' and obtain as large quotas of working capital as possible. The financial agencies, aware of this, strive on the other hand to reduce the quotas of working capital." This kind of planning is hardly calculated to lead to the establishment of the optimal quotas. It is more likely that some quotas will be too large and some too small.

The most interesting of the techniques used by managers to "secure" their supply of materials is the employment of special supply expediters called *tolkachi,* or "pushers." The table of organization does not provide for this occupation, yet so great is the need that firms manage somehow to employ these people. The chief job of the expediter is to make sure that his enterprise gets the materials it needs and when it needs them. Accordingly he spends most of his time on the road, visiting his enterprise's suppliers, handing out little gifts here and there to assure that his orders are well handled, picking up supplies of one kind or another that his firm may be able to use or trade for other goods. Much of their activity is associated with the black market, that is, obtaining materials for which no allocation order has been issued. This may be done either by wrangling an allocation order out of a reluctant government official by one means or another, or persuading an approachable enterprise official to sell him the things he needs without an allocation order.

Some *tolkachi* take up permanent residence in the city in which the chief suppliers are located, and only occasionally return to their home firms for consultations. To keep the record clean, they are carried on the books as "senior buyer," or "supply agent." If they are known to be particularly adept at their jobs, they may be asked by other firms to represent them. Nothing is known of their incomes, but there is no doubt that they earn many times their base pay. And they fully earn it, both because of the vital nature of their work, and because the risks they take make them vulnerable to prosecution.

How widespread is the use of these expediters? Again, we catch only occasional hints of their prevalence. The most recent outburst against them reports that the number of *tolkachi* who annually visit the typical large enterprise runs into the thousands, and their expenses into hundreds of thousands of rubles. These, however, are only the reported expenses. More often than not their expenses are not reported as such but are concealed under such rubrics as "exchange of technical information," or "contract negotiations." Our latest informant, who is a senior investigator for the State Control Commission of the USSR, is of the opinion that despite continued official criticisms of the use of expediters, their number has actually been increasing. One of the reasons he adduces is interesting. In 1956, along with a wave of measures designed to give more freedom to plant managers, an order was issued relieving managers of the need to report in detail on all minor expenditures. Travel expenditures were among the items exempted. The measure had the unintended effect of encouraging the increased use of expediters.

The economic effect of the use of expediters is difficult to assess. There is no doubt that they are of vital importance to individual enterprises, but from the national point of view much of their activity involves merely the transfer to one fortunate enterprise of resources that otherwise would have gone to another. Since the higher priority enterprises have less need for expediters, the chances are that the net effect of their activity is to cause more resources to flow to lower priority enterprises at the expense of higher priority ones. On the credit side, however, their wide knowledge of sources of supply, of who has what to sell, is of some importance, and they do arrange for the movement of supplies that otherwise would have lain idle in one plant while another had need for it. In short, the expediter possesses a certain kind of knowledge that may be as important to economic organization as the knowledge of the engineer or the machinist. The planning system is able to direct the bulk of the nation's resources with reasonable effectiveness, but substantial quantities of materials and equipment elude the main stream of planning. How to get these resources back into the system is a problem that has exercised Soviet economists for a long time.[1]

In summary, the incentives that motivate managers to strive for the

---

[1] Recently there have been numerous suggestions that enterprises and economic regions publish catalogs of the commodities they produce and the surplus materials and equipment they would like to sell. The expediters are rather like walking catalogs.

fulfillment of their production targets are the same incentives that motivate them to evade the regulations of the planning system. Because of the tightness of the supply system, which is deliberately engineered by the state, managers are compelled to defend their enterprises' position by overordering supplies, by hoarding materials and equipment, and by employing expediters whose function it is to keep the enterprise supplied with materials at all costs, legal or otherwise. The very planning system that serves to channel most of the nation's resources in directions desired by the state, serves also to misdirect a substantial volume of resources toward uses that are contrary to the wishes of the state.

Investment Decisions

If one were to ask what feature of the Soviet economic system accounts most of all for the rapid rate of growth, the answer would undoubtedly be the high rate of capital formation. The question at issue is whether it is as high as it might be, other things being equal. An examination of the system of managerial incentives will provide part, though by no means all, of the answer to this central question.

Management has a direct interest in obtaining new capital. It adds to productive capacity, and it is good for the record to show steady increases in production. Moreover fixed capital is provided to the enterprise as a free grant by the state, with no interest charge. The problem, therefore, has not been one of inducing management to accept more machines; it has rather been one of dissuading management from ordering too many machines. Far back in Soviet economic history one can find expressions of the problem similar to that recently uttered by Khrushchev in connection with the dissolution of the agricultural machine-tractor stations:

The machine-tractor stations accept any machine whether they need it or not. They don't grow flax, but they take flax-growing equipment. They don't grow cabbage, but they take cabbage-planting machines. Consequently many machines are not used for years and hundreds of millions of rubles worth of state resources are frozen.

The reason enterprises accept any piece of equipment they can get their hands on is similar to that discussed above in connection with materials hoarding. One can never tell when he may need just that kind of machine and not be able to obtain it. If one has a chance to get it now, order it by all means. It may come in handy some day for trading in return for something one might be able to use more readily. And above all, there is no charge for holding the equipment; there is no interest payment, and if the machine is not used there is no depreciation charge either. Hence there is everything to gain and nothing to lose by holding on to as much machinery and equipment as one can obtain.

How to induce managers to take a less cavalier view of capital has been a long-standing concern of economists. They look with some nostalgia at the effectiveness of the profit motive under capitalism in this respect. An eminent Soviet economist put it this way recently:

In order to increase his profit as much as possible, the capitalist strives to use his equipment to the fullest extent possible, and in no case will he buy a machine that he doesn't need at the moment, since every surplus machine slows down the turnover of his capital and reduces his profit. For the same reason he strives to keep his inventories down to the very minimum and to market his finished products as quickly as possible.

Recent economic literature contains a number of suggestions of ways in which Soviet managers might be induced to order only that amount of capital needed for production purposes. One of the more interesting is a proposal advanced by the author quoted above. He suggests that profit be calculated not as a ratio to total production cost (as has always been done), but as a ratio to value of invested capital. In this way the enterprise with too much idle capital will show a lower rate of profit, and profit is one of the principal indicators of overall performance. The suggestion is interesting because it proposes that return on capital be used as a criterion of performance, a rather "bourgeois" notion. It should not, however, be thought that the proposal envisages reliance on the "profit motive" as we know it. Profit is an important indicator of the efficiency of plant opera-tion, but the firm does not "own" its profit, although it shares in the profit in a minor way. As a personal incentive, profit is relatively unimportant in Soviet industry, certainly by comparison with the bonus.*

If the incentive system motivates managers to overorder and hoard equipment, the situation is quite the reverse with respect to technological innovation. Concern over managerial resistance to innovation is of long standing, but it has come to the fore in recent years in connection with increased emphasis on automation and modernization of plant and equip-ment. The reasons for managers' tendency to drag their feet in introduc-ing new products or production techniques are well understood by Soviet economists:

The explanation is, first of all, that the introduction of new technology in-volves certain risks and requires a considerable expenditure of time; secondly, after new technology has been introduced, more difficult plan targets are set and consequently there is less opportunity for fulfilling them and receiving bonuses.

When a manager has a well-running plant, when the workers have learned their jobs and have become experienced in using the existing equipment, he is reluctant to upset the cart by trying something new. A new production line means trouble. Production bugs have to be elimi-

---

* Editors' note: Reforms were adopted in 1965 under which interest is now charged on the enterprise's capital, profitability is calculated in relation to capital, and the enterprise retains a larger share of its profits. See Part IV of this book for some of the details of the reforms.

nated, workers have to be retrained, time is lost, and spoilage is high. The chances are that plans will be underfulfilled and the precious bonuses lost, particularly in view of the tendency for plan targets to be raised to the rated capacity of the new equipment. It is courting disaster to try new things. If the old machines are wearing out, it is safer to repair or even rebuild them rather than introduce the more complicated new models. Outlays on the rebuilding of old machines often exceed the price of a new modern machine.

There is another reason why managers shy away from innovation. Even if the potential gains from new technology are great, it usually takes a number of years before they are realized. But it is Soviet policy to shift managers around from plant to plant every few years. Therefore managers have a strictly short-run point of view. Why take on all the headaches of introducing a new line when one is not likely to be around to enjoy whatever benefits may eventually accrue? Capital investment policy is by its very nature a matter of long-term planning, and therefore does not commend itself to the short-run horizon of management.

How does the state combat managerial resistance to innovation? One technique is direct pressure. Pressure exerted on and by their own superiors explains much of the innovation that does occur. Enterprise managers may drag their feet for a long time, but when the direct order comes down that the new automatic line must be installed in the next six months, it is eventually acted upon. Pressure is also exerted through the Communist Party; if the Party officials in the enterprise are under direct orders from Moscow that automation must be accelerated, they are in a position to force the manager to move faster than he otherwise might. Such pressures are important, although it must be noted in passing that both the manager's bosses and the local Party people often try to shield the enterprise from such pressures. They are as dependent for their careers upon successful plan fulfillment as are the plant managers themselves.

Direct orders from above are one way of getting management to innovate. But innovation would proceed more rapidly if managers could be made to wish to innovate, instead of waiting until they are forced into it. The literature of the past few years is full of suggestions on how this can be accomplished. It is suggested, for example, that attractively high prices be set on new machines, in order to stimulate the producers of those machines to put them into production more rapidly. While this measure might ease the financial strain on the innovating firm, it will not remove the risk that the production plan may be sacrificed. And production is much more vital to the success of the enterprise than finance.

More to the point are the suggestions that the bonus system be employed as an incentive for innovation. Soviet economists seem to have enormous confidence in bonuses as a device for getting management to wish to do what the state wishes them to do. But how to adapt the bonus system to this purpose is more difficult. In the course of years a variety of special bonuses have been introduced for one purpose or another, in addition to the major bonus that comes from fulfillment of the production plan. There are special bonuses available for economizing certain critical materials, for reducing the volume of goods in process, for conserving fuel, for increasing labor productivity, for keeping the plant clean, for reducing the volume of spoilage, for operating the plant without stoppages, for winning "socialist competitions," and many others.[2]

This dilution of the bonus system may actually weaken its power as an incentive. If the special bonuses are small, they will not be very effective. If they are large they may detract effort from what is, after all, the main objective of the state: fulfillment of the production plan. For it is interesting to note the evidence that the relative size of the bonus for this or that special purpose often determines the manager's decision to concentrate on this or that objective. There are two types of innovation: relatively small measures such as organizational improvements or inexpensive alterations, and the more dramatic large-scale changes in production techniques. The former are included in the overall enterprise plan each year, under the name of the plan of organizational and technical measures (Orgtekhplan). It happens that there are certain bonuses available for the design and introduction of the large-scale innovations, but none for the fulfillment of the Orgtekhplan. The consequence is that research and managerial personnel concentrate on the large items and pay little attention to the small ones, even though the latter could result in great savings with relatively little cost and effort. Thus the very potency of the bonus as an incentive militates against its use for too many special purposes which may compete with each other.

To conclude this discussion, the unreliability of the supply system and the absence of a charge for the use of capital motivate management to order more fixed capital than they need and to hoard machines and equipment. This tendency deflects a certain amount of currently produced capital goods from being put directly into production in their best uses. On the other hand, the incentive system discourages management from taking the risks associated with innovation. Direct orders from above lead to a substantial volume of innovation, and in many cases management may consider certain forms of innovation to be to their interest. The provision of special bonuses for innovation, if they were large enough to compete with the production plan bonus, might help provide an incentive for innovation, and much of the current discussion in the Soviet Union seems to point to this as the next phase.

SOME COMPARATIVE OBSERVATIONS

The preceding section has shown that Soviet managers are motivated to make a variety of decisions that are contrary to the interest of the state. Since the state's interest is paramount in the Soviet scheme of things, we

---

[2] Not all these types of bonus are available to the director himself, but they are available to different groups of managerial personnel.

may properly conclude that the incentive and decision-making system is "relatively inefficient," or "less than perfectly efficient." Let me caution the reader once more against inferring from this that Soviet managers do not do a good job. They do. There is no doubt that their system works well. If I have chosen to concentrate on the "pathology" of Soviet management, the purpose was not to create the impression of ineffectiveness, but to illuminate the gap that every economy shows between the actual and the ideal.

A comparison of Soviet and American management will help drive the point home. No one doubts that American management does a good job. But it would be fatuous to allege that it operates with perfect efficiency. An exploration of the inevitable gap between the actual and the ideal in the case of American management will help to place the corresponding gap in the USSR in proper perspective.

A comparison of Soviet and American management is difficult for a curious reason; namely, we don't know enough about the more intimate aspects of American managerial practice. A moment's thought will make the reason clear. The American firm is a private enterprise in the full sense of the word. Its internal affairs are no one's business but its own. No one has the right to pry except with special cause. To be sure, the laws of the land have, over the years, required enterprises to disclose more and more of their private affairs to public and governmental perusal. But large sectors of the enterprise's internal operations are protected from the eyes of curious outsiders.

One of the most striking differences in the conduct of American and Soviet management is precisely in this matter of privacy. The Soviet enterprise is a public enterprise in the fullest sense of the word. It has no right to conceal its operations from any officially recognized agent of the state. And a great range of such agents have been deliberately endowed by the state with the obligation of keeping close watch on management and disclosing any irregularities or sources of inefficiency that come to their attention. These agents include the "home office" of the firm (the ministry), the state bank, the local governmental body, the central government's State Control Commission, the Finance Department (the tax collector), the local Communist Party boss and his staff, the Party secretary of the enterprise itself, and indeed just about anyone in the enterprise who enjoys the extracurricular activity of attending meetings to discuss the affairs of the enterprise (the *aktiv*).

If we can imagine an American business executive suddenly placed in charge of a Soviet firm, it is this public character of the enterprise which above all would drive him to distraction. It means that any government official can at any time demand to examine any aspect of the firm's operations he wishes to, that at any time he can be called on the carpet by the local Party boss to explain a charge made by an irate customer, that any member of his staff (perhaps bucking for his job) can write a letter to

Pravda exposing him for having made an irregular deal on some supplies, that any scatterbrained worker who wants to "get his picture in the papers" can rise at a public meeting that the director is obliged to attend and compel the director to explain why he hasn't yet installed the new assembly line. The point is that the result of this authorized prying often finds its way into the published Soviet economic and political literature, which gives us an insight into the more intimate operations of the Soviet firm that we cannot have in the case of the American firm. But in view of this committee's expressed interest in comparisons of the United States and Soviet economies, I have attempted certain comparisons below which appear to be highly suggestive.

Managers and Owners

The original form of modern business organization was the small firm in which the owner was also the manager. The owner-manager was responsible to no one but himself for his business decisions, and his interest as manager could not conflict with his interest as owner. The development of the modern giant corporation, however, had led to that separation of management and ownership first elaborated in the work of Berle and Means.[3] Under the new conditions the private interests of the hired managers (and the controlling group) need no longer coincide at all points with the interests of the stockholder-owners. This is precisely the relationship between the hired Soviet manager and the owner-state.

Berle and Means concluded from their study that "the controlling group, even if they own a large block of stock, can serve their own pockets better by profiting at the expense of the company than by making profits for it."[4] This is precisely what Soviet managers do when they produce unplanned commodities that are advantageous to their firms but not to the state, when they overorder and hoard commodities, and when they resist innovation. Because of the differences between the two economic systems, we should expect that the precise forms that the owner-manager conflict takes would be different in the USSR and the United States. In the United States they are to be found in such decisions as the awarding of subcontracts, the accounting of profit in such way as to benefit the claims of the controlling group, the awarding of bonuses and other benefits to management, and in dividend payment policy. As in the Soviet enterprise, the accountant is of crucial importance in handling the books of the enterprise in such ways as make the best possible case for the manager; it is he, for example, who figures out the best way to distract the state's attention from the large expenditures on *tolkachi*. The accounting techniques are, of course, different in the United States; they

---

[3] Adolph A. Berle, Jr., and Gardiner C. Means, *The Modern Corporation and Private Property* (New York: The Macmillan Co., 1945).

[4] *Ibid.,* p. 122.

involve "the charging or the failure to deduct depreciation; charging to capital expenses which properly should be charged against income account; including nonrecurrent profits as income though their real place is in surplus; and the creation of 'hidden reserves.' "[5]

A major difference between the Soviet firm and the American firm is that in the last analysis profit remains the criterion of managerial performance in the latter, whereas the Soviet manager is evaluated by a number of criteria that are sometimes mutually exclusive. Both systems have attempted to bring managerial interests into harmony with owner interests by some sort of profit-sharing system. In the Soviet case, it is clear that profit plays a very minor role, compared with bonuses, as a managerial incentive. In the United States the manager shares directly in profit to a very limited extent, and often follows other goals in his decisions. "The executive not infrequently tends to look upon the stockholders as outsiders whose complaints and demand for dividends are necessary evils . . ." concluded one American student of management.[6] In like fashion the Soviet manager often begins to feel like the "boss" and resents the intrusion into "his" affairs of the state, which after all is the owner. I have described above some of the ways in which the Soviet manager promotes the interest of "his" enterprise by means contrary to the interests of the owner-state. In the American corporation the forms are somewhat different. ". . . profits are reinvested in the business for the sake of bigness and to protect the company, and the interests of the stockholders may be given second place to the business leader's conception of what is best for the firm itself." Executives manifest a "general unwillingness to liquidate unsuccessful enterprises" and thus put themselves out of jobs, however consistent liquidation might be with the interests of the stockholders.[7] The dramatic growth of corporate self-financing in recent years has strengthened the power of management to expand their own enterprises without having to go through the "test of the marketplace" for capital.

It was observed earlier that the desire for "security" and for what the Russians call a "quiet life" motivates a wide variety of managerial decisions such as concealing production capacity and resisting technological innovation that might rock the boat. Students of American management have also noted the change from the adventurous business tycoons of earlier days to a more professionalized managerial climate in which "greater emphasis is placed on education, training, and a scientific approach, and less on rugged, venturesome, and frequently heedless individualism. The desire for security seems to have increased, and the concomitant of a growing emphasis on security is a diminishing desire for

---

[5] *Ibid.*, pp. 202–3, 335.

[6] Robert A. Gordon, *Business Leadership in the Large Corporation* (Washington, D.C.: The Brookings Institution, 1945), p. 309.

[7] *Ibid.*, p. 309.

adventure for its own sake."[8] There is indeed a remarkable parallel to this development in the change in the character of Soviet managers. There would have been a great affinity between the industrial empire builders of 19th-century America and the Soviet directors of the first two decades of the Soviet regime. Those directors were often men of little education who came out of the romantic conflict of revolution, who dreamed great dreams of building an industrial nation and who created an ethos of bold plans and adventurous undertakings. The old Commissar of Heavy Industry, Sergei Ordzhonikidze, would have understood the spirit of the ironmonger, Andrew Carnegie, and the man who built the great ZIL automotive works (now named after him) had the drives and the dreams of the bicycle mechanic, Henry Ford.

Time, and Stalin's purges, removed most of those old-timers and their place has now been taken by Soviet-educated young men born not of revolution but of bureaucracy. Organizations seem to develop "organization men" types, whether the organization happens to be communist or capitalist. An American reporter visiting with a group of Communist intellectuals reports that one of them had badgered him with questions about David Riesman's book, *The Lonely Crowd*. "The Communist had read Riesman's book and has been fascinated by it—not, he said, because of its application to life in the United States but because of what he maintained was its extraordinary relevance to the present conditions of life in the Soviet Union."[9] It is not, on reflection, very surprising that the job of running an industrial bureaucracy should place a common stamp on men of otherwise different backgrounds. The same would probably apply to the running of a large city or a large university.

Managers and the Laws

We have found that the Soviet manager is often compelled to evade regulations or even break laws. Part of the explanation is simply that there are so many laws. If a Chicago manufacturer fails to ship an order to a New York firm, and ships it instead to another Chicago firm, he has nothing to fear but the ire of the New York firm. But if a Kiev manufacturer fails to ship an order to a Moscow firm and ships it instead to another Kiev firm, he has injured a state enterprise and is subject to administrative action, a fine, or even criminal prosecution. If an American firm sells a substandard generator, he may lose money or his business. But if a Soviet firm sells a substandard generator, the director may go to prison. Thus, even if Soviet managers acted exactly as American managers do, we should expect to find more illegal or evasive activity in the Soviet Union than in the United States.

---

[8] *Ibid.*, p. 311.
[9] *The New Yorker*, April 6, 1955, p. 52.

With the growing complexity of our society, more and more legislation is enacted to protect the public from potential abuses. With the growth of such legislation, managers find their activities more and more circumscribed by laws and regulations. The Soviet manager apparently his firm (and his career and pocketbook). How does American management react when confronted by a spreading web of restrictive legislation?

It is not easy to find out very much about American managerial practice in this respect. Unlike the Soviet press, which throws its pages open to reports of the irregular activities of managers in order to warn others, the American press is likely to shy away from this kind of reporting. Moreover the private nature of American business keeps this sort of activity from coming to light as easily as it might in Soviet industry. Nor is it the sort of thing that businessmen are inclined to talk about very readily. If it is true that a businessman would more readily be interviewed on his private sex life than on his private business activity, then we should require the late Dr. Kinsey to help provide the answers to the extent of unlawful or quasi-lawful business activity.

Prof. E. H. Sutherland, the eminent American criminologist and sociologist, made a bold attempt to investigate the phenomenon he refers to as "white-collar crime." His study is based on the decisions of a limited number of courts and administrative commissions against the 70 largest industrial-type corporations in the country. In the period 1935 to 1944 these 70 corporations were convicted 585 times for such practices as restraint of trade, misrepresentation in advertising, patent and copyright infringements, unfair labor practices, granting of rebates, and a few others.[10] The average was 8.5 convictions per corporation. These data provide some idea of the extensiveness of such practices but they clearly understate the magnitude for a variety of technical reasons. Sutherland's conclusion is that "a great deal of scattered and unorganized material indicates that white collar crimes are very prevalent."[11]

The point I wish to make is that when American management finds itself in a position approximating that of Soviet management it tends to react in ways similar to those of its Soviet counterparts. Sutherland's unique study notes many aspects of American managerial practice that are astonishingly similar to those one might find in the literature on Soviet management. "These crimes are not discreet and inadvertent violations of technical regulations. They are deliberate and have a relatively consistent unity."[12] It is in precisely this way that the Soviet manager deliberately misappropriates earmarked funds or decides to shave on the quality of production. There is evidence that the Soviet manager, aware of the fact

---

[10] Edwin H. Sutherland, *White Collar Crime* (New York: Dryden, 1949), p. 26.
[11] *Ibid.*, p. 10.
[12] *Ibid.*, p. 217.

that "everybody does it" and that the investigating agencies have restricted budgets, counts on the law of averages (and his own superior shrewdness) to get away with it. So a member of the Federal Trade Commission wrote that "about the only thing that keeps a businessman off the wrong end of a Federal indictment or administrative agency's complaint is the fact that, under the hit-or-miss methods of prosecution, the law of averages hasn't made him a partner to a suit," and "Samuel Insull is reported to have remarked during his trial that he had only done what all other businessmen were doing."[13]

Similarities in managerial practice are paralleled by similarities in attitude to such violations and toward the administrative agencies enforcing the laws and regulations. The Soviet manager does not think it is "wrong" to use influence to obtain materials unlawfully, or to fudge his reports to the government. Success is the important thing, and if you are successful you can get away with all sorts of violations. There is evidence that the Soviet manager feels contemptuous of government planners and of Party hacks who try to tell him how to run his business but who themselves had "never met a payroll." Sutherland's picture of American management's attitudes contains strains of the same kind.

The businessman who violates the laws which are designed to regulate business does not customarily lose status among his business associates. Although a few members of the industry may think less of him, others admire him. . . . Businessmen customarily regard government personnel as politicians and bureaucrats, and the persons authorized to investigate business practices as "snoopers."[14]

In the first section of this paper, it was pointed out that a managerial career carries a great deal of prestige in the Soviet Union and attracts a large number of the better students. These youngsters have been raised in Soviet schools and have absorbed the incessant propaganda of the Communist regime. Many of them enter industry as green novices fresh from school, filled with high ideals about building the socialist fatherland and working for the common welfare. One wonders about the process by which the naive, idealistic young Komsomol member is transformed into the hard-headed manager who knows all the angles for survival in the Soviet business world. Numerous incidents such as the following provide a key to the answer. A young Soviet chemist had been assigned to the quality control department of his enterprise. He was quite pleased with himself when his test showed that a sample of production, which had previously been declared acceptable by his laboratory chief, turned out to contain an excess of phosphorus. He reported the "error" and expected to get a bonus for it. Instead, his boss obtained a new sample, gave it to an outside chemist for analysis, and submitted a report showing that the

---

[13] *Ibid.*, p. 218.
[14] *Ibid.*, p. 220.

batch of production was acceptable after all. The young chemist protested, was transferred to another shop, and was finally fired on trumped-up charges.

What happens to such young people? Some never quite get the point and remain ordinary engineers in the plants. Others learn to adapt themselves after a few buffetings and, when they decide to play the game according to the real ground rules, begin to rise in the managerial hierarchy.

It is interesting to note that Sutherland's interviews with American businessmen turned up accounts rather similar to that narrated above. His explanation of the process by which the naive American youngster is initiated into the business of selling used cars, settling insurance claims, covering up irregularities in clients' accounts—indeed, toning down the results of chemical analysis—helps explain the process of transformation of the young Komsomol member:

> In many cases he is ordered by the manager to do things which he regards as unethical or illegal, while in other cases he learns from others who have the same rank as his own how they make a success. He learns specific techniques of violating the law, together with definitions of situations in which those techniques may be used. Also he develops a general ideology. This ideology grows in part out of the specific practices and is in the nature of generalization from concrete experiences, but in part it is transmitted as a generalization by phrases such as "we are not in business for our health," "business is business," and "no business was ever built on the beatitudes." These generalizations . . . assist the neophyte in business to accept the illegal practices and provide rationalizations for them.[15]

Summarizing, the economic world in which the Soviet manager operates compels him to engage in a variety of illegal or evasive practices. Since the Soviet business world is enmeshed in a much greater web of laws and regulations than the American, the Soviet manager finds his interest in conflict with the laws and regulations more often than his American counterpart. But when American managers' interests conflict with the laws, they too are prepared to take the chance of violating them. Both American and Soviet managers justify their actions by an attitude of contempt for governmental controls and investigating personnel, and by a hardheaded view that "business is business" and "everybody does it." Young people in both systems who wish to achieve managerial prominence have to learn to play the game according to the rules or disqualify themselves from the tough competition for the top.

Managers and Overfull Employment

Many of the peculiarities of Soviet management spring from the fact that the economic system works under conditions of perpetual overfull

---

[15] *Ibid.,* p. 240.

employment. By "overfull" employment I mean a condition in which there are not merely as many jobs as employables (as under full employment), but the demand for labor far exceeds the available supply. The same applies to other factors of production: materials, equipment, and commodities in general are demanded in far greater volume than the current rates of production. The ability of the Soviet government to maintain, through the planning system, a condition of permanent overfull employment is one of the greatest economic assets of the regime. We err when we interpret evidence of shortages in the Soviet economy as signs of economic weakness; they are rather indications that the economic engine is racing with the throttle wide open.

But just as an engine does not work at its maximum efficiency when it is working at its maximum capacity, so the Soviet economy pays a certain price for the advantages of overfull employment. It is the perpetual shortages of supplies that account in large measure for the losses due to overordering and hoarding. The hunger for goods by both firms and consumers encourages the deterioration of quality. The "sea of ink" associated with materials allocations, price fixing, priorities, and all the rigamarole of a controlled economy nurtures the spread of the *tolkach* and the use of influence for personal gain.

The normally functioning American economy does not confront our managers with this kind of problem. Hoarding makes no sense when materials are in adequate supply. Competition and consumer resistance force the quality of production up to standard. The role of influence is narrowly circumscribed when the bureaucratic machinery of government controls is removed. The biggest problem of American managers under normal conditions is marketing, not purchasing. The energy spent by the Soviet firm on obtaining materials is spent by the American firm on selling and advertising.

Thus, the major differences between the practice of American and Soviet management are to be ascribed to the differences in the economic environment. The interesting question is, How do American managers behave when placed in an environment that approximates that of the Soviet manager? The obvious test case is war. During World War II the national emergency forced us into a state of overfull employment. Along with this came the total immersion of government into economic life, with a great burgeoning of materials allocation, price fixing, cost-plus contracting, and a prevailing shortage of supplies.

It is interesting to note that the rate of growth of production during the war rose to levels rivaling the current rates of Soviet economic growth. The implication of this fact is important; it means that there is no magic in the Soviet economic system. Our economy could grow as rapidly as the Soviet economy does if our people would consent to being pushed around as totally as the Soviet people are.

But like the Soviet economy, we paid for our high rate of production in various forms of waste. One of the first consequences of the introduction of materials controls was the rise of the black market. The only full-scale study of the black market, to my knowledge, confirmed what many people felt to be the case at the time:

> During the war at least a million cases of black market violations were dealt with by the government. Illegal profits ran into billions of dollars. Business interests and government vied with one another in estimating the seriousness of the black market, business estimates, curiously, often being higher than those of the government. Such extensive conniving in the black market in illegal prices and rationed commodities took place among so many businessmen, ordinary criminals, and even the average citizen that serious questions might be raised as to the moral fiber of the American people.[16]

To understand the position of the Soviet manager, we must realize that the American black market flourished at a time when the nation was fighting for its life and public indignation acted as a restraint. But if the economic controls that led to violations could not be justified by a national emergency, they would be thought of as just irritating obstacles, as so many hurdles that the resourceful manager must overcome as part of the risks of the game. There is good evidence that the Soviet manager takes just this amoral attitude toward economic controls, and it is therefore quite understandable that the evasion of controls would be more widespread.

The high quality of American production in normal times is a byword in international markets. But the effect on the economy of shortages was similar to that in the Soviet economy. One of the techniques used by Soviet managers is to represent lower quality merchandise as of higher quality, and to sell it at the higher price. In the United States during the war "upgrading was one of the most difficult violations to detect, particularly where no professional investigator was available who could appraise the grade or where there were no State or Federal grades stamped on the commodity."[17] The reports of government investigators read like some of the indignant letters of complaint we read in the Soviet press: men's shorts made of cheesecloth, water-resistant baby's pants which permit a third of a glass of water to leak through after one laundering. "If you pick up a board by both ends without breaking it in the middle, it's No. 1 Select," testified an American businessman.[18]

One of the features of Soviet managerial life which helps protect the manager is the feeling of "mutual support" among various officials whose fortunes depend on the success of the enterprise. The Communist Party secretary doesn't report the manipulations of a successful director because the Party benefits from the success of the enterprise; the people in the

---

[16] Marshall B. Clinard, *The Black Market* (New York: Rinehart & Co., Inc., 1952), p. vii.

[17] *Ibid.*, p. 224.

[18] *Ibid.*, p. 45.

"home office" (the Ministry) are reluctant to fire a director who violates the laws in order to get the materials his plant needs, for while the next director may be more law-abiding, he may not succeed in fulfilling his plan. This tendency to maintain a solid front against authority is a source of great irritation to the government, which periodically inveighs against it but has not been able to eradicate it. A similar sense of common front prevailed among groups of businessmen.

Nothing better illustrates the degree of organization and consensus among businessmen than their reluctance to testify against each other. . . . Some businessmen felt that the trade would disapprove of behavior that might undermine the solid front against the government as well as interfere with supplies.[19]

One of the major differences in the position of management in the two countries is the nature of the penalty for failure. Under ordinary conditions the unsuccessful manager loses his job. But the Soviet manager faces many more situations in which the action necessary to get the job done carries with it the threat of criminal action. Indeed, whenever the Soviet government has found some managerial practice too damaging to its interests and too intractable to the normal sanctions, it has turned to the criminal courts. Immediately after the death of Stalin the punishment for economic transgressions was relaxed, but the new regime has not been able to continue operating without the courts. One of the severest economic problems following the decentralization of industry was the tendency toward "localism": that is, each economic region tended to favor the plants in its "own" region, and would discriminate against plants in other regions. When all exhortation failed, the government had to turn to the law. Today, a manager who fails to honor the orders of plants outside his own region is subject to "administrative action, fines, or even criminal punishment."

Financial penalties, such as fines, have rarely proved successful as restraints on Soviet managerial behavior. American managers seem to have reacted the same way to the fines imposed for black-market violations. "They don't hurt anybody." "It just comes out of profits, like a tax." "They make so much money on the black market they can afford to pay steep fines." But imprisonment was another matter. "Jail is the only way; nobody wants to go to jail." "A jail sentence is dishonorable; it jeopardizes the reputation." This would not be quite the same in the case of the Soviet manager. At least during Stalin's lifetime some of the best people served their time in jail, and it definitely did not destroy their reputation among their neighbors; although the neighbors might be wary of associating with them. One has the impression that large numbers of Soviet managers feel the chances are fair that some day they will do their stretch, hopefully for a minor transgression.

The wartime economy of shortages injects the government into busi-

[19] *Ibid.,* pp. 306–7.

ness life not only as an agency of control but also as the largest customer of many firms. In the Soviet case we have noted the importance of the *tolkach*, the expediter, the peddler of influence. We might note in passing that the economic system of Nazi Germany, in which government had also assumed a dominant role, also gave rise to this chap. The Germans called him the "contact man." As described by an American student of the German economy:

To influence the powerful agencies of control, however, he [the German businessman] has good use for what might suitably be called a private relations department. Under the Nazi system of control of business by an absolute government, the contact man, or graft, or both, take the place of the public relations executive.

The contact man is primarily a political figure. His job is to pull wires. He knows the influential members of the all-pervading Nazi Party in a position to bring pressure successfully to bear upon the men in charge of controlling agencies. . . . Two types of contact man are known to be used: one is an independent agent whom the businessman hires, or attempts to hire, whenever necessary; the other is carried on the payroll of the business in a more or less permanent capacity.[20]

The words might well have been written about the Soviet economy. In that sector of the U.S. economy in which government plays a dominant role as customer, the symbols of the mink coat or Dixon-Yates, depending upon one's political persuasion, come to mind. "Washington," wrote Senator Paul Douglas, "is indeed full of lawyers and 'representatives' whose primary commodity is 'influence.' "[21] The techniques of the American influence-peddler differ little from those of his colleagues in the Soviet or Nazi economy. Gifts and *quid pro quo* favors are standard among Soviet *tolkachi*. Another way in which Soviet enterprises manage to exert influence is to have one of "their" men placed in other organizations that can be of use, rather like the unusually high employability in industry of retired military personnel. During the war the problem was particularly acute because of our government's desperate need for skilled managerial personnel, many of whom were on loan from corporations with which the government placed contracts. But the use of influence is not confined to government-business relations, as Senator Douglas pointed out in his critical defense of the ethics of government personnel:

As a matter of fact, the abuses which have been exposed and properly denounced in the field of government are quite widespread practices in private business. Thus the "padding" of expense accounts is so common that they are often referred to as "swindle sheets." Purchasing agents and buyers frequently exact toll from those who seek to sell them, and their Christmas presents and

[20] L. Hamburger, *How Nazi Germany Has Controlled Business* (Washington, D.C.: The Brookings Institution, 1943), pp. 94–95.

[21] Paul H. Douglas, *Ethics in Government* (Cambridge, Mass.: Harvard University Press, 1952), p. 56.

other perquisites appreciably increase their income. Business managers and directors think nothing of awarding contracts, insurance, and underwriting privileges on the basis of friendship and relationship rather than the quality and prices of the goods and services supplied. All this is taken as a matter of course in private business, although it obviously increases costs and intercepts gains which should go to stockholders and consumers.[22]

While gifts, payoffs, and bribery play their role in the Soviet scheme of things, the subtler and much more pervasive technique of influence is known as "blat." To have good blat with someone means that one has an "in"; one can always count on him for a favor because of friendship or family ties or some other relationship of confidence. Blat may be used to obtain everything from a new apartment to a carload of coal. The prominent British observer, Edward Crankshaw, has called blat the most significant word in contemporary Russia.[23] The way in which the American equivalent of blat is cultivated is described in one final quotation from Senator Douglas:

Today the corruption of public officials by private interests takes a more subtle form. The enticer does not generally pay money directly to the public representative. He tries instead by a series of favors to put the public official under such feeling of personal obligation that the latter gradually loses his sense of mission to the public and comes to feel that his first loyalties are to his private benefactors and patrons. What happens is a gradual shifting of a man's loyalties from the community to those who have been doing him favors. His final decisions are, therefore, made in response to private friendships and loyalties rather than to the public good.[24]

Summarizing, many of the differences between Soviet and United States managerial behavior spring from differences in the economic climate in which they operate. The stress on quality and appearance, the drive for innovation and technological development, and the interest in cost reduction reflect the force of competition and the buyer's market. Such similarities as have been observed in managerial behavior spring from features of the economic environment that are common to the two systems, such as large-scale organization and the intrusion of government into the economy. Under wartime conditions our economy takes on more of the features of normal Soviet economic life, and the consequence is that our managers adopt more of the normal practices of Soviet management.

---

[22] *Ibid.*, p. 25.

[23] *New York Times Magazine*, June 3, 1951, p. 35.

[24] Douglas, *op. cit.*, p. 44.

10| THE SOVIET LABOR MARKET

Emily Clark Brown

The allocation of the Soviet labor force is accomplished by a combination of central planning and the use of market forces. The distribution of the labor force by region, branch of the economy, occupation, and skill level is centrally planned in physical terms. However, the planners rely primarily on wage differentials in a largely free labor market to draw labor into the jobs created by the plan. The characteristics of the Soviet labor market are examined by Emily Clark Brown in the following article. It depicts the labor market of recent years, after the stringent controls over job choice in the Stalin era were eliminated and after forced labor (which is not discussed in the article) was sharply curtailed.

This article does not devote much attention to trade unions. In the Soviet Union, trade unions are instruments of the state (the employer of their members), and their main function is to increase production and enforce labor discipline. They do not bargain collectively on wages, fringe benefits, or job security, and strikes are illegal. The trade unions administer the social insurance system and operate recreational facilities for their members, and they offer the worker some protection against abuses by individual managers in job classification, working conditions, and housing.

Emily Clark Brown is Professor Emeritus of Economics at Vassar College. The selection is reprinted by permission of the author and publishers from Emily Clark Brown, *Soviet Trade Unions and Labor Relations* (Cambridge, Mass.: Harvard University Press, 1966), pp. 11–47. Copyright 1966 by the President and Fellows of Harvard College. Citations to Russian-language sources are omitted.

ALTHOUGH the concept of the labor market is foreign to their philosophy of planning, Soviet planners have long dealt with the theoretical and practical problems of labor force distribution and remuneration. Various combinations of planning and reliance on market forces have been used, including central and decentralized planning, planned training and recruitment, direction of labor and control over turnover, and voluntary self-direction under the influence of wage and other incentives, social pressure, advertisements, and local and country-wide methods of recruit-

196

ment. After Stalin, changes in manpower policies gave workers increased freedom to respond to market forces.

EMPLOYMENT AND UNEMPLOYMENT

Following the Twentieth Congress of the Communist Party in 1956, study of these problems increased. Economists and labor law experts in the institutes, universities, and state planning agencies spoke frequently of "deficiencies in labor resources in some areas" and "surplus" or "over-plan" workers in others, and of "the need for redistribution of workers freed from some enterprises." Beginning in 1959, annual conferences on labor resources brought together representatives from all parts of the country. It was recognized that the economic plans called for labor forces beyond the expected population growth and that wartime losses would still be felt. Although the situation improved after 1961, shortages in certain areas continued to pose difficulties. The eastern and central parts of the country, where intensive development was planned, were rich in natural resources, but they were underpopulated. The rapidly developing oil and chemical industries needed labor. More workers were needed also in the service occupations. It was expected that in spite of growth in productivity, "the demand of all branches of the national economy for labor will grow faster than the number of able-bodied population of working age."

At the same time, mechanization and automation were decreasing the need for unskilled hand labor and displacing workers from old skilled occupations.[1] In some areas the demand for labor was reduced by changing industrial structure. Surpluses of skilled workers were foreseen especially in old enterprises in heavy industry centers and in small cities where it was not expedient to build up new large industry.

The demand for labor in the growing fields and regions was expected to be met in part by released industrial workers and by large numbers not needed in agriculture because of mechanization and improved organization. Another source was the small part of the "able-bodied population" of working age (men 16–59, women 16–54) not working or studying—a little more than 10 percent, according to the 1959 census of population. Most of these were women occupied at home in household work and caring for children. There were also members of the families of peasants or workers engaged in private subsidiary farming—7.7 percent of the labor force.[2] It was hoped to draw many from these groups into employ-

---

[1] The proportion of hand labor was still very high. In 1959 in all industry 40.7 percent of workers in basic production were reported to be engaged in hand labor, compared with 61.3 in 1925. In auxiliary work, transport, maintenance, and the like, 68.1 percent was hand labor in 1959, and 91.4 in 1925.

[2] Another source was the able-bodied pensioners. Incentive to return to the labor force was given in a March 1964 decree liberalizing pension laws. In a broad list of fields and occupations pensions would be paid in addition to wages, up to 75 percent

ment in the public economy. It was argued also that new enterprises should be located with more attention to availability of labor.

Differences among regions were reported in 1962 by one expert. Labor resources were found insufficient in the Northwest, Siberia, the Far East, and Kazakhstan, but generally adequate in the Urals, the Volga region, and part of the Baltic area; there were surplus labor reserves in a majority of the regions of the European part of the country, and in republics of Middle Asia, especially Uzbekistan. Another expert complained, however, that current statistical reports on labor resources failed to show how many of those not employed in the public economy were actually engaged in household work, how many could be brought into jobs, or how many were "in need of placement"[3]—the Soviet euphemism for "unemployed."

Soviet theory holds that distribution of manpower is "by planned recruitment, preparation, and distribution of the labor force," in contrast to a market economy where labor is "a commodity, bought and sold in the market." Nevertheless, market influences are admitted, since wages are said to be "one of the economic instruments of the planned distribution and redistribution of labor forces." Thus the labor market depends on planned economic and legal measures and on individual choices in response to them.

The legal setting is the citizen's constitutional duty to work and guaranteed right to work. The duty to work means his obligation to engage in "socially useful labor" and neither to live on "unearned income" from private profit or speculation nor to be idle. Only for women with young children is it generally approved for people of working age not to participate in the labor force; and it is considered preferable if facilities provided for the care of children are enough that these mothers can work. Laws against "persons who avoid socially useful labor and lead a parasitic way of life," adopted in most of the republics from 1957 to 1961, permit exile of "parasites" for stated periods with the obligation to work; or they may be sent to work in their own locality.[4]

---

of the pension in the Urals, Siberia and the Far East, 50 percent in other regions; for agricultural work and underground work in mines, 100 percent. A million were expected to return to work.

[3] The Central Statistical Administration collects detailed reports on employment and makes them available to all government and economic agencies, but these are limited to the occupied population. Apparently there is no regular system of studying the extent and make-up of any people not currently employed but available for work.

[4] The sentence of exile is given by public meetings of citizens or in some republics only by the People's Courts or the executive committees of local soviets. There is concern among jurists over abuses in practice. Many problems are reported in handling the exiles in places to which they have been sent. R. Beerman, "The Parasites' Law," *Soviet Studies*, Vol. XIII, No. 2 (October, 1961), pp. 191–205, also Vol. XV, No. 4 (April, 1964), pp. 420–29; Harold J. Berman, *Justice in the USSR* (Cambridge, Mass.: Harvard Univ. Press, 1963), pp. 291–298. For the text of the law in the RSFSR see U.S. Bureau of Labor Statistics, *Principal Current Soviet Labor*

As to the right to work, Soviet spokesmen insist that in their system "there is not and cannot be unemployment." Experts argue that the socialist economic system ensures full employment by so organizing the distribution of labor "that each citizen has the possibility to work at his specialty and qualifications and in accordance with social needs." Under conditions of technological displacement and shifts of industry, increased attention turned to the need for "insuring full and rational employment of the able-bodied population in all regions." Solution of the problem is recognized as requiring carefully planned action.

It is apparent that at times Soviet workers do experience problems in finding work. References to "unoccupied people" and to citizens needing "labor placement" appear frequently, although these people are not called unemployed. The concept of frictional or seasonal unemployment is not explicitly recognized. Only rarely does the Soviet press mention difficulties in getting jobs. The most numerous reports, in 1956–1958, concerned young persons, especially minors leaving school after seven or ten years. Occasionally other reports of "being out of work" have appeared, especially as to people unable to find jobs for some months after being illegally discharged and before being reinstated.

Soviet authorities are concerned over loss of time between jobs, whether the turnover is voluntary or involuntary, but they consider the problem one of instability of labor forces or defects in the organized distribution of manpower. Failure to employ seasonal workers throughout the year is discussed as a problem of waste of labor. Shortage of workers is felt to be the main problem. If a man is out of work, an economist insisted, "approximately suitable jobs are available, even if not exactly what the worker thinks he should have."

Displacement by technological or other changes in industry, rather than causing an unemployment problem, is relied on as a major source of workers for expanding fields. One Soviet expert, writing in 1959, held that in most cases a decrease of workers in one department was compensated by expansion in others. He also considered redistribution of workers between enterprises "a healthy process" which should be more used, since "overplan numbers of workers" in many enterprises adversely affected productivity. Under the Labor Code of 1922 and later regulations,[5] when reducing its staff an enterprise is obligated to shift workers with their consent to other suitable work in the plant or related plants. A labor economist, who said flatly that management is required to find jobs for

---

Legislation (Washington, D.C., 1962), pp. 125–127. It has been reported that in 1961 in Moscow 2,000 persons were exiled as parasites and 8,000 were sent to work in Moscow; see George Feifer, *Justice in Moscow* (New York, 1964), pp. 196–97.

[5] The text of the Labor Code of the Russian Soviet Federated Socialist Republic, which became the basic standard of labor law for the entire Soviet Union, is available in U.S. Bureau of Labor Statistics, *Principal Current Soviet Labor Legislation* (Washington, D.C., 1962), pp. 1–34.

workers displaced by mechanization, emphasized the "moral principle that people need to have work, not only for the money involved," and so "it is not easy to fire people," even if they are not needed. A management official in the Bashkir autonomous republic wrote, "Is it thinkable that under our conditions party and trade union organizations would agree to discharges of thousands of people, as a result of automation, without finding jobs for them? Of course not."

A new term, labor-placement, which appeared with increasing frequency in Soviet publications after 1959, was defined as "assistance of government and public organs to different categories of citizens in receiving suitable work in the shortest time and without delay; one of the additional guarantees of the right to work." In several instances the government specifically required local authorities to find jobs for groups who were being displaced.[6] It is said also that administrative agencies are obligated to arrange transfers from enterprises with overplan numbers on their staffs to other enterprises where workers are needed. However, as one expert points out, there is no general governmental system to ensure that the shifts of people displaced are entirely painless. Even when retraining is at government expense, as when railroads shifted to electric operation, pay during training may be less than previous wages, and difficulties may be even greater when people shift by their own decisions.

Freedom of citizens to choose fields for training and the place and type of their work is a major Soviet principle.[7] On the whole, workers could select their work and move by their own choice during most of the Soviet period up to World War II; yet there were many exceptions. In 1919–1920 conscription was used extensively, and again during and after the war. Starting in 1928 young graduates of higher education and later of trade schools were directed to jobs. Efforts to curb wasteful mobility culminated in 1938 in the system of permanent labor books, giving the worker's employment record, and without which he could not be hired. A month's notice was then required for leaving jobs.[8] Youths were drafted for industrial training in Labor Reserve Schools from 1940. Finally, in 1940, harsh legislation prohibited workers from leaving jobs

---

[6] Notably for those displaced in the abolition of central ministries in 1957, for women removed from underground work in mines, workers who lost jobs in the reorganization of the machine tractor stations, released members of the armed forces, and amnestied persons.

[7] Penal labor is not included in the scope of the present study. The largest use of such labor is believed to have been in the late 1930's. The number of forced laborers is not known, but a recent estimate concludes that there may have been 3 million in 1937 and 3.5 million in 1940 and perhaps in 1950, and 2 million in 1955. Amnesties after Stalin's death released large numbers. Abram Bergson, *The Real National Income of Soviet Russia Since 1928* (Cambridge, Mass.: Harvard Univ. Press, 1961), pp. 96, 447.

[8] Solomon M. Schwarz, *Labor in the Soviet Union* (New York, 1952), pp. 98–103. For the early history see also Margaret Dewar, *Labor Policy in the USSR 1917–1928* (London, 1956).

without permission of the director and permitted compulsory transfer of skilled workers and experts, with severe criminal penalties for "truancy." Use of coercion declined in the early 1950's, until, with the complete repeal of the 1940 laws on April 25, 1956, freedom of choice of jobs again came to the fore. Workers could then leave jobs on two weeks' notice.[9]

This change of policy is held to have reestablished voluntary labor contracts as the chief way of entering jobs, on "the principle of genuine freedom of contract"—meaning "strict voluntarism in entrance on work, freedom to shift to other work, and freedom to remain at work by choice of the worker . . . , permitting transfer to other permanent work only with the agreement of the worker." The aim is said to be to combine protection of the interests of the individual and of society and to assure both satisfaction in work and high productivity. Wage differentials and a variety of other incentives are used to influence workers to go to jobs and to stay as stable members of the labor force where needed. In addition, constant propaganda seeks to educate workers as to the needs of the state and to enlist their cooperation.

PLANNING FOR LABOR RESOURCES

Central planning determines the nature and location of jobs, and seeks to provide the needed labor. Annual production plans include "limits" on the number of workers to be employed, the wage fund, average wages, and expected increases in labor productivity. Data from analyses at lower levels make possible nation-wide planning for needed training and shifting of workers. Each area is responsible for estimating its labor resources and demand. Planning starts in the enterprise, which is expected to study its own labor, the expected demand, and sources for new workers. Then the sovnarkhoz—the regional economic council—works out the balance for meeting the needs of its plants for all types of labor; and administrative and government agencies work out the combined balance for the cities, regions, and republics. Each industry needs attention, and also various groups of workers—women, youths, and specialists of all levels of training. Thus, the experts claim, the national economic plan provides for the mobile labor resources needed for fulfilling plans and for full employment.

Many regions, however, are said to be lax in their analysis, especially in planning for the full use of available labor. There is particular concern with the questions of surplus labor that should be shifted, of seasonal

[9] The law of June 26, 1940, provided penalties of imprisonment for two to four months for leaving jobs without permission, and lesser penalties for absenteeism or lateness without adequate excuse. For experience under the law see Schwarz, pp. 106–155, and Jerzy G. Gliksman, "Recent trends in Soviet Labor Policy," *Monthly Labor Review*, Vol. 79, No. 7 (July, 1956), pp. 767–75. For the text of the repeal see *Principal Current Soviet Labor Legislation, op. cit.*, pp. 63–65. The draft of youth for the Labor Reserve Schools had been repealed in March, 1955 (*ibid.*, p. 58).

workers not utilized the year around, and of women who could be drawn into employment.

Labor surpluses result when population growth supplies more new workers in a locality than needed; when the chief industry provides jobs mainly for one sex—women in textiles, men in heavy industry; and when an industry or big enterprise shuts down, or there is large scale automation. Local authorities are often remiss in planning for needed shifts of labor to other areas or for the development of new industry. When coal mines closed in an area 1,500 miles from Moscow because of a changeover to gas in Moscow and other cities, it is said that new factories were brought in, some miners were retrained for the new industries, and some moved to other coal fields. But when a somewhat similar problem arose from automation in the Bashkir oil industry, an administrative worker complained that no plan had been made for released personnel and that other types of industry were lacking; as a result large numbers of unneeded workers were kept on the payrolls.

Individual plants often have unnecessary workers. This sometimes arises from poor organization and lack of mechanization, especially in materials and product handling. On the other hand, surpluses result when mechanization has not been accompanied by adequate shifting and retraining of workers. Economists insist there is no real difficulty in the transfer of young workers, since other jobs are available locally or in other areas, and there are facilities for retraining. Older people, however, are more likely to be kept on though not needed and though productivity is adversely affected. One expert complained, also, of a tendency to underestimate the difficulties of providing employment for released workers; a time lag in the expansion of other job opportunities often led to maintaining surplus staffs.

Planning for full use of seasonal workers is another problem. Many are said to be "temporarily not working" in off-seasons; they are not called unemployed, as it is assumed that, typically, seasonal work is well paid and other off-season work at lower pay is available. The American Social Security Delegation in its 1958 examination of pension records, however, found numerous instances of seasonal unemployment, with extended periods of low earnings or none.[10] It has been recognized that there is underutilization of such workers, and therefore high turnover, in areas where the general supply of labor is inadequate. Regional authorities are urged to develop supplementary industries to provide off-season jobs for workers in fishing, mining, prospecting, agriculture, food processing, and other industries.

Underutilization of the potential labor of women continues. Employment of women varies greatly in different regions. In 1962 they were 51 percent of all employed in Russia, but 40 percent or less in most of the

---

[10] U.S. Department of Health, Education and Welfare, *A Report on Social Security Programs in the Soviet Union* (Washington, D.C.: U.S. Government Printing Office, 1960), pp. 8–9.

republics of the East. It was not known how many women were not working simply because of lack of jobs for women or lack of facilities for child care. Sample studies in Novosibirsk, Kemerovo, and Krasnoyarsk found many thousands of women, many with vocational training and experience, who would take jobs in industry if available and if their family duties were lightened by provision of more kindergartens and nurseries, and improvements in housing, public catering, and other consumers' services, or if they could work part-time. In many areas of heavy industry there was a lack of light industries that would offer more jobs for women and help to meet the need for better supplies for consumers.

The effectiveness of manpower planning is deeply affected by decisions on distribution of resources, location of industry, and provision for satisfaction of workers' needs. Complaints continue of labor shortages on one hand, of surpluses of labor on the other, of wasteful turnover and other problems. Although there is no large scale unemployment, full and productive employment of the entire potential labor force has not yet been achieved.

PLANNED TRAINING

A major means of providing industry with manpower is planned education and the job placement of workers on completion of their courses. The educational system was reorganized under the 1958 law "on strengthening the relations of schools with life."[11] Final decisions on numbers of students and on educational facilities are made by Gosplan and the USSR Council of Ministers. Plans for fields requiring training in specialized technical schools, institutes, and universities are under the Ministry of Higher and Specialized Secondary Education. A State Committee on Vocational-Technical Training assists the republics in planning and organizing vocational training and job placement of youths. Educational and planning authorities at the local level work with enterprises and other agencies to relate education to the needs of the local economy.

The 1958 school law provided free education at all levels, compulsory through the eighth grade, with secondary and higher education combined for the most part with "socially useful labor." Secondary "polytechnical"[12] schools were to provide general education through the eleventh grade, and training for selected occupations. Their graduates could continue education or more usually go directly to work, preferably in the

[11] For the English text, Nicholas DeWitt, *Education and Professional Employment in the USSR* (Washington, D.C.: U.S. Government Printing Office, 1961), pp. 556–574. For later discussion see his "Education and the Development of Human Resources: Soviet and American Effort," Joint Economic Committee, Congress of the United States, *Dimensions of Soviet Economic Power* (Washington, D.C.: U.S. Government Printing Office, 1962), pp. 235–268.

[12] "Polytechnical" is a term used for basic instruction in mathematics, science and technology and in production techniques, with specific training in some specialized occupational skill.

place of their practical training. Children finishing eighth grade have the right to enter one of these schools or go to work; or they may attend one of the vocational schools, with terms of one to three years, that replaced all former trade schools.[13] Some are admitted to specialized secondary schools for semi-professional training. Admission to higher education is competitive, based on entrance examinations and recommendations from the lower schools and from the place of work, and with preference in most fields for those who have worked two years in production jobs.

It was thought desirable that a substantial part of education beyond the eighth grade should be in evening and correspondence courses carried on while working. Facilities for full-time study were limited, young workers were needed, and the combination of study with work was considered educationally sound. Most eighth-grade graduates, it was expected, would go directly to work, but according to scattered reports they have not done so, although graduates of secondary schools go to work in relatively large numbers.[14] In 1963, of all in specialized secondary and higher education, 55 percent were studying while working. Young workers who study in evening and correspondence courses have shorter hours, additional vacations, and paid leaves for final projects and examinations. Students who are getting part of their training in industry are paid, under government regulations, for work done. Full-time students in specialized middle schools and higher education, who also have periods of production work, receive state stipends, varying with the fields of study, provided their work is satisfactory.

---

[13] The earlier system of vocational education included full-time factory schools, which until 1940 were the basic form of preparation of young skilled workers for mass production and which continued to serve the needs of light industry; and from 1940 the Labor Reserve Schools for skilled trades in heavy industry, mining, construction, and railroads, and later in agriculture. For details see DeWitt, *Education and Professional Employment, op. cit.,* chs. ii, iii. The Labor Reserve system, established in 1940 as one of the measures that tightened control over labor before the war, provided for a draft of urban and rural youth for two-year trade schools and six-month factory schools. Desertion was a criminal offense. Graduates were required to work for four years where sent.

To what extent the quotas given collective farms and cities in early years were filled by volunteers is not known, though officials later described the compulsion as having been on the villages, rather than on individuals. Later, the enrollments were said to have been entirely from volunteers. The draft was repealed in 1955. The schools served as a route by which rural children and others could get a start toward industrial jobs and opportunity for further education. In the middle 1950's increasing mechanization and the rising level of general education led to two-year mining schools and full-year schools for operators of agricultural machinery. Technical schools for secondary school graduates were established to prepare highly qualified personnel and junior technicians for industry.

[14] In the Ukraine in 1961 more than two-thirds are reported to have continued study. In Moscow, in 1960, of all eighth-grade graduates, 75 percent entered the ninth grade. In Leningrad in 1962 two school directors interviewed said that 15 percent or less went to work, most of the rest to eleven-year schools, and a few to vocational schools, while the most able went to specialized technical schools. *The New York Times,* August 13, 1964, stated that 40–50 percent of eighth grade graduates have been taking full time jobs.

Problems developed in this ambitious effort to tailor education to the needs of the planned economy. Most secondary schools were poorly equipped for production training, and practice in the plants was poorly organized. Good teachers were scarce. Frequently there was preparation only for traditional skills, and too few pupils could get training for the new and growing occupations. Many children were dissatisfied with their practice work. There were also too few vocational schools, especially in the East. Educational plans for regions and republics were said to be insufficiently related to the needs of the area. Young workers often had to be retrained or shifted to other industries or regions.

In practice, the right of young citizens to choose their fields of study and work was limited by the availability of educational facilities. Youngsters finishing eighth grade were helped in considering opportunities and were urged to choose carefully, but severe competition for some schools limited choices. Often fields of training were restricted to the needs of a nearby plant or farm. School officers insist, however, that a child is not bound by his secondary school training, and that there is ample chance for any able and energetic young person to shift fields later. Many young people have had to begin in evening and correspondence courses, since the number of openings for full-time study in the specialized and higher educational institutions was limited, though growing. Preference was given to young workers chosen by enterprises to be sent to study. On recommendations of their enterprises, they could transfer to full-time study for the later stages of their courses.

Many difficulties were found in the combination of work and study. Managements did not always provide the necessary conditions, and in spite of the generally strong drive to get education, not all workers were interested. There was concern also that the combination of general education with production training was weakening preparation for advanced study. By 1964 dissatisfaction had led to extensive discussion, and changes began to be made in the 1958 law. Secondary schools were reduced to a basic ten-year program, with less time for production training. Increased numbers of the most able were permitted to enter higher education directly from secondary school without two years' prior work. Educational policy was to continue as a key part in planning for the manpower needed in a modern economy.

Training on the job by enterprises themselves is still the predominant means of preparing skilled workers. Among applicants for apprenticeship training, ordinarily for six months, preference is given youths who have completed eight-year or eleven-year schools, although included also are recruits from collective farms, women without experience in industry, people sent by local soviet executive committees, and workers wanting to learn a second trade. Short term courses provide retraining to meet the needs of changing technology. Contracts with educational authorities provide for training for students. Training by the enterprises is thought useful for its close relation to current needs but is criticized as tending to be too narrow. There is hope that in the future increased numbers will be prepared in the vocational and higher schools, especially for the more complex jobs in automated industry.

Progress in developing manpower resources appears in the rising level of education reported. According to the Central Statistical Administration, people with seven or eight years of education increased from 83 per thousand inhabitants in 1939 to 281 in 1959 and 308 in 1963. Among wage-earners, 44 percent had at least this level of education in 1963. The number with secondary specialized education who were working in the national economy rose from 1.5 million in 1941 to 6.3 million in 1963. Those with higher education increased from under one million to 4.3 million. The average level of general education of industrial workers increased from 3.5 years in 1929 to 5.9 years in 1959, and according to a preliminary estimate would reach 7.5 years in 1965. Broader educational facilities, free education, stipends, and the drive for education to promote both individual and social interests, all contributed to this upsurge. Financial inability does not prevent able young people from getting the education they want, although low family incomes sometimes result in youngsters going directly to work rather than to full-time education. Local unions encourage the young to study, and their officers sometimes boast that every third worker is engaged in advancing his general or specialized education.

JOB CHOICE AND PLANNED PLACEMENT

Measures designed to direct or influence job choices and placement vary for different groups. The extent of these groups was shown in a report on expected sources of additional workers in 1962 in the industries of 11 economic regions. Only 15 percent were to come from vocational and other schools, and twice as many from people hired and trained by enterprises themselves. More than half were to be people shifting from other plants, including a small group trained in other enterprises. Only 2 percent were to come through organized recruitment systems.[15]

For young people finishing or leaving school, job placement is not left to chance. The state seeks to guarantee jobs for graduates of general education or for school leavers, with opportunity for further training. Difficulties have arisen when managements prefer not to hire such youths because of shorter hours and other privileges required. Children of fifteen can be hired, but only with the consent of the union committee and for four hours work daily. Sixteen and seventeen year olds are permitted to work only six hours but are paid for a full day, and there are other

---

[15] The 11 regions included 6 in Russia, 3 in the Ukraine, and Uzbekistan and Armenia. The percentages expected from each source were as follows: released from other enterprises, 48.1; individual and group training in enterprises, 31.2; vocational schools, 10.4; secondary schools with production training, 3.0; specialized technical schools, 2.1; prepared in other enterprises and *sovnarkhozy*, 2.5; from organized recruitment systems, 2.0; other, 0.7.

regulations on conditions of work and further study. School directors are obligated to know whether their graduates and others who left are working or studying, or both. Most children find their own jobs. If not, the child is referred to the executive committee of the local soviet, which has responsibility for placing young workers or assigning them to vocational schools.

District soviets in the cities have commissions on labor placement (*trudoustroistvo*) or on the affairs of minors, which should see that jobs are available for youths, with opportunity to continue study. Since 1957 they have had the obligation to assign to enterprises quotas of the number of youths to be hired. Under 1962 and 1963 decrees of the Council of Ministers, quotas of from 3 to 5 percent of the enterprise's number of workers are to be assigned, to assure jobs, in accordance with their training, for all leaving the eight and eleven-year schools and vocational schools. An enterprise may not legally refuse to hire the boy or girl sent with the commission's order of placement. On the other hand, it is not compulsory for the young person to take the job.

Difficulties of these young, partially trained, new workers in finding jobs were not entirely solved by the 1958 school reorganization and the assignment of quotas for their hiring. Mistakes were made in planning types of training, but the cost to the enterprise in hiring and training such youngsters was also a factor. There were reports in 1964 of refusals to hire boys and girls sent with placement orders from the commissions. Not over 15 percent of secondary school graduates are said to begin work in the fields for which they were trained. Local agencies were urged to see that all who finished school could get jobs according to their abilities.

Graduates of vocational schools are distributed to jobs by the schools, under plans approved by the republic councils of ministers. Graduates of specialized secondary and higher education are directed to jobs by state commissions including representatives of the schools and their social organizations and of economic administrations, under plans approved by the USSR Council of Ministers and Gosplan. In general, graduates of specialized and higher education have an obligation to work for three years where placed. Managers are forbidden to hire one of these graduates without a certificate directing him to the job, unless he has received formal permission to find his own work. Thus the state seeks both to assure jobs to all the young people according to their choice of fields and training and to see that they are used where most needed.[16]

------

[16] The system of directing graduates to work with a term of obligatory work for three years where sent was established in 1928. The 1940 adoption of the Labor Reserve System provided for placement and an obligatory four year term of work for graduates of the Labor Reserve Schools. Before the repeal of the 1940 laws these young graduates like all other workers were liable to harsh criminal penalties if they left jobs without permission or failed to take the jobs assigned. To what extent such penalties may have been used against refusal to accept work assigned, we have no evidence. In the later years they had been replaced by moral pressure. The obligatory term of work for vocational school graduates seems to have been dropped.

Planned placement of new entrants is one of the major methods of achieving the desired distribution of the labor force. Soviet spokesmen insist that the temporary limitation on free choice for "young specialists" does not mean compulsion, and that there are no penalties for refusal to take jobs assigned. Many young people tell how they declined jobs offered and found preferred work or opportunity to continue study. Yet there seems to be a strong sense of moral obligation to work where needed, after education at the government's expense, and this is heightened by social pressure from youth organizations and the public. The student can present objections to the proposed assignment, and often is given a choice or may be permitted to find his own job. The commissions consider the student's wishes and health and family circumstances. Regulations issued by the Ministry of Higher and Specialized Secondary Education put specific obligations on authorities carrying out the distribution and on the employing agencies; but they lay down only general obligations on the graduates to take the assignments and work for the stated term. If a graduate does not take the job assigned or leaves it ahead of schedule, he is expected to repay any sums given him for his journey to the place of employment; if he leaves the job without an acceptable excuse, his record of continuous work is broken.

Many criticisms are made of the way this system operates. There is concern over the number of young specialists who refuse to go where assigned and over those who do not continue in the occupation for which they were trained, or who exercise their right to return home after the required period. Enterprises are criticized for failing to use graduates according to their training and with proper living and working conditions; when conditions do not meet required standards, the young specialists have the right to refuse the work. Efforts were made in 1963 to improve the distribution and use of these specialists, and to put pressure on them to fulfill their obligations. Jobs were to be assigned a year in advance, and practice work was to be carried out in the enterprise of future work when possible. Only temporary certificates were to be given on graduation from higher and specialized education, diplomas to be issued after one year's work.

The needs of enterprises for young workers and specialists are expected to be met, in general, by local and regional educational systems. When the numbers of youth exceed the local need for additional labor, shifts of young people for work or training in other areas are possible through coordination at the republic level. Even secondary school graduates can be sent, with their consent, to other districts within the republic, or, with permission of the USSR Council of Ministers, to other regions of the East or North where they are needed.

The problem of finding jobs arises also for adults, especially peasants who leave for industry, women who wish to enter or return to the labor market, people whose construction jobs or other temporary work have terminated, and workers released by technological change or other causes of staff reduction. Others who need to find work include any who have been discharged for disciplinary reasons, or have left jobs by their own choice, or who for family or other personal reasons have come to the locality; also demobilized soldiers and persons released by an amnesty or after serving a sentence, or any brought into the labor market by warnings under the "anti-parasite laws."

Local employment exchanges went out of existence early in the 1930's, as there was said no longer to be any unemployment. When economists were asked in 1959 why there was no coordinated local organization for recruiting and placing workers, their answer was in effect, "There is no need. There is no unemployment. It is a question of choosing jobs, not finding jobs." The enterprises themselves have the largest role in local recruiting. Methods used include "open door days" for youths finishing general education schools, group and individual talks with workers about to be released from other enterprises or with demobilized soldiers, and different forms of publicity. People generally find jobs for themselves through notices at factory gates, newspaper and radio ads, and street bulletin boards, and through the spread of job information by friends and fellow workers. In many cities in 1955, 1959, and 1962 large bulletin boards on the streets showed numerous unfilled demands for all types of workers.

Although there are no coordinated job information and placement services, regional economic councils are expected to arrange placement of workers released from other jobs. In the larger cities, commissions on labor placement of the district soviet executive committees may aid any who come to them for help, but these are seldom mentioned except for their responsibilities for youths and demobilized service personnel. Their work is said generally not to be based on the labor balance of the area, nor to have enough contact with enterprises. Moscow has a Department of Resettlement and Organized Recruitment, and an Information Bureau with street kiosks. All of these may supply information on job openings. City party committees were reported in 1959 to have lists of people not employed, whom they tried to place. Trade unions may help to find jobs for their members. A complaint appearing in 1957, however, probably continued to be typical:

In a city, job placement is handled to some extent by everyone—special committees of local soviets, officials of various public organizations and militia departments. This results in an immense waste of time, and unnecessary phone calls and paper work. This lack of coordination does not help those who honestly want to work but for some reason have not been able to find a job.

A growing body of expert opinion has called for improved placement machinery, in order to avoid the wastes of lack of full information among plant managers on the availability of workers, and among workers on openings in their fields. Some argue also for strengthened obligations to find jobs for workers displaced. No unanimity had developed on these questions. Many believed that no further machinery was needed, or feared bureaucratic interference with local management of labor placement. Development of a well-coordinated system of employment exchanges to meet the needs of the dynamic economy appeared to have been hindered by the official dogma that there is no unemployment.

In a 1965 book, however, a leading authority of the Institute of Economics, M. Ya. Sonin, argued that good organization of the process of distribution of labor resources was not so simple as thought by some who "master only that truth" that under socialism there was no objective basis for unemployment. He insisted that it was wrong "to hide behind our advantages" and to decline active organized work on this "great and complicated business" which to this time proceeds "with great costs for society." He proposed a system of organs from the national to regional and local levels, relating the work of authorities in technical-vocational education, organized recruitment, and planning. Their duties would be to study labor resources and work out proposals for their use, to provide for meeting the needs of enterprises for workers and of youths and others for job placement, to help enterprises and administrations in the retraining and placement of workers displaced by mechanization, and to provide information on opportunities and conditions in other areas and arrange for recruitment.

ORGANIZED RECRUITMENT

Only for major recruitment needs for distant areas has there been a coordinated system—the Administration for Organized Recruitment of Workers, or Orgnabor—supplemented after 1953 by mass appeals and recruitment by the Komsomol, the Young Communist League, for work in the East. Orgnabor originated in 1931. The great flow of labor from the villages to industry was handled through Orgnabor contracts made by enterprises with collective farms and individual peasants, under governmental regulation. Quotas for the number of peasants to be released for industry were established by the planning authorities. From 2½ to 3 million came to industry each year from 1932 to 1940 through this chief form of recruitment for the major branches of industry.

After 1947, to avoid competition between industries in the same village, the Central Administration for Organized Recruitment made contracts with ministries for leading industries to recruit planned numbers of workers. Later, responsibility was given to the councils of ministers of the republics. Plans for interrepublic shifts of labor must be approved by Gosplan and the USSR Council of Ministers.

The role and significance of Orgnabor changed after the war. It became chiefly an agency for planned redistribution of labor between branches of industry and regions. By 1956, two-thirds of the recruits came from the cities. Recruitment for the old industrial centers fell sharply, though it increased for the North and East. The average annual number signed up for permanent work through Orgnabor fell to little over 500,000 for 1956–1958; seasonal workers signed up were about 200,000 each year. For the country as a whole, Orgnabor in 1958 supplied only 5.8 percent of those hired in manufacturing, compared with 13 percent in 1950; for construction, only 9.3 percent as against 29.8 percent in 1950. It continued to have an important role in supplying forces for developing industries and big construction projects in the East and North. Orgnabor also handled resettlement of whole families, especially collective farmers, for permanent residence and work on the new farms in the sparsely settled areas of the East. Some returned home, dissatisfied with conditions; others left the farms for industry, helping to fill the need for industrial labor. Beginning in 1958 it also recruited skilled workers and engineers on requests from sovnarkhozy.

Local Orgnabor offices, under republic Administrations for Organized Recruitment and Resettlement, conduct information programs, check on requests for labor, and sign up workers for jobs in other areas. Contracts are made in the name of enterprises for short period seasonal work, or for one to three-year terms, or more recently for permanent work. Cost of transfer is paid, suitable housing and training when needed are guaranteed, and additional lump sum benefits are given for work in distant areas. On completion of the term, cost of the return journey is paid. The worker may also sign for further terms, or, in many cases, he may stay for permanent work.

Some economists believe that Orgnabor has outlived its usefulness. As it concentrated on short term contracts, most of those recruited ultimately returned home. It was criticized for not adjusting to changes in the character of the labor force and the needs of industry. Complaints were made of poor selection, of sending "floaters" or "undisciplined workers." Skilled recruits were often sent to jobs without regard for previous training and experience. Since Orgnabor usually recruited for one enterprise, in only one or two districts, it had limited ability to find the skills needed by industry and to offer workers a choice of openings in their present fields. The result was loss of skills and need for retraining. Recruitment was often carried out in disregard of available local resources. Enterprises often failed to use recruits according to their qualifications and to provide proper housing and working conditions, knowing that Orgnabor would supply more workers on request.

It is generally thought that while improvements in its methods are needed, Orgnabor still has a place, especially in supplying workers for big construction projects and in facilitating shifts of workers released by technological change. If wasteful mobility is to be avoided, however, there is need for increased local responsibility for full use of labor resources, and more attention to providing suitable living conditions and consumers' services in the areas to which people are sent.

Starting in 1954, Orgnabor was overshadowed by the mass appeal, "public call-up," carried out by the party and especially the Komsomol for work in distant areas. The huge drives for agriculture in the "new lands" of Kazakhstan, and for construction and industry in the East and North were conducted, on the whole, by such mass appeals to young men and women. Meetings were held in plants, newspapers were filled with reports and appeals, and the Komsomol took special responsibility for encouraging volunteering, clearing applications and arranging for placement and transfer of those chosen. Party discipline could require volunteering, if necessary, and at times the pressure of "public opinion," with the possibility of reprisals against "slackers," amounted to coercion to "volunteer." There was also the appeal of adventure and pioneering, and of patriotism. Young people signing up received benefits similar to those under Orgnabor.

Hundreds of thousands responded. The number of volunteers was said to be always larger than the number sent. In 1959 the secretary of the Komsomol reported that over one million had gone to work in agriculture, and on new construction projects in the East—hydroelectric stations, steel plants, and others. Hardships were often severe when housing and other facilities were not ready or when farms and enterprises did not provide the promised training or use the recruits effectively. Retraining was often required when there were unnecessary shifts of occupation. In spite of the high morale with which many volunteers came, many left. It is said, nevertheless, that no other method of recruiting could in so short a time have met the needs for huge numbers of new workers in these areas and that these recruits proved much more stable, as permanent members of work forces, than those sent by Orgnabor.

During the seven-year plan, this method of mass appeals continued to have an important role in providing workers for developing areas. Efforts were made to improve its effectiveness by setting up special recruiting commissions with members from the party, the Komsomol, local soviets, and representatives of the sovnarkhozy and enterprises wanting workers, and by recruiting at enterprises and organizations with workers above the planned numbers. Administrative organizations were enjoined to do more to provide proper living conditions, cultural facilities, training, and other needs.

Thus the Soviet system, with its ideology of the right to work and the duty to work, its planning, and its propaganda, developed characteristic forms of recruitment and placement that met, at least to a degree, the basic requirements of the developing industries and areas. The need continued for better methods of assuring the voluntary and prompt shift of people to enterprises and areas where needed, and inducements for them to remain there on a stable basis.

UNPLANNED MOBILITY AND THE PROBLEM OF TURNOVER

Excessive turnover of industrial labor was a problem during the period of rapid industrialization.[17] Under conditions of great labor shortages, with an inexperienced labor force and inadequate working and housing conditions, efforts of workers to better themselves by shifting jobs could not entirely be suppressed, even if this had been desired. Measures to promote stability included incentives, penalties, compulsion, and attempts to develop "self-discipline and responsibility." The problem came to the fore again after the 1956 repeal of the 1940 law prohibiting any leaving of jobs without permission.

At the party congress in 1961, concern was expressed over the costs of unnecessary turnover, and the problem continues to receive attention. No comprehensive turnover statistics are published currently, but rates seem not to have been excessively high in general, and to have decreased from prewar rates. After 1957, turnover is said to have decreased under the influence of reduced hours, improved housing and living conditions, and changes in wage systems. The percent leaving jobs in industrial enterprises by choice or on disciplinary discharge is reported to have fallen by 1956 to one-fourth that of 1932, and by 1960 to one-half the 1956 figure. A Western scholar estimated in 1961 that average rates of turnover per month had ranged recently between 3 and 4 percent in most regions and industries—rates not far from those in the United States and the United Kingdom. The Institute of Labor of the State Committee on Labor and Wages reported in 1963, on the basis of an extensive study of turnover, that currently in the majority of enterprises 85–90 percent of the labor force was stable, but that monthly turnover in some amounted to 1.5 to 2 percent of the average force. This meant a substantial loss to the state, since the time between jobs for many workers amounted to 10–15 days or more. Workdays lost by newly hired workers had varied from about 15 days in Moscow up to over 30 in several of the more distant regions where interregional migration was a major influence. An average loss of time of 30 days is frequently mentioned. Unnecessary turnover results not only in loss of worktime, but also in lower initial productivity on new jobs, and in costs of retraining the many who change occupations when they shift jobs. For all industry and construction the annual loss from turnover is estimated at almost 3 billion rubles.

The extent of turnover varies between regions, with disastrously high rates in construction and in other industries in the East and North. A Siberian study found that while 700,000 came to Siberia from 1956 to

---

[17] For an excellent study see R. Fakiolas, "Problems of Labor Mobility in the USSR," *Soviet Studies,* Vol. XIV, No. 1 (July, 1962), pp. 16–40; also Mary Harris, "Social Aspects of Labour Turnover in the USSR," *British Journal of Industrial Relations,* Vol. II, No. 3 (November, 1964), pp. 398–417.

1960 through organized recruitment programs, and a still larger number came independently, more left than came in. Three cities of the Krasnoyarsk area lost within three years about half of those arriving from 1956 to 1960. A construction trust in Kemerovo in 1962 hired 13,000 and lost 8,500 workers. Such reports are numerous.

Much of the turnover is caused by workers shifting to enterprises, industries, and areas where they are needed, or leaving for study. This is recognized as corresponding to social interests. But when workers move to better themselves, it is said that the individual movements "far from always answer the interests of society."

The Central Statistical Administration includes in its figures of "instability of personnel" (*tekuchest' kadrov*) all who leave by choice or on disciplinary discharge; this is criticized by Institute of Labor experts, who consider that many who leave by their own choice belong in reality with the group of "organized" shifts, and that accordingly current figures of instability should be reduced by about one-third to indicate the extent of harmful turnover.

Ways to decrease the wasteful shifts have been sought through a number of studies of the causes of turnover. The most extensive, by the Institute of Labor, covered 70,000 workers from 670 enterprises in a wide range of industries and regions. One, by the Siberian Division of the Academy of Sciences, covered 4,700 workers who left 60 enterprises in Krasnoyarsk. Another, by the Leningrad Public Institute of Social Research, studied almost 11,000 newly hired workers in 25 enterprises of 12 major industries who had shifted jobs. The Institute of Labor found that about 17 percent of all shifts were through organized channels—Orgnabor, recruitment by public organizations, distribution of young specialists, and contracts with sovnarkhozy. Of the rest, the "unorganized shifts," the great majority were influenced directly or indirectly by state plans, especially investments in industrial, housing and other construction, and planned wage differentials. In the separations by the workers' own choice, in most industries 20–25 percent left for study, temporary family reasons, or to go on pension. Significant numbers went independently to work in the developing industries of the East and North, sometimes because there were overplan numbers in their own enterprises. Many young people shifted to be nearer educational institutions where they were studying. The Leningrad study found more than 25 percent of the movement related to study, or placement after graduation, and a significant part related to other social changes and shifts in industrial structure.

Separations by the worker's own choice were about 60 percent of all, according to the Institute of Labor's extensive study. Of these leavers, the great majority were young workers, 50 percent of them under 25 years and 85 percent under 35. Most of them were unskilled, 22 percent in common labor jobs. Most had worked not over three years, and almost a third of these had shifted twice or more during that time. In the Institute's sample, and also in the Leningrad and Krasnoyarsk studies, dissatisfaction with wages was not the main reason for quitting, though it was important in the low paid groups. Dissatisfaction with the work and working conditions was of far greater importance. Living conditions, including the character of housing and its distance from the job, and lack of places for children in kindergartens and nurseries ranked high in the reasons for quitting, especially in some localities. The Institute of Labor and Krasnoyarsk studies, which included all leavers, not only those newly hired as in the Leningrad study, showed very large groups leaving the region, or stopping for education, pensions, or temporary reasons. The Leningrad study of newly hired workers who had shifted jobs showed disciplinary discharges, but they accounted for only 1.4 percent of the job shifts. These three studies of reasons for turnover in areas with differing conditions are summarized below:

Reasons for Leaving Jobs	Institute of Labor %	Krasnoyarsk %	Leningrad %
Wages	13.8	17.5	23.5
Work and working conditions	17.4	13.9	37.4
Living conditions	15.9	19.4	29.9
Leaving the region	25.4	17.5	—
Stopping work	18.3	—	—
Education	—	5.2	—
Disciplinary discharge	—	—	1.4
Other	9.2	26.5	7.8
	100.0	100.0	100.0

It is clear from these and other reports that reduction of unwanted turnover requires more attention to working and living conditions. Some of the deficiencies can be removed only by added assignment of resources for improvements; some can be done by enterprises themselves. It is also clear that in many plants workers leave because of heavy unmechanized labor, irregular work, inequalities between enterprises in pay for equal work, lack of opportunities to improve skills; and because of arbitrary managements, inadequacies in the introduction of new workers to their jobs, and failure to provide young workers with proper living conditions and opportunity to study. Mistakes in distribution of housing, especially lack of housing near the place of work, cause many shifts. Managements and unions, planning and educational organs, Orgnabor and other recruitment systems, all are urged to work on these problems. The Leningrad study, which gave details of reasons for quitting in different industries and occupations, and for groups of young workers and women, was able to direct attention especially to improvements that should be made by plant managements in the interest of stabilizing their labor forces.

To a degree, job shifting is inhibited by indirect influences. The requirement of a passport, registered with the police and presented to the new employer along with the labor book, may prevent unauthorized movement to the old centers, although this requirement is not always successfully enforced, at least in Moscow. Difficulty in finding housing is a major check on mobility. The control by enterprises over allotments of land for gardens, and the possibility of their loss may hinder movement. In some of the older centers increased difficulty in finding other jobs may make work forces more stable.

Direct inducements meant to promote job stability included shorter hours and longer vacations for work under potentially harmful conditions; additional vacations for long service in major industries; preference in housing and variations in disability benefits and pensions related to length of continuous service. New wage systems introduced from 1956 on, however, reduced the former supplements to wages for long uninterrupted service in major industries as not decisive in holding workers and as interfering with the other aim of tying earnings to "the quantity and quality of labor." Wage benefits for long service were maintained primarily only for workers in a number of branches of heavy industry, and especially for underground workers.

Since the repeal of the 1940 restrictions on changing jobs, only two weeks' notice of intention to leave is required, and the record of uninterrupted work is preserved to those leaving by choice if a new job is taken within thirty days; it is preserved, also, for any period if the worker leaves for education or other approved reason. At first, with some exceptions, persons leaving by choice lost the right to temporary disability pay until they had worked six months on a new job, but this limitation was dropped on January 25, 1960.

These varied influences, and inducements, have more impact on older, established workers than on the young. It is not surprising that the larger part of the job shifts are among younger workers who have not yet settled down to the rather permanent attachment to an enterprise that is characteristic. Efforts to promote stability, accordingly, are directed especially toward young workers, as well as toward those who are considered "flitters and self-seekers," putting their own interests above those of society.

Continuous efforts are made through the press, the unions, the party, and older workers in the plants, to promote habits of stability, and to censure those who move irresponsibly. From 1962 to 1964, there was much talk about possibilities of reducing turnover by further rewards for long service and penalties for shifting jobs without adequate reason. Delay in adopting any such proposals suggests that authorities were concerned with the reaction of workers to any limitation of their freedom to change jobs. The fact that, as one union leader said, "The workers would not like it," probably held back changes in the laws. Also the investigations were making clear that basic reasons for turnover were to be found in working and living conditions.

Union committees in many plants sought to reduce turnover by giving more attention to the conditions of young workers and to removing causes of dissatisfaction. Some of them arranged to talk with every worker who applied to leave. Often they could learn the sources of discontent and eliminate them so that the worker was willing to stay. This form of social pressure seems to have brought constructive results in improving conditions and stabilizing work forces.

WAGES AND THE DISTRIBUTION OF MANPOWER

Wage differentials based on the principles of "the material self-interest of workers in the results of their work" and "pay according to the quantity and quality of labor" are an important means of influencing workers' decisions in choosing fields and jobs, and managers' decisions in hiring and utilizing workers. The structure of differentials is designed to compensate for differences in training, skill, and effort, and for difficulties or dangers in working or living conditions. In addition, differentials are used to promote employment in occupations, industries, and regions of special national significance. A major incentive for the Soviet worker to work where and as the government wants, is his opportunity in this way to increase his earnings and acquire a claim to a larger share of the still scarce consumers' goods.

Since wages are too important to be left for determination by market forces and private decisions, wage standards are centrally established. Before 1957, with administration of wages mainly in the hands of central industrial ministries, there were great variations and inequalities between industries. Reorganization of industrial administration put wage planning and administering largely under regional economic councils. At the same time, standards for differentials of all types came under strong central control. In 1955 a State Committee of the Council of Ministers on Questions of Labor and Wages was set up to strengthen state control and insure uniformity in regulating wages. The entire wage structure was revised gradually in a nation-wide wage reform that was completed for industry by 1962.

The structure of wage rates consists of the base rates (*stavka*) for the lowest wage grade and the schedules (*setka*) of percentage increases for the higher grades, for each occupation. These are determined by the government—the Council of Ministers in key cases, and in others by the State Committee on Labor and Wages in agreement with the Central Council of Trade Unions. Job evaluation handbooks approved by the State Committee and the CCTU set rules for allocation of jobs and workers by wage grades. Earnings are determined by wage rates and incentive systems. Wage systems, production standards, and details of premium systems established in the plants are expected to conform to central standards.

Wage differentials are intended to be large enough to induce entrance into more difficult and needed occupations and to provide incentives to increase skills. Differentials for skill became very large under the pressure of great scarcity of workers as industrialization proceeded.[18] Before the wage reform, base rates for the top grade in many schedules ranged from 1.8 to 4 times the rate for the lowest grade. In order to attract and hold workers, managers also established low production standards and piece rates that permitted high earnings. Actual earnings of skilled workers were sometimes 4 to 8 times the base rates for the unskilled. Such extreme differentiation became unnecessary as levels of education and skill increased and as mechanization reduced the differences in skill required. Minimum wages were raised and base rates were adjusted to give substantial increases in the lower grades. In most branches of industry the new schedules adopted after 1956 provided a range of rates giving the most skilled group only 1.8 or 2 times the lowest rate. Special higher rates are provided in crucial cases and for work under hot, arduous, or harmful conditions. While no comprehensive wage statistics are available, a 1961 study reported that differentials in earnings have been decreasing since the early 1950's, especially since the wage reform. It was expected that differentials for the most skilled could be reduced in the future to 80 percent or even 60 percent above the lowest rates and still give incentives for doing more complex work.

Industrial and regional differentials also are used to attract workers. During the early 1920's, consumers' goods industries led in earnings, but the drive for industrialization brought greater increases in heavy industries. Even before the war, wage levels in the coal, iron and steel, oil, and machinery industries were brought to the top. In these, and others important for war production, and in regions where climatic and living conditions created hardships, further increases were given during and after the war. Differences in average wages between branches of industry increased during the 1950's. In 1960, the ranking of a group of 17 industries by average wages showed coal at the top, then iron ore, iron and steel, oil, paper and pulp, chemical, machinery, and electric power production. Further down were textiles, woodworking, printing, footwear, and at the bottom, food processing and garment manufacture. Levels of average earnings reported for eleven industries in 1959 ranged from 182.7 for the coal industry, compared with all industry as 100, to

---

[18] Cf. Murray Yanowitch, "Trends in Soviet Occupational Wage Differentials," *Industrial and Labor Relations Review*, Vol. 13, No. 2 (January, 1960), pp. 166–91.

65.8 for the sewing industries. The gap between industries was said to be narrowing as the reform increased wages for the lower-paid workers.[19]

Under the post-1955 central regulation of wages, attempts are being made to develop scientific criteria for determining wage levels for different jobs and industries. Differentials are said to take account of difficulties in working conditions, complexity of the work and the skill required, territorial distribution, and national economic significance of the industry. Studies in the Institute of Labor have tried to estimate the relative effect of these factors on wage levels, but it is not clear to what extent the actual planning of wage changes has been based on such considerations. Differentials between industries are expected to decline further under the policy of raising low wages, the decreasing necessity for extreme differentials for skill, and improving conditions. In addition, the industries of national economic significance are no longer under so much pressure of labor shortages. It is said that labor supply is now basically a regional, not branch, problem.

Regional differentiation continues to be emphasized to stimulate shifts of workers to the rapidly growing areas by compensating for differences in living conditions, prices, and availability of consumers' goods and public services. A great variety of practices had grown up under regulation by the industrial ministries, each with its own wage zones and supplements for work in difficult regions. The result was a hodge-podge, with inequities between industries and between workers of similar skills in the same regions. In 1956, a start was made toward a more uniform system. Regional coefficients were approved, providing additions to the base rates in coal and other industries as their new wage systems were established. The coefficients ranged from 1:00 in the central, south, and western European parts of the Soviet Union, to 1:10–1:20 in the Urals, southwest Siberia, Kazakhstan, and Middle Asia; more for other remote regions and up to 1:50–1:70 for the Far North. The highest coefficient, for the Far North, was said to represent about 10 points for differences for the arduousness of work, 40 points for differences in living conditions, including higher prices, and 10 points for the relatively smaller supplements to wages from government services.

For personnel in the Far North, further incentives are given, under a law of February 10, 1960, which replaced the earlier variety of benefits. On top of the regular zone coefficients, workers receive supplements to

---

[19] The relationship of average wages in 1959 was as follows: all industry 100; coal 182.7; iron and steel 128.9; oil 103.9; paper 102.7; machine tool and metal fabrication 99.8; chemical 92.7; woodworking 85.7; leather, fur and footwear 82.9; textile 78.8; food 73.8; sewing 65.8. A report published in 1964 gave average wages for a few industries, compared with the food industry as 100; for textiles 107, machine tools 135, iron and steel 166, coal 230. This indicates a little narrowing of the gap, as the 1959 level for iron and steel and coal, according to the data above, was respectively 175 and 247 in comparison with the food industry.

monthly pay depending on length of service, in addition to extra vacations and increased disability pay. Special benefits are provided for those transferring on Orgnabor contracts for five years, or other similar transfers. One year of work in these regions from 1945 to 1960 is counted as two years, and from March 1960 as a year and a half, for the record of service that determines pension rights.

Except for the Far North, not all workers and industries are covered by the new zonal wage system. Inequities, not yet entirely eliminated, still limit the effectiveness of regional differentials as a means of assuring stable work forces. In addition, higher wages and money benefits are not enough to hold workers in the East and North when normal living conditions are lacking. An expert from the State Committee on Labor and Wages suggested that major differences in conditions, in some regions, should be compensated by additional expenditures from public funds on housing and communal and cultural services. Regional additions to wages could then be reduced, except in the Far North, although some differentials would continue to be needed because of variations in prices and climatic conditions, and temporarily for rapidly growing industries in these areas.

The Soviet planned wage system is not entirely different in its operations from that of a free labor market. It has necessarily responded to changing conditions of demand and supply, although both were influenced by planning. When unskilled labor was abundant, wages for the less skilled were very low. During the rapid growth of industry, wage differentials played a role in attracting labor. As education and experience increased the relative amount of skilled labor, and decreased that of unskilled, large differentials were less needed, earnings at the lower levels increased, and enterprises tended to avoid classifying workers in the lowest wage grades. General increases were made later in minimum wages and in rates for the lower wage grades. Higher wages continued to be paid in occupations and regions with labor shortages. Earnings thus responded to changes in the demand and supply of labor and to the rise of productivity. Groups strategically placed in relation to demands obtained higher earnings, in part according to plan, and in part by manipulations in the incentive systems. However, when unjustified differentials resulted in unwanted mobility, rigidities in the centrally determined standards limited the freedom of managers to adjust earnings. Soviet experts hope that scientific bases for all differentials will make these "levers" more effective in the future for the planned distribution and redistribution of the labor force.

ACHIEVEMENTS AND PROBLEMS

Over the years, for training and distributing its labor force, the USSR developed methods and institutions on the whole fitting the needs of the centrally planned economy with its principles of the duty of citizens to work and their right to work. Growth of the economy and of modern industry was accompanied by the development of an increasingly educated, skilled, and experienced working class. Harsh controls over labor were modified to allow more freedom of job choice. A combination of planning with a degree of freedom to respond to market forces served, to a workable extent, the interests both of the state and of individuals.

Many unsolved problems continued and were under study. Among the difficulties of planning for a huge country and an increasingly complex economy, are those of forecasting needs for labor and of long-range planning for training in a time of dynamic changes in technology. Deficiencies in analysis and planning in the regions limited the success of efforts to achieve full and productive use of labor. Continuing inadequacy of resources to meet all needs has had adverse effects on manpower problems. Inefficient managements have failed to provide the conditions under which workers would settle down as stable members of the work force. There were wastes when huge numbers moved to, and from, new areas and enterprises and also when needed shifts were not adequately planned and facilitated. The efficiency and economy of job finding and recruiting appeared still to be limited by lack of local employment centers and a good system of clearance between areas.

The claim of the Soviet Union to have no unemployment rests in part on terminology. By definitions used elsewhere there is evidence both of unemployment and underemployment. Seasonal lack of work, frictional loss of time between jobs, and lost time in the plants are recognized problems. Technological unemployment is probably felt temporarily in some cases, or it takes the form of underutilization of workers no longer needed. There is underutilization of labor resources also when women are unable to work because of the structure of local industry or inadequate provision of services.

Large scale unemployment is avoided by the continuing growth of the economy and by planned training and retaining, placement, and recruitment; by reluctance to displace workers; and by underemployment of workers inefficiently and unproductively employed on farms, in factories, in street work, public housekeeping, and other fields. Soviet workers do not suffer from mass unemployment, and the Soviet state avoids the waste and tragedy of such failure to use its human resources. Yet the cost of failure to use the whole labor force fully and effectively is spread over the entire population in the form of lower incomes resulting from the low level of productivity. This may be called the "Soviet equivalent of unemployment."[20] And any who are involuntarily out of work for a time are without unemployment insurance protection.

---

[20] I am indebted for this phrase to Dr. Robert J. Myers of the United States Bureau of Labor Statistics.

Freedom of citizens to choose their fields of training and their jobs is enough on the whole to serve the interests of individuals and of the state. Educational opportunities have greatly expanded, though they are still not enough to meet the demands of Soviet youth, and political and other forms of discrimination are possible. The ideal of equality of opportunity has wide enough effect, in practice, to open the door both for individuals to develop their capacities and for the economy to develop its human resources and the needed skills. Public interest in the distribution of labor, and individual interests in finding satisfactory work, are both served in the long run by freedom to choose jobs and to change jobs under the influence of planned incentives and political and economic conditions. Although turnover is a problem in many fields and a source of loss to the state, it also serves a social purpose. By changing jobs, workers express disssatisfaction and force attention of authorities to unsolved problems. The party and the state have continued to emphasize incentives for steady work and the development of responsible attitudes.

The Soviet labor market is not, and could not be, a free market. The planned elements are large and facilitate adjustment to change. At the same time workers are able to promote their own interests. Although official dogmas at times make realistic analysis more difficult, serious study of practical problems can be expected to lead toward pragmatic solutions in the interest both of the state and of individual workers.

11| KHRUSHCHEV'S AGRICULTURAL POLICIES

Jerzy F. Karcz

Soviet agriculture is backward both in comparison with Soviet industry and in comparison with agriculture in North America and Western Europe. The low level of productivity and the slow growth of output are attributable in part to unfavorable natural conditions of temperature, soil, and rainfall. The principal causes, however, are the low level of investment in agriculture and the lack of incentives for peasants on collective farms. The contrast in agricultural price policy between the Soviet Union and the United States is striking. While low procurement prices have led to food shortages in the Soviet Union, high price supports have contributed to agricultural surpluses in the United States.

Among the key features of Stalinist economic policy were the neglect of investment in agriculture and the imposition of a large share of the burden of industrialization on the peasantry through unfavorable terms of trade enforced by collectivization. Immediately after Stalin's death in 1953, his successors embarked on a broad program to raise agricultural output and marketings. Khrushchev is particularly identified with a number of dramatic steps affecting agriculture, including the "new lands" program, the abolition of machine-tractor stations, and the proclamation of extremely ambitious targets to "overtake and surpass" the United States in meat and milk production.

This selection carefully analyzes and evaluates Khrushchev's agricultural policies in a detailed case study of planning and administrative pressure in Soviet agriculture. It shows that the 1958 reforms, at the time widely regarded as "liberalizing" measures, in fact constituted a move back toward "command" methods, reversing the trend toward "marketization" which had begun in 1953. The selection concludes with a discussion of the continuing problems of Soviet agriculture and of the steps needed to achieve genuine improvements.

Jerzy F. Karcz is Professor of Economics at the University of California, Santa Barbara. The selection is excerpted from pp. 399–436 of his article, "Seven Years on the Farm: Retrospect and Prospects," in United States Congress, Joint Economic Committee, *New Directions in the Soviet Economy* (Washington, D.C.: U.S. Government Printing Office, 1966), Part II-B, pp. 383–450. Tabular material and most of the footnotes are omitted.

I. AGRICULTURAL POLICY, 1953–57

AT THE TIME of Stalin's death, Soviet agricultural output had stagnated for a period of some five years at about the level first reached in 1940. In per capita terms, the 1952 output was 4 percent higher, but conditions in agriculture were grim indeed. In 1952, the average cash and kind income received by a collective farmer from the socialized sector came to a startling 13 rubles a month, while the average wage for the rest of the economy was 66.6 rubles per month. Except for hogs, livestock herds were below levels of 1925. It was not surprising, therefore, that the new leadership undertook a revision of Soviet agricultural policy almost immediately after the dictator's funeral.[1] By the fall of 1953, its surviving members decided to lift partially the curtain of secrecy from the agricultural scene. In the winter of 1953–54, final touches were put to a "grand design for change" in Soviet agriculture.

The new design included the famous new lands program and ultimately also Khrushchev's attempt to adopt corn as a specialized feed-producing crop. The new lands venture can be viewed as a stopgap solution designed to increase grain supply rapidly and thus to gain time for the introduction of badly needed institutional reforms in the agricultural sector. The risks inherent in such a large expansion of acreage in a basically hostile natural environment were cushioned considerably by the rather surprising bequest left by Stalin. In 1952, Soviet grain reserves came to about 32 to 35 million tons, or to a level approximately equal to either the annual grain procurements, or to total government grain disposals for all purposes.[2] The existence of this reserve gave the new leaders a sense of security that may have strengthened their propensity to engage in risky ventures.

While preparations for the new lands campaign were going on, other new measures were being introduced. Farm prices were raised, first for grain in June of 1953 and in the fall for other products as well. By 1954, the total burden of direct taxes on the agricultural population declined by

---

[1] For a more complete analysis of policy since 1953, see the following: Jerzy F. Karcz and V. P. Timoshenko, "Soviet Agricultural Policy, 1953–62," *Food Research Institute Studies*, Vol. IV, No. 2 (May, 1964), pp. 123–63; Nancy Nimitz, "Agriculture Under Khrushchev: The Lean Years," *Problems of Communism*, Vol. XIV, No. 3 (May–June, 1965), pp. 10–22; Jerzy F. Karcz, "The New Soviet Agricultural Programme," *Soviet Studies*, Vol. XVII, No. 2 (October, 1965), pp. 129–61; and Frank A. Durgin, Jr., "Monetization and Policy in Soviet Agriculture Since 1952," *Soviet Studies*, Vol. XV, No. 4 (April, 1964), pp. 375–407.

[2] Nancy Nimitz, *Soviet Government Grain Procurements, Dispositions and Stocks, 1940, 1945–1963*, RM-4127-PR (Santa Monica, Calif.: The RAND Corp., 1964), p. 58.

about 53 percent (while that on the nonagricultural population dropped only by 24 percent). Compulsory deliveries from households were reduced in 1953; four years later they were eliminated altogether.

Substantial efforts also took place in the collective farm sector as such. The kolkhoz was designed primarily as an instrument of collection of farm products for the state. In some respects, the artel bears a striking resemblance to the prerevolutionary repartitional village (the mir). Both institutions were set up to assist the state in the performance of some of its functions.[3] In both cases equity was a major underlying consideration, though concern was shown primarily for an equitable distribution of poverty.[4] Neither institution in its original form had been particularly well suited for the task of securing rapid improvements in productivity and the concomitant rise in the level of output.[5]

In March 1955, planning procedures for collective farms had been simplified and a measure of genuine autonomy was granted to the farms, as direct planning of output by agencies of the state was replaced by a (physical) constraint of a sales quota assigned to each farm. Calculations of production costs on collective farms were introduced for the first time. Efforts were also made from 1956 on to introduce guaranteed labor remuneration on many farms. In 1958, state-owned machine-tractor stations were abolished and their equipment sold to collective farms. Simultaneously, the double-price system, which tended to perpetuate the backwardness of lagging farms, was also repealed. Under Stalin, barter-type transactions dominated exchange within the agricultural sector as well as many transactions between agriculture and the rest of the economy.[6] The greater monetization of agriculture, in conjunction with some of the other measures just discussed, increased the scope for greater (though still severely limited) autonomy in decisionmaking both at the household level as well as on the farm. Hence, the collective farm sector of Soviet agriculture during this period could be regarded as shifting slowly toward the market sector of the economy: as Gregory Grossman has recently shown, a movement of the sort offers substantial advantages to the ruling

---

[3] Both institutions assisted in the collection of taxes. The mir, of course, supported the military effort of the Russian state, while the kolkhoz that of industrialization.

[4] In the case of the mir, land distributions were based largely on the number of souls in the household. In the collective farm of the artel type, labor was remunerated on the labor-day basis. There are, of course, many other differences between these two types of institutions.

[5] Paradoxically, in both institutions the household had a direct interest in retaining as much as possible of the relatively abundant factor of production—labor. In the mir, this ultimately led to the acquisition of a greater acreage for use. In the collective farm, it enabled the household to devote more effort to the private plot or to outside employment.

[6] To wit: payments in kind, the milling tax, compulsory deliveries, and on the other hand the grants of machinery to MTS without any capital charges. Within the collective farm sector, the relative value of cash in total cash and kind value of the man-day was 36.5 percent in 1940 and 27.9 percent in 1952.

elite.[7] While all this was taking place, trends in output—that final measure of success—were very auspicious: in 1956 to 1958 (partly as a result of good weather), gross output exceeded the level of 1950–52 by 48.7 percent.

Yet, a closer consideration of these events reveals several discordant notes. It might not be improper to restate the obvious: all of the reforms just mentioned were introduced *ex cathedra* by the Communist Party. Adequate machinery for a truly meaningful consultation of the working masses or for the sampling of the opinion of experts did not exist in the USSR at that time. Given the fundamental nature of some of the reforms just mentioned, even extensive consultations with experts—from the groves of Academe or other levels of the government—could not guarantee enough honest and unbiased views. The Soviet intellectual had only recently been granted the right to express himself more freely in professional matters. With some outstanding exceptions, his advice would tend to be colored by what the adviser considered acceptable to the advisee. It is difficult to see how things could have taken a different course in the peculiar Soviet environment of the period. But the impact of all these features affected profoundly the very nature of the reforms: it made the resulting structure a good deal less appropriate for the hard tasks on hand and less resilient to external shocks than might otherwise have been the case. This statement applies with particular strength to the reorganization of the machine-tractor stations (MTS), pushed through with record speed.

Another flaw in the apparent picture of uninterrupted progress and liberalization may be detected in the attitudes toward the private sector. These revealed themselves in an increase in labor-input norms for the socialized sector (1954) and in serious restrictions on urban livestock holdings (1956).

More will be said on this issue presently. For the time being, though, we should note that much more is involved here than the simple Marxist antagonism toward private ownership of means of production (however limited) and toward the only remaining group of incipient capitalists in a socialist society. To be sure, political factors are relevant, but their importance tends to be exaggerated. Thus, for a Soviet organization man (Marxist or not) the private sector of the economy is an anomaly, if only because it is different from the others (just as much as the Volkswagen Corp. was an anomaly in the German Federal Republic prior to its

---

[7] Gregory Grossman, "Notes for a Theory of the Command Economy," *Soviet Studies*, Vol. XV, No. 2 (October, 1963), pp. 101–23. Among the advantages to the regime are (a) faster response from the market sector, (b) reduction in the burden of coordinative planning, (c) possibility of correlating incentives with results in the sector switching to the market, (d) higher morale and initiative in the sector located in the market area of the economy and (e) a possibility of shifting some costs and risks to this sector (this, of course, was taken care of in our case by the cooperative feature of the collective farm, regardless of the location of the sector in the market or the command area of the economy).

desocialization). Moreover, even though the urban consumer welcomes a chance to buy farm products on the collective farm market (and especially so when they are not available in the state store), he also resents high prices that peasants charge in these transactions. The resentment leads to the belief that particular peasants (though not necessarily the peasantry as a whole) grow too rich too fast. But again there is nothing exclusively Soviet in this attitude. The French *petit bourgeois* felt the same way during World War II about his neighbor on the farm, and so did an American college professor who looked with envy on a farmer driving a Cadillac in the immediate postwar period. Finally, there is the ambivalent attitude of the Soviet intelligentsia toward the peasantry as a whole (as well as toward the inhabitants of Soviet small towns—now regarded as "burghers" who are primarily interested in the ordinary business of living). The subject is much too complex to be analyzed here in detail. But the ambivalent attitude includes some resentment and is connected with the rationalization on the part of the intellectual of the relative achievements and failures of the Soviet regime. The upshot is that peasants as well as the "burghers" are viewed as failing to participate in the great task of constructing a "new society" based on a fuller, "more meaningful" life with the ultimate goal of a greater common welfare. From this standpoint, it is not material whether or not the attitude exists because of, in connection with, or in spite of the goals of the Communist Party. The important consequence is that the private sector of Soviet agriculture really has no friends outside of those who work the tiny plots of land in cities as well as in the villages. The best that can be said about those who do not object to it strenuously is that they tolerate it while the socialized sector fails to provide enough food at the present stage of the construction of communism.

It should also be borne in mind that in 1958, on 3.8 percent of total sown area (but with very considerable assistance from the socialized sector in the form of feed), the private sector produced the following percentage shares of the important farm products: potatoes, 66; vegetables, 45; meat, 52; milk, 53; eggs, 85; and wool, 22. At the same time, the importance of the collective farm market (including commission sales) in total sales of foodstuffs to the population was as follows (in percent): grain products (in grain equivalent), 8.4; potatoes, 65; vegetables, 36; milk, 10; meat, 22; eggs, 42. Thus, any measures directed against the private plot would affect the consumption of the nonagricultural population as well as that of households operating the private plot.

II. THE MTS REFORM AND GOALS OF THE SEVEN-YEAR PLAN

Measures Taken

The decision to lower machinery inputs in the agricultural sector under the seven-year plan was to have momentous consequences for

Soviet agriculture. A somewhat cryptic but revealing explanation of this decision has recently been supplied by A. A. Ezhevskii, presently chairman of the Association for the Supply of Agricultural Technology, who in 1958 was a director of the Gosplan department dealing with agricultural machinery. Ezhevskii states:

> When the plan for 1959–1965 was being constructed, these machines [in short supply] were "mortgaged." There were categorical objections from various departments of Gosplan against the proposed decline in the production of these types of agricultural machinery, since the existing supply did not allow for a timely conduct of work from the agrotechnical standpoint. The former chairman of Gosplan, comrad Kuz'min, categorically refused to agree [to proposals] for increasing the rate of growth of output of agricultural machinery. Certainly, he is not the only guilty one. As far as my own position on this issue is concerned, I should report to the Plenum directly and responsibly. At that time I personally urged an increase in production. Many here know the history of that problem, how matters stood, what unpleasantness there was when we tried to insist on the increase in output of agricultural machinery.

At the basis of this decision, states Ezhevskii, lay the belief that "after the sale of equipment to farms it would be used so much more efficiently that one could reduce sharply the output of these machines."

The connection between the decision to reduce machinery allocations to agriculture and the MTS reform of 1958 is supported by other evidence. The sixth five-year plan (1956–60) called for allocations of 1,650,000 tractors (in terms of 15-horsepower units) and 560,000 combines to agriculture. In December 1957, Kuz'min presented to the Supreme Soviet the annual plan for 1958. This gave goals for production of 155,000 tractors (or about 254,000 15-horsepower tractors) and 135,000 grain combines. Through the first quarter of 1958, output proceeded roughly at these annual rates. But the figure on the output of grain combines for the first six months of 1958 was not released in the semiannual plan fulfillment report; six-month allocations to agriculture came only to 37,000 combines. The MTS reorganization was decided upon in the spring of 1958. There is, therefore, no reason to suspect the validity of Ezhevskii's explanation (limited though it is) in other respects.

It will not be necessary to review in detail the rationale for MTS reorganization.[8] However, I would like to stress one point that is sometimes underestimated in this connection. The fact is that the MTS were simply not working very efficiently in the period 1955–57, and their crucial position as operators of mobile equipment endangered the very

---

[8] See Lazar Volin's exhaustive treatment of this question in United States Congress, Joint Economic Committee, *Comparisons of the United States and Soviet Economies* (Washington, D.C.: U.S. Government Printing Office, 1959), Part I, pp. 297–99. The reorganization eliminated dual management, strenthened the party apparatus in the countryside, and made it unnecessary to maintain duplicate agencies of control. Finally, the ability to purchase machines would offer an easy outlet for the collective farms' spending on investment.

balance of the agricultural sector in the performance of its tasks. Not only were there many complaints about inefficiency from the collective farms, but much capital was wasted on the stations (which turned out to be quite as willing as anybody else to accept a free factor of production until its marginal productivity was zero).[9] By November 1955, even Khrushchev seems to have given up hope of improving their operations within the existing framework:

No matter how we attempt to influence the MTS director, no matter what we tell him—it does not always get through to him. Apparently, reprimands alone do not suffice.

Early in 1957, the director of the All-Union Scientific Research Institute of Agricultural Economics, A. I. Tulupnikov, noted at the close of a conference that there was much that was obsolete in the relationship between the MTS and the collective farm. But, it was "now difficult to make well-founded proposals on new forms of this relationship though research should persistently seek these new forms."

The issue was not only delicate from the theoretical standpoint (it involved a transfer of state-owned property to collective farms) but also very complex. When Khrushchev first proposed publicly in January of 1958 that MTS equipment be sold to farms, a widespread debate ensued in which many voiced their apprehension about the ability of all collective farms to acquire machinery and to use it properly. Among those was K. T. Mazurov, now first deputy premier of the USSR. Khrushchev's impatience notwithstanding, it is clear that the issue could not and should not have been handled in a vacuum. A package deal was in order, covering also the existing system of procurement of farm products, the question of the level and structure of farm prices, and prices of the off-farm inputs that would in the future be purchased by collective farms. Khrushchev and his supporters sought to create the impression that economists objected to the reform primarily on obscure, theoretical grounds arising from Marxist-Leninist ideology. Actually, however, there was a good deal of opposition on relevant and more fundamental economic grounds. On the very eve of reform, the scientific council of Tulupnikov's institute came to the conclusion that the necessary conditions for sale of farm machinery to the collective farms simply did not exist. Under the circumstances, some unnamed but eminently sensible individuals proposed that weak collectives should receive machinery from MTS in the form of outright grants.

But all objections were brushed aside as Khrushchev argued successfully that the issue should be decided upon even before agreement on the level of prices at which the transfer should take place.

Ultimately, the total bill for the transfer of machinery and buildings to

---

[9] The complaints thus can be viewed in terms of the efficiency of MTS operation; this in turn is a separate problem from that of the existence of dual management.

collective farms came to 2.4 billion (post-1961) rubles, of which 1.8 billion was for machinery alone. Installment payments were allowed, and it was expected that rich farms would pay for the machinery within a year or two; average farms might take two to three years, while weak farms would liquidate their indebtedness within about five years. Khrushchev's time table in this respect turned out to have been remarkable principally for its boldness. Final results would obviously depend on the solution of the price and terms of trade issues relegated thoughtlessly to the near future.

In return, farms received machinery which was described in April of 1958 by a member of the Lenin Academy of Agricultural Sciences as consisting to the extent of "about three-fourths of machines and equipment which do not correspond to the contemporary level of technology and organization of production." The physical condition of the transferred machinery must have been far from impeccable. These two features account satisfactorily for the very high rate of retirement of agricultural machinery in 1958–60.

The issue of farm prices and farm terms of trade was handled in the summer of 1958. In June the government revamped the system of agricultural procurements and that of farm prices. Sales in the form of compulsory deliveries and the so-called state purchases were replaced by a system of (similarly compulsory) state purchases, quotas for which were to be established separately for each farm. This placed the relevant quota allocating authorities in the position of influencing to a very considerable extent the structure of output on an indidivual farm. Simultaneously, farms were no longer allowed to substitute one type of product for another in the fulfillment of state purchase quotas. Both features placed severe restrictions on farms, trying to exercise their recently acquired freedom to plan the structure of the output and the size of livestock herds.[10]

A single price system was also introduced, endowed with the provision of "flexible" prices for grains, sunflower, potatoes, and sugar beet. In anticipation of the record harvest, prices for these crops were immediately cut by 13, 15, and 10 percent, respectively.

The new price system turned out to be rather painful to collective farms, since the new level of aggregate farm prices was determined in a very peculiar way: the total procurement bill (on a comparable volume) was held down to the sum of the previous procurement bill and the expenditures on the maintenance of the machine-tractor stations.

---

[10] Some indication of the attitudes is provided by the statement of V. P. Mylarshchikov, directing the Agricultural Department for the RSFSR of the Central Committee of the Communist Party of the USSR, at the April 1958 session of the Academy of Agricultural Sciences. In one breath, Mylarshchikov declared that "we now have the new method of planning; no one plans sown areas or output (for collective farms), all problems are decided locally." A few moments later, he declared: "Comrades, this year there will be a major 'row' on the part of the party organization with respect to corn, and I will tell you honestly that it will be a violent row."

No significant effort was made to relate prices to costs in a meaningful way. On the whole, the new price structure favored producers of crops. In the livestock sector, the 1958 prices were much below the level of average costs. The new price structure was defective in other respects as well. While most prices varied regionally, within a given price zone (some of which were very large) the new prices allowed for a complete retention of rent and quasi-rents. Thus a much deplored feature of the pre-1958 double-price system continued to operate: most of the benefits would accrue to the prosperous farms, and the crucial task of eliminating the wide gap between performance of rich and lagging collectives would become more difficult.[11]

Nothing was done in 1958 to change the base upon which the tax on collective farm incomes was imposed. This continued to be computed on the basis of gross income. After the reform, the tax base was automatically expanded, since amounts previously delivered in the form of MTS payments in kind were now paid for by the state at prices that were high in relation to the earlier compulsory delivery prices.

Financial pressures on farms were also greater as a result of transfer of (relatively) higher paid MTS personnel, sale of many milk procurement points to collectives, and the planned rise in investment to 34.5 billion rubles in 1959–65, or to about 5 billion rubles annually. In 1952–58, collective farm investments came to a total of 13 billion rubles; even in 1956–58 collective farm investment proceeded at the annual rate of only 2.4 billion. Little was done to fill the rising needs by the allocation of additional government credits to agriculture. From 1957 to 1958 the allocation of gross credits to collective farms declined from 522 to 432 million rubles. Net long-term credits extended in 1958 were almost 50 percent below the level of 1956. (Their share in collective farm allocations to indivisible funds dropped from 18 percent in 1956 to 7.8 percent in 1957 and to 5.5 percent in 1958.) Short-term credit allocation in 1958 came to 375 million rubles: it had been 440 million in 1957 (as a percent of productive expenditures, short-term credit of the state bank advanced to collective farms came to 22.9 percent in 1957 but only to 11.9 percent in 1958). Moreover, the types of credit extended by the MTS were also eliminated with the stations themselves. Not the least advantage of these credits was the fact that a weak farm was able often to avoid repayment altogether, and received MTS services in the form of a de facto grant.[12]

Prices of off-farm inputs were also changed in 1958. In August, the Ministry of Agriculture of the USSR and its republican counterparts—in consultation with the USSR Ministry of Finance—established or re-

[11] Oddly enough, the Party was then well aware of the problem posed by the fact that significant achievements were reached only in a small number of farms. Mylarshchikov was quite explicit on this aspect.

[12] In 1950–53, over 16 million tons of grain were not paid by the collective farms for MTS work. This came to 19.6 percent of the total amount due to the MTS in this period.

viewed new prices for seeds, concentrated feed, fertilizers, machinery, and spare parts. Retail prices were now charged to collective farms for gasoline and concentrates. Machinery prices to collective farms increased from 5.6 to 69.5 percent. Prices of spare parts were raised by 100 to 120 percent.

Thus far we have been dealing with the impact of the 1958 reforms on collective farms as such. As far as the private sector was concerned, we note again the elimination of compulsory deliveries from the household plot which took effect at the beginning of the year. This was seemingly a beneficial measure, but it was accompanied by another regulation, which exerted a detrimental impact on operations of the private sector. From 1958 onward, the state discontinued sales of feed grains and concentrated feed to households; in 1953–56 these sales came to 700,000 to 750,000 tons annually.

Evaluation

Thus ended the most publicized and certainly the most important institutional reform of the Khrushchev era in Soviet agriculture, sometimes interpreted as the peak of his liberalizing efforts. With the benefit of hindsight, we must now give full credit to those Soviet economists who opposed the reform, for both their courage and the correctness of their analysis. There is no doubt that after the enactment of all the measures discussed above, the two most important sectors of Soviet agriculture— collective farms and private household plots—would operate in a very difficult environment. As a matter of fact, the 1958 reforms amounted to a reversal of the slow shift of agriculture toward the market sector of the economy. As the near future was to show, the most important consequence of these reforms consisted in the reintroduction of command elements into the agricultural sector. Given the tasks now imposed on farms, things could not have taken a different course. But here, as elsewhere, substitution of command for market-type controls was hardly conducive to greater efficiency.

Every schoolboy in the USSR knows that the collective farm is a cooperative organization and that its members are paid from products remaining on the farm after all other obligations are met. It should have been crystal clear therefore that the price of the mistakes associated with the MTS reform would be paid primarily by collective farmers.

Was this the intention of Khrushchev and those of his supporters who framed the final objectives of the seven-year plan? How can their actions be reconciled with the avowed aim of the plan to raise real incomes of collective farmers by "no less than 40 percent"? For obvious reasons, no clear-cut answer to this question can be made at this stage. But the economist can assist in the search for answers by formulating certain hypotheses that are at least not inconsistent with presently available evidence. Although all Soviet goals for increases in real incomes of peasant households should be viewed with skepticism, it seems to me that Khrushchev and his supporters deliberately altered the terms of trade of the farming sector and restricted the allocation of its inputs with the expectation that greater efficiency in the use of machinery (as well as greater enthusiasm of the masses for the task of construction of communism) would ultimately lead to rising productivity in agriculture, so that by 1965 output and peasant incomes would indeed climb to levels approaching those planned for 1965. As it turned out, this was a rather monumental miscalculation. But our hypothesis is quite consistent with several relevant considerations.

First, Khrushchev and those around him did on many occasions insist upon an almost immediate return (in the form of higher procurements, or output, or both) to greater allocations of machinery or government investment funds. The notion that a long gestation period may be necessary was evidently viewed with disfavor; indeed, Khrushchev made it clear that what ultimately convinced him of the necessity to increase output through expansion of sown area was the fact that the alternative required "a little too much time and too many resources."

Second, it also appears that by 1958–59, Khrushchev concluded that the relative standing of peasant and urban living standards had reached some kind of a satisfactory relationship (satisfactory, that is, to him).

Third, we know that in April 1958, in a speech to the Lenin Academy of Agricultural Sciences, the head of the Agricultural Department for the RSFSR of the Central Committee of the Communist Party of the USSR, V. P. Mylarshchikov, expressed no doubts about the ability of collective farms to function in the new environment. He did show some concern about the wisdom of producing defective or inappropriate machinery in large series, and he deplored the extraordinary long periods of time required for the performance of major agricultural tasks (such as sowing). But his speech is remarkably free of qualms about the quality of the on-farm machinery stocks and their size in relation to the task ahead. Earlier at the same session, Tulupnikov had enough courage to point out collective farm needs in the general area of credit and machinery supplies.

Fourth, it is difficult to reconcile measures affecting collective farms' terms of trade with any alternative hypothesis, except the one given above, or one even less favorable to the Soviet leadership: peasants were meant to pay for the success of the seven-year plan and the target for the rise in their income amounted only to window dressing.

Fifth, we must also consider the question of the abortive 1958 drive to revive the collective farm center or to set up a Central Council of Collective Farms. At least on one interpretation, associated with the weighty name of S. G. Strumilin, the agenda for the Council would include redistribution of income within the collective farm sector for the purpose of increasing the efficiency of weak and rundown farms. It is not known with certainty where Khrushchev stood on this issue in 1958, but at least one generally sympathetic observer believes that he probably endorsed the proposal.[13] The essence of this plan is strangely reminiscent of the "equitable distribution of poverty" which we find to have been characteristic of the mir and the Stalinist artel. If implemented, the proposal would have penalized efficient farms, might well have played havoc with the structure of farm incentives, and consequently exerted an adverse impact on trends in output. We should not wonder that those who opposed it had little trouble in making their views prevail in 1958 (as well as in 1959).

Sixth, there is no doubt that attitudes within the narrow circle of the top leadership were influenced heavily by the very real success in raising output during the years 1953–58. It is also clear that the causes of this success were imperfectly understood.

Finally, the hypothesis formulated here is fully consistent with long standing hostile attitude of the party toward the peasant sector. From this standpoint, Preobrazhenskii and Stalin are members of the same group.[14] So ultimately is Khrushchev, even though he did recognize quite clearly that Stalin had gone too far by 1952, and even though he was instrumental in raising the level of peasant incomes. He did so, I believe, not because his fundamental outlook was sympathetic to Narodnik ideology, but primarily because he considered this a necessary condition for further increases in output. Although the results of his policies (through 1957) were almost the same as could be expected of a genuine "liberalizer" the fundamental difference in outlook is of some consequence for the understanding of his policies in the subsequent period. Such weighty considerations apart, the heavy weight of tradition also suggested that if forced savings had to be extracted from anyone, it would better be someone in the peasant sector.

Two more questions remain to be considered before we proceed with the analysis of the 1959–65 period within the framework constructed thus far. The first deals with the consistency of the goals for agricultural policy with those of personal or disposable money incomes and household expenditures on food. Agricultural output under the seven-year plan was expected to rise by 70 percent and per capita output by some 56 percent. Abraham Becker's ingenious calculations of planned national income for 1965, taken in conjunction with our data, suggest that personal incomes were supposed to rise by 46 and disposable incomes by 53 percent. If

---

[13] Sidney I. Ploss, *Conflict and Decision Making in Soviet Russia* (Princeton: Princeton University Press, 1965), pp. 134–35. This book, which contains many valuable insights, suffers much from a fundamental defect of neglecting the merits of each issue. Its major conclusions are often distorted.

[14] Evgenii Preobrazhenskii, the outstanding economist of the "Left Opposition" of the twenties, argued that Soviet industrialization should proceed through the extraction of forced savings from peasants. This was to be done by raising prices of industrial goods (produced by state-owned industry) bought by the peasants. Preobazhenskii did not envisage massive collectivization of agriculture.

attention was paid to income elasticities of demand in 1958, the expectation probably was that expenditures on food would rise by some 48 to 50 percent. Hence, the plan contained a fairly comfortable margin to allow for the unpredictable impact of the weather, as well as for some increase in stocks and for exports.

But the decision to plan for such a large increase in output, given planned trends in the supply of off-farm inputs and the apparent disregard of peasant incentives in the short run, reveals a monumental unconcern for the true nature of the aggregate production function in agriculture, and a propensity to dismiss the results of dispassionate economic calculation in favor of the time-honored slogan: "Cadres Decide Everything!" In the end, all could be well if, and only if, the peasant obliged by working more with fewer machines while waiting patiently to reap the fruits of his additional effort in the more or less distant future.

We shall attempt to review the cost of an alternative policy in terms of the overall objectives of the seven-year plan in the concluding section. At this stage, we turn to the examination of trends and measures of agricultural policy from 1959 onward.

III. AGRICULTURAL POLICY, 1959–64

Problems Following MTS Reform

"No plan," runs a military maxim, "ever survives contact with the enemy." The dictum is applicable to economic as well as military plans, especially when the commander's staff does not fully agree with his decision on the conduct of the operation.

As was mentioned earlier, the largest Soviet academic institute of agricultural economics was opposed to the MTS reform in the form which it eventually assumed. There is a good deal of evidence that its concern was shared by other institutions and the USSR Ministry of Agriculture (this in turn explains various sardonic remarks of Khrushchev's about agricultural scientists, as well as the veritable phobia which he was to show toward the Ministry later). As we shall see presently, the scientific circles turned all their attention toward elaboration of practical measures that might be of assistance to farmers in their new environment. This may well have been the only thing to do at the time, but such activity may have been motivated by a desire to assist (and perhaps even shield) farms from the consequences of enacted policy measures.

The role played by the USSR Ministry of Agriculture in the setting of production targets for farms in 1958–60 is not quite clear. The USSR Ministry of Procurements continued to function as the State Committee on Grain Products after 1957, and we must assume that it concerned itself with more weighty matters than just the care and maintenance of grain elevators. But the voice of the Ministry of Agriculture was nevertheless influential.

At the time of MTS reorganization (as well as later in 1958), Khrushchev indicated the intention of the government to purchase grain primarily, if not exclusively, in low-cost areas. A firm decision to adopt this course immediately could have been the result of premature optimism, or perhaps Khrushchev expressed his views without the intent of seeing them implemented immediately. In any case, such a policy was quite consistent with, and, in fact, was a necessary prerequisite for, introduction of greater specialization in Soviet farm production. Because of the imposition of numerous procurement quotas for individual products, farms cannot take advantage of economies of scale and may often be forced into disadvantageous lines of production at too small a scale of output to allow for a reduction of costs and (perhaps) the realization of profits. Trends in grain procurements show a very clear tendency to lower procurement quotas for the more marginal grain production areas (such as the northwest, central, and Volga-Viatka regions of the RSFSR; the Baltic Republics; Transcaucasia; and Central Asia).

Whether or not the trend just mentioned began in 1958 is not entirely clear. It seems to have been in full swing by 1959 and reached its peak by 1960. These trends may have resulted from a conscious decision by the top leadership, but they could also reflect an attempt on the part of lower administrative echelons to ease the pressure on farms under the guise of conformity with the announced views of N. S. Khrushchev. In any case, the results were beneficial from the standpoint of rationality of overall resource allocation in the agricultural sector; they also relieved farms from the necessity of producing high-cost products, allowed them to sell more at higher prices on the collective farm market, and/or made it possible to obtain greater quantities of feed. In some instances, particularly in 1959–60, some of these marginal grain areas shifted much of their grain acreage to the production of feed and fodder crops.

While these trends were taking place, we should note some further difficulties resulting from the inadequate elaboration of the MTS reform. Much of the research concerned with farm operations in the new environment was only in an embryonic state: in the spring of 1958 work did begin on such important matters as the optimum composition of tractor and machinery stocks, the elaboration of a rational institutional structure for the allocation of machinery and spare parts to individual farms, the knotty problem of prices, and the most important problem of all—the elaboration of a system of "rational farming practices." Though many of these problems were "solved" by the top Soviet leadership in an arbitrary way during the summer of 1958, the work on the elaboration of various regional schemes of "rational farming practices" continued through 1959, and no less than 39 regional commissions were involved in the project. Paradoxically, this feature may have exerted an adverse impact on relations between farms and low-level administrators. Since no one knew as yet what the "rational farming practices" would consist of—the final blueprint was not completed until mid-1960—administrators found here an additional justification for continued intereference in farm affairs. Such a justification was not actually needed, as very high pressures for a considerable increase in procurements of animal products came from above. This was a direct result of the goal of surpassing the United States in the per capita production of milk and meat within the very near future (1960–61), announced by Khrushchev in May 1957. Since the fulfillment or overfulfillment of the procurement goals constituted a major success indicator for regional administrators, the latter were likely to seize upon any excuse for continued interference in farm affairs, regardless of the intent of existing legislation. The results were often paradoxical, but also detrimental to farms.

It should be noted that during 1958–59, the top leadership gave some very indirect signs of concern about the wisdom of their decision to impose additional hardships on the peasant in the short run. There are also signs of reaction against the Ministry of Agriculture and the academic specialists who continued to sound the alarm: in May 1959, Khrushchev brought up the subject of agricultural administration in terms that fore-shadowed his later views on the subject.[15] By June 1959, he sought further short-term insurance in another proposed extension of acreage, this time in the Far East and east Siberia. A similar proposal was also advanced by a professional economist, N. Anisimov, who wrote several short treatises on agriculture in the days of Stalin.[16] By the time of the December 1959 plenum of the Central Committee, several high-ranking individuals—iden-tified by Sidney Ploss as supporters of Khrushchev—came out in favor of the collective farm center. While only Polianskii explicitly favored the interfarm income redistribution in connection with this proposal, implicit assumptions in this context must have been made by others. As we have already implied, the scheme amounted to an effort to raise the collective farm sector by its own bootstraps, and its adoption in this form would have represented a retrogression from the standpoint of incentives and efficiency.

It came to naught, however, as a result of substantial opposition on the part of the Ministry of Agriculture, such academicians as could have made their voice heard, and some regional administrators. Some secre-taries of republican parties stressed the need for greater allocations of machinery and credit to agriculture at the 1959 plenum. On the last day, Matskevich, then USSR Minister of Agriculture, stated point blank that "we must increase shipments of machinery, trucks, and also prime mov-

---

[15] ". . . our agricultural organs . . . should become organizers of production." This statement, made in Kiev on May 11, 1959, sounds almost like those repeated by him frequently in March 1962.

[16] There was, of course, a shortage of labor in these areas.

ers and other machines, as well as other equipment, fertilizers, and chemical materials for the protection of animals and crops." We also know that more was going on behind the scenes: according to Khrushchev, "agricultural organs of the Central Committees of the Republics and of the RSFSR and Ministries of Agriculture prepared rather extensive proposals for the development of all branches of agriculture."

While the opposition was able to block the move toward a collective farm center that would prove to be another instrument of collection, the alternative program was not accepted. "We rejected these proposals," stated Khrushchev in January 1960. A few weeks earlier he went on record as approving heartily the statement by a foremost authority that it would be two or three years before the agricultural machine building industry would be able to supply agriculture with the required quantities of appropriately constructed machines.

Meanwhile, a vigorous campaign against the private sector of agriculture moved into full swing. Khrushchev appears to have been convinced that the relative living standards of workers and peasants had, by then, reached a desirable level. For some time he had been extolling the virtues of the collective farm in his own native village of Kalinovka, where farmers voluntarily transferred their private cows to the socialized sector. By June 1959, the offensive mounted: "Should we not think about passing a law forbidding the urban population to hold cows, goats, pigs, and other livestock? These goats are really the enemies of urban parks. . . . The ownership of livestock among a part of the urban population develops unhealthy, speculative tendencies."

The utterances of the First Secretary are of course reported in the press: as he himself stated on an earlier occasion, the Soviet citizen understands very well that what is printed in newspapers has approval from above. It was during 1959 that the campaign got into fuller swing and others joined the bandwagon. A number of articles deploring some of the features of the private plot—notably its disruptive effect on the supply of labor to the socialized sector—appeared in the technical journals. On February 20, 1959, in order to improve urban food supplies (but also to limit the collective farm market), the government allowed rural trade cooperatives to purchase farm products locally for the purpose of resale to urban population at prices not to exceed the government retail prices. Other restrictive legislation followed: in the RSFSR urban livestock holding in krai or oblast centers (and their suburban area) was to end on October 10, 1959; the legislation could be extended to smaller towns at the request of local authorities. Ever since 1956, collective farms had been empowered to reduce the size of household plots; the official pronouncements from the Kremlin must have added further fuel to the fire. Whether all these instructions were obeyed in toto or only in part is at present a moot question. In any event, the size of the private sector was very drastically reduced in 1959. Between January 1, 1959, and January 1,

1960, holdings of cattle declined by 13 percent, those of cows by 7 percent, hogs by 9 percent, and goats by 18 percent. Sown area in private plots in 1960 was almost 7 percent lower than it had been in 1959. A Soviet source notes that "in the majority of collectives (the land taken away from private holders) usually highly productive, turned into desert, became infested with weeds."

Beginning with January 1, 1960, the practice of selling grain at privileged prices to farms producing cotton, flax, hemp, tea, tobacco, cocoons, and some other technical crops was discontinued—ostensibly at the request of republican party and government authorities. Since such farms produce little grain, amounts purchased from state stocks were more often than not distributed to farmers and subsequently used as feed in the private sector. From 1960 on, farms would be able to purchase grain at state retail prices, but only if the appropriate authorities were able to make such grain available.

The grain situation—that persistent problem which may be found at the heart of so many Soviet policy decisions from 1918 onward—did not actually improve. That the 1959 harvest did not come up to the record level of 1958 was understandable because of weather. One could also disregard for the time being the alarming trend in the income elasticity of demand for food which manifested itself during that year, since no one could be sure whether earlier trends were altered in a fundamental fashion, or whether this was only a random kink in the series. But the drain on grain stocks continued unabated (in spite of the opportunity to replenish in 1958) and by January 1960 Khrushchev was forced to inform a group of agricultural experts from the satellite countries that:

> We still do not have the necessary grain reserves in order to fully satisfy the growing demand on the part of friendly socialist countries. We now have grain reserves, but they are not as large as we would like to see them. . . . Therefore, we would like to turn to you with a request that you take into account our abilities, that you do not show insistence, or stubbornness with which we sometimes meet from your side, that you do not make such demands on us which are onerous to fulfill.

These pressures may have contributed to the decision to raise machinery allocations to agriculture, taken in the summer of 1960. The goals for tractors were raised by 30 percent, those for grain combines by 35 percent, the targets for cottonpickers and corn-silo combines by about 50 percent, while those for smaller machinery by 25 to 52 percent. But there is no evidence of major concern on Khrushchev's part until the fall of 1960. By this time it was crystal clear that trends in output were very disappointing, and that the shift in income elasticity of demand for food and trends in disposable incomes were more permanent than they seemed earlier in the year.

Meanwhile, the economic position of the farms deteriorated still further as a result of the onerous financial and other obligations, and incomes of farmers dropped substantially: in the period 1957–60, the known decline in total income per man-day from the socialized sector ranged from 11 percent in Belorussia to 29 percent in Moldavia, and there are all indications that this was a general phenomenon. Under the circumstances, local administrators attempted to solve the problem of weak and lagging collectives by converting many of them to state farms. There is no doubt that this, rather than any ideological preference, was the main reason for the rapid conversions of 1959 and especially 1960: in these two years converted collective farms accounted for 15.6 million hectares of sown area and 1.7 million households (or almost 5 percent of total collective farm sowing and 9.2 percent of households in 1958). In 1959, the average collective farmer income per man-day (cash and kind valued at state retail prices) came to 57 percent of the state farm wage for a day's work (or to about 31 versus 53 rubles on a monthly basis). It is clear that conversions did not represent an "enserfment" of the rural population, but placed a rather heavy burden on the state budget.

Remedial Measures Attempted

In October, 1960, a remarkable memorandum under the title, "Against Placidity, Complacence, and Conceit over the First Successes in the Development of Agriculture," had been submitted to the Presidium of the Central Committee by Khrushchev. As the evidence of major difficulties accumulated rapidly, there were signs of a shift in the author's attitude. He noted the rising demand for food products, condemned certain administrative practices, insisted on strengthening cadres of farms, approved conversion of weak and lagging collective farms into state farms in Kazakhstan (and by implication everywhere else where a similar situation existed). He also suggested a shift of resources from industry to agriculture through transfer of funds resulting from overfulfillment of targets in the industrial sector and implicitly admitted the errors in the field of the state's contribution to capital formation in agriculture.

There must have been a good deal of argument among the top leadership as to the nature of the required remedial measures for the session of the Central Committee scheduled for December 13, 1960, was postponed until January 13, 1961. Before it met, Matskevich, whose earlier stands suggest that by 1959 he sided with hardheaded realists on all farm matters, was dismissed and relegated to the constructive task of improving agriculture in Kazakhstan. On January 5, Khrushchev advanced his theses for the development of agriculture to be discussed at the forthcoming meeting. The session itself was enlivened by the remarkable spectacle of the First Secretary interrupting speakers with acid and derogatory comments; for all practical purposes it amounted to window dressing that afforded to many an excellent opportunity to engage in self-criticism. The relevant decisions were taken three days before the Central Committee met.

The amazing feature of these decisions is that they were primarily concerned with the financial position of the farms, as if the USSR were a market economy and as if farms could have obtained the necessary implements and fertilizers by simply spending more money. (Financial relief did, of course, make it possible to arrest the decline in cash distributions to collective farmers.) Although Khrushchev now explicitly condemned the earlier decision (his own?) to reduce machinery inputs and to proceed slowly with the expansion of fertilizer and weed-killer production, there is little evidence of a substantial shift in the allocation of materials and fertilizers to agriculture (we now know that the technical reconstruction of agricultural machine building, begun in the late fifties, was not even completed by 1965). Thus, instead of treating the disease, the leadership dealt mainly with some of its symptoms. Four-fifths of collective farm income from animal husbandry was made tax-exempt for the next five years. Prices of spare parts (which had been raised again in 1959) were cut by 40 percent, as were those of gasoline. Smaller reductions were announced in prices of tractors (9 percent), trucks (17 percent), and other machinery (4.3 percent). This was at the time when labor productivity in agricultural machine building rose—from 1955 to 1961—about 60 percent, and when profitability norms for some machines came to 50 to 90 percent. The state bank was instructed to increase its lines of credit to collective farms at lower interest rates, while the installment payments for the loans associated with machinery purchases of 1958–59 were extended to a period of up to ten years.

This, however, was not all. For the pressures from the demand side, reflected in the high income elasticity of demand for food at home, and in the "insistent and stubborn demand" of the satellite countries on the foreign account, were increasingly felt: by June 30, 1961, grain stocks went down to some 11–16 million tons (from the high of 23–27 million registered on June 30, 1957). If we can say that by this time Khrushchev's analysis of the situation improved, his policies showed few signs of progress. The response to the challenge was threefold. First, the local procurement apparatus of the former USSR Ministry of Procurements, abolished in 1956 following the advice of Khrushchev himself, was now recreated in the guise of "inspectorates for agricultural procurements." If my judgment of the situation is at all correct, one of the most hated and despised institutions on the Soviet countryside was thus resurrected. Its task was to organize and control the fulfillment of the state procurement plan, supervise all state marketing operations involving farm products, and participate actively in the organization of collective and state farm production.[17]

Second, the policy of allowing grain procurements in the more marginal areas to decline was sharply reversed. Khrushchev made known his

---

[17] Jerzy F. Karcz, "Soviet Inspectorates for Agricultural Procurement in 1961," *California Slavic Studies*, Vol. III (1964), pp. 149–72.

displeasure with conditions in the central region of the RSFSR and Belorussia, where a number of areas shifted to the position of net buyers of grain from the government. From here until 1964, uncontrolled escalation occurred in this vital area.

Third, rural consumer cooperatives were allowed to purchase farm products at any price agreed to by the seller. This aimed in part at the increase in retail supplies of food which were to some extent controllable by the state and could be shipped to other areas. But the underlying hostility to the collective farm market and the private plot were obvious.

The consequences of these measures were simple enough. Since the price system, defective on many accounts, could not provide enough incentives for farms to sell their products (especially those of animal origin) to the government, resort was made to command. The failure of the seven-year plan to provide enough inputs and enough scope for the private sector reversed the trend toward the market sector which agriculture appeared to have been taking in 1953–57. But the application of command elements in this setting could only lead to a variety of vicious circles. The sharp increase in the size of the urban population and the increases in wages of low-income groups led to the need to increase the share of the state in total retail sales of food to households. In turn, given the slowly growing or even stagnating output, this could only mean a reduction in farm incomes in kind. This reduction, accompanied by all the measures taken against the private sector further reduced total incomes of collective farmers from the socialized sector. (It is of no consequence here that the monetary component of this income was growing: as long as the farmer was increasingly compelled to purchase a part of his food supply in the state and cooperative trade network, the pressures for more food to sell by the state would lead to pressure for a greater share of procurements in output. We would then come back to our main vicious circle.)

In turn, the reduction of incomes from the socialized sector could only mean further pressure either to leave the farm or to devote a greater number of man-days to the reduced but even more vital private plot. Since machinery inputs were not forthcoming in required quantities (or for that matter in proper assortment, type, or size), output could only stagnate further.

There were further repercussions elsewhere. Stagnating output made it more difficult to supply food through the state retail network. This, in turn, probably accentuated the existing pressures for further increases in money wages and might have contributed to what the Soviets would call "loosening of financial discipline" in enterprises, with all the inflationary consequences that this entails. We should recall that the increase in savings (and cash hoards) that begins around 1961–62 may well reflect shortages of desirable goods rather than a rise in the true propensity to save.

Other vicious circles can be mentioned briefly. The imposition of peculiar crop structures from above, accompanied by high procurement quotas, was reflected in the neglect of production of high quality seeds. In turn, the average quality of output declined. The policy of requiring individual farms to deliver a large variety of products on any given farm precluded specialization and often involved unnecessary financial losses for farms. The financial condition of farms was aggravated by outdated rules on depreciation allowances: since transferred stock of MTS machinery was carried on the books of collectives at depreciated values, and since prices for new machinery had been raised, depreciation allowances could not possibly approach the required replacement values for scrapped items.[18] It must have seemed to many uninitiated administrators that high goals for output of livestock products should be reflected in large herds; consequently, large herds in socialized sectors became a goal in their own right, in spite of difficulties of securing enough feed (which now had to be diverted from the much more productive livestock sector of the private plots).[19]

In the process, the last shreds of the "freedom to plan" acquired with great fanfare in 1955 were torn to pieces. "Freedom to plan," of course should be understood in a peculiar sense, as the term implies no limitations on the action of the highest party and government officials. Viewed in the larger context, the concept always allowed for the "right kind" of intervention by lower party and government officials. Numerous examples of this sort of advice had, of course, been furnished by Khrushchev throughout his career—he did not choose to alter his behavior in March of 1955. His disclaimers to the effect that he was only "offering advice" or that "I would be incorrect if I said that I excel in everything as far as agriculture is concerned, that I know everything there is to know," were disregarded as they were mostly meant to be. The consequences were often disastrous, as was the case with the extension of corn sowings into the Northwest of the RSFSR and Belorussia.

The harvest of 1961 was not much better than in 1960. Though domestic demand eased up a little as a result of the peculiar behavior induced by the effects of the 1960 monetary reform, the drain on grain stocks continued. So did the pressures on the collective farm market and the private sector of the economy; in many instances farms were forbidden to plan to sell on this market. Those that did were often castigated in

---

[18] This was not all. Since prices for repair work done in state-owned shops were set at a high level (perhaps because the shops themselves were not very efficient), it paid to conduct repair in small collective farm workshops at costs lower by one-third than the prices to be paid to larger (and potentially more efficient) state repair establishments.

[19] Oddly enough, when discussing Stalin's three-year plan for development of livestock (1949–51), Khrushchev remarked: "The plan reduced itself to the goal of having always more livestock of all kinds. But is the problem one of quantity of horns and tails? No dear comrades . . . ."

the press. In some (read: many) instances the markets were closed or converted to cooperative markets. This, too, accentuated pressures on the inadequate food supplies in the government and cooperative network. Another vicious circle was thus in progress when the Central Committee met again in the plenary session on March 6, 1962.

Ever since the fall, Khrushchev had been touring the country, inveighing against the *travopol'e* system of crop rotation introduced in the 1930's. Too much land had been left under unproductive grasses and clean fallow, he asserted: this must go. The attack was continued during the March 1962 plenum when the procurement goals for the grain and livestock products were escalated still further. The blessing was given to the demise of *travopol'e* and clean fallow: if official statistics are correct on this point, the area under grasses declined from 36 to 27 million hectares in 1962 and to 14 million hectares in 1963. The corresponding figures for clean fallow are: 1960, 17.4 million hectares; 1962, 7.4 million; 1963, 6.3 million. It was obvious that here, too, there was the beginning of another vicious circle, especially in the new lands. On comparable land in Saskatchewan, the Canadians fallow some 40 percent of their acreage.[20]

More came in the domain of administration: Khrushchev was unsatisfied with the inspectorates for agricultural procurements, and in April 1962 they were absorbed by a new agency, the territorial production administration (TPA), uniting for the first time state and collective farms of a given area under a common leadership. The TPA represents a curious blend of an earlier idea of "agricultural unions," voiced by Matskevich in June 1960, with the typically Khrushchevian drive of getting the specialist (and indeed the scientist as well) to dirty his feet in manure. But Matskevich (and those who elaborated this idea) envisaged the task of these unions quite differently. They were to organize repair work and supply other needed facilities on an interfarm, cooperative basis. The Khruschevian TPA, on the other hand, placed the main stress on the "correct kind of" interference in production matters of individual farms.

The March 1962 plenum decisions—which stressed the need to raise livestock production—were completely silent on livestock prices. The decision to raise these prices was discussed further within the more intimate circles of the leadership. The delay was understandable. Any further increase in farm prices without a matching rise in retail prices of meat would have increased the subsidy that the Soviet consumer was receiving since the early fifties while purchasing meat in a state store. When the moment of truth finally came on June 1, 1962, retail meat prices were also raised by 35 percent while those of butter rose by 10

---

[20] For an outstanding analysis and assessment of Khrushchevian agronomy, including the corn program, the reader should consult Naum Jasny, *Khrushchev's Crop Policy* (Glasgow: George Outram, 1965).

percent. The decision was greeted—in some known cases—by riots, and by general dissatisfaction of urban consumers.[21]

In his March 1962 speech, Khrushchev made it clear that machinery stocks in agriculture did not allow for the performance of agricultural tasks within the time period required by agronomic considerations. He also deplored trends in fertilizer allocations. One of his requests—to construct three new farm machinery plants—was not acted upon. In retrospect, it is easy to see why Khrushchev's colleagues were not eager to plunge into more costly and ill-conceived schemes; the refitting of the existing farm machinery plants, begun in the late fifties, was still not completed.

Khrushchev turned to other administrative reforms. In an unprecedented measure, the party organizations at local levels were split in November 1962. Henceforth, there would be a separate party unit for agriculture and another for industrial matters in each of the provinces, or republics.

Output trends in 1962 were somewhat better than in 1961, but this was chiefly due to the weather. A year later, harvest conditions were nearly catastrophic. Grain output declined by 23 percent and imports were required on a large scale to maintain unbroken food supplies for the population. For a while, it seemed as if the brush with catastrophe was a blessing in disguise: by October 1963 Khrushchev was arguing for a crash program of fertilizer production, which according to his initial estimates was to amount to 100 million tons in 1970 (1963 production was 19.9 million). Ultimately, the December 1963 plenum agreed to the expansion but at a reduced pace, with 1970 output planned at 70 to 80 million tons.

Overt signs of dissatisfaction with Khrushchevian policies in agriculture appeared at about that time. Early in 1964, a Gosplan economist wrote openly on the disadvantages of growing corn and sugarbeets for feed in certain areas. Many more must have objected to the even more restrictive tax measures imposed on the private plots in May 1963.[22] Khrushchev himself toned down the strength of the advice offered to farms and to their managers. In 1963, prices for cotton, sugarbeets, and potatoes had been raised, apparently against some opposition from Khrushchev. At the February 1964 plenum meeting on agriculture, some tentative measures were taken to handle the long overdue question of irrigation, and many measures were introduced in the spring of 1964 to handle the even more pressing problems of the financial condition of weak farms.

But heavy pressures from the demand side continued on the food

---

[21] Albert Boiter, "When the Kettle Boils Over . . ." *Problems of Communism*, Vol. XIII, No. 1 (January–February, 1964), pp. 33–43.

[22] Thus, a cow kept over the new norm (one cow or one goat) would cost the owner 150 rubles a year in extra taxes.

market, the government was understandably reluctant to raise its retail prices, and the impact of the more sensible measures just outlined would not occur immediately. Khrushchev, however, appeared firmly convinced that it is always better to do anything than to wait patiently. Once more he seemed to have searched for the answer in administrative measures: during the summer of 1964 he discussed openly the idea of forming branch-type productive administrations, patterned on the existing organization of the poultry industry. As is well known, he was unable to put this proposal before the Central Committee. When he next faced that body, it was to fight the lost battle for his political life.

IV.   THE NEW PROGRAM AND THE EIGHTH FIVE-YEAR PLAN

Khrushchev's successors lost little time in dealing with some aspects of his heritage. The extremely unpopular restrictions on the private plots were lifted in November 1964, while the party organizations at local levels were unified once again. Beginning with January 1, 1965, milk prices were raised to levels that compared favorably with 1964 collective farm production costs. Early in 1965, the USSR Ministry of Agriculture was reorganized; under the direction of Matskevich, recalled from the Kazakh steppes, it resumed operational leadership and control over state and collective farms.

Having accused Khrushchev of haste and impatience, the new leaders devoted more time to the elaboration of the "New Agricultural Program," announced in March 1965. I have analyzed this program in greater detail elsewhere,[23] and . . . I shall therefore confine myself to summary remarks alone.

Perhaps the most significant aspect of the new program is that several of its features make it possible for Soviet agriculture to begin once again a slow movement toward the market sector of the economy. It will be recalled that under Stalin agriculture was placed squarely in the command sector (with the notable exception of the collective farm market which depended on the private plots). From 1953 to 1957, farming seemed to be moving toward the adoption of market-type incentives, but the trend was arrested (intentionally, it appears) by various policy measures introduced in 1958. The market cannot, of course, provide the right kind of signals when the farm is forced to produce and to sell its output at a net loss, as was the case generally with livestock products and in some areas with crop production until 1965. In 1965, prices for livestock delivered by state and collective farms were raised by 30 to 36 percent. Also raised were prices of bread grains all over the country and of feed grains in the northwestern region. An interesting feature of the new prices is that they reflect a step toward pricing at the level of costs of marginal producers.

[23] Jerzy F. Karcz, "The New Soviet Agricultural Programme," *Soviet Studies,* Vol. XVII, No. 2 (October 1965), pp. 129–61.

Simultaneously, procurement goals for 1966–70 were reduced rather drastically; in the case of grain procurements a fixed overall quota has been established for the next five years. The latter feature is fully consistent with the introduction of greater autonomy in local decisionmaking at the farm level. It will also reduce the pressures on farms and enable many of them to adopt patterns of greater specialization in production. In March 1965, Brezhnev saw fit to declare that once the plans have been set, "no one has the right to change them."

The nature of the income tax on collective farms was altered drastically. Henceforth, it will be computed on the base of net rather than gross income. Net income will exclude collective farmer earnings up to the level of 60 rubles per month (or about 10 percent less than the lowest 1964 average wage in the lowest paid sectors of the economy—trade, health, communal services). Up to 40 percent of the existing short- and long-term indebtedness of collective farms has been written off, including the remaining portion of debt resulting from purchase of MTS equipment in 1958–59. Rural retail prices for certain categories of consumer goods, which had been higher than prices paid for identical commodities in urban areas, have been reduced to the urban level.

Moreover, machinery allocations have been raised substantially and the fertilizer supply targets have been cut back to a more realistic level of 55 million tons for 1970 (this is still almost twice as high as 1965 allocations). The state is assuming the burden of all major irrigation projects, which are to proceed on an unparalleled scale. Total investment in agriculture (productive and unproductive) may exceed 71 billion rubles within the next five years.

Thus, on the input side the eighth five-year plan is much more consistent with the announced production goals than was the case with the seven-year plan. Unfortunately, it is not possible to render the same verdict in connection with planned increases in money incomes and consumption of food.

The eighth five-year plan calls for an average annual increase of 25 percent in gross farm output over the level of 1961–65. The target is now put in a more sensible way that will avoid embarrassment in the future. But we do not know exactly the relation of planned figure for 1970 to the actual output of 1965; it might be as low as 118 percent or even higher than 125 percent. In any case, it is the lowest increase sought in any Soviet medium-term plan. A very rough calculation . . . indicates that disposable money incomes are likely to rise by 42 to 48 percent over the level reached in 1965. In 1970 disposable money incomes may be between 176 and 183 billion rubles. It also appears that planned household expenditures for food in 1970 may come to 75 to 83 billion (the lower limit of this range is based on the assumption of a 10 percent decline in food prices). This is an increase of 17 or 30 percent respectively over the likely level of such expenditures in 1965.

Apparently, the government hopes that the present high income elasticities of demand for foods will decline in the near future. If this is not to remain a pious hope, Soviet industry must supply adequate quantities of attractive and reasonable quality nonfood consumer goods. The government must also make good on its goal to raise the level of services by not less than 150 percent. Any dispassionate observer of the Soviet scene may be skeptical on this score. He is also compelled to note that plans based on the hope that all the optimistic assumptions of the planner will, in fact, be realized, are likely to go astray more often than not.

We also note that on the assumption of a 10 percent decline in prices of foods and nonfood products, total household expenditures in 1970 are likely to come to 171 billion. Given the existence of considerable cash hoards, this is likely to result in some inflationary pressures. These will be aggravated if major supply difficulties develop, especially if plans to raise wages or incomes would be implemented regardless of the conditions on the retail market.

We also note that planned average increases in state retail sales of foods during 1966–70 come to about 30 percent, while the planned increase in the total consumption of foods is somewhat higher (30 to 35 percent). Farm output is to rise by, let us even say, 25 percent. While there may be some increase in efficiency of marketing, this aspect of the plan is at best extremely tight. Some inconsistency in this context is much more likely. The increase in grain output is planned for only 30 percent over the level of 1961–65 (it is 44 percent over 1965). Yet the satellite demand for Soviet exports is likely to persist, and state grain stocks must also be replenished. Moreover, the planned increase in meat production (23 to 29 percent) will also cause an additional drain on grain supplies. The extent to which consumption plans will be met depends largely on the way these conflicting demands will be resolved.

The new plan also calls for specific increases in per capita consumption of major food categories. This type of planning calls for corresponding changes in the structure of state retail prices. Flexibility and willingness to experiment in this area have never been very pronounced in the USSR, and it will be interesting to watch future developments.

We should also note that although the "liberalizers" appear to be firmly in the saddle, the tug of war among the top leadership is by no means over. Thus, at the February 1966 plenum of the Central Committee, the matter of a guaranteed income for collective farmers, at the level of corresponding state farm wages, was apparently discussed. The summary of plan directives, issued in English by Tass, included the pledge to raise collective farmer incomes in this way. This was subsequently excluded from the Russian text printed in the Soviet press. In his speech to the XXIII Congress in March 1966, Brezhnev has once more reiterated it. Kosygin's wording a few days later was somewhat more ambiguous. The final published version of plan directives states that "guaranteed monthly labor remuneration for the collective farmers, in conformity with the level of wages of state farm workers, will be introduced gradually." The promise seems intended for the identical skills in identical regions; the meaning of "gradually" seems purposefully vague.

Moreover, although the 1966 procurement plans were not altered after the final results of 1965 became known, the state planning commission is proceeding on the assumption that the state will receive over-plan procurements of many products in 1966. The directives enjoin all farms "not only to fulfill fixed procurement plans but to sell to the state, in ever increasing amounts, over-plan quantities of grain at higher prices. They should also foresee over-plan procurements of sunflowers, cotton, flax, milk, wool, eggs, and other products." The line between such statements or assumptions and an actual increase in the procurement plan is rather thin in the present Soviet environment (there would have been none two years ago), and developments in this sphere too will have to be watched carefully.

We should also note that the higher farm prices introduced in 1965 do not always apply to the private sector (this is most likely the case for livestock, where the "premiums" rather than higher prices were introduced). Once more, it seems difficult to make a clean break with the heritage of the past.

V. CONCLUSIONS

When recent trends in Soviet agricultural policy are examined within the broader framework employed in this study several general conclusions immediately suggest themselves.

Fundamental Problems

It is clear that the highly disappointing recent trends in Soviet farm output can be traced directly to the inadequate performance of top Soviet decisionmakers during the years 1957–58. (We may note in passing that failure at the top occurs after Khrushchev consolidated his personal power within the party apparatus.) The two sets of decisions that were so patently harmful in retrospect involved the setting of goals for agricultural outputs and inputs under the seven-year plan and the reorganization of the machine-tractor stations.

All these decisions suffered from the apparent inability or unwillingness (or a combination of both) to accept the limitations imposed by available resources. The sense of haste and urgency which permeated these decisions can of course be traced further to certain psychological propensities of communist leadership. After all, the party has often violated similar constraints in the past and it has survived; the very seizure of power in November 1917 and the attempt to build socialism in one country must be viewed as willful (and successful) violation of the Marxian timetable for the transition from capitalism to socialism.

The causes of agricultural failures under the seven-year plan are basically the same as those that had been acknowledged as leading to the abandonment of the sixth five-year plan. Anybody doing research in Soviet capital formation, rationality of decisionmaking, efficiency of the construction industry, the lack of appropriate priority-setting for development of various sectors, and failures to reap the benefits of the division of labor, will be well advised to consult agricultural materials. The more fundamental reason for this state of affairs is that Khrushchev, who was able to de-Stalinize many aspects of Soviet life to a considerable extent, never succeeded in de-Stalinizing his own work habits or his own attitudes and outlook. The same may be said of many of his colleagues.

The consequences of these careless and overconfident attitudes would not have been so important, were it not for a basic difference between Soviet industrialization and that of the so-called Western economies. The latter was preceded by (or occurred concurrently with) a veritable revolution in cropping patterns and agronomical techniques.[24] As a result, Western agriculture was able to perform its main developmental task— that of supplying labor, food, raw material, and export surpluses to the industrial sector—in an entirely different environment, characterized by rising yields and sharply improving productivity. Nothing of the sort materialized in Russia—or Eastern Europe for that matter—prior to the inception of the industrialization drive. If the Soviets imported technology, the effort was largely restricted to the industrial sector; certainly, no comparable drive was made to import and implement modern Western farming techniques in a comparable manner. No Western country ever faced the crisis of "marketable grain surpluses"; yet, it was this very crisis that may well have tipped the scales in favor of the massive collectivization drive with all its consequences.

When the attitudes of the present Soviet leadership are examined in this context, they appear at first glance to be much more rational. The sense of urgency and haste have apparently yielded to the need for greater deliberation and reflection upon the merits of the underlying issues. The last debate on farming, conducted in March 1965 in the forum of the Central Committee, was no longer confined to largely

---

[24] One of the first references in the context of developmental economics to this phenomenon was made when Ragnar Nurkse referred to the role played by "the lowly turnip" in British agriculture in his *Problems of Captial Formation in Underdeveloped Countries* (New York: Oxford University Press, 1953), p. 52. See also the paper by William H. Nicholls, "The Place of Agriculture in Economic Development," in Carl Eicher and Lawrence Witt (eds.), *Agriculture in Economic Development* (New York: McGraw-Hill Book Co., 1964), pp. 18–19. Japanese experience is also relevant here; cf. Bruce F. Johnston, "Agricultural Development and Economic Transformation: A Comparative Study of the Japanese Experience," *Food Research Institute Studies,* Vol. III, No. 2 (November, 1962), pp. 223–52.

congratulatory slaps on the back, followed by stop-gap proposals and a series of camouflaged self-criticisms, beginning with that extremely useful word: "but . . ." Moreover, shortcomings have been admitted publicly with consequences to be elaborated presently.

It remains to be seen, of course, whether this change in attitudes is as fundamental as it must be in order to achieve the stated objectives. The task of modernizing Soviet agriculture cannot be separated from that of modernizing the Soviet economy as a whole. The latter requires a significant reduction in the number of existing "command" elements or sectors and their replacement by market-type incentives and controls. In this connection, the Soviet leaders face an arduous and protracted task. If the Yugoslav experience is at all relevant, the road ahead leads through many detours that will often take the traveler in the opposite direction. At any rate, the so-called reforms of the Soviet industrial sector, introduced in September 1965, do not go far enough. In fact, they fall far short of their Czechoslovak, East German, and Hungarian counterparts.

One other development must be mentioned in passing. The irrational Khrushchevian policies apparently led to the emergence of a type of "underground opposition," which involved not only farm managers but apparently also the republican government organs and the republican parties. Thus, peas were sown on paper only; Kazakh agriculture apparently succeeded in largely avoiding the order to sow legumes. Estonia evaded the restrictions on the private plot and Lithuania managed to minimize the impact of the antigrassland campaign. Anyone who has served in the armed forces or another large organization knows that orders must sometimes be neglected if the organization is to function at all. But what is interesting in the Soviet context is that, when the chips were really down, first loyalty went to the farm or to the republic—and not to the party. Violation of orders may have resulted from a conviction that the leadership ceased to represent the true will of the party. But attempts to determine for oneself the correct course of action in matters of major importance are also highly significant.

In thinking about the future it is well to bear in mind that the Soviet government is at present committed to a program of massive agricultural improvement, that the reasons for the sad state of agriculture have been aired in public, and that the program is fully in accord with the deeply ingrained sense of fairness that is characteristic of the ordinary Soviet citizen. In a sense, agricultural progress in the future will be looked upon as a test of the ability of the government to handle a persistent major difficulty. Thus, barring major upheavals of a random or foreign policy nature, there is no reason to expect a reversal of present policies toward those that have been properly labeled Stalinist in the past.

This does not necessarily mean that the new agricultural program is in any sense optimal. Preceding analysis suggests that the size and condition of machinery stocks on farms plays a crucial role in the aggregate production function of Soviet agriculture. Present trends do suggest that this factor is still underestimated at the Kremlin. The 1965 performance of agricultural machine building still leaves much to be desired, and machinery accounts for only 24 percent of total agricultural investment under the eighth five-year plan (1966–70).

Given the existing climatic conditions, rapid mechanization and electrification of Soviet agriculture are probably the most important necessary conditions for a rapid improvement of its performance and the resulting amelioration of Soviet diets. But machinery is also a substitute for labor. In thinking about the planned rate of mechanization, it is necessary to bear in mind the existence of the employment problem which appears to have assumed considerable proportions in the USSR.

The short-run interests of the economy as a whole and of the agricultural sector, viewed narrowly as just another industry, are not altogether identical. Thus, the relatively modest goal for the allocation of machinery to agriculture may not be due only to the priority of heavy industry. It may reflect the growing awareness of other limitations, including the difficulty of creating the required number of costly urban jobs in the very near future. Indeed, Kosygin and the final directives of the eighth five-year plan now speak of the need to locate industry in rural areas and of opening up seasonal branches of processing plants in the villages. In the meantime, the 1965 and 1966 measures aimed at increases in farmer incomes should help to slow down the exodus of the young and the able bodied to the cities.

Our analysis would not be complete if we failed to mention a fundamental and by now frequently forgotten assumption of Soviet agricultural policy. I refer to the desire to maintain self-sufficiency in the production of foods and raw materials, reinforced by the need to support the economies of other socialist countries of Eastern Europe with exports of grains. As Naum Jasny made clear,[25] Soviet agriculture is without doubt the most expensive food producer in the world. The reasons for this are many and some of them have been discussed in this paper. But it is also true that Soviet economic development has been taking place largely in isolation from world markets and without the benefit of correctives supplied by the foreign sector. The large size of the USSR, its rich resource endowment in industrial materials, the disregard of living standards and of efficiency in favor of rapid rates of growth, enabled the Soviet government to maintain (so far) the balance which Grossman calls a necessary condition for the very functioning of any economy.[26] But in the process of Soviet industrialization a great waste of resources has resulted and the Soviet economy is heavily populated with branches of industry

[25] "Production Costs and Prices in Soviet Agriculture," in Jerzy F. Karcz (ed.), *Soviet and East European Agriculture* (Berkeley: University of California Press, 1967), pp. 212–64.

[26] Grossman, *op. cit.*, pp. 101–02.

and plants that could not be maintained in a more open economy. It seems ironic that at the very time when a great debate on the need for greater efficiency in resource use is taking place in the USSR so little thought appears to have been devoted to the rationality of stressing the development of the agricultural sector.

It is impossible to state the issue in those terms without recalling that most other economies, including our own, are not without fault in this regard. The existence of many irrational programs in agriculture in virtually all Western economies testifies vividly to the fact that there is more to life than simple economic efficiency. But still, there are no indications as yet that the underlying assumption of autarky is being questioned in the Kremlin. Even a partial recognition of this problem, perhaps within the Comecon setting, would be most helpful at a time when new five-year plans are being drawn up and when very large investible resources are about to be sunk in a sector where Soviet production costs are bound to remain high by the standard of world prices for many years to come.[27]

One major issue remains to be considered. Soviet agriculture is often said to suffer especially from its internal organizational structure. In particular, it is sometimes argued that it is the very nature of socialized agriculture in the USSR that constitutes the greatest stumbling block on the road to greater agricultural productivity and toward a more affluent society.

This very complex issue lies on the far side of the imaginary line beyond which angels (let alone economists) fear to tread. While I do not wish to beg the question while pleading the excuse of lack of space, I must be very concise in stating my views on this matter. I shall also employ the favorite academic device of defining myself the views of the protagonists.

There is no doubt, of course, that the present size of Soviet farms, both state and collective, is far above any conceivable optimum. Some recognition of this fact has by now taken place in the USSR as well, and steps are now being taken to dismantle some unmanageable giants through an interesting process of deamalgamation. But it remains to be seen whether giantism as a disease of Soviet farming will ever be eliminated completely. It is a fact, however, that the optimum size of the farm cannot be determined offhand without a reference to the existing relative prices of inputs and outputs alike. Thus, this issue must necessarily be viewed in the much larger context of rationalizing the Soviet command economy. This fascinating subject does not fall within the frame of reference of this paper. But those who choose to ignore this factor can only proceed at their own peril.

What is also at stake here is the important issue of the relative

---

[27] We would have to take another look at this matter in the case of a major technological breakthrough, such as the introduction of hybrid wheat or other hybrid grains.

efficiency of the privately owned versus the socialized enterprise. We cannot enter into any detailed discussion of this question either. Any such comparisons, of course, must be made either between the existing actual systems or the underlying theoretical structures. Moreover, it is necessary to make a vital distinction between ownership as such and the related but still separate questions of autonomy in decisionmaking and the problem of incentives. When these distinctions are made, the entire issue appears in a very different light.

As far as agriculture is concerned, however, it is often claimed that some special conditions prevail that might even make the family farm an ideal (if not optimal) economic unit. Upon closer examination, however, it turns out that the specific characteristics of agriculture that are relevant in this context are confined largely (if not exclusively) to the relatively long production cycle, the dependence on the unpredictable weather, and the fact that most farms are multiproduct enterprises by definition. All that seems to be called for on this account is greater decentralization in decisionmaking. Ownership of land is not necessarily connected with the ability to make the right decisions at the right time. While Soviet experience with decentralization of decisionmaking is still in its infancy, this is a problem that appears in the economy at large and not only in agriculture. On a priori grounds, therefore, there are no reasons here to separate agriculture as a special case that stands in need of a different treatment. There are, of course, many other reasons that suggest that the solution of this particular problem is going to be more difficult for Soviet agriculture than for Soviet industry, but these reasons are environmental rather than theoretical in nature.[28]

On the other hand, Soviet experience with socialized farming cannot be separated from the role performed by agriculture in the special framework of Soviet economic development. To repeat, agriculture as a whole —and the collective farm sector in particular—served as an instrument of collection of forced savings to the detriment of its own internal efficiency. In the process, the level and the structure of incentives—a much more important matter than the question of ownership from the standpoint of economics—was grievously affected. The effects of the neglect of incentives on productivity are sufficiently well known so that further comment seems unnecessary.

But even in this difficult environment some Soviet farms—both state and collective—have done rather well. Given the nature of Soviet farm prices until 1965, once a farm passed a vaguely defined point of no return, the road toward relative affluence seemed wide open. It is not material here whether the farm was able to achieve this breakthrough because of

---

[28] Grossman, *op. cit., passim.* As Nancy Nimitz correctly points out, the Soviet farm is much more affected by administrative interference than a Soviet industrial firm. But this is still an environmental factor. Cf. Nimitz, *op. cit.* (in fn. 1), p. 21.

superior management or because of favoritism. Khrushchev's own native Kalinovka is indeed a case in point: it did well, as it turned out, because of extraordinarily high allotments of government investment funds and credits.[29] Indeed, this experience supports the view that output is largely determined by inputs even in the peculiar Soviet environment. If, in turn, inputs are available in the required quantities, the matter of incentives will probably be taken care of in an appropriate manner.[30]

The preceding paragraphs should not be misunderstood. Private property performs a variety of useful functions in the economy, not the least of which is the better care afforded to the capital stock, a greater sense of personal responsibility, and the fact that political and economic power tend to offset each other more readily when that revered and venerable institution is present. But it is one thing to argue in favor of private property on these general grounds, and it is another to argue—erroneously, I believe—that a specific form of private property is a necessary condition for the efficient performance of a given economic activity.[31]

Ultimately, therefore, the case against socialized farming is telescoped into the argument that farming of this type, especially when liberally seasoned with collective extraction of forced savings, has not been very efficient in the Soviet Union (one is indeed tempted to borrow Hayek's expression from the great debate on the efficiency of socialism and to say that socialist farming is not "particularly practicable"[32]). This, of course, is a very different argument than the one against which I have been taking the stand. Many cogent arguments can be advanced in its support and I would be the first to advance them were it not for the justified fear of exhausting the patience of the editor. Once more, however, we should be careful. Although there are some special costs of discrimination against the peasants, there is always a social cost of discrimination against any social group.

Having said this much, we must also say more. Recent research on the economic behavior of cooperatives, undertaken by Benjamin Ward and Evsey Domar, has shown that a cooperative (and thus the ideal collective farm) is simply not a very efficient form of economic organization when compared with the ordinary, labor-hiring and wage-paying firm, capitalist

[29] The share of the state in the formation of capital in Kalinovka was 80 percent. For all other farms in this (Kursk) oblast it was only 45 percent.

[30] Indeed, there are some indications that, in the environment of the Soviet countryside characterized by absence of many amenities, the supply curve of effort on the part of the farmers may begin to curve backward at a rather low level of earnings. On the Belorussian farm "Rassvet," this occurred when collective farmers received 2.5 to 3 rubles per labor-day.

[31] Thus, some American executives live in houses owned and staffed by the corporation and drive, or are driven in, company cars to work. They do not work less efficiently for all that, but they have full opportunity to own other property.

[32] F. A. Hayek, "Socialist Calculation: The Competitive 'Solution,'" *Economica*, New Series, Vol. VII, No. 26 (May, 1940), p. 149.

or otherwise.[33] Since the argument has just been clarified in the West, and since Ward's pathbreaking article has been largely ignored here, it seems premature to blame the Soviet leadership for failure to draw the necessary conclusions. In any case, the Soviet collective farm is still far removed from the conditions when limitations of this sort become important in practice.

In any event, desocialization of Soviet farming—in name as well as in fact—does not appear likely. At the moment, we have three examples of desocialization of agriculture in the socialist camp. These are (chronologically) Yugoslavia in 1952–53 and Poland and Hungary in 1956. The Hungarian experiment has been reversed since, so that we are left with the Polish and the Yugoslav cases. The Yugoslavs are trying hard to convince their individual farmers that the road to greater productivity leads through cooperation with the socialist sector that involves leasing of land to state farms for purposes of cultivation and/or harvesting. The Poles, on the other hand, are still unable to make up their mind as to the best and least explosive way of raising the issue except on a rather theoretical plane.[34] In both instances, however, socialization of agriculture remains the ultimate goal. It is difficult to see, therefore, how desocialization in name could be effected in the USSR. Moreover, such desocialization is not really necessary, since the Soviet socialized enterprises can well benefit from a variety of measures that would stop short of this exercise in brinkmanship á la communiste. In the process, a substantial amount of de facto desocialization can also occur.

Improvements Needed

The agenda for the improvement of the organizational structure of Soviet farms (collective as well as state) is fairly long. We list the most important points, since they might help to interpret future developments in Soviet agricultural policy:

1. Perhaps the most important single improvement that can occur in the near future is the introduction of rental payments. The issue is rather thorny from the theoretical Marxist standpoint, and Prof. Evsey Domar has recently pointed out to me that land has been granted to collectives in perpetual use on a "free of charge" basis. The latter difficulty might be overcome, however, by reinterpreting the terms of the grant to read that it was only marginal land that was granted to farms on this basis; consid-

---

[33] Cf. Benjamin Ward, "The Firm in Illyria: Market Syndicalism," *American Economic Review*, Vol. XLVIII, No. 4 (September, 1958), pp. 566–89; and Evsey D. Domar, "The Soviet Collective Farm as a Producer Cooperative," *American Economic Review*, Vol. LVI, No. 4 (September, 1966), Part 1, pp. 734–57.

[34] The so-called agricultural circles are the vehicle employed for this purpose in present day Poland. Cf. Andrzej Korbonski, "Peasant Agriculture in Socialist Poland since 1956: An Alternative to Collectivization," in Karcz (ed.), *Soviet and East European Agriculture*, pp. 411–35.

erations of equity might in fact require that rent be charged for better than marginal land (a lump-sum payment might be made to those farms that have undertaken substantial improvements of land on their own account).

The introduction of rental payments would go a long way in improving the pattern of resource allocation in agriculture, and indeed in the economy at large. It would then be possible to dismantle the existing structure of regional farm prices (the purpose of which is to extract at least a part of rent); prices would henceforth vary only to the extent of transportation costs.

Similar proposals, camouflaged in a variety of ways, have been advanced in the USSR, most persistently by Prof. M. Bronshtain. One difficulty results from the absence of a land cadaster (except in the Baltic republics) and Soviet specialists are still engaged in a weighty theoretical argument as to the appropriate nature of the cadaster. While the argument continues, precious time is being lost; as Kenneth Boulding once remarked, perfectionism and indolence have one thing in common—there is no output.

2. Farms must be free of undue administrative interference. While recent pronouncements by the top leaders are quite encouraging in this respect, it would be premature to expect that old attitudes will yield gracefully to those required on theoretical grounds. As long as the shift of farming as a whole from the command to the market sector of the economy continues, there will be less need, however, to engage in "administering." But there is many a slip between the cup and the lip in the entire matter of autonomy in decisionmaking in the Soviet Union. As Professor Grossman points out, positive steps are the result of top-level decisions, while retrogression occurs as a result of numerous actions by minor subordinates.

3. Procurement plans should be moderate; the nonsensical practices of procuring grain that must be borrowed again from the state in order to allow seeding must also be discontinued. Only in this environment will Soviet farming be able to reap the benefits of specialization. Given the present difficulties with grain supplies, this may not appear to be a very practicable solution at first glance. Yet, it turns out that only nine out of 24 major economic regions supply 90 percent of total grain procured by the state. Hence, the short-run cost of eliminating (or at least reducing further) grain procurements in marginal production areas would turn out to be much smaller than it appears at first glance. It might even be appropriate to make special allowances of foreign exchange to account for the necessary grain imports in the short run. Eventually, advances in productivity would more than offset these (admittedly heavy) costs.

Two items must be borne in mind in this connection. It may well be that the USSR finds itself on the threshold of a major breakthrough in yields. It was only in 1964 that fertilizers were available in sufficient quantities to allow for more than a token application in the production of grains. From here on, however, every ton of fertilizer supplied and used on the farm should have some effect in this respect. Presently contemplated irrigation projects have a similar impact, especially in conjunction with fertilizer application in dry areas. On the other hand, Yugoslav and (as Professor Montias remarks) Rumanian experience as well testify to the benefits that can be derived from proper seed selection and introduction of new varieties of crops. The new Soviet leadership does stress the need to follow the dictates of scientific achievements in farming. If deeds will correspond to intentions, much progress will be made on this account as well.

4. The existing network of repair facilities for machinery, rural construction enterprises, fertilizer warehouses, and indeed rural roads must be rapidly expanded. All these items (with the exception of roadbuilding, which should be reserved to the state) belong properly on the agenda for the Union of Collective Farms or the Kolkhoz Center. One should, however, keep in mind the fact that there is no real reason why state farms should not be allowed to avail themselves of these services, or (alternatively) why collectives should not be allowed to use state facilities on a reciprocal basis in areas where state farming predominates.

5. We have already noted that the present size of Soviet farms is by far too large. Steps should, therefore, be taken to break up these farms even before Soviet economists have had the time to work out in detail the optimal size of farms for many areas. "To fear mistakes," says Venzher correctly, "is to condemn oneself to inactivity." Total inactivity is probably a far greater mistake than those that might result from the creation of too small farming units. Within farms, of course, a movement is now afoot to restore the practice of forming the so-called links (*zven'a*) which might yield great improvements in productivity as a result of assignment of portions of farmland to individual links on what might even amount to a lease basis. From the standpoint of its effect on incentives, autonomy in decisionmaking, and the promotion of a sense of responsibility, the *zveno* is indeed a close enough substitute for private property in land. One difficulty is that once it is introduced, labor requirements per unit of land tend to decline sharply. It may thus not be practicable to introduce it on heavily populated farms, unless steps are also taken to provide other employment for the released labor.

6. Before attempting to overtake the United States in per capita production it would be well to bear in mind that the USSR must first narrow the gap in the supply of information to farms. This could be done by the adaptation of our agricultural extension service to Russian conditions. While Khrushchev has mentioned the subject on more than one occasion, he seemed unable to disassociate the agents from his own "inspector-organizers of farm production." A very substantial amount of experience has by now been accumulated in many countries to indicate that it is

example—and not command, no matter how camouflaged as advice—that is of essence here.

7. The state must also take steps leading to the creation of part-time or full-time employment opportunities in rural areas, through the creation of handicrafts (which it destroyed ruthlessly not too long ago) and construction of small-scale industry and service networks in the countryside. There are some straws in the wind to the effect that a major program for these purposes may not be long in coming.

It would be premature to say that the Soviets are belatedly adopting the Japanese pattern of industrialization, but they do talk of taking some steps in this direction.

To the extent that future policies will proceed in these directions one can expect substantial improvement in future trends in output. This in turn will be reflected in Soviet living standards and is very likely to have some international consequences, at least within the Soviet bloc. But all these policies will be inconsequential if there is not enough operational machinery on farms. After all, even the irrigated and the fertilized land must still be farmed; in Soviet climatic conditions it must also be farmed quickly. This can be done with human—rather than machine—labor only on small peasant farms which are not likely to return on the Soviet scene.

. . . .

The proverbial man from Mars, looking over the Soviet agricultural scene between 1958 and 1965 might well have asked himself this question: "Were all these hardships really necessary?" Any dispassionate observer would have to answer in the negative. Once again, the Kremlin has paid a heavy price for disregard of modern but not really complicated economic calculation. It remains to be seen whether the lesson has finally been learned.

12 | THE PROMISE OF ECONOMIC SELF-SUFFICIENCY UNDER SOVIET SOCIALISM

Leon M. Herman

The impact of foreign economic relations on the Soviet economy, as measured by the amount of trade or aid relative to GNP, is small. In part, this reflects the varied resource endowment of the Soviet Union and the size and structure of the Soviet economy. It is also the result of a conscious policy of autarky which seeks a high degree of self-sufficiency in order to avoid undue dependence on imports. Since 1950, however, Soviet foreign trade has increased significantly, both absolutely and in relation to GNP. This is true not only for intra-bloc trade with Eastern Europe but also for trade with non-Communist countries, both less developed and highly industrialized.

The following selection traces the development of the policy of national economic self-sufficiency in the USSR and the recent shift away from it. Leon M. Herman, who died in 1969, was Senior Specialist in Soviet Economics in the Legislative Reference Service, Library of Congress. His article is reprinted by permission from *Studies on the Soviet Union,* Vol. VII, No. 1, 1967, pp. 67–102. Statistical tables and references to Soviet sources have been deleted.

THE OCTOBER REVOLUTION in 1917 was a political undertaking motivated by many ambitions. The Bolshevik leaders of the revolution represented the overthrow of the weak and ill-defended Provisional Government not as an end in itself, not as a mere fulfillment of their own power ambitions, but as an historic act made inevitable by the patent need to break the chain of continuity with Russia's despised past. Without this abrupt break, Russia, though newly liberated from centuries of despotism, would, in their opinion, find it impossible to build its own new world. By the same token, the October Revolution was designed to help Russia execute a forward leap of historic proportions into the next stage of human development, into the age of socialism. In this sense, the revolution was perceived by its leaders as a ringing declaration of independence from the rest of the world, especially from "the exploiter nations," that is, the economically more advanced capitalist countries of the West. The implied warning was that the torch of economic leadership would thereafter be carried by the nation that had been propelled by this revolution ahead of the rest of the world into a new historical era.

Most immediately, according to the leaders of the revolution, the people of Russia would be liberated from their inherited condition of hopelessness, instilled over the centuries by class division, oppression, and exploitation. They would emerge into a new era of human history, characterized by social cooperation, communal prosperity, and free development of all members of society. "The social revolution of the proletariat," proclaimed the Programme of the Communist Party of Russia in 1919, "marks an end to the division of society into classes, and thereby liberates the whole of oppressed mankind, thus abolishing all forms of exploitation of one section of society by another."[1]

DESIGN FOR A NEW ECONOMIC ORDER

The early pronouncements of the Soviet regime were not, however, limited to hazy projections of the shape of things to come. They also contained a number of specific commitments to action. One such commitment was to the immediate pursuit of an historically new economic policy designed "to secure a universal increase in the productive forces of the country." This goal would be achieved, the Party Programme of 1919 promised, by following a new "governmental design" described briefly as including "the maximum centralization of production" in the sense of "consolidation of individual branches and groups of branches." On the plane of governmental action, this design began to take shape during the first months in which the Soviet state existed. The new rulers of Russia wasted no time in setting out to create the society of the future, seeing their way in violent divorce from Russia's past and defiant estrangement from the political and economic norms of the capitalist world. Only by breaking with the exploiter nations, ran the official argument of the period, was it possible to build an independent and efficient economic order, self-contained and self-renewing, and proof against the anarchy of the market ruling the economic affairs of the outside world.

In the realm of international cooperation, just one kind of effort was

---

[1] "Programme of the Communist Party of Russia, 1919," *The A.B.C. of Communism*, London, 1922, pp. 389–402 (Appendix).

provided for in the early plans of the Soviet government. This was the provision, in the words of the Party Programme of 1919, "to establish a unified economic plan in conjunction with those among [the nations] that have already established a Soviet system." An early act of symbolic commitment on the part of the Soviet leaders to economic isolation as a policy came in January 1918, in the letter and spirit of their decree on the cancellation of all foreign debts. It must have been quite clear to Lenin and his associates at this time that the countries most immediately affected by this kind of "nationalization" policy were precisely those that were Russia's most important actual and potential trade partners. These were, quite obviously, the countries to which the Soviet regime would have to turn if and when it ever felt the need to reinstitute any kind of normal exchange of commodities based on mutual economic confidence. It can only be assumed, therefore, that the new world that the Bolshevik leaders were planning to build in Russia was conceived of as a world without normal external economic relations, a world in which such legal and moral refinements as the inviolability of the economic rights of foreign owners would not longer have to be respected.

After the first flush of victory over Russian capitalism—"the weakest link in the chain of world capitalism"—the Soviet leaders were not inclined to be excessively impressed with the higher stage of economic development already achieved by the West. They were disposed, rather, to see in this highly advanced technical system a promise of growing internal social tension: over-production followed by under-consumption and unemployment at home and accompanied by frequent and fierce struggles for markets abroad. They foresaw a series of economic crises, and very little else, as "the inevitable outcome of the development of productive strength in bourgeois society," to use the language of the program. These were the symptoms and "the necessary conditions of the imminent social revolution." It followed, in their opinion, that the victorious proletariat of Russia could not conceivably be expected to build its future on a policy of extensive and continued economic cooperation, individual or collective, with the nations still clinging to the doomed economic and social order of the West.

Another significant commitment to economic isolationism came in April 1918, with the establishment of a state monopoly over foreign trade by the Soviet government. The intent behind this move, plainly enough, was to erect around the economic structure of Soviet Russia something like an insuperable administrative barrier against economic influences from the outside world. It was to be, more specifically, the kind of a barrier through which the government of the USSR alone could make, as a matter of exception, the necessary provisions required for a controlled exchange of goods with the economies of the outside world, in accordance with the changing economic conditions and interests of the Soviet state.

LENIN'S DESIGN FOR LIMITED ECONOMIC COLLABORATION

As long as internal economic conditions were in disarray, the Bolshevik leadership could not, understandably enough, proceed to foreswear active economic exchanges with the outside world. In the early period, following the seizure of power by Lenin and his monolithic Bolshevik Party, there were certain minimum requirements that had to be imported from abroad to help in the revival of economic life in Russia. There were, for example, such critical items as locomotives, generators, compressors, pumps, and trucks, which could, at that time, be procured only from outside the national economy. These critical shortages were rather generally characterized by Soviet officialdom of the period as strictly temporary in character, induced by a variety of passing emergency conditions. Faced by the persistence of these temporary shortages, however, Lenin declared himself ready to enter into any kind of contractual arrangements with private individuals and firms in the West, but only, in his own words, "in order to learn from the enemy" as quickly as possible. In spite of this, the principle of eventual economic disengagement from the capitalist world, from a "world plagued by endemic economic disorders," remained unchanged as a basic condition for building the new and unique socialist economy of the future.

Still, even in the balmy climate of the early years of the New Economic Policy (NEP) in Russia, Lenin argued vehemently against any attempt made by his associates to find a more efficient substitute for the cumbersome state monopoly instituted in 1918 to preempt all activity in the field of foreign trade. He rejected Nikolay Burkharin's well-reasoned proposal, which was, in effect, to replace the trade monopoly, along with the general condition of economic isolation fostered by it, with a system of high protective tariffs. He was especially stung by Bukharin's favourite epithet for the inflexible, largely negative state trading system, namely, *sistema glavzapora*, or literally, the system of the bolted gate. On this issue, Lenin took the position that "even a partial opening of the frontiers carries with it a most serious danger." He was prepared to agree with Bukharin, he said, that Russia had a lot to learn from its more advanced neighbors, and that some of these skills could be learned through the medium of foreign trade, but he was clearly not willing to open the door to a normal, legally regulated exchange of goods, and, at the same time, to the development of a process of economic interdependence between Soviet Russia and the outside world. Instead, Lenin continued to search for some form of *ad hoc* economic collaboration that would specifically benefit the industrial sector of the economy and that would remain at all times under the effective control of the Soviet government.

In the early years of NEP, the internal pressures for a more active form of economic intercourse with the industrial nations of Europe nevertheless continued to rise. In order to meet these pressures, Lenin came up with a proposal for the formation of a number of international "mixed companies," each dealing with a specific area of commodity trade. In these joint companies, he explained, "the foreign and the Russian merchants would work side by side," thereby helping to overcome the "bad work" of the state trading monopoly and to teach the inexperienced officials of the People's Commissariat of Foreign Trade the skills required for the conduct of international trade. Lenin concluded this proposal with the following blunt comment: "If we shall not be able even under these conditions to learn, and ultimately to master [the skills of foreign trade], then our nation is a completely hopeless nation of fools." Lenin's main concern during these formative years was to try to avoid, by any and all means, the kind of relationships with the economies of the outside world that might turn out to be open-ended. Almost any temporary system of cooperation, however radical, seemed to him to be preferable, under the circumstances, "in order to help us learn seriously and lastingly." He preferred such make-shift systems precisely because they could be terminated at any time by a unilateral decision of the Soviet government.

The need for international trade as a permanent condition of economic activity was considered by Lenin to be a uniquely capitalist phenomenon, arising directly out of the capitalist form of economic organization and, specifically, out of its "need of an over-expanding market" and its preoccupation with relative costs, fluctuating prices, and rates of profit. Such a need for ready access to foreign markets, Lenin assumed, was the motive force behind the public policy of all the major countries of Western Europe. It was this assumption, in fact, that served to keep alive his hopes for a rather easy and early political reconciliation with the rest of Europe, regardless of the character of Soviet internal economic and political institutions. He was convinced that the compulsive urge on the part of the trade-minded capitalists of Western Europe to enjoy the benefits of the "huge" Russian market would, in due time, compel the governments of these countries to accept the legitimacy of the Soviet regime, in spite of their strong antipathy for the political system of communism.

At the same time, however, Lenin did not perceive any comparable permanent pressures for external trade that were likely to develop in the kind of planned and inward-looking economy that he hoped to build in Russia. He regarded the observable need for foreign trade on the part of his government to be prompted by dislocations and imbalances in domestic supply brought about by years of living under abnormal economic conditions. Purchases made abroad at this time were considered to be justified on the grounds that they were unique and transitory, a function of the emergency conditions following the prolonged civil war. These purchases were limited, it was generally explained, to the kinds of implements and materials that would, eventually, in Lenin's words, "enable our factories to produce on their own all that is necessary."

Not all the principal leaders of the country during the mid-twenties, it should be noted, were convinced that economic isolation was indeed the most practical goal to be pursued by a country as backward in industrial development as Soviet Russia was at that time. This was particularly true of some Bolshevik leaders who had a close knowledge of the facts of international economic life. Such a man was Leonid Krasin, the first People's Commissar of Foreign Trade. Krasin was well aware that the progressive industrialization of a country tends to increase rather than diminish its need for and participation in world trade. In a speech delivered in November 1924, Krasin characterized as "completely mistaken" the popular notion that the division of labor among nations in the world market is mainly oriented towards exchange of goods between nations engaged exclusively in industrial production on the one hand and nations engaged primarily in agricultural and mineral production on the other. The most intensive growth of trade in the modern world, he pointed out, was actually taking place among the very highly industrialized nations of Europe, such as Germany, England, and France. His own knowledge of the world economy, he said, and his practical experience as a former businessman, brought him to the conclusion that "the industrial development of a country like the Soviet Union will hardly result in a decline of demand in the USSR for the products of foreign industry." Unlike many of his associates, Krasin was personally inclined, on the evidence at hand, towards a dynamic view of the process of industrialization. He argued that by the very nature of things, Soviet foreign trade agencies would always have to count on the appearance in the world market of "more complex machines, new chemical products, various patented products . . . which our own industry would not be in position to manufacture." There is no evidence, however, that he succeeded in winning Stalin over to his own pragmatic view of the value of keeping open the channels of external trade in the interest of sustaining a condition of balanced industrial growth in the Soviet Union.

FOREIGN CONCESSIONS VERSUS TECHNICAL AID CONTRACTS

In keeping with Lenin's preference for terminal forms of economic collaboration with the West, the Soviet government proceeded, even before the coming of NEP, to establish a system of "foreign concessions" under which duly qualified and licensed companies from abroad were permitted to operate a number of mining, industrial, and commercial enterprises in Soviet Russia. This arrangement was worked out by Lenin, who considered the concessions to be most suitable as a means of resolving the very real conflict between the immediate need for outside technical help and the long-term commitment to economic self-sufficiency. Under a decree, published on November 23, 1920, the Soviet government declared itself ready to conclude concession agreements with "reliable foreign firms" and to provide the necessary guarantees that property invested in such enterprises would not be nationalized, confiscated, or requisitioned. The decree further guaranteed that no arbitrary orders of any kind would be issued which might in any way adversely affect the concession agreements.

It seems unnecessary, in this context, to explore the reasons why Lenin's carefully devised program of foreign concessions failed to develop any real momentum or, eventually, to produce any significant economic results during the ten years of its existence. The fact is that by the end of 1929 there were only 59 foreign concessions in operation in the country, most of them small in size. The value of their aggregate output was only 44 million dollars, or no more than a fraction of one percent of the total annual product of state industry in the Soviet Union. It is even more to the point to recall that by this stage in Soviet history—that is, the late twenties—Stalin was already firmly in the saddle and that, as one might expect, he had his own ideas of the best way to proceed to transplant foreign technology onto the Soviet economic landscape under political conditions acceptable to him. Stalin's preferred method of economic cooperation with industrial firms from the West, as it turned out, was the "technical assistance contract." Under his leadership, therefore, the foreign concessions were gradually squeezed out of existence, largely by means of a variety of "labor disputes," long before the expiration of their legal duration, which usually ranged from 10 to 20 years.

Stalin had evidently changed his mind quite abruptly. He came out strongly in favor of a contract arrangement for technical assistance that was not only basically different in character from the concession agreement but also much shorter in duration. The technical aid contract appealed to him for a number of reasons. To begin with, it offered a direct choice to the Soviet government of the individual Western firm to be invited to assume a given set of obligations. These amounted typically to an undertaking to build and equip a complete new plant for a major branch of industrial production. Under such a contract, each Western firm was required, as part of the pattern, to place at the disposal of the Soviet government, among other things, "its technical processes and trade secrets." In addition, it was required to undertake "to send engineers and skilled workmen to the USSR to act as instructors, as well as to admit Soviet engineers to its own workshops." Contracts of this type, covering periods of two to five years, were arranged for most of the basic industries in the USSR. At the height of this phase of economic collaboration with the West, between 1928 and 1933, up to 2,000 technical experts from the United States alone—including designers, engineers, and mechanics— were employed in the USSR. No contract in this series, incidentally, is known to have been cancelled by the Soviet government prior to its legal date of expiration.

There is no reason to believe that Stalin ever regretted his choice of this method of accelerated technological transfer from abroad. He seems to have remained confirmed in his judgement that the technical assistance contract, which could be tailored to suit the current operational needs of every essential industry in the country, was by far the more appropriate instrument for the pursuit of the goal of eventual economic self-sufficiency in the USSR. At the same time, this method enjoyed the added advantage of involving the Soviet government in legal arrangements with outside firms that provided for short periods of duration and called for the fulfillment of a number of specified technical tasks. Meanwhile, the foreign trade monopoly continued to be managed by the leadership of the USSR in such a way as to "permit the Soviet state to utilize most fully the economic interest of the capitalist nations in [its] market." The obverse of this condition—namely, the interest of the Soviet state in the capitalist market—continued as before to be treated as a strictly short-term affair. It was regarded as motivated primarily by the need to strengthen Soviet industry until it could reach the stage of self-sustained growth.

STALIN'S DRIVE TOWARDS ECONOMIC DISENGAGEMENT

The objective of economic disengagement from the outside world remained high on the Soviet political agenda. Thus, for example, writing on the occasion of the tenth anniversary of the Bolshevik revolution, an authoritative commentator on foreign trade considered it appropriate to restate the standard formula for a successful national economic policy as follows: "Everything that can be procured or produced within the country must gradually disappear from the import plan." There was no hint in this formula that the Soviet government was giving any thought to the possible value of foreign trade as a means of arriving at a more effective utilization of the economic resources of the country. Nor is there any evidence in general that the economic planners of the country showed any interest during this period of relative international calm in discovering the areas of production in which the USSR enjoys a comparative advantage or in developing the channels necessary for the exchange of these competitive domestic goods through the world market for the products of the most efficient producers abroad. Foreign trade was perceived wholly as an operation oriented towards import substitution. The same writer, in fact, ended his survey of the economic situation in the comparatively quiescent year of 1927 with a call for "the strengthening of Soviet industry in order to diminish more and more our dependence on foreign countries."

The task of strengthening Soviet industry for technological self-sufficiency, through the medium of technical assistance contracts and foreign trade, was envisioned by Stalin as a readily attainable, short-term objective. He seems to have defined "modern technological capability" in strictly static terms. As he saw it, once Russia imported all the known important technical processes and innovations of the period, the goal of national technical and economic independence would be fully attained. In order to speed up the movement towards this objective, Stalin settled on a carefully screened list of "essential" industries that were in need of "strengthening" according to a clearly determined order of priorities. In due time, the branches of industry important enough to be included in this list began to enjoy the benefits of preferred treatment, from the standpoint of capital investment and modern technology. They were provided with the best productive equipment available abroad and introduced to the latest known foreign technological processes. They received, in addition, the benefit of the services of foreign engineers and technicians imported from the leading industrial countries of the West. These foreign technicians, working under the terms of technical assistance contracts drafted by Soviet specialists, were obliged, in the case of each individual selected industry, to elaborate an up-to-date construction design for an integrated industrial plant or complex of plants, to install the necessary equipment, and to supervise consequent production during a trial period of operations.

As a result, the period from 1926 to 1933 witnessed something of a high-water mark in economic cooperation between the USSR and the world industrial community at large. While it lasted, moreover, it was a cooperative undertaking of broad scope, designed to keep wide open the channels of technical communication with the outside world. As it turned out, the duration of this undertaking was limited, lasting only as long as it was considered officially necessary to fulfill the country's quota of import requirements as perceived at that moment in history. Owing to this drive to import technology, and partly because of the world-wide economic depression, the USSR emerged as the leading importer of machinery and equipment in the world at this time. In 1931, about one-third of the machinery moving in international trade, excluding automobiles, went to the Soviet Union. These imports were utilized, in keeping with official objectives, not for meeting the current capital needs of existing plants but "almost exclusively for the equipment of newly built enterprises in the heavy industrial sector." The will of history, in Stalin's view, seemed quite clear at this juncture: it called for a change in the direction of the systematic curtailment of foreign trade. Accordingly, a resolution adopted at the Seventeenth Party Congress held in 1934 stipulated that "during the Second Five-Year Plan the USSR must be converted into a country that is independent in a technical and economic sense, into the leading technological state in Europe."

After the passing of this water-mark, the People's Commissar of Foreign Trade, A. P. Rosengolts, was ready to explain how the government of the USSR viewed the future of its external economic relations now that the intensive industrialization program of the First Five-Year Plan had been brought to a satisfactory conclusion. He stressed two points:

(1) "our interest in imports has declined considerably" and (2) "we can now . . . display greater endurance than ever before by utilizing our considerable maneuvering possibilities." To this he deemed it appropriate to append the familiar official proposition that "Soviet interest in external trade is now less than the interest displayed in our orders by the capitalist countries." Against this background, the official press began around 1935, to pronounce the campaign for the industrialization of the country, partly with the aid of foreign imports, as an accomplished fact. Soviet spokesmen started assuring the public that the growth of industry had reached a stage where the nation could "sharply curtail imports without any loss whatsoever for the domestic economy." Henceforth, the official view ran, Soviet trading organizations would be authorized to engage in trade transactions only in cases where they were certain to receive especially attractive conditions, either on the export or import side of the trade. After the mid-thirties, in fact, Soviet foreign trade experts began to react somewhat defensively in regard to any observed increase in the level of trade, especially in the case of imports. When they reported "a certain increase" in the value of imports between 1935 and 1936, for example, they explained to their readers that "in a relative sense," that is, in relation to the rising level of industrial consumption in the country, such an increase was no real cause for alarm; it did not have to be considered as a serious deviation from the basic position of the Soviet government that the need for foreign trade had substantively diminished.

In keeping with this basic attitude, and with the new policy behind it, the organizational structure of the foreign trade in the country was ordered to be changed. Official spokesmen contended at the time:

. . . we must destroy the long-established practice under which our trading organizations sent people abroad in order to look there for buyers of our export goods and for sellers of import goods to us. . . . The Party has placed before us the task of so organizing our work as to make sure that foreign firms come to us and conclude transactions for export or import here, in Moscow, directly with our export and import organizations.

This shift towards Moscow as the main centre for the conclusion of foreign commercial transactions, ordered in June 1935, was greeted by the official press as the "organizational expression" of the end of Soviet dependence on imports from the economies of other nations. The specialists pointed with particular pride to the fact that the level of machinery imports into the USSR declined by nearly 90 percent between 1931 and 1937 from 2,076 million to 278 million rubles. In Stalin's opinion, made public in an address to graduates of the Red Army Academy in May 1935, this vigorously enforced control over imports, with emphasis on self-sufficiency, had advanced the situation to a point where "we have in the main outlived the period of famine in technical resources." One official commentator on the above Stalin text developed this idea still further, concluding with a flourish to the effect that "this was an import that has led to curtailment of imports, thanks to the colossally expanded, powerful, technically advanced Soviet heavy industry."

Once the Second Five-Year Plan had been completed, by the end of 1937, Soviet officials began to celebrate a dual achievement in the economic development of the USSR. They glorified both the completion of ten years of "scientific economic planning" in the country and the liquidation of its temporary "technical economic backwardness." Both achievements, it was asserted, were made possible as a direct result of the "innate advantages of the socialist order." Typically, the completion of the Second Five-Year Plan was hailed in the following language:

The USSR has fulfilled the grandiose plans of the Second Five-Year Plan, with the aid of an insignificant volume of imports, and in the future we can fufill our plans, without the need for imports. Nearly everything that is at all needed for a powerful country—everything—is being produced in the USSR.

In order to present evidence in support of this sweeping conclusion, Soviet experts in the field, academic as well as official, cited some comparative statistics on the importance of foreign trade to the major economies of the world. In these comparisons, Japan and the leading countries of Europe were shown to be exporting some 20–25 percent of their aggregate domestic product; even the United States was shown to have exported as much as 10 percent of its total national product before 1929. In contrast, they pointed out, "the dependence of the Soviet Union [on foreign economies] was less than that of any other country." The USSR, these figures showed, exported only 1.3 percent of its total national product in 1935; on the import side, Soviet involvement in the world market was even more insignificant, accounting for only one percent of the entire domestic product of the nation in the same year.[2] Such a development was no mere accident, according to the official experts: "This is a characteristic feature of the socialist economy, which bases itself entirely on the internal market." To be on the safe side, this Soviet writer proceeded to quote a dictum pronounced by Stalin in 1926. To no one's surprise, he used much the same words as the leader: "Our industry bases itself on the internal market." He did not, for his own good reasons, include the final qualifying phrase of Stalin's remark—"primarily the peasant market."

When the German author Marx-Reinhard suggested in a book pub-

---

[2] During this period, official opinion in the USSR tended to heap scorn on the claim of the Nazi government in Germany that it was leading a world-wide movement towards autarky. The Soviet view was that the German leadership was throwing "good money after bad" into a useless effort to stimulate production of synthetic raw materials. In the light of Marxist theory, it would seem, fascist economic policy was inherently incapable of producing real autarky, as long as it continued to base its economic activity on capitalist practices. "These fascist attempts to attain independence of imports in regard to the supply of raw materials have not, and could not, attain any major results, in view of the capitalist contradictions."

lished in 1930 that the Soviet Union, despite the rapid build-up of its own industrial plant, was likely to continue to import machinery from the West, citing as his reason the fact that it usually takes many decades to achieve self-sufficiency in the entire range of existing industrial equipment, he was ridiculed in the official Soviet literature on foreign trade. Specifically, he was accused of not understanding the socialist character of the economy of the USSR. According to one Soviet author, this was a case in which "the low-brow idealogues of capitalism" were not really to blame. Being culture-bound bourgeois intellectuals, they could "hardly have expected that the Soviet nation would be able to utilize the importation of machinery so effectively, with such exceptional goal-directedness, with such a profoundly conceived plan."

At the highest level of authority within the Party, it became fashionable towards the end of the thirties to associate a high level of foreign trade with a state of "backwardness and poverty," especially insofar as the Soviet Union was concerned. The Soviet success in liberating itself from backwardness, and at the same time from external commerce, was summed up as follows by A. Mikoyan, then the highest authority on foreign trade in the USSR:

> In the period when we were still backward and poor, when we did not have our own developed machine-building industry and we had to build industry at any cost, we were forced to export abroad a great deal of raw materials and foodstuffs, which we needed ourselves, and we exported these in order to obtain foreign exchange, and to use these earnings to buy machine tools for industry, equipment for tractor and automobile plants.

In the absence of any serious interest in the relative scales and costs of production, in the late thirties trade came to be regarded as something in the nature of a burden on the economy, a physical drain of commodities out of the country that ought normally to be consumed within the domestic economy. As one official text expressed it, with reference to this period, "the urgent need for large-scale imports disappeared," and it was no longer necessary "to expend vast resources that could be effectively applied toward socialist construction."

THE GRAND ILLUSION OF THE PARALLEL WORLD MARKET

The traumatic experience of the Second World War and along with it the massive economic support received by the USSR from the Western capitalist nations, brought little change in the fundamental bias of Soviet leaders in favour of autarky. For all their continued concern with reading the signs of history correctly, in the final analysis the rulers of the Soviet Union chose not to allow their post-war policy to be influenced in any way by the whole-hearted and massive support obtained from the West during the struggle for survival as a nation. If anything, their deep-seated urge towards isolation from the world economy was visibly reinforced by the consequences of the Second World War, if in a somewhat altered form.

In the wake of the westward advance of the Red Army, the Soviet Union moved rapidly to establish a broad belt of communist-ruled states as a means of achieving greater military security. At the same time, however, this enlarged domain served to bolster Soviet hopes for increased political and economic self-sufficiency. More particularly, the emergence of a group of communist nations in Eastern Europe appeared to Stalin to make his ceaseless quest for autarky more attainable at last. It helped to provide new impetus for the pursuit of the goal of economic self-sufficiency, this time on a broader territorial basis, i.e., no longer on the scale of a single nation but on the basis of a "new, socialist, world system of states."

It is clear from the authoritative remarks of the chief economic planner of the period, Nikolay A. Voznesensky, that the Soviet government had no intention of abandoning its apprehensive approach towards the world economy as a result of its shattering war experience. Nor did it see any reason for discarding autarky as an ideal. When called upon to spell out the economic policy of the Party for the first post-war five-year plan, Voznesensky followed closely both the reasoning and the language used by Soviet policy-makers and theorists before the war. He gave his official opinion in these words:

The USSR will continue in the future to maintain economic ties with foreign countries in accordance with the tested line of the Soviet government, which is directed towards the attainment of the technical and economic independence of the Soviet Union.

During the early years of the post-war period, it became evident to outside observers that Stalin had grown very infatuated with his own unique political creation, "the new and parallel world market," which extended over the territory of the USSR and the communist states that came into existence after World War II. He considered the creation of this rival market to be the most important political consequence of the war and a tangible result of his own activist policies in the post-war period. In the official language of the period, the international economy will never be quite the same again, for, it was said, "a world democratic market had arisen alongside the world capitalist market." The old, single capitalist world market, as Stalin saw it, had begun to disintegrate. Accordingly, the main thrust of Soviet foreign trade policy was to be directed towards "strengthening economic cooperation among the socialist countries." Henceforth, Soviet foreign trade would be assigned a new function: service as an instrumentality for the "planned link-up" of the economic development of these countries, "on the basis of the international socialist division of labor and fraternal cooperation and mutual assistance."

The advantages of the "world democratic market" were, in the Soviet view, economic factors of far-reaching political significance. It was at one and the same time a greatly enlarged political domain and a brave new economic world independent of the resources under the control of capitalism and sufficient unto itself. "The world democratic market has at its disposal," in the words of the official textbook, "sufficient resources to provide every country with everything necessary for its economic development."

If the men in power within the USSR were troubled by any shadow of doubt on this score, they made sure not to reveal it to the outside world. They all reported in unison that they were continuing to find their original assumptions about the innate superiority of the socialist world market validated by "the steady growth and consolidation" of this market. In other words, they were delighted to accept the results of their own arbitrary administrative orders for expanding intra-bloc trade as the judgment of history, as amounting to "irrefutable proof of the historic progressiveness" of the new, parallel world market. One of the major consequences of the establishment of the world socialist market, this theory stated, came in the form of an unprecedented body of benefits growing out of the economic cooperation between the Soviet Union and its new allies, the countries of Eastern Europe. "The experience of this cooperation," Stalin wrote in 1952, "shows that not a single capitalist country could have rendered such effective and technically competent assistance to the People's Democracies as the Soviet Union is rendering them."

By contrast, because of the lack of a similar climate for cooperation, the outlook for the major trading nations of the West was adjudged by Stalin to be rather hopeless. In the future the capitalist economies could expect to be confronted by increasingly severe competition, including an unexpected form of economic pressure from the countries making up the new, parallel world market. Indeed, as far as the immediate future was concerned, "it may be confidently said," Stalin predicted, "that with this pace of industrial development [among the communist countries], it will soon come to pass that these countries will not only no longer be in need of imports from the capitalist countries, but will themselves feel the necessity of finding an outside market for their surplus products."

Nonetheless, even under these circumstances—so dramatically new and so clearly favorable for the pursuit of ever closer economic cooperation within the socialist camp—official Soviet opinion, it should be noted, did not advocate a complete severance of commercial ties with the West. A measure of contact was still thought to be necessary for the socialist countries in the interest of "furthering the improvement of their economies." It was quite plain on the evidence, moreover, that continued commercial contact of this kind was favored primarily because of assumed strong interest on the part of the West in selling its "pressing surpluses" to the socialist market. It was reasoned that such an interest could, under proper conditions, be usefully engaged in any process of negotiation on economic or political matters. In the standard language of Soviet editorial comment of the period: "There need be no obstacle to the development of mutually beneficial trade with the nations of the capitalist camp." Such trade, however, was not a matter of particular significance on the Soviet side of the world-wide political barrier. "The development of trade relations among the nations of the two camps is of considerably greater significance for the capitalist countries, especially in connection with the continuous contraction of the world capitalist market."

The reorientation of Soviet foreign trade toward the socialist market, as shown by the record, had gone a long way by the end of the Stalin era. Some 60 percent of the entire foreign trade of the USSR was devoted to its European communist trade partners in 1953. By comparison, the same group of countries accounted for only 1.5 percent of Soviet foreign trade in 1938. Similarly, in 1953 trade with China had grown to a point where it represented 18 percent of total Soviet trade, as compared with only 4 percent in 1938. Taken together, all the communist-ruled countries accounted for 83 percent of the foreign trade of the Soviet Union in the last year of the long Stalin era. The degree of self-isolation within the confines of a regional market was most conspicuous; the large and diverse economies of the world industrial community had been successfully relegated to a peripheral role in the economic life of the USSR.

NIKITA KHRUSHCHEV'S OPENING TO THE WEST

After the death of Stalin, the external economic behavior of the Soviet Union began to suggest quite strongly that a serious revaluation of official policy on the part of the new leadership was under way. The severe degree of studied isolation from the international economy, which had been the hallmark of Soviet policy during the preceding eight years, diminished somewhat during the last months of 1953. By their action, if not by their words, the new leaders left no room for doubt that they had found some of the arguments used by Stalin in support of his policy of economic isolation rather unconvincing. He had argued, it will be recalled, that the West had entered its long-awaited phase of economic decline after the fatal blow that was delivered to its stability by "the great historic victories of communism" in Europe and Asia. As far as practical policy was concerned, it followed from this argument that the capitalist countries could be effectively helped along the road to oblivion if the Soviet government could continue to keep their access to the communist world market as limited as possible. The observable facts of international economic life, however, pointed clearly in the opposite direction, namely to a state of general economic good health among the nations making up the industrial West. By the early fifties, both foreign trade and industrial production in the major Western nations were showing a strong upward trend. Industrial production of Western Europe was 36 percent higher in 1952 than it was in 1948. Industrial employment increased by 8 percent. During the same four-year period, the export trade of all non-communist countries increased by one-third, from 60 billion to 80 billion dollars.

Three years later, at the Twentieth Party Congress, Mikoyan felt free to articulate the views of the new leaders on the basic issues related to the international economy. He reported that they had found Stalin's analysis of the economy of contemporary capitalism "hardly helpful or hardly correct." Stalin, he recalled, had forecast that "the volume of production in these countries [would] shrink." It was now quite clear to his successors that it was impossible to square Stalin's properly optimistic forecast with the hard facts as they had evolved around "the complex and contradictory manifestations of contemporary capitalism," especially "the fact of the growth of capitalist production in many countries after the war." To refute Stalin's highly doctrinaire analysis, Mikoyan noted, all you had to do was to look at the real world beyond the frontiers of the USSR. You would find, he contended, that throughout the post-war period, the developed capitalist countries were both expanding their economies and increasing their trade, among themselves as well as around the world. Evidently this was a case in which history itself was plainly not tending to its business. In these circumstances, it was argued, why should the Soviet Union deny itself the obvious benefits of a modest increase in trade with the highly productive and technologically sensitive economies of the industrial West?

The Imperatives of Technical Modernization

After he succeeded in eliminating his own peers and rivals from their positions of power, Party chieftain Khrushchev was left free to apply his prodigious energies towards the task of improving the operation of the domestic economy, as he perceived this task. One after another, he unveiled new initiatives designed to raise the operational efficiency of the domestic production plant, in the hope of thereby increasing the ability of the Soviet system to pay dividends, economic as well as political. In his new capacity as supreme leader, after June 1957, Khrushchev also tried hard, and not without a certain amount of success, to breathe a measure of new vitality into the old political slogans, to inject some variety into the flow of simulated optimism from the official media of opinion.

In the course of coming into closer daily contact with the operation of the domestic economic order, Khrushchev stumbled upon a number of unpleasant circumstances. Being a man of gregarious disposition, he often shared these findings with his captive audiences, and, in the process, helped to enliven his all too long and frequent official speeches. On one such occasion, in May 1958, he reported having learned that the entire procession of new techniques and products generated by the welter of discoveries made within the modern chemical industry had literally by-passed the Soviet economy, while its leaders were preoccupied with the pursuit of the will-of-the-wisp of "technical and economic independ-ence," i.e., with the protection of the domestic economy against possible negative influences from the outside world.

Information of this nature helped to steer Khrushchev in the direction of broadening his contacts with the business world of the West. In March 1959, for instance, Khrushchev took the initiative in delegating himself as "a representative of Soviet business circles," and travelled in that capacity to the Leipzig Fair in East Germany. Using the massive Soviet pavillion as his backdrop, he addressed a large group of businessmen for the West who were assembled there for his benefit. He dwelled in some detail on the advantages that awaited them if and when they decided to expand their commodity trade with the Soviet Union. He explained, in accord-ance with the standard Soviet formula on this subject, that he was thinking primarily of the economic interest of the capitalist countries. It is you, he informed them, who need the trade in order "to use your industries to capacity, to reduce unemployment, and to obtain normal income and profits."

About the time of this historic visit, Soviet economic relations with the industrialized countries outside the bloc became perceptibly more active as well as more purposive. The Soviet government revived an old tech-nique, not actively used since the late 1930's, for the promotion of its own economic development. It resumed the practice of importing complete industrial plants from the West, along with the patents and the engineer-ing services required for launching these units into production. After several decades of self-imposed isolation, this technique, plainly enough, still recommended itself to the Soviet leadership as the most effective means by which newly developed ideas embodied in these sets of equip-ment, technical processes, and finished products could be physically trans-planted onto the industrial landscape of the USSR.

As a man with a practical bent of mind and a competitive interest in building up an efficient production system at home, Khrushchev rated the acquisition of new, market-tested technology from the world market very high, considering it a direct stimulus to the economic development of the USSR. A campaign for systematic procurement of this type, he had previously explained with specific reference to the chemical industry, in his address to the May 1958 Plenem, would contribute directly "to the more rapid fulfillment of our program for the construction of new . . . enterprises without wasting time on the creation of designs and mastering the process of production of new types of equipment."

When it came to spending hard currency, Khrushchev was not a man given to impulsive behavior. He was willing enough to spend scarce foreign exchange, but only if he knew of no more promising alternative.

He had gradually become convinced that continued Soviet economic isolation from the world industrial community, under conditions of rapid technological change, would ultimately prove to be a costly exercise in political self-indulgence. He was too competitive a politician to permit the Soviet Union, under his leadership, to lose ground in the international economic race. Accordingly, after he had acquired the necessary practical experience in this sphere, Khrushchev began to suggest, in his numerous formal and casual remarks, that he was not impressed by the methods which the economic bureaucracy of the USSR was using to keep up with technical progress in the West. These methods consisted, in the main, of employing one, or both, of the following two approaches: (1) screening thoroughly the published technical literature of the West for the purpose of incorporating its findings into the current flow of Soviet industrial research, and (2) importing prototypes of more advanced models of foreign machinery for the purpose of imitating and eventually assimilating them into the production process at home. Both these approaches, Khrushchev discovered, left a great deal to be desired. Soviet industry lost a vast amount of valuable time and remained, for the most part, outside of the mainstream of technical modernization. Production equipment supplied to factories, and finished products, were, as a result, conspicuous by their display of a visible layer of technological dust.

Khrushchev was acutely aware of the direct bearing of continued technical modernization on the current efficiency of production. In keeping with this awareness, he never hesitated to compare Soviet equipment with that of the West, usually to the disadvantage of the former. On one occasion, for example, he reported that the Soviet aviation industry was producing engines that operated for only 500 hours, while British aircraft engines of the same class worked 2,500 hours. On all such occasions, he made it known that he had become too impatient to wait for the established, routine approach to technical innovation in the USSR to continue its familiar bureaucratic course. He declared himself willing, if necessary, to pay in cash for any foreign patents involved in order to acquire directly, and for immediate use, the most efficient industrial technology available. One practical outcome of this change in approach, begun under Khrushchev, was formal Soviet adherence, effective July 1, 1965, to the Paris Convention for the Protection of Industrial Property.

Thus, by the time of Khrushchev's displacement from power, the long-standing commitment to autarky as a practical goal for economic development had weakened perceptibly among the Soviet political elite. Khrushchev was a willful man, who pressed hard on this issue, and finally succeeded in convincing his associates of the importance of his own practical discovery that the modern tempo of technical progress had created an immense, world-wide reservoir of new production ideas fed from international sources and emptying continuously across national frontiers as part of the process of international trade. Given this situation, no single nation could afford either to reproduce this vast and ever-expanding reservoir on its own, or, still less, to isolate itself from it. Stalin, in his own, more "heroic" time, may have succeeded in imposing a state of economic self-isolation upon the USSR, while building his elaborate myth about the unique economic potential of his "parallel world market"; but working in a better informed, more skeptical environment, Khrushchev could not realistically undertake to turn his back upon the practical realities of contemporary international economic life.

The Changing Realities of the Socialist Market

During most of his years in high office, however, Khrushchev had no difficulty in accepting the second premise of Stalin's parochial foreign economic policy. This was the proposition that the Soviet state, given its "special role in history," should continue to pursue external economic relations primarily along political lines. Most immediately, of course, this meant the closest economic cooperation with the other communist-ruled countries of the world, those countries that had already "forever broken with the capitalist system." Khrushchev was quite naturally persuaded that a policy of utmost concentration of foreign trade activity within its own political orbit would enable the Soviet Union to achieve the dual purpose of "unifying and strengthening the socialist system of states," and, at the same time, deny the major trading nations free access to the markets, as well as the commodity resources, of the communist group of countries. The latter objective is generally expressed in official doctrine as "narrowing the sphere in which the principal capitalist countries have access to world resources."

The various putative advantages of growing trade within the bloc, as officially recited, are too numerous to be examined here. As might be expected, they cover the whole gamut of economic benefits considered to be attainable through the pursuit of the theory and practice of soviet economic development. In the context of this study, it is important to indicate that the advantages of maximum intra-bloc trade include, among others, benefits of a protective character. What this means, in effect, is that by maximizing intra-bloc trade turnover, the Soviet economy is assumed to be gaining added protection for itself against the unqualified evils of competition, anarchy of production, and economic exploitation holding uncontrolled sway over the capitalist market. Large-scale trade among communist partners, according to official doctrine, is certain to yield benefits bearing directly on the collective growth of the economic power of the communist camp. By their "collective, planned utilization of available resources, [they will be certain] to help develop the productive forces of the individual member countries and thereby increase the economic power of the socialist camp as a whole."

During the early sixties, however, it became quite apparent that

Khrushchev's devotion to the cause of the socialist market had begun to wane. His attempt to steer the regional economic organization of Eastern Europe (Comecon) in the direction of joint economic planning in June 1962 ended in failure.[3] He discovered that some of the member countries of Comecon were more interested in the feeling of pride and power they derived from their diversified industrial expansion programs than in the higher economic returns they were likely to secure from a more rational division of labor within the socialist market. He could not help being discouraged to find, for example, that the leaders of many of these countries were too bent upon the endless diversification of their under-sized industrial plant to be seriously concerned, as he was, over the persistence of small-scale, inefficient production in most of the national industries of the smaller countries in the region. Nor were these leaders as eager, as he was, to make a better showing in the economic competition with the Common Market or with the West in general. Instead, most of the smaller countries of Eastern Europe seemed rather to incline to give the Soviet Union a free hand in its efforts to solve the problem of competition between the two world political systems if their big neighbor would only give them in exchange the freedom to dispose of their economic resources in accordance with their own national interests, as they perceived them.

In the course of his search for ways to improve the climate for intrabloc cooperation, Khrushchev found the forces of economic nationalism and administrative inertia all too well entrenched in Eastern Europe. The leaders of the smaller countries of the region had been clearly over-educated in the fundamental Soviet approach to economic success. Like their earlier Soviet counterparts, they came to regard a rapid rate of industrial growth as the hallmark of successful economic development. Working with ambitious quantitative plans, in the manner of the Soviet Union, they had also become worshippers of "the cult of the ton." At the same time, the economic policies pursued by the smaller countries of Eastern Europe left little elbow room, and little real incentive, for the full play of the forces of innovation. As evident from Khrushchev's occasional public complaints, the managers of production in the command economy tended to be rather passive on this score; they had no incentive to exert any pressure upon their own research institutes either for machines or products of a better design. There were, plainly enough, no real rewards in the system for the time to be spent and the risk to be incurred in introducing a more efficient manufacturing process or a better quality product.

Khrushchev was perceptibly puzzled by the lack of incentive to manufacture products of a high standard of quality in the countries of the

---

[3] *A Background Study on East West Trade,* United States Senate, Committee on Foreign Relations, April 1965, pp. 26–38.

socialist camp. At times, in fact, he gave expression to his puzzlement in public, though he always sought to explain away this critical weakness of the quantity-oriented economies of Eastern Europe in the usual terms of "the temporary shortcomings of our dynamic economic system." For example, in the course of a tour he made through several factories in Hungary in 1964, Khrushchev digressed from the main topic of his speech to muse over a question that had apparently been long weighing on his mind. He reflected:

As a rule, the plants and factories in the capitalist countries turn out fine products. But these goods are made not by the capitalists but by men and women workers, by engineers. If the workers, engineers, and employees manufacture excellent goods while working for the capitalists, why then must we, the workers, engineers, and technologists in the socialist countries, work less well, producing goods of lower quality. After all, we are doing it all for ourselves, for our own people, for the building of socialism, for the building of communism.

In general, the momentum of intra-bloc commodity exchange has remained strong throughout the recent period. Trade between the USSR and Eastern Europe has continued to expand in volume. In 1965, for instance, the value of Soviet imports from Eastern Europe reached 4.7 billion dollars, a figure nearly three times the value of imports from the industrial West. It is most doubtful, however, whether Khrushchev, during his latter years in office, saw in this routine escalation of intra-Comecon commercial exchanges the making of a really self-sufficient regional economy in Eastern Europe, equal to and independent of the actively trading, cost-conscious industrial community of the outside world.

THE WITHERING AWAY OF THE SELF-SUFFICIENT STATE

Only three years have passed since the fateful power play, known formally as "the decision of the October 1964 plenum," that toppled Khrushchev from his position of supreme control. In most areas of policy-making, the style of leadership in the Soviet Union has changed conspicuously during this period. The official climate has come to be dominated by a mood of caution and a policy of general avoidance of new initiatives. As seen from the outside, the new men at the top of the Soviet power structure have succeeded in maintaining their collective leadership over a significant period of time, but they have done so largely by way of keeping open most of their options. This general mode of behavior cannot, however, be described as applying to the sphere of foreign economic policy. In regard to the issue of autarky, in particular, the post-Khrushchev leadership has not hesitated to show its hand, which indicates rather clearly that it favors a much more active engagement in economic intercourse with the world industrial community. Ever since

Kosygin's speech to the September 1965 Plenum, the new leaders have spoken and acted consistently in support of a more economically informed approach to foreign trade, both within and beyond the socialist market.

Through a More Expedient Approach to Socialist Trade

As part of the present reexamination of established policy, the whole subject of the utility of the socialist market has, for the first time, come to be viewed in a more sober light. While the rhetoric that suffuses all references to the realm of external trade has undergone little change, some of the practical issues involved in intra-bloc trade have begun to be aired in public discussion with a relative degree of candor. Foreign trade experts now feel free to discuss "the unresolved problems" that have arisen in commodity trade between the USSR and its socialist partners. These problems, it turns out, are quite fundamental, touching upon the stubborn facts of production costs and market prices. In its recent discussion of these issues, the Soviet economic press has begun to present evidence to the effect that the commodity structure of its trade with other Comecon members was ill-conceived, and has often been unprofitable for the USSR in a number of ways.

Soviet trade analysts now contend openly that the enormous volume of fuels, minerals, and other raw materials that the USSR exports annually to its socialist partners represents a growing burden on the capital resources of the country. Such exports require continued heavy outlay of new investment. Yet, the cost of this capital outlay, say the Russians, is not being recaptured by the prices currently in effect in the socialist market. While on this subject, the trade experts of the Soviet Union also make clear that they are quite dissatisfied with the other side of the bargain, i.e., with the fact that the merchandise that the Soviet Union imports from the other bloc members is all too heavily weighted on the side of machinery and consumer goods. Goods of this type, according to their calculations, require much smaller capital input for sustained expansion of their production.[4]

One Soviet economist has recently calculated that in order to obtain one "foreign exchange ruble" from the sales of some of its typical raw material exports to the Comecon countries, the USSR has to invest between five and eight times as much as is normally required to earn such income from its own machinery export items. Nor is this all. What also emerges from these recent, more candid discussions is that the machinery the Soviet Union imports from its socialist trade partners is overpriced in relation to its quality. The same Soviet writer volunteers the opinion,

---

[4] The share of machinery in total Soviet imports from Comecon countries was 45.5 percent in 1964. It had risen to this level from 43.6 percent in 1960.

with the kind of restraint that is generally indicated in all public discussions of intra-bloc problems, that "some socialist machines could be resold on the world market only at sharply reduced prices."

The new tone that has crept into these discussions in the mid-sixties suggests that Soviet officialdom has found it difficult to continue to ignore the salient fact that an exchange of goods that rests on a sound ideological base is not necessarily always a good economic bargain. In the present, less dogmatic political climate, the trade officials of the USSR have exhibited a strong tendency to pursue trade primarily for the opportunity it affords to obtain real and measurable economic benefits. It takes no rare political insight to recognize that the trade pattern now followed by countries of Eastern Europe among themselves is essentially a product of the cold war. As a matter of record, this trade assumed its particular commodity structure under the pressure of the political tensions that developed between East and West during the late 1940's. This, of course, was a period in which the Soviet Union was pressing relentlessly to expand westward by way of imposing minority governments on its weak neighbors immediately to the West. This display of expansionism, in turn, evoked a strong response on the part of the Western nations. One response, it will be recalled, took the form of barring the shipment of advanced types of machinery to Russia and its new captive alliance. The situation obviously called for a quick response in order to find a substitute source of imports, especially of machinery, needed to help rebuild the seriously demolished industrial plant of the USSR.

Faced by an urgent need for imported equipment, the Soviet leaders filled it, in large part, by directing the more industrially developed countries of Eastern Europe towards adaptation of their economies to meet the conditions of the cold war. In the early years after the war, it was a relatively easy matter for the Soviet leadership to impose a drastic change of domestic production patterns on some of its newly acquired weak allies, in particular Czechoslovakia and East Germany, two countries that were to initiate the production of a wide variety of heavy industrial equipment for export to the USSR. The USSR, for its part, was thereby enabled to keep its own basic production and trade pattern unchanged: it continued to provide, in its commodity exchange within Eastern Europe, roughly the same range of raw materials it had exported in the past to its highly industrialized trade partners in the West. Today, the economic rationality of this commodity exchange between the USSR and its small allies is clearly far less compelling. An exchange in which Russia imports from Poland, for example, 277 million dollars worth of machinery, while the flow of equipment in the other direction amounts to only 108 million dollars, can be explained only on the grounds of economic inertia. In time, however, a great deal of this kind of exchange pattern has come to be so patently indefensible that most of the trade partners within Comecon would like to find an escape. High Polish officials, such as Deputy Premier Jaroszewicz, have, on occasion, complained openly that the schedule of machines and vehicles assigned to the smaller trade partners for production, under the aegis of Comecon commissions, is altogether too long, with the result that these countries find it impossible to establish economically rational—that is, profitable—scales of production for most of the equipment on the list. As a result, the prices they receive from their socialist trade partners—these are generally world market prices based on the cost structure of large-scale producers in the West—do not pay back the full cost of their inputs of materials, labor, and capital, under their conditions of small-scale production.

The evidence at hand suggests that the present pattern of specialization and exchange among the Comecon group of nations is badly out of joint and in need of a searching review and modification. Soviet specialists in the field no longer hesitate to make this point explicit. They are now contending that in the past the approach to specialization has been all too broad, too superficial: for example, finished goods versus raw materials. In the future, it is said, the approach needs to be more selective, more oriented towards specific products. Ways should be found, it is recommended, to work out areas of national specialization within, rather than between, the individual branches of rapidly expanding processing industries: for example, those producing types of steel plate, generators, etc. At the same time, Soviet writers make the point that they would like to see a greater effort made towards specialization within the various branches of the more capital intensive industries, mining operations in particular, in the belief that "[this] would make it possible to increase the reciprocal exchange of raw materials among Comecon members." Such a drastic modification of the present commodity exchange pattern would obviously require a long and difficult process of negotiation and gradual readjustment.

Through a More Active Contact with the World Reservoir of Technology

Following the 1964 change in the personnel and style of leadership in the Soviet Union, Premier Kosygin emerged as the principal spokesman on issues involving the industrial and commercial policies of the Soviet government. In this capacity, he soon revealed himself as a man who is more concerned with the state of the industrial arts in the USSR than with the political image of Soviet socialism. Generally, his diagnosis of the state of affairs in domestic manufacturing has been, from the beginning of his accession to power, quite frank, within the limits of public discussion permitted in the USSR. In his now historic address of September 27, 1965, treating at some length all facets of the current economic reform, Kosygin summed up his own findings on the subject quite succinctly, if uninspiringly: "The pattern of production of machinery and equipment by many branches [of Soviet industry] does not conform to modern standards." His recommended remedy was equally straightforward: "In vigorously developing our machine-building industry," he advised, "we must make wider use of the achievements of engineering abroad." In the years that have passed since that address, Kosygin has continued to remind his associates in the Soviet leadership that they live in an efficiency-conscious world, distinguished by an incredibly fast tempo of technical change, and that it is neither in their interest nor in their power to turn their collective backs upon the existing world economic order. Rather, they must become more alert, availing themselves of all existing opportunities "to improve . . . production techniques" and "to satisfy . . . the needs of our export trade."

The most dependable way to keep in touch with the rapid pace of industrial change in the world, as seen by Kosygin, is to expand more widely than before the exchange of goods through the channels of international trade. This new faith in the healing power of external trade was made fairly explicit in the text of the Directives designed to govern the new, eighth Five-Year Plan, adopted at the Twenty-third Party Congress in April 1966. As might be expected, the formal statement on trade policy that issued from this Congress was replete with the familiar verbal formulas bestowing fulsome praise upon the official tenets of post-war Soviet foreign trade policy. At the same time, however, a number of new nuances of a significant character did come to the surface. Thus, the Congress, for example, placed itself on record as being wholeheartedly in favor of "an increase in the turnover of goods between the USSR and the other socialist countries," but this familiar objective was at once carefully qualified by a rather novel call for a more economic approach to this proliferating but rather slapdash commodity exchange. What was needed, the statement said, was "an improvement in the structure of exports and imports and the raising, on that basis, of the economic effectiveness of [this] foreign trade."

In the same statement, second place of honor, as usual, was again assigned to the newly developing countries. The latter were promised "more Soviet machinery and other types of industrial products needed for the creation of their national economy." To this was added the standard pledge that the Soviet Union would continue to render technical assistance to them, as well as train personnel and provide research facilities to assist in the creation of a domestic industry and in the improvement of agriculture, transport, communication, and geological prospecting.

The really novel and interesting element of official trade policy, in respect of the Directives of 1966, is to be found in the passages dealing with the need for a new approach to the third and last group of trade partners, i.e., "the industrially developed capitalist countries." Here, in new and strong language, one encounters a call for "a profound study of foreign markets" as the only way to develop a truly reciprocal relationship, based on the unique capabilities of the USSR in production, with the world economy at large. Here, one also finds an unusually clear affirmation of "the advantages of the international division of labor" and an expression of serious intent to make more complete use of them in the future. As a token of their seriousness in this respect, it should be noted, the Soviet leaders have gone so far in this statement as to direct the authorities at the level of the Ministry of Foreign Trade to introduce the kind of "improvements" (read: changes) in the commodity structure of Soviet trade, both on the import and the export side of the exchange, that would in fact make it possible for the USSR to take part in a rational division of labor on an international scale.

Most interesting of all, in the present context, is the clearly expressed judgment that previous Soviet practice in this regard has left a good deal to be desired. Past practice in planning domestic production, it is now recognized, has all too often resulted in the dissipation of economic resources, thanks largely to the enforcement of the principle of "universal production," to which official economic doctrine has long been dedicated. In the future, the new leaders indicate in their recent pronouncements, they will be guided, in ordering the structure of their domestic production, by the principle of comparative costs with reference to the world market. Specifically, they have committed themselves, in the words of the Directives of 1966, not to produce any longer but rather from now on to import "articles whose production inside the country entails greater costs and capital investment."

This new recognition of the value of close and continued cooperation with the international economy, through the exchange of products and technical processes, was expressed even more vigorously in the economic report delivered by Kosygin to the same Twenty-third Party Congress. In his own report, the Soviet premier related the growing official interest in trade with the West, more directly than it has ever been done in the past, to the principal imperative of the present inter-dependent world, that is, "the scientific and technical revolution unfolding in the contemporary world." This revolution, he asserted, "calls for more freedom of international economic intercourse, creates a basis for a broad economic exchange between socialist countries and the nations of the capitalist system." His judgment was based, he said, not on a mere theoretical perception of what trade with the West may bring in the future. This trade, he explained, had already expanded by some 50 percent during the preceding five years, under conditions of mutual economic advantage. What was more important, in his view, was the fact that the recent commodity exchange between Russia and the West had already helped "to solve a number of national economic problems." He could have added further weight to his argument by showing, on the authority of official Soviet data, that during the most recent period on record, from 1959–1965, trade with the industrial West grew more rapidly than did trade with the countries of the communist world system.

For all that, Premier Kosygin reported with disapproval, Soviet response to existing opportunities in world trade had been somewhat lethargic. There was still a serious educational job to be done, in his opinion. A great deal of bureaucratic inertia still remained to be overcome. He pointed in particular to the conservative disposition of the industrial managers who go about their accustomed rounds, absorbed in their day-to-day production schedules, indifferent to the varied and valuable contribution that a modest increase in external trade could make towards the modernization of their productive equipment as well as towards lowering the cost and raising the quality of their finished product. "We must change this essentially incorrect view, and strengthen our business contacts between industry and foreign trade." There is, in the view of Kosygin and his entourage, a very particular role that foreign trade can play in connection with the present campaign of economic reform. Trade, if properly utilized, can become a prime channel through which the higher layers of authority in the country can maintain systematic pressure upon the industrial managers, the kind of pressure that would serve to infuse ideas of cost-consciousness into the production process and thereby enforce a greater sense of discipline in the allocation of resources throughout the domestic economy.

In his own eminently pragmatic view of the future, Premier Kosygin seems to feel assured that many benefits would inevitably accrue to the Soviet industrial establishment as a result of an imaginative and sustained contact with the more industrially developed countries of the West. He is aware that Soviet industry in the years immediately ahead will need to be exposed, on a continuing basis, to a wide variety of new influences that could be helpful in the current drive to instill a sense of economic discipline among its managerial class, chiefly in the form of a compulsion to reduce costs to a minimum at every step of the production process. Above all, however, he knows his own environment well enough to realize that a national economy that is impelled, as Russia's has been over the past five decades, by a mission to catch up with the more advanced industrial nations in terms of physical output, enlarging its productive capacity at a forced pace, cannot at the same time be as sensitive as it should be to new processes of production, new manufacturing equipment, or new finished products. In this respect, the leaders of the country do not really have an acceptable choice at their disposal. They are faced by the alternative of either pursuing their economic growth on a narrow, purely national base of industrial research, or opting in favor of a much more systematic involvement in economic and technical exchanges with the growing community of technologically restless, industrially advancing nations of the world.

RETROSPECT

Among the many expectations raised by the Bolshevik Revolution and the founding of the first Soviet socialist state, the promise of economic self-sufficiency has long exercised a special fascination upon the minds of the ruling elite of the country, partly for reasons of national prestige and partly for reasons of security. Today, however, this promise is gradually but perceptibly evaporating into thin air. True, the foreign trade monopoly has never been allowed to lower its guard; it still mans the administrative barriers that protect the economic security of the USSR. The trade monopoly remains to this day deeply embedded in the institutional framework of the Soviet state structure, but the tantalizing prospect of economic independence from the rest of the industrial community of the world, which the monopoly trading institution was designed to achieve, continues to elude the USSR today as much as ever before. Even the enormous territorial expansion of the socialist camp, climaxed by the inclusion of Mainland China in 1949, accomplished precious little by way of creating an alternative, self-sustained reservoir of technological innovation.

Most discernible signs seem to point to the conclusion that the present generation of Soviet leaders has grown skeptical about the whole notion of a studied, politically justifiable isolation from the world industrial community. Their own experience of a lifetime has helped to make them aware that the scientific and technical revolution now under way in the world of production is concentrated among the actively cooperating economies of the industrially more developed nations outside the communist bloc. Having recognized this fact, the Soviet leaders are genuinely concerned over the danger of being cut off from this vital centre of technological change and economic progress. Accordingly, they no longer find it difficult to accept the proposition that in our time economic progress is in fact indivisible.

To this extent, then, it may reasonably be concluded that the Soviet political system has demonstrated its capacity to shed unworkable ideas, if given enough time and a clear record of negative results. The whole record of Soviet experience with the concept of autarky, national as well as regional, has indeed been demonstrably negative. A close reading of the current literature on this theme would suggest, in fact, that Soviet economic writers would like to forget about the whole thing. If possible, they would prefer to characterize the notion of autarky as some alien idea, invented by someone with an interest in keeping the Soviet Union in a state of economic retardation. "From an economic point of view," we read in a recent issue of the journal of the Ministry of Foreign Trade, "autarky is disadvantageous, because it tends to slow down the development of the productive forces, to brake the growth of labor productivity." The author of the article then goes on to explain, in the manner of a man who has just stumbled on a rare discovery, that any society which attempts to produce everything at home, without paying the closest possible attention to the comparative cost of production of the same article abroad, is inviting the waste of social labor. In light of this reasoning, he concludes, the Soviet Union and the other socialist countries now "do not believe in secluding themselves within the bounds of their national markets, or of the world socialist market, but are striving to utilize the advantages of the international division of labor on a worldwide scale."

The withering away of old ideas is obviously proceeding apace in Russia today. The present leaders of the Soviet government seem to be ready to accept the premise, now generally adopted among the economically more experienced nations, that the critical ingredient of an effective production system in our times is technology, and that the market for technological ideas must be as inclusive as the entire industrial community of the world. It is now quite clear to them that a national or regional market for technical innovation is, by definition, a needlessly impoverished storehouse of ideas. They are manifestly no longer willing to be confined to an economically retarding environment of this variety.

It is almost as if the rulers of Russia were now ready to agree with John Stuart Mill that it is the business of the state not to try to innovate but rather "to make itself an active circulator and diffuser [of experience] . . . to enable each experimentalist to benefit by the experiments of others, instead of tolerating no experiment but its own." The process of disillusionment with regard to the promise of autarky has been going on for a number of years in the Soviet Union. This goal, which once seemed within easy reach and full of glittering promise, is no longer held to be either attainable or desirable. The original urge to maintain the Soviet economy as an island, enjoying a state of splendid isolation from the main theater of economic activity and experimentation, is now clearly recognized as a fond illusion, as a condition which, if only partially attained, would deprive the Soviet Union, or any other nation in its place, of the right of free access to the growing abundance of the economic harvest made possible in our age by the studied application of human ingenuity and social cooperation.

III
SOVIET ECONOMIC GROWTH

Economic growth provides the products and services needed for higher standards of living, greater abundance of material things, and increased leisure. It is one of the goals human society has striven for as far back as we can trace human thought. It involves a massive effort on the part of society and individuals to wrest greater output from a niggardly nature. Not only is effort involved, but the social organization of that effort is significant.

In the American economy the proportion of total output plowed back for expansion is a decision largely made by millions of individuals and business firms when they decide to save a portion of their income rather than spend it on current needs. Many millions of other persons make decisions to invest. The two groups are brought together by the capital markets, to which savings flow and from which investment funds are obtained. The whole process depends on the individual motivations of many different people, although those motivations may be influenced by various types of public policy.

In our economy, this individualistic, market-directed pattern has resulted in about 20 percent of our GNP being used for investment in recent years. The corresponding figure for the Soviet Union is over 25 percent, and this is the chief reason why their economy has been growing more rapidly than ours. Another reason is that Soviet investment is directed by the planning system into growth-maximizing uses, while our market-directed system channels investment much more heavily into ultimate consumer uses.

Economic growth is seldom even and steady. In the United States the average annual increase in GNP between 1946 and 1953 was about 4 percent. It fell to about 2½ percent from 1953 to 1960 and rose to above 4 percent in 1960–68. In the period after 1953 fear that the Soviet Union would rapidly overtake the United States in economic strength became widespread, for the Soviet economy sustained its postwar surge until 1958. The slowdown in Soviet growth did not become clear until the early 1960's, primarily because of difficulties in evaluating Soviet economic data. The low point appears to have been reached in 1963, when even official Soviet data claimed a GNP growth rate of only a little more than 4 percent, compared with claims of over 10 percent for 1954–58. Western scholars usually discount these claims considerably.

During the 1960's the growth of the Soviet economy has picked up again, averaging something above 5 percent annually. But U.S. growth in the same period was almost as rapid, and American policymakers have stopped looking over their shoulders quite so frequently to see how fast the USSR has been catching up.

Part III examines Soviet economic growth patterns. It includes a brief evaluation of Soviet statistics; an analysis of the sources of Soviet growth, together with a series of international comparisons; and two selections that deal with consumption and living standards.

13 | A NOTE ON THE AVAILABILITY AND RELIABILITY OF SOVIET STATISTICS

Alec Nove

To what extent can we rely on Soviet statistics published in Soviet sources? To some extent we are in the position of the gambler who knew the roulette wheel was crooked but had to play it anyway: it was the only one in town. We are also hampered by the fact that statistics are often gathered for one purpose and used for another, with resultant difficulties in coverage, validity, and so forth. Finally, we are hampered by the natural wish of bureaucrats to make themselves look good by fudging their reports to statistical agencies of government.

Through all of the discussions of Soviet statistics three general conclusions emerge:

1. Soviet index numbers are dangerous. They tend to inflate the levels of output and the growth they are designed to measure. Use them with care.

2. Figures on units of output are much more reliable. The Soviet Union does not keep a double set of books. Production statistics reported by Soviet sources are generally the ones used by the planners themselves and are usually as accurate as the statistical agencies can make them.

3. When the Soviet government wants to conceal something, it doesn't publish false figures; it just refrains from publishing anything on the matter.

There are exceptions to these general rules, but you won't go far wrong by keeping these three points in mind. The following article presents an evaluation of Soviet statistics by an eminent British scholar, which gives the reasoning behind these conclusions.

Alec Nove is Professor of International Economic Studies at the University of Glasgow. His article is reprinted with permission from his book *The Soviet Economy: An Introduction* (2d rev. ed.; London: George Allen & Unwin Ltd., 1968; New York: Frederick A. Praeger, Inc., 1969), pp. 346–54. References to Russian-language publications have been omitted.

AVAILABILITY

A FEW YEARS AGO, it would have been easiest to make a quite short list of the few figures which were available. The fact that the contrary procedure is now the most convenient one is a measure of the "liberalization" achieved since the death of Stalin, or rather since 1956, when the systematic publication of economic statistics gradually began again after a long interval. However, there are still some conspicuous gaps, of which the following are the most important.

(a) Output figures for some *industrial products* are missing, among them non-ferrous metals, ships, aircraft, many chemicals, some machines, as well as military weapons.

(b) While more is now appearing about the breakdown of the *labor force*, including agriculture and the military services,[1] numbers in particular industries are not given in any detail.

(c) While since 1964 we have had some average wage statistics, there is nothing about average pay in different industries or as between different categories of workers, and hardly anything at all about actual earnings of peasants.

(d) There is no information given on the composition of turnover tax revenue, and only a few actual rates of tax are published.

However, let us give credit where credit is due. Gone indeed is the day when one had to search for statistics in leaders' speeches and make do with percentages of an unknown base. The statistical compendia on the economy as a whole, on agriculture, on various republics and localities, on transport, and so forth, together with the reports on the 1959 census, do give us a sizeable stock of statistics to work on, despite the remaining gaps. One difficulty is that many of the figures given are ill-defined; there is an unfortunate lack of explanatory notes; though minor attempts are being made to remedy this, we badly need longer explanations, and a new edition of a handbook on economic statistics is much overdue.[2] The lack of clarity about definitions, and especially changes in definitions, is a constant danger; it affects budget data, and also a number of the output figures and indices.

---

[1] Until it was decided to publish the numbers in the armed forces (1960), the number of peasants and the age and sex distribution of the population were unpublished, no doubt to prevent calculation by residual.

[2] There used to be such an explanatory handbook, but this was last published in 1948. Some notes do now appear at the back of the annual statistical volume.

CREDIBILITY: PHYSICAL OUTPUT FIGURES

Industry

Whatever the vagueness of definitions, the first question to ask is: are the figures true, or are they invented? Very few persons now believe that they are invented. The evidence against such a view is very strong. Despite captured documents,[3] despite the presence in the West of various Soviet officials who had defected, no evidence exists that the central Soviet statisticians invent figures to order, to produce propaganda effect. By this is meant that no one issues orders to print a figure of 400 knowing that the correct one is 350. Further support for this view comes from the fact that, when certain figures were discreditable, they were on occasion simply suppressed; many years later, they were published and showed that there was a fall in production in the "suppressed" year. If it were possible simply to invent, then such behavior would be pointless. Of course, we must note that selective suppression is a means of distorting a statistical table, but it is not invention. Not to tell the whole truth is not the same as telling a lie. Therefore we can legitimately conclude that when, for example, the Soviet authorities announce that 60 million tons of steel or 300 million pairs of shoes have been produced in a given year, this accords with the records of the central statistical office in Moscow.[4] However, there are several qualifications to be made. One of these relates, not for the last time, to ambiguities of definition. Footwear sometimes includes only leather footwear, sometimes all footwear; the definition of leather footwear can and does alter; handicraft production can be omitted from the base-year without this being stated. Furthermore, most commodities for which statistics are published are not homogeneous, are in reality many different kinds of goods aggregated under a single head for statistical convenience. The methodology of aggregation is often unspecified. Of course, this is often true of similar statistics in all countries. But the point is that rewards for growth are so important in Soviet industry that the definitional changes, and the adjustment to definitions at local level, can aim deliberately at whatever result looks best from the standpoint of statistical publicity. This point is also relevant to the reliability of aggregate indices, and we shall return to it.

The figures may correctly reflect the data available in Moscow, yet this data could be wrong by reason of statistical "padding" by the reporting agencies, especially the enterprises. They are interested in claiming plan

---

[3] Especially the *1941 Plan*, published in America by the American Council of Learned Societies, after it had been taken from the Germans.

[4] This is also the broad conclusion of G. Grossman in his searching examination of *Soviet Statistics of Physical Output of Industrial Commodities* (Princeton: Princeton University Press, 1960).

fulfillment, and this could lead them to exaggerate. Scattered reports of measures against directors who indulge in such practices confirm that such dangers exist, but measures are taken to minimize them. The close link between production and disposals (*sbyt*) puts a limit on the amount of likely cheating; to report nonexistent production which one would be called upon to deliver is asking for trouble. There are also some temptations to conceal output in order to keep extra stocks in hand or to cover up pilfering or some semilegal deal. Defective goods, on the other hand, seem frequently to be foisted on customers in the guise of standard products, the quality inspectors being overruled. On balance, one should expect some exaggeration in reporting, and no doubt the possibilities of getting away with it vary in different sectors and at different periods. Unless it can be shown that the *extent* of exaggeration changes, the rate of growth remains unaffected, for obvious reasons; this is the "law of equal cheating," which the author of these lines "invented" in 1956.[5] There seems no evidence one way or the other, in industry at least, to suggest that the rate of growth since, say, 1937 or 1950 has been affected by falsification from below.[6] However, it is maneuvring within the system of success indicators—without actually cheating—which seems much the most serious source of distortion.

Clearly then, care is needed in interpreting the various figures; exaggeration is possible. But an excess of scepticism can lead to unfortunate results. Thus a certain American commentator noticed that cotton and wool cloth output figures were below the previous year in physical terms while the official statistical report claimed an increase, and jumped to the conclusion that this was evidence of cheating. It was not; there had been a shift of statistical reporting from linear metres to square meters, the object of which was in fact to stop cheating by those who sought to fulfil plans by making cloth narrower. This illustrates the danger of using the "cheating" hypothesis. Far better is it to assume that the figures represent some aspect of reality, and proceed, on that assumption, to examine with care the coverage and definition of the figures cited.

Agriculture

For many years, until 1953, crop data were published in terms of "biological yield," for reasons which cannot be gone into here.[7] It is very much to the credit of N. Jasny to have been the first to have documented and calculated with great ingenuity and surprising accuracy the extent of the consequent exaggeration.[8] This was due partly to the

[5] In *Lloyd's Bank Review*, April, 1956, p. 3.

[6] This is also the conclusion of Grossman, *op. cit.*, p. 133.

[7] See A. Nove, "Some Problems in Agricultural Statistics," *Soviet Studies*, January, 1956.

[8] See his *Socialized Agriculture in the USSR*, and other works.

nature of the "biological" statistics, which purported to represent the on-the-root crop, and were therefore gross of the considerable harvest losses, and partly to the tendency of the inspectors to exaggerate the on-the-root crop estimates, since certain delivery obligations of *kolkhozy* (payments to the MTS)[9] were dependent upon them. In 1952, the grain harvest was said to have been 130 million tons. This has officially been revised downwards to 92 million tons, an exaggeration greater than many of the fiercest western critics thought possible.

Biological yield figures were dropped in 1953, and for several years no physical output data were published at all. Then they reappeared, and are now available in abundance, for every major farm product, down even to non-cow milk and non-sheep wool. However, there are several reasons for supposing that the "law of equal cheating" may fail to operate in agriculture. First, the large volume of unsold products makes it harder to keep track of reality. Second, a series of agricultural campaigns (grain, maize, meat, milk, and so on) have placed great pressures upon local officialdom, and we have Khrushchev's own word for it, at the January, 1961, plenum of the central committee, that it drove them into various kinds of simulation and exaggerated reporting (including the purchase of butter in the shops and its re-delivery to the state as new produce). Third, the much better prices now paid for produce probably led to a discouragement of various forms of evasion by which production remained unreported.[10] Finally, the very large proportion of meat and milk originating in the private sector is very inadequately counted, through a sample survey, and seems to be unreliable and possibly overstated. For all these reasons, there are grounds for supposing that both the absolute level of and the rate of increase in the output of some farm products are overstated, though we cannot tell by how much.

It is also noteworthy that the definition of meat includes offal, lard, rabbits, poultry, and so is wider than that usually adopted in the West. Maize figures included the grain equivalent of ensilaged cobs in the period 1955–64, but this has been abandoned. American analysts have claimed that milk sucked by calves is included in the Soviet milk statistics, but this has been denied.[11]

Foreign Trade

Very full data are published, but with some irritating omissions and one yawning gap in the figures. Two items which did appear before the

---

[9] Editors' note: The kolkhozy (collective farms) made payments in kind to the MTS (machine tractor stations) for services performed.

[10] An interesting parallel may be found in Great Britain, where an increase in the official buying price for eggs shortly after the war led to a spectacular rise in the *reported* number of eggs laid.

[11] See *Comparisons of the United States and Soviet Economies* (Washington, 1959), p. 236.

war are not there. These are, using the trade classification numbers which were entered in the prewar figures and which do not now appear at all:

> 28...."Objects of gold and precious stones"
> 31...."Pyrotechnical materials"

Does this mean that these items are no longer traded in, or rather that exports of arms and of some gold are kept out of statistical sight?

The gap mentioned above has become apparent since the USSR has divided its current trade statistics into three country categories: Socialist, capitalist-developed, and capitalist-underdeveloped. The first two present no problems at all: the figures for the obvious countries add up exactly to the import and export totals. The figures for the "underdeveloped" do not, as the following figures show:

	1962		1966	
	Import	Export	Import	Export
Total "underdeveloped capitalist countries"......	525.9	889.5	783.5	1090.6
Total of all countries given.................	522.8	484.4	779.7	758.3
Difference...............	3.1	405.1	3.8	332.3

The difference for imports is consistent with the fact that some minor trading partners are omitted from the returns. The export figures are clearly incredible. Obviously, some sales of something to someone have been statistically "dumped" into this category. No explanation has been forthcoming. But logically this entitles one to query the other figures, too, in which these not inconsiderable sums ought (somewhere) to belong.

INDICES: ARE THEY CREDIBLE?

According to the official statistics, gross industrial output rose almost twenty-one times between 1928 and 1955. The highest western estimate, by F. Seton, allows for a twelve-fold rise. The lowest, by W. Nutter, supports a much lower figure, a five-and-a-half-fold increase. There are some others in between. There is not the space here to comment in detail on the many western attempts to reconstruct an index of industrial production based on Soviet physical output series. The point is that all are unanimous in completely rejecting the official index, even while at odds with each other about the "correct" figure. My own view tends to favor the Seton index, because the much lower figures of Nutter and some other analysts seem to me inconsistent with what is known and accepted about Soviet fuel utilization and freight transportation. However, this still leaves the official index way up above the realms of possibility.

It is not that this index is deliberately "cooked." But all indices are conventional aggregations, necessarily lacking in accuracy. So much depends on price weights and on the treatment of new products, especially where, as in the machinery sector, these are extremely numerous. Anyone who wishes to make any such calculations should take an awful warning from A. Gerschenkron's calculations, in which he showed that, from 1899 to 1939, American production of machinery increased more than fifteen-fold with 1899 price weights, but less than doubled with 1939 price weights, and he emphasized the enormous difficulties due to changes in type and design. What is "truth" when such divergences are possible?[12] This is why the care and refinements of some attempts to aggregate all available physical output data for the USSR seem to me to lead to such uncertain results, which would remain uncertain even if there were none of the sizeable statistical gaps in the output series.

The official series suffers from the following defects:

(1) Until 1950, the weights used were those of 1926–27. Apart from giving "preindustrialization" weights to the fastest growing sectors of industry, the introduction of new products gave an opportunity (for directors) to maneuver so as to adopt for them high "1926–27" prices. Despite occasional efforts to check this practice, the big rise in costs in the thirties meant that the prices at which new products were introduced into the index were higher than they would have cost in 1926–27. There was then a tendency to concentrate on the production of items bearing high "1926–27" prices, even at the cost of underfulfilling plans for the less highly valued items, because plan fulfillment was measured in 1926–27 prices. All this led to a creeping inflation of the index, made easier by the fact that it was genuinely difficult to determine what is a new product and what it would have cost to produce in 1926–27.[13]

(2) It is a "gross" index. Therefore, it is affected by vertical disintegration.[14]

Several Soviet writers have claimed that the behavior of the authorities is affected by the knowledge that by dividing up production processes between enterprises they can artificially increase the growth rate, and thereby inflate the output of intermediate goods in relation to the final product.

(3) While since 1950 the index is no longer based on 1926–27 prices (it was calculated first in 1952 and then in 1955 prices), the growth rates

---

[12] *A Dollar index of Soviet machinery output* (Santa Monica: Rand Corporation, 1951).

[13] See A. Nove, "1926–27 and All That," *Soviet Studies*, October, 1957, pp. 117–30. Soviet journals have denied these exaggerations, but contemporary evidence, cited in the above-named article, is against them.

[14] Editors' note: The Soviet index is calculated by adding up the total output of all industrial enterprises. Therefore, if an enterprise is broken up into two enterprises, one producing component parts and the other assembling the final product, the index of production will show an increase even though output of the finished product may not have changed at all.

prior to 1950 were simply chained on to the new index and were not recalculated; or, if they were, the results have not been published. Much remains unclear about how the index is compiled. For instance, suppose that machinery output is expressed in 1955 prices, the problem of valuing new models remains, and, since in all countries such valuations are somewhat artificial, this makes possible the systematic selection of the highest of a range of possible figures, which can lead to distortion. It is only right to add that all analysts agree that the post 1950 indices are markedly less unreliable than those for earlier years. However, whatever the price base and whatever the regulations, the directors and local officials tend so to choose between possible alternatives as to be able to report a large increase in output. Because of the unavoidable imprecision of the regulations and of the definitions, the index can be affected by such choices in ways which are unlikely to arise in the West (where there is also a degree of imprecision and of arbitrary comparison), because increases in production as such are not vital "success indicators" in a western firm.

With so much room for more or less legitimate maneuver, Soviet statisticians can select the base and the weights which help them to show very large increases and omit to publish calculations which reflect less credit on the system. For instance, base-year weights give a larger increase in output than end-year weights, so, in discussing industrial production indices, one Soviet statistician went so far as to proclaim that end-year weights were contrary to science, a remarkable doctrine indeed. Yet, when Soviet statisticians calculate a cost of living index, they are careful to use end year weights, which minimize the increase in prices and so represent real wages in a more favorable light.

NATIONAL INCOME

The official index is at all times to be treated with a degree of suspicion. The official claim to a seventeen-fold increase in the period 1913–55, for instance, is utterly incredible. Thus it seems very widely agreed, by Soviet economists among others, that the national income of the Russian empire in 1913 was approximately a fifth of that of the United States. If the official claim were even remotely correct, the Soviet national income would now be well ahead of that of the United States, which, even allowing for the familiar vagaries of index numbers, just is not acceptable. Then it is decidedly odd that the national income can increase by seventeen-fold when one of its principal components, agriculture, showed a rise (in gross output) of only 70 percent. The computational methods are not properly explained. There seems to have been a substantial overstatement of the growth of the net product of trade and construction, at least during the period of "1926–27" prices.[15] But even in more recent years

---

[15] See A. Nove, "1926–27 and All That," already cited.

strange things happen to national income data. Thus an increase of 5 percent in 1964, given by several reliable Soviet sources, including Kosygin, was suddenly transformed into an increase of 7 percent in the statistical report published in *Pravda* on the 30th January 1965, and then converted into an increase of well over 9 percent in the statistical handbook for 1964, without (so far) a word of explanation. One can but show reserve in using official claims, and seek explanations where possible to clear up doubtful points.

SOME OTHER ITEMS

Housing data (in square meters) may be given in *living* space (excluding kitchens, corridors, etc,) or in *total* space (*obshchayaploshchyad'*). The former is roughly two-thirds of the latter, and the unwary are sometimes confused between them.

Real wage and other such figures are sometimes given by reference to the year 1940, or to some early post-war year. It should be noted that these were not good years for the consumer, and that a fairer picture of progress achieved requires a calculation based on some better year, say 1937 or 1928. This is never done by the official statisticians. It is important to distinguish data on real wages, which, allowing for the chosen base year, check well against other figures, from vague and barely credible claims about "real income per head"; these include estimates of the value of social services and such indirect "income" as the length of vacations with pay, and the methods used are never explained.

CONCLUSION

Despite some justifiable scepticism about certain Soviet data, it should be clearly stated that the published physical output series and many other figures must be taken seriously, that they generally represent an expression (though sometimes an ambiguous or distorted expression) of reality. Much greater doubt attaches to some of the index number series, which are in some instances just not credible. Yet these comments are by no means intended to deny that the Soviet system has achieved rapid growth. Undoubtedly it has, though not at the tremendous pace which the official indices allege. Its achievements have, indeed, been such that it is surely about time that some of the wilder claims were quietly buried.

14 | ANALYSIS OF THE SOVIET GROWTH MODEL

Stanley H. Cohn

What are the sources of rapid economic growth in the USSR? How does Soviet growth compare with economic growth in other advanced nations? These basic questions are examined and answered in the following selection by Stanley H. Cohn, reprinted by permission from Chapter VII of his recent book, *Economic Development in the Soviet Union* (Boston: D. C. Heath & Co., 1969).

Cohn examines the inputs into the Soviet economy since 1928, shows how they were directed into growth-producing uses, and points out which sectors of the Soviet economy tended to lag behind. Comparisons with other economies at comparable stages of their development reveal both Soviet accomplishments and Soviet deficiencies. Very slight changes have been made in editing the text; sources for data shown in the tables have been omitted (the interested reader can find them in Cohn's book); footnotes to Russian-language sources and some of Cohn's other writings have been deleted; and some footnotes have been combined. Copyright © 1969, by D. C. Heath & Co., a Division of Raytheon Education Co., Boston, Mass.

THE RECORD

Inputs and Efficiency—The Production Function

Our technique will be to examine the Soviet growth trend in terms of the economy's potential, i.e., the sum total of productive resources available for economic utilization. Since the Soviet system has been under chronic overstrain, the question of inadequate demand is hypothetical. The critical question has been the regime's ability to affect the supply of productive inputs; that is, the growth of inputs has determined the growth of output.

In the technical language of economists, the relationship between factor inputs and gross national product (GNP) is termed the production function.[1] Since it is not feasible to measure some of the more intangible inputs, such as management, or to obtain unambiguous data on others such as technology or scale of output, the explicit inputs are limited to the two most important—labor and physical capital. When data is available, education (human capital), land, and livestock may be included. Since not all inputs are included in empirical studies, the trend in GNP will always be larger than the trend in the inputs measured. If only one input is used, the difference will, of course, be even larger. The difference between the growth of inputs and the growth of GNP is termed *productivity*, i.e., the output per unit of a specific input or combination of inputs.

Productivity

The most common productivity measures are those for capital and labor (Table 1).[2] Productivity measures are often used as indicators of efficiency in the use of resources. The more rapid the rate of increase in labor productivity, the more efficient is the economy in its use of a limited supply of manpower. In our analysis of the Soviet growth record, we will distinguish between the system's success in infusing productive resources and in efficiently utilizing those resources. To provide perspective, the record of the USSR will be contrasted with that of other leading industrial powers at similar stages of development.

Table 1 provides the key to our understanding about trends in factor productivity or economic efficiency in the USSR since 1928. For pertinent periods since 1928, average annual rates of change have been computed for GNP in the aggregate and for GNP in terms of output per labor unit and per capital unit. Not shown in the table are rates of changes in employment and in capital stock. They may be found in Table 8. The productivity estimates are the quotients of average annual rates of change

---

[1] For those who have some background in economic theory, the production function used in my estimates is the conventional Cobb-Douglas function with the two inputs weighted according to their income shares as calculated by the author, plus trends in unmeasured inputs.

$$P = L^{.7} K^{.3} Z$$

where P = trend in GNP,
  L = flow of employment (man-hours) raised to its power of .7,
  K = flow of physical capital raised to its power of .3,
  Z = flow in unmeasured factors.

The coefficients represent the marginal productivities of the two inputs and in a two factor model add up to one, since they are assumed to exhaust the product. In the symbols used above, labor productivity = P/L and capital productivity = P/K.

For derivation of coefficients see my study, *Derivation of 1959 Value-added Weights for Originating Sectors of Soviet Gross National Product*, Research Analysis Corporation (TP-210), 1966, page 21.

[2] The difference between the two main magnitudes measures our degree of ignorance as to other inputs, particularly technology, which influence the production function. However, the concept of productivity is widely used as an expedient explanation of these unmeasured influences.

TABLE 1
Average Annual Growth Rates of Soviet Gross National Product
for Selected Periods
(in percent)

Period	Gross National Product		
	Aggregate	Per Employed Person*	Per Capital Unit
1928–1937†	4.8–11.9	1.8–8.0	−0.7– +1.0
1937–1940	3.6	−0.4	5.8
1940–1950‡	1.8–2.2	1.3–2.4	0
1950–1955	6.9	4.9	−2.6
1955–1958	7.4	7.4	−1.6
1958–1961	5.4	5.9	−3.5
1961–1965	5.2	3.2	−3.0

* Adjusted to account for less than full-time employment and changes in the length of the work year.

† Lower limit based on valuation of ruble factor cost in 1937 prices; upper limit on valuation in 1928 prices.

‡ Lower limit based on valuation of ruble factor cost in 1950 prices; upper limit on valuation in 1937 prices.

in aggregate GNP (expressed as index numbers) divided by the same rates of increase or decrease in employment and capital stock obtained from Table 8. The trends in GNP per employed person have been adjusted to represent the full time annual equivalent of persons employed corrected for changes in man-hours of annual employment.

A minus sign does not denote negative productivity, but declining marginal productivity. For most of the periods since 1928, additional units of capital have not meant a decline in GNP, but a reduced increment to GNP. More frequently the measure favored by economists is the inverse of the one shown in the right-hand column of Table 1 and measures the amount of capital required to obtain an additional unit of GNP. This ratio is termed the incremental capital-output ratio. The negative trends in the right-hand column indicate that the capital-output ratio has been rising almost continuously since 1928.

Comparative Growth Performance

By any international standard, the aggregate growth record of the USSR since 1928 is outstanding, although at similar or lower per capita levels the United States approached the lower 1928–1937 Soviet limit in 1870–1890[3] and Japan equalled it in 1890–1900 and surpassed it between 1920 and 1930.[4] In the postwar years the Soviet growth spurt in the early

[3] Angus Maddison, *Economic Growth in the West* (New York: Twentieth Century Fund, 1964), pp. 201–2.

[4] Michael C. Kaser, "Education and Economic Progress," in E. A. G. Robinson and J. E. Vaizey (eds.), *The Economics of Education* (New York: St. Martin's Press, 1966), p. 169.

TABLE 2

Comparative Trends in G. N. P., Employment, and Productivity
(average annual rates in percent)

Country	1950–58			1958–65		
	GNP	Employ-ment	Produc-tivity	GNP	Employ-ment	Produc-tivity
USSR.............7.1		1.7	5.3	5.3	1.7	3.5
France.............4.4		0.4	3.9	5.4	0.2	5.0
Germany...........7.6		2.4	5.1	5.8	1.1	4.6
Italy...............5.6		1.6	3.9	6.1	−0.9	6.5
United Kingdom......2.4		0.4	2.0	3.9	0.8	2.9
Japan..............6.1		2.1	3.8	12.0	1.4	9.2
United States........2.9		1.0	1.9	4.4	2.0	2.6

and middle fifties was high, but not unique, as more developed economies, such as West Germany almost matched it. These comparisons are shown in Table 2. Since 1958 the USSR growth rate has only been average among nations with relatively high levels of per capita GNP. The Japanese record has been much superior. The postwar growth position of the USSR testifies not only to the inability of the system to maintain growth superiority but also to the success of the market economies in maintaining high levels of employment and demand.

When the comparative basis for growth performance is cast in productivity terms relating GNP to some factor input or combination of inputs, the Soviet record is less noteworthy. As to its efficiency in utilization of the most important input, manpower, Soviet advances in GNP per man-hour in the first two five-year plans were exceeded at the lower limit by all of the major continental European economies and the United States in pertinent decades of the 19th century, as shown in Table 3.

TABLE 3

Comparative Historical Trends in Growth of GNP per Man-hour
(annual average rates in percent)

Country	Period	Rate
USSR....................1928–37		1.8–8.0
	1937–40	−0.4
France...................1880–90		2.5
	1890–00	2.2
Germany.................1871–80		2.5
	1880–90	2.4
	1890–00	1.9
United Kingdom...........1880–90		3.8
	1890–00	1.2
United States.............1871–90		2.7
	1890–00	2.2
Italy....................1900–13		2.6

In the early postwar years through the mid-fifties, the Soviet record of growth of man-hour labor productivity was the highest of any of the major powers, but since 1958 it has fallen behind Japan and the major continental economies (Table 2).

In its utilization of fixed capital the Soviet system has been glaringly inefficient, especially in the postwar years. The trend in marginal capital productivity (additions to GNP per unit of capital investment) has been steadily falling (Table 1). In perhaps more familiar language, the marginal capital-output ratio has been rising continually. Historical estimates for the United States[5] and postwar estimates for Western Europe[6] indicate that such a persistent negative trend is probably unique. One would intuitively expect that in an economy like the Soviet, with its extensive technological borrowing activities and the presence of a large corps of trained engineers, scientists, and managers, that the capital-output ratio would decline, or at least remain relatively constant. Since new capital would be more productive than older capital, the rise in the capital-output ratio would be offset. The postwar experience of Western Europe and Japan, where unlike the USSR capital-output ratios have tended to remain low and below historic trends, supports this hypothesis.[7]

It would seem from these two tests that efficiency in resource use has not been a strength of the Soviet system. Rather the key to Soviet success lay in the ability of the system to infuse vast inputs into the production process. A comprehensive test is to expand the production function described at the beginning of this section to include two additional inputs, farm land and productive livestock. In this way the unexplained residual factors in growth are reduced. In Table 4 the historical experience of the USSR is compared with that of the United States, from 1928 to the present for the USSR and since 1869 for the United States. The historical comparison is divided into pertinent developmental periods for each country.

For the USSR, except for the period 1950–58, the infusion of productive inputs has been more important than their utilization in explaining growth. By contrast, for the United States, except for the last two decades of the 19th century, the utilization of inputs has played a greater

---

[5] Simon Kuznets, *Capital in the American Economy* (Princeton, N. J.: Princeton University Press, 1961), p. 80, and John Kendrick, *Productivity Trends in the United States*, (Princeton, N. J.: Princeton University Press, 1961), p. 167.

[6] Edward Denison, *Why Growth Rates Differ* (Washington, D.C.: Brookings Institution, 1967), pp. 189–195. United Nations Economic Commission for Europe, *Incomes in Postwar Europe* (Geneva: 1967), chap. 3, p. 2.

[7] For a comparison of postwar non-residential, fixed capital-output ratios, see Stanley Cohn, "Soviet Growth Retardation," in U.S. Congress, Joint Economic Committee, *New Directions in the Soviet Economy* (Washington, D.C.: U.S. Government Printing Office, 1966), Part II-A, p. 120. If historical ratios of investment to output, as computed by Simon Kuznets, are compared with my postwar ratios, those for Germany and Italy prove to have been at historic lows after World II and those for Japan at the lowest level in this century.

role. The Soviet exception is probably explained by the spur to efficiency following relaxation of Stalinist controls after his death and the U.S. exception by the heavy immigration of the period. Since the Soviet productivity growth rate is no higher than that of the United States for most of the years covered, the superior Soviet growth margin is almost entirely explained by higher trends in the employment of productive factors. Other things being equal, the usual developmental pattern is for the lesser developed country to show higher productivity growth rates because of its advantage in assimilating the accumulated technology of older industrial economies.

The extent to which Soviet growth has mainly been a result of the regime's ability to increase the quantity of resources can be graphically illustrated by contrasting Soviet experience in increasing employment and

TABLE 4

Comparative Growth Contributions of Factor Inputs*
and Combined Factor Productivity
(annual average rates in percent)

	USSR			United States	
Period	Inputs	Productivity	Period	Inputs	Productivity
1928–37............3.7		1.0–7.9	1869–78 to		
1937–40............3.8		−0.2	1899–08............3.0		1.5
1940–50............0.6		1.2–1.6	1899–08 to		
1950–58............3.2		3.9	1929...............1.5		1.8
1958–64............2.9		2.3	1929–48............0.4		2.2
			1950–57............1.2		2.4
			1957–63............0.8		2.4

* Weighted inputs for man-hours, fixed capital, farm land, and productive livestock. Productivity = index of GNP ÷ index of inputs.

in accretions to fixed capital stock with that of other major economies. By any international standard the rates of growth in the Soviet labor force have been prodigious. No other economy has remotely matched the Soviet labor influx rate at comparable stages of development, especially during the period of the first three five-year plans (Table 5). In these years employment was increasing by over 3 percent per year, while even in the years of heavy immigration before 1914 U.S. employment was rising by about 2.5 percent on an annual average. At comparable stages of growth with presumably similar demographic and structural advantages, the major Western European economies and Japan had much lower employment growth rates.

During the postwar years demographic disasters stemming from the war and agricultural stagnation have prevented continuation of so high a rate of labor influx, but given the more limited untapped manpower reservoir, additions to employment have been unusually large.

TABLE 5

Comparative Historic Rates of Increase in Employment
(annual average rates in percent)

Country	Period	Rate
USSR....................	1928–37	3.7
	1937–40	3.0
United Kingdom..........	1821–1831 to 1851–1861	0.9
	1851–1861 to 1871–1881	0.7
Germany.................	1851–55 to 1871–75	0.7
	1871 to 1886–95	1.4
	1886–95 to 1907	1.7
United States.............	1874–89	2.8
	1889–1914	2.4
Japan....................	1883–87 to 1903–07	1.0
	1893–97 to 1913–17	0.6
	1918–22 to 1938–42	0.9
Italy....................	1861–81	0.2
	1881–1901	0.2
	1901–21	0.3
	1921–36	0.3

This accomplishment during the years 1928–40 was made possible by ability of an authoritarian state to move labor rapidly from the country-side to the city through the drastic reduction in agricultural real incomes under collectivization and through a policy of conscripting rural school graduates for employment in burgeoning industrial plants. Since most labor was provided only seasonal employment in agriculture, while activities continued throughout the year at capacity pace in industry, the transfer of labor, in effect, greatly increased the average number of hours worked per year. If we compare employment (in full-time equivalents) with the labor pool of the prime working age groups, we find that the ratio, termed the labor force participation ratio, rose sharply between 1928 and 1937—from 57 to 70 percent (Table 6). So rapid an increase in a comparatively short time span is historically unique. In fact, since 1913 the participation ratio has tended to fall in most West European economies.[8]

After the mid-fifties, when the natural increments to the labor force were drastically reduced by demographic factors, the regime managed to maintain the incremental employment rate at relatively high levels by again increasing the participation ratio from 71 percent in 1958 to 76 percent in 1965 (Table 6). Since the potentialities for transfers from agriculture were greatly diminished, the source of active manpower had to come from the remaining reservoirs of women and youths. By 1965 the Soviet participation ratio was the highest among the major industrial

---

[8] Maddison, *op. cit.*, p. 31.

TABLE 6

Trends in the Labor Participation Ratio in the USSR

Year	Work-Age Population (thousands)	Employed Population (thousands)	Participation Ratio (percent)
1928	87,000	49,400	56.8
1937	98,000	68,700	70.1
1950	115,100	82,500	71.7
1958	133,900	94,800	70.8
1964	140,100	106,600	76.1

powers.[9] It probably cannot be increased much further, thus restricting the economy in its principal traditional growth approach.

The extent to which the USSR has maximized the economic participation of its manpower resources is illustrated by the unusually large role played by the female population in productive life. The high general labor participation ratio is explained by this feature. The female proportion of total employment is not only much higher than in the economies of the West, but is higher in all of the principal economic sectors. Particularly striking is the large role of women in industry, agriculture, construction, and transportation. Even in the sectors in which heavy

TABLE 7

Comparative Female Labor Participation, 1960
(percent total civilian employment)

Country	Agriculture	Industry	Construction	Transport	Commerce	Services	Total
USSR	61.5	45.0	29.0	29.0	69.0	64.3	53.7
France	39.6	25.3	4.3	17.7	46.1	60.1	37.7
West Germany	53.6	25.3	4.5	23.0	48.8	49.9	36.5
Italy	33.5	24.0	1.2	7.2	32.5	39.7	29.8
United States	9.8	20.9	3.7	8.6	37.7	51.3	32.8

female employment is traditional in the West, such as commerce and the services, the Soviet proportions are still the highest. (Table 7).

Striking as has been the tendency for the Soviets to infuse labor massively into the production process, even more so has been the case with capital. As noted earlier there has been a steady upward trend in the capital-output ratio. Furthermore, such a persistent upward trend appears to be unique in international developmental experience. Normally rates of increase in capital stock exceed those in the labor force, since trends in the latter magnitude are constrained by population growth. Under the law of

---

[9] Cohn, *op. cit.*, p. 114.

diminishing returns, such disparate growth rates should lead to declining marginal productivity of capital, but such a tendency has been offset by technological progress. Technology has enabled the quality of capital to rise sufficiently to keep its marginal productivity rather constant, or inversely, to keep the capital-output ratio largely unchanged. Even though the USSR has been able to assimilate rapidly foreign technological developments, the expected productivity benefits have apparently been overwhelmed by the rapid rates of increase in capital stock. Except for the disrupted decade of the forties, increments to capital stock, exclusive of retirements, have been above an annual rate of 8 percent (Table 8). During the mid- and late 19th century, the comparable rates for the United States ranged between 4.5 and 4.8 percent.[10] Even in the boom conditions of the postwar period neither the United States nor any

TABLE 8

Annual Average Rates of Growth of Employment, Fixed Capital, and GNP
(in percent)

| Period | Employment | | Fixed Capital | GNP |
	Persons Employed	Man-hours Worked		
1928–37.	3.7	3.6	8.18–10.8	4.8–11.9
1937–40.	3.0	3.8	10.3	3.6
1940–50.	0.3	0.6	−1.7–2.2	1.8–2.2
1950–55.	2.5	1.9	9.8	6.9
1955–58.	1.4	nil	9.0	7.4
1958–61.	1.2	−0.5	9.2	5.4
1961–65.	2.4	2.0	8.5	5.2

Western European economy has approached the Soviet rate,[11] and Japan did so only between 1958 and 1961.[12]

The rise in the capital-output ratio (declining marginal productivity of capital) occurred not only because the expected technological offset was nullified by the high rate of capital formation, but also because the infusion of this input was disproportionately large compared with that of manpower. Even if the rate of capital formation had been relatively lower, the law of diminishing returns would apply if the growth rate for capital stock were greatly in excess of that of the labor force. Disparity in the Soviet case is evidenced in the high incremental capital-labor ratios[13]

---

[10] Kuznets, *op. cit.*, p. 64.

[11] Denison, *op. cit.*, p. 190.

[12] Shuntaro Shishido, "Japanese Experience with Long-term Planning," in Bert Hickman (ed.), *Quantitative Planning of Economic Policy* (Washington, D.C.: Brookings Institution, 1965), p. 214.

[13] Defined as the rate of increase in capital stock divided by the rate of increase in man-hours of employment.

TABLE 9

Incremental Capital-Labor Ratios*

USSR		United States	
Period	*Ratio*	*Period*	*Ratio*
1929–37............2.4–3.0		1869–79..............1.9	
1937–40............ 2.7		1879–89..............1.5	
1940–50............2.8–3.7		1889–99..............2.2	
1950–58............ 6.9		1899–09..............1.7	
1958–64............ 15.7		1909–19..............2.1	
		1919–29..............2.9	

* Increase in fixed capital, net of retirements, divided by increase in man-hours of employment.

shown in Table 9, as compared with U.S. experience at similar growth stages. With their strong fixation for rapid growth, Soviet leaders have indiscriminately channeled immense resources into capital investment, even though rapidly diminishing returns were the result of such a policy. Substitution of capital for labor was especially prominent after 1958 as the demographic pinch on manpower became acute. During the 19th century U.S. incremental fixed capital-labor ratios were far lower than anything experienced by the Soviets, except for the atypical war and recovery decade. Postwar computations for Western Europe indicate no ratio higher than the 5.5 for Germany between 1955 and 1962 with ratios for most countries in the 3.0 to 4.5 range.[14]

Undoubtedly the peculiar nature of the Soviet system of pricing played a role in the disproportionate infusions of capital because of the absence of an interest charge. In a market economy the imposition of interest charges would have led to low returns to capital investment long before attaining the investment rate reached in the Soviet economy. Determined as it was to foster rapid industrialization, the regime might have ignored the rising cost of investment, but at least it would have possessed an adequate criterion for reaching a judgment.

THE EXPLANATION

Resource Allocation Policies

We have noted thus far that a major explanation of rapid Soviet growth was the intensive exploitation of the nation's bountiful endowment of human resources through unusually rapid rates of increase in employment and high rates of capital formation. Productivity considerations were relegated to the aim of industrialization at a maximum pace.

[14] Denison, *op. cit.*, p. 193.

What policies enabled the state to sequester resources for this all-compelling purpose?

In general terms, rapid growth occurred because the regime could channel a large share of current output into investment. This policy, of course, meant that a relatively small share could be used to satisfy consumer needs, a share further reduced as defense claims burgeoned after 1937 and continued at a high proportion all through the postwar years (see Table 10).

Even in 1928 before the progressive squeezing of the consumer to direct resources into investment commenced, the share of GNP devoted to private consumption purposes was low by the historical standards of other major economies at similar levels of per capita GNP. Bergson's

TABLE 10

Trends in Allocation of Soviet GNP*
(percent of total)

End use	1928	1937	1940	1950	1955	1965
Private consumption...............	64.7	52.5	51.0	51.0	50.6	46.2
Communal consumption†............	5.1	10.5	9.9	8.0	8.2	9.9
Investment‡.......................	25.0	25.9	19.2	23.0	25.3	30.4
Defense§.........................	2.5	7.9	16.1	13.3	13.0	11.3
Other‖...........................	2.7	3.2	3.8	4.7	2.9	2.4
Total....................	100.0	100.0	100.0	100.0	100.0	100.0

* The estimates are in terms of factor cost; i.e., they exclude indirect taxes and subsidies. For an explanation of the differences between the prewar and postwar estimates, see Stanley H. Cohn, "The Soviet Economy: Performance and Growth," in Vladimir G. Treml and Robert Farrell (eds.), *The Development of the Soviet Economy: Plan and Performance* (New York: Frederick A. Praeger, Inc., 1968), p. 40, Table 11.

† Outlays for public education, health, and science.

‡ Fixed investment and inventories.

§ Budgetary category of defense, 1928–40; budgetary plus estimates of defense expenditures under other portions of state budget, 1950–65.

‖ Largely composed of governmental administrative expenditures.

estimate of 64.7 percent for 1928 compares with 83.0 percent for the United Kingdom in 1860–69, 82.6 percent for Germany in 1851–61, 79.7 percent for the United States in 1867–78, 84.1 percent for Italy in 1891–1900, and 82.0 percent for Japan in 1931–40.[15] Equally without historical precedent is the rapidity with which the proportionate claim of private consumption on GNP declined, reaching a share in 1937 of only 52.5 percent. No other major economy approached this low proportion in peacetime circumstances until Japan in the late 1950's. In the nine years following 1928, the USSR achieved a proportionate reduction in the share of private consumption in GNP by 12 points, an accomplishment which required 40 years in Germany, 50 in the United Kingdom and Italy, 30 in the United States, and over a half century in Japan.[16]

[15] Simon Kuznets, "The Share and Structure of Consumption," *Economic Development and Cultural Change*, January, 1962, Part II, pp. 72–74.

[16] *Ibid.*

TABLE 11

Comparative Trends in per Capita Private Consumption
(annual average rates in percent)

Country	Period	Rate of Growth
USSR......................	1928–37	−1.0 — +2.6
	1937–40	−1.0
	1940–44	−8.1 — −8.8
	1944–50	9.5
	1950–58	5.0
	1958–65	2.8
United Kingdom..............	1880–89 to 1890–99	1.7
	1890–99 to 1900–09	0.6
	1950–58	1.6
	1958–65	2.6
Germany....................	1851–60 to 1861–70	1.9
	1861–70 to 1871–80	1.4
	1871–80 to 1881–90	0.8
	1881–90 to 1891–00	1.8
	1950–58	6.3
	1958–65	4.8
Italy.......................	1861–70 to 1871–80	0.1
	1871–80 to 1881–90	nil
	1881–90 to 1891–00	1.2
	1950–58	3.1
	1958–65	4.5
United States...............	1869–79	4.2
	1879–89	2.0
	1889–98 to 1899–08	2.9
	1950–58	1.1
	1958–65	3.2

Another way of casting perspective on Soviet consumption policy is to compare rates of change in per capita private consumption levels in other major economies at similar levels of per capita income (Table 11). Depending on the base year prices used, Soviet per capita private consumption either declined from 1928 through 1941, or showed a moderate increase between 1928 and 1937 and then declined for the next four years.[17] If there were an increase, it was more nominal than real, as much of it reflects the costs of urbanization, i.e., the commercial purchase of commodities and services formerly supplied by the consumer himself in a rural environment. In no other historical instance did consumption decline in other economies under peacetime conditions, nor were increases so largely reflective of urbanization costs, as shifts out of agriculture were more gradual.[18]

With Stalin's demise, the policy of treating the consumer as a residual

---

[17] In either case per capita consumption declined from 1928 to 1937.

[18] There is divided opinion on whether or not per capita consumption levels fell in the United Kingdom during the early part of the Industrial Revolution; years prior to those shown in Table 11.

claimant ceased. Thanks in good part to the rehabilitation of agriculture in the mid- and late fifties, per capita consumption increased by 5.0 percent per year through 1958, but after that date with stagnation again prevailing in agriculture the rate of increase was cut almost in half and since 1961 has barely exceeded 2.0 percent annually, the lowest rate among the major industrial economies.

Investment Emphasis

The rapid rate of industrialization of the USSR after 1928 was ultimately a function of the high rate of investment, supported by a rapid increase in the urban labor force. As the ratio of private consumption to GNP was unusually low, so the ratio of investment was unusually high. Low income, underdeveloped economies customarily cannot invest a large portion of their national product, as consumption cannot be easily diverted from a population living close to the margin of subsistence. Through close control over resources, especially in agriculture, the Soviet state was able to sequester the savings which enabled the economy to enjoy a high rate of investment.

No other major economy similar to the Soviet Union of 1928–37 was able to invest anything like the quarter of GNP the USSR attained in these years. In the mid-19th century the British proportion was only about an eighth, the German ranging from a seventh up to a fifth toward the end of the century, the Italian a seventh early in the 20th century, the Japanese only as high as a sixth in the 1920's and 1930's, and the U.S. a fifth in the 1870's and 1880's, but at a higher per capita income level than the USSR in 1928.[19] It was only in the 1950's that some large market economies began to approach the high Soviet investment ratios, and none of these had relative defense burdens comparable to that of the USSR.

The ability of the Soviet economy to devote so large a share of product to investment at low per capita income levels appears all the more unique when it is realized that the entire burden of saving occurred within national boundaries. By contrast, other economies at the stage of development of the USSR in 1928–40 were able to draw on capital inflows from more highly developed nations. The United States was partially dependent upon European sources of financing until the 1890's, with foreign sources providing about 11 percent of net capital formation in the 1870's, and probably considerably more earlier.[20] Japan was heavily dependent on foreign investment until World War I, and Italy for most of the period under review. This dependence was particularly sharp for such countries as Canada, Australia, and Argentina.[21]

In addition to its large magnitude, Soviet investment has also been

---

[19] Simon Kuznets, "Long Term Trends in Capital Formation Proportions," *Economic Development and Cultural Change*, July 1961, pp. 10–11.

[20] Kuznets, *Captial in the American Economy*, p. 133.

[21] Kuznets, "Long Term Trends in Capital Formation Proportions," pp. 52 and 53.

distinguished by its concentration in growth supporting sectors. The most graphic illustration of this propensity has been the unusually small portion of fixed investment devoted to housing. Between 1928 and 1940 this proportion was only 15.5 percent compared with around 25 percent for the United States in the 1870's and 1880's, a third for Germany from 1851 to 1890, a quarter to a third for Italy from 1861 to 1915, and a quarter for Japan from 1887 to 1906.[22] The small Soviet proportion is even more significant, given the rapid rate of urbanization in these years. The combination of circumstances led to a drastic decline in housing standards with per capita availabilities falling from 5.8 square meters in 1928 to 4.6 in 1937[23] and rising only to 6.4 in 1964.[24]

During the period of relaxation following Stalin's passing, the share of housing in fixed investment increased to around 21 percent, just under the proportions for the United Kingdom, Germany, and Italy. However, with the resource and productivity constraint that developed after 1958, the regime chose to sacrifice housing in favor of maintaining the rate of productive investment. As a result, the housing share fell back below 20 percent, considerably below the proportions for all major economies other than the United Kingdom. In fact, there was an absolute decline in the annual volume of housing investment from 1959 through 1964. The Brezhnev-Kosygin regime, with its renewed concern for the interests of the consumer, has contemplated a restoration of the housing program, since the draft of the new Five-Year Plan (1966–70) shows an increase for housing investment some 2½ times that of productive investment.

Investment has been directed not only to productive sectors of the economy, but also toward those with the heaviest growth orientation. In the 1928–40 period Soviet investment was much more concentrated in industry and agriculture, and less in commerce and services, than was the case in mid-19th century United States. Within industry it has been more directed to the growth-inducing metallurgical and machinery branches.[25] In the postwar years Soviet investment has continued to be high in its orientation toward industry and agriculture among leading economies, with neglect for the service sectors and for transportation.

Defense Burden

The Soviet development model has been characterized not only by a high rate of investment and slow increases, and even declines, in consump-

[22] *Ibid.*, pp. 65, 73, 97, 116.

[23] Janet G. Chapman, "Consumption," in Abram Bergson and Simon Kuznets (eds.), *Economic Trends in the Soviet Union* (Cambridge, Mass.: Harvard University Press, 1963), p. 238.

[24] Timothy Sosnovy, "Housing Conditions and Urban Development in the USSR," *New Directions in the Soviet Economy*, Part II-B, p. 533.

[25] Norman M. Kaplan, "Capital Formation and Allocation," in Abram Bergson (ed.), *Soviet Economic Growth* (Evanston, Ill.: Row, Peterson, 1953), pp. 59, 63.

tion, but also by a large defense burden since the Third Five-Year Plan. Whatever the considerations which have prompted the regime to pursue policies of heavy defense expenditures, their continued prevalence (between 11 and 13 percent of GNP since 1950) alongside high shares of investment in GNP has further worsened the position of the Soviet consumer. In the postwar period only the United States has devoted as large a share of its resources to military purposes, but with a much lower investment ratio. By contrast, countries with investment ratios as high as the USSR, such as Germany and Japan, have had small or minuscule defense programs. Defense ratios amounted to 11.3 of GNP in the USSR and 10.8 in the United States in 1965, compared with 5 to 7 percent in the United Kingdom, France, and Germany. Investment ratios were 28.9 in the USSR, 36.1 in Japan, 29.1 in Germany, 26.6 in Italy, 23.4 in France, 18.2 in the United Kingdom, and 17.9 in the United States. Only an economy with the strong, centralized controls of the Soviet Union could tolerate so small a claim for the consumer out of available resources.

Not only the consumer bears the sacrifice of heavy defense spending, for the growth potential of the economy is also restrained. Those periods in Soviet history which have seen sharp increases in defense spending, such as 1937–40, 1951–52, and 1960–63, have also been periods in which rates of increase in investment have sharply declined. Furthermore, as defense expenditures are composed more and more of research and developmental outlays for aerospace and nuclear weapons, the greater becomes the demand for the scarce services of highly trained scientists, engineers, and managers. The absorption of a significant share of such personnel into military-oriented activities means that civilian-oriented investment is deprived of vital inputs. Part of the explanation for the sharp rise in capital-output ratios may be slower technological progress because of the drain of so many skilled personnel into defense production. If these personnel could be released into the civilian economy, they could devote their energies to research, development, and adaptation of civilian-oriented technology. If the pace of technological development and assimilation into the production process could be accelerated, there would be increased cost savings which would serve to prevent the inexorable rise in the capital-output ratio.

Education—Human Capital Investment

Concomitant with and of equal importance to the heavy emphasis on fixed capital investment has been the high priority which the Soviet leadership has placed on education, i.e., investment in human capital. At an early stage Soviet leaders were aware that their strenuous physical investment efforts would be for nought if not accompanied by provision for training a skilled labor force. In the prewar years the main objective of educational policy was mass literacy through universal elementary education and an extensive program of adult education. Since the war the emphasis has been on universal secondary education and rapid expansion of higher and technical education.

The USSR is the one country in Europe to have emulated the U.S. in goals of mass secondary and higher education. As of about 1960 the enrollment ratio, i.e., the proportion of a given age group enrolled in school, was just under half for the age group 15–19 compared with two-thirds in the United States and only about a sixth in the major West European countries. In the age group 20–24 years, the Soviet ratio was about a twelfth, compared to an eighth in the United States and only a twenty-fifth in Western Europe. Since Soviet per capita income is considerably below that of the principal countries of Northwestern Europe, its educational effort is disproportionately large. Furthermore, the present high ratio has been attained in a much shorter time period than in Western Europe.

While the increase in the ratio for most other economies was slow until after World War II, the Soviet ratio rose steadily during the years of comprehensive planning, reaching 3.3 by 1937, 4.7 by 1950, and 6.7 by 1964 (Table 12). Since 1932 the Soviet university enrollment ratio has been second only to that of the United States, with exception, perhaps, for Japan since 1958, even though its relative per capita income level would warrant a much lower ranking. The comparison in terms of university enrollments may somewhat understate the relative Soviet educational effort, as that country's program of training high-level technicians is much more advanced than those of the principal West European economies.

As in the case of physical capital, Soviet investment in human capital has also been narrowly channeled toward growth-supporting activities. At the elementary and secondary levels, Soviet students on the average are exposed to more instruction in science and mathematics than their American equivalents. In higher education, liberal arts curricula are unknown in the USSR, with students specializing narrowly in their major disciplines. In universities, graduates in engineering and the sciences comprise a much larger share of the total than in the United States. In 1960, for example, 38 percent of all Soviet graduates were in these fields, compared to only around 15 percent in the United States. By contrast, 31 percent of U.S. graduates majored in the humanities and social sciences other than economics, compared with only 3 percent in the USSR.[26]

Structural Transformation

The rapid industrialization of the Soviet economy after 1928, as previously emphasized, was accomplished by heavy infusions of man-

---

[26] Nicholas DeWitt, "Education and the Development of Human Resources: Soviet and American Effort," in U.S. Congress, Joint Economic Committee, *Dimensions of Soviet Economic Power* (Washington, D.C.: U.S. Government Printing Office, 1962), p. 259.

TABLE 12

Comparative University Enrollments

Country	Year	Full-time Students per 1000 Population
USSR...............................	1914	0.8
	1928	1.2
	1932	3.2
	1937	3.3
	1950	4.7
	1958	6.4
	1964	6.7
United Kingdom....................	1901	0.9
	1911	1.1
	1921	0.9
	1931	1.1
	1937	1.1
	1951	1.9
	1958	2.2
Germany..........................	1901	0.9
	1911	1.1
	1922	1.8
	1932	1.9
	1937	1.1
	1951	2.5
	1959	3.7
France............................	1921	1.1
	1931	1.5
	1954	3.3
	1959	3.7
Italy..............................	1881	0.4
	1901	0.8
	1921	1.3
	1941	3.2
	1951	3.1
	1958	3.4
Japan.............................	1890	0.3
	1910	0.9
	1920	1.3
	1930	2.5
	1940	3.2
	1950	2.9
	1958	7.1
United States......................	1870	1.3
	1890	2.5
	1910	3.8
	1920	5.6
	1930	8.9
	1940	11.3
	1950	17.6
	1960	20.0

TABLE 13

Agricultural Employment as Proportion of Total Employment
(percent of total)

Country	Year	Proportion
USSR	1928	71
	1937	54
	1940	51
	1950	46
	1958	41
	1964	34
France	1788	75
	1845	62
	1866	52
	1886	48
	1906	43
	1926	39
Italy	1861	62
	1881	57
	1901	59
	1921	56
	1936	48
Japan	1877–82	83
	1887–92	76
	1897–02	70
	1907–12	63
	1920	54
	1940	42
Germany	1882	42
	1895	36
	1907	34
	1925	30
	1939	27
England and Wales	1841	23
	1861	19
	1881	12
	1901	9
United States	1870	50
	1890	42
	1900	37
	1920	27
	1940	17

power and capital into productive industrial enterprises. This process was accompanied by rapid transformation in the structure of the system. In terms of the proportion of the labor force employed in agriculture, the Soviet economy of 1928 was far less industrialized than were the other major economies at comparable levels of per capita income (Table 13).

Within 12 years the transfer of labor from farm to urban occupations through collectivization and organized recruitment reduced the agricultural proportion by 20 percentage points. The shift was far more rapid than in the other major economies, with shifts of comparable proportions requiring 60 years in France, 65 in Italy, 40 in the United States, and 30 to

35 in Japan (Table 13). Yet, because of the huge initial size of the farm population and the rapid increase in population as a whole, agricultural employment actually increased by 2.4 million between 1928 and 1937 and by another 4 million between 1937 and 1940. The latter increase is largely explained by the territorial acquisitions of 1939–40.

The unbalanced nature of Soviet growth under the first three five-year plans is reflected in divergent productivity trends in the various sectors of the economy. In terms of man-hours, industrial labor productivity increased at an average annual rate (depending on the prices used to value output) of between 3.1 and 10.4 percent from 1928 to 1937 and at a rate of 2.7 percent from 1937 to 1940.[27] By contrast, in agriculture the rise of employment was coupled with a decline in production,[28] implying, of course, a fall in productivity. Historically, in other economies the transfer of labor out of agriculture has been accompanied by rising labor productivity trends at rates not too different from industry, especially since World War I.[29] In no instance has agricultural productivity declined. While the rapid reduction in the agricultural share of employment and the decline in production are not functionally related, both stemmed from the drastic collectivization campaign, with its emasculation of incentives and wholesale destruction of livestock.

The imbalance between industrial and agricultural development is the corollary of the policy of suppression of consumption in favor of investment and defense. Within the aggregate of industrial production, output of industrial raw materials and producer durables rose much more rapidly than that of consumer goods, inclusive of home-processed food and clothing. Within the broad category of services, production- and investment-oriented services increased more swiftly than did consumer services. This dichotomy makes generalizations as to output and productivity trends in the services sector meaningless as a guide to development policy.

In the years following Stalin's passing, the formerly unbalanced sectoral growth pattern was considerably rectified by rapid progress in agriculture through 1958. Since the rapid rise in output was extensive in nature, being partially based on an 18 percent increase in cultivated acreage,[30] farm employment actually increased by a million from 1950 to 1958.[31] Though the proportion of manpower on the farm continued to fall, the relative decline was far slower than the breakneck pace of 1928 to 1940. After 1958, with the cessation of acreage expansion, agricultural

[27] Raymond Powell, "Industrial Production," in Bergson and Kuznets, *op. cit.*, p. 178.

[28] Gale Johnson, "Agricultural Production," *ibid.*, p. 218.

[29] Deborah Paige, "Economic Growth: the Last Hundred Years," *National Institute Economic Review*, July 1961, p. 39.

[30] Douglas Diamond, "Trends in Output, Inputs, and Factor Productivity in Soviet Agriculture," in *New Directions in the Soviet Economy*, Part II-B, p. 353.

[31] Murray Feshbach, "Manpower in the USSR," *ibid.*, Part III, p. 786.

employment resumed its secular decline, but at a much more deliberate pace than in the prewar Stalinist years.

These were years of rapid growth and technological progress throughout the western world over the entire range of modern economic activity. In most industrial economies, productivity in agriculture since 1950 has risen more rapidly than in these economies as a whole.[32] In fact, one prominent economist has demonstrated that the ability of the principal continental economies to transfer redundant manpower smoothly from low-productivity agriculture and petty trade into burgeoning industrial sectors was the principal factor explaining rapid economic growth in the fifties and early sixties.[33] By contrast, in the USSR, except for the period 1950–55, rates of increase in agricultural man-hour productivity have continued to lag behind for the economy as a whole. For 1955–58, the respective rates for agriculture and the economy were 6.4 and 7.4 percent; for 1958–61, 3.9 and 5.9 percent; and for 1961–65, 1.7 and 3.2 percent.[34]

Role of Foreign Trade in Soviet Economic Development

The forgoing analysis of Soviet growth has assumed the existence of a closed economy. Compared with most other nations in the course of development, foreign trade played a minor role in the USSR, but nevertheless it was important at certain stages of Soviet development and should be evaluated, even in summary fashion.

Foreign investment and technology played a vital role in Czarist economic development.[35] Russian grain and other raw material exports financed the imports of machinery and of capital which were essential to industrial development in an agricultural economy. In 1913, about 12 percent of the grain crop, 25 percent of lumber, and 12 percent of petroleum produced was exported. Over a third of imports were comprised of machinery and textile raw materials. Exports amounted to about 10 percent of national product in 1913.

In the Soviet period the importance of foreign trade has been considerably less, though of considerable weight in particular periods. After falling to the vanishing point in the years immediately after the Revolution, foreign trade volume recovered slowly during the NEP period, but by 1927 only attained about 35 percent of the 1913 level of exports and 39 percent of the level of imports. Export volume was limited by the great reduction in the marketed share of the grain crop arising from the establishment of small, private farms in agriculture. Imports were, of

---

[32] Angus Maddison, "Soviet Economic Performance," *Banca Nazionale del Lavoro Quarterly Review,* March 1965, p. 13.

[33] Denison, *op. cit.,* p. 321.

[34] Douglas Diamond, *op. cit.,* pp. 352, 373.

[35] Data in this and the following four paragraphs are from Franklyn Holzman, "Foreign Trade," in Bergson and Kuznets, *op. cit.,* pp. 284–95.

course, limited by the economy's export capabilities, but by the late twenties their composition was already being shifted in the direction of growth- and reconstruction-supporting products.

With the onset of the First Five-Year Plan with its greatly increased requirements for industrial imports, foreign trade volume rose sharply, particularly through 1931. By 1930 the ratio of exports to national product had risen to 3.5 percent, a proportion not to be attained again since that date. What is of greater developmental significance is the composition of trade during these early plan years. Even though these were years of great privation in agriculture with sharply reduced grain and livestock product output, nearly half of total exports consisted of these agricultural products. The creation of such exporting capability may have been one of the purposes of the collectivization program. The composition of imports was closely geared to the frentic industrialization effort. In the early 1930's machinery and ferrous metals comprised nearly 75 percent of total imports.

During the Second Five-Year Plan, with the fruition of domestic productive capabilities in machinery and in metals, foreign trade volume fell not only relatively to national product, but absolutely. By 1938, exports were down to 62 percent of the 1929 level and the ratio of exports to national product to only 0.5 percent. During World War II exports declined drastically, but imports increased in the form of Allied military assistance. Since World War II, the role of foreign trade has again increased, reflecting first extensive trading relations within the Soviet Bloc and more recently wider economic relations with the industrialized market economies and the less developed nations. In recent years the ratio of foreign trade to national product has been approaching the 3.0 to 3.5 percent peak of the early plan years. For the most part, Soviet imports have been keyed in recent years to imports of prototype industrial plants from the industrialized market economies and specialized industrial machinery from the planned economies of Eastern Europe. Exports still heavily emphasize raw materials—oil, lumber, and metals to the industrial market economies, and industrial raw materials to the Eastern European economies.

If foreign trade has played a positive role in furthering economic development, the question arises as to why the Soviet leadership, commencing with the Second Five-Year Plan, pursued a policy of autarky. Politically this policy was consistent with the aim of the leadership to secure and maintain military and economic independence from the capitalist world. The experience of World War II in which the Soviet Union had to rely largely on its own resources confirmed the defense argument. The economic rationale for autarky is the desire of economic planners to control as many of the economic variables as possible. A large foreign trade sector would have considerably reduced the planners' independence in decisionmaking.

One of the costly legacies of the policy of minimization of foreign trade has been the perpetuation of an uneconomic agricultural sector. The nearly total dependence of the economy on domestic sources of supply of farm products has been a limiting factor on economic development. Perhaps if foreign trade were liberalized, the Soviets would find it to their comparative advantage to import a considerable portion of their agricultural requirements, such as feed grains, and to concentrate their exports on industrial products, the production of which has been the beneficiary of their tremendous technological efforts. Such a change would have to overcome the fixation of an adequate domestic grain supply as the cornerstone of defensive logistical capability.

While the constraints on foreign trade have been largely political in nature, they undoubtedly have had the effect of increasing the cost of economic development and thereby constraining growth. The new post-Khruschev leadership with its enhanced economic perception is aware of this limitation. In his general assessment of economic affairs in 1965, Kosygin berated Soviet planners for turning their backs on an efficiency-conscious outside world distinguished by an incredibly fast tempo of technological change. The new Eighth Five-Year Plan urges in several passages an enhanced Soviet interest in the potentialities of foreign trade. Among other statements, the Plan Directives decree "improvements in the commodity structure of Soviet trade, both on the import and export side of the exchange, that would in fact make it possible for the USSR to take part in a rational division of labor on an international scale." The Directives presage a sharp reversal of the policy of economic isolationism by urging that the structure of domestic production be guided by comparative costs in the world market and that the Soviet economy no longer produce but import "articles whose production inside the country entails greater costs and capital investment." Should these Directives be implemented, the Soviet economy will be taking belated advantage of efficiency gains it has long denied to itself in its development policies.

SUMMARY

From the vantage point of the mid-sixties, we have briefly surveyed the techniques and policies which enabled the Soviet Union to achieve its rapid rise to second position among the world's economies. This success stemmed from the determination of the regime to channel the country's prodigious resource endowment into economic growth and the building of the nation's international power position. The abundance of resources and the regime's ability to suppress consumer demands brought success, so long as these favorable conditions held. Meanwhile the economy was incurring deferred obligations in the form of housing, transportation facilities, consumer services, and consumer durables production. As the day of deferred payment drew closer, some sweeping modification in the traditional Soviet development model was becoming ever more compelling. The increasing recognition of the need for change on the part of the leadership has led to a permissive atmosphere, reminiscent of the twenties, in which Soviet economists have again engaged in intellectual controversies as to the future shape of the Soviet economic system. At the same time, the traditional Stalinist and post-Stalinist development model is evolving in directions which more closely resemble those which the advanced market economies of the West have followed.

15 | CONSUMPTION IN THE SOVIET UNION

Janet G. Chapman

When the Soviet leadership decided to push for rapid economic growth through massive industrialization it was forced into a policy of keeping living standards from rising. Every man-hour devoted to production of consumer goods was one man-hour which could not be used to produce investment goods. Every ton of steel used in automobiles or refrigerators was a ton which could not be used to produce tractors or turbines. The trade-off between living standards on the one hand and economic growth on the other was clearly understood, and Soviet policymakers have not masked their preference for the latter at the sacrifice of the former. The Soviet population has been required to work and produce more now, in order that future generations might benefit.

As a result of the emphasis on industrial growth, Soviet living standards have suffered. Clothing supplies are adequate, but prices are high relative to wages, and quality and style are inferior in comparison with both Western and Eastern Europe. The Soviet diet, though adequate in total caloric intake, is deficient in meat and dairy products, vegetables, and fruit. Although much new housing has been constructed in recent years, space, quality, and equipment are well below West European and U.S. standards. Perhaps the most striking difference from the West is in durable consumer goods such as home appliances and automobiles. On the other hand, the USSR has developed one of the most comprehensive welfare programs in the world, especially in the areas of health care, education, and social insurance.

After the death of Stalin, Soviet living standards improved substantially. The rate of growth slowed somewhat in the early 1960's but increased again after 1965. Patterns of change in Soviet consumption levels through 1965 are documented in the following selection by Janet G. Chapman, Professor of Economics at the University of Pittsburgh. It is reprinted with permission from *Applied Economic Papers*, Vol. V, No. 1 (March, 1964), pp. 1–9, and *Opinion*, Vol. IV, No. 51 (28th April 1964), pp. 14–17.

THE SOVIET UNION transformed itself in the course of a few decades from an underdeveloped, largely agricultural economy into an industrial and military giant. The effect that this fundamental change in the nature of the Soviet economy has had on the level and pattern of consumption is the subject of this paper. In considering consumption trends under Soviet planning it is of interest to note which aspects seem primarily a feature of the industrialization process, which are mainly related to the historical period and the level of technology prevailing when the industrialization took place, and which are attributable to the policies of the Soviet leadership.

TRENDS IN CONSUMPTION 1928–1958

The discussion is based on a number of indicators of Soviet per capita consumption shown in Table 1. The period covered is 1928 to 1958. The year 1928 was the initial year of the First Five Year Plan, and the year in which Stalin launched the industrialization drive. It also marks roughly the point at which the economy generally had recovered from World War I, the Revolution and Civil War. After a brief review of the changes in the level of consumption during the thirty years 1928–58, we will turn to the major changes in the pattern of consumption.

Level of Consumption

The policy of the Soviet leaders has been to hold down consumption in the interest of achieving a high rate of economic growth and a concentration on heavy industry and military power. As a result, the gain in consumption has been much less spectacular than Soviet advances in other areas. Measures of average real per capita consumption, both excluding and including communal services, are shown in the table. Per capita consumption refers to total household purchases of goods and services for consumption plus household consumption in kind, expressed on a per capita basis. Communal services are the education and health and related services provided (for the most part) without charge by the government. The measures shown (items 1, 2, and 3 in the table) are calculations of Abram Bergson in which consumption is valued at 1937 prices.[1] During the prewar period there was little, if any, gain in real per capita consumption. By 1940, as the table shows, real per capita consumption was slightly below the 1928 level if taken alone, but slightly above the 1928 level if the communal services are included. Actually, the 1937 and 1940 levels shown represent a recovery from a decline in consumption during the First Five Year Plan (a decline which has not been measured with any precision),

---

[1] Abram Bergson, *The Real National Income of Soviet Russia Since 1928* (Cambridge, Mass.: Harvard Univ. Press, 1962). Bergson's alternative valuation procedure leads to somewhat different results, as indicated in the notes to the table.

TABLE 1

Selected Indicators of Consumption, USSR
1928–1959

Indicator	·1928	1937	1940	1944	1950	1958	1958 in per cent of 1928
1. Real per capita consumption in 1937 adjusted market prices, index 1937 = 100[a]	103	100	96	66	114	191	185
2. Real per capita consumption and communal services in 1937 adjusted market prices, index 1937 = 100	91	100	96	69·	116	185	203
3. Real per capita consumption of communal services at 1937 factor cost, index 1937 = 100	29	100	101	86	131	154	531
4. Per capita industrial output of consumer goods, index 1937 = 100	68	100	92	43[b]	97	172	253
5. Per capita output of selected foods:							
a. Flour, kilograms	158	169	149	86[b]	121	159	101
b. Potatoes, kilograms	110	200	191	n.a.[c]	243	150	136
c. Meat, poultry, lard, kilograms	32	18	24	15[b]	27	38	119
d. Milk, kilograms	178	141	141	108[b]	145	224	126
e. Eggs, number	65	45	56	n.a.	59	105	162
f. Fish (catch), kilograms	5.5	9.7	7.2	6.4[b]	9.6	14.2	258
g. Sugar, kilograms	8.5	14.7	11.1	2.7[b]	13.8	26.2	308
h. Vegetable oil, kilograms	3.0	3.3	4.1	1.7[b]	4.5	7.0	233
i. Vegetables, kilograms	53	66	53	n.a.	41	55	104
j. Vodka, liters	3.7	5.4	4.7	2.5[b]	3.4	7.0	189
k. Beer, liters	2.6	5.4	6.2	2.3[b]	7.2	9.6	369
6. Per capita output of selected non-foods:							
a. Fabrics, meters	19.6	23.6	22.8	10.3[b]	24.5	35.9	183
b. Hosiery, pairs	0.4	2.5	2.5	0.5[b]	2.6	4.3	1075
c. Shoes, pairs	0.5	1.1	1.1	0.4[b]	1.1	1.7	340
d. Soap, kilograms	2.0	3.0	3.6	1.6[b]	4.5	6.6	330
e. Cigarettes, number	327	540	515	143	686	1120	343
7. Urban housing space, square meters per capita	5.8	4.6	4.5	3.9	5.0	5.5	95
8. School enrollment per 1,000 total population:							
a. Grades 1–4	65	128	110	116[b]	110	86	132
b. Grades 5 through university	15	64	85	47[b]	100	90	600
9. Medical care and health:							
a. Doctors per 10,000 population	4	6	7	n.a.	14	17	425
b. Hospital beds per 10,000 population	16	36	40	n.a.	56	73	456
c. Crude death rate per 1,000 population	24.2	17.8[d]	18.1	n.a.	9.7	7.2	30
d. Infant mortality, deaths under 1 year per 1,000 births	187[e]	n.a.	184	n.a.	81	41	22

a. At adjusted market prices of 1928, the 1928 index number is 82. At adjusted market prices of 1950, the 1928 index number is 99 and the 1958 index number is 185. Linking the 1928 index number valued at 1928 prices to that for 1958 valued at 1950 prices results in a 1958 index number of 226 percent of 1928.

b. 1945.

c. Not available.

d. 1938.

e. 1926–27. European Russia.

Source: J. Chapman, "Consumption," in A. Bergson and S. Kuznets, eds., *Economic Trends in the Soviet Union* (Cambridge, Mass.: Harvard Univ. Press, 1963), pp. 238–39.

resulting mainly from the very rapid increase in the level of investment and the disruption in agriculture and loss of livestock which accompanied collectivization. The war effort and heavy war losses meant a sharp decline in consumption. These losses were finally made good in the late 1940's and since then there has been a very rapid increase in consumption. By 1958, real per capita consumption was 85 percent higher than in 1928, taken alone, and including communal services real per capita consumption was more than twice as high as in 1928.[2]

Pattern of Consumption

With average real income today about twice what it was in 1928, how has the Soviet consumer's pattern of consumption changed? Although the stage of economic development by now achieved in the Soviet Union is advanced, consumer income is still at a low level characteristic, usually, of an earlier stage of economic development. Because of the low level of income the role of basic necessities in the consumer's budget is still very large. Food takes about 58 percent of the Soviet worker's family budget and food accounts for the labor of about two-thirds of the people engaged in the production and distribution of consumer goods. The Soviet diet today is adequate in calories, but the consumer gets less meat and milk than he would like, and his diet is still made up largely of bread and potatoes, a characteristic of a low level of income.[3] Per capita food consumption shows a more moderate increase over the thirty-year period than consumption of non-foods. This would, indeed, be expected in the course of economic development and rising incomes. However, the loss of half the country's livestock during collectivization in the early 1930's, further losses during the war and persistent difficulties in agriculture are more important factors here. The output of cloth for clothing increased by 83 percent on a per capita basis and the output of ready made clothes and shoes increased more substantially.

Concerning shelter, the third traditional basic necessity, urban housing construction always lagged behind the great increase in the urban population so that urban per capita dwelling space as late as 1958 was but 5.5 square meters and less than in 1928. The 1928 level has by now been

---

[2] In 1958, Soviet per capita consumption including communal services, at current prices was about 4800 rubles a year. Nancy Nimitz, *Soviet National Income and Product 1956–1958*, RAND Research Memorandum RM-3112-PR, (Santa Monica, California: The RAND Corporation, June, 1962). In terms of the currency in use since January, 1961, this is equivalent to 480 "new" rubles. At the official exchange rate, one "new" ruble is equal to $1.11.

[3] Although the table shows that the per capita level of meat consumption in 1958 had finally regained the 1928 level, more recent unfavorable developments in Soviet agriculture may mean a further deterioration in the quality of the Soviet diet. The poor harvest of 1963 and the shortage of fodder led to the slaughter of more livestock than usual, which reduced the number of cattle, sheep, and goats by a few percentage points and the number of pigs by over 40 percent.

exceeded as a result of intensified building activity, and urban per capita dwelling space was 6.5 square meters in 1961. The provision of household utilities, also, has lagged way behind the growth of urban population, except in the case of electricity. Today, 89 percent of the Soviet urban population is supplied with electricity but two-thirds of the urban population live in housing without running water or plumbing.[4]

In the realm of private personal consumption, prime emphasis of Soviet policy has, of necessity, been the more adequate provision of basic necessities. As the data in the table show, during much of the period, this policy was not very successful. Some luxuries, however, must be made available as incentives to make differentials in wages worth earning. And now that consumer income is somewhat higher, there is more leeway for luxuries. Output of clothing and some other consumer goods is beginning to be large enough so that the consumer can exercise some choice and is beginning to show some resistance to poor quality and unattractive design. Output of ice cream, beer, vodka, and cigarettes has increased substantially. There has been an almost five-fold increase in the publication of newspapers and an almost three-fold increase in the publication of books per capita. The average Soviet family sees 17 movies a year and goes to the theater or a concert about once a year. By now almost half the Soviet families own a sewing machine or radio, about 10 percent own a TV set[5] and a number own bicycles. Production of other, modern consumer durables has been increasing very rapidly in recent years, but total output is still so low that very few own a refrigerator or a car.

It is evident that the Soviet leadership has not only kept a limit on the total level of consumption but their policies have also played a role in the kinds of goods which are made available for private consumption. Books, radios, and movies have been made plentiful and cheap, and this is clearly related to Soviet policy on education. Beer, wine, soda water, and ice cream have been made more plentiful and cheaper than vodka. Output of most of the modern consumer durables was held off until the postwar years. In this, the iron curtain no doubt helped in shielding the country from the "demonstration effect."

A second major feature of the Soviet consumption pattern is the large and increasing role of communal consumption. As the table shows, per capita consumption of the communal services of health care and education increased five-fold over the period. Currently, health care accounts for about 5.5 percent and education for 10 percent of total household con-

---

[4] The percentage of the urban population supplied with water and sewage facilities has somewhat increased but the absolute number of people without such amenities has increased substantially. Timothy Sosnovy, "The Soviet City," in Joint Economic Committee, Congress of the U.S., *Dimensions of Soviet Economic Power* (Washington, D.C., 1962), p. 334.

[5] Imogene Erro, "Trends in the Production of Consumer Goods" in Joint Economic Committee, *Dimensions of Soviet Economic Power*, p. 379.

sumption plus the communal services. Health care in a sense comes under the heading of basic necessities in that basic necessities are whatever are necessary to maintain the health and working efficiency of the population and the reproduction of the race. As a matter of Soviet policy, health care has been furnished on a large scale and almost entirely by the government. The individual Soviet family can now count on free medical care whenever it is needed. And much has been done in the way of control and prevention of disease. As the table shows, there has been a large increase in the provision of facilities for medical care, and in the number of doctors, and there has been a very significant reduction in the mortality rate.[6] As hardly needs to be pointed out to an Indian audience, it was the advanced state of medical knowledge available at the time of Soviet economic development which has made it possible for the Soviet Union, in a way which would not have been possible in 19th century America or England, to make very large strides in public health with a direct, and relatively small, investment in health and medical care.

Education, too, has been a matter of high priority for the Soviet regime. All education in the Soviet Union is public and free (though students have to buy their books). The first eight years of schooling are compulsory, and beyond that level education is open to those who want it and can qualify for it. Even before the Revolution most Russian children received a free four-year education; so the increase in the proportion of the population receiving a primary education has not been large but, as the table shows, the number of people per thousand of the population enrolled in secondary and higher education has increased six-fold. Illiteracy has been abolished and the general level of education of the population raised significantly.[7] The need of an educated labor force for industrialization played a major role in Soviet policy here. And again, the policy was influenced by the advanced level of knowledge and technology available when the industrialization drive was begun. One feature of backwardness is the large gap between the level of education and way of life of the still largely agricultural population, and the level of education and way of life demanded by modern industry. Even the simplest jobs in modern factories required a minimum of education, and much more advanced education and research were crucial if full advantage was to be taken of the technological possibilities. Education and mass communication are increasingly important, also, for keeping contact with the masses and as a means of encouraging support for the regime and its programs. From these points of view, public expenditure on education (and on health, also) is investment rather than consumption. However, it can also

---

[6] The table shows the crude death rate. Adjusted for changes in the age composition of the population—towards a younger average age—the decrease in the death rate would be smaller.

[7] Half of the labor force had attained a secondary or higher level education by the end of 1963.

be considered as consumption, and the Soviet people appear to place a high value on education in itself, as well as on its role as the main path to advancement in income and status.

Other features of Soviet life which must be mentioned are such things as the 41-hour week with two or more weeks' paid vacation and social security. For wage earners and salaried employees, there is a complete system of social security providing for income during periods of inability to work, and for a pension in case of permanent disability and in old age. Social security is financed through a tax on the wage bill of the factories and institutions, rather than by a direct contribution from the individual worker. These social provisions were made shortly after the Revolution and, although of course there have been changes and modifications since, there has been no change in principle. But such provisions were certainly unknown to the American worker in the 19th century, at a stage of American economic development when the American worker's real wage was as large as the Soviet worker's real wage today. The short work week is presumably a general benefit of increasing productivity, and it and social security reflect greatly changed world standards on social matters. In part, too, this is a result of industrialization and an increasing appreciation that in an industrial world the care of the sick and the old cannot be left to their families as in a peasant society but must be handled publicly.[8]

To summarize, Soviet policy on the pace and direction of development meant few of the gains of industrialization went to the consumer until recently, but the postwar increase has brought average per capita consumption including communal services to something over twice the 1928 level. The low level of consumer income so far achieved means basic necessities still account for a very large share of Soviet consumption, though this share is beginning to lessen with the recent advance in income level. The low quality of the diet even today reflects long-standing difficulties in agriculture, some of which may be inherent in Russian soil and climatic conditions, but many of which are the results of the Soviet policy of forced collectivization and inadequate investment in agriculture. The urbanization accompanying industrialization has meant more processed food, more restaurant meals, and more ready-made clothing. It has required the construction of much urban housing and utilities (though there was never enough to keep up with the growth in urban population) and transport. The advanced level of knowledge and technology, available at the time the Soviet industrialization drive was launched, helps to explain such things as electricity in urban housing, automatic vending machines on the streets of Moscow, the widespread ownership of radios

---

[8] Collective farm members, the bulk of the Russian peasantry, are not included in the social security system but are still dependent upon their family and such provisions as their farm may be able to make for assistance to the needy. However, a law of July 15, 1964, effective in January, 1965, establishes a limited social security system for collective farmers.

and movie attendance, and the small but recently increasing supplies of modern consumer durables, as well as partially accounting for Soviet emphasis on, and success in, public health and education. Emphasis on the public areas of consumption appears to have some other roots also in the Soviet vision of utopia. This is perhaps an explanation for the construction of impressive public monuments, such as the Moscow Metro, and luxurious parks and "palaces" of culture, while private living quarters are cramped and unpleasant. Khruschev's outline of life in 1980, on the verge of "Full Communism," provides for a large further extension of the public areas of consumption.

THE SOVIET CONSUMER IN THE 1960'S

The Soviet people reaped very large gains during the 1950's. Their prospects for the 1960's appear dimmer, and there are many signs that the rate of growth in consumption is slowing down. By 1950, the severe wartime cuts in consumption had been made good, though Abram Bergson's calculations (in terms of 1937 prices) show that real per capita consumption, including free health and education services, was still only 27 percent above the level prevailing on the eve of the Soviet First Five Year Plan in 1928. The average annual net real wage of non-agricultural wage-earners and salaried employees was still below the 1928 level, by 25 to 42 percent (depending on the price weights used). During the 1950's, money incomes rose, and retail prices were reduced each year through 1954 and then remained very stable. As a result, both average real per capita consumption, including health and education services, and the average real net non-agricultural wage increased by some 60 percent during the eight years 1950–58.

The Seven Year Plan for 1959–65 provided for further substantial gains for the Soviet consumer, though the rate of growth envisioned was somewhat lower than had been achieved during the previous eight years. Average real income net of taxes and including benefits per worker, as the Soviets calculate this, was to increase by 40 percent in the case both of wage-earners and salaried employees and of collective farmers. (Wage-earners and salaried employees comprise virtually all the non-agricultural labor force and hired workers on state farms. They totalled about 66 million people in 1961 and, together with their dependents, make up about 72 percent of the Soviet population. Most of the rest of the population is made up of members of collective farms and their dependents.) A number of measures was to be taken to improve the lot of the consumer and to result in a more equal distribution of income. But progress on many of these fronts has been slowed down.

The first outward sign of difficulties was the raising of the prices of meat and butter by 25–30 percent in the summer of 1962. Incomes of collective farmers probably rose as a result but it meant an increase in the cost of living for urban workers of about 3 percent. The Seven Year Plan had stressed that most of the gains in real income were to come through increases in money incomes, rather than through price reductions, but had provided for a modest decline in retail prices.

The Plan provided for the abolition of income tax by 1965 in annual stages beginning in 1960. The Soviet income tax rates have never been high, it should be understood, reaching a maximum for wage-earners and salaried employees of 13 percent of income above 100 rubles a month. The Soviet government relies much more heavily on the turnover tax, a sales tax on consumer goods. In 1958, for instance, the turnover tax amounted to 30.5 billion rubles (almost 45 percent of the value of retail sales) while personal income taxes totalled only 5.2 billion rubles. Still, the abolition of the income tax would have provided a gain. During 1960 and 1961, the income exempt from income tax for wage-earners and salaried employees was raised from 37 to 60 rubles a month and tax rates were reduced for those earning between 61 and 70 rubles. But in September, 1962, just before the next cut in income tax was due, the government announced that there would be no more tax reduction until further notice.

A more significant provision of the Seven Year Plan was that for establishing a minimum monthly wage for all wage-earners and salaried employees of 40–45 rubles by the end of 1962, and of 50–60 rubles by the end of 1965. This program, too, has been slowed down. By the end of 1962 a basic wage rate of at least 40 rubles a month had been established for about two-thirds of the wage-earners and salaried employees. The workers now covered by the 40–45 rubles minimum wage are those in industry, construction, transportation and communications, and on state farms. These groups, except those on state farms, had been covered by a 1956 law providing a minimum monthly wage of 27–35 rubles a month. But workers in other branches—branches considered as "non-productive" such as trade, health, education, housing, municipal services, administration—were not covered by the 1956 minimum wage legislation and are not yet covered by the planned 40–45 ruble minimum wage. It was announced this January that the 40–45 ruble minimum wage will be introduced in these branches during 1964–65. These branches include some of the highest paid workers, such as university professors with monthly salaries of 400—600 rubles, but also the least well paid. Scattered data suggest that there are significant numbers in these branches with wages under 40 rubles a month, and some with wages of as little as 20 rubles a month. Monthly salaries of 30 rubles are in force for secretary-typists, electricians, custodial personnel in urban schools, and for children's nurses, cooks, assistant cooks, watchmen and doormen in kindergartens serving 100 children. In municipal water and sewage plants in the largest Soviet republic, the RSFSR (exclusive of Moscow and Leningrad), for wage-earners the grade 1 basic monthly wage rate is between 18.85 and 21.90

rubles and the basic wage rate exceeds 40 rubles a month only for the highest paid group (grade 7 piece-workers in the most important group of cities), whose basic rate is 42.92 rubles. The goal of a minimum wage for all of 50–60 rubles a month has evidently been postponed indefinitely.

Once the minimum wage of 40–45 rubles had been established, the Plan provided that the minimum old age pension for wage earners and salaried employees was to be raised from the present 25.5–30 rubles a month to 34–40 rubles, and in 1965, when the minimum wage was to have been 50–60 rubles, the minimum old age pension was to have been raised to 45–50 rubles. Evidently any rise in minimum old-age pension rates has been postponed until after 1965. Instead, in March of this year, it was made easier for an old person to receive his pension while continuing to work and receive wages. Previously, a pensioner working full-time was entitled to a pension of 15 rubles a month in addition to his earnings, if his earnings did not exceed 100 rubles a month, but received no pension if his earnings exceeded that. Now, in underground mining and on state farms, a pensioner can receive his full pension in addition to his earnings; and in other work, a pensioner can receive 50 percent of his pension (75 percent in the remote areas of Siberia) in addition to earnings. This should alleviate the financial position of those old-age pensioners who are able to work. It should help also to relieve the shortage of labor, particularly in the lowest-paid occupations where it has been difficult to recruit high school graduates.

The large imports of grain in 1963–64 were the Soviet government's immediate response to the bad harvest of 1963. The grain shortage meant scarcities of bread, at least in some areas, and also, by government order, a deterioration in the quality of bread. For lack of feed, an exceptionally large number of livestock was slaughtered. Meat must have been relatively plentiful in late 1963, but the reduction of the herds of cattle, sheep and goats by 2–5 percent and of the pig herd by over 40 percent foreshadows future shortages.

Although the overt indications of a slowdown on the consumer front I have outlined date from mid-1962, the difficulties apparently began earlier. The delay in implementation of the minimum wage provisions is attributed by one Soviet economist to the slowdown in the rate of growth in agricultural output during 1959–61—i.e., before the exceptionally poor harvest of 1963. Khrushchev's Virgin Lands program provided substantial extra quantities of grain during the late 1950's, but the signs are that the area is turning into a dust bowl and the program is now looked on as having been a temporary expedient. A real break-through on the agricultural front must, it is apparently finally being realized, be achieved by increasing productivity in the traditional agricultural areas.

Output of manufactured consumer goods continues to increase but Imogene Erro points out in *Problems of Communism* (Nov.–Dec., 1963) that the rate of growth in output of almost all major items in the textile, footwear, and clothing industries has declined each year since 1959. The revised 1965 goals for these items, announced in January, are below the original goals of the Seven Year Plan.

In housing, intensified efforts during the late 1950's to overcome the perpetual shortage succeeded for the first time in bringing the average urban per capita dwelling space beyond the 1928 level of 5.8 square meters and to 6.5 square meters per capita in 1961. But urban housing construction in 1963 was less, absolutely, than during the years 1959–62, and revised plans for 1964–65 indicate that urban housing construction during the whole period 1959–65 will total something like 560 million square meters of floor space, well short of the original goal of 650–660 million square meters.

The declining rate of increase in Soviet consumption is evident in the movement of the official Soviet measure of real consumer income. Real income, net of taxes and including benefits per worker, on the average for wage-earners, salaried employees, and collective farmers increased by 5 percent in 1959 and again by 5 percent in 1960, it was announced in the annual plan fulfillment reports. The 1961 plan fulfillment report failed to give this measure (an indication that the growth was not considered impressive), stating only that average money wages of wage-earners and salaried employees increased by 4 percent, and that income of collective farmers from their work on the collective farms (no mention of income from the farmers' private plots) increased "somewhat." From later reports, it can be deduced that the 1961 increase in average real income net of taxes and including benefits per worker was about 3.9 percent. The 1962 increase in this measure was said to be 3 percent. The 1963 plan fulfillment report stated only that real income net of taxes and including benefits per worker was 20 percent above 1958; as it was 18 percent above 1958 in 1962, the increase in 1963 was but 1.7 percent. The 20 percent rise in average real income per working-person claimed for the five years 1959 through 1963 is certainly impressive, but it is only half the gain of 40 percent originally planned for 1965. The text of the revised plan for 1964–65 omits any mention of the extent of gain in consumer income planned, beyond an implication that money wages of wage-earners and salaried employees will rise by less than 4 percent, and from this it may be assumed that the original goal has been quietly shelved.

All the indications are, then, that Soviet consumption has been increasing, but that the rate of increase has been very much lower than the rate achieved during the 1950's and well below the rate originally planned, and that it has been declining. The very small gain in 1963 may, however, be a temporary result of the 1963 crop failure and the next few years may show some improvement.

Beyond 1965, one may expect Soviet consumer income to continue to increase as long as total Soviet GNP continues to increase. The rate of increase in consumption will, of course, depend in part on the rate of increase in GNP. Prospects here are at the moment somewhat obscure. It will depend also on Soviet policy toward consumption and on the extent to which priority in resource allocation continues to be given to the conflicting goals of investment, defense, space exploration, and various foreign commitments. (In this connection, it may be recalled that butter was being shipped to Cuba shortly after the increase in the domestic retail price of butter.) Prospects for the consumer, however, will remain rather dim until a real solution to the long-standing stagnation in agriculture is achieved. Khrushchev is now laying great hopes on a crash program in the chemical industry as a solution to agricultural productivity. It is also to provide substitute materials for the consumer goods industries. The emphasis on the chemical industry has certainly been put forward as a means of increasing consumption, and it does seem to indicate a real concern for the consumer. But the increased investment required for this program may be one factor in the current slowdown in the rate of growth of consumption.

16 | RECENT TRENDS IN CONSUMPTION AND INCOMES

U.S. Congress, Joint Economic Committee

The previous selection suggested that the slowed growth of consumption levels in the USSR during the early sixties might well continue. In fact, the growth of per capita consumption speeded up in 1966–67, indicating that the post-Khrushchev leadership is attempting to provide a growth rate of close to 5 percent annually in consumers' real income—at least for the present. In addition, various measures have raised the income levels of lower income groups, reducing income differentials. If these policies are continued, they may lead to significant changes in the Soviet economy —such as lower rates of growth in total output as the proportion of resources devoted to investment is reduced, greater reliance on personal saving as a source of investment funds, and less use of income differentials as work incentives.

The following selection describes recent changes in consumer welfare in the USSR, and includes comparisons with the United States in the tables which follow. It is reprinted from United States Congress, Joint Economic Committee, *Soviet Economic Performance: 1966–67* (Washington, D.C.: U.S. Government Printing Office, 1968), pp. 89–95.

THE LEVEL of welfare of the Soviet population has improved conspicuously in recent years. Statistically, the rate at which consumer welfare improved during 1966–67 has been exceeded only by that of the early 1950's, which was a period when consumption was still recovering from effects of World War II. To review the record briefly, beginning in 1964 a series of welfare measures, aimed primarily at groups occupying the lower rungs of the economic ladder, has produced an increase in per capita money income of more than one-quarter. At the same time, per capita consumption, after a decade of declining rates of growth, also moved ahead at an accelerated rate after 1964, although at a slower rate than incomes. Notwithstanding the degree of real progress achieved, the level of living in the USSR today remains far below the levels of Western Europe and the United States. Moreover, the Soviet Union has made no progress since the late 1950's in the pursuit of its longstanding goal to catch up with the United States in per capita consumption.

TRENDS IN CONSUMPTION

USSR in 1966–67

During 1966–67 per capita consumption of all goods and services increased by almost 5 percent annually, which is more than 1½ times the rate recorded for the previous 5-year period (see table below). With the exception of health and education services, all major components of personal consumption grew at a more rapid rate in the most recent period.

USSR: Average Annual Rates of Growth in Per Capita Consumption
by Major Component, 1951–67*
(percent)

	1951–55	1956–60	1961–65	1966–67
Total consumption	6.0	4.1	3.1	4.8
Food products	4.9	2.5	2.0	3.5
Nonfood-products (soft goods and consumer durables)	10.9	5.4	2.1	7.7
Services, excluding health and education	5.3	5.9	5.5	7.2
Health and education services	3.3	3.4	5.1	3.6

* The base year for the calculations shown in each column is the year before the stated initial year of period, i.e., the average annual rate of increase for 1951–55 is computed by relating consumption in 1955 to base year 1950.

Consumption of soft goods and durables scored the biggest gain, growing at nearly four times the rate achieved during the first half of the decade.

Especially important to Soviet consumers was the large boost in supplies of meat and milk in 1966–67, permitting a substantial improvement in the quality of the diet. Although the average caloric intake of the population has fluctuated narrowly over the past decade—about 3100–3200 calories a day—there has been a decline in the share of calories provided by basic foods such as potatoes and grain products, along with an increase in the share of calories accounted for by quality foods such as milk and meat. Hence the share of calories derived from starchy foods, the so-called starchy-staple ratio, dropped from 63 percent in 1958 to 57 percent in 1965 and to 54 percent in 1967.

Increased supplies of agricultural raw materials for light industry, some improvement in quality, and better distribution of goods combined to effect a major boost during 1966–67 in the production and sales of clothing, footwear, and other soft goods. In addition to an improved supply from domestic sources, sales of soft goods in 1967 were enhanced by stepped-up imports ($100 million) of Western-made clothing, footwear, and fabrics. During the early 1960's a severe problem developed in the accumulation of inventories of soft goods in retail outlets. From 1958 to 1964 inventories of soft goods more than doubled, whereas retail sales grew by less than 30 percent. A major part of this problem had its origin in the growing consumer resistance to the low quality and lack of variety of clothing, fabrics, and shoes in the market. Beginning in 1965, however, inventories began to decline, both in absolute amount and as a share of sales. By the end of 1966 the value of inventories had fallen to 40 percent of annual sales, compared with more than 50 percent at the end of 1964. The decline in the ratio of inventories to sales was brought about largely by: (a) price cuts on several commodities such as certain types of cloth and clothing; (b) a 7-percent reduction in the price of goods in rural stores (making rural and urban prices equivalent); (c) rapid increase in the earnings of lower income groups who were willing to purchase low quality merchandise; (d) official emphasis on better quality soft goods rather than quantity; and (e) improved distribution, particularly to rural areas.

Although there has been a notable increase in retail sales of consumer durables in the USSR since 1955, available stocks of household appliances still remain very low, and a large pent-up demand exists for some types of durables, as shown by the long waiting lists at retail outlets.

The existing stock of housing increased by almost 3 percent annually in 1966–67. Although more housing was completed in 1967 than in any previous year, adequate housing space remains one of the most serious consumer problems. At the end of 1967, per capita living space was about 7 square meters (about 75 square feet)—far less than the officially designated minimum norm of 9 square meters and less than half the available space per capita in Austria or West Germany. Nevertheless, the current level represents a per capita increase of almost one-third since 1955 and has been accompanied by an appreciable improvement in individual privacy—fewer people per room and more apartments with private kitchens and baths.

U.S.–Soviet Comparison

In 1966 Soviet consumption per capita was approximately 30 percent of the U.S. level (see Table 1), the same as in 1958. Per capita consumption of food in the USSR is about 50 percent of that in the United States; health and education services, about 53 percent; other services, 24 percent; and nonfood consumer goods, about 13–14 percent (see Table 2). Although supplies of consumer durables have increased markedly in the USSR since 1955, stocks of home appliances are still far below those of

U.S. households in most instances (see Table 4). As shown in Table 5, the Soviet Union has made rapid advances in health and education services. The supply of these services, in terms of available medical and teaching personnel, has exceeded levels in the United States since the mid-1950's.

TRENDS IN DISPOSABLE MONEY INCOME

Per capita money incomes increased at an average annual rate of 7.5 percent since 1964 (see Table 6). In part, the increases were due to normal wage creep, brought about by an improvement in skills, higher labor productivity, and greater welfare payments in the form of stipends for education, pensions, and the like. More important, however, were wage and welfare reforms begun by Khrushchev in 1964 and continued and embellished by the Brezhnev-Kosygin regime. Welfare measures implemented in 1965 brought 25 to 30 million collective farmers and their families under a state social insurance program, raised by 20 percent the average wage of 18 million workers in the services sector, and increased the minimum monthly wage by more than one-third. Further increases in 1967 added approximately 15 percent a month to the incomes of 4.5 million workers in lumbering, consumer goods industries, and certain occupations on state farms.

These programs have narrowed income differentials among occupational and social groups. Thus while average earnings in industry have increased by one-third since 1955, average earnings in health and education have risen by about one-half and money payments to collective farmers have tripled. Part of the rapid increase in money incomes of collective farmers is the result of higher prices paid by the government for agricultural products, but a substantial part merely reflects policy to substitute cash wages for payments-in-kind. In-kind payments as a share of total income paid out by the collective farm to its members declined from about 60 percent in 1955 to approximately 20 percent in 1967.

The upward spiral of incomes is expected to continue as a result of new welfare measures being implemented in 1968 that will add 6 billion rubles annually to incomes. They include:

(a) Increase in the minimum wage to 60 rubles per month for both urban and rural wage and salary workers.

(b) Introduction of regional wage differentials for service workers and longevity payments for all workers in remote regions.

(c) Reduction of the eligibility age for retirement pensions of collective farmers by 5 years (from 65 to 60 years of age for men and from 60 to 55 years for women), thereby placing collective farmers on the same footing as wage and salary workers and adding 2½ million persons to the pension roles.

(d) Reduction of 25 percent in the income tax rates for persons in the lowest income bracket.

NOTES TO TABLES ON CONSUMER WELFARE

Consumption

The international comparisons shown in the following tables are subject to both statistical and conceptual limitations. Nevertheless, it is believed that the quantitative results are fairly reliable. With respect to nonquantitative factors, however, the comparisons undoubtedly are biased in favor of the USSR. Although every effort has been made to match goods of identical quality in the two countries, precise matching has not always been possible. In housing and health services, in particular, the allowances for differences in quality are probably inadequate. Further-

TABLE 1

USSR and United States: Total Consumption Per Capita, 1955, 1958, 1960–66

	1955	1958	1960	1961	1962	1963	1964	1965	1966
USSR (1960 = 100)............82		93	100	103	107	108	111	116	120
United States (1960 = 100).......93		94	100	100	104	107	110	116	121
USSR consumption per capita as a percent of United States.........26		30	30	31	31	31	30	30	30

TABLE 2

USSR and United States: Consumption Per Capita by Major Component, 1955, 1958, 1960–66

	1955	1958	1960	1961	1962	1963	1964	1965	1966
Food products:									
USSR (1960 = 100)..........88		97	100	102	105	104	105	111	113
United States (1960 = 100)....98		98	100	100	101	101	104	107	109
USSR as a percent of United States..............43		47	48	48	50	49	49	50	50
Nonfood products:									
USSR (1960 = 100)..........77		90	100	103	107	107	108	111	118
United States (1960 = 100)....98		92	100	99	105	110	117	125	132
USSR as a percent of United States..............11		14	14	15	14	14	13	12	13
Services, excluding health and education:									
USSR (1960 = 100)..........75		89	100	105	111	116	123	131	140
United States (1960 = 100)....91		95	100	101	103	106	109	114	116
USSR as a percent of United States..............17		19	20	21	22	22	23	23	24
Health and education:									
USSR (1960 = 100)..........85		92	100	105	107	114	119	128	132
United States (1960 = 100)....82		93	100	102	106	109	114	120	130
USSR as a percent of United States..............54		52	53	54	53	55	55	56	53

more, there are two characteristic deficiencies in the Soviet pattern of consumption that could not be measured despite the fact that they are undoubtedly significant: first, the observable lack of balance between supplies of particular kinds of goods and the demand for them that continues to be endemic; and second, the lack of variety and diversity and the resulting lack of choice on the part of consumers.

TABLE 3

USSR and United States: Availability of Food Products for Human Consumption, by Major Food Group; Selected Years, 1953–67
(calories per capita per day)

	USSR					United States			USSR 1966 as percent of United States 1909–13
	1953	1958	1962	1966	1967 preliminary	1909–13	1966	1967 preliminary	
Grain products, potatoes, and pulses..................	2,169	2,031	1,931	1,769	1,717	1,560	850	827	113
Fats and oils, including butter..................	209	246	288	346	369	408	529	528	85
Sugar..................	168	229	292	334	354	408	517	518	82
Meat and fish..................	139	170	186	211	217	555	599	626	38
Milk and milk products, excluding butter..........	220	320	305	334	347	328	396	391	102
Vegetables, fruit, eggs, and other foods..............	195	204	198	206	196	231	279	290	89
Total................	3,100	3,200	3,200	3,200	3,200	3,490	3,170	3,180	

TABLE 4

USSR and United States: Household Stocks of Selected Durables;
Selected Years 1955–66
(units per thousand persons)

	USSR			United States 1966	USSR as percent of United States in 1966
	1955	1960	1966		
Sewing machines...........	31	92	151	136	112
Refrigerators..............	4	7	40	293	14
Washing machines.........	1	10	77	259	30
Radios....................	66	130	171	1,300	13
Television sets............	4	22	82	376	22
Automobiles..............	2	3	5	398	1

Money Incomes

After a lapse of 30 years, the USSR Central Statistical Administration began in 1965 to publish average monthly wages by sector of the economy. . . . The official publication of wage levels has permitted estimates of disposable income to be made with greater confidence than was heretofore possible.

TABLE 5

USSR and United States: Comparative Indicators of Health and Education Services; Selected Years, 1950–66

	USSR			United States
	1950	*1958*	*1966*	*1966*
Doctors (per 10,000 persons)	13.2	16.8	21.6	15.6
Hospital beds (per 10,000 persons)	56	74	100	85
School enrollments (thousands)	34,752	31,483	48,170	48,987
Number of teachers (thousands)	1,475	1,900	2,530	1,788
Number of students per teacher	23.6	16.6	19.0	27.4

TABLE 6

USSR: Personal Disposable Money Income, 1960–67
(in billions of rubles)

	1960	*1961*	*1962*	*1963*	*1964*	*1965*	*1966*	*1967*
Total money income to the population	85.14	93.99	101.36	105.50	111.57	124.76	134.77	143.87
Gross earnings of wage and salary workers	59.59	65.95	70.65	74.11	79.25	88.24	94.89	101.72
Collective farm wage payments	4.94	6.00	6.63	6.79	7.68	8.90	10.60	11.40
Other earnings	9.66	9.97	11.40	12.24	11.53	11.81	12.11	11.75
Transfer payments	10.95	12.07	12.68	12.36	13.11	15.81	17.17	19.00
Total state deductions	5.95	6.16	6.38	6.74	7.22	8.24	9.06	9.86
Total disposable money income	79.19	87.83	94.98	98.76	104.35	116.52	125.71	134.01
PER CAPITA								
Disposable money income (rubles)	369.7	403.1	429.0	439.5	458.1	505.5	539.1	569.0
Increase over preceding year (percent)	4.9	9.0	6.4	2.4	4.2	10.3	6.6	5.5

IV
ECONOMIC CONTROVERSY AND REFORM

Economic planning in the USSR has never been static. The system has been changing and developing ever since the early days of the GOELRO plan for electrification in the early 1920's, before the adoption of the Five-Year Plans.

Nevertheless, the basic system of administrative planning which emphasized quantity of output, adopted in the late 1920's, has not been significantly changed until recently (if then). It brought rapid rates of growth in total output, enabled the state to build its military strength and emerge on the winning side of World War II, and served to strengthen the centralization of political power. By the late 1950's the planning system had begun to show some flaws, however. There were complaints about shoddy goods from both consumers and government procurement agencies. Substantial inventories of unsalable items began to pile up. More significantly, the nation's rate of economic growth began to slow down. Since high growth rates are most important to the Soviet leadership, some changes were sure to follow.

In the early 1960's Soviet economists began to discuss the problem, following an article in *Pravda* in 1962 by Yevsei Liberman which opened up for debate the whole question of planning methods. After a lull in 1963, the discussion heated up again in the following year, some experiments along Liberman's lines were begun, and in 1965 reforms were announced by Premier Kosygin.

The articles in this part of the book deal with the controversy about planning and the economic reforms of the 1960's. A paper by Marshall Goldman reviews the whole subject. It is followed by Liberman's key article of 1962, three other statements by Soviet economists on the issues raised by Liberman, and the sections of Kosygin's 1965 speech dealing with reforms in industry. These reforms are evaluated in Robert Campbell's article. The selection by Roger Clarke on agricultural reforms argues that changes in that sector were perhaps more fundamental than in industry. Alternative paths followed in Eastern Europe are sketched by John Michael Montias. The book closes with a thoughtful evaluation of the "convergence" hypothesis by three knowledgeable Dutch economists.

17 | ECONOMIC GROWTH AND INSTITUTIONAL CHANGE IN THE SOVIET UNION

Marshall I. Goldman

The economic reforms instituted in the USSR in the mid-1960's seek to eliminate some of the barriers to efficiency and economic growth which had become apparent to both economists and political leaders. In the 1930's and 1940's, the key task of planning was to draw more resources into economic growth uses, and efficiency considerations were largely ignored. But by the 1950's it became increasingly evident that the highly centralized system of physical planning could no longer maintain growth rates merely by increasing inputs. Attention therefore turned to raising efficiency—obtaining more output per unit of input—through better planning, greater autonomy for enterprise management, and new incentive schemes.

This basic economic problem was at the root of the Soviet economic reforms, but it was given greater urgency by two other developments. One was internal to the Soviet regime: consumers demanded a larger share of the economic pie. Unable to continue the extremes of Stalinist repression as a system of negative incentives, the Soviet leadership began to provide greater positive incentives in the form of higher living standards. This change meant that the economy had to respond to consumers' wants, rather than planners' wants, to a greater extent than ever before.

The second factor was external. The Yugoslav economy had abandoned Soviet-type central planning during the 1950's and there were movements for economic reform in various other East European countries which inevitably influenced economic thinking in the USSR.

It is within this framework that the Soviet reforms should be considered. This selection provides an overview of the debates through 1965. The author is Professor of Economics at Wellesley College. The article is reprinted by permission from Peter H. Juviler and Henry W. Morton (eds.), *Soviet Policy-Making: Studies of Communism in Transition* (New York: Frederick A. Praeger, Inc., 1967), pp. 63–80, with the omission of references to Russian-language sources.

I

SINCE NOVEMBER, 1917, Soviet economic institutions have been formed, reformed, and abandoned with a rapidity that has left many observers two or three changes behind. Most often, the endless series of alterations and proposals for change have aroused little comment, but occasionally a particularly far-reaching suggestion has provoked a period of exceptionally intense debate. One such controversy occurred in the early 1960's. It was precipitated by the arguments and proposals of an engineering economist from Kharkov named Yevsei Liberman. The debate itself yields some valuable insights into the nature of the new economic problems that face Soviet decision-makers. The issues brought out during the Liberman discussions not only anticipated the downturn in the economic growth rate of the Soviet Union but suggested that the Soviet economy was undergoing basic qualitative changes.

In the early days of the Russian Revolution, if not before, the decision was made to industrialize the country as rapidly as possible. Although Russia was not exactly an industrial wasteland in 1921, it could not be counted among the leaders of the industrialized world. Furthermore, the still immature industrial framework of the country had been severely handicapped by the destruction of World War I, and of the Russian Civil War (1918–21).

Realizing that economic growth could be obtained only through the country's own efforts, the Soviets set out to mobilize their resources in what Stalin and his advisers believed was the most effective way. They identified economic growth with industrialization. The kind of industry they wished to establish was to be large in scale and heavily capitalized. This was the pattern of the most efficient and productive firms in the capitalist world and clearly it was the wave of the future. To the extent that machinery could take the place of manpower, economic progress would not be unduly hampered by the shortage of skilled laborers. At the same time, there were many other projects—such as dams and subways—that could absorb the mass of unskilled labor. Since capital was in such short supply and unskilled labor so abundant, it was perhaps only natural that both capital-intensive and labor-intensive projects should be constructed side by side.

To accomplish all this, it was necessary to mobilize and manage the entire agricultural and industrial resources of the country. Toward this end, in the late 1920's, the Soviets inaugurated the Five-Year Plans for industry and collectivized agriculture. By rounding up all the peasants into large farming units, Stalin assumed he would have greater political and economic control over the agricultural sector and, therefore, would be able to extract a marketable surplus much more efficiently. This surplus could then be used to feed the rapidly growing urban population and to earn foreign exchange in overseas markets. Similarly, the nationalization of all private business and the subordination of all production to central planning were meant to ensure compliance with major industrial aims and to hasten the industrialization of the country.

Soviet policy-makers recognized that it would take more than brute force and state directives to speed up industrialization. While the planners could dictate physical targets in terms of steel tonnage and machine-tool production, there were other, more subtle techniques that could also be utilized to mobilize the support of plant managers. For example, with central control the traditional cost-price relationship could be manipulated so that certain desirable decisions would be taken by the managers. Prices of many producers' goods were held constant or reduced below direct and indirect labor costs while prices of consumers' goods were generally doubled. To the extent that producers' goods, such as coal, appeared to be cheap, industrial consumers were induced to increase their use. Although the low prices often meant that producers had to receive state subsidies, the reductions in price increased the demand for such commodities and helped spread them throughout the industrial system. At the same time, the high prices on consumers' goods served to absorb consumer income, so that real consumption fell. To ensure that the high prices would not generate excess profits for state enterprises, the state imposed a turnover tax (a hidden sales tax) on consumers' goods that eventually averaged 50 percent of the retail price. This proved a convenient method for diverting resources from consumption to investment.

Marx's doctrinal prohibition against charging interest on capital also served to reinforce the trend toward heavy industry. If the enterprise did not have to pay interest on its capital, then capital was virtually a free good. Plants therefore sought the techniques that were most capital intensive. This facilitated the introduction and extensive use of advanced methods in industrial production.

II

The central planners' manipulations had the desired effect. Despite civil strife, political repression, and World War II, the economy of the Soviet Union grew rapidly. By the time of Stalin's death, a solid industrial base had been forged. It was widely agreed that by the mid-1950's, the Soviet Union had become the world's second largest industrial power, with an impressive core of heavy industry.

Onto this expansive scene strode Professor Liberman in 1956. In an article in the Communist Party's official journal, *Kommunist*, he suggested that perhaps all was not well and that a change in planning procedure was needed. He was not alone in his concern, but his suggestions, like those of other critics, generally had little practical effect. The Soviet economy was growing as rapidly as ever. According to official figures, Soviet national income was growing at an annual rate of 10–12 percent, and even American estimates showed a rate of 7–8 percent.[1] While most economists agreed that there were shortcomings in the existing program, no basic reforms were attempted. No one wanted to run the risk of ruining a good thing.

The prevailing system of physical planning had brought rapid industrialization to the Soviet Union. The main body of economists continued to argue that the best way to stimulate the factory manager and his workers was to tie premiums and bonuses to plan-fulfillment. Each factory and department was assigned a production plan and urged by word and material incentive to fulfill it. The goal of the plan was invariably set in some quantitative terms, such as number of units produced or weight. Each year, the goal was increased. The operating success of an enterprise was judged by how well the plan was fulfilled or overfulfilled. The success indicators of other societies, such as profits, were considered to be of secondary importance. This was reinforced by divorcing the bulk of employee bonuses from all yardsticks but amount produced.

If the economy lacked flexibility, it was a small price to pay. The task was to produce and then produce some more. In effect, it was decided to turn on the switch and let the production line pour out goods. Whatever was produced was in demand somewhere. If the products were inappropriate and inefficient, there was no cause for alarm. A "good" factory manager would find a way to utilize the supplies. The important thing was to produce and avoid "down time"—that is, production interruptions that are necessary if adjustments must be made for style and customer specifications. For example, most factories simply took it for granted that they would have to rework the metal they received from the steel-rolling mills. To speed up production, the steel mills set their rollers at one thickness and simply ran the ingots through until it was necessary to replace the rollers. By eliminating much of the down time that would have been required to readjust the rollers, the steel mills increased their output, although some of the manufacturing work was pushed off onto the fabricator. In the production of consumers' goods, the purchaser of a pair of ill-fitting shoes was usually forced to do the best he could, since the alternative sometimes was to go shoeless.

It was Liberman's contention, however, that major reforms were required in the planning system. The methods of economic development that had been so suitable heretofore, he argued, were too gross and unsophisticated for a developed economy. The minor shortcomings inherent in a system of physical planning were gradually assuming major proportions.

------

[1] Abram Bergson and Simon Kuznets (eds.), *Economic Trends in the Soviet Union* (Cambridge, Mass.: Harvard University Press, 1963), p. 336.

Liberman's pleas did not receive any special notice until 1962. Then, in September, *Pravda* carried an article by him that contained his previous arguments. This time, however, his message received careful attention—from both the economists and the politicians. By 1962, Khrushchev and the other members of the Presidium were doubtless bothered by the fact that the rate of increase in national income had fallen off continuously after 1958. Subsequently, official Soviet figures indicated that whereas national income increased by more than 12 percent in 1958, it increased by less than 6 percent in 1962. With this in mind, Khrushchev gave his official sanction to a debate over Liberman's proposals.

As recounted in the pages of *Pravda*, *Voprosy ekonomiki*, and *Ekonomicheskaya gazeta* from 1962 to 1964, Liberman and most of his fellow reformers argued along five major lines:

1. As long as almost all goods were in short supply, the reformers stated, it did not matter too much if supplies did not fit specifications perfectly. Since there were usually no substitutes, the goods were accepted willingly. If they could not be refashioned or refinished by the customer, there was always the possibility of barter with someone who had a complementary deficiency.

Gradually, however, as supplies and stocks increased, customers started to reject the thick paper and nails, the wrong-gauge steel, the ill-fitting sizes. If the product did not meet specifications, customers learned they could look around and find something that did. Nevertheless, the manufacturers kept on producing unwanted items. Since performance was judged on the basis of production, not sales, the manufacturer was not penalized if his unsold goods ended up in a warehouse. Technically, he was fulfilling his plan and his duty. But, as V. Dymshyts, then chairman of the USSR Sovnarkhoz (Economic Council), stated: "The time for striving for quantity at the expense of quality has passed."

2. Capital, the reformers argued, will inevitably be misdirected in a system with no interest rate to act as a guide for allocation. In Stalin's time, except for a few of his schemes, misallocation had been no more serious than some of the other problems facing the economy. Most of the country's investment projects ultimately proved to be successful, for there was so much to do that it was hard to go wrong. But the more lucrative projects were gradually completed, and continuation of economic growth required closer scrutiny over capital utilization. Too many projects had been undertaken and not completed. Also, because the projects were often so large, capital was tied up too long, and projects did not begin to pay for themselves for several years. Liberman and his colleagues were critical that a cement plant and canal could take more than ten years to complete, and pointed out that Khrushchev had decided it was better to build thermal-electric plants because they were less capital intensive than hydroelectric facilities. Khrushchev, in fact, even suggested a moratorium on all new investment projects for 1964 so that the available

capital could be concentrated on completing existing projects. Liberman and his supporters pointed out that while the absence of an interest rate may have facilitated the introduction of large-scale capital projects in earlier years, the needs of the country were no longer the same. Growth was coming more slowly now, and some economic mechanism had to be found that could automatically provide discipline and guidance in the allocation of capital.

3. Except for products and processes that were assigned military priority and those promoted in nationwide crash campaigns, the reformers continued, there was a dearth of innovation. Because experimentation might result in the underfulfillment of the physical plan, there were few planners or managers who were willing to venture off the beaten track. Since the production of steel had been mastered, it was easier to increase steel capacity and production than to switch to other materials, such as plastics, even though they might be suitable. As Khrushchev put it so colorfully: "The production of steel is like a well-traveled road with deep ruts; here even blind horses will not turn off because the wheels will break. Similarly, some officials have put on steel blinkers; they do everything as they were taught in their day. A material appears which is superior to steel and is cheaper but they keep on shouting, 'Steel, steel!' "

In some cases, new products were not even proposed. In other cases, there might be proposals but no implementation. Thus the expansion of the chemical industry had been proposed long before December, 1963.[2] In fact, sizable investment funds had been set aside as early as 1958, and there had been a considerable increase in chemical production. Yet Khrushchev could still complain that out of the funds that had been allocated to the Soviet chemical industry from 1958 to 1963, close to $777 million had been left untouched. The planners simply ignored the proposed projects and shirked their responsibility. And when they did submit proposals, the plans were not necessarily the best. Khrushchev found that when planning bureaucrats took their plans out of the closets and onto the construction fields, the blueprints were often filled with worthless detail. This he ascribed to the fact that the state was paying for its blueprints by the page! The reformers maintained that some other method of promoting innovation and change was necessary.

4. The operation of the economy, the reformers argued, was further complicated by the fact that the economy had become so large. Not only were there more products and factories to plan for, but the various

---

[2] Khrushchev's response to the lag in the chemical industry was to introduce another crash campaign. Since the normal planning procedures did not facilitate the introduction of unmastered and sophisticated techniques, the blitz-krieg campaign was necessary again. To many Soviet economists, this game of leapfrog offered little long-run promise. It always seemed that while the Soviet Union was caught up in the midst of one campaign, the rest of the world had leaped ahead to some other area of technology, and that another campaign and another diversion of resources would be required if the Soviets were to catch up.

products were becoming more sophisticated and complex. The interactions between various sectors had been increasing at virtually multiple rates. Thus, unless changes were made, by 1980 the entire adult population would have to be employed in planning, with no one left for production. While this might be the way to deal with those who found themselves unemployed because of automation, it suggested that existing planning methods were no longer adequate.

5. Finally, Liberman and his adherents were concerned about a wholly unanticipated phenomenon. There were faint, but nonetheless real indications that the Soviet system was not immune to the woes of underconsumption. Who would have predicted such a turn of events? After all, in the 1920's and 1930's, everything possible was done to discourage consumption in order to aid investment and capital formation. This explains the usefulness of the turnover tax and the resulting high prices on consumers' goods. But just as supply-and-demand conditions in industry had altered, so had the pressures on consumption. Although there still were depressing shortages of food and many nonfood products, the consumer was better off than ever before. He no longer had to buy "just any" shoes. In fact, since he already had several pairs of shoes, he could wait until he saw what he wanted. The shoes might even be of Czech, Italian, or English origin. The same applied to such items as fabrics, clothing, watches, cameras, bicycles, radios, and sewing machines. This did not mean that the average citizen had as much in his closet or suitcase as the West European, but it did mean he was no longer compelled to take whatever was shoved at him.

As a direct result of this, inventories piled up, sales plans were underfulfilled, and deposits in savings banks were soaring. Despite numerous promotional techniques—such as clearance sales, advertising, and installment credit—excess inventories of consumers' goods totaled close to $4 billion in 1964. Sales targets in the early 1960's were often underfilled by 1 percent or more, even though projected increases were lower than in many previous years. New deposits in savings banks amounted to more than $1.5 billion a year, which represented as much as 3 percent of total retail and restaurant sales.

Such developments had important implications for the future. Several economists, such as Ya. Orlov, complained about the accumulation of the unsold merchandise. Wages had been expended and loans extended for the production of these items. While increased exports and style changes (planned product obsolescence) were partial solutions, it was necessary to cut back the rate of expansion in some of these industries. Sometimes, when inventories had piled up too much, production was actually reduced. Thus, sewing-machine sales and production fell close to 20 percent in 1963 after a series of price markdowns and other sales campaigns failed to clear out the warehouses. What happened to the workers and raw materials? They might have been shifted to bicycle production.

But bicycle sales also fell. Fortunately since there were enough shortages of such items as refrigerators and washing machines—and, of course, automobiles—there could still be found many alternative uses for the displaced resources. Yet the number of items in short supply might conceivably diminish day by day, and then what would happen? Liberman and the reformers argued that something had to be done to make the production system more responsive to the consumer. Consumer tastes must be catered to, and production adjustments anticipated and made as painless as possible.

III

In the hope of resolving these shortcomings, Professor Liberman resubmitted his proposals. He and his supporters were not the only economists who had sensed impending trouble. There was almost no one in the USSR by 1962 who would have insisted that no further improvements might be made in the planning system. Debates over the need for price reform had been going on for years. Other economists, including L. V. Kantorovich, the director of the Laboratory for Economical and Mathematical Methods and the originator of linear programming, argued that cybernetics and electronic computers would provide the answer to everything. The Workers' Councils of Yugoslavia were even mentioned as a possible remedy for the Soviet Union's problems. And there were other proposals for either increasing or decreasing the amount of centralized control. Academician V. S. Nemchinov suggested the use of an auction method for matching bids and offers, and his colleague A. Arzumanyan criticized the stress given to heavy industry. Liberman's proposals were especially interesting because he was one of the few to offer a comprehensive and far-reaching scheme that incorporated several suggestions at once.

Essentially, Liberman sought more authority for the factory manager and less interference from the central planners with their plans. If instead of trying to cope with the contradictions of a central plan, the manager could concentrate on producing what his customers wanted and using his resources more effectively, the economy would be better off. Liberman did not go so far as to advocate the abolition of all central plans (and this created its own contradictions, as will be shown), but he did suggest that seven or so existing planning indices might be eliminated and never be missed. For the guidance previously provided by the several plans, Liberman wanted to substitute greater reliance on profits.

Liberman's emphasis on profits is sometimes misunderstood. The use of profits in the Soviet Union is nothing new. Where possible, a Soviet manager has always sought to earn a profit and avoid a loss. A profit-and-loss system, called *khozraschet* ("economic accounting"), in which certain costs are subtracted from revenues, has long been in use. Liberman proposed that the *khozraschet* profit figure of a plant be compared with a base consisting of the plant's fixed and working capital. The resulting percentage would be called the "profitability rate." This figure would then be compared with a "profitability norm" that would be set up for plants in comparable positions. Since the profitability rate would be the sole determinant of the manager's and the plant's bonus fund, it would be the chief index for guiding managerial action.

There was no thought that this would mean turning over the factories to private ownership. It would not be much different from the system of awarding bonuses for profitable operations to the hired manager of a local Chevrolet assembly plant. But Liberman hoped that his scheme would provide certain important benefits: (1) More decision-making power would be delegated to the manager and much of the excess planning bureaucracy, which was discussed earlier, would be eliminated. (2) Since the profitability rate would be increased if costs were reduced, the manager would run his plant more "economically" than in the past. (3) Because of the diminution of the role of planning, the manager would be given increased responsibility for ensuring that his products were sold. Because failure to sell would reduce revenue and thus the profitability rate, presumably the manager would only produce what the consumers wanted. (4) Since the denominator of the profitability rate is capital (working and fixed), ideally the manager would earn a higher bonus if he could either reduce or maintain the capital at his disposal. As a disguised capital charge (interest rate), this would promote the conservation of capital funds and the completion of long-delayed proejcts. (5) Adjusting the profitability norm for various plants would make it easier for those who might attempt to innovate, and this could stimulate the introduction and production of new products. (6) Making it harder to earn premiums for plants that set their targets too low might induce the managers to raise their sights and increase their own goals. This would eliminate the tug of war that exists when the manager fights to pull down his targets and the planner tries to pull them up.

Inevitably, Liberman's proposals and those of his allies attracted considerable criticism. However, it is interesting to note that the exchanges were conducted without acrimony and in what seemed to be a scholarly spirit. Few economists, if any, rejected everything Liberman had to say. They simply disagreed with him on what corrective steps should be taken.

Most Soviet economists were elated at the chance to conduct a debate on the extent to which, and the methods by which, the system of central planning should be dismantled. Several were convinced that Liberman was definitely on the right track. Like good managers the world over, they accepted the idea that "what was good for the firm was good for the country." Some even felt that Liberman had not gone far enough. What he really was trying to do, they argued, was to recognize that capital was a source of value. Rather than beat around the bush, the late well-known V. S. Nemchinov, an academician at the USSR Academy of Sciences, V. Kotkin, then assistant director of the Technical Administration of the Belorussian Sovnarkhoz, and E. Slastenko, a member of the group at the

USSR Academy of Sciences that was studying the effects of material stimulation on production, all urged the introduction of a straight 10 percent capital charge (interest rate).

Such proposals were bound to evoke a frightened response from more conservative economists. In tempered tones, some conservatives said they felt the implementation of Liberman's plan would be tantamount to switching to capitalism. Others, such as L. Alter of the Economic Research Institute of the USSR Gosekonomsovet (State Economic Council), protested that the spirit of Communism had been lost. "No one speaks of obligations any more. Today, nobody asks what he can do for the state, only what the state can do for him."

There were other, more serious complaints about the proposals. Radical changes like these could result in the rejection of economic planning and all that the Soviet Union stood for. Conceivably, the state would be unable to implement special projects or care for special needs that might arise. As argued by G. Kosyachenko, if a project could not be justified according to the principles of profit maximization, then presumably it would not be attempted. Long-range projects and heavy-investment opportunities, which had made the Soviet Union what it was, would be abandoned. Instead, it was likely that resources and investment would be shifted to the production of consumers' goods. Four decades of neglect virtually assured that there would be enormous profits in the production of automobiles and the construction of homes and apartments. Heavy industry, the keystone of the Soviet economy, would be sacrificed for the production of trifles and the promise of high profits.

Even if they agreed that there was nothing holy about heavy industry, several critics, like Kosyachenko, argued that the transition to a Liberman-type system would be chaotic. Since profits depend on prices and costs, a fundamental price reform would be needed before anything could be done. Naturally, each manager would seek to push his prices up as much as he could in the hope that his profitability rate would be high, at least in the short run. The unrealistically low prices on heavy-industrial products would have to be raised the most, and this would further hamper the growth of heavy industry.

There were others, such as D. Onika and V. Chernyavsky, who recognized that some sort of change in the direction suggested by Liberman was necessary but who felt that Liberman's plan contained too many inconsistencies. Because of technical flaws, for example, it appeared that Liberman's method of determining profitability might make it possible for a firm to expand its capital stock and receive a bonus even though its profits had not increased. This was clearly the opposite of what was intended. But the objection refers more to a mechanical problem than to anything basic in the proposals.

More important, therefore, was the criticism that there would still be too much dependence on bureaucratic planning. As A. G. Zverev, formerly the Minister of Finance, pointed out, if Liberman planned to leave decisions to agencies outside the plant, the manager would inevitably find himself frustrated and once again in the midst of those so-called bureaucratic battles that Liberman presumably wanted to avoid. Indeed, Liberman had suggested that the profitability norm be adjusted to fit the circumstances of each factory. The norm should reflect differences among industries and such varients as location and efficiency among plants in a particular industry. It should also reflect the number of new projects being introduced. Since new projects normally necessitated extra operating expense, plants that experimented would be assigned norms that were easier to meet. However, his critics argued, since the norms would be set by some sort of bureaucrat, there would probably be trouble. Life would no doubt be more comfortable for the factory manager if, instead of concentrating his efforts on the efficient operation of his factory, he could convince the bureaucrats that his factory deserved an easier norm. Hence, the bureaucratic juggling would be no different from what it was before.

Similarly, Liberman planned to retain at least three of the physical planning targets for the plant—quantity, quality, and destination—since he did not want to surrender all power to the plant manager. Thus he tried to anticipate those who would argue that his plan meant the abdication of state control and the introduction of competitive anarchy in the Soviet economy. But, Liberman's opponents pointed out, the continued existence of physical planning targets was a serious contradiction that would mean the retention of the worst aspects of the old system and might even eliminate the positive benefits of the new system. There would still be outside interference and there would still be the temptation to concentrate on reducing the targets rather than on increasing production.

For those with great expectations who were willing to experiment and did not automatically reject all attempts at reform, it soon became evident that Liberman's plan was not the solution it initially promised to be. On balance, it seemed to them that his system would be an improvement over existing procedures but at the same time might give rise to unpredictable problems. For example, it would be hard to determine precisely what a price reform of the scope suggested might entail when combined with an increase in the decision-making power of the manager. Could Soviet managers be entrusted with greater power? And would their power really be increased if some form of centralized control was retained?

IV

What have been the results of the debate? In mid-1963, just when the Western press began to proclaim that the profit motive was finally taking over in the Soviet Union and that the next logical step would be the emergence of capitalism, Liberman and his proposals faded into the background. However, planning difficulties continued to hamper the growth of the Soviet economy, and in mid-1964 Liberman and an enlarged core of supporters reappeared on the scene. Liberman's re-emergence was heralded by his somewhat unfair attack on a correspondent from *Time* magazine. Liberman alleged that the correspondent had distorted his original proposals and their significance. It seemed as though Liberman felt the attack was necessary to show Soviet critics both economic and political that he was not a capitalist lackey and that he was writing, not for Western publicists, but for Soviet economists.

With the ideological air purified and the "noncapitalistic" nature of the plan re-established, the debate was resumed amid some intriguing experiments. Apparently as a direct by-product of the Liberman debate, the Soviet Government announced the formation of what were called "firms." These turned out to be units composed of several factories producing the same product. Primarily, these have been formed by the horizontal combination of like enterprises under a common management. There have also been vertical mergers of both supplier enterprises and retail outlets. Patterned after the large integrated American company, the firm is an attempt to generate the administrative and operative economies of scale the Soviets see in the United States. It is, in addition, a means of focusing more of the decision-making power within the operating unit. Thus, the firm may eliminate some of the outside interference that so concerned Liberman. Then, too, the firm makes it possible for the managers to obtain feedback from their customers. The Soviets apparently believe it is easier to communicate product desires and complaints if suppliers and buyers are merged under a common management. This explains why some of the factories that have not been incorporated into firms, have opened up their own retail outlets. Presumably, the fewer the bureaucrats in the way, the more flexible and responsive the manufacturer can be to changes in consumer tastes.

With the explicit approval of the USSR Sovnarkhoz and its chairman, V. Dymshyts, two plants were singled out for an even more radical experiment. As of May 1, 1964, the textile plants Bolshevichka, in Moscow, and Mayak, in Gorki, were given complete independence from central planning. The only plan handed down to these firms from above was the investment plan. This arrangement even went beyond what Liberman had proposed. The firms themselves draw up their own plans for procurement, production, assortment, quality, and labor productivity. These plans are passed on to industrial ministries (formerly to the Sovnarkhoz), but only as information, not for confirmation. The finished products are then shipped to the retail outlets according to contracts drawn up at frequent intervals. The stores take only what they can sell. Profits of the firm and its associated stores are based on what the ultimate consumer buys and no longer on what the factory produces. A portion of the firm's profits is then directed to the factory incentive fund. From 10 to 50 percent of an employee's salary can be matched by a supplemental payment from the incentive fund. The exact amount is to be determined by the manager in conjunction with the trade union. As before, 4 percent of the profits will go into the manager's fund. A further innovation, however, is that the plant director and the store manager can themselves set their prices within a limited range. This applies to both increases and decreases in price.

In this experiment, however, some features of Liberman's original plan were not included. There was no profitability rate nor any explicit scheme to stimulate the manager into raising his goal. Instead, in order to earn a bonus, the firm not only must make a profit but must fulfill its "delivery plan." Apparently, it was still too soon to do away with all central control.

After six months of the Bolshevichka and Mayak experiment, it was announced that the scheme was being extended to include 31 percent of all ready-to-wear factories and 33 percent of all shoe factories in the USSR. Moreover, the new system was being pushed back to the raw-material suppliers. About 17 percent of the textile factories that supply the clothing-makers and 10 percent of the leather factories that supply the shoe manufacturers were to be affected. Thus, about 400 firms in all were put on the new experiment.

Liberman, who served as a consultant on reorganization for the USSR Sovnarkhoz until its dissolution in 1965, said that somewhat less ambitious experiments were also being conducted in heavy industry. Between late 1964 and mid-1965, two coal mines near Lvov (Lwów), a truck factory, and a television assembly plant were converted to the new system, along with several meat packing plants, some dairies, and a candy factory. Even more suggestive of what was to follow was the call for the adoption of the new methods in the whole machine-tool industry. As introduced in heavy industry, however, there were some adjustments in the experiment. In addition to the profit and sales plans, these enterprises were required to fulfill a production plan that spelled out the units of production just as before. This was a retreat from some of the flexibility introduced earlier, but it appeared to be a compromise that was necessary to pacify those who feared that heavy industry would be dissipated if all controls were removed.

The most significant aspect of this last set of reforms was that they began in May, 1964, under Khrushchev's patronage and continued after his ouster, in October of that year. It seems fair to assume that the issue of the reforms was not, as some originally suggested, a cause of Khrushchev's removal. The movement for economic reform even gained momentum in the months that followed. Clearly, Kosygin and Brezhnev have supported the new measures.

What seemed to be the culmination of the experiment was introduced without warning at the September, 1965, plenary session of the Central Committee of the CPSU. Kosygin announced that reforms in economic administration would be implemented throughout the whole of Soviet industry. As before, there were some steps backward toward increased control, but there were also steps forward toward increased flexibility. Plants in light industry were again granted the greatest autonomy. Most enterprises would be allowed to operate as had the 400 firms put on the experiment a year earlier.

The situation in heavy industry was somewhat ambiguous. There were profit, sales, and production plans to be fulfilled, as mentioned above. Furthermore, some central control over factory supplies has been retained, which means that there will also be control over factory deliveries. This system cannot match the effect that greater reliance on profits would have. However, it is interesting to note that this is a return to the proposals originally made by Liberman. In his 1962 plan, Liberman wanted to retain three physical planning targets. Although they were not included in the Bolshevichka and Mayak experiment, they were now adopted despite the fact that it meant considerable inconsistency and a moving at cross-purposes which had been criticized before. The changes in heavy industry seemingly represent a retreat, but another reform was introduced in September, 1965, that clearly is an economic advance. Kosygin declared that henceforth enterprises would be evaluated by a profitability rate. This, of course, was a direct throwback to Liberman's original proposals. Furthermore, there was to be a capital charge (interest rate) on capital lent out by the state bank. These features had all been omitted from the experiment at Mayak and Bolshevichka and at the 400 plants. In many ways, the introduction of the interest rate was the most radical move of all. Marx had not taken a stand against profits, but he had denied that capital had value. The Soviet Union has now been forced to acknowledge that it does. At the Twenty-third Party Congress, Kosygin announced that by early 1967 one-third of the Soviet industrial labor force, including much of that in heavy industry, would be working under the new system.

To ensure that the local plants are not given too much power, an organization reform intended to secure some increase in centralization was announced in conjunction with the incentive reforms. All the sovnarkhozy at both the local and republic levels were abolished, and their power was transferred to reconstituted industrial ministries. This was an attempt to replace territorial with branch administration. Theoretically, the net effect of all this should be that the reforms will provide needed flexibility for the firm, while the return to the ministerial system should provide an offsetting restraint. It will be interesting to see if Soviet theory approaches practice any more successfully than it has in the past.

Institutional reforms are clearly not the only significant result of the debates. If the past suggests any pattern, undoubtedly the reforms themselves will shortly be reformed. Of much greater significance is the official recognition by the Soviet government that the nation has reached an important economic crossroad.

Central planning served its purpose in the Soviet Union. But as the demands of both industry and the consumer became more sophisticated, central planning as it once existed became a fetter. Although the debates and reforms were initiated under Khrushchev, they have continued under Kosygin and Brezhnev. Apparently it is too late to return to the old methods. The core of a new economic structure has been completed. As Marx postulated so long ago, economic growth necessitates institutional change. The Soviet experience has proved to be no exception.

18| THE PLAN, PROFITS AND BONUSES

Yevsei Liberman

The following selection presents Liberman's own statement of his proposals for reforms in the planning and management of the Soviet economy. While enterprise managers would have greater freedom and flexibility in the use of inputs, they would still have to meet centrally fixed output, assortment, and delivery assignments. In addition to setting these targets, the central authorities would still retain control of "all the basic levers of centralized planning," including prices, finance, and large capital investments. Enterprise performance would be assessed in terms of profitability, and a portion of profits would be devoted to an "incentive fund" from which bonuses would be paid. In this way, Liberman hopes to mobilize the initiative and knowledge of the enterprise to produce greater output of needed goods more efficiently, rather than conceal its production capabilities and resist technological change and the introduction of new products.

The author is Professor at Kharkov Engineering and Economics Institute. This article originally appeared in *Pravda,* September 9, 1962. The translation is reprinted with permission from *The Current Digest of the Soviet Press,* Vol. XIV, No. 36 (October 3, 1962), pp. 13–15, with some omissions. *The Current Digest of the Soviet Press* is published weekly by the American Association for the Advancement of Slavic Studies at Ohio State University. Copyright 1962.— The Editors.

IT IS necessary to find a sufficiently simple and at the same time well-grounded solution to one of the most important problems set forth in the Party Program: the formation of a system for planning and assessing the work of enterprises so that they have a vital interest in higher plan assignments, in the introduction of new technology, and in improving the quality of output–in a word, in achieving the greatest production efficiency.

In our view, it is possible to accomplish this if the enterprises are given

360

plans only for volume of output according to assortment of products, and for delivery schedules. These must be drawn up with the maximum consideration for the direct ties between suppliers and consumers.

All other indices should be given only to the economic councils; they should not be apportioned among the enterprises.

On the basis of the volume and assortment assignments they receive, the enterprises themselves should draw up the final plan, covering labor productivity and number of workers, wages, production costs, accumulations, capital investments, and new technology.

How is it possible to entrust the enterprises with the drafting of plans if all their calculations are, as a rule, far lower than their true potentials?

It can be done if the enterprises have the greatest possible moral and material interest in making full use of reserves not only in plan fulfillment but also in the very compilation of plans. To this end, planning norms of profitability must be worked out for each branch of industry and must be firmly established for an extended period. It would be most expedient to confirm these norms through a centralized procedure in the form of scales fixing the amounts of incentive payments to collectives of enterprises in accordance with the level of profitability achieved (in the form of profits expressed as percentages of production capital).

In the first place, this principle means that the higher the profitability, the more the incentive provided. . . . This guarantees a powerful material stimulus for the enterprise to increase productivity. At the same time, the amount of income for the state would increase relatively much faster . . . There is no danger whatever to budget revenues. On the contrary, there is reason to expect a substantial increase in state revenue under the influence of a powerful material interest on the part of enterprises in increasing profits generally.

In the second place, the principle means that the enterprises would be granted incentives on the basis of a share in the generated income: The higher the profitability plan drawn up by the enterprise itself, the greater the incentives. If the plan for profitability is not fulfilled, the enterprise would receive an incentive payment, based on the same scale, in accordance with profitability realized. If the profitability plan is overfulfilled, the enterprise would receive an incentive based on the same scale but at a rate midway between plan and actual profitability. Let us say that the enterprise plans for a profitability of 10 percent but achieves a profitability of 15 percent. It would then receive an incentive payment based on a profitability of 12.5 percent, i.e., the figure midway between planned and actual profitability. This means that it will be an extreme disadvantage for enterprises to draw up plans that are too low. At the same time, the system retains a stimulus to overfulfill plans. Of course, when the volume of output, the assortment, and delivery schedules are not met, the enterprise would be deprived of the right to bonuses.

On this basis it is possible to simplify radically and at the same time to improve low-level planning. In fact, an enterprise would receive only one assignment for output in the proper assortment and, in addition, would proceed in its plans from a set table of incentive payments for profitability.

In order to achieve a high level of profitability, an enterprise must strive to place the fullest load on equipment and capacity when working out plans under our conditions and at plan prices (after all, profits will be computed as a percentage of capital!). This means it will be in the enterprises' interests to increase the number of shifts and the load on existing equipment, to stop asking for excess capital investments and machine tools and creating unneeded reserves. While all these surpluses now serve the enterprises almost as a free reserve, under the new system they would "drain the pockets" by cutting down the size of incentive payments. Consequently, the "struggle" waged by an enterprise to obtain lower plan figures would disappear. After all, such plan figures would never give the enterprise a sufficiently high level of profitability.

Also, the enterprise would strive to reduce production costs as much as possible, to be thrifty and to avoid artificial increases in norms for the expenditure of materials, fuel, tools, and power. Reduction of expenditures would lead directly to increased profitability regardless of what norms manage to "creep" into the plan or orders. Therefore, profitability expressed as a percentage of fixed and working capital of the enterprise is an objective criterion. It does not depend on what kind of plan the enterprise has tried to get for itself.

The last and main point is that the enterprise will strive for the maximum increase in labor productivity. They will stop requesting and hiring surplus manpower. These surpluses reduce profitability and consequently the incentive funds.

The incentive fund is formed in accordance with the level of profitability achieved and must be the single and sole source of all types of bonuses. It is important to tie individual and collective material incentives together in one single system. Let the enterprises have somewhat more freedom in using "their" part of the profits!

One might naturally ask if the centralized basis of our planning would be retained and strengthened under this system.

There is every reason to assert that the proposed system would relieve centralized planning from petty tutelage over enterprises and from costly efforts to influence production through administrative measures rather than economic ones. The enterprise alone knows and can discover its reserves best. But in order to do this, they should not have to fear that through their own good work they will put themselves in a difficult position in the following year. All the basic levers of centralized planning —prices, finances, budget, accounting, large capital investments—and finally all the value, labor, and major natural indices of rates and proportions in the sphere of production, distribution, and consumption will be determined entirely at the center.

Their fulfillment will be assured and guaranteed because obligatory annual control figures on all important indices will be presented to the economic councils (and to the executive committees of local Soviets). The economic council would no longer be just an intermediate agency (as it often still is, unfortunately) but a center or hub at which all the lines of planning converge. Generalized state assignments for the economic region as a whole would be sent to it from above. From below, the economic council would receive the plans prepared by the enterprises themselves, which would take account of the obligatory assignments for the quantity and assortment of goods. Since enterprises, when compiling their plans, will have a vital interest in providing maximum output with a minimum of current and capital expenditures, it is possible to say with reasonable confidence that the sum of the plans for the enterprises in the economic council will suffice to fulfill and even overfulfill the assignments from the center.

The enterprises will not "meet with fixed bayonets" the economic council's proposals concerning the improvement of certain indices, because the basis of incentives will not be altered at all. The scale for the deductions will remain exactly the same. If the plan is improved upon, the scale will only promise the enterprise a higher incentive payment. As things are now, any change in the plan (and there are scores every year!) evokes demands by the enterprises that all the interrelated indices be revised.

Many economists assume that enterprises can be spurred to uncover reserves by improvement of the accounting base, a centralized system of technical norms, and so forth. There is no arguing the point that accounts and norms are necessary. But these should be left up to the enterprises themselves. This is necessary so that the enterprises will have a material interest in the progressiveness of these norms.

Thus the proposed system proceeds from the principle: What is profitable for society must be profitable for each enterprise. And conversely, what is unprofitable for society must be extremely unprofitable for the collective of any enterprise.

Some economists say that profit should not be made too conspicuous, that this is supposedly a capitalist index. This is not so! Our profit has nothing in common with capitalist profit. Where we are concerned, the essence of such indices as profit, prices, and money is something else entirely, and they successfully serve the cause of communist construction. Our profit, where planned prices for the products of labor exist and net income is used for the benefit of society as a whole, is the result and at the same time the measure (in monetary terms) of the actual effectiveness of labor expenditures.

Fears exist that the enterprises will start to make only profitable output and to abandon unprofitable production. But in the first place, the enterprise would be deprived of all incentive payments if the assignment for a given assortment of goods is violated. In the second place, it is a very bad thing that some of our types of output are highly profitable because of shortcomings in price formation while others are losing propositions. It follows from the decisions of the 22nd Party Congress that the task of price formation is to render the complete assortment of goods profitable.

People fear also that the enterprises will start to raise the prices of new products artificially. But right now, this is one of the most difficult things to control from the center or from the economic council. After all, the consumer is rather indifferent to the suppliers' calculations; the consumers need their deliveries at any price, as long as the price has been approved at some point. The system we propose would change this situation. Any increase in prices for the goods delivered would reduce the profits of the consumer. This means that they would be extremely demanding about checks on the prices set by the suppliers. This would help the economic councils and the state planning committees in carrying out effective, not formal, control over price formation.

At present, profitability is reduced if the enterprises are mastering many new products and a great deal of new technology. For this reason, we have worked out a scale of supplements to and reductions in incentive payments in accordance with the proportion of new products in the plan. The incentive payments will be somewhat reduced for the output of items long established in production and raised substantially for the introduction of new products.

Besides this, the very process of price formation must be flexible. Prices for new products that represent more efficiency in production or consumption should be set to begin with so that the manufacturer can cover his additional expenditures. The consumer would not suffer from this at all but, on the contrary, would reap benefits for himself and for the national economy. In this way profitability incentives might become a flexible weapon in the struggle for rapid introduction of new technology and for increased quality (durability, reliability) of products. The present incentive system for inducing enterprises to reduce production costs and to increase output above the plan, or above the figure for the previous years, is a direct impediment to increasing product quality or mastering new products.

In quest of a solution to this, economists look for good new "indices." There is no disputing that some indices need correction. But even "ideally" conceived indices are not worth anything in themselves. This is a matter not of indices but of the system of relations between the enterprises and the national economy and of methods for planning, evaluating, and providing incentives for production collectives. We already have the example of a new index provided for the clothing industry to replace the gross value of output index. This is the index of "normative value of processing."[1] It was meant to prompt the clothing factories to produce clothing from cheap textiles rather than expensive ones. What has come of it? The result has been the factories now willingly make old-line articles from cheap textiles, for which the "normative value of processing" has become advantageous, but are quite reluctant to make new, fashionable articles from more expensive textiles. And the population wants these very things. Therefore, it follows that any indices will be distorted when they are imposed on the enterprises from above.

Instead of doing this, we must make it possible for the enterprises to compute for themselves the optimum combination of indices, with the final result being the best products, ones the consumers really need and that can be produced with the greatest profitability. Without this "freedom of economic maneuvering" it is impossible to increase sharply the efficiency of production. Without it, we can talk as much as we like about increasing the rights of enterprises, but we shall not accomplish this.

Therefore the current plan must be freed from the function of a standard yardstick for determining the degree of incentive, and at the same time there must be an increase in the importance of the plan as a production regulator for ensuring production growth and increased production efficiency.

Far be it from us, of course, to think that the proposed method is some sort of panacea, that by itself it will remove the shortcomings. Clearly the organizing, educational, and controlling job done by the Party and economic apparatus will remain a decisive force. But this force will grow many times if it is supported from below by a firm stake in the success of the cause, and not for the sake of "indices," but in the name of true production efficiency. Then the apparatus of the administration will decrease sharply.

Let us note that the proposed procedure forces the enterprises to put out only products that are capable of being sold and of paying their way. Further, the enterprises will calculate the efficiency of new technology with some care and will stop thoughtlessly ordering any and all kinds of new equipment at state expense.

It is now common practice to assume that any evaluation of the enterprises' work and any incentive for them must proceed from plan fulfillment as the most trustworthy yardstick. Why is this so? Because the plan creates supposedly equal conditions for enterprises, takes into account different natural conditions, different degrees of mechanization, and other "individual" circumstances. In actuality, the plans of enterprises are now set according to the so-called "record basis," i.e., proceeding from

---

[1] Editors' note: Essentially "planned value added," in contrast to "gross value of output."

the level attained. What this creates is completely unequal conditions, privileged for those who work poorly, and strenuous for those enterprises that really uncover and use their reserves. Why strive for good work in these conditions? Is it not simpler to try to obtain a "good" plan? It is time to amend this system!

Is it not clear that truly "equal conditions" can be created if there is the single standard of profitability for enterprises finding themselves in roughly the same natural and technical conditions? It is less dangerous to ignore a few differences in these objective conditions than to level off the quality of economic guidance. By such leveling, we are preserving backward methods of production. Let the enterprises themselves, having the production program from the center and the long-term standard of profitability to go by, show what they are capable of doing in competition for the best results. It is right that we have no rivalry, but this in no way means that we have no competition for the best methods of leadership. On the contrary, such competition must receive full scope here.

And so, what specifically is proposed to improve the situation?

1. To establish that the plans of enterprises, after concurrence on and confirmation of the volume and assortment program, are composed entirely by the enterprises themselves.

2. To guarantee conscientiousness toward state interests and a stake in the maximum efficiency of production on the part of enterprises, to establish a single fund for all types of material incentive depending on profitability (from profits calculated in percentage of production assets).

3. To confirm centrally, as standards for long-range activity, incentive scales depending on profitability for various branches and groups of enterprises having approximately the same natural and technical conditions.

4. To improve centralized planning by carrying obligatory assignments (control figures) only as far as the economic councils (executive committees, departments). To eliminate the practice on the part of the economic councils of making assignments among enterprises according to "the level attained." To instruct the economic councils to check, evaluate, and improve, on the basis of economic analysis, the plans independently worked out by the enterprises, without thereby changing the scales of profitability as a basis for the enterprises' incentive payments.

5. To work out a procedure for using single incentive funds accumulated out of profits of enterprises, keeping in mind the expansion of the enterprises' rights in the expenditure of funds for their collective and personal incentive payments requirements.

6. To establish a principle and procedure of flexible formation of prices for new goods, taking into account that the more effective goods must be profitable both for the producer and for the consumer, that is, for the national economy as a whole.

19 | CRITICISMS OF LIBERMAN'S PROPOSALS

V. S. Nemchinov
A. G. Zverev
G. Kosiachenko

Although Liberman had published important critiques of the planning mechanism as early as 1955, it was not until his 1962 article that the "Liberman controversy" really got started. The discussions in 1962 were particularly far-ranging, while those in 1964–65 were devoted more heavily to specific propositions about plant management, incentives, cost controls, and the proper degree of centralization. We present here relatively short statements of three rather different reactions to Liberman's 1962 article:

(a.) V. S. Nemchinov agreed with Liberman's diagnosis of the problem, and wanted to go well beyond Liberman's remedies. Academician Nemchinov, now deceased, was Chairman of the USSR Academy of Sciences' Scientific Council on the Interdisciplinary Problem of the Scientific Foundations of Planning and the Organization of Social Production. His statement was published in *Pravda*, September 21, 1962, and translated in *Problems of Economics*, Vol. VII, No. 3 (July, 1965), pp. 9–13.

(b.) A. G. Zverev, former USSR Minister of Finance, recognized that improvements in planning could be made, but felt that Liberman's proposals would create more difficulties than they would eliminate. His article is from *Voprosy ekonomiki*, No. 11, 1962. It was translated in *Problems of Economics*, Vol. V, No. 12 (April, 1963), pp. 15–18.

(c.) G. Kosiachenko, director of the USSR Financial Research Institute, also opposed Liberman's ideas. He thought that there was little fundamentally wrong with the existing system and that a series of administrative reforms could solve the problems. His article appeared in *Voprosy ekonomiki*, No. 11, 1962, and was translated in *Problems of Economics*, Vol. V, No. 12 (April, 1963), pp. 21–23.

The translations are reprinted by permission of the International Arts and Sciences Press, Inc., White Plains, New York.

19a | THE PLAN TARGET AND
MATERIAL INCENTIVE

V. S. Nemchinov

PLANNING AND material incentive are two most important factors in the development of the socialist economy. For the first time in the entire history of the development of the productive forces of society, social ownership of the means of production, constituting the basis of socialist relationships in production, eliminates the antagonism between the interests of the individual enterprise and those of society. The socialist mode of production unifies hundreds of thousands of enterprises into a structured system, operating and directed in accordance with a single national economic plan that has been discussed by the people as a whole and has the force of law.

Thus, planning is an inseparable component of the socialist economy. With respect to material incentive, however, the situation is somewhat different. The role played by material incentive with respect to growth of production has differed at various stages in the development of our economy. During the period when the economic chaos inherited by the Soviet state from the old system was being overcome, in a period when the question of "who will win over whom" was being resolved in the economy, when it was necessary to establish our own industry and a collectivized agriculture in a historically brief period, the interests of society as a whole often did not permit complete consideration of the interests of the individual enterprise. The years of World War II and the period of rebuilding the economy that had suffered from the fascist attack also required the concentration of all the strength of the Soviet people.

However, the concentration of the economic efforts of the Soviet state as a result of these circumstances never meant abandonment of the principle of material incentive. As we know, Lenin repeatedly emphasized the immense role of material incentive in the building of socialism. And current economic experience constantly reminds us of this. Socialist social production has attained a level of development at which all the available economic resources and hidden possibilities cannot be mobilized adequately and effectively utilized without an improved system of material stimuli.

368

In the past year, the economic literature has repeatedly published the statements of managerial, planning, and scientific personnel on matters of improving the management of production.

What is responsible for the appearance of these articles? The answer is that fulfillment of the vast program set forth by our party for establishing the material and technical base of communism and creation of the world's most powerful industry are possible only if there is continuous improvement of the forms of management of social production and a constant search for new economic techniques for controlling it.

The practical experience of recent years indicates that the plan targets for a large number of indices by no means always stimulate growth of production and assure mobilization of unutilized resources and the introduction of new technology. Planning that is based on the level of gross output, the cost of production, and the labor productivity already achieved by an enterprise inevitably leads to an effort on the part of managerial personnel not to reveal all their productive capacities and resources.

Naturally, such a situation begins to inhibit the operation of the irrevocable law of economic activity formulated in the Program of the Communist Party—*to assure maximum results with minimum expenditures,* inasmuch as part of the economic resources remains unutilized.

As a consequence, a broad discussion is now unfolding with respect to the most important economic problem of our contemporary economic science: how to improve the planning system so that enterprises and their personnel will have a material interest in increasing output, cutting production costs, and introducing new, highly productive equipment, so that they will have an interest in higher targets under the plan.

Comrade Liberman's recommendations are based upon introducing long-term norms into planning. This proposal is certainly of interest, for the establishment of such norms should serve to eliminate the harmful striving of heads of enterprises to be given understated plans, and will at the same time directly stimulate a more intensive development of production. That is why the experiment of the Economics Laboratory of the Kharkov Economic Council, whose data provided the basis for Comrade Liberman's article, has attracted the attention of the USSR Academy of Sciences' Scientific Council on the Interdisciplinary Problem of the Scientific Foundations of Planning and the Organization of Social Production. A report by Comrade Liberman, the head of the laboratory, was discussed at a plenary session of the council in April 1962. The council gave its support to the initiative of the man from Kharkov and recommended greater experimentation in this direction, turning its special attention to the elaboration of proposals to stimulate the production of new types of output and introduction of the achievements of technological progress.

It is necessary to note that the planning of the final rather than intermediate results of economic activity is acquiring increasing significance at the present time. Objections to the use of *gross output* as a planning index are being raised more and more often by managerial personnel. This index is a poor reflection of the results of the economic activity of the individual production team because it includes the value of raw materials, fuel, and other materials received from the outside. When planning is based on this index, it is found to be advantageous to utilize more expensive materials and services. By consuming more expensive materials and employing more costly services, one can overfulfill the plan for gross output. As a result, increases in gross output are derived from the intermediate product. On the whole, however, *society is interested in the growth of the final product rather than of the intermediate product.*

From the viewpoint of the national economy, the final product is characterized by the material composition of the newly produced national income. For the individual enterprise, however, the final product is the output sold and shipped. However, the volume of net income created in the sphere of material production remains the general and sole index of the ultimate economic result of the efforts of all components of the national economy. *Enhancement of the material and cultural level of life of the population and further expansion of social production come solely from this net income.*

This is why the index of the profitability of the operation of all units in the national economic system acquires decisive significance. Consequently, one of the basic planning indices must be the planned profitability target for the enterprises and economic agencies. The index of profitability must be determined in percent of the fixed and circulating assets. In planning profitability, a rigorous delimitation of two stages is needed:
a) determination of the plan target with respect to profitability
b) establishment of a scale of material reward for production personnel relative to the actual level of profitability (approximately the type of scale presented in Comrade Liberman's article)

The plan target for profitability should be defined in the form of plan charges on fixed assets. These charges should be designed to cover the expenditures of society upon expanded reproduction of fixed assets, associated with the growth of the social product.

The results of the economic activity of each enterprise and combination of enterprises should be determined not only by factory production costs, but also by total outlays of the national economy.

The time has come to eliminate the situation in which fixed assets allocated by society to any given production entity are given without charge. Society constantly and continuously reproduces its fixed assets on an expanded scale. And each enterprise should participate in this process of reproduction in proportion to the fixed assets granted to it by society to make possible its functioning. This participation should be expressed in standardized charges on fixed assets, just as the partial participation of the enterprise in social expenditures is reflected in charges on wages.

The coefficients of reproduction of fixed assets with various material compositions are not identical. The material composition of fixed assets varies from one branch of industry to another and from one enterprise to another. Therefore, the norms of charges on fixed assets should be differentiated by branches and groups of enterprises, with consideration of the material composition of fixed assets and the coefficients of reproduction of various types of assets. These norms should be standardized over a ten to fifteen year period. If the plan norms of charges are changed from year to year, such planning of profitability can only have negative consequences.

It should become the chief concern of economists and planners to study the causes of failure of individual enterprises and branches to meet these long-term norms. Every failure to meet a profitability norm should be regarded as a loss and be reflected in the national bookkeeping as a grant or subsidy by the government to the given production unit. The major duty of economists and planners is to develop, in good time, measures that will eliminate such losses. In the majority of cases, *improvement of planned prices and selection for the enterprise of an appropriate assortment of output would make it possible quickly to liquidate the operation at a loss of many branches and enterprises.*

The most important task in reorganizing planning is to bring about a radical change in the situation that now usually comes into being in relations between enterprises and planning agencies. The enterprises must offer the planning agencies alternative plans for increasing their output capacity and alternatives with respect to the volume and possible assortment of products, showing the cost to the economy as a whole, including planned charges on fixed assets in accordance with long-term norms. The planning agencies should select the enterprises to which it is economically advantageous to issue a particular order for commodity deliveries of various products.

It is necessary for each enterprise to seek to obtain from the planning agencies the largest possible plan target for commodity deliveries, in which case a situation opposite to that now existing will come into being. This is entirely possible if fulfillment of the order will be profitable not only to the state but also to the individual production unit.

Toward this end, *the enterprise must possess a fund for material incentive, the size of which must depend upon the actual level of profitability.* This attained level of profitability should include the actual payment of minimal planned charges on fixed assets, as well as economies in factory production costs calculated by comparison with the preceding period (on the condition that there is no reduction in quality of output).

This incentive fund should be calculated as a percentage of the difference between the level of profitability planned and actually achieved, the former being determined as the charges on the fixed assets in accordance with norms fixed for a long period. As in the scale presented by Comrade

Liberman, these percentages paid into the incentive fund should be long-term norms, diminishing logarithmically as the level of actual profitability increases. Moreover, contributions of specific size to the incentive fund must be made from standardized receipts on account of charges on the fixed assets.

The incentive fund should be expended in accordance with definite rules: as bonuses to plant personnel and as an addition to the total wage fund, issued over and above basic individual pay rates. A portion of the incentive fund might be spent on improving the living conditions and communal life of the personnel of the given enterprise, particularly on housing construction and on bonuses in the form of apartments with greater conveniences.

The procedure for building and expending the entire incentive fund and that portion of it constituting the joint wage fund must be regulated by a special law of the Supreme Soviet of the USSR.

With such a system of planning material incentives for the personnel of enterprises, one may be confident that the relationship between planning agencies and state and cooperative enterprises will change radically. Under such circumstances it will not be the planning agencies that will press enterprises to accept particular plan assignments but, on the contrary, enterprises will seek to obtain the highest possible plan assignment from planning agencies.

It is usually held that under such a system enterprises will seek to obtain more profitable orders and avoid less profitable ones. But why should that which is profitable and necessary to the state be unprofitable to the enterprise? This occurs only because of defects in planned price formation and shortcomings in planned guidance. It is unfortunate that our planning agencies very often permit such powerful economic means for stimulating production as price planning and assignments from profits to the enterprise fund to escape their control. Quite often there is no need whatever to raise the price for products in short supply. It would do merely to increase the percentage of profit on such products that goes into the enterprise fund.

In funding means of production, under which material resources are dispersed among an enormous number of holders of innumerable physical funds, a "metabolic" sickness inevitably develops in the economic organism of society. The constant shortage of material resources is a manifestation of this disease of economic exchange. Such a situation is inevitable when, for example, marketable funds for surfacing materials and paints are doled out per million rubles of new construction and when it is necessary to begin to "time" these funds so that they do not come in response to that quarter million rubles expended at the initial stage of construction, i.e., when these materials are as yet virtually unneeded.

It has long been time to organize materials supply along the lines of state trade, and to cease to distribute commodity resources in accordance with the infinitely complex system of physical funds. Conversion to state trade in the field of materials supply would doubtless make it possible, in quick order, to eliminate the situation in which there is a constant shortage of material resources. This would also be facilitated by the planning of profitability, accompanied by elimination of the gratuitous provision of fixed assets and by introduction of long-term norms in the area of material incentive.

The need for a reorganization of planning has certainly matured. It is essential that the plan be fully harmonized with the principle of material incentive.

Management of the economy must be built on a proper combination of planning and material incentive—the two basic principles of socialist social development. Coordination of these social principles assumes the introduction of long-term plan norms, an increase of the enterprise funds (in particular, of the incentive fund), and expansion of the rights of enterprises in the expenditure of these funds.

Improvement of the price mechanism, introduction of long-term norms of profitability and of material incentive, expansion of the rights of the enterprises and abandonment of petty supervision over them—these are the principal landmarks to be followed in the reorganization of planning that has now become urgent.

19b | AGAINST OVERSIMPLIFICATION IN SOLVING COMPLEX PROBLEMS

A. Zverv

THE PARTY and government are carrying out a comprehensive program of democratization of state and social life. Important changes in the management of industry and the reorganization of management in agriculture have increased the role of the working people in economic management and in all other spheres of our country's state and social life. This is one of the important factors determining the steady rise in the effectiveness of social labor, the successful progress along the road of communist construction.

Further improvements in the utilization of labor, material and financial resources in production, a consistent reduction in expenditures of social labor per unit of output and a steady increase in labor productivity constitute a law of the socialist economy, the importance of which has grown still more in the period of the creation of the material and technical basis of a communist society.

Economic incentives for increasing and improving output, personal material incentives for the working people to improve the results of production and economic activity (in combination with moral factors) play a highly important role in implementing production and other economic plans as far as both quantity and quality are concerned. At present the state spends several billion rubles a year on premiums to workers at enterprises and other economic organizations. In addition, about 80% of profits over and above the plan remain at the enterprises. Considerable sums allocated to enterprise funds from planned profits are utilized for improving material standards and cultural services for the workers of these enterprises. Thus tremendous sums are spent on providing material incentives for workers to improve and increase output. If these sums are correctly utilized, much can be achieved to heighten the interest of workers in the effectiveness of production.

Unfortunately, there are still many shortcomings and violations in the

374

utilization of these funds. There are also shortcomings in the system of building up premium funds and in the indices which are used to evaluate the results of the work of an enterprise, a group of workers and individual workers, as well as in the indices according to which premiums and other material rewards are paid. It is necessary to improve in every possible way the system of material incentives for improved production indices and results of economic activity. Material and moral factors should be used fully in solving the problems of expanding socialist production and in raising its efficiency.

It goes without saying that economic planning must also be improved in all its aspects, freeing it from many minor faults and eliminating excessive patronage over economic branches and, all the more so, over individual enterprises. Excessive, uncalled-for interference of planning and other bodies in the work of economic branches and enterprises should be stopped. The state plan should be freed of unnecessary indices and provisions for petty patronage. This will benefit planning and economic management. It will make it possible to strengthen the fundamental role of state planning in the development of the socialist economy in the period of the full-scale building of communism and will improve the quality of economic planning.

If the problems raised by E. Liberman in his article in *Pravda* are approached from these positions, we may note certain positive aspects. The author attempts to identify the correct criteria for the evaluation of plant operations, criteria which would facilitate the best utilization of productive forces and raise production efficiency. In any case, the questions posed by him have attracted widespread attention and sparked a lively discussion of many vital problems. Undoubtedly this will considerably accelerate the search for, and elaboration of, the best methods of material incentives.

As for the basis of the concept which E. Liberman advances, it seems to me to be dubious, insufficiently thought out, and inconsistent. He takes an oversimplified and sketchy approach to the solution of an extremely complex problem.

Any innovation should be implemented only if it is really progressive, if it moves things ahead and facilitates the development and improvement of production and raises its efficiency. What are Comrade Liberman's new proposals? First, he suggests that to "improve" planning we should no longer plan from above enterprise targets for reduction of production costs, increases in labor productivity, utilization of raw materials, fuel and other supplies, that we stop planning employment figures for enterprises and wage funds. All this should be planned by the enterprises themselves. The only centralized targets handed down to the enterprise should be the volume and composition of production. Second, he believes that the enterprises should decide for themselves the amount and direction of investment. Third, he thinks that we should stop drawing up yearly plans of profitability and profits, and establish average, long-term profitability standards according to an appropriate centralized scale. Fourth, E. Liberman suggests that enterprises and their workers be awarded premiums for fulfillment of the fixed profitability standard, with higher premiums for overfulfillment of profitability indices. In his view the best utilization of all manpower, material and financial resources of an enterprise, the rational distribution of capital investments and their greater effectiveness will be ensured by discontinuing centralized planning of investments and production cost quotas, and by introducing a stable profitability scale which will be fixed for an enterprise for a long period as a percentage of total fixed and current assets.

It should be noted, first of all, that E. Liberman falls into a contradiction. He bases his new system of planning on the premise that the State Planning Committee and the economic councils are less informed as to the capabilities of the enterprise than the enterprises themselves. At the same time he considers that the state plan and the plans of the economic councils should specify volume and composition of production, as well as the suppliers and consumers of the finished product. The question then is, how can the State Planning Committee and the economic councils establish the volume and composition of production for enterprises if they know the production capacities so poorly? Actually this is not the case. The planning organs and the economic councils are obligated to know, and actually do know, the production capacities of enterprises. Without this they would be unable to plan and the economic councils would be unable to direct the work of enterprises.

E. Liberman claims that his proposed system of planning and material incentives precludes the possibility of understatement and "concealment" of plant capacities from the planning authorities and the economic councils. However, his system of material incentives does not preclude the possibility of enterprises understating their production capacities so as to overfulfill the production plans and the fixed profitability rate, thus receiving more premium funds.

Furthermore, E. Liberman suggests that the enterprises themselves draw up their investment plans, except for "large-scale" investments. But investments are the main aspect of the process of enlarged socialist reproduction. Furthermore, it is necessary to ensure the necessary proportions in developing different branches. Under socialism this balanced development must be reflected and grounded in the state economic development plans. It can best be achieved when the amount and direction of investments are determined by a state plan and not decided by an enterprise. The enterprises are ignorant of the various national economic interrelations, and even if they wanted to establish the balance of the economy they could not do it. Even now we have mistakes in planning that result in disproportions in the national economy; what would happen if every individual enterprise would engage in this work? There can be no doubt that it would give rise to still greater mistakes, with more serious discrepancies in planning investments and more serious disproportions in industrial development.

In the USSR the development of the productive forces, and of industry in particular, takes place not within territorial or national boundaries but according to the principle of the best utilization of natural and other resources so as to achieve the greatest effect from investments for the benefit of the society as a whole and each member individually. An example is Kazakhstan, where the Soviet state has been investing material and financial resources far in excess of the national income produced by the republic. This is of advantage to the state and the people. Implementation of this extremely important principle of Soviet economic policy, which ensures a steady rise in the efficiency of social production, is possible only if state planning discipline is observed, only as a result of better planning on a national scale, not by transferring the planning of investments from the State Planning Committee to the economic councils and enterprises.

We should not forget that some republic, regional, and plant executives display parochial tendencies. The results are misappropriations of investments, disruption of economic balance, and disorganization and weakening of the planned basis of the economy. The ending of capital investment planning by the State Planning Committee and the economic councils, and the transfer of these functions to the enterprises, would only intensify these negative tendencies and in no way improve the utilization of resources for capital investments and the observance of balance in the development of the economy.

It is necessary to improve state planning, including the planning of investments, to accelerate the commissioning of new enterprises and to raise the economic effectiveness of investments. At the same time the rights of the republics, economic councils, and enterprises in economic management must be observed.

E. Liberman's views on production costs seem very strange. If we are to believe him, it is not planned cost assignments and control on the part of the respective organizations and authorities over their fulfillment that will guarantee the fulfillment of quantitative and qualitative indices but the average rate of profitability. How can we end the planning of cost targets for enterprises? If we discontinue the centralized planning of production costs, what use will the economic councils have for these indices? And why then should the State Planning Committee consider problems of costs if the indices drawn up by it will be obligatory to no one? We must not forget that production cost is the basic qualitative index of any production plan. The effort to reduce production costs means a daily search for ways and means of reducing the expenditure of social labor per unit of output.

The same must be said about the planning of labor. The correct distribution of manpower resources in the economy is a prerequisite for the growth of the national income. The increase in labor productivity determines the possibilities and rates of enlarged socialist reproduction, the rise of the material and cultural standards of the working people and the implementation of other state and social tasks. High labor productivity and low production costs are the basis for the development of the productive forces of the socialist society at a higher rate than under capitalism. Comrade N. S. Khrushchev noted that the higher the labor productivity and the lower the production costs, the faster will be the rise of living standards, the greater the accumulations of the economy, and the faster we forge ahead to our cherished goal, communism. The steady growth of labor productivity on the basis of technological improvement, the better organization of operating techniques, and the systematic rise in the skills of workers are prerequisites for the building of communism. High rates of enlarged socialist reproduction and a steady improvement in living standards are inseparable from a more rapid growth of labor productivity than of wages.

Tremendous importance must be attached to the correct and economical utilization in production of raw materials, fuel, power, and other supplies. All these elements are linked with production costs and expenditures. The economical utilization of all these elements raises the effectiveness of production, reduces the expenditure of living and materialized labor, increases accumulations in the economy, and, consequently, the reserves for further enlarged reproduction and satisfaction of the growing requirements of the population.

Comrade Liberman suggests that all these great and difficult problems be solved by a simple method: by introducing a long-term average rate of profitability for every enterprise, a material incentives scale, and by discontinuing the planning of investments and cost assignments for enterprises.

Obviously, to improve the organization of production and promote technical innovation, to steadily increase labor productivity and reduce production costs, it is necessary to improve the system of material incentives for better work. But for this purpose the power of state planning must be utilized. Taken by itself, the average rate of profitability established for enterprises for a long period, and the material incentives scale drawn up by the author, cannot solve the great and difficult problems of production. These questions require a thorough study and a premium system which would really raise the effectiveness of social production.

It seems to me that in his proposals E. Liberman oversimplifies the problems and views them too schematically. In his view the premium scale should be drawn up in a centralized manner. But such a scale can be drawn up only on the basis of production costs. Consequently the average rate of profitability for the scale must also depend on costs. The only difference is that at present production costs are studied for each enterprise and cost reduction and profitability targets are fixed with due consideration for all circumstances on the basis of production conditions. The author, however, suggests that the average profitability for a group of enterprises be found, that is, a quantity which will not correspond to the objectively possible profitability of every enterprise in the various groups of the scale. As a result, some enterprises will be receiving higher profitability quotas, which will serve to reduce their premium funds, while other enterprises will be overfulfilling their targets because of understated profitability rates and will receive unduly high premiums. This shows how erroneous is the scale of average profitability indices and premiums.

It should not be forgotten that in industry one enterprise or another is constantly improving its machinery, organization, and techniques. This drastically changes labor conditions and raises productivity. Conditions of fuel and power supplies, the quality of raw materials, haulage distances of raw materials and supplies, and many other conditions change. In many cases these changes may not depend on the enterprises; yet as a result their actual profitability may change. What is to be done? Comrade Liberman might say that in such cases it would be necessary to revise the profitability rates. That is so, but in view of the tremendous scale of our industry and the constant changes taking place in it, the revision of profitability indices of enterprises will be a mass and continuous activity. It will be carried out by some special authorities with whom the enterprises and other organizations will inevitably engage in unnecessary disputes. In revising profitability it will be essential to take into account the production costs of each enterprise under conditions in which these will be determined by each enterprise for itself. Moreover, some organization will have to establish at what enterprises the profitability indices must be changed in view of new conditions. Those enterprises in which the conditions of achieving the established profitability have worsened will immediately raise the question of their revision, while those in which the profitability is higher may not "realize" that it is time to ask for a revision to raise their profitability quotas.

Is such an "innovation" necessary or useful? I think not. It is impossible to replace the role and power of state planning by establishing an average profitability rate for all enterprises. This is an "innovation" which can be detrimental to the economy.

Discontinuing the planning of production costs for enterprises would reduce the attention paid to this basic economic question of production; in any case, control over the production expenditures of enterprises would be reduced. Average profitability cannot replace the control functions of higher organs. Disputes would be inevitable in establishing new profitability rates. The possibility of receiving higher profitability quotas and the related possibility of industrial executives concealing their reserves are not precluded, particularly since the profitability quotas would be set for long periods.

Elimination of planned production cost quotas for enterprises would make it more difficult, and in some cases impossible, to plan the net income of society and finances, for the enterprise which sets its own costs would be unable to take into account possible changes in production conditions and would proceed from the profitability indices established for a long period. Difficulties would appear in drawing up the overall financial plan of economic development; additional difficulties would appear in the distribution and redistribution of the national income on a branch and territorial basis; the role of the State Planning Committee, the economic councils and financial organs in planning costs and bringing the quotas down to the enterprises would be reduced, which would serve to weaken to some extent the drive for higher production efficiency.

In conclusion, it should be noted that the author's understanding of profitability and profit contradicts generally accepted theoretical concepts, according to which profit is the main part of the surplus product created by the workers' surplus labor. According to E. Liberman's conception, it seems that profit is created not only by the workers' labor but also by the fixed and current assets. It is hardly necessary to prove the erroneousness of such a "theory." In questions of price formation, which constitute a large and independent economic area, the author's ideas lead to the conclusion that the methodological basis of price formation in a planned socialist economy should be the price of production, which is characteristic of the capitalist system of economy.

These are by no means all the considerations against the advisability of accepting E. Liberman's suggestions. However, the facts above are sufficient to reject his theory and his recommendations.

19c | IMPORTANT CONDITION FOR IMPROVEMENT OF PLANNING

G. Kosiachenko

THE 22ND CONGRESS of the CPSU has posed important tasks in the sphere of improving the management of the national economy. Hence the need to improve planning and material incentives for industrial enterprises. These two problems are closely connected, for any principles that are employed as a foundation for material incentives, as well as any bonus systems, will be useless unless they are connected with the formulation of the enterprise's plan and with the quality of this plan.

The main shortcoming in the field of planning is the neglected state of norm-setting. Norm-setting, which was unsatisfactory even earlier, has deteriorated in recent years. Hence the weak technical-economic foundation of the plans established for enterprises, the lack of coordination between production and supply plans, the constant alteration of plans—all of which leads to a lack of confidence in them among enterprise workers and undermines their attitude to the plan as law, as a directive that should be carried out unconditionally.

In order to eliminate these shortcomings it is necessary, in our opinion, to improve norm-setting. In his speech at the 22nd Congress of the CPSU, Comrade N. S. Khrushchev said that it is necessary to have "progressive planning norms for the utilization of all types of instruments of labor, raw and other materials, for technological methods and time limits for various jobs; it should be law for every manager to introduce these norms and abide by them strictly."

It is impossible to prepare a well-grounded plan without proper norms. It is said that economic councils prepare unsatisfactory plans for enterprises, compiling them by mechanically working out targets based on the level of production attained by the enterprise in the preceding year. However, this is explained not only by the lack of sufficient qualifications of the economic council staff but also by the fact that they do not have at their disposal the necessary instrument that would enable them to prepare a more firmly grounded plan. Progressive norms are such an instrument. They should be calculated not for each enterprise separately but for a whole branch of industry, or at least for a group of similar enterprises whose technical level of production is more or less the same. Such norms should reflect the achievements of leading enterprises and promote the advance of lagging enterprises, orienting them in such a way that they will make fuller use of their capacity, more economical use of raw and other materials per unit of production, etc.

The question arises: who should work out the norms? As we know, this job is being done by the Research Institute of Planning and Norms. However a single research establishment, even if it does have the support of several branch research institutes, is unable to solve this problem. This work should be directed by Union and republic organs, agencies that are more closely connected with the actual work of management and planning of industry. The branch departments of the State Committees of the Council of Ministers of the USSR, in particular, could render great aid in working out the technical norms for the corresponding branches.

In order to eliminate the shortcomings in economic planning it is also necessary to introduce proper order in the material and technical supply system; this should also be based on technically substantiated norms, balance accounts, and an improved supply organization.

In working out plans we must ensure a concrete approach to each enterprise and take into account its specific features in the coming planning period. This means that in each individual case it is necessary to provide for measures, which should be taken by a given enterprise if, for example, it is undertaking the production of a new item, or is entering the stage of mass production of this item. It is also necessary to consider the degree to which technical norms have been adopted, the extent to which the enterprise is provided with raw materials for the coming year, how its production capacity is being utilized, etc.

But such a concrete and comprehensive assessment of all the conditions of an enterprise's work is possible only if a number of plan indices are worked out. That is why there can be no single universal index which could be used as a basis for assessing the work of an enterprise. Even such a summary index as the level or growth of profit relative to the preceding period cannot replace all the other indices in assessing the work of an enterprise, for profit, as we know, also includes elements of redistribution of net income.

Some economists propose that enterprises be granted bonuses not for the fulfillment and overfulfillment of the plan, but for the actual growth of output or the actual reduction of production costs in comparison with the preceding year. These indices are certainly of basic importance in assessing an enterprise's work, but if used alone they do not give us a correct picture of the enterprise's work, for they do not reflect the concrete conditions under which the results in question were achieved.

Proposals are also being made to grant enterprises bonuses, depending on the way in which a given enterprise fulfills or overfulfills the norms of utilization of production assets and labor set for the branch. The degree of fulfillment of technical norms is, naturally, an important index in assessing the work of an enterprise. However there are either no such norms or very few of them. That is why the job of working out norms should now be tackled in real earnest. But this is not all. In applying uniform branch norms at a given enterprise, to assess its work we must also introduce substantial corrections, taking into account the enterprise's specific features: its technical level, composition of output, etc.

Some economists are of the opinion that in order to make general norms applicable to the peculiarities of individual enterprises, we must differentiate branch norms and work out group norms. There is no doubt that group norms are necessary. However, average norms should not be replaced by individual ones. In evaluating the work of an enterprise, a concrete approach is required. For this purpose we must use a definite system of indices, rather than a single one, however important it may be. It is necessary to proceed from such a system in preparing a plan and in assessing the results of its fulfillment. Furthermore, in addition to certain common indices for all branches (for example, the fulfillment of the plan for composition of output and production costs), it is necessary to establish specific indices for each branch of the economy. All these indices can be embraced only by a plan. That is why only the plan proper and the degree of its fulfillment are generalized indices on the basis of which an enterprise's work can be assessed. Consequently bonuses should also be granted for the fulfillment and overfulfillment of the plan. We must raise the significance of the plan. It must be a mobilizing factor but also realistic. It is only on the basis of a plan that a bonus system can be set up, a system that will play a substantial role in achieving economies of living and past labor.

At the same time we must improve individual plan indices, particularly value indices, and apply them with more attention to specific features, taking into account the special characteristics of economic branches and endeavoring to have them reflect as precisely as possible the actual achievements of each enterprise.

We must also find a more effective method of utilizing bonus funds. In particular, it is our opinion that it would be wise to grant larger bonuses for the fulfillment of plans than for their overfulfillment; correspondingly the allocations to the enterprise fund should be larger from planned profits than from above-plan profits. It is important to raise somewhat the role of individual bonuses from the enterprise fund. It is also desirable to increase incentives for certain categories of workers for raising the quality of output, for mastering the production of new types of goods, for improvements in production technology that ensure substantial economies.

The plan should also reflect more fully the degree of utilization of fixed assets, particularly the time limits for mastering production capacity at new enterprises. We must establish higher depreciation rates at enterprises with superfluous fixed assets and treat these as expenditures connected with the enterprise's work, i.e., as losses. This will reduce somewhat the zeal of managers prone to hoarding.

We must raise the role and responsibility of the heads of enterprises and economic councils for the fulfillment of profit plans. Among other factors this should be one of the criteria for granting bonuses to certain categories of managerial personnel. In general it is necessary to define more precisely the indices whose fulfillment would give the right to receive a bonus. It is clear that these indices cannot be absolutely identical for all branches of industry.

The whole system and conditions of material incentives should reflect in the fullest possible way the specific features of production in different branches of the economy. For this purpose it is necessary to raise the role of the economic councils in assessing the work of individual enterprises and in granting bonuses with due regard for the degree of difficulty of plans.

In analyzing E. Liberman's proposals we have come to the conclusion that he actually denies the significance which a plan has for an enterprise and makes everything depend on changes in profits. It follows from his conception that it is hopeless to raise the quality of the plan for an enterprise and therefore it is not worth attempting to improve plans. The only means possible, according to him, is to have the enterprise share in the profits and to set for it only the volume and composition of production. All other indices are to be worked out by the enterprises themselves in such a way as to ensure maximum profit. This is the only criterion which, in Comrade Liberman's opinion, will ensure automatically and by itself the full utilization of fixed assets and the economical utilization of raw materials, fuel, and other materials per unit of output, and will ensure the wage fund and will promote a rational allocation of capital investment, etc.

N. Antonov, one of the supporters of this conception, develops it in his article in *Pravda* (issue of September 14, 1962). He declares that profit should be the basic and the most important index and not a derivative of the volume of output production costs. This means that production will be subordinated to changes in profits. In this case a wide range is opened up for the law of value and, rather than bringing any benefits, this will only harm the planning system.

In this connection we must also examine the proposal made by Academician V. S. Nemchinov, who considers that the time has come to replace the funding of materials by trade. True, it is wise to shift to trade in certain goods or materials, whose supply meets the requirements of the national economy. But given the relatively limited quantities or even lack of substantial reserves of many major materials, we cannot change over to other distribution by trade rather than by direct authorization.

Academician V. S. Nemchinov feels that the main reason for the shortage of materials lies in shortcomings in the supply system. True, shortcomings in the material and technical supply system make shortages more acute, but they are not its main cause. It is sufficient to cite, for example, the resources of agricultural raw materials which still restrict the growth of certain branches of the light and food industry, the resources of metal which restrict the scope of production in certain branches of machine building, etc. A shift to trade in metal will inevitably lead to a somewhat different trend in the utilization of metal compared to that envisaged in our annual and long-range plans. This should not be forgotten.

Let us take another example from the sphere of construction. In planning the material and technical supply of construction projects, preference is given to projects of special importance to the national economy. However, there are also non-centralized investments from local funds. The sum total of these funds is greater than the volume of capital construction which could be supplied with material resources. There are two possibilities: either material funds (not counting local resources) should be allotted at reduced norms for non-centralized construction, or the volume of non-centralized construction should be restricted and brought into conformity with existing resources. As a result, in the first case there would be a sharp increase in the volume of construction and, as a consequence of this, a scattering of resources and a growth in the number of uncompleted construction projects. This is unacceptable. There remains, consequently, the other way—that of ensuring strict conformity between the volume of non-centralized investments and material resources. The question arises: how will such conformity be ensured if, as Comrade Liberman suggests, investments connected with the reconstruction of existing enterprises (not counting new ones) are to be determined by the enterprises themselves? It can be said with complete certainty that this will lead to a marked deterioration of capital construction in the country. However, capital construction is a national economic problem and not an isolated issue concerning only individual enterprises. That is why it must be solved in a planned manner, in close connection with national economic targets, and proportions established for the economy as a whole.

We must also examine the question of planning the wage fund. E. Liberman holds that no targets for labor productivity and increased wage funds should be set for an enterprise, for it will naturally be interested in lowering production costs and raising profits. However, an increase in profit can be achieved by economizing on past labor, while permitting a considerable growth of wages. As far as the reduction of production costs and increases in profits are concerned, it does not make any difference whether the latter increased as a result of economies of past or living labor, but for the national economy it does make a difference. This question hinges on proportions whose significance goes far beyond a single enterprise: it depends on the relationship between Department I and Department II of social production, between accumulation and consumption, between money incomes and expenditures of the population, etc.

In this connection there is another question of great importance. Suppose that the additional growth of wages (compared with the calculations used as the foundation of the national economic plan) is accompanied by a corresponding additional increase in production. But in this case it is important to know at what enterprises this takes place—at those which produce consumer goods or at those producing means of production. In the first case the growth of money incomes of the working people will be accompanied by a growth in the market commodity stocks of goods; in the second case (particularly in branches producing the means of production for means of production) the growth of the wage fund in excess of the planned increase in turnover of goods and services can lead, in the absence of sufficient reserves of commodity stocks, to certain pressures and unjustified currency issue. Consequently, additional market stocks of goods will have to be found for the additional wage fund. That is why under no circumstances should we reject the regulation of the growth of the wage fund on a national scale and permit enterprises to solve this problem themselves.

20 | ON IMPROVING MANAGEMENT OF INDUSTRY

Alexei Kosygin

On September 27, 1965, Premier Kosygin reported to the Plenary Meeting of the Central Committee of the CPSU "On Improving Management of Industry, Perfecting Planning, and Enhancing Economic Incentives in Industrial Production." His long speech laid out the major aims of the economic reforms subsequently introduced. The changes announced by Kosygin had been preceded by considerable discussion among Soviet economists, as well as by experiments in the consumer goods sector of the economy (see Selections 17–19, above). The changes were accompanied by new measures in agriculture (see Selection 22, below), and were followed by reforms in the pricing system (see Selection 7, above).

Kosygin's speech covered new planning methods, incentives, and administrative arrangements. The first two are described in the sections of his speech reprinted here. The administrative changes (not covered in the portions reprinted) consisted of the abandonment of the scheme of regional organization introduced by Khrushchev in 1957 and a return to a more centralized organization of the state sector according to branch of industry. Thus, the 1965 changes involved shifts in two directions. On the one hand, performance indicators were revised to increase responsiveness to customers' needs, the authority of enterprise managers was extended somewhat, and new incentives were provided. On the other, administrative controls over the planning process were strengthened.

The selection is reprinted from *New Methods of Economic Management in the USSR* (Moscow: Novosti Press Agency Publishing House, n.d.), pp. 26–49, with some omissions.

ON THE IMPROVEMENT OF INDUSTRIAL PLANNING AND ON THE EXPANSION OF THE ECONOMIC INDEPENDENCE OF ENTERPRISES

IN ORDER to expand the economic independence of individual enterprises it is proposed to reduce the number of indices demanded by higher bodies.

387

At the same time those indices that are retained in the plan should be aimed at raising production efficiency.

As seen from experience, the index of overall volume of output does not stimulate the enterprises to produce goods which are really needed by the national economy and the public and in many cases tends to limit the improvement in the assortment of goods produced and their quality. Not infrequently our enterprises are producing low-quality goods which the consumer does not want and which therefore remain unsold.

Instead of using an overall volume of production index, it is proposed that the plans for enterprises should incorporate assignments for the volume of goods actually sold. Enterprises will then have to allot greater attention to the quality of goods they produce in order to be able to fulfil their assignment for marketed produce. An enterprise that produces low-quality goods will experience difficulties in selling its goods and, consequently, will not be able to fulfill its plan. Under the existing system of evaluating the activities of an enterprise on the basis of overall volume of output, such an enterprise would have been considered to have fulfilled its plan.

However, it would be not sufficient to appraise the work done by an enterprise only on the basis of the volume of goods sold. The national economy requires definite items of production for satisfying social needs. For this reason assignments for the more essential assortments of goods must be retained in the system of planned indices.

When economic ties between enterprises are well organized and the contract system is well developed, it will be possible to reduce steadily the assortment of goods produced according to the state plan, and to substitute for it a group, or enlarged list of commodities.

The assignment for goods sold is aimed at establishing a closer link between production and consumption; and to orientate the enterprise towards raising efficiency, it would appear to be better to use the profit index, the index of profitableness. The amount of profits characterises, to a considerable extent, the contribution made by an enterprise to the country's net income, which is used to expand production and raise the people's well-being.

It goes without saying that profit assignments do not tend to lessen the importance of the need for lower production costs but, on the contrary, increases it. One of the most important tasks of economic managers is to lower production costs. The production costs index should command special attention in the technical, production, and financial plan of the enterprise.

The state is interested in constantly increasing accumulations by means of lowering the cost of each particular item of production, and also as a result of increasing the quantity of goods produced, of expanding and modernizing the range of manufactured goods and raising their quality. Profit reflects all these aspects of the production activities of an enterprise in a much more complete way than the production costs index. What is important in this case is to take into account not only the amount and increment of profit obtained, but also the level of profitableness that has been attained, i.e., the amount of profit per ruble of productive assets.

Substantial changes are also envisaged in the planning of work at enterprises. At present higher bodies request four labor indices from enterprises—the productivity of labor, number of workers, level of average wages, and the size of the wage fund. From now on it is proposed to cut down the number of these indices to one—the wage fund. This, of course, does not mean that the other indices have lost their significance. The indices of labor productivity, the number of workers employed, and that of average wages remain, as before, important elements in the national economic plan and the production plan of the enterprise itself. But is it really necessary to hand down all these assignments to an enterprise from above? We have discovered from experience that such a system of planning hampers the initiative of the enterprises in searching for a way to increase labour productivity.

There have also been proposals not to have the wage fund of an enterprise assigned from above. But to discard the planning of the wage fund would be premature. The necessary balance between the quantity of consumer goods manufactured and the population's purchasing power must be guaranteed in the national economy. And the population's purchasing power is determined in large measure by the wage fund.

In future, when we are able considerably to expand the production of consumer goods and accumulate necessary reserves of these goods, it will be possible to abolish the system of predetermining the wage fund for enterprises. This is planned, first of all, for industries producing consumer goods.

Thus, an enterprise will have the following indices set from above:
the volume of goods to be sold;
the main assortment of goods;
the wage fund;
the amount of profits and level of profitableness;
payments into the state budget and allocations from the state budget.

Besides these, the following indices will be set:
the volume of centralized capital investment and exploitation of production capacities and fixed assets;
the main assignments for introducing new technology;
material and technical supplies.

All other indices of economic activity will be planned by the enterprise independently, without endorsement by a higher organization. This will relieve the enterprises of excessive control and will permit them to adopt the most economical decisions in the light of actual production conditions.

While extending the economic independence of enterprises, the state will continue to observe a unified policy in the sphere of technical progress, capital investment, labor remuneration, prices and financing, and will organize the compilation of accounts and statistical returns according to a unified system.

It is proposed to establish the five-year plan as a basic planning form, including the annual distribution of the more important assignments, so that the enterprises may implement their production and economic activities on the basis of the plan.

ON INCREASING ECONOMIC STIMULI FOR ENTERPRISES AND STRENGTHENING THE COST-ACCOUNTING SYSTEM

Improvement of the forms and methods of planning will make it possible to tackle the problem of strengthening and developing the system of cost accounting in a new way. Lenin stressed that each enterprise must work on a paying basis, i.e., its income should be sufficient to cover the expenditures and still make a profit.

The enterprises operating on the cost-accounting system and their managers must bear full responsibility for the economic results of the work they do. Lenin's ideas on the cost-accounting system must become firmly entrenched in our economic activities. In the consistent implementation and further development of the idea of cost accounting we see the way to the solution of many of the current problems of communist construction at the present stage.

What must be done in order to strengthen and develop cost accounting in the new conditions?

First, it is necessary to create conditions whereby enterprises will be able to solve their problems of improving production independently, where they will be interested in utilizing to the utmost the productive assets assigned to them for increasing output and making bigger profits. It is therefore necessary to leave the enterprises more of the profits they derive in order to develop production, improve their techniques, materially encourage their workers, and improve labor and living conditions of the wage and salary earners on their staffs. The profits to be left to an enterprise should be in direct proportion to the effectiveness with which it utilizes the productive assets assigned to it, the increase in volume of the goods it sells, improvements in the quality of its goods, and the increased profitableness of the enterprise. At the same time financial grants made by the state to enterprises for capital investment must be restricted and the credit system expanded.

Second, it is necessary to strengthen the cost-accounting system in inter-enterprise relations to guarantee that enterprises adhere strictly to consignment deliveries as stated in concluded contracts and to increase their material responsibility for discharging their obligations.

Third, on the basis of the cost-accounting system, it is necessary to provide material incentives for the entire personnel and every shop and section of the enterprise to make them interested in fulfilling not only their own individual assignments but also in improving the overall results of the enterprise. In doing this, incentives must be provided so that enterprises will be interested in working out and fulfilling higher planned assignments, and in better utilizing internal resources.

In short, it is necessary to orient all the activities of the enterprise towards seeking out means of improving the economics of production, of increasing its own incomes, and thereby increasing the overall national income.

Under the existing system, capital investments are almost exclusively allocated according to the central plan, and in the main are devoted to the construction of new enterprises. In many cases operating enterprises do not have the necessary means at their disposal and thus cannot replace obsolete equipment quickly enough. The result is a tendency towards slowing down the growth of labor productivity, improvement in the quality of the goods produced, and increase in the profitableness of production.

It is proposed that every enterprise should have a production development fund to be formed from deductions from its profits. Such funds will also be supplemented by part of the amortization fund which is intended for the complete replacement of fixed assets. At present this part of the amortization fund is totally directed in a centralized manner towards financing capital construction and enterprises cannot use these means at their own discretion.

When these measures are implemented, the size of the production development fund—which the enterprises will be free to use for technical improvements in production—will comprise a much larger sum than is the case nowadays.

The strengthening of the cost-accounting system and the economic stimulation of production depends on the basis on which the state grants means to the enterprise, and the way in which enterprises transfer part of their income to the state budget.

At present no charge is made for financing capital investments from the state budget. Enterprise managers are not much concerned with the cost of the reconstruction of the enterprise or how effective the additional capital investment will be, because their enterprises are not obliged to refund sums granted them. Hence we need such a system that will induce our economic managers to be more concerned as to how to use investment funds in the most effective manner, so that new installations and workshops will be built with a minimum of capital investments, put into operation in good time, and working at planned capacity as quickly as possible.

One way of tackling this problem is to switch from the free allocation of means for capital construction to long-term crediting of enterprises. It is suggested that the credit system will, first of all, be introduced for capital investments in already operating enterprises. As for new construction work, it appears that it might be expedient to introduce long-term credit for those construction sites where expenditures might be refundable in a comparatively short period of time.

Of great importance in making production more efficient is the correct and economical use of the working capital allocated to an enterprise. At present, any deficiency in working capital is refunded to the enterprise from the state budget. We cannot, therefore, speak of a genuine cost-accounting system if the enterprise does not, essentially speaking, bear any economic responsibility for the utilization of the working capital allocated to it. It is proposed to abolish the practice of providing free supplements to the working capital of enterprises from the state budget and instead, where necessary, to grant them credits for these purposes. Such a system will encourage enterprises to use the working capital allocated to them more thriftly.

A change in the system by which enterprises make payments to the state budget from their incomes is also envisaged.

At present the size of the deductions made from the profits of enterprises in favor of the state budget does not depend on the value of the fixed assets assigned to them. That is one of the reasons why enterprises attempt to obtain more money from the state for capital investments, and for supplementing their working capital, without taking necessary measures on their part for their rational use. It sometimes happens that an enterprise purchases equipment for which it has no need, merely in order to spend the funds allocated to it.

As has already been said, the efficiency of using productive assets has recently declined in a number of branches of industry. It is most important, therefore, to interest enterprises in increasing their output and raising not only the sum total of their profits but also the percentage of these profits in relation to productive assets assigned to them. To do that it is necessary to credit the state budget with charges against the profits of enterprises in proportion to the value of fixed assets and working capital allocated to them, calculating these deductions as payments for productive assets.

The norms of payments for fixed assets and working capital will be established for a prolonged period of time—several years—so that a normally functioning enterprise will have profits left, after making its payments, for setting up incentive funds of its own and providing for planned expenses. Those enterprises which make better use of their fixed assets and working capital will retain more profits for setting up incentive funds, and thus provide the necessary material encouragement for the better use of state money allocated to the enterprise.

New machines, newly installed equipment, and shops or enterprises just put into operation, cannot in every case produce their maximum effect immediately and enterprises might experience certain financial difficulties in this connection. Therefore it is proposed that deductions for fixed assets be made only after the end of a period envisaged to permit the full utilization of these capacities.

It must be stressed that these payments are not proposed as additional payments to the state budget over and above payments which enterprises are making now; the idea is that a considerable portion of these payments to the state budget be obtained through new channels. Looked at in perspective, payments for fixed assets will become the most important part of state income, and the importance of other payments, including the turnover tax, will be correspondingly reduced.

It is also planned to introduce cost accounting on a broader scale in inter-enterprise relations. At present the economic responsibility of an enterprise in its dealings with other enterprises is most inadequate. Contracting has not as yet acquired the importance it deserves in relations between enterprises.

It is proposed to increase an enterprise's or organization's material responsibility in cases of non-fulfilment of contract obligations for deliveries of goods so that, as a rule, the party at fault will make good any losses incurred. Rail, water, road, and other transport organizations should bear greater responsibility for delays in moving goods from enterprises and retarding their delivery to the customer. It is also necessary that design organizations should be accountable for errors they make in projects, technical drawings, and designs, when these errors lead to material losses and additional expenditures during the building or commissioning of a project.

The introduction of the sales index makes the position of producing enterprises and the size of their funds dependent on payments by customers. It goes without saying that every enterprise must itself bear full responsibility for making payments and settling accounts with suppliers on time. A cost-accounting relationship between enterprises demands that payment discipline be tightened. Simultaneously the role of state credit in economic turnover must be intensified with the aim of guaranteeing unhindered settling of accounts between suppliers and their clients.

ON MEASURES TO STIMULATE THE MATERIAL INTERESTS OF WORKERS IN IMPROVING THE WORK OF ENTERPRISES

At present, the material incentives provided for production collectives and for individual workers to make them interested in improving the over-all results of their enterprise's work are quite inadequate. Enterprises possess very limited opportunities for raising the remuneration of industrial and office workers from the sources of income created by the enterprise itself.

About 50 percent of industrial enterprises do not possess funds created from their own profits, and in those cases where enterprises do possess them, these funds are very small and sums paid out from them for encouraging workers are insignificant. Nearly every kind of bonus and other stimuli are being paid out not from profits but from the wage fund. The achievements of the enterprise in increasing profits and profitability of production do not have any direct effect on the wages of the staff of the enterprise.

It is necessary to change this system in order to give the workers a greater material incentive. It is necessary to introduce a system under which the enterprise's opportunities for increasing the remuneration of its workers would be determined, above all, by the growth of production, improved quality, increased profits, and greater profitableness of production. The basic wages and salaries of factory and office workers will continue to be raised by central impetus as before. At the same time the enterprises must have at their disposal—in addition to the wage fund—their own source for stimulating the workers to individual achievements and to high overall results for their enterprises.

This source must be a part of the profits obtained by the enterprise. Out of this profit the enterprise will not only pay bonuses to the factory and office workers for high labor achievements in the course of the year, but also a lump sum at the end of the year. In doing this the length of uninterrupted service of the worker at the enterprise will be taken into account, which will have a positive effect on the stabilization of manpower.

Under the existing system of material incentives, the enterprises are not interested in providing for the utmost utilization of their internal resources in their plans, because the entire appraisal of the enterprise's work and the system of material incentives for the workers are mainly based on encouraging overfulfilment of the plan. Such a system encourages enterprises to strive for lower plan assignments in terms of volume of production, for growth in labor productivity, and lowering costs of production, and for higher assignments in terms for the wage fund, the number of workers, capital investments, and material funds, so that it will be easier for them to overfulfil the plan. This makes it more difficult to compile realistic plans. How is this system to be changed?

A fund for the material stimulation of the workers will be set up at each enterprise from the profits obtained by the enterprise. Allocations made to the material stimulation fund should be made according to stable norms, established for a number of years and in such a manner as to ensure that the volume of the material incentive funds is dependent on an increase in the volume of goods sold or in profit and on the level of profitableness envisaged by the plan. The sums for stimulating overfulfillment of the plan will be relatively less than the sums paid for achievement of the planned indices. This will tend to indice enterprises to find reserves in sufficient time and to agree to larger planned assignments.

The material stimulation fund will also increase, depending on the share taken up by new goods and on additional income derived by the enterprise from higher prices for better quality goods. The enterprises will be interested in mastering the production of new models as quickly as possible and in improving their quality.

Because the pattern of production, the cost of production, and the ratio between profit and wages are not the same in different branches, a differentiation is suggested in the norms for deductions made to the stimulation funds according to the branch of industry and perhaps even according to separate groups of enterprises with due account to the wages fund.

A fund for financing social and cultural undertakings and for housing construction must also be set up at enterprises. This fund will go for new housing (over and above the centralized resources allocated for this purpose), for building and the upkeep of pre-school children's institutions, Young Pioneer camps, rest-homes, sanatoriums, and for other social and cultural needs.

Consequently, the better an enterprise functions the more opportunities it will have not only for raising wages but also for improving the living conditions of its workers and for cultural and health-protection undertakings.

The transition to new forms and methods of economic stimulation of industrial production demands the improvement of the system of price formation. Prices must increasingly reflect expenditures of socially necessary labor, and must cover production and turnover outlays and secure the profits of each normally functioning enterprise.

The existing neglect of economic levers in planning and managing the national economy, and the weakening of the system of cost accounting, are to a great extent connected with the considerable shortcomings in the system of price formation. If prices are not substantiated, then economic calculations lose their dependability, which in turn encourages the adopting of subjectivist decisions.

At present, when wholesale prices are determined for industrial goods, it is becoming absolutely necessary to substantiate scientifically the calculated level of profitability in the branches of industry. Normally functioning enterprises must obtain their profits from the sale of their produce at wholesale prices; in this way they must derive an opportunity to set up stimulation funds and to dispose of the necessary means for expanding their activities, for paying for their fixed assets and for making other transfers to the state budget.

Price must also play a major role in tackling the problems connected with the raising of the quality of goods and improving the length of service and durability of goods. Thus, when prices are determined for new improved models, they must reflect the additional expenditures made by the manufactures and the economic effect which the customers will get from using better quality goods. In such a situation, manufactures will be more interested in improving their produce and it will be economically more advantageous for consumers to purchase such goods.

In the course of preparing for this Plenary Meeting, the Presidium of the CPSU Central Committee and the Council of Ministers of the USSR have decided to set up a State Committee for Prices attached to the USSR State Planning Committee. This Committee is entrusted with working out and presenting, by January 1, 1966, proposals relating to the main trends in the evaluation of wholesale prices for industrial goods, basing its decisions on the need to bring prices as near as possible to levels of expenditure of socially necessary labor. These prices must guarantee the implementation of the planned measures for the improvement of planning and the economic stimulation of the enterprises.

Improvements in the system of price formation and in the methods of determining wholesale prices will help in improving the economic organization of the work of industry, in finding additional reserves and in securing systematic and constant reduction in the cost of production. There can be no question but that retail prices can be reconsidered only with the aim of reducing them.

Experience shows that the task of establishing wholesale price levels for all kinds of goods, and the preparations of new price lists for all branches of industry, take considerable time. It will probably be possible to introduce the new prices in 1967–1968.

At the same time, the State Planning Committee, the Ministry of Finance and the Committee for Prices will have to introduce—for those branches of industry where the transition to new forms of economic stimulation will take place at an earlier date—the necessary amendments to operating prices in order to eliminate unjustified differences in profits derived from goods made by those branches.

Such is the general outline of the main proposals for improving planning and the stimulation of industrial production. The proposed system of planning and stimulation is also applicable, in its main features, to construction work, railway transport, and certain other branches of national economy. But it must not be extended to those branches mechanically, without taking into account their specific economic features and the tasks facing them. Work in this direction will be carried on gradually.

21 | ECONOMIC REFORM IN THE USSR

Robert Campbell

How are the Soviet economic reforms to be evaluated? Are they the first steps toward a drastic reformulation of the Soviet economic system? Or are they merely administrative changes that do not significantly alter the essential elements of the system as a whole? Most scholars who study the Soviet economy do not believe that the reforms herald a new system, but many argue that they should not therefore be dismissed as inconsequential. There is general agreement, however, that they do not constitute a shift toward "capitalism."

A somewhat tentative, but nevertheless balanced, evaluation is presented in the following article by Robert Campbell, Professor of Economics at Indiana University. It is reprinted by permission from the *American Economic Review,* Vol. LVIII, No. 2 (May, 1968), pp. 547–58. References to Russian-language publications have been omitted.

INTRODUCTION

MANY OF US have surely grown skeptical of the possibility of really reforming the Soviet economy or changing its essential nature in any important way. Considering that the Russians have been engaged in economic reform for the last fifteen years and that the problems do not seem to change much, one wonders whether economic reform is not something of a hoax. The rationale for this paper must be some presumption that this time the Russians are serious about economic reform, and one of the tasks of my paper must be to consider that question. I also find it difficult to interpret the current reform measures as a movement from the command economy model to the market socialism model, and a second goal of my paper is to ask whether the Soviet leaders might not be moving toward a kind of system distinct from either of these. Finally, I want to explore a bit the political implications of the reform.

PRINCIPAL FEATURES OF THE REFORM

A plenary session of the Central Committee in September, 1965, approved guidelines for dissolving the ramshackle structure of planning and administrative agencies which Khrushchev had set up and restoring the ministerial principle of organization, reforming the system of prices according to new principles, and altering the system of planning and controlling enterprise behavior. The general goals of these reforms might be summarized briefly as an attempt to give enterprise decision-makers more freedom to make decisions about resource use and to give them a reformed set of incentives and signals that would encourage them to use this new freedom in ways consistent with the general welfare. The "new system" can be most easily described in terms of an altered decision-making environment for the firm; the reform then involves the gradual transfer of enterprises and branches to this new system, a process which will not be completed until the end of 1968.

The new system alters somewhat the constraints and goals confronting the firm. The total number of plan indicators assigned from above was cut and output is now measured by sales rather than by gross output. Rationalized incentives and independence are sought through a system of three incentive funds.

1. A "Fund for Material Stimulation" is formed in part from the enterprise's planned payroll as in the past, but that source is now supplemented with a portion of the profits earned by the enterprise, the amount depending on profit increases or sales increases over the previous year and on the rate of profit achieved. (Actually only a small fraction of the firms will have profit increases as the relevant indicator and for most, sales increases will be the success indicator.) For each percentage point increase in profit (or sales where that is the accepted success indicator) over the previous year, an amount equivalent to x percent of the enterprise's payroll is deducted into the fund. In addition, for each percentage point of profitability (i.e., net profit figured as a percentage of the annual average stock of capital employed in the enterprise) a second amount equal to y percent of the wage fund is deducted into the incentive fund. This dual system was established to permit the *normativy* to operate for several years. An enterprise might be expected to achieve big increases in profits in the first year or two after being put on the new system, but might find it rather harder to attain further profit increases in subsequent years, in which case the first component might soon be generating very small flows. In the process, however, the enterprise would have raised its profitability to a high rate, so that it would now be getting substantial flows from the second component.

2. A "Fund for Social-Cultural Measures and Housing Construction" is formed on the basis of the same success indicators, but with a distinct pair

of *normativy* applied to the payroll. As its title suggests, this fund is to be used as a source of socialized bonuses in kind.

3. A "Fund for the Development of Production" is created from three sources, one of which is another pair of *normativy* tied to the same success indicators as those for the other incentive funds, but applied to the value of the firm's capital rather than to the payroll. A second source is a portion of the depreciation earned by the firm, which heretofore had been extracted into a central pool of investment resources. This fund also receives any revenue received from the sale of fixed assets. In combination with the fact that incentive deductions are tied to the rate of profit, this last provision is intended to induce enterprises to divest themselves of underutilized hoards of assets. They seem to have done so on a very large scale, even when, as often happened, they had to give the assets away! The Fund for the Development of Production then becomes a source out of which the enterprise can finance investment at its own discretion and on its own initiative, for adding a new production line, replacing obsolete machinery, and so on.

The discretionary investment potential provided by the Fund for the Development of Production is augmented with easier access to long-term bank credit, though there is still to be a considerable degree of centralized control over much of the investment financed by bank credit. Under the new system enterprises will also have easier access to short-term bank credit to cover working capital needs. In both cases, firms will be partially self-regulated in their resort to bank credit by the fact that they will have to pay interest to the bank on the borrowed funds.

Most enterprises under the new system pay to the treasury each year an amount equal to 6 percent of the average annual value of the assets, circulating and fixed, at undepreciated value, shown on their balance sheets. Certain assets are omitted from this total, and there is provision for the use of a 3 percent rate in some branches and complete remission of interest payments in others. Rent charges have also been established to extract the extraordinary profits of specially advantaged enterprises in branches where there is great cost variation among enterprises because of differences in situation. These rent charges differ somewhat from a Western conception of rent, since they are charges per unit of output rather than lump-sum amounts.

Under old prices, enterprises did not everywhere generate enough profit to pay the new charges and to finance the new system of incentives. Hence the new system was applied in the first instance to individual enterprises and subbranches where profits were already high enough to support it, and the final transfer of all enterprises to the new system has only now been made possible by an economy-wide price reform on July 1, 1967. Although the price reform was conditioned in large part by the financial needs of the new system, it has also been used as the occasion to accommodate some new conceptions of how prices should be set to serve as guides to rational decision-making. In addition to the inclusion of rent and interest charges already described, these new ideas include a more sophisticated understanding of proper price relationships between substitutable goods, and the relevance of demand considerations. Reforms in economic institutions and practices over the past decade and a half have been paralleled on the theoretical and analytical plane by a revolution in economic theory, culminating in the adoption of standard modern value and allocation theory by at least a portion of the economics profession in the USSR. The new school of economists seems to have played only a modest role in the process of institutional and planning reform so far, but the conception of rational prices—referred to as the "prices of the optimal plan"—has been important in the thinking of the groups that have worked out the new price systems for individual branches.

In the beginning, apparently, this new system was intended only for the industrial sector of the economy. Since then, however, the same general principles have been extended in supplementary decrees to at least some of the enterprises in numerous other sectors as well—automobile transportation, retail trade, including eating establishments and consumer service establishments, railroads, water transportation, the Moscow Metro, construction, and state farms. Analogous reforms have been made in scientific research establishments. The details differ, but in each case the same principle is followed of setting up incentive funds and decentralized investment funds based on successful performance according to some profit or sales indicator, and giving the management of the enterprise a smaller number of planned indicators and more room for independent decision making.

CRITIQUE OF THE NEW SYSTEM

We need waste little time in a detailed critique of the measures described above or in trying to evaluate their success as shown by the performance of enterprises transferred to the new system. Much of the experience under the reform so far is surely transitory. . . . But I want to offer just enough of a critique to establish one crucial proposition, namely, that the reform measures so far introduced constitute neither a coherent system, nor a sufficient departure from the norms and behavior of the command economy to really solve the ills that prompted the reforms.

The independence and initiative from below that the new system is supposed to stimulate is much constrained by the fact that decision making still takes place in a context of physical rationing. In responding to the call to increase profit or sales, managers still have very little freedom with respect to the input or output mix. Although the number of indicators planned for the enterprise from above has been reduced, one of those retained is the output assortment in physical terms. On the input side, freedom to improve efficiency through substitution or to choose the cheapest source of supply is severely restricted by the fact of physical rationing. Centralized allocation is similarly a hindrance to "realizing" the new investment resources. The new system provides money but, as one manager explains, the true test of the procurement department's skill is still its ability to spend money without *fondy* and *nariady*.[1]

The enterprise objective function under the new system is not the simple maximization of profit that might conceivably make what is advantageous for society also advantageous for the individual *kollektiv*. My original description of the new success indicator system was over-simplified—in its full complexity it is an insanely baroque creation. The established *normativy* are tied to the planned magnitudes of the success indicators, and in the event a plant overfulfills or underfulfills the targets, the *normativy* are adjusted by another set of coefficients. Given the trade-offs which this system sets up, an enterprise may find it to its advantage to propose an easy plan in order to overfulfill it, or an over-ambitious plan that it knows it will be able to fulfill only in part. It is claimed that tying the normative to the wage fund has discouraged cost-cutting reductions of the work force. Outsiders have usually objected that it would be more sensible simply to covenant with the enterprise to let it have some fixed proportion of whatever profit it earns, and then shift attention to rationalization of prices. Soviet commentators are now beginning to draw the same conclusion from the experience of enterprise response to the success indicator system.

For all the innovations it embodies, the new price system is still a hurriedly constructed and makeshift device. The reform was incomplete because its designers accepted a number of rather artificial constraints, e.g., that the terms of trade with agriculture and with households should not be altered under the new prices. This meant, for example, that the new relative prices of diesel fuel, gasoline, and residual fuel oil worked out earlier in a very sensible way by oil industry economists could not be achieved while simultaneously coordinating the price of residual fuel oil with coal and gas, and keeping the bill for motor fuel to the agricultural sector unchanged. So the notorious underpricing of diesel fuel continues.

The new charge for capital is a clumsy instrument. As a quasi rent, the return to embodied capital should be price determined rather than price determining. If, as one suspects, there has been serious past misallocation of capital in the Soviet economy, true quasi rents probably depart very considerably from the marginal efficiency of investment. In one of the relatively few contributions that the new economists seem to have made to the discussion of price reform as a concrete policy measure, L. V. Kantorovich made the very sensible suggestion that it would be much

---

[1] Editors' note: *Fondy* are quotas of material inputs the enterprise is authorized to buy. *Nariady* are allocation certificates covering specific transactions.

better to set prices according to some notion of the shadow prices of an optimal allocation, and then let the payment for capital emerge as a residual—perhaps zero in some cases. He argues this for railroads on the traditional decreasing cost basis, but also for machinery using a somewhat more complicated rationale. Machinery prices which omit interest on the tremendous capital accumulated in the industry as a result of overinvestment in the past would both encourage growth from the demand side and force the machinery producers under the new system to get the extra output by better utilization of the capital they already have. With such prices they could not afford new investment on which they would have to pay the true opportunity cost of free capital. The decision to have a mostly uniform rate means that a subtle but powerful use of prices to improve decision making has been lost.

Levying the capital charge on the undepreciated value of assets may also have serious adverse consequences. For example, it is hard to think of a more literal case of sunk costs than past investment in an oil well, or a better illustration of the proposition that only variable costs are relevant to continued use of an asset. But since interest will have to be paid on old wells at 6 percent of their original cost, it will often be greatly to the advantage of an oil field administration to shut them down and get them off its balance sheet, to be replaced with new wells in more productive parts of the fields under its jurisdiction.

Overriding everything else, finally, is the fundamental difficulty that reformed prices are still administered prices and not an item for negotiation in an environment of lateral negotiations between firms which the designers of the new system hope to create. Centrally fixed prices powerfully inhibit improvements that require joint decisions by more than one firm.

UNRESOLVED ISSUES IN THE REFORM

The above is not intended as a balanced analysis of the new system since in my view it is fruitless even to attempt any comprehensive evaluation. What clearly emerges from studying these two years' experience is that no new system exists, in the sense of a coherent set of new institutions, mechanisms, and policy instruments for which a blueprint exists and toward which the leaders are building. What is taking place is a revolution, partially guided by the leaders, but not founded on a clearly understood strategy. One of the most interesting questions about the reform concerns the dynamics of this process. During the two years that the Russians have been implementing the reform many things have happened also that don't fit in very well with the new system as originally expounded. The dynamic interaction of these forces and ideas creates a revolutionary potential in the reform and gives us some clue as to what kind of system might finally emerge.

The reform has created the conditions for a new allocation of powers between the ministry and other units under its general supervision—the *glavk*, the trust, the combine, the enterprise. If we take the original decrees at face value, it would appear that the leaders were junking Khrushchev's organizational innovations to return to the tested branch system in its traditional form. The rationale for the reversion to ministries was that the development of branches required strong, unified leadership, and the ministry was the kind of organ to which the central planners could assign responsibility for branch innovation, investment, growth, and productivity. As the Russians have proceeded through the multifarious concrete measures required to put the reform into effect—such as drafting statutes on rights and responsibilities, assigning enterprises to ministries, and deciding whether firms should be consolidated—it has become clear that there is a strong pressure against recreating the pre-1957 system. If fully implemented, the new system would mean greatly increased autonomy for the enterprise, but those with a stake in strong powers for central organs are arguing very strongly that the enterprise cannot use independence wisely because it cannot see the whole picture. It is too small, for example, to do market research or to make sensible decisions on investment since it can't forecast demand and technical changes. But this argument is now being employed in a novel way to suggest that enterprises must be merged into larger units. The Russians had already been experimenting with such consolidations, though this campaign has waxed and waned. Many of the units formed were later dissolved. But there is now a renewed push for this kind of consolidation, sometimes through the creation of combines along the previous lines, sometimes by a process that makes what was formerly a supervisory organ such as a *glavk*[2] into a head office with *khozraschet*[3] independence. If all this weren't being discussed in the Russian language and the command economy jargon, we would have no hesitation in labeling it an oligopolistic "rationalization" movement. One would predict that both enterprises and ministries would have ambivalent reactions to such a cartelization movement. Despite its obvious threat to the enterprise, strong firms may still see it as a chance for increasing their power and gaining real autonomy vis-à-vis the party, their customers, or resurgent ministries. Higher agencies and officials, though they may see it as second best to the kind of power they would like to have, may sense that the old type ministry is gone and that this is their best hope against plant-level autonomy. The concern that many officials have about this reform is clearly revealed in a statement by the minister of the merchant marine in

---

[2] Editors' note: Main administration—an intermediate agency through which a ministry supervises its enterprises.

[3] Editors' note: Units with *khozraschet* ("business calculation") status are expected to cover all current and some capital expenditures from their sales revenue, rather than being financed by budget grants.

Pravda in which he lauds the reform, explains how they have put every ship on *khozraschet*, but then spends most of the article explaining the great potential advantages of having the comings and goings of the merchant marine controlled through a computerized center in the ministry.

The price reform affected or threatened to affect the distribution of power and prestige and shows the interaction of economic reform and politics. Considering the power-distributive implications of the Kantorovich proposal for freight rates and machinery prices mentioned above, for example, it is not difficult to understand why this line of argument got such short shrift. There are numerous other incidents illustrating the potential of the reform for redistributing power and prestige, but I will describe only one in some detail.

The oil industry got out of the reform a greatly improved pricing system. Crude oil was previously sold under a system of settlement prices differentiated to meet cost variations among producers. The rent generated in this industry was collected by turnover tax only at the point of sale of finished products. Under the new system rent is being collected where it originates, i.e., largely in extraction, by establishing uniform regional purchase prices for crude oil. The price for any region is based on costs of the highest cost fields in that region that have prospects for expanding output. The new prices make possible rational internal margin calculations at the level of the individual field (when to abandon wells, whether intensification measures are worthwhile, etc.) and will lead the refineries and other consumers within the sector to make more rational decisions about their consumption of crude oil and intermediates. There was a problem in extending that system to Azerbaidzhan, where some producers have extremely high costs. If the Azerbaidzhan regional price had been set to cover the costs of the marginal producer, it would have been far out of line with other regional prices. At the insistence of the Azerbaidjanis it was finally decided to permit them to use the old system of settlement prices, so that the regional price would be set at something like average cost of all producers, with individual producers paid according to cost. The Azerbaidjan producers must have sensed that in the new kind of environment a marginal cost price would expose their oil as uneconomic and threaten their growth prospects.

This incident is but one of many suggesting that the Russians are edging up to the normal situation in which money is power and distributes power so that prices become important. If the former ideological obstacles to rational pricing have been eroded, the political difficulties have become much more important, and the sensitivity of this issue is well shown in the reluctance with which it is discussed. The position taken by N. P. Fedorenko in a review of the progress of the reform that enterprises which cannot cover their current costs ought to be reconstructed or shut down is almost unique.

Implementation of the reform has revealed an acute need for an improved system of contract law. An enterprise used to have a kind of filial relationship to its "system" and faced the rest of the economy half hidden by the skirts of its *almum ministerstvo*.[4] But it now faces increasingly the prospect of being out in the cold scrambling to make sales and profits—determinants of success from which there is going to be little appeal. It will have to look out for its own interests through obligations expressed in contracts and guaranteed by a legal system that will protect it against customers who won't pay up, suppliers who won't fulfill supply contracts, a superior organ which directs it to do things which are neither in its or society's interest. The present system of state and intrabranch arbitrage has either too circumscribed a jurisdiction to handle all problems or is a creature of the ministry in which it is hopeless for the enterprise to appear as plaintiff against its bosses. The most recent development is an attempt to try to fill the gap with a decree establishing draconian sanctions against suppliers for delayed or incomplete shipments and goods below the quality specified in contracts, those who fail to pay bills on time, against railroads for upsetting shipping schedules. It is hard to believe, however, that this decree is an adequate answer—it will put a crushing burden on Gosarbitrazh[5] and make the bank a battleground for intraenterprise disputes, and is likely to open the door to a frightful outbreak of traditional Russian litigiousness.

At the time of the introduction of the reforms it was stated that the system of material-technical supply (i.e., rationing) would be retained, but that an eventual transition to a system of "wholesale trade" was intended. This promise is cautiously reiterated from time to time, but nothing like a tangible blueprint has ever been offered, and this is one area where there has been a palpable absence of bold experimentation.

The only exception that has come to my attention is the "no-limit system" for distribution of petroleum products (in operation since July, 1966, in Voronezh, and extended in July, 1967, to nine additional regions).

Under this system the customers are supposed to advise the supply organization in advance of the amounts they expect to buy in a given quarter but are not obligated to take the whole amount requested or to stay within it. Very substantial reductions in amounts sold are reported, and this is explained by the disappearance of the temptation to fight for big allocations and to use up current allocations, wastefully if necessary, so that they will not be arbitrarily cut in a subsequent period. The significance of this experiment is its implication that rationing of petroleum products could be abandoned without fear of shortages. We have

---

[4] Editors' note: Maternal ministry.

[5] Editors' note: Gosarbitrazh is the system for settling legal disputes between enterprises over nonfulfillment of contracts.

often been tempted to explain the Soviet material balance system as a consequence of the seller's market caused by the overcommitment of resources flowing from the ambitiousness of Soviet growth goals. But this experiment suggests that the seller's market may be a myth, created and sustained by the material balance system that was established to cope with it.

One might argue that this conclusion might not have universal validity, i.e., that there may objectively be a surplus of petroleum products but not of all commodities. However, the conclusion certainly fits in with what a lot of separate studies have hinted at, namely, that the real drag on Russian growth is leakage of gross output into inflated intermediate consumption. A buyer's market would be a wonderful solvent for many of the sticky residues of the past: it would stimulate innovation and quality improvements, would generate commercial solicitude for the customer, and so on. But I repeat that the issue of rationing continues to be treated very evasively in discussions of the reform, and one suspects that it is so politically and ideologically sensitive a topic that only some very adept maneuvering will get it on the agenda for open discussion. Moreover, it will probably remain politically sensitive. If the final outcome of the reform is to be a cartelized production system, cartel managers probably prefer a seller's to buyer's market.

CONCLUSION

In concluding, I want to return to the questions raised at the beginning of my paper. If this is not a well-controlled transition to a clearly outlined new system, what will the end product be? Also, how does the reform affect political power and the political processes of the Soviet system?

I am not a very bold prophet, and on the first point will limit myself to the suggestion that it is not very productive from either the explicative or predictive point of view to continue our discussion in terms of the polar alternatives of a return to the command economy (perhaps in a computerized, optimal planning version) or an ultimate adoption of Lange-style market socialism. I doubt that it is possible to return to the command economy now, and for all its didactic usefulness in explaining the idea of decentralization through prices, the market socialism model is too full of ambiguities to permit reformers to pattern real institutions on it, and correspondingly for us to use in interpreting actual developments. (I have in mind here such traditional objections as its failure to explain how to make socialist managers abide by the rules when they have any significant degree of market control.)

The Soviet developments seem to offer confirmation of the idea of those who have studied the Eastern European reforms that reformed socialism may end up with a kind of industry cartel as its dominant institution. The industry level cartel would make investment and pricing decisions, handle marketing and forecasting, determine income distribution among its constituent publics, control innovation, and so on. It would capture much of the present planning machinery for itself and although it would still work within a framework of central planning institutions, the policy instruments available to the latter would be much different from those now used and would involve such things as price regulation, tax policy, legal controls, chartering and licensing functions, and the like. (Note that I am not talking here about macroeconomic instruments in the usual sense.) As a kind of socialist version of "the new industrial state," this is not a very attractive kind of system for economists to try to cope with. It is much more difficult to create neat simple models when the parameters confronting the main decision-makers are not prices, but legal controls over market power, or fiscal influences on decision making, and when the objective functions of the main decision-makers involve not only some simple measure like profit or output, but are an internalized amalgam of these with social conscience, ideology, and political ambition.

Closely correlated with this view of what the outcome may be is the other conclusion, i.e., that economic reform cannot help but be an active reagent in the process of political change. Interim steps in the reform (such as successive versions of the price reform) are less the result of moving toward a design the leaders know they must satisfy by a certain date than *ad hoc* reactions to pressures and difficulties that grow out of preceding steps and this situation offers a continuing chance for aggrandizement on the part of various groups. Traditional power relationships are being disturbed—relative power of big and little producers, of the entrepreneur and the rentier, the countryside in relation to the towns. Politically or socially determined status is to be challenged by the cash nexus. In short, things that count are up for grabs, and this probably includes the really fundamental thing: political power. This suspicion has been voiced by many observers. One of the things that I had hoped to do but have hardly succeeded in doing was to analyze in detail how the reform might redistribute political power. Unfortunately, the economist who looks to the political scientists for some clear-cut model of Soviet politics must come away rather confused. But students of Soviet politics have always viewed the managerial class as a kind of competitor with the party for whatever it is that political power consists of. A recent book by Jeremy Azrael, *Managerial Power and Soviet Politics*,[6] provides considerable substance for the proposition that the party has always seen the managerial class as a serious rival for power, and that it has never been able to solve that issue as clearly and permanently as it would like to. It does seem obvious that reform upsets whatever equilibrium had previously been achieved in this rivalry. There are many symptoms in addition to those already mentioned. In the recent changes in statistical

---

[6] Cambridge, Mass.: Harvard University Press, 1966.

reporting rules, the steel industry and oil industry received what seem to me some very special concessions—a number of indicators formerly reported monthly now are reported only quarterly, including for the steel industry the blast furnace and steel furnace utilization figures, and for the oil industry drilling indicators. Considering the role these have played as planning and control indicators, this is a real revolution. The exemption of the coal industry from the normal interest charges already mentioned is only one element in the generally distinctive application of the new system which the coal industry obtained. The decision to have a reform itself reflects the willingness of the party to hand over an area of decision making to the technical experts, but the reform as it progresses intensifies the process and calls for its extension into new areas, such as law and sociology. These examples may sound a bit farfetched and insufficient warrant for an assertion that the Party's monopoly of political power is being diminished. I must agree that they are only small symptoms, but they do involve the substance of what power consists of in the Soviet system, and I believe they are only symptoms of more significant but still unrevealed acquisitions of power already made by the managers and of still greater ones to come.

22 | SOVIET AGRICULTURAL REFORMS SINCE KHRUSHCHEV

Roger A. Clarke

The development of agriculture has been a major concern of the post-Khrushchev leadership. Its program of agricultural reforms was announced in March 1965, six months before the reforms in the industrial sector. The broad package of measures involves administrative reorganization, increases in prices and investment, guaranteed pay for collective farmers, easing restrictions on private plots, and authorization for farms to create subsidiary industrial enterprises to provide off-season employment and raise incomes.

In this article, Clarke reviews and evaluates the various measures, analyzing their effects on output, sales, and incomes. In doing so, he shows the kind of complex calculations needed to estimate peasant cash and in-kind incomes and income differentials in the USSR. He argues that these reforms in agriculture have had greater practical consequences than the more widely publicized industrial reforms—particularly in regard to worker incentives and managerial autonomy.

The author is Lecturer in the Institute of Soviet and East European Studies at the University of Glasgow. The article is reprinted by permission from *Soviet Studies,* Vol. XX, No. 2 (October, 1968), pp. 159–78, with the omission of citations of Russian-language sources.

DURING the last three years the economic reform, or "new economic system," which involves predominantly the industrial sector, has probably been the principal single subject of attention of analysts of the Soviet economy. Yet it is by now substantially clear that the extent of the change brought about by the reform is considerably less than was initially hoped or even expected. The continued practice of ministerial intervention in the form of frequent changes to enterprises' plans, and the imposition of "old" plan targets now supposedly dropped, and above all the persistence of administrative allocation of all important supplies, are well

409

documented,[1] and provide ample evidence that the degree of change has not really been very large.

In contrast, the changes in the agricultural sector seem, after the initial package deal of the March 1965 Plenum, to have been relatively neglected. Yet there have been a number of other measures of major significance for agriculture since then, and there is also now evidence indicating that the changes brought about by the initial measures of the new leadership have indeed had results which are arguably of much greater importance than the industrial reform. The aim of this article is—after briefly summarizing the earlier measures[2]—to describe those taken since mid-1965 and to examine the results which can now be seen. It seems to me that this will support the contention that the most important economic reforms since Khrushchev have been in agriculture. It is, of course, far from my intention to imply that all the problems of Soviet agriculture are now solved, or even on the way to solution. Many still remain untouched.

PRINCIPAL MEASURES TAKEN

Administrative Organization

By the end of the Khrushchev period the administrative structure of Soviet agriculture was in considerable confusion as a result of his frequent reorganizations. Among the earliest actions of the new leadership, in late 1964, was the abolition of the "territorial production administration," whose boundaries corresponded to no other administrative units, and the reversal of Khrushchev's agricultural/industrial division of the local party committees. This restored the raion as the basic local unit of agricultural administration. A few months later, on March 1, 1965, the USSR Ministry of Agriculture was reorganized and put in overall charge of both kolkhoz (collective farm) and sovkhoz (state farm) agriculture. It had gradually been reduced by Khrushchev to advisory and research functions only, and the administrative responsibility for agriculture had been divided between various other agencies. The consequence of this had been that no one central government department had full responsibility for agriculture, and although the party's role in agriculture has always been of greater direct importance than in other sectors, the restoration of a single government agency should have made for greater administrative clarity.[3]

---

[1] See Gertrude Schroeder, "Soviet Economic 'Reforms': A Study in Contradictions," *Soviet Studies*, Vol. XX, No. 1 (July, 1968), pp. 1–21.

[2] These are fully described and analyzed in Jerzy F. Karcz, "The New Soviet Agricultural Programme," *Soviet Studies*, Vol. XVII, No. 2 (October, 1965), pp. 129–61.

[3] On Khrushchev's agricultural reorganization see Alec Nove, "Some Thoughts on Soviet Agricultural Administration," in Roy D. Laird and Edward L. Crowley (eds.), *Soviet Agriculture: The Permanent Crisis* (New York: Frederick A. Praeger, Inc., 1965).

Prices and Investment

The measures announced at the March 1965 Plenum are examined very thoroughly by Karcz, and will simply be listed here. Procurement prices for virtually all products were increased, with particularly big increases for livestock, which had often been completely unprofitable for farms to produce. There were changes in the planning of procurements, with lower targets, set in advance for the whole period to 1970, and overplan deliveries were to be paid 50 percent above the basic procurement prices. The share of investment going to agriculture was to be raised, the irrigation and drainage program was expanded, and plans for the supply of trucks, tractors, and agricultural machinery were stepped up. At about the same time, the kolkhoz income tax was reformed, reducing its incidence on poorer farms particularly and changing the tax base from gross to net income, that is, excluding payments to kolkhozniki (collective farmers) for all farms; at the same time a considerable portion of kolkhoz debt was cancelled. Prices of some machinery, and of electricity, were cut, and a start was made on the abolition of the rural surcharge on retail prices, which was to be completed in 1966. The increased agricultural investment program and the rises in the planned supplies of equipment, in contrast to the decline in the years after 1958, have been examined by Karcz, and little further detail has become available since, though the fertilizer program has had to be scaled down from a 1970 deliveries target of 70–80 million tons to 55 million tons. The final important measure taken by the new leadership soon after taking over power was the relaxation of the stringent restrictions on the size of private plots and on private livestock ownership, by which Khrushchev had presumably hoped to force the peasants to devote more time and effort to the collective farms.

Guaranteed Pay for Kolkhozniki

The next major step in the new agricultural policy came a year later, in the middle of 1966. This was the decree introducing guaranteed pay in cash and produce for kolkhozniki.[4] It was intended to take effect from July 1, 1966, and although towards the end of the year a *Pravda* editorial criticized some farms for delay in the introduction of guaranteed pay, it was reported in January 1967 to have been implemented in the majority of farms by the end of 1966. Instances of failure to adopt the new rules for money payment have been reported again since then, but early in 1968, according to one source, 93 percent of kolkhozy had then adopted

---

[4] A few kolkhozy had already introduced guaranteed monthly pay. One in Amur oblast introduced it in 1963; Estonian kolkhozy in particular had also been moving in this direction earlier.

guaranteed monthly pay, and another gave a figure of 34,000 for kolkhozy which had already introduced it.[5] There can be little doubt that the system is now in general operation.

Kolkhozniki were now to be paid at least monthly, whereas previously many farms had paid their members considerably less frequently, and a few had paid no advances at all during the year, but only a single end-of-year payment. The pay of kolkhozniki also became the first charge on the farms' income, and the allocation to the notorious indivisible fund was to be decided after paying the peasants and after meeting taxes and social insurance fund contributions. Pay for kolkhoz peasants was to be at the rates already in operation for similar types of work in sovkhozy, and the poorer farms, which would not be able to afford this out of their revenue immediately, were to get five-year loans, with repayment to start after three years. The guaranteed pay rate was the total, and the proportion of cash and produce comprising it was for the farms to decide, but there was to be a guaranteed fund of produce (a fixed proportion of the gross harvest) for distribution. In addition to the basic guaranteed pay at sovkhoz rates, there were to be bonuses linked to the quantity and quality of output produced; for this purpose farms were to form a *nadtarifnyi fond*, consisting of net income in excess of that required to pay the basic rates. Farms whose income was insufficient to do this could either simply pay at basic rates with bonuses only when they overfulfilled production and revenue plans, or they could divide the basic wage fund into a part for monthly payments and a second part to be distributed according to quantity and quality of production.

An example of how the new pay operates in practice is provided by a kolkhoz statute on pay, published towards the end of 1967. In the first place 60 percent of this farm's gross income is allocated for pay. (The farm's income is adequate to cover pay at sovkhoz rates; so it does not need credits.) During the year 45 percent goes on the basic guaranteed pay, and the remaining 15 percent is used for payments according to results at the end of the year. The statute also provides for 20 percent of the gross harvest to be set aside for distribution to the kolkhozniki, and there are bonus distributions for overplan production: 10 percent of crop production in excess of the previous three years' average, and 20 percent of overplan livestock production. Soon after its introduction it was estimated that the adoption of the guaranteed pay would mean an overall increase of 20–25 percent over the 1965 level in the pay of kolkhozniki; in fact, the increase was 16 percent in 1966 and a further 6 percent in 1967. The fact that the rise in 1966 was somewhat less than anticipated may well be due to some delays in implementing the new pay arrangements in some farms. It is probable that kolkhoznik incomes from the farms will still be somewhat below the wages of sovkhoz workers, but the difference

---

[5] There were 37,100 kolkhozy at the end of 1966.

may be made good by more income from their private plots and livestock. A detail worth noting is that rich kolkhozy which previously paid out more than the corresponding sovkhoz rates will not reduce the amount they pay their members, but the extra amount will be paid in performance-related bonuses.

It is important to understand the nature of what is guaranteed by the new system of kolkhoz pay. Whilst, not surprisingly, perhaps, the point does not appear to have been made explicitly in Soviet sources, it seems fairly clear that what is guaranteed for an individual kolkhoznik is not a definite amount per month, but a definite amount for the work that he does and the fact that he will be paid monthly what he has earned. It is not clear whether this still means that when in winter there is no work available kolkhozniki are not paid; farms may establish a minimum level which they pay members monthly as advances against future earnings.[6] In any case, as well as the increase in the level of pay, the fact that kolkhozniki now know how much they will get for their work when they do it, and that they will get paid fairly soon for it, is a very big improvement on the old *trudoden'* system, under which the ultimate money value of the units being earned was unknown, and more work might simply result in less money per unit.

The Sovkhoz Reform

At around the same time as the announcement of the guaranteed pay for kolkhozniki, the USSR Minister of Finance, Garbuzov, wrote in an article that his ministry had prepared plans for the transfer of sovkhozy to full economic self-reliance (*polnyi khozraschet*). No more was heard of this proposal for some time, though there were many criticisms of the illogical arrangement whereby sovkhozy were paid lower prices for their produce than kolkhozy while, even after the 1965 price increases, they received large budgetary grants to cover their investment requirements.[7] There were also frequent complaints about the extent to which sovkhoz managers' freedom of action was circumscribed. One director objected that although they had difficulty in disposing of all the fruit and vegetables they produced they were ordered to increase output, *and* not allowed to sell it in a nearby city in a different oblast, even if it was refused in their own oblast.

This was the background to the publication in April 1967 of the decree initiating the transfer of sovkhozy to full economic self-reliance. In the first place 390 sovkhozy[8] were to be put on to the new system experimen-

---

[6] I was told that this was the case by a Soviet economist, in private conversation, but I have not seen it stated explicitly in print.

[7] According to D. Kondrashev, the difference in prices paid was 15–20% overall, but the state in fact paid out considerably more than this to the sovkhozy.

[8] The actual number transferred was later reported to be 406.

tally. They would be expected to cover all their production costs, productive capital investment (but not housing or cultural and social amenities), increases in working capital, the formation of incentive funds, and due repayment of bank credit out of their own revenue. In order to enable them to do this, they would receive for the produce they supplied to the state the same prices as those established in 1965 for kolkhozy. The need to extend the autonomy of sovkhozy was recognized and the plan targets set by superior organs were limited to the following: sales to the state of major products (in physical terms), the total wages fund, total profits, and allocations from the state budget and payment for agricultural productive fixed capital. Total planned profit was to be determined by the farms and confirmed by superior organs. Plans would cover capital investment, and the supply of tractors, vehicles, machinery, equipment, fertilizers, and building materials. Sovkhozy would pay the state an annual charge of 1 percent of the value of their capital (excluding livestock and perennial plantations), but this would not be applied to sovkhozy whose profit rate on direct cost was less than 25 percent. After payment of the capital charge, farms would form the same three incentive funds as industrial enterprises under the reform, and in addition an insurance fund. The calculation of these funds is much simpler than in industry; the material incentive fund (the source of profit-related bonuses) is 15 percent of planned profit, and a smaller proportion of overplan profit (to discourage efforts to get an easy plan), but must not exceed 12 percent of the wages fund. The social-cultural and housing fund and the enterprise development fund are each to take 10 percent of planned profits, and the insurance fund 20 percent. The rest of profit is to be used for augmenting working capital, financing centralized investment, repaying credits, and other purposes; there is no remainder which must be paid to the budget, as there is in industry.

The sources of finance for various types of investment are described in some detail, but the position may be summarized by saying that the main sources of investment finance are to be profits and long-term credits, with a sharp reduction in state budgetary financing, which will basically be restricted to housing, schools, hospitals, clubs, and other social amenities, and also irrigation, land improvement, and electric power transmission lines. This too is similar to the new arrangements in industry, with corresponding exemption from the capital charge of capital financed by loans still being repaid, and, for the first two years after coming into operation, capital financed out of profits. Farms are to be free to plan their own production program, but as this must accommodate the sales targets for major products, the degree of freedom may not actually be large. They are also free to plan the number of workers they employ, which would appear to be a potential source of difficulty, as in many rural areas the sovkhoz must be the only local employer. The directors' rights also include that of selling unused equipment which the superior organ does not wish to re-allocate, and that of selling perishable produce which is refused by the procurement organizations to state and cooperative trade organizations, and on the markets, both within and outside their own oblast, krai or republic, at mutually agreed prices. Such sales are to be counted towards fulfillment of sales plans, except for sales on the markets.

By the autumn of 1967 the first appraisals of this sovkhoz experimental reform were appearing in the Soviet press. In his speech on the economic plan for 1968, 1969, and 1970, Baibakov referred confidently to the benefits the extension of the reform would bring, and an article in *Ekonomicheskaya gazeta* claimed general success for the new system, and said that all sovkhozy must prepare to adopt it. A second group of 400 was transferred to full *khozraschet*, on the same terms as the initial group, from the second quarter of 1968. The well-known and controversial economist Lisichkin reported on the experiment in *Pravda* on November 20, 1967. Three farms in Rostov oblast which he visited expected profits to be 60 percent above plan and had increased their area under the crops they could grow most profitably without infringing their procurement sales plan. When the procurement agency refused vegetables from one of the farms, the farm sold them to a canning factory on its own initiative. Another farm had refused to accept machinery it did not need, whereas previously, Lisichkin claimed, it would have taken it without question. The problems to which he drew attention were, first, that retained profits could often be unusable because of the impossibility of getting materials for minor investment projects for which there are no allocations, and secondly, the increasing importance of relative prices, where farms' production patterns were being influenced directly by prices paid. He also reported that 10 of the 400 farms were experimentally being given special rights to alter their wage funds, and said that the provision that the material incentive fund must not exceed 12 percent of the wage fund could prevent already successful farms from continuing to reward further success. Towards the end of 1967 and in 1968 reports of the success achieved by sovkhozy on the new system became frequent.

There seems little doubt that the new sovkhoz arrangements as outlined above are being extended with little alteration to apply to all sovkhozy. The financial aspects of the reform in particular seem likely to bring a considerable improvement in efficiency. Previously it was a matter of relative indifference to the management of a sovkhoz whether it made a profit or a loss, as in the former case the profit was taken by the state, and in the latter the loss was covered by a state subsidy. Now failure to make profits will mean loss of bonuses and probably shortage of funds for investment. The produce of the sovkhozy will cost the state more, because of the higher prices, but there will be a saving on subsidies to loss-making sovkhozy, and the result should be redistribution from inefficient to efficient producers. The inevitable doubts about the extent of the change center on the degree of management independence to decide production patterns which is permitted by the sales targets (and whether in fact output targets are not also likely to be imposed, although supposedly "illegal," as happened in the 1950's with kolkhozy, and has been happening frequently in reformed industrial enterprises). The meaningfulness of leaving decentralized investment funds to the farms is also questionable, when they are experiencing, and are likely to continue to experience, difficulties in obtaining any materials with these funds. Whilst in view of what has happened with the industrial reform one is bound to be somewhat pessimistic on these counts, this sovkhoz reform, although it will probably prove less radical than it appears on paper, is nevertheless an improvement of considerable significance.

The Decree on Subsidiary Enterprises

Later in 1967 another decree was published which is potentially of great importance for the future development of Soviet agriculture. This was the decree on the further development of subsidiary enterprises in agriculture. Union-republican, ASSR, krai and oblast government organs, and the Ministry of Agriculture were given the right to extend subsidiary enterprises in kolkhozy and sovkhozy, so long as this was not done at the expense of agricultural production. The aim was to make full use of seasonal surpluses of labor and of materials available on the farms. Particular attention was to be paid to the processing of agricultural produce and wild fruits and berries, etc., to the production of local building materials and consumer goods, and the development of production links with industrial enterprises. The farms with subsidiary enterprises will be responsible for compiling their production plans, which will not be subject to higher approval. The output will be sold on the basis of contracts with the consumer cooperative and state retail trade networks, and industrial enterprises, and also on the markets. Prices will be determined by mutual agreement between the contracting parties, and in the case of goods sold on the markets the seller will naturally be free to set them. The cooperative and state retail trade networks are allowed to sell non-food goods from these sources at uncontrolled prices, but the prices at which they sell food must not exceed state retail prices. This provision will obviously limit the prices the farms' subsidiary enterprises can negotiate with the trade networks. Arrangements are specified for the subsidiary enterprises to obtain equipment, waste metal, packing, and other necessary materials; industrial enterprises are allowed to sell their unwanted materials to them, and the state bank is to provide farms with credit for the construction and equipment of such enterprises.

In his plan speech Baibakov said that experience had shown that subsidiary enterprises could become a serious source of increase in the output of various consumer goods, artistic goods, and building and other materials. Their expansion would also increase rural employment in the off-peak season, make use of remnants of raw materials and agricultural produce, and increase the farms' incomes. Clearly these are all desirable effects, and the decree on subsidiary enterprises is very much to be welcomed as providing a useful channel for some local initiative. The intention to expand these enterprises was announced at the Twenty-third Party Congress, and their number was reported late in 1967 to have increased by 2,000 in kolkhozy alone since then. However, they are not an entirely new development and some farms have had them for a decade. The annual increase in output of industrial products (excluding food-processing) by farms was said late in 1967 to have been 7.8–5.1 percent in sovkhozy and 10.4 percent in kolkhozy, and output of many food products had risen greatly. A number of accounts of rapid progress achieved by individual farms' subsidiary enterprises have since appeared.

In the long term, if its provisions are fully implemented, the decree could lead to a marked improvement in the rural standard of living, by increasing employment and incomes, and at the same time improving the availability of processed foods and at least the simpler types of non-food goods, many of which are unobtainable in the countryside because of the weakness of the distribution system and the low priority attached to their production in any case. The early results cannot be expected to be very striking, as the setting up of new enterprises of this kind takes time, and, despite the decree's provisions, there are bound to be difficulties in getting supplies of equipment and such materials as cannot be made locally, since the priority enjoyed by their users will almost inevitably be low. Indeed, this has already been the subject of criticism; in 1966 farms in the Ukraine ordered 234 sets of brick-making equipment, but were allocated 54, and 2500 saw frames, but received 520. Requirements of equipment for canning were only 20–25 percent satisfied. On the other hand, the freedom for the farms to decide the production plans of subsidiary enterprises without higher approval and the right to negotiate sale prices freely, subject only to a retail ceiling in the case of food, are quite impressive as indications of a serious intent to release and encourage initiative and response to demand. If these points are adhered to, the subsidiary enterprises will in fact be producing for the market (though of course their choice of product will obviously be restricted to a narrow range by the nature of the materials available to them), as they will only be able to purchase such things as packaging and waste metals, and control can be exercised through the equipment with which they are supplied. Nevertheless, the decree is potentially of great importance within a limited sector, and it is to be hoped that conservatism and fears that initiative might get out of hand do not stifle a sensible and promising measure.

PERFORMANCE SINCE 1964

The first part of this article has described the various changes introduced in Soviet agriculture by the post-Khrushchev leadership. There will presumably be general agreement that they represent a substantial improvement in Soviet agricultural policy. We now turn to an examination of the achievements of agriculture since the new policy began.

Output

Table 1 shows the annual increase in gross agricultural output, and production of the major products for the period 1960–67.

TABLE 1
Soviet Agricultural Output, 1960–67

	1960	*1961*	*1962*	*1963*	*1964*	*1965*	*1966*	*1967*
Gross agricultural output (% increase on previous year)	2.3	3.0	1.2	—7.5	14.4	2.0	9.8	1.0
Grain (million tons)	125.5	130.8	140.2	107.5	152.1	121.1	171.2	147.6
Cotton "	4.3	4.5	4.3	5.2	5.3	5.7	6.0	6.0
Sugar beets "	57.7	50.9	47.4	44.1	81.2	72.3	74.0	86.8
Potatoes "	84.4	84.3	69.7	71.8	93.6	88.7	87.9	95.0
Vegetables "	16.6	16.2	16.0	15.2	19.5	17.6	17.9	19.8
Meat "	8.7	8.7	9.5	10.2	8.3	10.0	10.8	11.4
Milk "	61.7	62.6	63.9	61.2	63.3	72.6	76.0	79.3
Eggs (billions)	27.4	29.3	30.1	28.5	26.7	29.1	31.7	33.7
Wool (thousand tons)	357	366	371	373	341	357	371	395

It is only three years since Khrushchev's dismissal, and the effects of policy changes cannot be expected to show up immediately. It is therefore difficult to draw conclusive lessons, as an apparent trend may be due to the influence of climatic conditions. However, it is surely not without significance that the 1967 output of all the major products except grain was a record. Even the grain harvest was the third-best ever achieved and was only 3 percent below the 1964 crop. The record harvest of 1966 clearly owed a lot to exceptionally favorable weather and could not be expected to be repeated in 1967. In view of this the planned rise of gross agricultural output for 1967[9] was probably overoptimistic, and although the 1 percent increase actually achieved is somewhat disappointing it is not really discreditable. On the other hand, one is bound to say that achievement of the 7.4 percent planned increase for 1968 seems highly improbable, unless the weather is extremely favorable.

It is the output of livestock products which shows most clearly the

[9] The plan for 1967 published in *Pravda*, December 16, 1966, gave 4 percent for this figure, but the plan fulfillment report (*ibid.*, January 25, 1968) gave 3 percent.

improvement starting in 1965. The high level of meat production in 1963 was a result of exceptional slaughtering because of the disastrous harvest of that year and was offset by a sharp drop in 1964 (it is noticeable that this phenomenon did not recur in 1965–66). If, therefore, we average meat production in 1963 and 1964, we find that for all except wool the 1965 output itself was already the highest achieved, and the two subsequent years both showed further increases. There can be no doubt that the substantial procurement price increases announced in March 1965 were largely responsible for this improvement. Lisichkin attributed the 1966 success mainly to the new policies, principally to the price increases and the increase in farms' autonomy permitted by the lower procurement plans. He stated that as incomes rose the supply of labor to the farms increased. This would have been of great importance for the successful gathering of the exceptional harvest.

The Private Sector

One of the major fallacies of Khrushchev's agricultural policy after 1958 was his idea that by tightening the restrictions on the size of private plots and numbers of private livestock the peasants could be made to work harder on the kolkhozy. The new leadership repudiated this policy almost immediately, by relaxing the regulations and by saying that, for a considerable time to come, at any rate, the private sector of agriculture had an

TABLE 2
The Private Sector, Selected Years, 1958–67

	1958	1960	1964	1965	1966	1967
Sown area (million hectares)	7.3	6.8	6.3	6.6	6.7	n.a.*
Livestock ownership (millions at end of year)						
Cattle	29.2	23.0	25.1	27.9	29.3	28.4
of which Cows	18.5	16.3	16.2	16.6	17.1	17.1
Pigs	15.1	15.4	14.5	18.2	16.5	13.6
Sheep	28.6	28.1	26.0	27.6 }	33.3	33.5
Goats	7.8	6.0	4.5	4.7 }		
Production						
Potatoes† (million tons)	57.1	53.2	56.2	55.9	56.3	n.a.
Vegetables† ” ”	6.7	7.1	7.6	7.2	7.5	n.a.
Meat ” ”	4.0	3.6	3.5	4.0	4.4	4.4
Milk ” ”	31.1	29.1	27.0	28.7	30.2	30.6
Eggs (billions)	19.6	22.1	19.7	19.6	20.9	21.9
Production as percentage of total						
Potatoes	66	63	60	63	64	n.a.
Vegetables	45	44	39	41	42	n.a.
Meat	52	41	42	40	42	39
Milk	53	47	42	39	40	39
Eggs	85	80	73	67	66	65

* Not available.
† Calculated from percentage share.

essential role to fulfill. Statistical evidence now shows that these were not mere words, but have indeed led to practical, if limited, results. Table 2 indicates the trends in the private sector's sown area, livestock ownership, and production in physical units and as a percentage of total production of products for which it is of substantial importance. With very few exceptions there was a fall after 1958 to a low point in 1964 or 1965, and a modest but significant upturn in 1965 or 1966. The share of the private sector in the total fell again in 1967, but the actual level of private output continued to rise for livestock products. In the long run the share of the private sector must decline if the socialized sector becomes more efficient. The 1967 livestock ownership figures for total cattle (but not cows) and pigs also dropped again, for which the reason is not clear, though it could

TABLE 3

Urban Kolkhoz Markets, Selected Years, 1958–67

	1958	1960	1964	1965	1966	1967
Agricultural produce sales (index)						
total (except cattle)................100	100	83	70	72	77	85
Crop products......................100	100	92	77	79	82	n.a.*
Livestock products.................100	100	69	57	59	70	n.a.
Price index (all commodities except cattle). 100	100	100	126	118	119	n.a.
Crop products......................100	100	97	121	113	119	n.a.
Livestock products.................100	100	103	139	129	118	n.a.

* Not available.

be that the increased pay for work on the farms is reducing the attractiveness of private livestock. It is noteworthy that the number of private cows did not fall, as it is probably cows above all which are important for peasant households. In any case, the overall total of livestock in the country did not rise during 1967, and the overall number of pigs fell by 12 percent. Certainly there does not seem to be any evidence of a renewal of restrictions on the private sector.

Another source of evidence on the activity of the private sector is statistics on kolkhoz market trade. Table 3 shows very clearly the fall in sales and the rise in prices on the markets between 1958 and 1964 which resulted from Khrushchev's restrictions on private plots and livestock. In 1965 the trends of both sales and prices changed direction, and sales have continued to increase since then at a substantial rate. Prices of vegetables and potatoes, and to a lesser extent fruit, rose somewhat in 1966, and sales of potatoes actually dropped 1 percent. Sales of fruit and vegetables increased; so the reason for the rise in their prices was presumably greater demand. Altogether, the statistics on kolkhoz market trade are a clear indication that the restrictions on the private sector have indeed been relaxed, and in 1966 and 1967 peasant incomes from sales of private produce should have risen appreciably. The proportion of market sales which consists of kolkhoznik as opposed to kolkhoz produce is not known but may very well have risen since 1964, and the figures in Table 3 would thus understate the effects on the private sector.

Farm and Peasant Incomes

The increases in procurement prices in 1965 led to a reported 16 percent rise in the gross income of kolkhozy in that year, which was followed by a further rise of 15 percent in 1966, as a consequence of the record harvest and the extensive overplan procurements, which are paid at 50 percent above the basic prices. The 1967 rise was only 5 percent, but this on its own contrasts favorably with the total increase between 1958 and 1964, both good harvest years, of 15.4 percent, and comparison with this latter figure highlights the exceptional increases of 1965 and 1966. On this basis, kolkhoznik incomes in money and produce from the farms rose 16 percent in 1965, 16 percent in 1966, and 6 percent in 1967. There has thus been a slight increase in the proportion of kolkhoz income distributed, but most of the rise in peasant incomes from the farms has been the result of the greater revenue of the farms themselves.

Statistics on kolkhoznik incomes are not published systematically, so that no official national average figure is available. We can, however, make a reasonable estimate of the present level of kolkhoznik incomes from the farms and will have to be content with a rough approximation for the rest of peasant incomes. The average monthly pay of kolkhozniki from the farms was recently reported to have been little more than half the pay of sovkhoz workers in 1960, but to have reached three-quarters of the sovkhoz level in 1966 and slightly more than this in 1967. Average monthly sovkhoz pay in 1960 was 53.9 rubles, and in 1966, 79.8 rubles, so this gives us figures for kolkhoznik pay from the farms of about 27 rubles a month or 325 rubles a year in 1960, and about 60 rubles a month or 720 rubles a year in 1966. Applying the official percentage increase of 6 percent to this figure, we get an estimate of 763 rubles per year, or 63–64 rubles per month for 1967 for incomes in money and produce. The share of produce in this is probably less than the 26 percent it was officially reported to be in 1962, as in 1966, at least, the money component of the total income rose much more than the total, by 28 percent as against the combined figure of 16 percent, and this has been the general trend. This is still well below the average sovkhoz worker's earnings, which were probably about 1,000 rubles in 1967, or 83–84 rubles a month, and in fact corresponds to the level of sovkhoz pay about 1962. (It is also just above the new minimum wage, established from January 1, 1968, although this legislation only applies to the state-employed labor force.) Like all averages, of course, these figures conceal wide variations, and the typical pay of peasants engaged in horse and manual labor is certainly considerably lower. At this point we should also note that the rise in average sovkhoz workers' pay between 1960 and 1966 was 48 percent, more than any other category, and two and a half times the overall increase for all state employees from 80.1 to 99.2 rubles monthly. This, however, has not been specifically associated with the post-Khrushchev leadership, as the rate of increase was actually a little faster in 1960–63 than in 1963–66.

We cannot leave the question of kolkhoznik pay here, because, of course, income from the farms is a smaller proportion of total income for kolkhozniki than for sovkhoz workers. Unfortunately, we do not have sufficient information to make the necessary adjustments with any precision. Recently it was stated that the pay of the working members of kolkhoznik families was about two-thirds of total income. If we relate this to our figure of 763 rubles for average pay from the farms in 1967, we would get a total figure of 1,144 rubles per year. However, this certainly gives too high an estimate of average income per working peasant. The first reason is the inclusion of highly-paid senior administrative staff and mechanized workers in the average figure. The second reason is that the figure of two-thirds, cited above, is the proportion of pay from the farms in family income, not just in the income of kolkhozniki who work on the farms, and there are some working members of kolkhoz families who do not work on the farms. Thus, whilst total kolkhoz peasant income from all sources is about half as much again as income from the farms, this total must be divided into a larger number than the income from the farms, so average working peasant income is less than half as much again as average kolkhoznik pay from the farm. There is no basis for quantifying this at all, though there is some ground for thinking that a figure of around 1,000 rubles a year for 1967 for the overall average total money and produce income of kolkhozniki (again including highly-paid senior administrative staff and mechanized workers), although nothing more than a very rough approximation, is of the right order. This was the level of annual average pay of all sovkhoz workers in 1967 (which is also an average covering a similarly wide range), and one or two Soviet articles have suggested that there is now little difference between the incomes of kolkhoz and sovkhoz peasants. For both, the average figures above are considerably higher than the incomes of the majority of unskilled peasant laborers, as the differential between field-workers and mechanized workers is 1:3 or 1:4; for senior administration the ratio is larger still.

Lisichkin, in a review of the new agricultural policy (in which he attributed the success of 1966 largely to the price increases and the greater farm autonomy introduced in March 1965, and said that, as kolkhoznik incomes rose, the supply of labor to the farms increased), gave the impression that kolkhoz and sovkhoz peasants were now in approximately the same financial position. He said specifically that their lack of payment in produce put sovkhoz workers at a disadvantage compared with kolkhozniki because of the state of the trade network. He also cited figures for Krasnogvardeiskiy raion, Crimea, showing that there, even by 1965, kolkhoznik pay was about 6 percent above that of sovkhoz workers. This, however, is only for one raion and in an area where kolkhozy would be expected to enjoy above-average prosperity.

We can reach the same approximate figure of 1,000 rubles per annum by another rough calculation, starting from the statement in a Soviet article that in the RSFSR as a whole the incomes of kolkhozniki were 65 percent of those of workers and employees. The year to which this referred was not stated, but since the article appeared early in 1966, and the tense used was the present, 1964 seems the most likely. The figure applies to the RSFSR, but the USSR as a whole is unlikely to be very different. If we relate this 65 percent to the published national average wage for 1964 of 90.1 rubles per month, we get 58.5 rubles for the kolkhozniki, and, applying the reported increases since then, which total 42.5 percent, we get 83.5 rubles per month, or 1002 rubles per annum for 1967. Of course, this too is an extremely crude approximation, but the various approaches together tend to reinforce each other to some extent. In general, the average kolkhoznik income is still a long way below the 1967 overall national average of 1,236 rubles per year, but after increases in 1965–67 amounting to 42.5 percent in pay from the farms, and an unknown increase in income from sales of private produce, the huge gap once separating them has been substantially reduced.

Evidence of Other Changes

One of the most famous, and most criticized, of Khrushchev's agricultural policies was his drive to increase the importance of maize. Statistics now show that this was promptly curtailed by his successors, as can be seen from Table 4. The area under maize was actually reduced in 1964, although production that year exceeded 1963 because of the very low yield in 1963, and it was cut in 1965 to a level below that of 1958, and less than half the 1961–63 peak. The maize area will presumably remain at around this level, and the criticism has never intended to imply that it should be eliminated, but simply that it can only be grown economically in certain limited areas. It is noteworthy that the 1963 harvest disaster brought an enormous drop in the maize yield, whereas in 1965, on the much smaller area, the yield was very slightly below 1964 and 1966.

Parallel to the relative demise of maize has been the revival of oats, a crop which Khrushchev regarded as unprofitable and the area of which he insisted on drastically reducing.[10] Modest increases in the sown area and the output of this crop occurred in both 1965 and 1966, and may continue, since the old level of 1961 and before has by no means been reached. Finally, the Virgin Lands area under grain has been cut slightly from the 1962–64 peak level, presumably indicating some increase in

---

[10] See Naum Jasny, *Khrushchev's Crop Policy* (Glasgow: George Outram, 1965), chap. III.

concern about the dangers of wind erosion and weed infestation. The latter part of Table 4 provides some confirmation that the declaration of intent to step up supplies of industrial inputs to agriculture has indeed been followed by action. Fertilizer delivered in 1967 was fully 50 percent above the 1964 level, and the increases for other major items were also substantial, particularly for lorries.

CONCLUSION

In the three years 1965–67 gross agricultural output has increased by 2 percent, 10 percent, and 1 percent successively, making a total rise of 13.3 percent, or over 4 percent annually. This compares with a total rise of 13 percent in 1958–64. This contrast serves to summarize the advance

TABLE 4

Selected Indicators Relevant to Agricultural Output, Selected Years, 1958–67

	1958	1960	1961	1962	1963	1964	1965	1966	1967
Area sown to maize (for ripe grain) (million hectares)...............	4.4	5.1	7.2	7.0	7.0	5.1	3.2	3.2*	n.a.†
Production of maize (million tons)....	10.2	9.8	17.1	15.5	11.1	13.8	8.0	8.4	n.a.
Area sown to oats (million hectares)...	14.8	12.8	11.5	6.9	5.7	5.7	6.6	7.2*	n.a.
Production of oats (million tons).....	13.4	12.0	8.9	5.7	4.0	5.5	6.2	9.2	n.a.
Total grain sown area of Virgin Lands (million hectares)‡.........	60.2	60.3	60.5	65.9	65.0	65.8	63.9	62.6	n.a.
Total deliveries Mineral fertilizer (thousand tons of conventional units)...........................	10.6	11.4	12.1	13.6	16.0	22.0	27.1	30.5	33.7
Tractors (thousands).............	n.a.	n.a.	n.a.	(annual average)	"	668	(annual average)	"	806
Trucks "	n.a.	n.a.	n.a.	"	"	255	"	"	362
Agricultural machinery (million rubles).......................	n.a.	n.a.	n.a.	"	"	3,942	"	"	4,667
Cement for social construction in kolkhozy (thousand tons).......	n.a.	n.a.	n.a.	"	"	11,900	"	"	17,042

* Sown areas of maize and oats for 1966 are calculated from production and yield data.
† Not available.
‡ In 1953, the area was 36.1 million hectares.

which has been achieved and about which there can be little dispute. However, it obviously does not mean that the difficulties besetting Soviet agriculture have now been overcome. In his plan speech in October 1967, Baibakov reported that agricultural investment plans were not being fulfilled, and announced the establishment of a union-republican Ministry of Agricultural Construction. This administrative measure may help to simplify procedure and organizations, but will not in itself solve the problem, which is presumably related to the shortage of materials and the traditional lack of priority of agriculture. The effects of this are particularly serious on smaller investment requirements, which, although undramatic, are nevertheless highly important for increasing efficiency and productivity. Unfortunately, it is by now a habit of mind which will probably be difficult to eradicate.

We have not so far mentioned the question of migration from country to town. During Khrushchev's later years, as a result of the fall in peasant incomes after 1958 and the squeeze on the private sector, what has become known as the flight from the land reached extremely serious proportions. Naturally, this had a highly adverse effect on the quality of the agricultural labor force.[11] In view of the rise in incomes, and Lisichkin's statement that this had brought an increase in the supply of labor to the farms, we may surmise that the rate of movement to the towns has probably slowed. A continued secular decline in the proportion of the occupied population in agriculture is to be expected, with increasing mechanization, but it is essential to retain some good-quality labor to operate a mechanized agriculture. This involves what seems to me one of the most formidable of all long-term problems for Soviet agriculture, namely the whole question of communications, amenities, and the quality of rural life. Very heavy investment in roads, and in amenities, cannot be avoided eventually, and the returns will inevitably be slow to appear. Yet without it the flight from the land must surely accelerate again.

The immediate prospects would appear to be for a continuation in the growth of output at a modest rate, with a parallel rise in rural incomes. The 1965–67 rate of increase of output seems rather unlikely to continue, so that the draft five-year plan target for 1970, if it still stands,[12] implying an annual average growth rate of about 4.5 percent, will probably not be fulfilled. Nor does the 1968 projected increase of 7.4 percent seem very realistic. Rises of this size may be achieved for livestock products, but are surely most improbable for crops, especially grain. In the same way, the very large increases in peasants' pay in 1965 and 1966 represent a once-for-all redistribution of income and will not be repeated, though it may continue to rise somewhat faster than the overall average, as in 1967.

Finally, a few remarks seem appropriate on two aspects of the organizational structure of agriculture. The first is the distinction between kolkhozy and sovkhozy. The guaranteed pay for kolkhozniki, following the introduction of pensions (actually announced by Khrushchev in 1964, to take effect from the beginning of 1965), and, on the other hand, the 1967 sovkhoz reform, which involved the adoption of kolkhoz procurement prices in place of the lower sovkhoz delivery prices, have diminished sharply the difference between the two types of farms. The independence of sovkhoz managers to decide production patterns within the bounds set by sales targets, if it is in fact observed, will place them in a very similar position to kolkhoz chairmen with procurement plans. The

---

[11] At the March 1965 CPSU Plenum it was stated that in some parts of the country the average age of able-bodied kolkhoz members was over 50. At about the same time a kolkhoz chairman wrote that 30 percent of the households on his kolkhoz consisted of single elderly people—presumably mostly women.

[12] The revised plan for 1970 published in *Pravda*, October 11, 1967, gives no target for agriculture for 1970.

former practice whereby kolkhozy used to pay higher prices for some inputs than sovkhozy has been abolished. There will still be differences in that a larger proportion of total production will be accounted for by planned sales in sovkhozy, as they have no arrangement corresponding to the guarantee of a proportion of the harvest to kolkhozniki, though they may be permitted to sell a small proportion of output to employees at delivery prices. Kolkhozniki will, for the present at least, presumably retain their larger private plots, and will continue to derive a lower, though probably gradually increasing, share of their total income from the farms. Despite the recent rise, however, the long-term trend of the private sector's share in total output must be downwards. Both kinds of farms will now receive and pay the same prices, including for labor, have more or less the same degree of autonomy (somewhat more for kolkhozy), and for both the ultimate financial responsibility will rest with the state. (It will, of course, be some time before we see what happens if some of the kolkhozy now being given loans to cover members' pay are unable to repay these later, but a return to the situation where the peasants bear the responsibility seems out of the question.)

Lastly, attention should be drawn to what seems to be a promising development in the intrafarm organization of labor, namely the system of *zven'ya*. This is an arrangement whereby small groups of peasants are given an area of land, told what to sow, and left to look after it themselves. There have been a number of reports of successful extension of this arrangement. Average output and earnings for *zveno* workers were nearly double those of other workers on four sovkhozy in Volgograd oblast, and at least one of the farms was entirely organized on the *zveno* system. More than 3000 *zven'ya* were organized in kolkhozy and sovkhozy in Novgorod oblast, according to the obkom first secretary, with very good results, and he emphasizes the importance of the feeling of personal responsibility created. This point was also stressed by another commentator, who regretted that the ending of personal ownership of land had been accompanied by the loss of the feeling of love for the land. He described the *zveno* system tried in a kolkhoz in Voronezh oblast. A group of 12 peasants, mainly neighbors, were given 750 hectares, seed and equipment, and instructions on what to sow. There would be no interference, and they would themselves decide when they worked. They were paid 64 rubles per month each, with a final settlement on the basis of results. The first year the results were very successful, with higher yields and revenue per worker, although they had twice as much land per worker as the rest of the farm. The second year early frost ruined the harvest, so the results seemed inconclusive, but the writer emphasized the feeling of involvement created, and called for the arrangement to be continued, giving land to *zven'ya* for longer periods, although he deplored the fact that many people were not convinced of the system's success. Despite this, the other reports do seem to imply that the system is being tried out more extensively and that generally, where it is used, it is found to give very encouraging results. This is entirely understandable, and it is to be hoped that the arrangement will gradually be instituted more widely and that the promise of most of the early results will be fulfilled.

In the introductory remarks to this survey, I contended that the agricultural reforms which have taken place since Khrushchev's dismissal were the most important ones in the whole economy. We have now examined the measures taken, the rises in procurement prices and cuts in procurement targets, the relaxation of restrictions on the private sector, the reforms in kolkhoz pay and in the system of sovkhoz operation, and the increased industrial supplies and investment plans for agriculture. We have seen the results achieved in total output, in the revival of the private sector, and the big rise in agricultural earnings, particularly of kolkhoz-niki. The crucial change, it seems to me, to which there is no parallel under the industrial reform, is the big rise in incomes and thus in the incentive to work. In contrast, industrial workers are receiving only a marginal material benefit from the industrial reform, which is involving some redistribution in favor of manager and technical staffs. Secondly, there does seem to be reliable evidence that the degree of autonomy of farm managers has increased. Kolkhoz procurement targets were set stable at a lower level than before and have not been raised. (The 1967 level of procurements was only slightly above the constant target set in 1965, and *was* reported as an overfulfillment.) Lisichkin cited examples of increasing management initiative in sovkhozy. In contrast again, it is generally agreed that the independence of industrial managers under the reform has really increased very little, if at all. Taken altogether, the catalogue of changes introduced, and the results achieved, seem to provide ample evidence that the real reforms in the Soviet economy since Khrushchev have been in agriculture rather than in industry.

23 | EAST EUROPEAN ECONOMIC REFORMS

John Michael Montias

The reforms planned or undertaken in the East European countries have varied widely. Hungary has gone far beyond the USSR in decentralization, reliance on the market, and the use of profit-based incentive systems. Other countries, such as Poland, have adhered much more closely to the Soviet model. In Czechoslovakia the economic reforms became associated with political changes unacceptable to the USSR, and the Soviet intervention of 1968 resulted.

These alternative patterns of economic reform are described by John Michael Montias, Professor of Economics at Yale University. The article is reprinted from United States Senate, Committee on the Judiciary, Subcommittee on Antitrust and Monopoly, *Hearings on Economic Concentration* (Washington, D.C.: U.S. Government Printing Office, 1968), Part 7, pp. 3785–92. Some footnotes have been omitted.

INSTITUTIONAL REFORMS designed to transform an entire economic system are so complex and so difficult to comprehend in their entirety that they offer unlimited scope for more or less gratuitous speculation. One may easily draw up plausible conjectures about the motives for the reforms of the East European economic systems or criticize this or that illogical aspect of their construction. It is more difficult, if it is possible at all, to answer the fundamental questions one would like to pose about their eventual effects. Can they be expected to increase the efficiency of the socialist economies, either in their static allocation or in their growth-generating capabilities? Are they systematic enough to take hold, as they did in Yugoslavia, or will they be neutralized and rendered ineffectual by centrifugal counterforces in the same manner as previous half-hearted attempts at changes in the system that were limited to a partial remolding of the command economy? I cannot answer these pivotal questions, but I

428

hope that my remarks will narrow down the area where possible answers might lie.

BACKGROUND

Much can be learned about the reasons for the present reforms and about the factors likely to condition their success or failure from a study of the evolution of the East European economic systems.

There is evidence that the highest authorities in the more developed countries of the area began to recognize the disadvantages of overcentralization almost as soon as replicas of the Soviet planning system were set up and began to function in the late 1940's and early 1950's in their respective economies. They found from experience that it was inefficient to try to centralize the operational management of the economy in any detail. As early as 1952, the Czechoslovak Planning Commission issued instructions to ministries, central administrations, and enterprises with the aim of carrying out a simultaneous "decentralization of national economic planning and of economic management." Only the methodology for drawing up plans at lower levels and the stipulation of "basic targets" were to remain centralized. A similar although more tentative attempt to delegate planning and executive functions to lower organs—mainly to the ministries—occurred in Poland in 1953–54. More far-reaching moves in the same direction were made in Poland, Czechoslovakia, and East Germany in 1958–59. While the early efforts at breaking the bureaucratic logjam in the central coordinating organs fell far short, both in their scope and in their internal coherence, of more recent attempts, both the earlier and the later reforms were meant to fulfill the same broad purpose: to enable the central coordinating authorities to concentrate on essential tasks—particularly on maintaining an overall sectoral balance in the course of rapid development—by freeing their personnel from work required to reconcile the supply and demand for a myriad of commodities and from the exigencies of detailed surveillance and control of plan execution.

It need hardly be stressed that the formal institutional arrangements of an economic system may not reflect its real mode of operation and may give a false image of the real extent of central control over producers' decisions. In the usual state of a command economy, the congestion of communication channels between the center and producing enterprises and the inability of the center to take certain decisions in time to affect the operations of the enterprise force producers to exercise their own initiative. The central planners must reconcile themselves at all times to a certain degree of *de facto* decentralization. The cumulative effect of decisions escaping central direction may even on occasion cause important lapses from plan fulfillment and seriously thwart the planners' will. Thus the nominal delegation of decision-making authority to lower organs may only express the recognition of an existing state of affairs. Decentralization will only impair the coordination of the supply and demand for individual materials and items of equipment, to the extent that the center previously did coordinate input and output decisions for these goods. In the same vein it may be argued that a more systematic balancing of aggregate inputs and outputs by the Planning Commission, accompanied by the devolution of coordinating decisions for individual commodities onto lower organs, even if these organs entertain an imperfect view of the overall market, may be an improvement over ritualistic but ineffective attempts at meshing the supply and output plans for thousands of individual items. The reforms attempted in Eastern Europe in the 1950's failed in the sense that overcentralization persisted or recurred in spite of the ostensible delegation of planning and executive authority to ministries and to still lower organs of the state apparatus. The reasons for this retrogression are instructive in the light of current developments.

The first and most obvious explanation is that entrenched bureaucrats resisted the delegation of decision-making powers and undermined the reforms. This argument is not fully convincing for, up to the late 1950's, none of the reforms could be said to have seriously disturbed the bested interests of the planning or managerial bureaucracy. Executive titles were reassigned; responsibilities were shifted; nevertheless, politically loyal bureaucrats with experience in planning and high-level management stood an excellent chance of keeping their jobs in the administration or of finding an equivalent niche if their old posts were abolished. Upper-level functionaries, may, however, have impeded the reforms by their unwillingness or inability to change their style of work, in particular by maintaining their petty tutelage over enterprises instead of encouraging managers to exercise their own initiative in matters that did not seriously affect state interests.

To find a more satisfactory explanation for the failure of the early reforms, we must look deeper into the nature of a command economy and consider the impact of a partial decentralization of decision making on these systems. The East European economies were partitioned along functional lines according to sectors—industrial, transportation, and so forth—whose main criterion of success was the volume of their output or, if they produced a service, the value of their activity at centrally fixed prices. Each sector claimed as much capital and labor and as much of the materials and services produced by other sectors or imported from abroad as it could, since the more inputs were made available to producers in the sector the greater the output they were capable of turning out. The chief organ responsible for dividing up scarce resources and assigning them to competing uses according to the priorities laid down by the Communist party was the Central Planning Commission. When, in the course of institutional reforms, ministries were assigned certain planning and executive functions formerly exercised by the Planning Commission, they made their decisions from the narrow viewpoint of their sector, instead of defending nationwide interests. In the end, intersectoral conflicts had to be resolved by the Planning Commission. Since input and output decisions in any modern economy tend to be highly interdependent, conflicts of interests among enterprises belonging to different sectors were the rule rather than the exception; and central authorities were deluged with appeals which had to be resolved expeditiously, if not efficiently, if the economy was to move forward with a minimum of disruption toward established goals. It should be noted, incidentally, that intersectoral conflicts tended to be more acute when development plans were excessively ambitious and resources were grossly inadequate to fulfill them, for the disproportions inherent in the plans had to be corrected on an *ad hoc* basis by the Planning Commission. In such situations, there was hardly any chance at all that spontaneous coordination between representatives of the various sectors could supplant the need for coordination from above during the period when the plans were ostensibly being carried out. In sum, the failure of the system was in its inability to substitute indirect inducements for direct commands, so as to cause enterprises to moderate their appetite for additional resources.

Given the type of price system in effect at the time, one may wonder whether any incentive scheme could have been devised that would have harmonized sectoral interests with central policy. The prices of goods traded among socialized enterprises, far from equating supply and demand and from expressing the relative scarcities of the goods to which they were attached, diverged significantly from production costs for reasons that had more to do with administrative inertia than with the state of their demand. As revisions of wholesale price levels were made only every three to five years and average wages tended to creep upward despite central controls, the production costs of goods exhibiting lower-than-average gains in labor productivity had every opportunity to rise above their established prices.

Indeed, the occasional revisions of centrally administered prices were not coordinated in any way with the partial reforms in the system that were promulgated prior to the 1960's. Under these circumstances, attempts to substitute macroeconomic directives—limits on costs, approved wage bills, gross output targets, sales quotas—for targets expressed in physical terms and for centrally ordained rations foundered on the conflicts of interests I have already described: enterprises complying with the letter of the directives rather than with their spirit disrupted the intersectoral flow of output and upset microeconomic proportions by biasing the assortment of their output or the makeup of their orders for inputs. They did this, of course, with a view to swelling their profits, adding to the value of their production, or otherwise qualifying for the bonuses awarded to managers on the basis of one or more of the success criteria established by higher authorities.

CURRENT REFORMS

We may now consider whether the economic reforms presently being carried out in the Soviet Union and in Eastern Europe are well enough designed and go sufficiently far to check the centripetal tendencies that nullified previous efforts in this direction. Whether a particular reform will take root depends largely on the nature of the price system and of the incentive schemes that will be instituted, for these two institutional parameters will determine the extent to which the planners will be able to use prices, as well as monetary and fiscal policy, to guide managers to decisions compatible with centrally established goals, instead of setting targets for individual commodities and of rationing out materials and equipment to producers.

With the exception of Yugoslavia, which has recently taken further steps toward the liberalization of its socialized economy, the countries of Eastern Europe have all retained important elements of the command economy in their reformed systems. Administrative rationing of key resources and centralized price setting for basic producer goods are still in evidence from Vladivostok to Prague. The amalgamation of enterprises into very large units monopolizing production in each subsector—a common feature of all the reforms—has practically eliminated competition as a source of efficiency. It is extremely unlikely under these conditions that the central planners will be able to mobilize and channel the initiative of plant managers—operating under the tutelage of enterprise directors and of the heads of sectoral administrators—precisely toward the goals mapped out by party authorities. The reforms may nonetheless bring about a net improvement if enterprises under the influence of these decentralized inducements happen to choose inputs and outputs acceptable to the central decision makers even though the resulting pattern of allocation may diverge from that which was initially expected or planned for by these authorities. The latter, by abstaining from administrative interference with producers' decisions, by resisting centripetal tendencies, and by pressing for further consolidation of the decentralized institutions created by the reforms, will reveal their preference for the new patterns of inputs and outputs, and, more broadly, for the overall performance characteristics of the institutionally renovated economy. It is this ultimate ratification by high officials in the Communist party and in the government which previous reforms never received.

After these general considerations, it may be in order to list the chief common features and differences among the reforms, as they are contemplated or actually being put into effect at the present time in Bulgaria, Czechoslovakia, East Germany, Hungary, Poland, Romania, and Russia. This descriptive listing, it should be noted, is confined to the industrial sector, and, within that sector, to socialized enterprises. (Except in Poland where experiments are going on with the leasing of state property to private operators in certain retail services, including gas stations, the reforms hitherto do not offer substantially wider scope to private enterprise.)

Similarities among Countries

The common features are these:

1. The chief coordinating organs—the Planning Commission, the Ministry of Finance, and the Ministry of Foreign Trade—will resort to financial inducements to guide socialized enterprises to desired goals and will restrict the scope of target setting and of physical quotas for materials, capital investments, and imports.

2. Enterprises will be given more autonomy in drafting their plans and in the course of plan execution with respect to the volume and composition of their output and their finances. They will have more choice in the selection of their suppliers (in the case of wholesale and retail establishments) and of their contractors and subcontractors (in the case of producing enterprises). Contracts between enterprises will no longer merely ratify and fill in the decisions of superior authorities as to who should supply whom with what. The financial independence of enterprises will be enhanced by permitting them to retain an appreciably larger part of their profits than in the past.

3. In industry, enterprises are to be organized in "associations" or "sectoral directorates" exclusively responsible for the management and development of a specified range of industrial production.

4. The national bank and the specialized investment and trade banks, wherever they lead a separate existence, will exert greater influence over enterprises via the extension of short-term credits to cover a large part of their working capital and long-term credits to finance a substantial share of their long-term investments. The banks will discriminate in the allocation of short- and long-term credit according to the ability of enterprises to repay loans (although the criterion of social return, if it differs from the criterion of profitability for the enterprise, is still expected to dominate credit allocation).

5. Prices of producer goods are to be revised—if one of the periodic revisions has not recently taken place—with a view to making them conform more closely to "socially necessary costs." (Although complete information is lacking on details of price formation, in certain countries, including Bulgaria and Romania, a general tendency to interpret "socially necessary costs" more flexibly—for example to include capital charges and rents—may be discerned.) The need to revise prices more frequently in line with changing costs and demand conditions is recognized everywhere, but the practical conclusions that will be drawn from this consideration are likely to differ from country to country.

Differences among Countries

The main differences are these:

1. In only two countries (Czechoslovakia and Hungary) will enterprises and associations be allowed to set prices for any significant proportion of output for standardized producer goods (as distinguished from goods produced on special orders). In Hungary, where "free prices" for producer goods are slated to comprise a much larger share of total sales than in Czechoslovakia, 28 percent of sales for domestically produced raw materials and 85 percent for processed goods (including all timber and paper goods and all construction projects) will be free of direct price controls.

2. Bonuses to management hinge on the fulfillment of profit plans in Poland and East Germany; on profit and sales plans in the Soviet Union; on "gross income," equivalent to value added, in Czechoslovakia; on total profits irrespective of plan in Hungary; and on the growth of labor productivity and profits in Bulgaria.[1] In Romania bonuses will undoubtedly be tied to plan fulfillment, but it is not yet apparent whether the link will be to profits or to some other "indicator."

3. The number of binding directives issued to enterprises by ministries and other authorities varies from country to country. In Czechoslovakia and Hungary where the changes introduced are the most profound, binding directives will, wherever possible, be abolished, although some physical targets are retained in the yearly plans and a number of scarce materials are still on the ration list. But the wage bill, at least in Czechoslovakia and Hungary, will not be directly set by the center; it will be indirectly influenced by progressive taxes on wages, which will discourage the excessive disbursement of profits for this purpose. In the Soviet Union, as well as in most of the remaining countries, the wage bill will still be subject to direct control.

4. The degree to which investments will be decentralized in particular will be initiated and financed by enterprises from their own funds supplemented by bank loans differs significantly from country to country. It is interesting that the Czechoslovak authorities, mindful of their adverse experience of the late 1950's when investments were too rapidly "decontrolled" and inflationary pressures were released, adopted a fairly conservative policy in this regard, although they are likely to give enterprises more leeway in investment policy than the less developed nations of the

---

[1] The size of the bonus depends on the growth in labor productivity, but the bonus is financed from plan profits. Note that labor productivity is defined as the ratio of the enterprise's gross output to its labor force and that incentives thus still hinge indirectly on gross output, which includes the value of materials processed. This type of bonus, which induces the squandering of material inputs, has now been rejected in the majority of East European countries.

area, which are still bent on marshaling the greatest possible financial resources for the construction of new factories.

5. Some reforms, including the Hungarian, call for the delegation to the enterprise of certain import and export decisions and for the right of the enterprise to retain a part of its foreign-currency earnings. In Bulgaria, extra allotments of foreign currency can be obtained only if an enterprise's exports exceed plan. In Czechoslovakia, which has suffered an acute shortage of convertible foreign currency in recent years, the provisions in this regard are less liberal; nevertheless, a few very large exporting enterprises like the Škoda Works in Pilsen will be brought closer to their foreign markets by the creation of special foreign-trade enterprises operating in the framework of the same industrial association as the producing enterprise.

6. In the Soviet Union, Bulgaria, and East Germany the reforms were introduced piecemeal, starting with "experimenting enterprises," and were gradually extended to cover the bulk of industrial output. In the other countries the reforms were put into effect in all industrial enterprises simultaneously.

Since the reforms everywhere in Eastern Europe are open-ended in character and undergoing constant modification in the light of experience, there is no reason to believe that the similarities and differences I have listed will continue to prevail. There can be no question, however, that the Communist leaders of Czechoslovakia and Hungary have so far endorsed a more profound institutional transformation than other East European states. Perhaps the most radical departure from the previous system they have ratified consists in giving free scope to producer goods' prices for an appreciable number of commodities and in severing managerial incentives from plan fulfillment. There is still some hesitation on the subject among Communist officials and among economists in these two countries, but the moment cannot be far off when decisions of enterprises based on considerations of profitability will be held valid, even if they cause deviations from approved plans. At the other end of the scale, the Romanian government has been the most tardy in scheduling systematic changes and the most guarded in framing reforms when it finally decided to do so late in 1967. If one were to grade the remaining countries according to the intensity of the reforms being carried out (all lying between the extremes already listed), East Germany and Bulgaria would come out slightly ahead of the Soviet Union and Poland.

Timing and Scope of Reform

Our sample of experimenting economies is too small to account convincingly for the intensity of a country's reforms by its level of development or other special circumstances. Nevertheless, several factors seem to have influenced the timing and the scope of the reforms.

In general, the economies that are high on the intensity scale are relatively highly developed, export manufactures on a large scale, and have grown at relatively slow rates since the beginning of the 1960's.[2]

East Germany stands lower on this scale than we should expect, since it fulfills all three of the above conditions; but it may be supposed that its extraordinarily repressive dictatorship works against economic liberalization, which could easily spill over into the political arena. Walter Ulbricht's unwillingness to tolerate the kind of free-for-all discussion about the best "model" for a socialist system that has blossomed out in Hungary and Czechoslovakia since 1963 may also have retarded the adoption of more radical measures.

While a high level of development and economic dependence on the export of manufactures are to some extent correlated in Eastern Europe, it is at least suggestive that Hungary and Bulgaria are both more intensively engaged in exports of manufactures than one would expect from the level of development they have achieved and are also more committed to reform than Poland and Romania, which may be taken as their respective counterparts in development.[3]

It is easier to find convincing reasons why levels of development and of manufactured exports should be related to the intensity of reforms than to establish the statistical relation among these variables. The gist of the argument is that a centralized system of the Soviet type is a suitable vehicle for "extensive growth"—a rapid expansion of industrial output accomplished by dint of massive injections of labor and capital, using mainly established techniques—but that it is not capable of maintaining smooth and rapid "intensive growth" at a later stage of development based on technical progress, improved organization, product development, and new combinations of inputs capable of yielding increases in output with only moderate net additions to total inputs. If this argument is accepted, it will be at least as evident that a system where production is determined by central authorities vested with the responsibility for distributing the capital and the materials required by enterprises to fulfill

---

[2] From 1961 to 1965, the year-to-year increase in national income, according to official estimates, averaged about 2 percent in Czechoslovakia and East Germany, 4–5 percent in Hungary, a little over 6 percent in Bulgaria, Poland, and the Soviet Union, and 9 percent in Romania.

[3] In 1965 Hungary exported per capita a value of $81 of manufactured goods (not including foodstuffs); Bulgaria, $56; Poland, $34, and Romania, $16.5. Yet, according to Hungarian estimates, the national income per capita of Hungary was more or less on the same level as that of Poland and only 20 percent larger than that of Romania. In 1964 Bulgaria's national income was estimated to be $470 per capita as against $498 in Poland and $423 in Romania. Note also that Czechoslovakia, with a national income per head less than twice as great as Romania's, exported more than seven times as much per capita in manufactured goods. (Exports of manufactures were computed from official trade statistics converted at the official exchange rate, a procedure yielding meaningful results inasmuch as the trade of Comecon countries is carried on at "foreign-exchange prices" approximating prices prevailing in world trade.)

their output targets hardly provides a proper environment for exporters of manufactured goods competing on world markets for orders depending crucially on the quality, servicing, and technology of their products. The situation in the Comecon Market, which was isolated for many years from the competition of manufacturers in capitalist economies, has changed radically in the past decade. The Czechs and the East Germans must now supply technologically advanced capital goods to win orders from their less developed customers in the Soviet area if they wish to meet the competition of Western suppliers. Exporters must have a considerable degree of financial and organizational autonomy to develop products that will preserve or widen their markets, both in Eastern and in Western Europe. What makes this competitive struggle so crucial is that the more developed countries of Eastern Europe are highly vulnerable to fluctuations in the world demand for their manufactures, due to the hypertrophied expansion of their heavy industry: lacking the raw materials basis for their industrial complex and suffering from a shortage of domestically produced farm products, they must increase their exports of manufactures at least as fast as their industry grows in order to pay for their imports of materials and foodstuffs.

It would be an error to infer from the conjectured need for more thorough reforms in the highly developed East European economies that the institutional changes will be more successful wherever they happen to be more systematic and more profound. For there are also greater obstacles to success in a country like Czechoslovakia than in Bulgaria or Romania. To extent that most prices, even where the reforms are most far-reaching, will be linked to past production costs reflecting an inefficient state of affairs, they will not offer a reliable guide to determine which production lines should be curbed and which developed, which factories should be closed down and which expanded. But even if it turned out that prices did emit the right signals, it is doubtful whether the painful structural changes to which they would point would be systematically undertaken. In 15 to 20 years of extensive development, hundreds of inefficient plants have mushroomed forth in Czechoslovakia, especially in rural, less developed areas, which can only prosper as long as their inefficiency is concealed behind the more or less profitable operations of the multiple-plant, monopolistic enterprises to which they are subordinate. The elimination of inefficient units would create temporary pockets of unemployment with undesirable social and political side effects. (Whatever the demerits of the old system, it had the advantage in the eyes of workers of protecting them from this liability.) These structural problems are less acute in countries such as Poland, Bulgaria, and Romania, industrial late comers where the introduction of borrowed technologies has been so rapid that obsolete productive capacity built up in earlier years contributes only a relatively small share of industrial output.

The paramount importance of prices correctly reflecting relative scarcities—or at least coming closer to this norm than prereform prices—is that this will make it possible to calculate meaningful costs and returns and thus provide an *impersonal measure of efficiency*, which had so far been absent. Anyone today may, with some justice, deny that an enterprise should be wound up or a product line discontinued because none of the indicators at hand provides totally convincing evidence of the inefficiency of these operations. Costs are so distorted by subsidized raw material prices, by deviations from opportunity cost in foreign trade, and by the absence or the inadequate levels of capital charges that no firm conclusions about the inefficiency of a given operation can be inferred from them. An incontrovertible measure of efficiency would equip "rationalizers" of production with a weapon that, while it might not be proof against political lobbying by threatened interests, would permit them to offer a good deal more resistance against arbitrary intereference than in the recent past.

THE ORGANIZATION OF INDUSTRY IN THE CONTEXT OF THE REFORMS

The trend in Eastern Europe since the late 1950's has been toward the merger of small enterprises and especially toward the creation of powerful associations reminiscent of cartels or holding companies.[4] Integration is generally proceeding along horizontal lines in Eastern Europe, except in Hungary and East Germany where at least some enterprises have been integrated vertically—from raw materials to finished products.

The planners in authority are counting on a number of distinct advantages from the consolidation of enterprises and from their association in sectoral directorates with a monopoly of planning and production for a range of products in each industry. First they hope to facilitate the coordination of individual inputs and outputs within the broader framework of the consolidated balances for groups of commodities prepared by the Planning Commission. The schema the authorities have in mind would require the procurement organization attached to each association to communicate its requirements for materials and capital goods, within the aggregate limit imposed by the plan directives, to the sales organizations of the associations capable of supplying them with these inputs. Negotiations between suppliers and their customers would go on until every enterprise had fully committed its output and had contracted for sufficient supplies to produce this output in the desired assortment.

The advocates of mergers and associations do not explain why lateral liaison should work in the present setup when all previous attempts to bring it about failed in the past. The obstacle to spontaneous coordination

---

[4] The most recent reforms in Czechoslovakia, for example, merged 1,371 old into 713 new industrial enterprises. These enterprises are grouped into 85 "productive economic units" with wide-ranging powers over their "subjects."

lay, and still lies, in the mutual interdependency of production programs: No producing plant can specify its inputs until its output-mix has been pinned down, but its own output-mix depends on the demands from enterprises that directly or indirectly supply it with material inputs. Several revisions of the contracts between suppliers and their clients, at a considerable cost in time wasted and energy, would be required to achieve anything like consistency in the production programs of all plants.

Second, the designers of the reforms believe that research and development can best be carried on within very large enterprises or by agencies whose management will be close enough to the production problems of an industrial sector to guide research toward concrete and relevant objectives but which will have a wide enough *vue d'ensemble* to avoid the duplication of R.&D. efforts typical of more fragmented organizations. Similar considerations about the need for ensuring close ties between producers and their foreign clients and suppliers militated in favor of the type of monopolistic organization that was generally adopted in Eastern Europe.

The Czech and Slovak writers who have given a good deal of attention of late to issues of market organization have thrown up a number of objections to the "monopolistic management" of production sectors. First and foremost, those among them who favor the creation of a full-fledged socialist market economy deplore the elimination of competition. They argue that initiative and drive, which were stifled under the old system, can only be recaptured in a competitive climate. A second point that is often made is that the monopoly management of a production sector (corresponding to a given range of goods) tends to perpetuate the old bureaucratic procedures for allocating materials and capital goods—especially the mechanical distribution of the quotas of rationed materials available to the sector on the basis of "standard" shares for each region and for every enterprise within a region, thereby "embalming" the negative features of the old system. Third, the monopoly position of an enterprise or of a group of enterprises distorts the nature and direction of technical progress, especially if the prices of the outputs are set by a centralized agency. For it has been observed, at least under present Czechoslovak conditions, that R.&D. efforts are biased toward innovations capable of raising output and cutting costs in preference to those that might improve the quality of the product or the range of choice open to consumers. Finally, and most obvious of all, a sales monopoly in a line of products invites open price increases wherever prices are free to move and covert increases where they are not.

There has also been increased recognition among Czechoslovak economists that the net effect of the positive and negative elements of monopoly management may differ appreciably from one sector or product line to the other. The trouble, according to some analysts, is that organizational forms are cut from a single pattern by central authorities, ignoring the need for differentiation. Eugene Löbl, the eminent Slovak economist and intellectual leader, argues that there is a natural symbiosis between large and small firms, the latter subcontracting for the former or filling the interstices of market demand that the giants cannot easily satisfy. Small independent enterprises are more "resonant" to market signals than large; they make more efficient use of market information

Granted that a mixed solution is optimal, with a very few large enterprises carrying on most of the R.&D. and many small independent units adjusting flexibly to market demand, how should such a state be brought about? Are the system managers located in Prague or Budapest capable of working out an optimal scheme of organization and then of decreeing its adoption? Or should they encourage the spontaneous formation of enterprises—by merger, spin-off, or the creation of new ventures —until some sort of institutional equilibrium will have been reached?[5] In short, does decentralization of the decision-making process, which so far has only been extended to the choice of inputs and outputs within bounds set by the center, require the decentralization of organizational forms as well?

These far-reaching questions open up a host of related problems about the role of the center as arbiter or regulator of independent enterprises, about short- and long-run managerial incentives and their relation to profit maximization over a variable horizon, about the incidence of risk and the responsibility of managers to society—matters which as far as I know have not been thought through by the economists crusading for more profound reforms. But the fact that they have been raised at all and that the reforms in most East European countries, including the Soviet Union, are considered open-ended, augurs well for the future evolution of economic institutions in these socialist states.

---

[5] So far the central authorities in the Soviet Union and in the East European countries under discussion have retained the exclusive power to create, to merge, and to wind up enterprises. In Yugoslavia, by contrast, there has been a substantial delegation of organizational powers to republics, communes, and even to existing enterprises.

24 | CONVERGENCE OF ECONOMIC SYSTEMS IN EAST AND WEST

H. Linnemann,
J. P. Pronk
J. Tinbergen

For a number of years there has been considerable discussion among scholars about whether the Soviet and East European social- ist planned economies and the Western capitalist market economies are becoming more alike. Strong differences of opinion have been expressed. In the following article, three scholars at the Netherlands Economic Institute at Rotterdam (Tinbergen is director of the Insti- tute) argue that the two systems are indeed "converging" insofar as their economic aspects are concerned. However, they leave as open questions (1) whether ideological polititions are being depolarized, and (2) whether political accommodation between the two blocs can be achieved.

This article is reprinted by permission from Emile Benoit (ed.), *Dis- armament and World Economic Interdependence* (Oslo: Universitets- forlaget, 1967), pp. 246–60. Most of the footnotes have been omitted.

1. Introductory

This study tries to summarize the changes in the social systems of East and West in the last few decades, with the main emphasis on the socio- economic aspects. Other important aspects such as the political or group decision-making and the cultural aspects will be neglected; one argument for doing so may be that economic forces are among the most fundamen- tal. The main criteria used will therefore be taken from the theory of economic policy. This implies that the aims and means of that policy will be taken as the main characteristics of the systems and their changes.

The subject seems important for two reasons. On the one hand, changes in economic systems may entail changes in political and cultural order, at least according to Marxist views. On the other hand, changes in the socio-economic order of East and West will exert influence on the systems chosen in the South, the uncommitted developing world. The importance of the subject stands out if, as the authors believe, a converging movement can be observed.

The arrangement of this report is based on what the authors consider to be the most important elements of any socio-economic order. As already stated, a distinction must be made between aims and means. Together with the main aims we will discuss, in Section 2, their fulfillment as observed so far. The means will be subdivided into qualitative means or institutions and quantitative means or instruments of socio-economic policy. The former will be discussed in Sections 3 through 6 and the latter in Sections 7 through 10. Section 11 offers a theoretical explanation of the observed changes, using the analytical instruments of welfare economics. Section 12 summarizes our findings and makes an attempt at predicting further changes.

2. Aims, Fundamental and Derived, and Their Fulfillment

The aims of any socio-economic system can be expressed in very general or in more specific terms; the latter give a more precise picture. Means are used to attain the aims, and they do so along a causal chain, which may be short or long. The shortest chain occurs when a means coincides with one of the aims. Thus, if increased health is among the aims, a hospital constitutes a means which almost coincides with this aim. In the case of longer chains, we may say we pass from the means proper to intermediate aims first and reach the ultimate aim afterwards. Reasoning backward the latter may be called the fundamental aim and the former (or intermediate) aim the derived aim. A well-known tendency in real life is to consider some means (or derived aims) as "ends (or aims) in themselves." An example of a longer causal chain is provided by investments, which (1) raise production, hence (2) income, (3) consumption, and finally (4) human satisfaction. The latter constitutes a fundamental aim, while higher production represents a derived aim. An example of a means which became an end in itself is entrepreneurial freedom; economists of the liberal school (in the European sense of that word) argued that this freedom raises efficiency and hence general well-being, but for many businessmen it constitutes an end in itself. Marx argued that public ownership eliminates exploitation, while many communist politicians identify it with an end in itself.

The fundamental aim of Eastern systems is often formulated as the elimination of exploitation; more specifically this signifies the elimination of unearned income for people in the productive age class. The fundamental aim of Western systems is often formulated as the maximum of well-being, specified as a combination of a high average consumption and equity in distribution or social justice. Opinions and interpretations diverge more in the West than in the East, diverging in particular whenever it comes to defining social justice and to choosing the weights given to the components of average consumption and its distribution.

Among the derived aims the following stand out for Eastern systems: (1) community property of the means of production, (2) a high level of investments, (3) priority to capital goods industries, (4) a high level of education. Moreover it is characteristic for these systems that they specify their production and trade pattern in great detail.

The derived aims of the more advanced Western systems have often been formulated as (1) high and stable employment, (2) a fairly high level of investment, (3) a reduction of income inequality, (4) stable prices, and (5) as much freedom as possible.

The main features of the degree of fulfillment attained are, for the East: (1) an overwhelming portion of the means of production is owned by the community in the Soviet Union, smaller portions in people's democracies, with probably the lowest figure in Yugoslavia, where it has been estimated to be one-half; (2) investment, measured with Western methods, is at about one-quarter of national income; (3) growth rates of capital goods industries as a percentage of those of consumer goods industries at about 170 in the thirties and 107 for 1965; (4) education enrollment at levels near those of the United States and clearly surpassing those of Western Europe.

For the advanced countries of the West fulfillment may be characterized by saying that (1) unemployment in Northern and Central Europe is negligible but not in the United States; (2) investment is between 15 and 20 percent of national income (and 30 percent in Japan); (3) income inequality after tax may have fallen from 0.75 to 0.55 (expressed as the average absolute deviation from the mean); (4) prices are not stable but rise by about 3 percent per annum in Western Europe and 2 percent per annum in the United States; (5) freedom decreases for the ruling classes but is still characteristic for many activities of the majority of the people.

In an attempt to compare and to appraise the aims and their fulfillment in East and West we should add that some aims of the West are considered self-evident for the East (for instance, high and stable employment and stable prices) and vice versa (for instance, a high level of education). We may also add that levels of living are higher in the advanced Western countries than in Eastern countries, but that the rate of increase in GNP is higher in the East. For the fifties it is estimated by Western experts to be 7 percent per annum as against 5 percent in Western Europe, 3 percent in the Anglo-Saxon countries and some 9 percent in Japan. Recently the rate of growth in the Soviet Union declined and the 1964 figure is estimated at some 4 percent. In this connection Alexeyev stated that the moment of overtaking Western economies has been postponed somewhat. The decline in the rate of growth of the Soviet Union may be interpreted as another example of convergence alongside the ones to be discussed below.

Most important perhaps is the statement that, their differing formulation notwithstanding, the fundamental aims of East and West are not so far apart anymore. The elimination of exploitation in essence constitutes a change in income distribution and in this formulation also ranks high in Western societies. Though by other means, these societies have arrived at an income distribution (after tax) which probably compares favorably with that of Eastern economies. High average consumption is increasingly becoming a main objective also in Eastern economies. The existing differences in level must be understood partly as a result of historical data: Eastern countries started their development later.

3. Qualitative Means or Institutions; Planning

A socio-economic order consists of a number of institutions, each of them handling their instruments of policy. We may make a subdivision into concrete and abstract institutions, the latter constituting legal rules. Concrete institutions are production units (factories, farms, shops), the transportation system, schools, banks (central and other), insurance institutions, the tax administration, police and army, planning agencies, and organizations such as trade unions, political parties, and other associations. They all have certain tasks, usually well known. The task of the tax administration is not always completely understood; not only does it collect money to finance public expenditures, but it also regulates, by so doing, the level of demand that can be exerted by private consumers.

Abstract institutions are property rights, markets, and the degree of decentralization in production decisions and pricing.

Some of the main differences in institutions between East and West are that the planning agencies are much larger in Eastern countries since they have to plan many more details from a central point; that private property rights are restricted in the East to consumer goods and a small portion of capital goods; that markets are less regulated in the West than in the East; and that production and pricing decisions are considerably more decentralized in Western than in Eastern countries. In Eastern countries, large numbers of decisions take the form of orders by central agencies, for instance decisions on what to produce and to whom to sell or from whom to buy.

Both types of systems have changed, however; some changes have been temporary and have been followed by opposite changes later. Others seem to have been of a more lasting character. In this and in the following section, the main changes will be described and appraised.

We will start this description by summarizing some of the characteristics of planning in both systems.

Eastern, especially Soviet, planning is overwhelmingly carried out by government institutions. There are various levels: the all-Union and lower ones. In 1957 a major reform consisted of the establishment of the then about 100 sovnarkhozy or geographical subdivisions, whose planning units took over considerable portions of the sector planning, formerly under the responsibility of central ministries for a number of industries. The number of sovnarkhozy was later reduced to some 50, with some grouping into 17 bigger units. Lower organs down to single production units have their part to play in the process too. The number of civil servants in the central agency (now again Gosplan) is several thousands. In Yugoslavia the number declined from over 1,000 to a few hundreds after 1952.

The tasks of the planning apparatus consist of drawing up plans for different time units, up to 20 years. Among these the annual plan has great operational significance. This plan specifies a few thousands of production figures, but the number is declining. The plan also specifies investments, foreign trade, and, remarkably, which factory has to supply which other factory. Quite recently, this begins to change (cf. Section 5). In the late fifties, some 6 percent of all production was planned at the Union level, 71 percent at the Republic level and 23 percent at the local level. Similarly, there is a size limit to the projects appraised at the center. Planning for consumption is indicative only, as rationing was abolished years ago already; agricultural production is not planned completely: only the deliveries to the non-farm sector.

In the early phases of Soviet planning targets were formulated, not in macro-economic terms, but in quantities of the main commodities. Later on, money was introduced as a common denominator, and in recent years national income concepts are increasingly used, though defined differently from Western concepts. The growth rates of capital good industries were chosen higher than those of consumer good industries, the ratio of the growth rates being 1.70 in the period 1929–40, 1.00 in 1933, 1.30 in 1964, and 1.07 in 1965.

The complicated hard core of planning was indicated as the balance method, approximately identical with what Western economists now call the input-output method, but the use of mathematics was avoided until 1956. The method was not used in the traditional Western way where the final bill of goods is considered given, and production volumes are unknowns. This facilitates corrections to a considerable extent. Today the study of mathematical methods is in full swing, continuation of the older methods of trial and error becoming increasingly more difficult with the rise in number of products and qualities.

The procedure of planning seems to be one of trial and error, too, in that the following succession of steps is taken:
(1) formulation of some general targets by the government,
(2) scrutiny of the consistency of these targets by Gosplan,
(3) announcement of these targets to all lower levels,
(4) preparation of draft plans by single factories, shops etc.,
(5) fitting together of such draft plans by higher levels, while consulting

various types of agencies (lower authorities, research agencies, sector authorities, group organizations), repeating the contacts as long as discrepancies occur, and finally

(6) fixing the plan.

The number of revisions in the light of new evidence was large, giving the impression of a high degree of trial and error in the procedure and entailing considerable difficulties. The natural conclusion seems to have been drawn, namely to decentralize larger portions of the decisions. This means less items to be planned at the center, more at lower levels, down even to the single factory (cf. Section 5).

Western planning started in large enterprises and was virtually absent at government level before 1914. The two wars and the great depression brought government intervention, which gradually required coordination; and so planning then started also from the top, mainly for broad policy measures, but during the most difficult periods also directed at detailed allocation of scarce resources. After post-war reconstruction was over, a number of countries maintained some central planning, mostly in order to give indirect guidance to the economy (United Kingdom, the Netherlands, Norway, and France, soon followed by the United States). Planning in France was in more detail than elsewhere. The main emphasis in the other countries mentioned was on employment policy, balance of payments equilibrium, income distribution, and price stability. French planning was also directed at development aims and later the other countries also included this aim in their planning. Italy, Sweden, Denmark, and Belgium followed. Part of the planning activities was induced by the Marshall Plan. In the last few years there has been an increased tendency to plan for development and to do so sector-wise, using indirect instruments for the private sector but affecting the public sector directly.

4. The Degree of International Centralization

As long as the Soviet Union was the only communist-ruled country, the degree of centralization in decisions on the interregional division of labor in the Eastern world was relatively high—the main decisions were taken in Moscow. After World War II the scene changed. Even though the Soviet Union had overwhelming power to impose its will, formal and increasingly also actual power to decide was partly handed over to the "people's democracies" of Eastern Europe. China anyway followed its own course. Soviet experience in governing a "socialist economy" played a considerable part, however, in shaping the other countries' policies and so autarky was given emphasis even for small countries, as much as possible. One argument in its favor was that planning can be more consistent, another that national independence can be furthered. The creation of steel industries everywhere is a well-known consequence of that view. Trade was considered a secondary device to get rid of surpluses and fill up the worst deficiencies; it was, in the beginning, negotiated only after the national plans had been drawn up. Gradually the use of international exchange was recognized and some coordination envisaged, resulting in the creation of Comecon. Until 1963 trade agreements were kept in bilateral equilibrium, however. This was believed to be a necessary element of the system. But planning of the international exchange of goods was integrated with national planning and became more systematic. As criteria for an international division of labor became necessary, the concept of comparative advantages began to play a role. This required cost comparisons, and prices and exchange rates reflecting the real cost structure (cf. also Section 9). Considerable revisions of price structures took place, including the revaluation of the ruble. It was finally discovered that multilateral equilibrium represented a higher welfare for all concerned, so the condition of bilateralism was given up in 1963. Even so the bilateral component still represents a large portion of trade between the communist countries, as is the case in Western Europe. In 1964 an International Bank was created. While planning is formally kept an issue of national autonomy, some supranational elements in planning can already be found. Interestingly enough, however, the communist-ruled world is as little internationally minded as the Western world, or probably somewhat less so.

In the Western world, international trade has always been given considerable emphasis. Many economists and some governments have gone in for free trade. Most governments have stuck to some degree of protection, partly for fiscal reasons, partly in order to protect their economies against sudden changes in competitive power, and to some extent for nationalistic reasons. Thus it was considered necessary to produce a certain minimum of indispensable consumer goods at home. The two world wars tended to reinforce national isolation. After World War II Western European countries first followed a policy of trade and payments control which often resulted in bilateral equilibria. Under OEEC trade was increasingly multilateralized and trade impediments were reduced. EEC and EFTA continued the process of reduction of barriers inside their groups. The criterion of the international division of labor applied is the one of free competition, which for many industries is almost identical with the one of comparative advantages. This is not true for trade with the outside world, however, since the outer tariffs or levies are considerable for some types of goods, particularly agricultural products in EEC. In recent years proposals have been discussed envisaging some supranational planning by EEC.

Even so, the similarity in development of views on and practices of trade policies within their own area between East and West are striking, East having lagged somewhat behind West in this respect.

5. The Degree of Internal Centralization: General

Having discussed the degree of centralization in production and exchange planning already in Section 3 we shall now turn to the degree of centralization in the execution of production and exchange of commodities and services, including their pricing. The role of the single production unit (factory, shop, etc.) is of paramount importance for any discussion of this subject. It should not be overlooked, of course, that even during the period of highest centralization, a large number of decisions had to be taken by management. Even so its freedom was very restricted compared with Western standards. Formally at least the volume and assortment of production, the quantities to deliver to various customers, and the prices were all fixed by the central plan. Factually there was a limit to what could be specified, however, and there were numerous complaints about the wrong specifications being produced. Moreover, actual production did deviate from the plan, and plan overfulfillment was among the instruments of economic policy almost from the start, while underfulfillment was frequent enough, too.

A long time ago, the pure war-type command economy had been loosened by the introduction of a number of stimuli to management as well as to employees. The well-known example is the director's fund, later called enterprise fund, fed by contributions dependent on the unit's performance. The definition of performance requires a choice among various "success indicators."

In recent years discussions have increased considerably and measures have been taken both with regard to decentralization of decisions and with regard to the calculation of success indicators. Leading in these discussions have been Liberman, Nemchinov, and Trapeznikov. Among the decisions at stake, the choice of assortment was one of the most important. In recent years, a number of clothing and footwear factories have been given the right to discuss directly with the department stores selling their products which styles and qualities are desired. Comments on this experiment are generally favorable, and it has been decided to extend this practice to textiles and leather factories, as a second step. This will no doubt reinforce the position of managers in the more restricted sense of that phrase.

In a more general way, the authors quoted have advocated more freedom for managers in order to enhance productivity. The question of the success indicators is narrowly connected with it, since they must be a partial substitute for the orders from above governing managers' activity before. In recent discussions, profit has been indicated as the most suitable composite success indicator. One of the conditions that it actually is a good indicator evidently is that prices must reflect the relative scarcity of the product. This subject will be discussed later (Section 9), since it constitutes a quantitative means of policy.

Among the qualitative aspects of pricing we may now discuss the role of the market. So far, this institution has been used in the Soviet Union or, for instance, Poland, in a very limited way only; mainly for a portion of agricultural production. Lange, while favoring decentralization even to the extent that he recommends expansion of the private sector, does not favor the market as a price-fixing institution. Only Yugoslavia has introduced almost free markets on a large scale; but some of the drawbacks mentioned by Lange have indeed shown up, namely instability of some markets.

In Western economies the situation some fifty years ago was still close to the free-enterprise–free-market system as described in their text books. In the meantime important changes have taken place, some of them shifting with the environment—two wars and the great depression—but generally leaving a clear trend. Characteristic for that trend is on the one hand, a decline in the power of pure owners in favor of managers; and, on the other hand, increased centralization in decisions, whether private or public, and increased central regulation. Large cartels have developed, limiting competition within branches, although not so easily between branches. Manager freedom with regard to decisions on labor conditions has been increasingly reduced by social legislation and growing power of trade unions, while freedom to spend has been reduced by progressive taxes, taking as a rule about one-half of profits. Pricing by the market has been eliminated in a number of unstable markets, mainly agricultural and mining markets. Decisions on the main issues of socio-economic policy are often taken in central organizations of employers and employees and by governments in close contact with these organizations.

6. The Degree of Internal Centralization: Agriculture

Agriculture may be called the biggest single industry; during the past decades about one-half of the population of the Soviet Union was still rural. In Western countries farmers are more influential than their numbers would suggest: witness the protective agricultural policy of EEC. In the East, the farmer's psychology was one of the most difficult obstacles to communist policies. Crude factual evidence on the developments in Eastern and Western countries may be summarized by stating that the West is permanently producing more and the East less than needed. This statement may somewhat neglect the fact that demand has risen more quickly in Eastern countries than in Western.

Eastern agricultural policy has been characterized by frequent changes, partly of a trial-and-error type. The doctrine of centralized decisions is most difficult to apply in agriculture because of the space-consuming nature of this industry. The well-known forms in which it has been tried out were collective and state farms, machine and tractor stations, and forced deliveries of part of the crop at fixed prices. Alongside this policy one of opening up large virgin areas with the help of mass-production techniques has been tried out. The machine and tractor stations were abolished again; in Poland and Yugoslavia collective farms have been abandoned. In the Soviet Union and elsewhere the regime has been loosened and numerous incentives have been introduced. Prices of forced deliveries have been raised; supplementary deliveries to the authorities at better prices were introduced; and sales directly to the public admitted, where prices were the result of market forces. Farmers in collective farms have their private plot, the significance of which was recently underlined by Party Secretary Brezhnev. Specialized state farms for vegetables and fruits have their own trade channels.

Western agriculture is overwhelmingly in private hands; cooperatives have been successful in auxiliary activities such as buying, selling, process- ing, and joint operation of machines, but have not entered the field of production. Large farms have been more successful than small ones; there is convincing evidence of increasing returns to scale and a corresponding tendency towards larger units, but the tendency is slow. Almost all agricultural markets are now considered inherently unstable and hence are regulated by national or international schemes. Moreover, considerable support is given to agricultural prices in many Western countries, to the detriment of a number of developing countries.

7. Quantitative Means or Instruments: Investment and Education

After having discussed some of the main changes in institutions, we shall now discuss the role of and changes in some of the main instruments of economic policy in East and West.

Probably the most important quantitative means (or instrument) of Eastern socio-economic policy has been the level of investment expendi- tures. We include in this item both material investment (in fixed capital goods and stocks) and education (or investment in human beings) in its broadest sense. The percentage of national income devoted to investment (both measured according to Western definitions, for reasons of compari- son) has been estimated at about 25 percent. Not much change in this percentage has been reported. Education expenditures and other measures of educational activity (enrollment figures) have also been high; at about the level of the United States. Of this, a larger percentage than in the latter country was devoted to education in the sciences and technology.

In this field, changes have been more outspoken in the West. For decades the percentage of national income saved was estimated at 11 to 12 percent (averages over cycles) in the United Kingdom and the United States. In Continental Europe it may have been somewhat higher, say 15 percent. After World War II, the latter area invested up to 20 percent and Japan almost 30 percent (net) of their national income. Education activity also increased as a percentage of national income or of the population. Levels in Western Europe seem to be lower than in the United States or the Soviet Union, however. The impact of education on productivity has been estimated in recent years; Denison estimates that for the United States out of an average rate of increase in product per capita of 1.6 percent (over the period 1929–57) some 0.6 percent is due to increased volumes of education.

8. Income Distribution and Incentives

The central aim of all socialist action, whether formulated as the elimination of exploitation or otherwise, has always been to make income distribution more equal. It is perfectly understandable, therefore, that in the early phases of communist rule an attempt was made more to equalize incomes by decree. The economic function of income inequality was insufficiently understood, however, and only experience taught the Soviet authorities that this aim cannot be reached at short notice or by decree. Measures in the field of education and taxation have to accompany any such policy. Without them, reducing income inequality by decree disrupts a number of equilibria, namely those between supply of and demand for labor of different quality, and becomes inconsistent with rapid economic growth which the Soviet authorities understood they had to go in for. Hence, as early as in the thirties they introduced payment according to productive contribution, which was then announced as a socialist wage policy, in contradistinction to a communist wage policy aimed at in the long run. Egalitarian principles were, from that moment on, denounced as dilettantism and petit bourgeois. This important change constituted one of many further steps meant to create material incentives to further productive effort, to replace pure command or an appeal to idealism which only works under special circumstances and with a minority of people. The problem still exists to some extent, as is illustrated by the recent contention (1962) that in Poland wages in the machine industry were too equal.

Incentives have been created for managers, workers, and peasants in different forms. Both managers and workers share, although at different rates, in additional income obtained from overfulfillment of plans. Various types of premiums have been introduced and some experimenting goes on, remarkably parallel with Western experiments. Thus, there was a time when piece rates were considered a good stimulus and a time when this was carried too far. In 1962, time rates again took the place of piece rates in a number of occupations. Premiums were tried at the individual and later at a group level, experimenting with the size of the group. We already briefly hinted at the price increases for agricultural products

(Section 6) as an incentive to farmers. Quite recently Trapeznikov emphasized the necessity of creating incentives for producing better qualities.

The results of more education begin to show up, increasing the supply of qualified and reducing that of unskilled people and hence changing the equilibrium rates in the various compartments of the labor market. This made it possible to attain more equality again; the degree of inequality is estimated to be the same in 1960 as in 1930, before the switch away from egalitarian wage scales.

Income distribution in Western countries, very unequal in the nineteenth century, has become more equal gradually. One of the causes was unearned income, which has never been abolished so completely as in Eastern countries. Instead of all-out nationalization, the West had a gradual increase in public ownership (now at perhaps 20 or 25 percent of all means of production) and the introduction of increasingly progressive income and wealth taxes. The higher amount of national wealth in Western countries is responsible, in addition, for a greater relative scarcity of labor, and gradually education played the role already discussed. In all probability, income inequality is comparable in East and West; but this is easier to attain in more than in less developed countries.

Incentives have always played a role in Western societies, and their nature is very similar to the ones which have gradually developed in the East. We already noted the similarity in recent experiments on both sides. We may add that, more recently, incentives for education have quickly developed in the West; apart from exemption of admission and tuition fees financial assistance to students was expanded considerably. A powerful incentive to entrepreneurs, with less desirable side effects, is capital gains, a natural consequence of private ownership. Recently, some attempts have been made in Western countries to limit these gains (capital gains taxes; land agencies).

9. Pricing and Investment Criteria

In communist countries, and particularly in the Soviet Union, prices have been fixed in a highly centralized way, even though not all of them by central government agencies. For goods of a regional or local character, prices were fixed by lower authorities; in a very few cases even by producers themselves (goods of a unique character; and the free agricultural commodities). They were kept constant for a considerable period; thus most prices of durable producer goods had been fixed in 1955 and will be revised in 1966 only. They were not always used to clear the market; this was also done by planning allocations.

Pricing was based on Marxian concepts, meant to reflect long-term influences, and based on the labor theory of value. This implied relatively low prices for capital-intensive products, such as electricity prices. Gradually elements comparable with interest rates were introduced to reflect capital scarcity—although not yet completely or correctly. In a way the profit margin recognized as an element of correct pricing in the CPSU party program represents such an element already; the recoupment period used in investment decisions (cf. below) another. In Hungary and Poland interest rates are used as cost elements and rightly so; of course, this does not imply any income payment to private capital owners.

Another feature of Soviet pricing is that prices are based on average rather than marginal costs; presumably this does not distort the price structure too much, however. Even if the elements mentioned did distort it (and some surely did), this was of no consequence as long as all allocations were planned. With the abolition of consumer rationing and as a consequence of technological development, choices are now more and more made in a decentralized way, that is, by consumers and producers; hence, the need for a better pricing method has become clear. Trapeznikov, Nemchinov, and Liberman all stressed certain needs for changes based on arguments familiar to the Western economist. In the 1963 revision of metal product prices, interesting new elements were introduced, such as the relationship with prices of similar products, changes in wages in mining, changes in productivity or in materials available (including synthetics).

While more flexible prices are advocated, this is not done for all goods; also in Czechoslovakia some prices are kept constant or fixed by the government, while the intention was expressed to introduce free prices in markets with a sufficient intensity of competition.

A related subject is the appraisal of investment projects. Here again the purpose is to arrive at the best use of available scarce resources. In recent years, extensive discussions have been held on the criteria to be used. The central criterion is now the recoupment period; that is, the ratio of additional investments to savings in costs obtained by them. In Poland and Hungary, a uniform upper limit is applied in all industries, with corrections for differences in gestation period and life-time equipment—this latter because of the possibilities of obsolescence. In other Eastern countries, uniformity of the upper limit accepted does not yet seem to exist. This would seem to entail a non-optimal allocation of capital.

Also in Western countries, numerous cases can be found where investment decisions are not optimal; often enough private profit of the producer concerned decides, instead of the gains to the economy as a whole, on the selection of some project. Wherever external effects exist, or market prices do not reflect real scarcities, corrections are necessary.

10. Tax Systems

We already observed that taxes have not only the function of financing public expenditure, but also the one of regulating the nation's purchasing power, and hence the level and the movements of total demand. The main difference between Eastern and Western tax structures is that direct taxes play a much larger part in Western countries than in Eastern. In the West, these are the substitute for what public ownership of the means of production accomplishes in the East: an instrument to reduce unearned income. These taxes have been introduced under mainly socialist pressure; their disadvantage is that they require a complicated administration and may reduce incentives to higher production. Their advantage is that they offer possibilities to build in some incentives for investment.

Another difference between East and West consists of the differential treatment, in the East, of consumer and producer goods. In contradistinction, Western countries differentiate more between necessities and luxuries. There is some differentiation, however, also in communist countries among the "turnover tax" rates for different consumer goods; thus, textiles have always been taxed relatively high and consumer durables relatively low. Also, no tax is levied on vegetables and fruits.

11. Welfare Economics in the Optimum Regime

So far our emphasis has been on observed facts, particularly on the changes in both systems. We will now take up a question of a theoretical or deductive character: are we able to present any theory on the changes to be expected in the socio-economic systems of East and West?

We think the chapter of Western economic science known as welfare economics has to offer a tentative outline of a theory. Welfare economics tries to define the situation of maximum welfare attainable under the constraints of given initial quantities of the factors of production and given production laws, without assuming any particular social structure. Rather, the social institutions occur as the unknowns of the problem which have to be fixed in such a way as to maximize welfare. To be sure, the welfare concept to be used must be considered given. Since this concept represents the aims of the economy considered, and since we have already stated that the ultimate aims of East and West are not so different (cf. Section 2), we may start from a welfare concept not too different from both sets of aims. Theoretically, we may then derive the institutional structure of the optimum order. Elsewhere we have made a first crude attempt to do so.[1] Summarizing very briefly we found that a "mixed order" seems to be optimal showing the following structure:

(a) A public sector of considerable extent takes care of all activities showing external effects or indivisibilities of some importance, while activities that show

---

[1] J. Tinbergen, "The Theory of the Optimum Regime," in *Selected Papers* (Amsterdam, 1959), p. 264, and "The Significance of Welfare Economics for Socialism," in *On Political Economy and Econometrics, Essays in Honour of Oskar Lange* (Warsaw, 1964).

neither of these characteristics can be carried out by a private sector. The latter should contain at least small and medium production units.

(b) The degree of centralization in the handling of instruments of socio-economic policy should be such that no instrument shows considerable external effects: this principle distributes the policy tasks over authorities of different "levels".

(c) The regulation of total demand, of the level of total investment, of unstable markets, and of income redistribution is among the tasks of the public sector; income redistribution should aim at equalization of marginal utilities among the individuals and no taxes on marginal efforts are permitted.

The precise nature of the optimum order has not yet been determined and, moreover, remains different under different circumstances or with different social welfare preferences.

The main arguments in favor of the features just enumerated are these:

(a) If production decisions on activities showing either external effects or indivisibilities are left to private firms, they will be different from the production required by the optimum. This danger does not exist for activities not showing these characteristics, as was shown by a large number of economists from Adam Smith to modern mathematical economists. The information needed for a proper choice of production patterns may even be more readily available to the production units themselves than to high-level authorities. While private activity will imply unearned income to some extent, it will probably also show, especially for small units, higher productivity than public activity.

(b) Handling of instruments of socio-economic policy at too low a level will imply external effects, that is, effects on the outside world, which are insufficiently taken into account by the policymakers at these lower levels and may lead to erroneous decisions. Handling such instruments at too high a level will imply unnecessary bureaucracy and for that reason be undesirable.

(c) If the regulation of total demand is left to the business community, the danger of business cycles will exist. If the level of total investment is left to the individual savers, a too low rate of growth may obtain. Income redistribution can only be organized at a sufficiently large scale by public authorities. The taxation of marginal efforts will tend to keep total production below the optimum.

Assuming, for the time being, that (1) an optimum of about this nature exists and (2) economic forces are predominant in shaping and moving the social order, we may conclude that societies showing deviations from the optimum will tend to move towards the latter. Clearly, both Eastern and Western society deviate from the optimum as just sketched. As long as they do, we expect them to change. Since their deviations in most elements are on opposite sides from the optimum, a tendency for convergency can be expected.

However, though dominant, economic forces are not the only ones making for changes in socio-economic order. Cultural preferences will play a certain part, even if their pursuance may keep welfare below the optimum. Actually, welfare can be defined broadly enough to contain these cultural preferences, and it then follows that the optimum will somewhat deviate from the "pure socio-economic" optimum. Thus, the West may attach an autonomous value to some types of entrepreneurial freedom not necessary for maximum welfare; or the East may attach an autonomous value to public ownership not necessary for maximum welfare in the pure sense. The wealthier a community, the more it can afford to have such "hobbies." On the other hand, their competition narrows down the leeway they can give to these autonomous preferences, particularly if the latter are not shared by those whom East and West try to impress with their system, that is, not only their own population but also the uncommitted world.

12. Preliminary Conclusions

From our preceding survey of the changes in Eastern and Western socio-economic systems we conclude that, first of all, these changes mostly took place as a consequence of the experience each society had with its own system, rather than out of a desire to imitate the other. Even so, most changes represent a converging pattern. The speed of this convergence should not be overestimated, however, and there have also been movements in the opposite direction.

Quite generally, there is a tendency towards decentralization in the East and one towards centralization in the West. Central planning tends to be reduced in the former and to be strengthened in the latter type of society. More freedom is being given to Eastern managers and less to Western managers. Education and investment in Western countries are stepped up and tend to approach Eastern figures. International trade tends to grow more rapidly in the communist group than in the non-communist. Income distribution becomes increasingly equitable in Western as well as Eastern countries. Costs and investment criteria in the East are more and more calculated in a way similar to the Western way.

A convergence of ideas could also be noted in the advice given to developing countries, which is especially clear in the contributions made by the United States and the Union of Soviet Socialist Republics to the United Nations Conference on Science and Development held in 1963.

For an appraisal of the changes, their persistency is important. While some previous changes in Eastern policy have been temporary and should be seen as tactical moves, persistency can be expected whenever (a) changes have been maintained for a considerable period; (b) they have been incorporated into the party program with the epithet "socialist"; (c) they are irrelevant for the basic aim of socialism; (d) they are motivated by changed circumstances, such as the level of development or the existence of nuclear arms; or finally (e) they are based on their effect on economic performance.

Thus, the introduction of material stimuli and the present wage system may be considered as definitive changes for the reasons mentioned under (a) and (b); the introduction of multilateral trade or less rigid prices for the reasons mentioned under (c); the recent loosening of central planning and increased freedom of managers for the reasons under (d). Outside the realm of economics, the Soviet Union's willingness to conclude the nuclear test stop can be seen as a consequence of changed circumstances which Khrushchev explicitly mentioned as a ground to depart from even Marx's or Lenin's views. Most of the economic changes in communist-ruled countries can, moreover, be understood for the reasons mentioned under (e), also implicit in our theoretical analysis in Section 11. From this analysis we can even derive expectations regarding further changes—in East and West—tending toward the optimum order. Thus, we may expect more freedom for managers and scientists and less central planning of production and central pricing, together with some more international integration on some macro economic issues. In the West we may expect more central planning, further restrictions on unearned income, and further financial aid in education. The West may also change its attitude toward feudal Southern countries and require reforms more emphatically.

The process of convergency raises two very fundamental questions. The first is whether the process of dedoctrinization it represents will spread to other areas of thinking and policy. Expert opinions diverge widely, from those who deny this to those who offer evidence in its favor. Spulber, Brzezinski, and Huntington, and Prybyla belong to the first group; Zebot, Sorokin, and Goodman to the second.[2] Further development and more thorough observation may be needed.

The second question is simpler but no less important. Doesn't the process kill the official argument of both the left-wing East ("Stalinist") and the right-wing West (capitalist) that the two economic systems cannot be reconciled and that the main reason for the East-West controversy is socio-economic? We think it does; in other words, it does rule out the idea that for socio-economic reasons East and West cannot cooperate. Even so, there would remain the other reason, believed by the West to be the most important controversy, namely the one about political system or group decision making. This question goes beyond our topic; suffice it to say that also there we must do our utmost to analyze the contrast in the hope of finding a way to cooperation. But it remains important to state that the foundations of both "Stalinist" and capitalist views are being gradually undermined.

---

[2] N. Spulber, in Reviews of Landauer, *American Economic Review*, LIV (1964), p. 1139; Z. Brzezinski and S. P. Huntington, *Political Power: U.S.A./U.S.S.R., Similarities and Contrasts; Convergence or Evolution* (New York, 1964); J. S. Prybyla, "The Convergence of Western and Communist Economic Systems: A Critical Estimate," *The Russian Review* 23 (1964) no. 1, p. 3; C. A. Zebot, *The Economics of Competitive Coexistence* (New York, 1964); P. A. Sorokin, "Soziologische und Kulturelle Annäherungen zwischen den Vereinigte Staaten und der Sowjetunion," *Zeitschr. für Politik* 7 (1960), p. 341; E. Goodman, "Reflections on the New Soviet Party Program," *Russian Review* 21 (1962), p. 109.

SUGGESTIONS FOR FURTHER READING

SUGGESTIONS FOR FURTHER READING

The selections included in this book have been chosen to present, in a relatively small collection, an introduction to various facets of the Soviet economy. For the reader who is interested in exploring the Soviet economy further, there is a wide variety of material to choose from.

GENERAL WORKS ON THE SOVIET ECONOMY

There are a number of textbooks which deal with the Soviet economy from different points of view and at different levels. Harry Schwartz, *An Introduction to the Soviet Economy* (Columbus, Ohio: Charles E. Merrill Publishing Co., 1968) is a brief elementary survey. Robert W. Campbell, *Soviet Economic Power: Its Organization, Growth and Challenge* (2d ed.; Boston: Houghton Mifflin Co., 1966), is a relatively short, essentially nontechnical book which concentrates on the factors affecting the growth and performance of the Soviet economy. Nicolas Spulber, *The Soviet Economy: Structure, Principles, Problems* (rev. ed.; New York: W. W. Norton & Co., Inc., 1969), considers the organization, operation, and performance of the various sectors of the economy. Alec Nove, *The Soviet Economy: An Introduction* (2d rev. ed.; New York: Frederick A. Praeger, Inc., 1969), emphasizes the structure and problems of the economy, with much institutional information and many specific illustrations from Soviet publications. Howard J. Sherman, *The Soviet Economy* (Boston: Little, Brown and Company, 1969), deals with ideological and historical aspects, as well as contemporary planning problems. Edward Ames, *Soviet Economic Processes* (Homewood, Ill.: Richard D. Irwin, Inc., 1965), is somewhat more theoretical in its orientation and also more difficult, making some use of differential calculus and matrix algebra.

The Joint Economic Committee of Congress has issued two important types of publications on the Soviet economy—compendia of articles, and collections of up-to-date statistics. The most recent example of the first is *New Directions in the Soviet Economy* (Joint Economic Committee, 89th Cong., 2d sess., 4 parts; Washington, D.C.: U.S. Government Printing Office, 1966). The statistical collections are published irregularly, approximately biennially, with varying titles. The *Economic Survey of Europe* and the *Economic Bulletin for Europe,* both published by the

United Nations Economic Commission for Europe in Geneva, also contain extensive statistical data on the Soviet and East European economies. Franklyn D. Holzman (ed.), *Readings on the Soviet Economy* (Chicago: Rand McNally & Co., 1962), includes a large number of older articles on the Soviet economy. Harry G. Shaffer (ed.), *The Soviet Economy: A Collection of Western and Soviet Views* (2d ed.; New York: Appleton-Century-Crofts, 1969), presents matching Western and Soviet articles on various features of the Soviet economy.

There are several useful periodicals. *Soviet Studies* (published quarterly at the University of Glasgow, Scotland) is an interdisciplinary journal with many articles on the Soviet economy. Its *Information Supplement* contains concise digests of important items on the economy in Soviet journals and newspapers. *Problems of Communism* (published bimonthly by the U.S. Information Agency, Washington, D.C.) is an interdisciplinary journal on world communism with nontechnical articles on the Soviet economy and Soviet foreign economic relations. *The Current Digest of the Soviet Press* (published weekly at Ohio State University by the Joint Committee on Slavic Studies) contains translations and digests from Soviet newspapers and magazines, including speeches, reports, and articles about the economy. *Problems of Economics* (published monthly by the International Arts and Sciences Press, White Plains, New York) consists of translations of articles from Soviet economics journals.

HISTORICAL BACKGROUND

There are several important books on the history of Soviet economic development. Alexander Baykov, *The Development of the Soviet Economic System* (New York: The Macmillan Co., 1947), deals in great detail with the period from 1917 to the end of the 1930's. Maurice Dobb, *Soviet Economic Development Since 1917* (rev., enlarged ed.; New York: International Publishers Co., 1966), concentrates on the same period, although it also discusses Russian economic development before the Revolution and developments immediately after World War II. Naum Jasny, *Soviet Industrialization, 1928–1952* (Chicago: The University of Chicago Press, 1961), is an economic history of the Stalin era. A more specialized work dealing with the controversy in the 1920's over the strategy of economic development is Alexander Erlich, *The Soviet Industrialization Debate, 1924–1928* (Cambridge, Mass.: Harvard University Press, 1960). Much of the important literature of this controversy has been translated in Nicolas Spulber (ed.), *Foundations of Soviet Strategy for Economic Growth: Selected Soviet Essays, 1924–1930* (Bloomington, Ind.: Indiana University Press, 1964). This material is summarized and appraised in a companion volume by Spulber, *Soviet Strategy for Economic Growth* (Bloomington, Ind.: Indiana University Press, 1964). A detailed analysis of the decisions about the collectivization of agriculture and their implementation appears in Moshe Lewin, *Russian Peasants and Soviet Power:*

A Study of Collectivization (Evanston, Ill.: Northwestern University Press, 1968). The accomplishments and problems of the Soviet economy during the first decade after the death of Stalin are examined in Harry Schwartz, *The Soviet Economy Since Stalin* (Philadelphia: J. B. Lippincott Co., 1965). A brief historical survey of the highlights of Soviet economic development may be found in Anatole G. Mazour, *Soviet Economic Development: Operation Outstrip, 1921–1965* (Princeton, N.J.: D. Van Nostrand Company, Inc., 1967).

HOW THE ECONOMY OPERATES

Economic planning in the Soviet Union is appraised in Abram Bergson, *The Economics of Soviet Planning* (New Haven: Yale University Press, 1964), which presupposes some acquaintance with welfare economics and with the main characteristics of the Soviet economy. On material balances and input-output analysis in Soviet planning, see J. M. Montias, "Planning with Material Balances in Soviet-Type Economies," *American Economic Review*, Vol. XLIX, No. 5 (December, 1959), pp. 963–85; Herbert S. Levine, "Input-Output Analysis and Soviet Planning," *American Economic Review*, Vol. XLIX, No. 5 (December, 1959), pp. 963–85; Herbert S. Levine, "Input-Output Analysis and Soviet Planning," *American Economic Review*, Vol. LII, No. 2 (May, 1962), pp. 127–37; and Michael J. Ellman, "The Use of Input-Output in Regional Economic Planning: The Soviet Experience," *Economic Journal*, Vol. LXXVIII, No. 312 (December, 1968), pp. 855–67. Planning strategy is discussed in Holland Hunter, "Optimal Tautness in Developmental Planning," *Economic Development and Cultural Change*, Vol. IX, No. 4 (July, 1961), Part I, pp. 561–72.

Two recent Soviet accounts of the planning system are Mikhail Bor, *Aims and Methods of Soviet Planning* (New York: International Publishers, Co., 1967); and G. Sorokin, *Planning in the USSR* (Moscow: Progress Publishers, 1967).

A comprehensive survey of the financial system is given in U.S. Bureau of the Census, *The Soviet Financial System: Structure, Operation, and Statistics*, by Daniel Gallik, Cestmir Jesina, and Stephen Rapawy (International Population Statistics Reports, Series P-90, No. 23) (Washington, D.C.: U.S. Government Printing Office, 1968). The basic study of Soviet taxation is Franklyn D. Holzman, *Soviet Taxation: The Fiscal and Monetary Problems of a Planned Economy* (Cambridge, Mass.: Harvard University Press, 1955). Inflation in the Soviet Union is analyzed in Franklyn D. Holzman, "Soviet Inflationary Pressures, 1928–1957: Causes and Cures," *Quarterly Journal of Economics*, Vol. LXXIV, No. 2 (May, 1960), pp. 167–88; and Robert M. Fearn, "Controls Over Wage Funds and Inflationary Pressures in the USSR," *Industrial and Labor Relations Review*, Vol. 18, No. 2 (January, 1965), pp. 186–95.

Industrial management in the Soviet Union is the subject of several monographs. David Granick, *Management of the Industrial Firm in the USSR* (New York: Columbia University Press, 1954), is still useful and pertinent, although the materials on which it is based deal mainly with the 1930's. Joseph S. Berliner, *Factory and Manager in the USSR* (Cambridge, Mass.: Harvard University Press, 1957), based primarily on interviews with Soviet émigrés, is a classic work. David Granick, *The Red Executive: A Study of the Organization Man in Russian Industry* (Garden City, N.Y.: Doubleday & Co., Inc., 1960), is a nontechnical and popular, but solid and well-researched, book which compares the Soviet industrial manager with his American counterpart. Barry M. Richman, *Soviet Management—With Significant American Comparisons* (Englewood Cliffs, N.J.: Prentice-Hall, Inc., 1965), is based in part on interviews at 16 Soviet enterprises. Also relevant is Barry M. Richman, *Management Development and Education in the Soviet Union* (East Lansing, Mich.: Michigan State University Institute for International Business, 1967).

Broad studies of labor in the USSR include Arvid Brodersen, *The Soviet Worker: Labor and Government in Soviet Society* (New York: Random House, 1966); and Robert Conquest (ed.), *Industrial Workers in the USSR* (New York: Frederick A. Praeger, Inc., 1967). More specialized are S. Swianiewicz, *Forced Labor and Economic Development: An Enquiry into the Experience of Soviet Industrialization* (London: Oxford University Press, 1965); and Norton T. Dodge, *Women in the Soviet Economy—Their Role in Economic, Scientific, and Technical Development* (Baltimore, Md.: Johns Hopkins Press, 1966). Contrasting views of efficiency in the use of the labor force may be found in Gertrude Schroeder, "Labor Planning in the USSR," *Southern Economic Journal,* Vol. XXXII, No. 1 (July, 1965), pp. 63–72; and Efim Manevich, "The Management of Soviet Manpower," *Foreign Affairs,* Vol. 47, No. 1 (October, 1968), pp. 176–84. On wages, see Gertrude Schroeder, "Industrial Wage Differentials in the USSR," *Soviet Studies,* Vol. XVII, No. 3 (January, 1966), pp. 303–17; and United Nations Economic Commission for Europe, *Incomes in Post-War Europe (Economic Survey of Europe in 1965,* Part 2) (Geneva, 1967), chaps. 7–11.

Soviet agriculture is discussed from various points of view in Roy D. Laird (ed.), *Soviet Agricultural and Peasant Affairs* (Lawrence, Kan.: University of Kansas Press, 1963); Roy D. Laird and Edward L. Crowley (eds.), *Soviet Agriculture: The Permanent Crisis* (New York: Frederick A. Praeger, Inc., 1965); Jerzy F. Karcz (ed.), *Soviet and East European Agriculture* (Berkeley, Calif.: University of California Press, 1967); and Robert Conquest (ed.), *Agricultural Workers in the USSR* (New York: Frederick A. Praeger, Inc., 1969). The formation of agricultural policy is examined in Sidney I. Ploss, *Conflict and Decision-Making in Soviet Russia: A Case Study of Agricultural Policy* (Princeton, N.J.: Princeton University Press, 1965). The private plot is analyzed in C. A. Knox Lovell, "The Role of Private Subsidiary Farming during the Soviet

Seven-Year Plan, 1959–65," *Soviet Studies*, Vol. XX, No. 1 (July, 1968), pp. 46–66; and Karl-Eugen Wädekin, "Private Production in Soviet Agriculture," *Problems of Communism*, Vol. XVII, No. 1 (January–February, 1968), pp. 22–30. Many useful insights into the conditions and problems of Soviet agriculture are provided in Soviet literature, as shown by Alastair N. D. McAuley, "Kolkhoz Problems in Recent Literary Magazines," *Soviet Studies*, Vol. XV, No. 3 (January, 1964), pp. 308–30; and Ronald Hingley, "Home Truths on the Farm: The Literary Mirror," *Problems of Communism*, Vol. XIV, No. 3 (May–June, 1965), pp. 22–34. An outstanding example available in English translation is Fyodor Abramov, *The New Life: A Day on a Collective Farm* (New York: Grove Press, Inc., 1963).

Various aspects of Soviet foreign trade are examined in Alan A. Brown and Egon Neuberger (eds.), *International Trade and Central Planning* (Berkeley, Calif.: University of California Press, 1968); and P. J. D. Wiles, *Communist International Economics* (Oxford: Basil Blackwell, 1968). Soviet trade with Communist countries in Eastern Europe is analyzed in Frederic L. Pryor, *The Communist Foreign Trade System* (Cambridge, Mass.: M. I. T. Press, 1963); and Michael Kaser, *COMECON: The Integration Problems of the Planned Economies* (2d ed.; London: Oxford University Press, 1967). Soviet-Chinese economic relations are discussed in Chu-yuan Cheng, *Economic Relations Between Peking and Moscow, 1949–63* (New York: Frederick A. Praeger, Inc., 1964); and Alexander Eckstein, *Communist China's Economic Growth and Foreign Trade* (New York: McGraw-Hill Book Co., 1966), chap. 5. Marshall I. Goldman, *Soviet Foreign Aid* (New York: Frederick A. Praeger, Inc., 1967), considers aid to both Communist and non-Communist countries. Soviet trade with the industrial West is examined in Gunnar Adler-Karlsson, "Problems of East-West Trade—A General Survey," *Economics of Planning*, Vol. 7 (1967), No. 2, pp. 119–82; Phillip Grub and Karel Holbik (eds.), *American-East European Trade: Controversy, Progress, Prospects* (Washington, D.C.: National Press, Inc., 1968); and Gunnar Adler-Karlsson, *Western Economic Warfare, 1947–1967: A Case Study in Foreign Economic Policy* (Stockholm: Almqvist & Wiksell, 1968).

ECONOMIC GROWTH

Some of the statistical problems involved in assessing Soviet economic growth are analyzed in Gregory Grossman, *Soviet Statistics of Physical Output of Industrial Commodities: Their Compilation and Quality* (Princeton, N.J.: Princeton University Press, 1960). Difficulties in comparing the Soviet with other economies are discussed in the articles by Hans Heymann, Jr., and Robert W. Campbell in *Comparisons of the United States and Soviet Economies* (Joint Economic Committee, 86th Cong., 1st sess.; Washington, D.C.: U.S. Government Printing Office,

1959, Part 1, pp. 1–30); and Abraham S. Becker, "Comparisons of United States and USSR National Output: Some Rules of the Game," *World Politics,* Vol. XIII, No. 1 (October, 1960), pp. 99–111.

Concise explanations and assessments of Soviet economic growth include Raymond P. Powell, "Economic Growth in the USSR," *Scientific American,* Vol. 219, No. 6 (December, 1968), pp. 17–23; and Abram Bergson, *Planning and Productivity under Soviet Socialism* (New York: Columbia University Press, 1968).

The results of a number of studies measuring different aspects of Soviet economic growth are presented in Abram Bergson and Simon Kuznets (eds.), *Economic Trends in the Soviet Union* (Cambridge, Mass.: Harvard University Press, 1963). Basic works on Soviet economic growth include Abram Bergson, *The Real National Income of Soviet Russia Since 1928* (Cambridge, Mass.: Harvard University Press, 1961); G. Warren Nutter and others, *The Growth of Industrial Production in the Soviet Union* (Princeton, N.J.: Princeton University Press, 1962); Richard Moorsteen, *Prices and Production of Machinery in the Soviet Union, 1928–1958* (Cambridge, Mass.: Harvard University Press, 1962); and Richard Moorsteen and Raymond P. Powell, *The Soviet Capital Stock, 1928–1962* (Homewood, Ill.: Richard D. Irwin, Inc., 1966).

Consumption is discussed in Janet G. Chapman, *Real Wages in Soviet Russia Since 1928* (Cambridge, Mass.: Harvard University Press, 1963); and Philip Hanson, *The Consumer in the Soviet Economy* (London: Macmillan, 1968). On Soviet retail trade, see Marshall I. Goldman, *Soviet Marketing: Distribution in a Controlled Economy* (New York: The Free Press of Glencoe, 1963). Social welfare programs are examined in Bernice Q. Madison, *Social Welfare in the Soviet Union* (Stanford, Calif.: Stanford University Press, 1968).

The decline in Soviet economic growth after 1958 is analyzed in Robert W. Campbell, "The Post-war Growth of the Soviet Economy," *Soviet Studies,* Vol. XVI, No. 1 (July, 1964), pp. 1–16; Judith Thornton, "Factors in the Recent Decline in Soviet Growth," *Slavic Review,* Vol. XXV, No. 1 (March, 1966), pp. 101–19; Herbert S. Levine, "Industry," in Allen Kassof (ed.), *Prospects for Soviet Society* (New York: Frederick A. Praeger, Inc., 1968), pp. 219–317; and Norman Kaplan, "Retardation in Soviet Growth," *Review of Economics and Statistics,* Vol. L, No. 3 (August, 1968), pp. 293–303.

ECONOMIC CONTROVERSY AND REFORM

Comprehensive discussions include Eugene Zaleski, *Planning Reforms in the Soviet Union, 1962–1966* (Chapel Hill, N.C.: University of North Carolina Press, 1967); and George R. Feiwel, *The Soviet Quest for Economic Efficiency* (New York: Frederick A. Praeger, Inc., 1967).

The Liberman proposals have been analyzed in various articles, including Marshall I. Goldman, "Economic Controversy in the Soviet Union," *Foreign Affairs*, Vol. 41, No. 3 (April, 1963), pp. 498–512; Alec Nove, "The Liberman Proposals," *Survey*, No. 47 (April, 1963), pp. 112–18; Harry G. Shaffer, "What Price Economic Reforms? Ills and Remedies," *Problems of Communism*, Vol. XII, No. 3 (May–June, 1963), pp. 18–26; and Alfred Zauberman, "Liberman's Rules of the Game for Soviet Industry," *Slavic Review*, Vol. XXII, No. 4 (December, 1963), pp. 734–44.

Evaluations of the Kosygin reforms include James H. Blackman, "The Kosygin Reforms: New Wine in Old Bottles?" in Vladimir G. Treml and Robert Farrell (eds.), *The Development of the Soviet Economy: Plan and Performance* (New York: Frederick A. Praeger, Inc., 1968), pp. 249–89; Marshall I. Goldman, "Economic Revolution in the Soviet Union," *Foreign Affairs*, Vol. 45, No. 2 (January, 1967), pp. 319–31; and Gertude E. Schroeder, "Soviet Economic 'Reforms': A Study in Contradictions," *Soviet Studies*, Vol. XX, No. 1 (July, 1968), pp. 1–21. An evaluation by Liberman may be found in Yevsei Liberman, "The Soviet Economic Reform," *Foreign Affairs*, Vol. 46, No. 1 (October, 1967), pp. 53–63.

Translations of important Soviet articles, speeches, and decrees appear in Myron E. Sharpe (ed.), *Planning, Profit and Incentives in the USSR*, Vol. I, *The Liberman Discussion—A New Phase in Soviet Economic Thought*, and Vol. II, *Reform of Soviet Economic Management* (White Plains, N.Y.: International Arts and Sciences Press, 1966).

Michael Gamarnikow, *Economic Reforms in Eastern Europe* (Detroit, Mich.: Wayne State University Press, 1968), is a general survey, with emphasis on political aspects. More specialized is Gregory Grossman (ed.), *Money and Plan: Financial Aspects of East European Economic Reforms* (Berkeley, Calif.: University of California Press, 1968). Reforms in Czechoslovakia are discussed concisely in articles by Václav Holešovský and Boris Pesek in the latter volume; a much more detailed treatment is George R. Feiwel, *New Economic Patterns in Czechoslovakia: Impact of Growth, Planning, and the Market* (New York: Frederick A. Praeger, Inc., 1968). The most comprehensive account of the Hungarian reform is István Friss (ed.), *Reform of the Economic Mechanism in Hungary* (Budapest: Akadémiai Kiadó, 1969). On Polish reforms, see Leon Smolinski, "Planning Reforms in Poland," *Kyklos*, Vol. XXI (1968), Fasc. 3, pp. 498–512.

Evidence for the convergence of Communist and Western economic systems is presented and evaluated in Jan S. Prybyla, "The Convergence of Western and Communist Economic Systems: A Critical Estimate," *Russian Review*, Vol. 23, No. 1 (January, 1964), pp. 3–17; Zbigniew Brzezinski and Samuel P. Huntington, *Political Power: USA/USSR* (New York: Viking Press, 1964), especially pp. 409–36; and Peter Wiles, "Convergence: Possibility and Probability," in Alexander Balinky and others, *Planning and the Market in the USSR: The 1960's* (New Brunswick, N.J.: Rutgers University Press, 1967), pp. 89–118.